Software Test Automation

Effective use of test execution tools

ACM PRESS BOOKS

This book is published as part of ACM Press Books – a collaboration between the Association for Computing (ACM) and Addison Wesley Longman Limited. ACM is the oldest and largest educational and scientific society in the information technology field. Through its high-quality publications and services, ACM is a major force in advancing the skills and knowledge of IT professionals throughout the world. For further information about ACM, contact:

ACM Member Services
1515 Broadway, 17th Floor
New York, NY 10036–5701
Phone: 1-212-626-0500
Fax: 1-212-944-1318
E-mail: acmhelp@acm.org

ACM European Service Center
108 Cowley Road
Oxford OX4 1JF
United Kingdom
Phone: +44-1865-382388
Fax: +44-1865-381388
E-mail: acm_europe@acm.org
URL: http://www.acm.org

Selected ACM titles

Component Software: Beyond Object-Oriented Programming *Clemens Szyperski*

The Object Advantage: Business Process Reeingineering with Object Technology (2nd edn) *Ivar Jacobson, Maria Ericsson, Agneta Jacobson, Gunnar Magnusson*

Object-Oriented Software Engineering: A Use Case Driven Approach *Ivar Jacobson, Magnus Christerson, Patrik Jonsson, Gunnar Overgaard*

Software for Use: A Practical Guide to the Models and Methods of Usage Centered Design *Larry L Constantine, Lucy A D Lockwood*

Bringing Design to Software: Expanding Software Developments to Include Design *Terry Winograd, John Bennett, Laura de Young, Bradley Hartfield*

CORBA Distributed Objects: Using Orbix *Sean Baker*

Software Requirements and Specifications: A Lexicon of Software Practice, Principles and Prejudices *Michael Jackson*

Business Process Implementation: Building Workflow Systems *Michael Jackson, Graham Twaddle*

Interacting Processes: A Multiparty Approach to Coordinated Distributed Programming *Nissim Francez, Ira Forman*

Design Patterns for Object-Oriented Software Development *Wolfgang Pree*

Software Testing in the Real World: Improving the Process *Ed Kit*

Test Process Improvement: A Practical Step-by-Step Guide to Structured Testing *Tim Koomen, Martin Pol*

Requirements Engineering and Rapid Development: An Object-Oriented Approach *Ian Graham*

Software Test Automation

Effective use of test execution tools

MARK FEWSTER

DOROTHY GRAHAM

ACM Press
New York

An imprint of **Pearson Education**

London • Boston • Indianapolis • New York • Mexico City
Toronto • Sydney • Tokyo • Singapore • Hong Kong • Cape Town
New Delhi • Madrid • Paris • Amsterdam • Munich • Milan

PEARSON EDUCATION LIMITED

Edinburgh Gate
Harlow CM20 2JE
Tel: +44 (0)1279 623623
Fax: +44 (0)1279 431059
Website: www.pearsoned.co.uk

First published in Great Britain 1999

ISBN: 0-201-33140-3

British Library Cataloguing in Publication Data
A catalogue record for this book can be obtained from the British Library

Library of Congress Cataloging in Publication Data
Fewster, Mark, 1959–
    Software test automation / Mark Fewster, Dorothy Graham.
        p. cm.
    "ACM Press books" – CIP facing t.p.
    Includes bibliographical references and index.
    ISBN 0-201-33140-3 (pbk. : alk. paper)
    1. Computer software–Testing–Automation. I. Graham, Dorothy,
1944–   .   II. Title.
QA76.76.T48F49 1999
005. 1´4–dc21   99–35578
                                                              CIP

The programs in this book have been included for their instructional value. The publisher does not offer any warranties or representations in respect of their fitness for a particular purpose, nor does the publisher accept any liability for any loss or damage arising from their use.

Many of the designations used by manufacturers and sellers to distinguish their products are claimed as trademarks. Pearson Education has made every attempt to supply trademark information about manufacturers and their products mentioned in this book. A list of the trademark designations and their owners appears on page xviii.

10 9 8 7

Typeset by Pantek Arts, Maidstone, Kent.
Printed and bound in Great Britain by Biddles Ltd, King's Lynn, Norfolk

The Publishers' policy is to use paper manufactured from sustainable forests.

Contents

Foreword

In a better world than ours, there would be magic. If you had a problem, you'd approach a wise old magician who embodied the experience of years of study and practice. You'd give the magician some money. In return, you would receive a magical object to make your problem go away. We don't have magic, but we do have technology. And, as Arthur C. Clarke famously wrote, 'any sufficiently advanced technology is indistinguishable from magic.'

That brings us to test automation. As a tester or test manager, one of your problems is that developers keep changing the product. They introduce new bugs in what used to work. You're responsible for finding those bugs. To do that, you re-execute tests you've already run. The yield (bugs found per test) is low. You need a way to make the cost (human effort) correspondingly low. Only then can you escape the trap of spending so much time re-running old tests that you have no time to create new ones.

So why not give your money to a magician (test automation tool vendor) and receive a magical object (testing tool) that will make the problem go away? Simply create the test once and let the tool take it from there. Why not? The technology isn't sufficiently advanced. In untutored hands, the magic object won't work. Without the magician's touch, it will be dead . . . rotting . . . a destructive distraction from the job of finding bugs.

That's where this book comes in. It will teach you how to make automated testing tools useful, instead of a big rat hole down which to pour your precious time and budget. It embodies the experience of a fantastic number of people who have suffered through trial and error. Reports about what they've learned have been too scattered: a conference paper here, a few pages in a book there, a conversation over beers somewhere else. Mark Fewster and Dorothy Graham have taken that scattered experience and made it accessible, concise, specific, and systematic.

I wish I'd read this book in 1981. I'd have spent less time trying and much less time erring.

Brian Marick
Principal SQA Practitioner,
Reliable Software Technologies

Preface

What this book is about

This book describes how to structure and build an automated testing regime that will give lasting benefits in the use of test execution tools to automate testing on a medium to large scale. We include practical advice for selecting the right tool and for implementing automated testing practices within an organization.

An extensive collection of case studies and guest chapters are also included, reflecting both good and bad experiences in test automation together with useful advice.

Who is this book for?

This book is intended to be of most help to those starting out on the road to automation, so they do not have to spend time discovering the hard way the most likely problems and how to avoid them.

The target audience for this book includes:

- potential and recent purchasers of test execution automation tools;
- those who already have a test execution automation tool but are having problems or are not achieving the benefit they should;
- people responsible for test automation within an organization;
- anyone who is building an in-house test execution automation tool;
- technical managers who want to insure that test automation provides benefits;
- testers and test managers who want to insure that tests are automated well;
- management consultants and test consultants;
- test tool vendors.

Why should I read this book?

If you want to automate testing (not just automate a few standalone tests) then this book will be useful to you. Specifically:

- if you automate on a small scale, you will pick up some useful tips;
- if you automate hundreds of tests, this book will help you do so efficiently;
- if you automate thousands of tests, you will be more certain of long-term success if you follow the advice given in this book (or have discovered it for yourself).

You do *not* need to read this book:

- if you plan to run all your tests manually, forever;
- if you only hope to automate a few tests, say up to a dozen or so;
- if your tests will only be run once and will never be needed again;
- if you don't care that your test automation actually takes longer and costs more than manual testing.

The more tests you automate, the more benefit you can gain from this book.

Spaghetti tests?

An analogy for the main subject of this book is structured programming. Before structured techniques were used, there was little discipline in software engineering practices. It appeared that all you needed to know was a programming language and how to work the compiler. This led to serious problems with 'spaghetti code,' i.e. code that was difficult to understand, hard to test, and expensive to maintain. The search for a solution led eventually to a disciplined approach, where requirements were analyzed and software designed before the code was written. The benefits of a structured approach included greatly increased maintainability, understandability, and testability of the software produced.

Today, test execution tools are very popular, particularly capture replay tools, but there is little discipline in the design of the test automation in many organizations. The obvious benefits of test execution tools are in automating a tedious but necessary task, that of regression testing. However, there is an assumption that all you need to know is a scripting language and how to work the test execution tool. This approach leads to 'spaghetti tests' that are hard to understand and difficult and expensive to maintain, thereby negating the benefits of automating testing. This book is about 'testware design techniques' that are parallel to the 'software design techniques' of 20 or more years ago.

What this book does not include

We do not include any information about specific tools currently on the market (except where they are mentioned in the case studies in Part 2). This is intentional, for two reasons. First, this book is about techniques that are applicable using any test execution tool, available now or in the near future. This book therefore contains generic principles that are not restricted to any existing specific tools. Second, the test execution tool market is very volatile, so any specific information would soon become out of date.

This book does not include techniques for testing, i.e. for designing good test cases. Although an important topic, it is outside the scope of this book (that's our next project).

This book covers the automation of test execution, not the automatic generation of test inputs, for reasons explained in Chapter 1.

How to read this book

This book is designed so that you can dip into it without having to read all of the preceding chapters. There are two parts to the book. Part 1 is technical and will give you the techniques you need to construct an efficient test automation regime. Part 2 contains case studies of test automation in a variety of organizations and with varying degrees of success, plus some guest chapters giving useful advice. Any chapter in Part 2 can be read on its own, although there are two sets of paired chapters. A guided tour of the content of the case studies is given in the introduction to Part 2.

We have used some terms in this book that are often understood differently in different organizations. We have defined our meaning of these terms in the Glossary at the end of the book. Glossary terms appear in bold type the first time they are used in the book.

The table on the next page shows our recommendations for the chapters that you may like to read first, depending on your objectives.

Guided tour to Part 1: techniques for automating test execution

Each chapter in Part 1 concludes with a summary, which contains an overview of what is covered in that chapter. Here we outline the main points of each chapter.

Chapter 1 is a general introduction to the content of the book. We discuss testing and the difference between the testing discipline and the subject of this book, and we explain why we have concentrated on test execution automation.

If you have not yet experienced the difference between post-purchase euphoria and the grim reality of what a tool will and will not do for you,

If you are:	Read these chapters first
Shopping for a test execution tool	1, 2, and 10
A manager wondering why test automation has failed	1, 2, 7, and 8
Using a test execution tool to automate tests, i.e. you will be writing scripts, etc.	2, 3, 4, and 5 (and then 6, 7, 8, and 9)
Concerned with achieving the best benefits from testing and test automation	1 and 8
Having difficulty persuading other people in your organization to use the tools you already have in place	1 and 11
Wanting to know what other people have done	Any chapter in Part 2
Wanting to know why we think we know the answers to the problems of test automation	12
Having problems with maintenance of automated tests	7, then 3 and 5
Wanting to know what other people advise	22, 24, 26, 27, and 28
Interested in 'failure' stories	19, then 13

Chapter 2 will open your eyes. A simple application ('Scribble') is tested manually and then taken through typical initial stages of the use of a capture replay tool.

Chapters 3–9 contain the technical content of the book. Chapter 3 describes five different scripting techniques. Chapter 4 discusses automated comparison techniques. Chapter 5 describes a practical testware architecture. Chapter 6 covers automation of set-up and clear-up activities. Chapter 7 concentrates on testware maintenance. Chapter 8 discusses metrics for measuring the quality of both testing and of an automation regime. Chapter 9 brings together a number of other important topics.

The next two chapters deal with tool evaluation and selection (Chapter 10) and tool implementation within the organization (Chapter 11).

Acknowledgments

We would like to thank the following people for reviewing early drafts of this book: Yohann Agalawatte, Steve Allott, Ståle Amland, Hans Buwalda, Greg Daich, Peter Danson, Norman Fenton, Dave Gelperin, Paul Gerrard, David Hedley, Bill Hetzel, Herb Isenberg, Ed Kit, David Law, Shari Lawrence-Pfleeger, Aiden Magill, Pat McGee, Geoff Quentin, David Ramsay, Krystyna Rogers, Hans Schaefer, Melanie Smith, Graham Titterington, Otto Vinter, Jelena Vujatov, Stuart Walker, Robin Webb, and Kerry Zallar.

We are particularly grateful to the authors of the case studies, for taking the time out of their busy schedules to prepare their material. Thanks to Keiron Marsden for bringing up to date the case history in Chapter 12, Marnie Hutcheson for sharing insights and lessons learned, and Clive Bates, Peter Oakley, Paul Herzlich, Simon Mills, Steve Allott, Bob Bartlett, Susan Windsor and Lloyd Roden for chapters on automation in various UK industries. Special thanks to Marnie Hutcheson and Ståle Amland for sharing experiences that were not as successful as they might have been, and to all the authors for their honesty about problems encountered. Thanks to two sets of authors who have given us a description and experience story of using what we consider to be good ways of achieving efficient and maintainable automation: Hans Buwalda and Iris Pinkster for the 'Action Words' approach, and Graham Freeburn, Graham Dwyer, and Jim Thomson for the 'RadSTAR' approach. We are particularly grateful to the US authors of the final three chapters: Linda Hayes has kindly given permission to reproduce a number of sections from her *Test Automation Handbook*, Chip Groder has shared his insights in building effective test automation for GUI systems over many years, and Angela Smale gives useful advice based on her experiences of automating the testing for different applications at Microsoft. Thanks to Roger Graham for his support and for writing our example application 'Scribble'. Thanks to Sally Mortimore, our editor, for her support, enthusiasm, and patience over the past three years.

We would also like to thank those who have attended our tutorials and courses on test automation and have helped us to clarify our ideas and the way in which we communicate them.

Some parts of this book first appeared in different forms in the following publications:

The CAST Report, Cambridge Market Intelligence, 1995 (Chapters 10 and 11)
The Journal of Software Testing, Verification and Reliability, 1991, Sigma Press, now published by Wiley (Chapter 12)
Proceedings of the International Conference on Testing Computer Software, 1991 (Chapter 12)
Proceedings of the EuroSTAR conference, 1993 (Chapter 7).

Please accept our apologies if we have not included anyone in this acknowledgment that we should have.

Mark Fewster and Dorothy Graham, May 1999
http://www.grove.co.uk

Mark Fewster

Mark has 20 years of industrial experience in software engineering, half of this specializing in software testing. He has been a software developer and manager for a multi-platform graphical application vendor, where he was responsible for the implementation of a testing improvement programme and the successful development and implementation of a testing tool which led to dramatic and lasting savings for the company.

Mark spent two years as a consultant for a commercial software testing tool vendor, providing training and consultancy in both test automation and testing techniques.

Since joining Grove Consultants in 1993, Mark has provided consultancy and training in software testing to a wide range of companies. As a consultant, Mark has helped many organizations to improve their testing practices through improved process and better use of testing tools.

Mark serves on the committee of the British Computer Society's Specialist Interest Group in Software Testing (BCS SIGIST). He has also been a member of the Information Systems Examination Board (ISEB) working on a qualification scheme for testing professionals and served on the BCS SIGIST working party that drafted the Software Component Testing Standard BS7925-1. He has published papers in respected journals and is a popular speaker at national and international conferences and seminars.

Dorothy Graham

Dorothy has worked in the area of Software Testing for more than 25 years, first for Bell Telephone Laboratories in New Jersey and then with Ferranti Computer Systems in the UK. Before founding Grove Consultants she worked for the National Computing Centre developing and presenting software engineering training courses.

She originated the *CAST Report* on Computer-Aided Software Testing Tools, published by Cambridge Market Intelligence, and is co-author with Tom Gilb of *Software Inspection* (Addison-Wesley, 1993). She has written articles for a number of technical journals, and is a frequent and popular keynote and tutorial speaker at national and international conferences and seminars.

Dot was Programme Chair for the first EuroSTAR Conference in 1993. She is on the editorial boards of the Journal for *Software Testing, Verification and Reliability* and the *Software Testing & Quality Engineering* magazine, and is a board member for the International Conference on Testing Computer Software (an annual conference in Washington DC USA) and the Information Systems Examination Board for Software Testing (ISEB).

Grave Consultants' Web site: www.grove.co.uk

PART ONE

Techniques for automating test execution

Trademark notice

TestFrame™ is a trademark of CMG Automator; QA™, QA Centre™, QARun™ are trademarks of Compuware; SQA Robot™, SQA Team Test™, SQA Manager™, V-Test™ are trademarks of Cyrano (formerly Systems FX); DEC VMS™ is a trademark of DEC Digital Test Manger; (DTM)™ is a trademark of Digital; RadSTAR™ is a trademark of IMI Systems Inc./Integrated Computer Technologies Ltd; 123™ is a trademark of Lotus; WinRunner™, XRunner™ are trademarks of Mercury Interactive; Windows®95, Windows®98, NT, 3.1™, Word®, Excel™, FoxPro™, IE3™, IE4™, Source Safe™ are registered trademarks and trademarks of Microsoft Corporation; Oracle™, Personal Oracle™ are trademarks of Oracle; PSenterprise™ is a trademark of Peterborough Software; PRODIGY™, Gremlin™ are trademarks of Prodigy Services Company; QA Partner™, AutoTester™ are trademarks of Segue Software Inc; SQL Anywhere™ is a trademark of Sybase; QEMM™ is a trademark of Quarterdeck International Ltd; SPSS® is a registered trademark of SPSS (UK) Ltd.

Permissions acknowledgment

The publisher and the authors would like to thank the following for permission to reproduce material in this book.

Paul Godsafe for the Experience Report (p. 41) about Squat the robot dog, from his presentation 'Automated testing', at the *British Association of Research Quality Assurance 13th International Conference*, May 1998, Glasgow; Computer Weekly for the Experience Report (p. 61) *Bug in jet engine downs Microsoft's high-flyer*, published on 10 September 1998, Computer Weekly, Quadrant House, The Quandrant, Sutton, Surrey SM2 5AS UK; Herb Isenberg, for the Experience Report (p. 97) adapted from 'Flexible testing systems', published in *Dr Dobb's Journal*, June 1995, pp. 88–95. Dr Dobb's Journal, P.O. Box 56188, Boulder, CO 80322–6188 USA; Robert Glass for Experience Report (p. 282) 'Testing automation, a horror story', originally published in *The Software Practitioner*, Mar–Apr 1995, published by Computing Trends, 1416 Sare Road, Bloomington, Indiana 47401 USA; Chris Kemerer (p. 284), for information from 'How the learning curve affects CASE tool adoption', published in *IEEE Software*, May 1992, IEEE Service Center, 445 Hoes Lane, Piscataway, NJ 08855–1331 USA.

The section supplied by Susan Windsor and Bob Bartlett is gratefully received from SIM Group Ltd as a small representation of the many fascinating success stories SIM Group has achieved with automated testing over the years. The fact that SIM Group have consistently made significant differences to projects through the use of automated testing is reason enough for this book to exist.

The Publishers and the Authors wish to thank Angela Smale (nee McAuley) for permission to include details of her experience as a Test Manager at Microsoft Corporation in Chapter 28.

CHAPTER ONE

Test automation context

At first glance, it seems easy to automate testing: just buy one of the popular **test execution tools,** record the manual tests, and play them back whenever you want to. Unfortunately, as those who tried it have discovered, it doesn't work like that in practice. Just as there is more to software design than knowing a programming language, there is more to automating testing than knowing a testing tool.

1.1 Introduction

Software must be tested to have confidence that it will work as it should in its intended environment. Software testing needs to be effective at finding any **defects** which are there, but it should also be efficient, performing the tests as quickly and cheaply as possible.

Automating software testing can significantly reduce the effort required for adequate testing, or significantly increase the testing which can be done in limited time. Tests can be run in minutes that would take hours to run manually. The case studies included in this book show how different organizations have been able to automate testing, some saving significant amounts of money. Savings as high as 80% of manual testing effort have been achieved. Some organizations have not saved money or effort directly but their test automation has enabled them to produce better quality software more quickly than would have been possible by manual testing alone.

A mature test automation regime will allow testing at the 'touch of a button' with tests run overnight when machines would otherwise be idle. Automated tests are repeatable, using exactly the same inputs in the same sequence time and again, something that cannot be guaranteed with manual testing. Automated testing enables even the smallest of maintenance changes to be fully tested with minimal effort. Test automation also eliminates many menial chores. The more boring testing seems, the greater the need for tool support.

This book will explain the issues involved in successfully automating software testing. The emphasis is on technical design issues for **automated testware**. **Testware** is the set of files needed for ('automated') testing, including scripts, inputs, expected outcomes, set-up and clear-up procedures, files, databases, environments, and any additional software or utilities used in automated testing. (See the Glossary for definitions of terms used in this book, which appear in bold the first time they are used.)

In this introductory chapter we look at testing in general and the automation of (parts of) testing. We explain why we think test execution and result comparison is more appropriate to automate than test design, and describe the benefits, problems, and limitations of test automation.

A regime is a system of government. This book is about how to set up a regime for test automation. A **test automation regime** determines, among other things, how test automation is managed, the approaches used in implementing automated tests, and how testware is organized.

1.2 Testing and test automation are different

1.2.1 Testing

Testing is a skill. While this may come as a surprise to some people it is a simple fact. For any system there is an astronomical number of possible test cases and yet practically we have time to run only a very small number of them. Yet this small number of test cases is expected to find most of the defects in the software, so the job of selecting which test cases to build and run is an important one. Both experiment and experience have told us that selecting test cases at random is not an effective approach to testing. A more thoughtful approach is required if good test cases are to be developed.

What exactly is a good test case? There are four attributes that describe the quality of a test case; that is, how good it is. Perhaps the most important of these is its defect detection effectiveness, whether or not it finds defects, or at least whether or not it is likely to find defects. A good test case should also be exemplary. An exemplary test case should test more than one thing, thereby reducing the total number of test cases required. The other two attributes are both cost considerations: how economical a test case is to perform, analyze, and debug; and how evolvable it is, i.e. how much maintenance effort is required on the test case each time the software changes.

These four attributes must often be balanced one against another. For example, a single test case that tests a lot of things is likely to cost a lot to perform, analyze, and debug. It may also require a lot of maintenance each time the software changes. Thus a high measure on the exemplary scale is likely to result in low measures on the economic and evolvable scales.

So the skill of testing is not only in ensuring that test cases will find a high proportion of defects, but also ensuring that the test cases are well designed to avoid excessive costs.

1.2.2 Test automation

Automating tests is also a skill but a very different skill from testing. Many organizations are surprised to find that it is more expensive to automate a test than to perform it once manually. In order to gain benefits from test automation, the tests to be automated need to be carefully selected and implemented. Automated quality is independent of test quality.

Whether a **test** is automated or performed manually affects neither its effectiveness nor how exemplary it is. It doesn't matter how clever you are at automating a test or how well you do it, if the test itself achieves nothing then the end result is a test that achieves nothing faster. Automating a test affects only how economic and evolvable it is. Once implemented, an automated test is generally much more economic, the cost of running it being a mere fraction of the effort to perform it manually. However, automated tests generally cost more to create and maintain. The better the approach to automating tests the cheaper it will be to implement them in the long term. If no thought is given to maintenance when tests are automated, updating an entire automated test suite can cost as much, if not more, than the cost of performing all of the tests manually.

Figure 1.1 shows the four quality attributes of a test case in a Keviat diagram. A test case performed manually is shown by the solid lines. When that same test is automated for the first time, it will have become less evolvable and less economic (since it has taken more effort to automate it). After the automated test has been run a number of times it will become much more economic than the same test performed manually.

For an effective and efficient suite of automated tests you have to start with the raw ingredient of a good test suite, a set of tests skillfully designed by a **tester** to exercise the most important things. You then have to apply automation skills to automate the tests in such a way that they can be created and maintained at a reasonable cost.

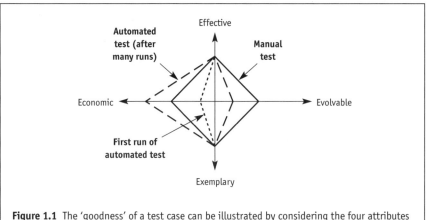

Figure 1.1 The 'goodness' of a test case can be illustrated by considering the four attributes in this Keviat diagram. The greater the measure of each attribute the greater the area enclosed by the joining lines and the better the test case.

The person who builds and maintains the artifacts associated with the use of a test execution tool is the **test automator**. A test automator may or may not also be a tester; he or she may or may not be a member of a test team. For example, there may be a test team consisting of user testers with business knowledge and no technical software development skills. A developer may have the responsibility of supporting the test team in the construction and maintenance of the automated implementation of the tests designed by the test team. This developer is the test automator.

It is possible to have either good or poor quality testing. It is the skill of the tester which determines the quality of the testing.

It is also possible to have either good or poor quality automation. It is the skill of the test automator which determines how easy it will be to add new automated tests, how maintainable the automated tests will be, and ultimately what benefits test automation will provide.

1.3 The V-model

Having made the important distinction between testing and automation, we return to the topic of testing in more detail. Testing is often considered something which is done after software has been written; after all, the argument runs, you can't test something that doesn't exist, can you? This idea makes the assumption that testing is merely test execution, the running of tests. Of course, tests cannot be executed without having software that actually works. But testing activities include more than just running tests.

The V-model of software development illustrates when testing activities should take place. The V-model shows that each development activity has a corresponding test activity. The tests at each level exercise the corresponding development activity. The same principles apply no matter what software life cycle model is used. For example, Rapid Application Development (RAD) is a series of small Vs.

The simplified V-model in Figure 1.2 shows four levels of development and testing activity. Different organizations may have different names for each stage; it is important that each stage on the left has a partner on the right, whatever each is called.

The most important factor for successful application of the V-model is the issue of *when* the test cases are designed. The test design activity always finds defects in whatever the tests are designed against. For example, designing acceptance test cases will find defects in the requirements, designing system test cases will find defects in the functional specification, designing integration test cases will find defects in the design, and designing unit test cases will find defects in the code. If test design is left until the last possible moment, these defects will only be found immediately before those tests would be run, when it is more expensive to fix them.

Test design does not have to wait until just before tests are run; it can be done at any time after the information which those tests are based on becomes available. Then the effect of finding defects is actually beneficial rather than destructive, because the defects can be corrected before they are propagated.

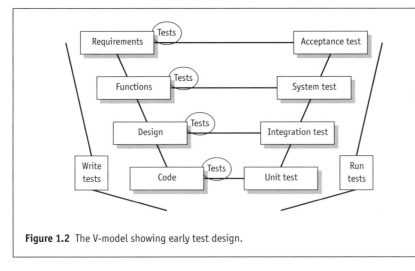

Figure 1.2 The V-model showing early test design.

Of course, the tests cannot be run until the software has been written, but they can be written early. The tests are actually run in the reverse order to their writing, e.g. unit tests are written last but are run first.

1.4 Tool support for life-cycle testing

Tool support is available for testing in every stage of the software development life cycle; the different types of tools and their position within the life cycle are shown in Figure 1.3, using alternative names for development stages.

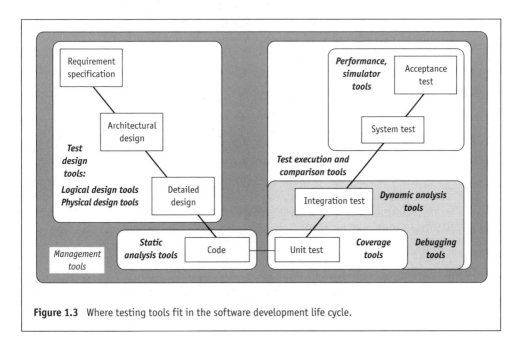

Figure 1.3 Where testing tools fit in the software development life cycle.

Test design tools help to derive **test inputs** or **test data**. Logical design tools work from the logic of a specification, an interface or from code, and are sometimes referred to as test case generators. Physical design tools manipulate existing data or generate test data. For example, a tool that can extract random records from a database would be a physical design tool. A tool that can derive test inputs from a specification would be a logical design tool. We discuss logical design tools more fully in Section 1.8.

Test management tools include tools to assist in test planning, keeping track of what tests have been run, and so on. This category also includes tools to aid traceability of tests to requirements, designs, and code, as well as defect tracking tools.

Static analysis tools analyze code without executing it. This type of tool detects certain types of defect much more effectively and cheaply than can be achieved by any other means. Such tools also calculate various metrics for the code such as McCabe's cyclomatic complexity, Halstead metrics, and many more.

Coverage tools assess how much of the software under test has been exercised by a set of tests. Coverage tools are most commonly used at unit test level. For example, branch coverage is often a requirement for testing safety-critical or safety-related systems. Coverage tools can also measure the coverage of design level constructs such as call trees.

Debugging tools are not really testing tools, since debugging is not part of testing. (Testing identifies defects, debugging removes them and is therefore a development activity, not a testing activity.) However, debugging tools are often used in testing, especially when trying to isolate a low-level defect. Debugging tools enable the developer to step through the code by executing one instruction at a time and looking at the contents of data locations.

Dynamic analysis tools assess the system while the software is running. For example, tools that can detect memory leaks are dynamic analysis tools. A memory leak occurs if a program does not release blocks of memory when it should, so the block has 'leaked' out of the pool of memory blocks available to all programs. Eventually the faulty program will end up 'owning' all of the memory; nothing can run, the system 'hangs up' and must be rebooted (in a non-protected mode operating system).

Simulators are tools that enable parts of a system to be tested in ways which would not be possible in the real world. For example, the meltdown procedures for a nuclear power plant can be tested in a simulator.

Another class of tools have to do with what we could call capacity testing. **Performance testing** tools measure the time taken for various events. For example, they can measure response times under typical or load conditions. **Load testing** tools generate system traffic. For example, they may generate a number of transactions which represent typical or maximum levels. This type of tool may be used for **volume** and **stress testing**.

Test execution and comparison tools enable tests to be executed automatically and the **test outcomes** to be compared to **expected outcomes**. These tools are applicable to test execution at any level: unit, integration, system, or acceptance testing. Capture replay tools are test execution and comparison tools. This is the most popular type of testing tool in use, and is the focus of this book.

1.5 The promise of test automation

Test automation can enable some testing tasks to be performed far more efficiently than could ever be done by testing manually. There are also other benefits, including those listed below.

1. Run existing (regression) tests on a new version of a program. This is perhaps the most obvious task, particularly in an environment where many programs are frequently modified. The effort involved in performing a set of regression tests should be minimal. Given that the tests already exist and have been automated to run on an earlier version of the program, it should be possible to select the tests and initiate their execution with just a few minutes of manual effort.

2. Run more tests more often. A clear benefit of automation is the ability to run more tests in less time and therefore to make it possible to run them more often. This will lead to greater confidence in the system. Most people assume that they will run the same tests faster with automation. In fact they tend to run more tests, and those tests are run more often.

3. Perform tests which would be difficult or impossible to do manually. Attempting to perform a full-scale live test of an online system with say 200 users may be impossible, but the input from 200 users can be simulated using automated tests. By having end users define tests that can be replayed automatically, user scenario tests can be run at any time even by technical staff who do not understand the intricacies of the full business application.

   When testing manually, expected outcomes typically include the obvious things that are visible to the tester. However, there are attributes that should be tested which are not easy to verify manually. For example a **graphical user interface (GUI)** object may trigger some event that does not produce any immediate output. A test execution tool may be able to check that the event has been triggered, which would not be possible to check without using a tool.

4. Better use of resources. Automating menial and boring tasks, such as repeatedly entering the same test inputs, gives greater accuracy as well as improved staff morale, and frees skilled testers to put more effort into designing better test cases to be run. There will always be some testing which is best done manually; the testers can do a better job of manual testing if there are far fewer tests to be run manually.

   Machines that would otherwise lie idle overnight or at the weekend can be used to run automated tests.

5. Consistency and repeatability of tests. Tests that are repeated automatically will be repeated exactly every time (at least the inputs will be; the

outputs may differ due to timing, for example). This gives a level of consistency to the tests which is very difficult to achieve manually.

The same tests can be executed on different hardware configurations, using different operating systems, or using different databases. This gives a consistency of cross-platform quality for multi-platform products which is virtually impossible to achieve with manual testing.

The imposition of a good automated testing regime can also insure consistent standards both in testing and in development. For example, the tool can check that the same type of feature has been implemented in the same way in every application or program.

6. Reuse of tests. The effort put into deciding what to test, designing the tests, and building the tests can be distributed over many executions of those tests. Tests which will be reused are worth spending time on to make sure they are reliable. This is also true of manual tests, but an automated test would be reused many more times than the same test repeated manually.

7. Earlier time to market. Once a set of tests has been automated, it can be repeated far more quickly than it would be manually, so the testing elapsed time can be shortened (subject to other factors such as availability of developers to fix defects).

8. Increased confidence. Knowing that an extensive set of automated tests has run successfully, there can be greater confidence that there won't be any unpleasant surprises when the system is released (providing that the tests being run are good tests!).

In summary, more thorough testing can be achieved with less effort, giving increases in both quality and productivity.

1.6 Common problems of test automation

There are a number of problems that may be encountered in trying to automate testing. Problems which come as a complete surprise are usually more difficult to deal with, so having some idea of the type of problems you may encounter should help you in implementing your own automation regime. Most problems can be overcome, and this book is intended to help you deal with them. We describe some of the more common problems below.

1. Unrealistic expectations. Our industry is known for latching onto any new technical solution and thinking it will solve all of our current problems. Testing tools are no exception. There is a tendency to be optimistic about what can be achieved by a new tool. It is human nature to hope that this solution will at last solve all of the problems we are currently experiencing. Vendors naturally emphasize the benefits and successes, and may play down the amount of effort needed to achieve lasting benefits. The effect of optimism and salesmanship together is to encourage unrealistic expectations. If management expectations are unrealistic,

then no matter how well the tool is implemented from a technical point of view, it will not meet expectations.

2. Poor testing practice. If testing practice is poor, with poorly organized tests, little or inconsistent documentation, and tests that are not very good at finding defects, automating testing is not a good idea. It is far better to improve the effectiveness of testing first than to improve the efficiency of poor testing.

Automating chaos just gives faster chaos.

---

3. Expectation that automated tests will find a lot of new defects. A test is most likely to find a defect the first time it is run. If a test has already run and passed, running the same test again is much less likely to find a new defect, unless the test is exercising code that has been changed or could be affected by a change made in a different part of the software, or is being run in a different environment.

   Test execution tools are 'replay' tools, i.e. regression testing tools. Their use is in repeating tests that have already run. This is a very useful thing to do, but it is not likely to find a large number of new defects, particularly when run in the same hardware and software environment as before.

   Tests that do not find defects are not worthless, even though good test design should be directed at trying to find defects. Knowing that a set of tests has passed again gives confidence that the software is still working as well as it was before, and that changes elsewhere have not had unforeseen effects.

4. False sense of security. Just because a test suite runs without finding any defects, it does not mean that there are no defects in the software. The tests may be incomplete, or may contain defects themselves. If the expected outcomes are incorrect, automated tests will simply preserve those defective results indefinitely.

5. Maintenance of automated tests. When software is changed it is often necessary to update some, or even all, of the tests so they can be re-run successfully. This is particularly true for automated tests. Test maintenance effort has been the death of many test automation initiatives. When it takes more effort to update the tests than it would take to re-run those tests manually, test automation will be abandoned. One of the purposes of this book is to help you make sure that your test automation initiative does not fall victim to high maintenance costs.

6. Technical problems. Commercial test execution tools are software products, sold by vendor companies. As third-party software products, they are not immune from defects or problems of support. It is perhaps a double disappointment to find that a testing tool has not been well tested, but unfortunately, it does happen.

   Interoperability of the tool with other software, either your own applications or third-party products, can be a serious problem. The technological environment changes so rapidly that it is hard for the vendors to keep up. Many tools have looked ideal on paper, but have simply failed to work in some environments.

The commercial test execution tools are large and complex products, and detailed technical knowledge is required in order to gain the best from the tool. Training supplied by the vendor or distributor is essential for all those who will use the tool directly, particularly the test automator(s) (the people who automate the tests).

In addition to technical problems with the tools themselves, you may experience technical problems with the software you are trying to test. If software is not designed and built with testability in mind, it can be very difficult to test, either manually or automatically. Trying to use tools to test such software is an added complication which can only make test automation even more difficult.

7. Organizational issues. Automating testing is not a trivial exercise, and it needs to be well supported by management and implemented into the culture of the organization. Time must be allocated for choosing tools, for training, for experimenting and learning what works best, and for promoting tool use within the organization.

An automation effort is unlikely to be successful unless there is one person who is the focal point for the use of the tool, the tool 'champion.' Typically, the champion is a person who is excited about automating testing, and will communicate his or her enthusiasm within the company. This person may be involved in selecting what tool to buy, and will be very active in promoting its use internally. More detail on the role of the champion is given in Chapters 10 and 11.

Test automation is an infrastructure issue, not just a project issue. In larger organizations, test automation can rarely be justified on the basis of a single project, since the project will bear all of the start-up costs and teething problems and may reap little of the benefits. If the scope of test automation is only for one project, people will then be assigned to new projects, and the impetus will be lost. Test automation often falls into decay at precisely the time it could provide the most value, i.e. when the software is updated. Standards are needed to insure consistent ways of using the tools throughout the organization. Otherwise every group may develop different approaches to test automation, making it difficult to transfer or share automated tests and testers between groups.

Even a seemingly minor administrative issue such as having too few licenses for the people who want to use the tool can seriously impact the success and the cost of a test automation effort.

Perceptions of work effort may also change. If a test is run overnight, then when the testers arrive in the morning, they will need to spend some time looking through the results of the tests. This test analysis time is now clearly visible as a separate activity. When those tests were run manually, this test analysis time was embedded in the test execution activity, and was therefore not visible.

Whenever a new tool (or indeed any new process) is implemented, there are inevitably adjustments that need to be made to adapt to new ways of working, which must be managed. Chapter 11 discusses ways in which you can insure successful implementation of test automation within an organization.

EXPERIENCE REPORT: SPURIOUS DEFECT PRESERVED

A client had a geographical information system that produced maps showing various underground structures, both artificial and natural. The company had an automated testing system that it was very proud of, as it had been in continuous use for over three years. Every release of the software had to pass the automated tests before it could be released.

The client was somewhat mystified at an error reported by a customer, where there were structures shown on the map produced by the software that should not have been there. Further investigation revealed that three spurious circles were included in the expected outcome for that particular map. The automated tests had insured that the defect had been preserved over all releases of the software for three years.

1.7 Test activities

In this section, we describe testing activities, since these are the activities that we may want to automate. There is wide variation in the way in which these activities are carried out in different organizations. Some organizations will perform all of these activities formally. Others may be informal to the point of being almost chaotic. In any case, the core activities are still carried out more or less in the sequence described in Figure 1.4.

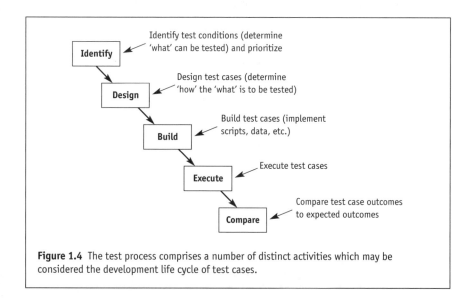

Figure 1.4 The test process comprises a number of distinct activities which may be considered the development life cycle of test cases.

In an ideal world, testing should start with the setting of organizational test objectives and test policy, the setting of test strategies to meet test objectives, and policies and strategies for individual projects. Test planning at the management level would include estimating the time required for all test activities, scheduling and resourcing of test activities, monitoring the progress of testing, and taking any actions required to keep the entire test effort on track. These high-level activities should be done at the beginning of a project and continued throughout its development.

Test cases will typically be developed for various functional areas of the system to be tested. Each of these test cases will go through five distinct development activities (not including re-testing). The five test development activities are sequential for any one test case, i.e. the test conditions must be identified before a test case for those conditions can be designed, a test case must be designed before it can be built, built before it can be run, and run before its results can be compared. The five steps may be done formally, with documentation at each step, or all five steps may be done informally when the tester sits down to test.

Note that there are many variations of terminology in testing. We have defined what we mean by each term in the Glossary.

1.7.1 Identify test conditions

The first activity is to determine 'what' can be tested and ideally to priori-tize these test conditions. A **test condition** is an item or event that could be verified by a test. There will be many different test conditions for a system, and for different categories of test, such as functionality tests, performance tests, security tests, etc.

Testing techniques help testers derive test conditions in a rigorous and systematic way. A number of books on testing describe testing techniques such as **equivalence partitioning**, **boundary value analysis**, cause–effect graphing, and others. A bibliography about books on testing and other topics can be found on the authors' web site (http://www.grove.co.uk). These include Kit (1995), Marick (1995), Beizer (1990, 1995), Kaner *et al.* (1993), Myers (1979), and Hetzel (1988).

Test conditions are descriptions of the circumstances that could be examined. They may be documented in different ways, including brief sen-tences, entries in tables, or in diagrams such as flow graphs.

Note that the activity of identifying test conditions is best done in paral-lel with the associated development activities, i.e. on the left-hand side of the V-model.

1.7.2 Design test cases

Test case design determines how the 'what' will be tested. A **test case** is a set of tests performed in a sequence and related to a **test objective**, i.e. the reason or purpose for the tests. Test case design will produce a number of tests comprising specific input values, expected outcomes, and any other information needed for the test to run, such as environment prerequisites.

Note that the expected outcomes include things that should be output or created, things that should be changed or updated (in a database, for example), things that should not be changed, and things that should be deleted. The set of expected outcomes could be of considerable size.

An example test case is given in Table 1.1. Note that the tester performing this test case would need to understand the purchase order system at least to the extent that he or she would know how to create a new order, verify a purchase order, print a new orders report, and so on.

The following three test conditions are exercised by this test case:

- order created for a single item (VB10);
- order quantity of 100 (VB23);
- order cancelled (V8).

The tags in parentheses at the end of each condition are used for cross-referencing between test conditions and test cases. The tags used here represent test conditions derived using equivalence partitioning and boundary value analysis. VB10 is the 10th Valid Boundary, VB23 is the 23rd Valid Boundary, and V8 is the 8th Valid **equivalence partition**.

Table 1.1 An example test case. This comprises five steps (each of which may be considered a single 'test') and exercises three different test conditions.

Test case: POS1036

Prerequisites:
- logged into the purchase order system as a data entry clerk with the main menu displayed;
- database system must contain the standard Data Set;
- there must be no other new purchase order activity on the system.

Step	Input	Expected outcome	Test conditions
1	Create a new order for any one standard order item, setting order quantity to exactly 100	Order confirmation message displayed	VB10 VB23
2	Confirm the order	Purchase order printed with correct details	VB10 VB23
3	Print a new orders report	New orders report printed showing just this one new order	VB10 VB23
4	Cancel the order	Purchase order cancellation notice printed with correct details	V8
5	Print a new orders report	Report printed showing no outstanding purchase orders	V8

This example test case is taken out of a larger set of test cases. It is assumed that we have already tested other aspects such as the correct printing of purchase orders. In this example test case, we are therefore using some 'trusted' functionality in order to test different aspects. In the last column we have noted the condition tags covered. Steps 2 and 3 also exercise the same tags as step 1, and step 4 and step 5 exercise V8.

Note that this style of test case is what we will define in Chapter 2 as a 'vague manual test script.'

Each test should specify the **expected outcome**. If the expected outcome is not specified in advance of it being run, then in order to check whether or not the software is correct, the first **actual outcome** should be carefully examined and verified. This will, of course, require a tester with adequate knowledge of the software under test to make a correct assessment of the outcome. If correct, it can then become the future expected outcome, i.e. the outcome to which future actual outcomes from this test can be automatically compared. This approach is referred to as **reference testing**. The validated expected outcome is sometimes referred to as the **golden version**.

Test case design (ideally with expected outcomes predicted in advance) is best done in parallel with the associated development activities on the left-hand side of the V-model, i.e. before the software to be tested has been built.

1.7.3 Build the test cases

The test cases are implemented by preparing test scripts, test inputs, test data, and expected outcomes. A **test script** is the data and/or instructions with a formal syntax, used by a test execution automation tool, typically held in a file. A test script can implement one or more test cases, navigation, **set-up** or **clear-up** procedures, or verification. A test script may or may not be in a form that can be used to run a test manually (a manual test script is a **test procedure**). The test inputs and expected outcome may be included as part of a script, or may be outside the script in a separate file or database.

The **preconditions** for the test cases must be implemented so that the tests can be executed. For example, if a test uses some data from a file or database, that file or database must be initialized to contain the information that the test expects to find.

A test case may require special hardware or software to be available, for example a network connection or a printer. This would also form part of the environment needed to be set up before the test case could be run.

The expected outcomes may be organized into files for automation tools to use. For manual testing, they may simply be notes on the manual test procedure or script. Setting up expected outcomes for automated comparison may be considerably more complex than setting up expected outcomes for manual testing. The tools require everything to be spelled out in great detail, so much more rigor is required than for manual testing.

Any aspects of the test building activity that can be prepared in advance, i.e. on the left-hand side of the V-model, will save time later.

The software under test is executed using the test cases. For manual testing, this may consist of the testers sitting down and possibly following a printed manual procedure. They would enter inputs, observe outcomes, and make notes about any problems as they go. For automated testing, this may involve starting the test tool and telling it which test cases to execute.

Test execution can only be done after the software exists, i.e. it is an activity on the right-hand side of the V-model.

1.7.5 Compare test outcomes to expected outcomes

The actual outcome of each test must be investigated to see if the software being tested worked correctly. This may be informal confirmation of what the tester expects to see, or it may be a rigorous and detailed comparison of the exact actual outcomes with expected outcomes. The comparison of some outcomes such as messages sent to a screen can be performed while the test is being executed. Other outcomes, such as a change to database records, can only be compared after the test case execution has completed. An automated test may need to use a combination of these two approaches. See Chapter 4 for more about comparison techniques.

The assumption is that if the actual and expected outcomes are the same, then the software has passed the test; if they are different, then the software has failed the test. This is actually an oversimplification. All we can say is that if the actual and expected outcomes do not match, then something needs to be investigated. It may be that the software is incorrect, or it could be that the test was run in the wrong sequence, the expected outcomes were incorrect, the test environment was not set up correctly, or the test was incorrectly specified.

There is a difference between comparing and verifying; a tool can compare but cannot verify. A tool can compare one set of test outcomes to another, and can flag any differences between the two. But the tool cannot say whether or not the outcomes are correct – this is verification, and is normally done by testers. It is the testers who confirm or insure that the results being compared are in fact correct. In some special circumstances, it is possible to automate the generation of expected outcomes but this is not the case for most of the industrial testing done using commercial test execution tools. See Poston (1996) for a discussion of automated oracles, reversers, and referencers.

1.8 Automate test design?

1.8.1 Activities amenable to automation

As shown in Figure 1.5, the first two test activities, identify test conditions and design test cases, are mainly intellectual in nature. The last two activities, execute test cases and compare test outcomes, are more clerical in nature. It is the intellectual activities that govern the quality of the test cases. The clerical activities are particularly labor intensive and are therefore well worth automating.

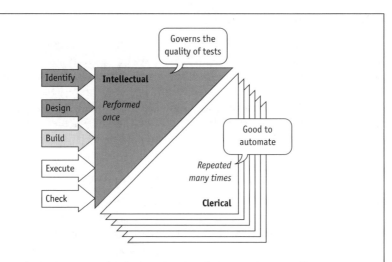

Figure 1.5 The testing process breaks down into five distinct activities. The first two are predominantly intellectual while the last two are predominantly clerical. The intellectual activities govern the quality of the final test cases but as a whole are performed only once. The clerical activities are usually performed many times, making them ideal candidates for automation.

In addition, the activities of test execution and comparison are repeated many times, while the activities of identifying test conditions and designing test cases are performed only once (except for rework due to errors in those activities). For example, if a test finds an **error** in the software, the repeated activities after the fix will be test execution and comparison. If a test fails for an environmental reason such as incorrect test data being used, the repeated test activities would be test building, execution, and comparison. If tests are to be run on different platforms, then those same three activities would be repeated for each platform. When software is changed, regression tests are run to insure that there are no side effects. A regression test will repeat the test execution and comparison activities (and possibly also test building). Activities that are repeated often are particularly good candidates for automation.

All of the test activities can be performed manually, as human testers have been doing for many years. All of the test activities can also benefit from tool support to some extent, but we believe it is in automating the latter test activities where there is most to gain.

The focus of this book is on the automation of the test execution and comparison activities. However, we cannot ignore the automation of test design activities in a book on test automation, since the output of such tools may (or may not) be in a format that can easily be used by a test execution tool. The next section discusses different types of test design automation tools. (Skip to Section 1.9 if this topic does not interest you.)

1.8.2 Automating test case design

Can the activities of test case design be automated? There are a number of ways in which testing tools can automate parts of test case design. These tools are sometimes called test input generation tools and their approach is useful in some contexts, but they will never completely replace the intellectual testing activities.

One problem with all test case design approaches is that the tool may generate a very large number of tests. Some tools include ways of minimizing the tests generated against the tester's specified criteria. However the tool may still generate far too many tests to be run in a reasonable time. The tool cannot distinguish which tests are the most important; this requires creative intelligence only available from human testers. A tool will never be able to answer questions such as: 'If we only have time to test 30% of what we could test, which are the most important test cases to run?' Even if the testing is automated, there may still be insufficient time to run 100% of the automated tests.

All test generation tools rely on algorithms to generate the tests. The tools will be more thorough and more accurate than a human tester using the same algorithm, so this is an advantage. However, a human being will think of additional tests to try, may identify aspects or requirements that are missing, or may be able to identify where the specification is incorrect based on personal knowledge. The best use of test generation tools is when the scope of what can and cannot be done by them is fully understood. (Actually that applies to the use of any tool!)

We will look at three types of test input generation tools, based on code, interfaces, and specifications.

1.8.2.1 Code-based test input generation

Code-based test input generation tools, shown in Figure 1.6, generate test inputs by examining the structure of the software code itself. A path through the code is composed of segments determined by branches at each decision point. A profile of the logical conditions required for each path segment can therefore be produced automatically. This is useful in conjunction with coverage measurement. For example, some coverage tools can identify logical path segments that have not been covered.

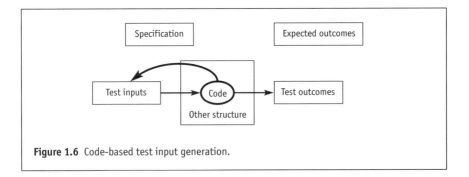

Figure 1.6 Code-based test input generation.

This approach generates test inputs, but a test also requires expected outcomes to compare against. Code-based test case design cannot tell whether the outcomes produced by the software are the correct values – it is the specification for the code that tells you what it should do. So this approach is incomplete, since it cannot generate expected outcomes. A **test oracle** is the source of what the correct outcome should be; code-based test input generation has no test oracle.

Another problem with this approach is that it only tests code that exists and cannot identify code that is missing. It is also testing that 'the code does what the code does.' This is generally not the most useful kind of testing, since we normally want to test that 'the code does what it should do.' (We once saw a defect report dismissed with the phrase: 'software works as coded' (not 'as specified').) This approach cannot find specification defects or missing specifications.

Another type of code-based test design automation can generate tests to satisfy weak mutation testing criteria. **Mutation testing** is where the code or an input is changed in some small way to see if the system can correctly deal with or detect this slightly mutated version. This is used to assess the fault tolerance of systems and the adequacy of test suites. For more information, see Voas and McGraw (1998).

1.8.2.2 Interface-based test generation

An **interface-based test** input generation tool, shown in Figure 1.7, is one that can generate tests based on some well-defined interface, such as a **GUI** or a web application. If a screen contains various menus, buttons, and check boxes, a tool can generate a test case that visits each one. For example, a tool could test that a check box has a cross in it when checked and is empty when not checked (similarly fundamental tests can be automated on other graphical interactors). Other examples include selecting each field and seeing if *Help* works, trying to edit data in all display-only fields, performing a spell check in help text and legends, and checking that something pops up when each menu item is selected.

A similar function is found in tools to test internet and intranet pages. The tool can activate each link on a World Wide Web page, and then do the same for each of the pages linked to, recursively.

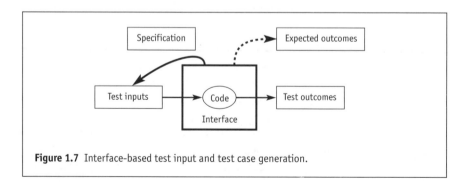

Figure 1.7 Interface-based test input and test case generation.

An interface-based approach is useful in identifying some types of defect (for example, any web page links that do not work can be identified). An expected outcome can be partially generated, but only in a very general sense and only negatively, i.e. a link should be there (correct result), not broken (incorrect result). This type of automated test generation cannot tell you whether working links are in fact linked to the right place.

This approach can therefore perform parts of the test design activity, generating test inputs (one test for each interface element identified by the tool), and can be a partial oracle, which enables some errors to be identified. It can be very useful in performing 'roll-call' testing, i.e. checking that everything which should be there is there. This type of testing is tedious to do manually, but is often very important to do thoroughly.

Tool support of this nature will probably increase in the future, and may help to free testers from tedious tasks so that they have more time to perform the intellectual testing activities.

1.8.2.3 Specification-based test generation

Specification-based test tools can generate test inputs and also expected outputs, provided that the specification is in a form that can be analyzed by the tool. This is shown in Figure 1.8. The specification may contain structured natural language constructs, such as business rules, or it may contain technical data such as states and transitions. Tools can derive tests from object-oriented specifications, if they are sufficiently rigorous. Hence these tools do have a test oracle.

For example, if the allowable ranges for an input field are rigorously defined, a tool can generate boundary values, as well as sample values in valid and invalid equivalence classes. For more information see Poston (1996).

Some specification-based tools can derive tests from structured English specifications, or from cause–effect graphs. This can identify some types of specification defect such as ambiguities and omissions.

A benefit of a specification-based approach is that the tests are looking at what the software should do, rather than what it does do, although only within the limited scope of the existing tool-examinable specification. The more tedious it is to derive test cases from a specification, the higher the potential for this type of tool.

Expected outcomes can be generated if they are stored in the specification, assuming that the stored specification is actually correct.

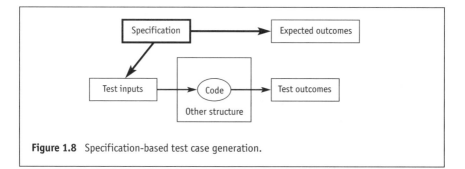

Figure 1.8 Specification-based test case generation.

1.8.2.4 *Summary of test design automation*

Summary of the benefits of automated test case generation:

- automates tedious aspects of test case design, such as activating every menu item or calculating boundary values from known data ranges;
- can generate a complete set of test cases with respect to their source (code, interface, or specification);
- can identify some types of defect, such as missing links, non-working window items, or software that does not conform to a stored specification.

Summary of the limitations of automated test case generation:

- code-based methods do not generate expected outcomes;
- interface-based methods can only generate partial expected outcomes;
- code-based and interface-based methods cannot find specification defects;
- specification-based methods depend on the quality of the specification;
- all methods may generate too many tests to be practical to run;
- human expertise is still needed to prioritize tests, to assess the usefulness of the generated tests, and to think of the tests that could never be generated by any tool.

It is our contention that the automation of the intellectual part of testing is much more difficult to do, and cannot be done as fully as automation of the more clerical part of testing. When we refer to 'automating software testing' in the rest of this book, we mean the automation of test execution and comparison activities, not the automation of test design or generation of test inputs.

1.9 The limitations of automating software testing

As with all good things, nothing comes without a price. Automated testing is not a panacea, and there are limitations to what it can accomplish.

1.9.1 Does not replace manual testing

It is not possible, nor is it desirable, to automate all testing activities or all tests. There will always be some testing that is much easier to do manually than automatically, or that is so difficult to automate it is not economic to do so. Tests that should probably not be automated include:

- tests that are run only rarely. For example if a test is run only once a year, then it is probably not worth automating that test;
- where the software is very volatile. For example, if the user interface and functionality change beyond recognition from one version to the next, the effort to change the automated tests to correspond is not likely to be cost effective;

- tests where the result is easily verified by a human, but is difficult if not impossible to automate; for example, the suitability of a color scheme, the esthetic appeal of a screen layout, or whether the correct audio plays when a given screen object is selected;
- tests that involve physical interaction, such as swiping a card through a card reader, disconnecting some equipment, turning power off or on.

Not all manual tests should be automated – only the best ones or the ones that will be re-run most often. A good testing strategy will also include some **exploratory** or **lateral testing**,[1] which is best done manually, at least at first. When software is unstable, manual testing will find defects very quickly.

1.9.2 Manual tests find more defects than automated tests

A test is most likely to reveal a defect the first time it is run. If a test case is to be automated, it first needs to be tested to make sure it is correct. (There is little point in automating defective tests!) The test of the test case is normally done by running the test case manually. If the software being tested has defects that the test case can reveal, it will be revealed at this point, when it is being run manually.

James Bach reported that in his (extensive) experience, automated tests found only 15% of the defects while manual testing found 85%.

Source: Bach, 1997

Once an automated test suite has been constructed, it is used to re-run tests. By definition, these tests have been run before, and therefore they are much less likely to reveal defects in the software this time. The test execution tools are not 'testing' tools, they are 're-testing' tools, i.e. regression testing tools.

1.9.3 Greater reliance on the quality of the tests

A tool can only identify differences between the actual and expected outcomes (i.e. compare). There is therefore a greater burden on the task of verifying the correctness of the expected outcomes in automated testing. The tool will happily tell you that all your tests have passed, when in fact they have only matched your expected outcomes.

It is therefore more important to be confident of the quality of the tests that are to be automated. Testware can be reviewed or inspected to insure

---

[1] Testing should be systematic, rigorous, and thorough in order to be effective at finding defects. However, there is also a valid role in testing for a more intuitive approach to supplement a rigorous approach. This is referred to in most testing books as '**error guessing**.' We prefer to call it 'lateral testing,' after the laterial thinking techniques of Edward De Bono.

its quality. Inspection is the most powerful review technique, and is very effective when used on test documentation. This technique is described in Gilb and Graham (1993).

1.9.4 Test automation does not improve effectiveness

Automating a set of tests does not make them any more effective (or exemplary) than those same tests run manually. Automation can eventually improve the efficiency of the tests; that is, how much they cost to run and how long they take to run. But it is likely that automation will adversely affect the evolvability of the test, as discussed in Section 1.2 and shown in Figure 1.1.

1.9.5 Test automation may limit software development

Automated tests are more 'fragile' than manual tests. They may be broken by seemingly innocuous changes to software. The techniques described in this book will help you produce automated tests that are less fragile than they would be otherwise, but they will always be more vulnerable to changes in the application software than manual tests.

Because automated tests take more effort to set up than manual tests, and because they require effort to maintain, this in itself may restrict the options for changing or enhancing software systems or applications. Software changes with a high impact on the automated testware may need to be discouraged for economic reasons.

1.9.6 Tools have no imagination

A tool is only software, and therefore can only obediently follow instructions. Both a tool and a tester can follow instructions to execute a set of test cases, but a human tester, given the same task, will perform it differently. For example, if a human tester is given the task of running a prepared test procedure, he or she may follow that procedure to begin with, and will check that the actual outcomes are correct. However, the tester may realize that although the software conforms to the expected outcomes, both are wrong. The human tester can also use his or her creativity and imagination to improve the tests as they are performed, either by deviating from the plan or preferably by noting additional things to test afterwards.

Another way in which human testers are superior to testing tools is when unexpected events happen that are not a part of the planned sequence of a test case. For example, if a network connection is lost and has to be re-established, a human tester will cope with the problem in the middle of the test, and do whatever is necessary. Sometimes, the tester will do this without even realizing that the test has deviated from the plan. However an unexpected event can stop an automated test in its tracks. Of course, the tools can be programmed to cope with some types of event, but just as astronauts have discovered, there is nothing like human ingenuity to overcome problems.

25

Summary

Summary

Test tools aren't magic – but, properly implemented, they can work wonders!

Source: Hayes, 1995

Test automation is not the same as testing, and the skills needed to be a good test automator are not the same skills needed to be a good tester.

Testing should fit into the software development process at every stage. Test cases are best identified and designed early (on the left-hand side of the V-model), but can only be executed and compared after the software is available for testing (the right-hand side of the V-model).

Tool support is available for all types of test activities throughout the development life cycle, though none of them can (or will ever be able to) make any testing activity completely automatic.

The automation of testing holds great promise and can give significant benefits, such as repeatable consistent regression tests that are run more often, testing of attributes that are difficult to test manually, better use of resources, reuse of tests, earlier time to market, and increased confidence. However, many problems typically arise when attempting to automate testing, including unrealistic expectations, poor testing practices, a false sense of security, maintenance costs, and other technical and organizational problems.

Although there are ways to support test case design activities, we consider that automating the more clerical and tedious aspects of testing generally gives more benefit than trying to automate the more intellectual test activities. This book therefore concentrates on the test activities of executing test cases and comparing outcomes. This is what we mean by automating software testing.

Test automation has its limitations. It does not replace manual testing, and manual testing will find more defects than automated testing. There is a greater reliance on the correctness of expected outcomes. Test automation does not improve test effectiveness, and can limit software development options. The testing tools have no imagination and are not very flexible. However, test automation can significantly increase the quality and productivity of software testing.

CHAPTER TWO

Capture replay is not test automation

If you don't know better, it is tempting to think that the quickest way to automate testing is to simply turn on the record facility of a capture replay tool when the tester sits down to test. The recording can then be replayed by the tool, thereby repeating the test exactly as it was performed manually. Unfortunately, many people also believe that this is all there is to test automation. We will show why this is far from the truth.

This chapter describes the way test automation typically evolves when a capture replay tool is brought in for the first time. Using an example application, we examine the manual testing process, which is where the automation will start. The automation of test execution is normally accompanied by the automation of test verification, but even this leaves a lot to be desired in terms of a fully automated testing regime. This chapter shows why automating tests is not the same as automating testing.

2.1 An example application: Scribble

Our example application is called Scribble. It is a very simple word processor, for the purpose of illustrating the points we wish to make. Real applications will be far more complex, and that makes the problems of automating their testing correspondingly more complex as well.

2.1.1 Example test case: editing a List in Scribble

A feature of Scribble is that a document can include a structure known as a List. The example test case that we use in this chapter exercises some of the List editing functions. The way it works is illustrated in Figure 2.1.

Starting from the initial state with just one item in the List (Netherlands), we add a new item, Belgium (using the *Add Item* function), which is added to the end of the List. Next we sort the List, which changes

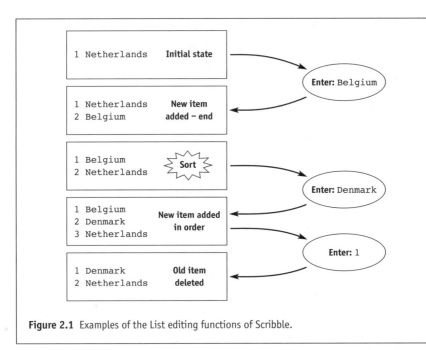

Figure 2.1 Examples of the List editing functions of Scribble.

the order of the two items. When we add the third item (Denmark), it is inserted into the List in the correct place, since it is now a sorted rather than an unsorted List. Finally, we delete the first item in the list (Belgium) by selecting *Delete item* and entering the position number.

2.1.2 The test for a Scribble List

Now we are ready to test (manually) our application. We will test the editing of a List in a document called countries.dcm (the suffix 'dcm' stands for 'document'). The starting state is a sorted List of three items. The test case will perform the following:

- add two new items to the sorted List;
- move an item (which makes the List unsorted);
- add an item to the unsorted List;
- delete an item;
- try to delete an item which isn't there (invalid position number).

The edited document will be saved as countries2.dcm.

This is not a very rigorous test case and of course there will need to be others to adequately test this functionality. However, we have chosen the above test case as being reasonable for our purposes.

The execution of the test case is shown in the series of screen shots in Figure 2.2.

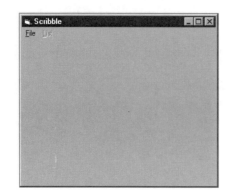

Screen 1 Invoke Scribble.

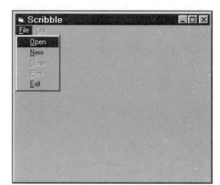

Screen 2 `File` menu: `Open`.

Screen 3 Select `countries.dcm` to open.

Screen 4 Countries file opened.

Screen 5 `List` menu: `Add Item` selected.

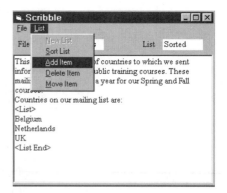

Figure 2.2 The screen shots for our example test case for Scribble.

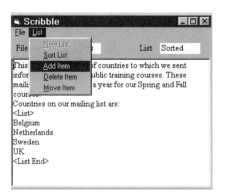

Screen 6 `Add Item`: Sweden.

Screen 7 Sweden added in order.

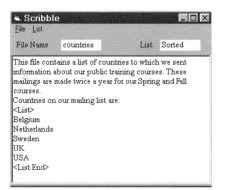

Screen 8 `List` menu: `Add Item`.

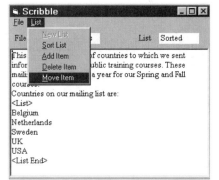

Screen 9 `Add Item`: USA.

Screen 10 USA added in order.

Screen 11 `List` menu: `Move Item`.

Figure 2.2 Continued

Capture replay is not test automation

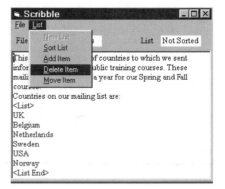

Screen 12 Move from position 4 to 1.

Screen 13 UK now at top (list unsorted).

Screen 14 List menu: Add Item.

Screen 15 Add Norway to unsorted list.

Screen 16 Norway added at end.

Screen 17 List menu: Delete Item.

Figure 2.2 Continued

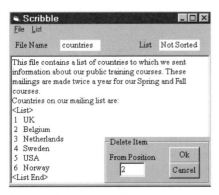

Screen 18 Delete item at position 2.

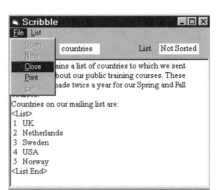

Screen 19 Belgium deleted.

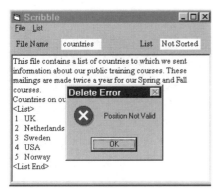

Screen 20 `List` menu: `Delete Item`.

Screen 21 Try to delete position 7.

Screen 22 Error message: invalid position.

Screen 23 `File` menu: `Close`.

Figure 2.2 Continued

Screen 24 Wish to save?

Screen 25 Save as `countries2`.

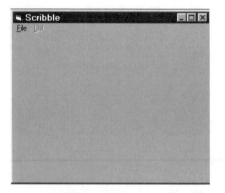

Screen 26 Scribble main menu.

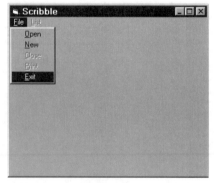

Screen 27 `File` menu: `Exit`.

Figure 2.2 Continued

In the test case above, we have entered input to take the application from its initial invocation to completion, entering specific data to perform the test case. The specific key presses and/or mouse actions that we have performed are shown in Table 2.1. Note that we have described our actions in terms of the logical elements on the screen rather than their physical locations, for example, 'List menu' rather than 'bit position (445, 120).' Note also that all mouse clicks listed are left mouse button.

Table 2.1 What was actually entered to run the Scribble test.

Action/input

1 Move mouse to Scribble icon	23 Move mouse to *List* menu	45 Move mouse to *List* menu
2 Double click	24 Click	46 Click
3 Move mouse to *File* menu	25 Move mouse to *Move Item*	47 Move mouse to *Delete Item*
4 Click	26 Click	48 Click
5 Move mouse to *Open* option	27 Type '4'	49 Type '7'
6 Click	28 Press TAB key	50 Move mouse to *OK* button
7 Move mouse to countries.dcm in file list	29 Type '1'	51 Click
	30 Press Return key	52 Move mouse to *OK* button
8 Double click	31 Move mouse to *List* menu	53 Click
9 Move mouse to *List* menu	32 Click	54 Move mouse to *File* menu
10 Click	33 Move mouse to *Add Item*	55 Click
11 Move mouse to *Add Item*	34 Click	56 Move mouse to *Close*
12 Click	35 Type 'Norway'	57 Click
13 Type 'Sweden'	36 Move mouse to *OK* button	58 Move mouse to *Yes* button
14 Move mouse to *OK* button	37 Click	59 Click
15 Click	38 Move mouse to *List* menu	60 Type 'countries2'
16 Move mouse to *List* menu	39 Click	61 Press Return key
17 Click	40 Move mouse to *Delete Item*	62 Move mouse to *File* menu
18 Move mouse to *Add Item*	41 Click	63 Click
19 Click	42 Type '2'	64 Move mouse to *Exit*
20 Type 'USA'	43 Move mouse to *OK* button	65 Click
21 Move mouse to *OK* button	44 Click	
22 Click		

2.2 The manual test process: what is to be automated?

The test case that we have just carried out manually in the example above is the test case that we will now try to automate using a **capture replay** tool. The amount of effort it takes to automate a single test case depends on a number of things and varies widely. Experienced automators typically report it takes between 2 and 10 times the effort required to run the test manually, and occasional reports have said it is as high as 30 times the manual test effort. Thus, a test case that takes half an hour to perform manually may well take between 1 and 5 hours to automate, but could also take as much as 15 hours. When you start automating, expect it to take at least five times longer to automate a test than to run it manually.

Some of the things that affect the amount of effort required to automate a test case include the following:

- The tool used. Tools provide a variety of facilities and features designed to make creating automated tests easy, and increasingly allow testers to specify during recording more about how the test should behave when being replayed.

- The approach to test automation. There are a number of different approaches we can use to create automated tests, though the first approach most people use is to record the test being performed manually and then replay this recording. Other approaches require additional effort to modify recorded scripts or prepare scripts manually. While this does take longer initially the idea is to make it easier to implement new tests and reduce maintenance costs.

- The test automator's level of experience. Clearly, people who are very familiar with using a testing tool will be able to use it more quickly and with fewer mistakes. They should also be able to avoid implementations that do not work well and concentrate on those that do.

- The environment. Where the software to be tested runs in specific environments that are difficult to replicate precisely for testing, it can be more difficult to automate testing. For example, embedded software and real time software are particularly troublesome as these can require specialized tools or features that may not be commercially available.

- The software under test. The tests for software applications that have no user interaction, such as batch programs, are much easier to automate providing the environment in which they execute can be reproduced. This is because user interaction has to be 'programmed' and this can be a lot of work. Although this can be recorded it does not result in a cost-effective solution in the long term. A batch program has no user interaction but is controlled from information passed to it when invoked or read from files or databases during execution.

  There are also many facets of software applications that can make testing, and in particular automated testing, more difficult. There are many testing issues to consider when designing software applications and often it is the design of the software itself that will make or break automating testing.

- The existing test process. When automating testing we are automating some of the five activities that make up the test process (identification of test conditions, design of test cases, build the tests, execution, and comparison of expected outcomes with actual outcomes) as described in Chapter 1. The consequences of this are our next point of discussion.

The effect of the existing test process on the effort required to automate testing is immense. If test cases are not documented but the testers make them up as they go, then automating the test cases will involve designing them as well. At the other extreme, if the test cases are documented in great detail such that every input and comparison is noted, then automating them will require less effort.

In the following subsections we describe three broad categories of test process: ad hoc testing, where the test cases have not been designed or documented, vague manual scripts, where the test cases are documented but not all the details have been specified, and detailed manual scripts, where every input and comparison is noted. Your own test processes should fit, more or less, into one or more of these categories.

2.2.1 Ad hoc testing: unscripted

Ad hoc or unscripted testing implies simply sitting down at the computer and trying things. The tester may or may not have a mental plan or checklist of things to test, let alone any specific values to try. He or she thinks up what to test, trying this and that, and thinking 'I wonder what will happen if I do this.' The tester's ideas and actions are probably not logged or documented, so what is done cannot be accurately repeated.

This is usually the case when a software development project is running late and little or no thought has been given to testing. Typically there are no specifications, the requirements are still changing, and the manager is saying 'there is no time to document, just test.' This is not a good place to be, but if that is where you are now, you have no choice about it. You have our sympathy, but don't try to automate this kind of testing – it will only slow you down even more.

The way in which automation of ad hoc testing often proceeds is described in this section, and illustrated in Figure 2.3.

The steps of unscripted testing, illustrated in Figure 2.3, are:

1. think what to do, what to test;
2. think up specific inputs;
3. enter the inputs that have just been thought up;
4. check that the software worked correctly, by watching the responses that appear on the screen.

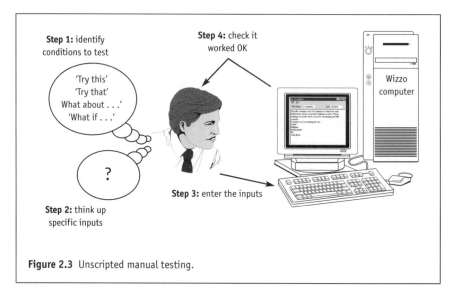

Figure 2.3 Unscripted manual testing.

It is hard to think of many advantages for unscripted testing. The one aspect that is most often mentioned is that it should save time, since we do not need to spend any time in planning and test design activities, we can just start testing. This is analogous to the 'why isn't Johnny coding yet?' syndrome that characterizes unsophisticated software development. This approach always costs more in the long term (both in writing software and in testing it) as more mistakes will be made and they will cost more to correct when they are found.

The disadvantages of unscripted ad hoc testing include:

- important areas that should be tested may be overlooked;
- other areas may be tested more than is necessary;
- tests are not repeatable, so fixes cannot be confirmed with certainty (in some cases defects may not be reproducible);
- it is usually both ineffective and inefficient.

Automating ad hoc testing relies on the automator deciding what is to be tested. This means that the tester must have the necessary skills to automate tests or the automator must have the necessary skills to define good test cases. Either way, it relies on individuals designing and implementing tests without any independent assessment of the quality of the tests.

2.2.2 Vague manual scripts

Vague manual scripts contain descriptions of the test cases without going into the detail of specific inputs and comparisons. For example, a vague manual script might say 'try some invalid inputs' or 'add some items to the list.' The test conditions may be implied (some invalid inputs), rather than stated explicitly (for example invalid inputs that are too large, too small, or the wrong format).

Our description of the example test case is also an example of a vague manual script:

- add two new items to the sorted List;
- move an item (which makes the List unsorted);
- add an item to the unsorted List;
- delete an item;
- try to delete an item which isn't there (invalid position number).

This type of manual script usually includes a vague description of the expected results and a place to tick to indicate when a test has passed (to be filled in each time the test case is run). Therefore, the test script for our test case may look something like that shown in Table 2.2.

Table 2.2 Example of a vague manual test script based on our test case for Scribble.

Step	Input	Expected result	Pass
1	Run up Scribble	*File* menu displayed	
2	Open file with sorted list	File contents displayed	
3	Add some items to List	Items added in order	
4	Move an item	Item moved, List now unsorted	
5	Add an item	Item added at end of List	
6	Delete item from List	Item deleted	
7	Use invalid position number to delete an item	Error message displayed	
8	Save changes in new file	End of test	

The steps of manual testing from a vague script, illustrated in Figure 2.4, are:

1. read what to do;
2. think up specific inputs;
3. enter the inputs that have just been thought up;
4. check that the software worked correctly, by watching the responses that appear on the screen.

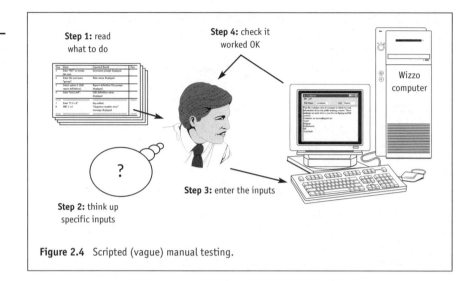

Figure 2.4 Scripted (vague) manual testing.

Vague manual scripts have many advantages over unscripted ad hoc testing:

- different testers have a reasonable chance of finding similar defects following the same script;
- the conditions identified will all be tested if the script is followed;
- the script documents what is to be tested;
- the test cases can be reviewed or inspected;
- the testing performed is likely to be more effective and more efficient than ad hoc testing (depending on how well the test design process is carried out).

However, vague manual scripts also have a number of disadvantages:

- the test input is not precisely defined;
- different testers will perform slightly different tests using the same script;
- it may not be possible to reproduce problems reliably.

When a test is run from a vague script, the tester still has to decide exactly what input to use in order to test the identified conditions. For example, in our example test case there are many different ways to have an invalid input: a number could be out of range, either above or below, it could be alpha instead of numeric, it could be a negative number or a space.

Automating vague manual test scripts relies on the automator deciding what specific inputs to use and possibly being able to decide whether or not the actual results are correct. This means that the automator does not have to invent the test conditions but must have an adequate understanding of test cases does not denigrate their quality.

2.2.3 Detailed manual scripts

A detailed manual script contains exactly what will be input to the software under test and exactly what is expected as a test outcome for that input. All the tester has to do is what the script says. This is the level that is the closest to what the test tool does, so automation is easiest in many ways from this level. However, this is also the most tedious and boring for human testers; they have no scope for creativity. Using a vague manual script, at least they can choose what inputs to use for each test.

If the vague script said 'enter some invalid input' or, slightly less vague, 'enter an invalid position number' or 'enter a position number too large,' the detailed manual script would say 'enter invalid position number 7.' Here, 7 is invalid based on the context of the test.

Our detailed manual script might look like Table 2.3.

Table 2.3 Example of a detailed manual test script based on our test case for Scribble.

Step	Input	Expected result	Pass
1	Click on Scribble icon	Scribble opened, *File* menu enabled	
2	Move mouse to *File* menu, click	Options available: *Open*, *New*, *Exit*	
3	Move mouse to *Open* option, click	Filenames displayed, including countries.dcm, filename prompt displayed	
4	Move mouse to countries.dcm, click	Text plus List of three countries: Belgium, Netherlands, UK, *File* and *List* menus displayed	
⋮	⋮	⋮	
7	Enter 'Sweden'	Item added as number 3 in List	
⋮	⋮	⋮	
12	Enter '7'	*Position not valid* message displayed	
⋮	⋮	⋮	

Detailed scripts come in many 'flavours.' The example shown in Table 2.3 is typical of a very thorough manual script that can be performed by staff with relatively little knowledge of the application or its business use. The script's expected results are shown here as exact (as the most detailed form of detailed script). In this case, if the software is relatively stable, the test script could actually show the screen shots as expected results. The detailed script would then look like Figure 2.2. A slightly less detailed format for the expected results might say 'error message displayed' instead of giving the exact text of the expected error message, for example.

The steps of manual testing with a detailed script, illustrated in Figure 2.5, are:

1. read exactly what to do;

2. enter the exact inputs in the script;

3. check that the software worked correctly, by watching the response that appears on the screen.

The advantages of detailed manual scripts are:

- testers will run exactly the same tests (i.e. as exact as manual regression testing can be) from the same scripts (subject to human error, of course – which is not insignificant when people are bored);

- software failures revealed by the tests are much more likely to be reproducible;

- anyone can run the test, since the instructions are full and detailed;

- it is easier to automate since all the information about inputs and expected outcomes is given in the script.

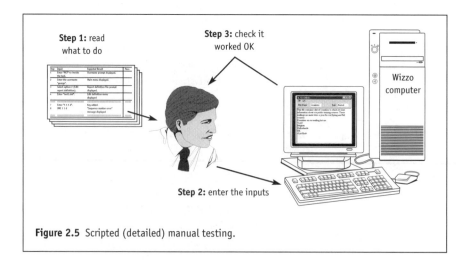

Figure 2.5 Scripted (detailed) manual testing.

The disadvantages of detailed manual scripts are:

- they are expensive to create (requiring a lot of effort);
- there is often a lot of redundant text (e.g. the word 'Enter' appears many times) though strictly there need not be so;
- scripts tend not to lend themselves to reuse of common actions;
- they are verbose, making it hard to find information and hard to maintain;
- they are very boring to run, since the tester has no scope to think or be creative, therefore mistakes are more likely.

Because a detailed test script contains detailed information about how to perform each test case, the tester does not need any knowledge of the application. Test tools have no knowledge of the applications they test; in fact test tools have no intelligence at all. They are, however, superb workhorses. They never complain, never become bored or distracted, and never want a holiday or sick leave, but will work all day and all night throughout the year. Unfortunately, they do need to be told in painstaking detail everything that they are required to do.

EXPERIENCE REPORT

In a conference presentation, the test tool was likened to a robot dog (called Squat). A dog is not as intelligent as a human tester, and robots are even less so. Some of Squat's characteristics are:

- he gets sick if he is not fed properly (i.e. good quality scripts, with error recovery built in, for example);
- he gets unfit if he is not exercised (if left for a long time without being used, he won't do very much when he is eventually woken up again);
- he gets bored if he is not taught new tricks (need to keep developing the automated regime over time).

Source: Paul Godsafe (Instem-Apoloco), 'Automated testing,' British Association of Research Quality Assurance 13th International Conference, Glasgow, May 1998.

A detailed script is, therefore, in theory a good starting point for automation because all of the details are specified. However, detailed manual scripts are not usually written in a form that any test tool can understand. There is then an overhead associated in translating the manual scripts into automated scripts that a test tool can process. The information is therefore documented twice, once in the manual scripts and again in the automated scripts. Although unavoidable when automating existing detailed tests, this is a duplication that would be wasteful if new tests were documented in the same way.

For efficiency, a new form of test documentation is required, one that can be read and understood by humans and used directly by a test tool.

Automating detailed manual test scripts frees the automator from responsibility for the quality of test case design, allowing him or her to focus on how best to automate the tests. The automator does not have to understand the application, the business or the test cases because all the information is documented.

2.3 Automating test execution: inputs

It is natural to assume that automating test execution must involve the use of a test execution tool, but in fact this is not the only way to achieve at least some test execution automation. For example, batch programs and other programs that do not involve user interaction are perhaps the easiest to automate. A simple command file can be used to set up data, invoke the program, and compare the outcomes. Although it will lack most of the additional facilities offered by modern testing tools it will automate the essential chores. Other options may be applicable to those for whom a commercial tool does not exist, is not suitable, or is not available; for example, post-execution comparison, described in Chapter 4, pre- and post-processing, described in Chapter 6, or changing the application so it can run in 'test mode.'

2.3.1 Automating test input

In the rest of this section, we will assume that a commercial test execution tool will be used to automate testing, since this is what most people will do. We turn on the record or capture facility of our test tool while we perform all of the actions for the manual test case shown in Table 2.1.

The tool will record all of the actions made by the tester and will write them to a script in a form that the tool can read. Our recorded script will contain the test inputs (including text and mouse movements). The tool can then repeat the tester's actions by reading the script and carrying out the instructions in it. The script will be held in a file that can be accessed and edited.

Scripts can also be created manually, but because they are generally written in a formal language that the tool can understand, writing (or editing) scripts is best done by people with programming knowledge. This makes a test tool's capture facilities appear very attractive indeed since the script generated during the recording of a test case performed manually is the same script needed by the tool to perform exactly the same test case.

Let us assume that we have recorded our example test case being performed manually and now wish to replay it. Figure 2.6 depicts what will happen. The test script (that we have named countries.scp) is read by the tool, which then invokes Scribble and drives it as though it were a real person at the computer keyboard. The actions the test tool takes and the information it effectively types into Scribble are exactly as described in the test script. During execution of the test case, Scribble is caused to read the initial document countries.dcm, output information to the computer screen, and finally output the edited document as a file called countries2.dcm.

The test tool creates a log file countries.log containing information about what happened as the test case was run. Logs usually include details such as the time it was run, who ran it, the results of any comparisons performed, and any messages that the test tool was required to output by instructions within the scripts.

2.3.3 Automated scripts are not like manual scripts

Exactly how the script looks will depend on the test tool being used and the implementation of the application.

Table 2.4 gives an idea of what a recorded script may look like for our Scribble test. What is listed here is a pseudo-code version of the minimum information that a tool would produce, but this should give you an idea of the complexity of a script for a rather simple test.

The scripting languages for the commercial tools do basically the same thing, but often in different ways. To give you an idea of what some scripting languages look like, Figure 2.7 shows a portion of the Scribble test in a commercial scripting language. Actually, this may not be exactly correct, as

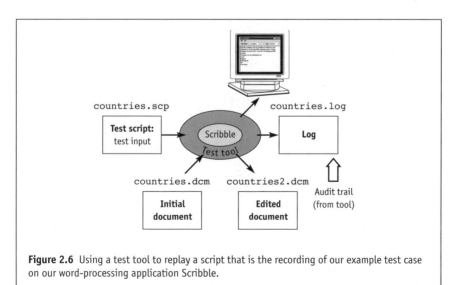

Figure 2.6 Using a test tool to replay a script that is the recording of our example test case on our word-processing application Scribble.

Table 2.4 Pseudo-code recorded script for the Scribble test.

```
LeftMouseClick 'Scribble'          SelectOption 'List/Add Item'
FocusOn 'Scribble'                 FocusOn 'Add Item'
SelectOption 'File/Open'           Type 'Norway'
FocusOn 'Open'                     LeftMouseClick 'OK'
Type 'countries'                   FocusOn 'Scribble'
LeftMouseClick 'Open'              SelectOption 'List/Delete
FocusOn 'Scribble'                 Item'
SelectOption 'List/Add Item'       FocusOn 'Delete Item'
FocusOn 'Add Item'                 Type '2'
Type 'Sweden'                      LeftMouseClick 'OK'
LeftMouseClick 'OK'                FocusOn 'Scribble'
FocusOn 'Scribble'                 SelectOption 'List/Delete
SelectOption 'List/Add Item'       Item'
FocusOn 'Add Item'                 FocusOn 'Delete Item'
Type 'USA'                         Type '7'
LeftMouseClick 'OK'                LeftMouseClick 'OK'
FocusOn 'Scribble'                 FocusOn 'Delete Error'
SelectOption 'List/Move Item'      LeftMouseClick 'OK'
FocusOn 'Move Item'                FocusOn 'Scribble'
Type '4'                           SelectOption 'File/Close'
Type <TAB>                         FocusOn 'Close'
Type '1'                           LeftMouseClick 'Yes'
LeftMouseClick 'OK'                FocusOn 'Save As'
FocusOn 'Scribble'                 Type 'countries2'
                                   LeftMouseClick 'Save'
                                   FocusOn 'Scribble'
                                   SelectOption 'File/Exit'
```

the example has been constructed rather than recorded. Also, the tools may have changed their scripting languages since this book was written. However, it does give an idea of what a script might actually look like.

Some scripts may look quite different, but regardless of what our script language looks like, each is automating only one thing: the actions performed.

Depending on the format of the recorded test, there may also be a great deal of redundant information contained in the captured script, such as the pauses between entering data (while reading the manual script, for example), and any typing mistakes that were corrected (backspacing over incorrect characters before typing the correct ones).

In order to make a recorded script usable, or indeed even recognizable, comments should be inserted in the script. Despite some vendor claims, no recorded scripts 'document themselves.'[1] We expand on these matters in Chapter 3.

---

[1] We feel that the comments produced in 'self-documenting' scripts are about as useful as an ashtray on a motorbike.

```
;          Select "&List~&Add Item" from the Menu
           MenuSelect "&List~&Add Item"
           Pause 3 seconds

; Use the dialog window
Attach "Add Item ChildWindow~1"
           Type "SWE{Backspace}{Backspace}"
           Pause 2 seconds
           Type "weden"
           Button "OK" SingleClick

; Use the parent window
Attach "Scribble MainWindow"

;          Select "&List~&Add Item" from the Menu
           MenuSelect "&List~&Add Item"
           Pause 2 seconds

; Use the dialog window
Attach "Add Item ChildWindow~1"
           Type "USA"
           Pause 1 seconds
           Button "OK" SingleClick
```

Figure 2.7 Script segment from a commercial testing tool.

All scripting languages allow you to insert comments into the scripts. However, just as when commenting code, you must conform to the syntax or the test tool will try to use your comment as a test input (just like a compiler will try to compile your comment in source code if it does not conform to comment syntax).

2.3.4 Benefits and uses of automating only test input

A raw recorded script (of what a tester did) does have its place within a test automation regime, but it is a much more minor place than most novices to test automation give it.

One advantage of recording manual tests is that you end up with a form of replayable test comparatively quickly. Little or no planning is required and the tool can be seen to provide benefit more or less right away (well, at least in theory). However, recording ad hoc testing is a bit like writing software without a specification. You may end up with something similar to what is actually required but is unlikely to be any better than unspecified software. The end product will probably do some things correctly, some things incorrectly, not do some things, and do others that are not required.

One benefit of capturing and recording test inputs is that this can automatically provide documentation of what tests were executed. This provides an audit trail, which is useful if you need to know exactly what was done. This audit trail does not necessarily make a good basis for an effective and efficient automated testing regime, but it has its place as a way of getting started and for special tasks. For example, if you have invited users in for 'playtime' and they manage to crash the system, you can at least see what was typed in. The audit trail may also contain a lot of useful information that is not normally available from manual tests, for example detailed statistics on timing or performance.

The set-up of test data is often a long and tedious task and for this reason is sometimes avoided, resulting in fewer runs of a set of test cases than there should be. If the data set-up can be recorded the first time it is performed then, providing the software's user interface does not change, the set-up can be replayed much more reliably and usually a lot faster by the tool. For example, adding the details of one new client isn't too bad, but adding the details of 100 new clients is best automated. Even if the next version of software has user interface changes that invalidate the recording, it may still be worth doing, since the additional effort to record the data set-up the first time will soon be repaid by the effort saved with the first or second replay. This is only true if the recording does not need editing; where editing is necessary the costs are much greater.

There are some other uses of recording manual tests, or at least recording of user interaction, such as making the same maintenance change across large numbers of data files or database(s). A recording can also serve as a demonstration. For multi-platform applications a script may be able to be recorded on one platform and played back on a number of other platforms with no or only minor changes. If complicated sequences need to be typed accurately, and this is error-prone if done manually, replaying them as one step in a manual test can save time. Automated execution is much more accurate than manual execution, and therefore the test input is repeatable. Exact reproduction of inputs is particularly useful in reproducing bugs. If the cause of the bug has been recorded, playing it back should reproduce it, and playing it back after it has been fixed should confirm that it was fixed correctly (or not).

However, in most circumstances, automating only test execution has little benefit. Manual verification is error prone, wasteful, and very tedious. Yet some people end up with a test execution tool which produces stacks of paper that has to be checked by hand – this is nonsense if we are talking about automating testing. In order to claim any real test automation, we should therefore also automate comparison of the test outcomes.

It is important to appreciate that we are not suggesting that test result comparison for all test cases should be automated. As we have already discussed in Chapter 1, not all test cases should be automated, and not all comparisons should be automated either.

2.3.5 Disadvantages of recording manual tests

The disadvantages of record and playback only become apparent as you begin to use the tool over time. Capture replay always looks very impressive when first demonstrated, but is not a good basis for a productive long-term test automation regime.

The script, as recorded, may not be very readable to someone picking it up afterwards. The only value of an automated test is in its reuse. A raw recorded script explains nothing about what is being tested or what the purpose of the test is. Such commentary has to be inserted by the tester, either as the recording is made (not all tools allow this) or by editing the script after recording has finished. Without this information any maintenance task is likely to be difficult at best.

A raw recorded script is also tied very tightly to the specifics of what was recorded. Depending on the tool, it may be bound to objects on the screen, specific character strings, or even screen bitmap positions. If the software changes – correction: *when* the software changes – the original script will no longer work correctly if anything to which it is tightly bound has changed. Often the effort involved in updating the script itself is much greater than re-recording the script while running the test manually again. This usually does not give any test automation benefit. For example, the values of the inputs recorded are the exact and detailed values as entered, but these are now 'hard-coded' into the script.

The recording is simply of actions and test inputs. But usually the reason for running a test is to look at the test outcome to see whether the application does the right thing. Simply recording test inputs does not include any verification of the results. Verification must be added in to any recorded script in order to make it a test. Depending on the tool, it may be possible to do this additional work during recording (but it takes additional time and effort) or during the first replay, otherwise it will be necessary to edit the recorded script. This is described in more detail in Section 2.4.

2.3.6 Recommendation: don't automate testing by simply recording

It should be the aim of every professional testing organization to implement an efficient and effective test automation regime appropriate for their objectives. Simply recording manual tests will not achieve this for the following reasons:

- Unscripted (ad hoc) testing is not usually very effective (it can be effective in some cases if you have a person who either knows the system well and has experienced the weaknesses of previous versions, or has a good understanding of how the software works and is able to identify likely defective areas). Automating ad hoc testing will at best result in faster, but nonetheless not very effective, testing.

- Recording only input does not result in an automated test. The outcomes of a test have to be checked to insure they are as expected; if this is not automated, this is not an automated test, only automated input.

- Re-recording when the software changed is inefficient. Almost any change to the user interface of software will result in changes to the test inputs or their order or both. Editing recorded scripts is neither easy nor pleasant. It is often easier and quicker to simply re-record the test but this usually incurs an unacceptably high cost anyway.

We recommend that if you currently perform only ad hoc manual testing, you will achieve far more benefit from improving your testing process than from attempting to automate it. The use of testing techniques, for example, may well double your test effectiveness. (See the threefold improvement in Chapter 12.) This will save you much more money than trying to run ineffective tests faster and will lead to better quality software.

2.3.7 Automated execution, with manual verification?

As it stands we have a script that was generated by recording our example test case being performed manually, and this can now be replayed by our test tool as often as we wish. However, all we have automated are the test inputs. In order to determine if the test case produced the correct results, we still have to check the expected outcomes manually. The tool will not do any checking for us yet because we have not instructed it to do so; so far, it knows only how to enter one set of test inputs, the inputs of our one test case.

There is a certain novelty value in having a tool type the inputs in for you, especially at first. There is a tendency for 'coffee parties' to gather around the screen. Remarks such as 'I wish I could type that fast' may be overheard. However, the novelty will soon wear off when the testers realize that they still have to sit there watching the test in order to verify that it worked (or not). The idea of overnight and weekend testing will not be popular with testers if automation has only reached this stage as yet.

Manually checking that our test case has worked correctly could involve having to watch the screen as the tool replays the script. It would also be a good idea to take a look at the edited document (countries2.dcm) after test execution to insure that the data was saved as it had appeared on the screen. (See the Experience Report in Section 2.5.2.)

So do we have automated testing? Well, we have some automation: the inputting has been automated. However, we still have very much a manual process in checking that the software did the right thing.

2.4 Automating test result comparison

It is unlikely that the entire outcome of a test case will be compared (including not only what has changed but also everything that has not changed), since it is often impractical and unnecessary. Usually, only the most important or most significant aspects need to be compared. Some outcomes such as the outputs to the screen can be performed while the test is being executed, this is known as **dynamic comparison**. Other outcomes such as some outputs to a file or database can only be compared after the test case execution has completed, this is known as **post-execution comparison**. An automated test may need to use a combination of dynamic and post-execution comparisons. This topic is discussed in more detail in Chapter 4.

There are a number of design decisions that need to be taken when deciding how to implement automated comparison. We will illustrate with an example.

2.4.1 Deciding when to compare the outcome of a test case

The first design decision is to decide when in a test run a comparison should be done. As an example, take a single input from our Scribble test, to add an item (Sweden) into a sorted List. Let us assume that we are recording the manual test once again but this time we will insert a few dynamic comparison instructions as we go. We arrived at the point in the test case where we are going to add the country 'Sweden' to the list. Figure 2.8 shows the screen as it might appear at this stage, before and after entering 'Sweden'.

At this point, we should check the screen as it now appears (Screen 7) whenever this test is run in the future, so we need to add a comparison to the test script now.

The first step is to manually verify that this screen is indeed correct for the input of 'Sweden'. Next we will want to capture what is on the screen to compare against the next time this test is run. This will insure that the application performs in the same way at this stage of the test case each time it is run. The next step is to decide how much to compare.

2.4.2 How much should be compared?

We now have some options for what to capture as the future expected output:

- the whole screen;
- the absolute minimum;
- something between these two extremes.

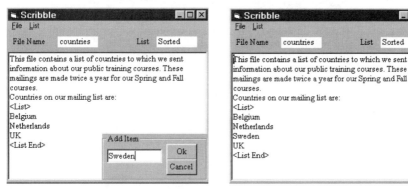

Screen 6 Add Item: Sweden.　　　　**Screen 7** Sweden added in order.

Figure 2.8 Screen images at the point when the list item 'Sweden' is added.

Capturing the whole screen is often the easiest to do. However, if there is any information on the screen which is likely to have changed the next time the test is run, then the easiest choice now will cause us significant grief later. Sometimes a screen will be displaying the current date or time. The next time the test case is run, we certainly do not want the test to fail because the test was not run on exactly the same date or at the same time it was recorded. In our example, we may have changed the text outside the List, but that is not important for this test, which is concerned only with whether an item can be added in the correct order to the List.

Capturing whole screens can be quite greedy of disk space for tests. Particularly when graphics are involved, the space needed to store a whole screen can run into tens of megabytes.

What about other options? We could perhaps capture only a single character, say the letter 'S.' Or we could capture the line containing the new entry, which would make sure that all of the new entry had gone in correctly. In Figure 2.9, we show this option as the shaded area.

Our first try at capturing an expected outcome seems sensible: it is a fairly minimal set. However, there is one error that may occur which this option will not find. Suppose the next version of the software ends up overwriting the third entry instead of moving UK down and inserting Sweden as the new third entry. The screen would then appear as shown in Figure 2.10.

The tool will pass this test, since all it is checking for is the line containing Sweden, and that looks exactly as it was told to expect it to look. So by making our comparison more robust (from things we are not interested in), it has become less sensitive to unexpected errors. (These terms are explained more fully in Chapter 4.)

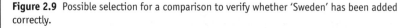

Figure 2.9 Possible selection for a comparison to verify whether 'Sweden' has been added correctly.

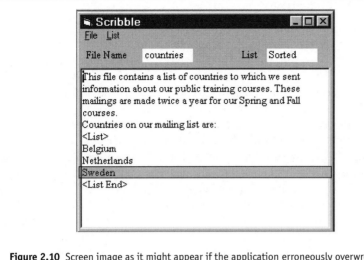

Figure 2.10 Screen image as it might appear if the application erroneously overwrote the third list entry with 'Sweden'.

A better option may be to compare not only the newly inserted entry, but also the entry that was 'pushed down.' This will catch the error shown (but may well miss still others). Our improved test comparison area is shown in Figure 2.11.

We have looked at the choice between comparing a little versus comparing a lot at a time. There are a number of other choices for comparison, which are discussed in more detail in Chapter 4.

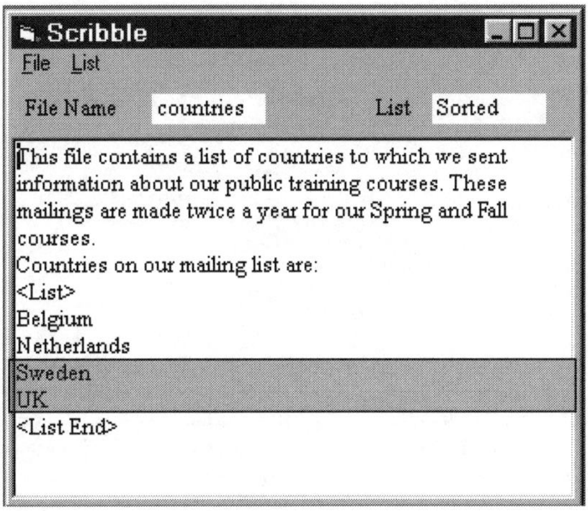

Figure 2.11 Improved selection for comparison.

2.4.3 Dynamic comparison

Let us now assume that we have included some dynamic comparison instructions as we recorded our example test case being performed manually, including the comparison for Sweden outlined above. Figure 2.12 depicts what will happen. The test script now contains additional instructions that tell the tool which outputs are to be compared and the expected result to which they are to be compared. At each comparison point, the tool will capture the actual output from the software as it executes the tests and it will then compare that with the corresponding expected output. Every time a comparison is performed a message is written to the log file indicating whether or not differences were found. The test script may now look something like the example shown in Figure 2.13.

Note that even if a comparison reveals differences, the tool will continue to run the test case. This is both sensible and useful since not all differences imply catastrophic failure so it usually is worth running a test case right to the end to see if any other problems can be revealed. However, this characteristic is something of a double-edged sword. If a detected difference really does imply catastrophic failure, the tool will continue to run the test case anyway, unaware of the potential havoc doing so may cause. It may be that for a more complex system than our example word processor, test cases that do not go according to plan are best aborted to prevent undesirable outcomes such as data being incorrectly changed or deleted, large volumes of data being created or printed, or just hours of machine time being wasted.

Fortunately, where such potential damage could occur, it is usually possible to instruct the test tool to abort the test case. It will be necessary to edit the script though, inserting appropriate instructions to detect an undesirable situation (or perhaps more easily, not a specific desired situation)

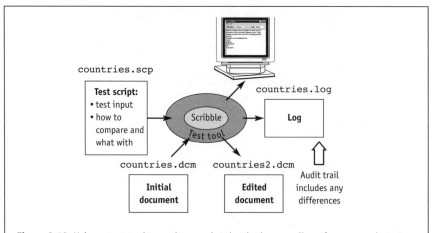

Figure 2.12 Using a test tool to replay a script that is the recording of our example test case on our word-processing application Scribble, but now including dynamic comparison instructions.

```
;          Select "&List~&Add Item" from the Menu
           MenuSelect "&List~&Add Item"
           Pause 3 seconds

; Use the dialog window
Attach "Add Item ChildWindow~1"
           Type "SWE{Backspace}{Backspace}"
           Pause 2 seconds
           Type "weden"
           Button "OK" SingleClick

; Use the parent window
Attach "Scribble MainWindow"

;          Text check on Scribble
           Check("SCRIBBLE.CB", "ADD_1" )

; Use the parent window
Attach "Scribble MainWindow"

;          Select "&List~&Add Item" from the Menu
           MenuSelect "&List~&Add Item"
           Pause 2 seconds

; Use the dialog window
Attach "Add Item ChildWindow~1"
           Type "USA"
           Pause 1 seconds
           Button "OK" SingleClick
```

Figure 2.13 Script segment from a sample commercial testing tool showing a dynamic comparison instruction in bold. This instructs the test tool to perform a comparison according to instructions stored in the file SCRIBBLE.CB under the label ADD_1. These instructions would have been previously set up in the tool's dynamic comparison database.

and then the action to take. This is 'programming' the script, and brings with it not only endless possibilities of tailoring test cases to detect all sorts of situations and deal with them accordingly, but also unconsciously to make errors that will cause the test case to fail through no fault of the software under test. This can lead to much wasted effort, instead of the intended saved effort.

2.4.4 Post-execution comparison

In the previous subsection we looked at how the use of dynamic comparison affects our example test case. Here we will look at the effect post-execution comparison would have on it as an alternative to dynamic comparison. A comparator tool for post-execution comparison is sometimes supplied bundled with a capture/replay tool and in any case most computer systems offer some utility program or other that can perform simple independent comparisons.

Figure 2.14 depicts what happens with our example test case when we use post-execution comparison. The test script is back to its simplest form: a straight recording of the inputs. The log file contains just the basic information including start and end times, who ran it, etc. but no information about the results of comparisons (though this will depend on the implementation). The expected outcomes are now held in a separate file called countries2.dcm, the same name as the output file with which it has to be compared, but in a different directory, rather than being embedded in the script. We could have used a naming convention such as Expcountries2.dcm to distinguish our expected results file from the actual results file. Using the same name is what we recommend, for reasons outlined in Chapter 5. After the test case has been executed the comparison process can begin. This will take the actual outcome of the test case and compare it with the expected outcome, possibly generating another log file (not shown in the figure) and/or a report of the differences found.

Here we have shown the edited output file (countries2.dcm) as the only outcome being compared. Whether or not this is sufficient depends on the purpose of the test case. This may be all that we consider necessary to compare, as it insures that the edits to the input file are reflected correctly in the new version of the file. While this may be a reasonable approach for positive testing, i.e. testing valid inputs such as adding Sweden correctly, it would not be appropriate for testing invalid inputs such as trying to enter an invalid position number. Showing that the screen display is updated correctly is more difficult to do in post-execution comparison, but it is not impossible. For these kinds of test, other outcomes would need to be captured in another file or files for later comparison.

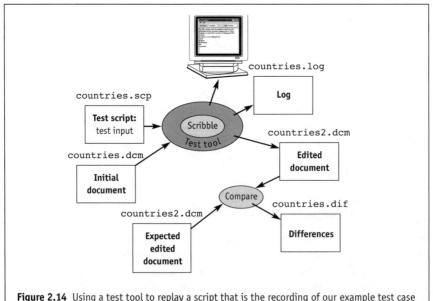

Figure 2.14 Using a test tool to replay a script that is the recording of our example test case on our word-processing application Scribble, with post-execution comparison.

the first executes the test case while the second process performs a comparison. It is this aspect that makes post-execution comparison a more difficult facility to automate well (Chapter 4 shows how to overcome these problems). Commercial testing tools usually provide much better support for dynamic comparison than they do for post-execution comparison.

2.4.5 Automated comparison messages have to be manually checked

So far we have described the automation of our example test case starting with a simple recording and then adding dynamic comparison and post-execution comparison to verify the actual outcome. Now, in order to determine whether or not our test case is successful every time it is run, there are some additional tasks we may have to do, depending on the tool and the implementation of post-execution comparison when used.

First we should look at the log file to make sure that the test case was executed right through to the end. It is quite possible for automated test cases to fail to start or be aborted part way through (for example, due to insufficient disk space). Where dynamic comparison has been used we may also need to check the log file for any 'failed' comparison messages. Where we have used post-execution comparison, we may have to look at one or more other files for information about any differences between the actual and expected outcomes.

Clearly, this is a manually intensive task. Having to repeat it for only a few test cases will not be too arduous, but it will be impractical where there are tens, hundreds, or thousands of test cases. Of course, it may be a relatively simple matter to write a small utility program to search through all the log files, doing a text match on the word 'fail,' wouldn't it? That utility program would need to know the names of all the log files, and where to find them. It may also give some spurious results, such as a test that writes text to the log file containing the word 'fail,' e.g. 'This is test 325B.43 Communication Link Failure Test.'

This additional utility should be produced if we want testing to be automated, but this does represent an additional task that is normally not anticipated.

At the time of writing, some commercial test tools do provide an acceptable summary of the information, or at least can be made to do so. However, where post-execution comparison has not been integrated well with the execution of the test cases, obtaining a report that takes into account the results of post-execution comparisons can be far more difficult. When we invoke a set of automated test cases we would really like to be presented with a single report at the end that takes into account all of the comparisons and simply states how many test cases ran successfully, how many failed, and then which test cases failed. (Our recommendations for the content of such a report are discussed in Chapter 9.)

2.4.6 Automating test comparison is non-trivial

2.4.6.1 There are many choices to be made

There are a number of aspects to automating comparison that must be designed into the automated testing regime. Whether and when to do dynamic comparison and post-execution comparison is one example. It is not a case of one alternative being better than another; each alternative has advantages and disadvantages, and each will be more suitable in some circumstances than in others. Usually a combination of the two should be used to give the best results.

Other choices include comparing a lot of information at once versus comparing only a little piece of information each time, and performing many comparisons versus performing only a few. (These and other issues are discussed further in Chapter 4.)

Many of the choices come down to trading off the resilience of the tests to changes in the software, with the ease of finding defects when the tests find a discrepancy.

2.4.6.2 Scripts can soon become very complex

Incorporating comparison into test cases is essential in order to be able to fully automate testing. If dynamic comparison is embedded in the script, as we have seen in the example, this can make the script more complex, since the comparison instructions and possibly the expected output will now be contained within the script.

The more information the script contains, the more susceptible it will be to changes, either changes in the software being tested, or changes in the test cases themselves. For example, if the error messages changed their wording slightly, all expected outputs embedded in scripts would need to be edited. This can increase the cost of maintaining the scripts considerably. Ways to reduce such script maintenance costs are addressed in Chapter 3.

2.4.6.3 There is a lot of work involved

Tool support is essential, not only to automate testing, but also to help automate the automation! In order to produce an effective and efficient automated testing regime, effort needs to be invested upfront, so that effort is continually saved later on. The speed and accuracy of *use* of the testing tools is important. The effort involved in setting up this regime will be paid back many times on all of the numerous occasions when the automated tests are re-run. The more reuse of automated tests you need, the more important it is to build them correctly.

2.5 The next steps in evolving test automation

Surely having put all this effort into automating test execution and comparison, we must be ready to tell the test tool to run our test cases so we can then put our feet up, right? Unfortunately, we have only just begun. What happens next? Typically, what is shown in Figure 2.15.

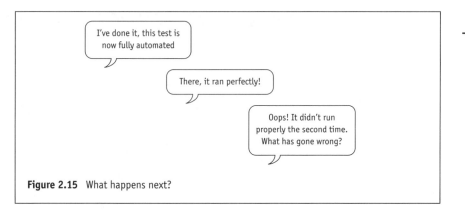

Figure 2.15 What happens next?

2.5.1 Why tests fail the second time (environmental trip-ups)

The first time our test ran, it used as its input the file countries.dcm. It created the file countries2.dcm as the edited document file. This is no problem when running the test for the first time, either manually or automatically. The final steps of our test script are shown in Figure 2.16.

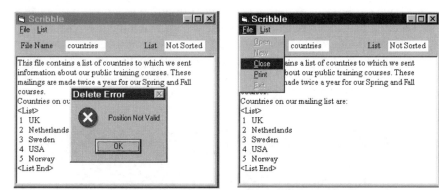

Screen 22 Error message: invalid position.

Screen 23 File menu: Close.

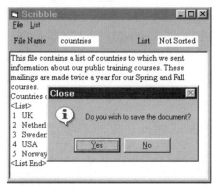

Screen 24 Wish to save?

Screen 25 Save as countries2.

Figure 2.16 The end of our original test.

Screen 26 Scribble main menu.

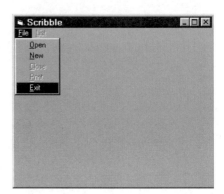

Screen 27 File menu: Exit.

Figure 2.16 Continued

What happens the second time we run this exact test? Screen 25 will actually be different, because both countries.dcm and countries2.dcm will be shown in the file list. The tool, however, will not 'notice' this! The next input is to type in countries2. The next screen that appears is now not the one shown on Screen 26, but a new one containing a dialog box that was not seen the first time the test was run. This is shown in Figure 2.17.

If this happens when you are testing manually, you would naturally put in the additional step of answering 'Yes' (and you would also probably have noticed the file in the list on Screen 25), and then select *Exit* from the *File* menu. You may not even realize that you had put an extra step into the test.

Figure 2.17 The screen at the end of the test the second time it is run.

However, when the tool comes to replay the exact input, after sending countries2, the next thing it sends is an attempt to select the *File* menu. Since this is not a valid input to this screen, Scribble will beep and redisplay the same screen. The automated test then tries to select the *Exit* option, causing Scribble to beep again and redisplay the same screen. The tool now thinks it is finished and exited from Scribble, so it may go on to start the next test case in the sequence. You can see how the automated testing will soon reach a state in which it will achieve nothing useful and might actually do some damage by deleting or changing data files that it should not.

The test tool is essentially 'blind' to what is really happening. All it can know about is what it has been told. Anything you want the automated test to know about, you have to tell it explicitly.

Again, the problem outlined here is but one of many possible ways in which a test can be tripped up. As with all such things, the problem is not insurmountable, but it takes time and effort to surmount it.

There are a number of alternative ways to overcome this problem. Here are three:

- Alter the script to respond to the extra prompt. The test case will now run the second and subsequent times, but will fail the first time, or if countries2.dcm has been deleted for any reason.

- Alter the script to check for the extra prompt and respond whenever it occurs. This enables us to have a script which will run regardless of whether countries2.dcm exists or not. Our script will contain an additional 'if' statement along the lines of: 'if countries2.dcm exists, hit "Y".' Note that this will make our script more complex again.

- Alter the script to check for the file, and delete it if it exists before running the test case. Rather than 'hard-coding' the check for the existence of this file into the script at the point where the problem occurs, another possibility is to anticipate the problem at the beginning of the script. This may be better from a maintenance point of view, since something buried at the end of the script is more easily overlooked.

  In this case, we could put the check for the existence of the file at the beginning of the test script, and delete the file if it exists, so that the rest of the script will now run correctly. Now we don't have to check for the extra screen because we know it will not come up. Our script may now contain something like: 'if countries2.dcm exists, delete file countries2.dcm.'

This example is typical of a number of things that can occur to trip up a test. It may be more efficient to collect all such similar things for a set of test cases into one place, where all the environment factors can be dealt with either for one test case or for a set of tests. This could be done as a separate script in the testing tool language, or it could be done as a completely separate exercise, possibly implemented in a command file or whatever is most familiar to the software engineers or testers. This is called pre-processing and is discussed in Chapter 6.

Which solution is best? This is another area where there are no answers, but choices to be made. The chosen solution will be a trade-off of many factors, including:

- implementation effort;
- future maintainability;
- test case failure analysis effort;
- debugging effort;
- this test case's ability to handle similar situations;
- robustness;
- what is done for other automated test cases.

2.5.2 Other verification requirements (often overlooked)

Having taken the environment considerations into account, our test is now finished, right? Well, what we now have is certainly a long way forward from our first attempt of simply capturing inputs.

The next question to ask is: is it a good test case?

Actually, this is the very first question we should have asked before we started automating it. As we discussed in Chapter 1, there is no point in automating poor test cases. However, the point we wish to make now concerns the comparisons we have implemented. Have we checked everything that we should? Will they reveal all the defects that could be found by this test case?

Often there are many facets to the outcome of a test case that we could check, which go beyond what we could illustrate with our simple Scribble example. Testers performing test cases manually will be making a multitude of checks, some consciously and probably many unconsciously. Automated tests will only check what they are programmed to check so it is important that we consider exactly what is programmed in and what can be left out.

Some of the outcomes we could consider for a lot of systems include:

- files that may have been created or changed (Were the correct files created? Were the correct files changed? Were they changed in the right way?);
- databases that may have been altered (Were the correct records altered? Were any alterations made to other records which should not have been touched?);
- other outputs, such as to printers, networks, or to other communication equipment (Were the right things sent to the right places? How can you be sure?);
- screen attributes may have been changed, possibly ones that are not visible such as whether a field is protected or not (Have the correct attributes been changed to the right new values?);

- internal data structures may have been created or altered, perhaps stored briefly before they are used by another program (Has the right information been put into that temporary storage? How can you check it?).

EXPERIENCE REPORT: BUG IN JET ENGINE DOWNS MICROSOFT'S HIGH-FLYER

Reports of a potentially serious bug, which corrupts database records in the Microsoft Access application, have caused concern among its millions of users, writes Tom Forenski.

The bug is activated when editing database records and causes the edits to be posted to a record other than the one being viewed. The bug can be created simply by running one of Microsoft's own wizards. 'The bug is particularly devious in that everything appears to work correctly', reports Allen Browne. 'It is only when a record is checked later that the results become apparent. In addition, it only occurs when the form contains more than 262 records, so that the database works correctly initially, and the bug only surfaces as more data is added.'

The steps needed to reproduce the bug are:

delete a record on a form

without closing the form, search for a different record using the bookmark properties of the form and recordset clone objects using the combo box wizard option 'Find a record on my form based on the value I selected in my combo box'

make data changes in the found record

The changes are then saved to a different database record than the intended one.

Microsoft has posted information on a workaround, and a fix would be released in the next service pack for Access, said a Microsoft representative.

Source: *Computer Weekly*, September 10, 1998.

2.5.3 Ways of verifying file or database changes

How can we verify that these additional items have been correctly handled by the software? There are some choices for how we handle this.

One option is to add more verification to the script. We could check data values stored in a file or database by doing an additional read after we have modified something, to see whether the right information has been stored. This would be checked against the way we would expect to see that data displayed.

This does make the script more complex (again), and also more vulnerable to changes. If the layout of the display from the database were changed, all scripts that used this method would need to be updated, increasing the test maintenance burden.

Another possibility would be to use a comparison tool to search for differences between the correct version of the file and the actual file. This means that we would need to save a copy of the file as it should appear, in order to do the comparison. If this were a database, this may not be feasible.

As with many aspects of test automation, there are choices to be made, and the choice will affect many things. An effective test automation regime will have a good balance of checking things in a way that will be resistant if not immune to changes.

2.5.4 Where will all the files go?

There is one last thing to consider in implementing our example automated test case. In the process of creating the automated test case for Scribble, we have created several files. For example:

- countries.scp, our test script;
- countries2.dcm, our expected output for post-execution comparison;
- countries2.dcm, our actual output;
- countries.dif, the list of differences produced by the comparator (if not in log);
- countries.log, the audit trail of what happened when the test ran.

All of these files must be given a home. Where should we put them? This is yet another decision to be made, and the results of that decision will affect the future maintainability of the tests. These issues are discussed in Chapter 5.

2.6 Conclusion: automated is not automatic

When you start implementing automated tests, you will find that you are running the (supposedly automated) tests manually. Automating some part of test execution does not immediately give automatic testing; it is but the first step along a long road.

There are many different approaches to automating testing, and generally speaking, the more elaborate the approach, the greater the end productivity (quicker to add new automated tests, less maintenance involved, etc.). Conversely, the simpler the approach, the less the end productivity. However, simple approaches have the advantage of comparatively low start-up costs and some benefits can be achieved fairly quickly, while elaborate approaches incur much larger start-up costs and the benefits are usually a much longer time coming.

It is important to choose an approach (or approaches) appropriate for the objectives of test automation. For example, if the tests are short term (perhaps because the software is to be used once and then thrown away) there is no point in using an approach that is designed to minimize long-term maintenance costs at the expense of upfront effort.

There is more to a test than just running it. Often there is some set-up and clear-up involved. This additional work also needs automating. Unfortunately, the easiest solution is often not the best solution. A standard approach is required in order to get the best balance between many alternative ways of solving the problems.

There is usually more verification to be done than first meets the eye. Automation can lead to better testing, if a comparator is used to compare things that might otherwise be overlooked if testing was done manually. However, this is by no means guaranteed.

The 'testware' must be designed to be maintainable and of high quality in order to achieve effective and efficient test automation, just as software must be designed to be maintainable and of high quality for effective and efficient use. This testware design process involves balancing many decisions concerning comparison, scripting, where files are stored, etc.

The commercial test execution tools are generic; one size fits all. However, each individual user is unique, and some parts of the generic solution may fit well, some not so well, and some may be downright damaging. In order to build an automated testing regime, you must tailor the generic tools to suit your own situation.

The key characteristics of a good automated regime are:

- it is very easy to select sets of tests to be run (the proverbial 'touch of a button');
- those tests take care of all their own housekeeping such as environmental set-up and clear-down, i.e. the tests are self-sufficient;
- it is easier to add a new test to the automated pack than to run that test manually.

This can only be achieved through continuous improvement of the entire regime.

Summary

We have taken a very simple example test case for Scribble, our primitive word processor.

We looked at the different alternative starting points for automating this test, in terms of the current type of test documentation: ad hoc or unscripted, a vague manual test script, or a detailed manual test script.

Testing can be automated from any of these starting points, but is easiest from the detailed script. Recording is one way of getting the detailed test inputs into a form that a test execution tool can use, and can be used from any of the starting points. However, we do not recommend that you attempt to automate ad hoc testing, as it will not give you effective testing. Automating a chaotic process will just give you faster chaos.

We looked at the stages that you will go through in beginning to automate testing. The first step, especially if you have a capture replay tool, will be to capture a test. What you actually capture is only the test inputs, however. Although this does give some advantages over typing the input manually, the test process still includes checking the screen manually as the test runs in order to see if the software is working correctly, as well as checking other things such as the file that was created.

Test comparison is normally also automated. This can be done by dynamic comparison within the script, or by post-execution comparison after the test has completed. With dynamic comparison, there are a number of choices to be made. The decisions made will affect how easy the tests are to maintain, how easy it will be to identify defects found by the test, and how likely the test is to miss defects that could have been found (unexpected changes).

Automating comparison still does not provide a good automated test, however. Other aspects must be taken into consideration. In our example, the file that was created by the test caused the test to fail the second time it was run automatically. This can be overcome, but this must also be built in to the test automation.

There may be other things that need to be verified in addition to what we can see on the screen, such as files or databases which have been altered by the test. We also need to decide where the files used and produced by the automated test will go.

In a good test automation regime, tests are easy to run and self-sufficient, and it is easier to add a new automated test than to run that same test manually.

Scripting techniques

3.1 Introduction

Much of this chapter may seem familiar to anyone who has ever read a 'How to write maintainable programs' book. The techniques for producing maintainable scripts have many similarities to those for producing maintainable programs. Yet it seems that people who abandoned 'spaghetti code' many years ago end up producing 'spaghetti test scripts.' This chapter aims to insure that any test scripts that you produce, if they are not simply to be thrown away after a single use, are properly engineered.

3.1.1 Similarities with programming

Test scripts are a necessary part of test automation for interactive applications and, in some cases, non-interactive applications. As we demonstrated in Chapter 2, the information contained within a script can be extensive, and the more information there is the more there is to go wrong, update, and manage. Writing scripts is much like writing a computer program. Most test execution tools provide a scripting language that is in effect a programming language; thus, automating tests is a case of programming tests.

Of course programming tests correctly is no less difficult than programming software applications correctly and is usually about as successful. This means that no matter how clever we are at programming or testing there will be defects in the automated tests. The more programming, the more defects there will be. For the tests to work properly it is necessary to spend time testing the tests, debugging, and fixing them. This can become very time consuming, particularly because it is not limited to the first time the tests are automated. Changing the software usually forces some of the tests to be changed, for example, to cope with new options in the user interface, menu changes, user interactions, and changes to the expected results.

Test automation would be so much easier and quicker if it were not for the need to produce test scripts. This is a bit like saying that programming would be much easier if we did not have to write source code! However, this is exactly what we have been heading for during the past three or four decades. Third generation languages (3GLs) save us having to write a lot of assembler code, and fourth generation languages (4GLs) save us having to write as much 3GL code. We don't really want to have to write the code; rather we would prefer to only say what the system has to do and let it go ahead and do it (not having to tell it how to do the job). So it is with automated tests. We do not want to have to tell the tool down to every last keystroke how to run each test case, at least not all the time. Rather, we wish only to tell the tool what to do by describing the test case and not have to tell it how to execute it (a descriptive approach, not prescriptive). However, in the same way that 4GLs have not replaced 3GLs, and 3GLs have not entirely replaced assembler code, there are occasions when it is appropriate and necessary to write a script that specifies each individual keystroke. For example, when testing a real-time application, it can be useful to specify specific time delays between particular keystrokes.

The purpose of 3GLs and 4GLs is to increase productivity and make programming easier. There are different scripting techniques that seek to do the same (increase productivity, make test automation easier). Although test scripts cannot be done away with altogether, using different scripting techniques can reduce the size and number of scripts and their complexity. This chapter describes a number of different approaches to scripting, explaining the advantages and disadvantages of each technique and when it may be appropriate to use one in favor of the others.

3.1.2 Scripting issues in general

3.1.2.1 What test scripts are used for

Recording a test case being performed manually results in one (usually long) linear script that can be used to replay the actions performed by the manual tester. Doing the same for a number of test cases will result in one script for each test case. So if you have thousands of test cases you will end up with thousands of scripts. The script is really a form of computer program, a set of instructions for the test tool to act upon. Having one such program for every test case is not efficient since many test cases share common actions (such as 'add new client,' 'query client details,' etc.). This will lead to higher maintenance costs than the equivalent manual testing effort because every copy of a set of instructions to perform a particular action will need changing when some aspect of that action changes.

Most tools use a scripting language that offers far more power and flexibility than would ever be used by recording, but to benefit from it you have to edit the recorded scripts or write scripts (or rather, code scripts) from scratch. One of the benefits of editing and coding scripts is to reduce the amount of scripting necessary to automate a set of test cases. This is achieved principally in two ways. One way is to code relatively small pieces of script that each perform a specific action or task that is common to several test cases. Each test case that needs to perform one of the common actions can then use the same script. The other way to reduce scripting is to insert control structures into the scripts to make the tool repeat sequences of instructions without having to code multiple copies of the instructions. Although these approaches inevitably cause us to code several more scripts initially, they are much smaller and therefore easier to maintain. Eventually, however, once a reasonably comprehensive set of scripts has been coded, new test cases can be added without the need to add more scripts so we enter a stage where thousands of test cases are implemented by hundreds of scripts.

Scripts may contain data and instructions for the test tool, including:

- synchronization (when to enter the next input);
- comparison information (what and how to compare, and what to compare with);
- what screen data to capture and where to store it;
- when to read input data from another source, and where to read it from (file, database, device);
- control information (for example, to repeat a set of inputs or make a decision based on the value of an output).

The actual content of a script will depend on the test tool being used and the scripting techniques employed.

Like software, scripts are very flexible. There will usually be many ways of coding a script to perform a given task. The way a script is written usually depends on the skill of the person coding it but should also depend on its objective. A 'quick and dirty' approach may be to record as much as possible, or perhaps to copy parts of other scripts and cobble them together. A more thoughtful approach may involve some design work and coding from scratch.

Some scripting techniques involve elaborate constructs and logic while others are much simpler. The more elaborate the scripting technique used, the more upfront work there will be and the more effort will be needed on debugging the scripts. However, there will also be greater end productivity because there will be more reuse of scripts and they will involve less maintenance. The more tests you automate, the more worthwhile it is to put the effort into the more elaborate scripting techniques. This is illustrated in Figure 3.1.

However the scripts are created, what should concern us most is the cost of producing and maintaining them and the benefits we can obtain from using them. If a script is going to be reused by a lot of different tests that are expected to have a long life, then it will be worth ensuring that the script works well and is easy to maintain. If, however, the script is to be used for only one test case that will be discarded as soon as the testing has been completed, then there is little point in spending much effort creating it.

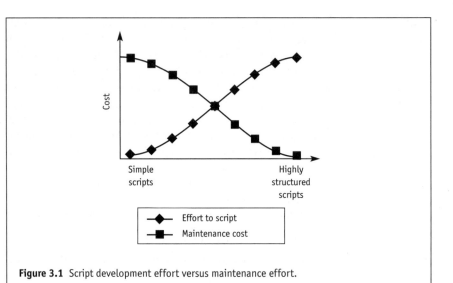

Figure 3.1 Script development effort versus maintenance effort.

It is worth considering which scripting techniques you are likely to use when you are choosing a tool so you can check for appropriate support (see Chapter 10).

3.1.2.2 Good versus bad scripts

Since scripts form such a vital part of most test automation regimes, it seems sensible that we should strive to insure that they are good. Certainly we can be sure that nobody would wish to be associated with bad scripts. So what is a good script?

The easy answer to this question is 'a script that is fit for purpose,' but that doesn't amount to a very comprehensive answer. Does this mean that a good script is one that does what it is supposed to do reliably and is easy to use and maintain? Often yes, but there are circumstances when scripts do not have to be particularly easy to use or maintain (such as the one-off automated test cases described earlier) though it is difficult to think of any circumstances when scripts need not do what they are supposed to or be unreliable. If you are not concerned with ease of use or maintainability for any of your scripts then much of what we have to say in this section will be of little interest to you.

Given that good scripts should be easy to use and maintain we can describe a few characteristics or attributes that will have a significant bearing on how easy to use or maintain a script really is. Rather than consider individual scripts, we will compare two sets of scripts that perform the same set of test cases in Table 3.1.

When test automation begins, you will start out with a small number of scripts and it will not be difficult to keep track of them, but this task will become more difficult as the number of scripts increases. Ways of organizing scripts are described in Chapter 5.

Table 3.1 Comparison of good and poor sets of test scripts that perform the same set of test cases.

Attribute	Good set of test scripts	Poor set of test scripts
Number of scripts	Fewer (less than one script for each test case)	More (at least one script for each test case)
Size of scripts	Small – with annotation, no more than two pages	Large – many pages
Function	Each script has a clear, single purpose	Individual scripts perform a number of functions, typically the whole test case
Documentation	Specific documentation for users and maintainers, clear, succinct and up-to-date	No documentation or out-of-date; general points, no detail, not informative
Reuse	Many scripts reused by different test cases	No reuse; each script implements a single test case
Structured	Easy to see and understand the structure and therefore to make changes; following good programming practices, well-organized control constructs	An amorphous mass, difficult to make changes with confidence; spaghetti code
Maintenance	Easy to maintain; changes to software only require minor changes to a few scripts	Minor software changes still need major changes to scripts; scripts difficult to change correctly

3.1.2.3 Principles for good scripts

What is it that makes a script 'easy to use' or 'easy to maintain'? There is bound to be a subjective element to the answers to these questions, as different people will have varying preferences as to the style, layout, and content of scripts. However, in our view the following principles provide a guide.

Scripts should be:

- annotated, to guide both the user and the maintainer;
- functional, performing a single task, encouraging reuse;
- structured, for ease of reading, understanding, and maintenance;
- understandable, for ease of maintenance;
- documented, to aid reuse and maintenance.

These basic principles apply whatever scripting technique is used, but they may be implemented in different ways. For example, all scripts should be annotated, but the annotation may differ in style and format from one regime to another.

3.1.2.4 'Easy to read' scripts?

Occasionally a tool vendor will claim that its tool generates recorded scripts that are 'easy to read' or even 'self documenting.' Such claims are misleading and very short-sighted. Let us deal with these claims once and for all.

A 'raw' recorded script consists of a whole sequence of inputs for the test and may also include some verification. Some tools under user instruction can insert the verification instructions as the recording takes place. The end result is usually a long script, perhaps hundreds of lines covering several pages, that does not have a useful structure. It could be likened to a book that has no chapters or section headings but just page after page of text. Finding a particular topic in such a book would be tiresome to say the least, as you would have to read through it until you found the required text. So it is with a recorded script. The reason we would wish to look at a recorded script anyway is usually because we need to make a change to it, perhaps to insert some verification or control instructions, or to change a particular sequence of actions to reflect changes in the software under test. In order to make these changes correctly it will be necessary for us to find the relevant part of it, and the longer the script is, the more difficult this will become. It would also be wise for us to gain an understanding of the script as a whole, to help insure that any changes we make will not have adverse affects on other parts of the script or indeed any other scripts that use this one.

Of course, finding things in a script and gaining an understanding of it will be easier for us if we are familiar with the scripting language. It will also be easier if there is some useful documentation in the script telling us what it does and how it does it. Script annotation, comments embedded throughout the script that say what is happening at each stage, will be the most helpful. Some tools automatically embed comments in the scripts they generate while recording and this is sometimes what the tool vendors allude to when they claim their tools' scripts are 'easy to read.'

However, 'easy to read' can be taken to mean different things. Scripts usually comprise keywords that are the same as they appear in the English language, such as 'Type,' 'Button,' and 'Click.' Fair enough, but is this 'ease to read' what we want? Certainly we do not want 'difficult to read' scripts (perhaps using acronyms and symbols rather than proper words, although this would depend on the person doing the reading, since an experienced author may prefer familiar abbreviations and acronyms for ease and speed of typing and reading).

When we wish to make changes to the script, its readability becomes very important, but readability in this sense means easy to understand. This leads us to the second common claim.

3.1.2.5 'Self-documenting' scripts?

'Self documenting' is a rather mythical term. To document a script means to give written information supporting or detailing it. We interpret this as written information that is useful and in addition to what is already there. The information that can usefully be written down somewhere includes the following:

- the raw content of the script (inputs and sometimes expected outputs);
- the purpose of the script (what this script does, the actions it performs);
- user information (what information has to be passed to the script, what information it returns, what state the software under test has to be in when the script is called, and what state the software will be left in when the script ends);
- implementation information (additional information helpful to maintainers, such as an explanation of why it was implemented in a particular way or references to similar scripts that may also need changing);
- annotation (comments embedded throughout the script to say what is happening at each logical step in terms of the actions being performed on or by the software under test).

It is only the first item above that a tool can generate. The only annotation that can be generated 'automatically' is limited to 'click the OK button', 'focus on window "Payments"', and 'input the string "John Doe" in the field "name"'. Such information is often rather obvious anyway, so the annotation is generally not adding any value. This type of annotation certainly is not sufficient if the script is to be used and maintained effectively and efficiently.

None of the other information can be generated automatically. But if you want understandable scripts, someone must produce this information, generally a job for the script's author. To add this information to the script, this person needs to be able to edit the script itself so he or she needs to have some technical skills (unless the tool supports easy insertion of comments during script creation). If the people recording the scripts are not technical, then adequate support must be provided to them.

Simply recording a long test is not by any means the end of the story; there is a lot more work to be done. However, a recording is often the place where test automation starts and is sufficient in a few instances.

3.1.3 Test case design and implementation

3.1.3.1 Test case design

There is not always a direct relationship between an automated script and a test case. In fact, what is taken to be a test case can vary enormously. For some people a single test case may last only a few seconds or minutes but for others a test case can last for several hours. Long test cases can usually be considered as a series of individual tests, as shown in Figure 3.2. The rectangles in this figure each represent a single test case and include 'in' and 'out' activities such as invoking the software under test and terminating its

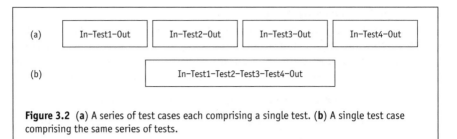

Figure 3.2 (**a**) A series of test cases each comprising a single test. (**b**) A single test case comprising the same series of tests.

execution. In Figure 3.2(a) each test is implemented as a separate test case, whereas in Figure 3.2(b) a single test case executes all four tests. It is important to realize that tests 2, 3, and 4 are performed under different conditions, so, strictly speaking, they are different tests. However, the inputs and expected outcomes would be the same for the tests, whichever way they were performed.

We use the term 'test case' to mean a series of one or more tests that can be meaningfully distinguished from other such series. For example, running one test case on our Scribble program may involve starting the program, opening a particular document, performing some edits, saving the document, and exiting the program. However, some people's perception of a test case would not include starting and exiting the program. Thus, if a set of test cases were performed, the program could be started, all the test cases run and then the program terminated.

It may be helpful to think of a single automated test case as being the shortest sequence of tests that collectively are assigned a single status. Commercial test tools typically assign a 'passed' or 'failed' status to some amount of testing but they are not so consistent when it comes to naming this unit of testing. For example, test case, test procedure, and test script are used by different tools to mean the same thing. We will use the term test case.

3.1.3.2 Test case implementation

Regardless of how long or short, complex or simple test cases are, there is not necessarily a direct relationship between the test cases and the scripts used by the test tool in performing them. Although a few tools force their users into defining separate 'scripts' for each test case, this is not generally helpful when implementing a test automation regime of any substance.

At first it may seem sensible to implement each test case using a single script. Indeed, this is actually encouraged by some tools. However, as we shall show, this is not going to lead to an effective and efficient test automation regime. Implementing automated tests in this way will always be costly, and the cost of maintaining them will continue to grow and probably become greater than the cost of performing the same tests manually.

The following section describes a number of scripting techniques that take us into script programming. It is only by breaking the 'one test case one test script' relationship that we will ever achieve a good automated testing regime.

We recommend that the documentation for each script is placed in the header of the script itself and that it should be as concise as possible. These two points will help whenever the script is changed, since whoever is making the change will be more likely to update the documentation as well as the body of the script. The layout of the script documentation is a matter of style that may already be governed by existing coding standards or conventions (if these work well then use them; if not then change them). In our view it is important that everyone who writes or edits scripts conforms to the same conventions. Everyone will know what information to include in the documentation, where to put it, and how to present it. They will also know where to look for particular information. Another advantage of everyone conforming to the same standards or conventions is that it makes it easy to copy the information from each script into a separate document such as a catalog of all shared scripts. Such a task can be automated easily using one or two suitable text manipulation tools, and indeed it is best automated since it can be run 'at the touch of a button' to produce an up-to-the-minute catalog.

We suggest a script header layout like that shown in Figure 3.3. This can be used as a template for all scripts or it can be adapted for different types of scripts (though we do prefer to see one common header for all scripts). The actual layout is not as important as the content but we do recommend all our scripts are laid out in a consistent way. Note that the semicolon at the start of each line in Figure 3.3 is used here as a comment marker to tell the test tool to ignore the whole line. How comments are identified in your scripts will depend on the tool you use.

```
;                        Test Automation Script
;                        ----------------------
;    SCRIPT:
;    AUTHOR:
;    DATE:
;
;    PURPOSE:
;
;    PARAMETERS:
;
;    PRE- AND POSTCONDITIONS:
;
;    MAINTENANCE
;
;------------------------------------------------------------
;    AMENDMENTS:
;    <id> <name> <date> <what & why>
;------------------------------------------------------------
```

Figure 3.3 Our suggestion for a script header. This contains all the information necessary to understand what a script does and how to use it. It also contains any information that would benefit someone who has to maintain the script.

Everything in this template has a purpose but they will not all be relevant to everyone. The template contains a series of keywords which serve to remind the script writer what information to document (and where to put it) and make it easy to automate the task of copying the information into a separate file. The title 'Test Automation Script' simply tells us what this is. It may seem like overkill but it can be useful in environments where there are a lot of different types of file and all with numerous uses. It would be improved if it included the name of the test tool (particularly if the scripting language is unique to the tool). Similarly, the keyword 'SCRIPT' should be followed by the name of the script. This will be redundant if printouts automatically have the filename included. The purpose is to avoid the problem of finding a printout without the filename on it – it can be time consuming, if not difficult, to find out the script's name.

The 'AUTHOR' and 'DATE' keywords should be followed by the name of the scriptwriter and the date when it is written. Having the author's name clearly makes it possible to identify who wrote the script, something that can be useful to know (to ask questions or to ask for help, for example). The date may be redundant, particularly if there is a good configuration management system in place that can provide this information.

A brief statement as to the purpose of the script should follow the 'PURPOSE' keyword. Usually this will not need to be more than a single, short sentence. If it is any more then it is likely that the script is performing too much and may be better divided into two or more smaller (and possibly more reusable) scripts. We prefer the keyword 'purpose' rather than the ubiquitous 'description' since it discourages totally worthless statements like 'This is a script.'

The 'PARAMETERS' keyword heads up a section of the header that describes any parameters that are accepted or returned by this script. It may be helpful to distinguish between parameters that are passed in and those that are passed out or returned. The 'PRE- AND POSTCONDITIONS' section informs users of the script what state the software under test has to be in at the time the script is called and what state the software will be left in when the script has completed. This is particularly important information if users of the script are going to be able to use it correctly first time, every time. For example, the script may expect the software application to have a specific dialog box displayed but will leave a different one displayed when it exits. If the person using this script did not know this, the script may be called when the required dialog box was not displayed. This could cause the test case to fail (but not necessarily at the point the shared script was called, thereby making it more difficult to identify and correct the problem).

The 'MAINTENANCE' section contains any information that would be useful to people who will be maintaining the script. Most of the time this will be blank (rather than removed altogether) since the user information given in the rest of the header together with the script annotation will be sufficient. However, sometimes scripts have to be implemented in a strange or unusual way in order to avoid some problem or other (such as a tool featuːe that does not work correctly or an idiosyncrasy of the software application).

The 'AMENDMENTS' section contains details of all changes made to
the script since it was first completed. The 'id' can be used to mark all the
lines in the script that are altered or added in order to make the amendment. Again, this section may be redundant if there is a good configuration
management system in place that can provide this information.

The 'AMENDMENTS' section contains details of all changes made to
the script since it was first completed. The 'id' can be used to mark all the
lines in the script that are altered or added in order to make the amendment. Again, this section may be redundant if there is a good configuration
management system in place that can provide this information.

3.2 Scripting techniques

We now look at some different scripting techniques and their uses. These
techniques are not mutually exclusive. In fact, the opposite is true – they
can, and most likely will, be used together. Each technique has its own
advantages and disadvantages that affect the time and effort it takes to
implement and maintain the test cases that the scripts support.

However, it is not which techniques are used that is most significant;
rather, it is the overall approach taken by the whole regime in implementing test cases supported by the scripts. This has the greatest impact. There
are two fundamental approaches to test case implementation, prescriptive
and descriptive. These are discussed later in this chapter, after we have seen
what different scripting techniques look like.

In the rest of this section, we use simple example scripts to illustrate the
points we wish to make, using a pseudo-scripting language which should be
understandable to all readers, whether or not you have actually used a tool.
In reality, the actual tool scripts would be more complex than the examples
we show. For simplicity, we show only the minimum script features that
allow us to explain the different scripting techniques.

The scripting techniques described are:

- linear scripts;
- structured scripting;
- shared scripts;
- data-driven scripts;
- keyword-driven scripts.

3.2.1 Linear scripts

A **linear script** is what you end up with when you record a test case performed manually. It contains all the keystrokes, including function keys,
arrow keys, and the like, that control the software under test, and the
alphanumeric keys that make up the input data. If you use only the linear
scripting technique – that is, if you record the whole of each test case –
each test case will be replayed in its entirety by a single script.

A linear script may also include comparisons, such as 'check that the
error message *Position not valid* is displayed.' Adding the comparison
instructions may be done while the test case is being recorded (if the test
tool allows this) or it may be done in a separate step afterwards, perhaps
while replaying the recorded inputs from the script.

Note that a test case that takes 10 minutes to run manually may take anywhere from 20 minutes to 2 hours to automate with comparison. The reason for this is that once it is recorded, it should be tested to make sure it will play back – it is surprising how often this is not the case! Then it may need to be played back again while the specific comparison instructions are added, and the new script with comparison embedded should also be tested. If it is not correct, the test script then needs to be debugged and tested again. The more complex the application and test case, the longer this process is likely to take.

3.2.1.1 Advantages of linear scripts

Linear scripts have advantages that make them ideal for some tasks. The advantages are:

- no upfront work or planning is required; you can just sit down and record any manual task;
- you can quickly start automating;
- it provides an audit trail of what was actually done;
- the user doesn't need to be a programmer (providing no changes are required to the recorded script, the script itself need not be seen by the user);
- good for demonstrations (of the software or of the tool).

3.2.1.2 When to use linear scripts

Almost any repetitive action can be automated using a linear script. There are some situations where a simple linear script is the best scripting technique to use. If a test case will only be used once, for example, to investigate whether a test execution tool works in a given environment, then there is no point in investing any more effort than necessary in such a script since it will be thrown away.

Linear scripts can be used for demonstrations or training. When you want to show the features of the software to a potential customer, and don't want to have to be concerned with typing in exactly the right keystrokes when you are feeling a little nervous anyway, replaying a recorded script will reproduce the keystrokes exactly.

Linear scripts can be used to automate edits to update automated tests. Any given update will probably only be done once, so a throwaway script is all that is needed. Linear scripts can be used to automate set-up and clear-up for tests, or to populate a file or database by replaying an input sequence.

Linear scripts can be useful for conversions. If some part of the system has been changed but without changing the working of the system from the user's perspective, recording live data one day, replacing the software or hardware, and then replaying the day's traffic can give an initial level of confidence that the new system generally works. This approach has been used successfully for benchmark testing for Year 2000 conversion.

3.2.1.3 Disadvantages of linear scripts

Linear scripts do have a number of disadvantages, particularly with respect to the building of a long-term test automation regime:

- the process is labor-intensive: typically it can take 2 to 10 times longer to produce a working automated test (including comparisons) than running the test manually;
- everything tends to be done 'from scratch' each time;
- the test inputs and comparisons are 'hard-wired' into the script;
- there is no sharing or reuse of scripts;
- linear scripts are vulnerable to software changes;
- linear scripts are expensive to change (they have a high maintenance cost);
- if anything happens when the script is being replayed that did not happen when it was recorded, such as an unexpected error message from the network, the script can easily become out of step with the software under test, causing the whole test to fail.

These disadvantages make the sole use of linear scripts to automate testing an impractical approach for long-term and large numbers of tests. Every test to be automated will take as much effort as the first, and most scripts will need some maintenance effort every time the software under test changes.

3.2.2 Structured scripting

Structured scripting is parallel to structured programming, in that certain special instructions are used to control the execution of the script. These special instructions can either be control structures or a calling structure.

There are three basic control structures supported by probably all test tool scripting languages. The first of these is called 'sequence' and is exactly equivalent to the linear scripting approach we described earlier. The first instruction is performed first, then the second, and so on. The other two control structures are 'selection' and 'iteration.'

The selection control structure gives a script the ability to make a decision. The most common form is an 'if' statement that evaluates a condition to see if it is true or false. For example, a script may need to check that a particular message has been displayed on the screen. If it has it can continue; if it has not it has to abort. In this example the condition is whether or not a particular message has been displayed.

The iteration control structure gives a script the ability to repeat a sequence of one or more instructions as many times as required. Sometimes referred to as a 'loop,' the sequence of instructions can be repeated a specific number of times or until some condition has been met. For example, if a script were required to read records containing data from a file, the sequence of instructions would perform the read and process the information in some way. This sequence can then be repeated until all the records in the file have been read and processed.

In addition to the control structures, one script can call another script, i.e. transfer control from a point in one script to the start of another sub-script, which executes and then returns to the point in the first script immediately after where the sub-script was called. This mechanism can be used to divide large scripts into smaller, and hopefully more manageable, scripts.

Introducing other instructions for changing the control structure gives even more opportunities for not only increasing the amount of reuse we can make of scripts but also increasing the power and flexibility of the scripts. Making good use of different control structures leads to maintainable and adaptable scripts that will in turn support an effective and efficient automated testing regime.

Making good use of different structured scripting techniques does require programming skills. It is not necessary to have years of programming experience or indeed knowledge of numerous programming languages. We would suggest that the minimum requirement is someone who is interested in learning and is given both the time and resources (such as training) to learn. If experienced programmers can be brought into the test automation project, so much the better.

Figure 3.4 shows a script for part of our Scribble test. After entering the filename and clicking the *OK* button in the *Save As* dialog box, the script then checks to see if there has been a *Replace existing file?* message output. If there has, it will click the *OK* button, but if not it will continue in the normal way.

This example has been simplified. In practice a script may have to wait a few seconds to give Scribble time to display the message. The script probably would also need to move the focus to the message box before it

```
Part of the Scribble test script
SelectOption 'File/Close'
FocusOn 'Close'
LeftMouseClick 'Yes'
FocusOn 'Save As'
Type countries2
LeftMouseClick 'Save'

If Message = 'Replace existing file?'
    LeftMouseClick 'Yes'
Endif

FocusOn 'Scribble'
SelectOption 'File/Exit'
```

Figure 3.4 This script fragment contains a check for a *Replace existing file?* message using an 'If' instruction (shown in bold). If this message is displayed the OK button will be clicked. If the message is not displayed the script will continue as usual.

could read the message. These considerations further complicate the script but this may be well worth doing since it makes the script more flexible and robust.

The main advantage of structured scripting is that the script can be made more robust and can check for specific things which would otherwise cause the test to fail, even though the software was working correctly as shown in Figure 3.4. A structured script can also deal with a number of similar things that need to be repeated in the script, using a loop. A structured script can also be made modular by calling other scripts.

However the script has now become a more complex program and the test data is still 'hard-wired' into the script.

3.2.3 Shared scripts

Shared scripts, as the name implies, are scripts that are used (or shared) by more than one test case. Of course, this implies that we require a scripting language that allows one script to be 'called' by another but this is more or less standard across all test execution automation tools.

The idea of this is to produce one script that performs some task that has to be repeated for different tests and then whenever that task has to be done we simply call this script at the appropriate point in each test case. This gives two distinct advantages: first, we do not have to spend time scripting (writing or recording the actions required); and second, we will have only one script to change in the event that something concerning the repeated task changes.

One of the features of current development tools is the ease with which graphical development environments can change the user interface to a system. However, the aspects that make this so attractive to users and developers are also the aspects that can be most destabilizing to automated testing. The use of shared scripts is one step towards building automated tests that can keep up with rapidly changing software, i.e. that will not require extensive maintenance.

For example, rather than have the navigation repeated in a number of scripts, when the commands to navigate to a particular place in the application are identical, there can be a single shared script that does the navigation for all tests. The shared script contains the inputs to the application that cause it to navigate to a particular screen which is the starting point for a number of tests. Each of the tests calls the navigation script and then runs the detailed test. When the tests are completed, a common script would be called to navigate back out to the main menu.

3.2.3.1 Going from a linear to a shared script: example
An example of shared scripts for our example Scribble test case is shown in Figure 3.5. A shortened linear script Scribble1 shown on the left has been divided into the three separate scripts shown on the right-hand side. The first of these new scripts, ScribbleOpen, invokes the Scribble application and causes it to open a document, the name of which is passed into the script at the time it is called. Similarly, the last of these new scripts, ScribbleSaveAs, causes

Shared script:
ScribbleOpen (FILENAME)

```
LeftMouseClick 'Scribble'
FocusOn 'Scribble'
SelectOption 'File/Open'
FocusOn 'Open'
Type FILENAME
LeftMouseClick 'Open'
```

A shortened original linear script:
Scribble1

```
LeftMouseClick 'Scribble'
FocusOn 'Scribble'
SelectOption 'File/Open'
FocusOn 'Open'
Type 'countries'
LeftMouseClick 'Open'
FocusOn 'Scribble'
SelectOption 'List/Add Item'
FocusOn 'Add Item'
Type 'Sweden'
LeftMouseClick 'OK'
FocusOn 'Scribble'
SelectOption 'List/Add Item'
FocusOn 'Add Item'
Type 'USA'
LeftMouseClick 'OK'
FocusOn 'Scribble'
SelectOption 'File/Close'
FocusOn 'Close'
LeftMouseClick 'Yes'
FocusOn 'Save As'
Type 'countries2'
LeftMouseClick 'Save'
FocusOn 'Scribble'
SelectOption 'File/Exit'
```

New script: Scribble1

```
Call ScribbleOpen ('countries')
FocusOn 'Scribble'
SelectOption 'List/Add Item'
FocusOn 'Add Item'
Type 'Sweden'
LeftMouseClick 'OK'
FocusOn 'Scribble'
SelectOption 'List/Add Item'
FocusOn 'Add Item'
Type 'USA'
LeftMouseClick 'OK'
FocusOn 'Scribble'
Call ScribbleSaveAs ('countries2')
```

Shared script:
ScribbleSaveAs (FILENAME)

```
FocusOn 'Scribble'
SelectOption 'File/Close'
FocusOn 'Close'
LeftMouseClick 'Yes'
FocusOn 'Save As'
Type FILENAME
LeftMouseClick 'Save'
FocusOn 'Scribble'
SelectOption 'File/Exit'
```

Figure 3.5 A shortened version of the original linear script Scribble1 shown on the left has been divided into the three separate scripts shown on the right-hand side.

Scribble to save the current document using a name that is passed into it at the time it is called. The third script (the new Scribble1) first calls ScribbleOpen then performs the testing actions before calling ScribbleSaveAs to finish.

Of course it will take longer to implement the shared scripts version of the test case since we have to create three scripts instead of just the one. If we create them by editing a recorded script, the two shared scripts will need to be changed so the filename they enter is not the one used at the time they were recorded but can be specified at the time the script is called. This is usually achieved by replacing the literal filename with a variable name (here we have used the variable name FILENAME), which can be thought of as a place marker that will be substituted for the real filename by the test tool when the script is called. The new test script Scribble1 will also have to be edited to insert the calls to the two shared scripts.

Scribble2 (linear)

```
LeftMouseClick 'Scribble'
FocusOn 'Scribble'
SelectOption 'File/Open'
FocusOn 'Open'
Type 'countries'
LeftMouseClick 'Open'
FocusOn 'Scribble'
SelectOption 'List/Add Item'
FocusOn 'Add Item'
Type 'France'
LeftMouseClick 'OK'
FocusOn 'Scribble'
SelectOption 'List/Add Item'
FocusOn 'Add Item'
Type 'Germany'
LeftMouseClick 'OK'
FocusOn 'Scribble'
SelectOption 'File/Close'
FocusOn 'Close'
LeftMouseClick 'Yes'
FocusOn 'Save As'
Type 'test2'
LeftMouseClick 'Save'
FocusOn 'Scribble'
SelectOption 'File/Exit'
```

Scribble2 (using shared scripts)

```
Call ScribbleOpen('countries')
FocusOn 'Scribble'
SelectOption 'List/Add Item'
FocusOn 'Add Item'
Type 'France'
LeftMouseClick 'OK'
FocusOn 'Scribble'
SelectOption 'List/Add Item'
FocusOn 'Add Item'
Type 'Germany'
LeftMouseClick 'OK'
FocusOn 'Scribble'
Call ScribbleSaveAs ('test2')
```

Figure 3.6 The second and subsequent test cases can be implemented much more easily since the shared scripts can be reused.

Actually, calling the two shared scripts 'shared' is a bit misleading at this time since they are not shared at all! Only one script calls them. However, as soon as we start to implement another similar test case we can use them a second time. Figure 3.6 shows a new control script, Scribble2, that implements a slightly different test. This is much shorter than the linear script for this test case so it should not take as long to implement. We can carry on implementing more test cases that each call these two shared scripts and others beside. If the user interface of Scribble changes such that one of the shared scripts needs changing we will have only the one script to change. Had we used different linear scripts to implement the whole of each test case then we would have to change every one.

This approach is useful for any actions that are done often or that are susceptible to change. Navigation is one example, but any scripted activity that is repeated often may well be better in a common script, particularly if it is a complex or lengthy sequence.

3.2.3.2 Types of shared scripts

There are two broad categories of shared script, those that can be shared between tests of different software applications or systems, and those that can only be shared between tests of one software application or system. Some examples of these two categories are given in Table 3.2. Note that application-independent scripts may be more useful long term, and are worth putting additional effort into.

Table 3.2 Types of shared scripts.

Application-specific scripts	Application-independent scripts
Menus	Login and logout
Individual screen/window routines	Synchronization
Non-standard controls	Logging
Navigation	Input retrieval
	Results storage
	Error recovery
	Data-driven shell
	Checking or comparison

3.2.3.3 Advantages and disadvantages of shared scripts

The advantages of shared scripts are:

- similar tests will take less effort to implement;
- maintenance costs are lower than for linear scripts;
- eliminates obvious repetitions;
- can afford to put more intelligence into the shared scripts. For example, on login if the network is busy, wait 2 minutes and try again. It wouldn't be worth doing that in hundreds of scripts, but is well worth doing in one.

The shared scripting approach is good for small systems (for example, simple PC applications and utilities) or where only a small part of a large and stable application is to be tested using relatively few tests (a few tens of tests, certainly no more than a few hundred).

There are also some disadvantages to shared scripts:

- there are more scripts to keep track of, document, name, and store, and if not well managed it may be hard to find an appropriate script;
- test-specific scripts are still required for every test so the maintenance costs will still be high;
- shared scripts are often specific to one part of the software under test.

3.2.3.4 How to get the best out of shared scripts

In order to reap the benefits of shared scripts, you have to be disciplined. You have to insure that all tests actually do use the shared scripts where they are appropriate. We were once told that programmers will look for a reusable function for up to two minutes before deciding to implement their own version. We are sure this is much the same for automated test script writers. Knowing that there is, or at least should be, a reusable script to do a particular job is one thing; being able to find it is another. If it cannot be found quickly people will write their own version of it and then we will have a much more difficult task with maintenance updates. When the script needs changing the person undertaking the maintenance will believe that it is only the shared script that needs changing. The fact that there is another script that needs editing may not be realized until the tests are run. Even then it may not be obvious what the problem is.

Some form of reusable script library will help matters considerably. This has to be set up and managed, and although it will not be a full-time job, it is likely to take a significant amount of effort in the early days. Script libraries are an aspect of testware architecture, which is covered by Chapter 5.

Another aspect of shared scripts that needs careful attention is their documentation. The scripts need to be documented in such a way that makes it easy for testers to determine what each one does (to tell whether this is really what they need) and how to use it. Software documentation in general is notoriously poor. Where it exists it is often out of date or just plain wrong. If these traits are carried into the documentation of our scripts then automation will suffer from unnecessarily high implementation and maintenance costs.

A good way to try to avoid these problems is to adopt conventions and define standards for scripts. These will form a part of the overall test automation regime. They will not only help insure documentation is considered but also will guide new script writers as to how to go about creating scripts (and how to make new shared scripts available for others to use).

3.2.4 Data-driven scripts

A **data-driven** scripting technique stores test inputs in a separate (data) file rather than in the script itself. This leaves the control information (e.g. menu navigation) in the script. When the test is executed the test input is read from the file rather than being taken directly from the script. A significant advantage of this approach is that the same script can be used to run different tests.

For example, one test for an insurance system will enter the details of a new insurance policy and verify that the database has been updated correctly. A second test would do the same thing except it would use a different insurance policy. It therefore requires the same instructions but different input and different expected outcomes (the values that describe a different insurance policy). These two tests can be implemented using a single test script and a data file.

3.2.4.1 Data-driven example 1: using the same script with different data
Figure 3.7 shows how this could work with our Scribble test case at a basic level. (Figure 3.8 shows a more sophisticated approach.) Rather than having one script for each test case we can now implement numerous test cases with a single script. We will refer to this single script as the control script because it controls the execution of a number of test cases. Note that each of the test cases we are showing here only adds two names to the list of names in the file 'countries.' This is because we have shortened the original

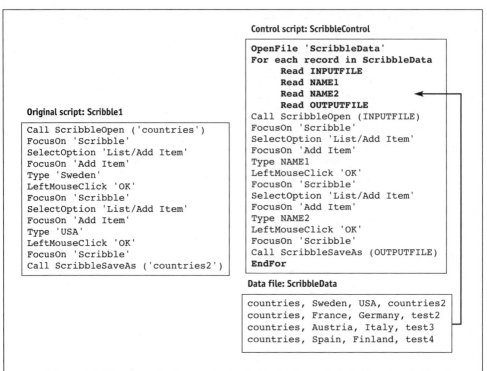

Control script: ScribbleControl

```
OpenFile 'ScribbleData'
For each record in ScribbleData
        Read INPUTFILE
        Read NAME1
        Read NAME2
        Read OUTPUTFILE
Call ScribbleOpen (INPUTFILE)
FocusOn 'Scribble'
SelectOption 'List/Add Item'
FocusOn 'Add Item'
Type NAME1
LeftMouseClick 'OK'
FocusOn 'Scribble'
SelectOption 'List/Add Item'
FocusOn 'Add Item'
Type NAME2
LeftMouseClick 'OK'
FocusOn 'Scribble'
Call ScribbleSaveAs (OUTPUTFILE)
EndFor
```

Original script: Scribble1

```
Call ScribbleOpen ('countries')
FocusOn 'Scribble'
SelectOption 'List/Add Item'
FocusOn 'Add Item'
Type 'Sweden'
LeftMouseClick 'OK'
FocusOn 'Scribble'
SelectOption 'List/Add Item'
FocusOn 'Add Item'
Type 'USA'
LeftMouseClick 'OK'
FocusOn 'Scribble'
Call ScribbleSaveAs ('countries2')
```

Data file: ScribbleData

```
countries, Sweden, USA, countries2
countries, France, Germany, test2
countries, Austria, Italy, test3
countries, Spain, Finland, test4
```

Figure 3.7 The Scribble test case implemented using the data-driven technique. Note that the data file ScribbleData actually contains the input of four test cases. These are all implemented using just the one control script (here called ScribbleControl) and the one data file.

script to accommodate it in the example. Whether the four test cases we have defined here would be useful is not the point of the example; rather it is to demonstrate the technique of data-driven scripts.

The control script shown in Figure 3.7 contains an almost exact copy of the script for a single test case. The only differences are that instead of literal data in the script we have used variable names. (You will remember from our discussion of shared scripts that a variable name can be thought of as a place marker that will be substituted for the real data by the test tool when the script is executed.)

In addition to these changes we also have to insert some additional instructions, which are shown in bold type. The first instruction *OpenFile* basically tells the test tool that it will be reading data from the file ScribbleData. The second instruction is actually one of a pair of instructions that implement an iteration control structure. The other half of this pair is the *EndFor*, the very last statement in the script. All the instructions in between this pair are executed once for every record in the data file ScribbleData. The next four instructions each read one value from the current record in ScribbleData and store the value in a different variable name (the variable names used are the same as those used in the next part of the script).

3.2.4.2 Data-driven example 2: more sophisticated data-driven script

Figure 3.8 shows a more sophisticated approach to using data-driven scripts. Here we are building in some knowledge of our application into our control script. Each column of the data table now represents a type of input. The first column is the filename (to open or save to), the second column is the data to add to a list, the third and fourth columns are the location in the list to move from and to, respectively, and the fifth column is the position number to delete.

We have two data files. The first is the complete test we performed in Chapter 2. (This form of scripting is a very concise way of showing what our test was.) The second script adds a couple of different countries, does a few more tests of the 'move' function, and deletes the first item of the list, saving to the file 'test2.'

We can see that our control script now contains 'if' statements that check each column to see if it is blank. If not, then it processes the data in a

Control script: ScribbleControl

```
OpenFile 'ScribbleDataX'
Read INPUTFILE
Call ScribbleOpen (INPUTFILE)
Go to next record (ie row)
For each record in ScribbleData
    Ignore first field if blank
    Read ADDNAME
    IF ADDNAME not = Blank THEN
        FocusOn 'Scribble'
        SelectOption 'List/Add Item'
        FocusOn 'List Add Item'
        Type ADDNAME
        LeftMouseClick 'OK'
    Read MOVEFROM
    Read MOVETO
    IF MOVEFROM not = Blank THEN
        FocusOn 'Scribble'
        SelectOption 'List/Move Item'
        FocusOn 'Move Item'
        Type MOVEFROM
        Type <TAB>
        Type MOVETO
        LeftMouseClick 'OK'
    Etc.
EndFor
```

Data file: ScribbleData1

INPUTFILE	ADDNAME	MOVEFROM/TO		DELPOS
countries				
	Sweden			
	USA			
		4	1	
	Norway			
				2
				7
countries2				

Data file: ScribbleData2

INPUTFILE	ADDNAME	MOVEFROM/TO		DELPOS
countries				
	France			
	Germany			
		1	3	
		2	2	
		5	3	
				1
test2				

Figure 3.8 A more sophisticated data-driven script.

specific way depending on the column position in the table. So the script 'knows' that column 2 contains things to add to a list, that column 5 contains the position number to delete, etc. This makes the control script more complex. (Note that you can't put 'Etc.' in a real script!)

In fact, the control script needs to be designed as the small software module that it has now become. There are a number of design decisions that need to be made. For example, should the two filenames be in the single data file, or would it be better to have another data file containing only filenames, with the main data file containing only the input data? Should the processing of the filename be inside or outside the main control loop (for each record)? Should the read of 'moveto' be done inside the 'if' statement when 'movefrom' is not blank? Should the column headings be included in the data file? (Yes, they definitely should!) But then the control script needs to ignore the first record. If one column is not blank, should the script check that all other columns are blank? What if they aren't? (The control script would actually handle a data file that contained a list item to be added and a 'move item' test in the same row.) These design decisions are not difficult (for an experienced programmer) but they all do need to be made.

Whatever design decisions are made about the control script, the data file must correspond to it. This means that if we change either the control script or the format of the data table, we need to make sure they are still 'in synch.' Note also that because different columns represent different types of data, our table has a lot of blank spaces. Our last scripting technique, keyword-driven, overcomes these problems.

3.2.4.3 Why make things so complicated?

These additional instructions do make the script more complicated to implement and maintain, and it is definitely a task that requires programming skills. In using this approach we are opening ourselves up to a vast array of errors that can be easy to make but very difficult to find. It is extremely unlikely that we will always write the scripts correctly the first time around so it will become necessary to test the tests and debug them before we can actually use them to test the software.

For all this additional difficulty, it is often well worth the effort since the benefits can greatly outweigh the costs. Once the control script has been implemented, new test cases, similar to the first one, can be added much more quickly and without any additional scripting. To add new test cases we simply have to add new data records into the data file, or add new data files in the same format that can be read by the control script.

3.2.4.4 Advantages of data-driven scripts

At the data-driven scripting level we can now really start to benefit from test automation. Using this technique it is possible to implement many more test cases with very little extra effort. This is because all we have to do is specify a new set of input data (and expected results) for each additional test case. We will not have to implement any more scripts. For example, Figure 3.9 shows a set of regression tests (represented by the crosses) each exercising a different part of the software under test. Let us assume that these are all the regression tests that we could afford to run manually. They would clearly be a good target for automation. If we automated them using linear or shared scripts then initially these are all we may automate. However, using the data-driven technique we could easily add many more test cases around each of the original regression tests. Because they would be using exactly the same script instructions, the only aspects that we can readily change are the input data and the expected outcomes. However, this is sufficient to enable us to produce numerous other test cases. They are unlikely to be test cases that we would necessarily consider performing if they had to be done manually but because they can now be implemented and run so cheaply, we can justify the effort.

A major advantage of the data-driven technique is that the format of the data file can be tailored to suit the testers. For example, with a little more sophistication in the scripting, the data file can be allowed to contain comments that the script will ignore but that will make the data file much more understandable and, therefore, maintainable. Another approach to this is for the testers to use a different format altogether to specify the test input. For example, it is common for testers to use a spreadsheet package. Once the spreadsheet has been completed it is converted to a more neutral format (typically a comma-separated text file, as used for the data file in Figure 3.7). The spreadsheet is kept as the master version and any changes required are made directly to the spreadsheet rather than the data file. Whenever changes are made the data file is regenerated from the spreadsheet.

The benefits of this ability for you to choose the format and layout of your test data should not be underestimated. Much effort will be spent in implementing automated tests and maintaining them. It is well worth investing a little time experimenting with different formats and layouts in order to find one that makes it really easy for your testers (not necessarily the automators) to edit the test data. The easier it is, the quicker and less error prone it will be – a goal worth striving for.

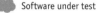

Software under test

Key automated regression test cases

Additional automated regression test cases
made possible by data-driven scripting technique

Figure 3.9 An advantage of the data-driven scripting technique is that many additional test cases (represented here by ●) can be used. These would not be undertaken without the data-driven technique since the cost of implementing and running them would be too high. The data-driven technique makes them cheap to implement and maintain and therefore worthwhile.

In addition to the test input, the expected results are also removed from the script and put into the data file. Each expected result is directly associated with a particular test input, so if the inputs are in the data file, the results to compare to must also be in the data file. A lot of test execution automation tools encourage this by providing mechanisms for capturing information on the screen and storing it somewhere as expected results for comparison with new results generated by a later run of the test.

EXPERIENCE REPORT

One company needed some maintenance effort for its automated scripts before they could be run. However, the company was unable to bring in the programming effort in time (due to pressure of other work on the programmers). Unable to use the automated tests, it had to test the new release of software manually.

Summarizing the advantages of the data-driven approach:

- similar tests can be added very quickly;
- adding new tests can be done by testers without technical or programming knowledge about the tool scripting language;
- there is no additional script maintenance effort for the second and subsequent tests.

3.2.4.5 Disadvantages of data-driven scripts

Writing these control scripts does need to be done by someone with a technical (programming) background and this is often a stumbling block. If your testers are not comfortable with programming automated test scripts then the skill has to be brought into the team, though not necessarily full time. If the programming skill is not available full time it is important to insure that it can be called on at very short notice.

The initial set-up will take some time but the benefits gained (faster to add new tests and less maintenance) will vastly outweigh this upfront cost when you have hundreds rather than dozens of tests. When a reasonably comprehensive set of test scripts is available, many more tests can be implemented and run. In practice, organizations that have done this find themselves implementing considerably more tests than they would have even thought about running manually. They also run these tests many more times within a single software release cycle, mostly as regression tests.

If you don't have many tests, this approach will entail more work, and will seem excessive. So for small systems this may not be appropriate. However, for large systems that are expected to live a long time and change frequently, you will appreciate this approach and gain far more in saved effort than you put in.

The disadvantages of the data-driven approach are:

- initial set-up takes of lot of effort;
- specialized (programming) support is required;
- it must be well managed.

3.2.5 Keyword-driven scripts

3.2.5.1 Keyword-driven scripts incorporate application knowledge

'**Keyword-driven** scripts' is the name we have given to what is really a logical extension of the more sophisticated data-driven technique. A limitation of the data-driven technique is that the navigation and actions performed have to be the same for each test case, and the logical 'knowledge' of what the tests are is built into both the data file and the control script, so they need to be synchronized.

However, there is nothing to say that we cannot take out some of the intelligence from the script and put it into the data file. Taking a literal approach to this would permit a single control script to support a wider variation in what the associated test cases could do but the vastly increased complexity of the data file (due to the scripting instructions it would now contain) would most likely outweigh any benefits. Furthermore, the job of debugging an automated test case implemented in this way could be seriously more difficult.

As we explained in Chapter 2, one of the reasons scripts can be so complex is that every single action has to be specified in the finest detail. For example, to specify an automated test using a linear script we would say: Enter 'John Smith' into the first field, press the tab key, enter '38 Yellow Brick Road' into the second field, press the tab key, etc. To specify the same test using a data-driven approach we would say: Enter 'John Smith' into the name field, enter '38 Yellow Brick Road' into the street field, etc. If we were writing the instructions for a human tester rather than a test tool, we could simply state the action: 'Enter the following client details: John Smith, 38 Yellow Brick Road.' We do not have to tell the human tester exactly how to enter the client details. In other words, we can assume that the human tester has some knowledge about the system under test or at least how to navigate a computer program.

The keyword-driven technique combines the data-driven technique with the desire to be able to specify automated test cases without having to specify all the excruciating detail. We expand the data file so it becomes a description of the test case we wish to automate using a set of keywords to indicate the tasks to be performed. The control script then has to be able to interpret the keywords but this is implemented outside of the control script itself. This additional level of separation from the implementation (tool) level does require an additional layer of technical implementation. Although this sounds as though it would be more difficult, we believe that it is actually much easier in the long run. The trick is to identify the right keywords.

An example of a keyword-driven script is shown in Figure 3.10. Rather than a data file we now have what we can call a test file since it describes the test case. The control script reads each keyword in the test file in turn and calls the associated supporting script. The supporting script may require more information from the test file, and this can either be read directly or passed on by the controlling script. The control script is no longer tied to a particular feature of the software under test, nor indeed to a particular application or system. Figure 3.10 also shows two test files associated with a different application, a drawing package called Doodle.

Note that we said the test file *describes* the test case; that is, it states *what* the test case does, not *how* it does it. At the start of this section on scripting techniques we said that there are two fundamental approaches to test case implementation, prescriptive and descriptive. Up until now all the scripting techniques we have described are used for a prescriptive approach to implementation. Keyword-driven scripting allows us to take a descriptive approach. To implement an automated test case we have only to provide a description of the test case more or less as we would do for a knowledgeable human tester.

The effect of this descriptive approach is that we build knowledge of the software under test into our test automation environment. This knowledge is contained in the supporting scripts. They 'know' about the software under test but they do not know anything about our test cases.

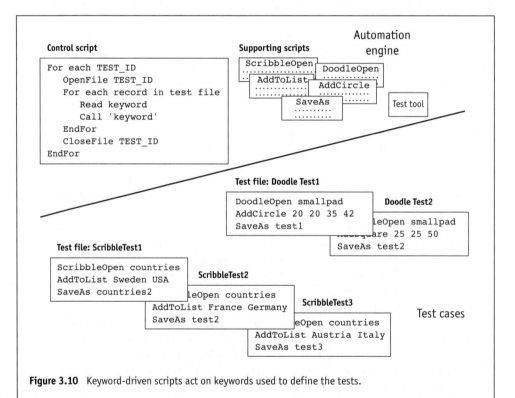

Figure 3.10 Keyword-driven scripts act on keywords used to define the tests.

Thus it is possible to develop the test cases separately from the test scripts and vice versa. People with business knowledge and tester skills can concentrate on the test files while people with technical knowledge can concentrate on the supporting scripts. Of course they cannot work completely independently since the supporting scripts have to support the keywords used in the test files.

3.2.5.2 Advantages of keyword-driven scripts

The advantages of this approach are immense. Generally the number of scripts required for this approach is a function of the size of the software under test rather than the number of tests. Thus, many more tests can be implemented without increasing the number of scripts, once the basic application supporting scripts are in place. This greatly reduces the script maintenance cost and not only speeds up the implementation of automated tests, but also makes it possible to use non-programming testers to implement them. We should be able to implement thousands of test cases with only a few hundred scripts.

The automated tests can be implemented in a way that is tool independent (and platform independent). So if we have to change the test tool (tool vendor goes bust, political pressure from parent company, or whatever) we can do so without losing any of our investment in the test cases. We would have to re-implement the supporting scripts, but that is all. Similarly, if the software under test has to be tested on different hardware platforms that are not all supported by the same test tool, we will not have to change our tests, merely the supporting scripts.

The way in which tests are implemented can be tailored to suit the testers rather than the test tool, using the format and tools that the testers are most comfortable with (e.g. text editor, spreadsheet, or word processor).

It is then possible to optimize the format so that new automated tests can be implemented as quickly as possible and yet in the safest way (i.e. least prone to error), avoiding many of the mistakes that can cause excessive debugging of tests.

Furthermore, simple tools can be implemented to perform static analysis on the automated test definitions. While this facility is not unique to programmed scripts, it is perhaps more easily implemented on them.

3.2.5.3 Example implementations of keyword-driven scripting

This book contains two extensive examples of good implementations of the keyword-driven scripting technique. Hans Buwalda from CMG has developed a method of scripting using Action Words, which are what we call keywords. He calls the supporting scripts 'navigation scripts' (although they are not concerned with navigation to specific points in the system menu structure, rather they interpret the Action Words).

This approach has enabled the users of the 'TestFrame' method to separate out the business-level test concerns (the business users construct test files called 'clusters' and the technical people program the scripts). This also gives independence from any specific commercial tool, since a different navigation script, i.e. supporting script, can implement the Action Words in different tool scripting languages.

This method has been very successful, and we recommend that you read Hans Buwalda's chapter, Chapter 22, which describes the method very clearly, and also Chapter 23, Iris Pinkster's case history of using Action Words.

The second example is a slightly different approach to implementing the keywords, described by Graham Freeburn. The approach taken here is to use additional data tables to implement the keywords. This means that the supporting scripts are standardized rather than being specific to an application. These standardized supporting scripts are bundled into the tool called RadSTAR.

This approach also provides the benefits of separating tester concerns from technical concerns, and has been implemented using a number of different commercial test execution tools.

This method is described in Chapter 24, and Chapter 25 contains a case history using the RadSTAR tool and its associated methods.

If there are additional methods or tools that also implement a keyword-driven approach, we apologize for not being aware of them at the time this book was written. The authors would like to be informed of any other implementations.

3.2.5.4 Implementing keyword-driven scripting

Some tools provide support for reading data from some other source, such as a spreadsheet (usually in the form of a comma-separated file). If you have this facility, you can use it directly. If you do not, you will need to develop your own approach. This initial development only needs to be done once, and will then become part of your overall regime.

You may want to develop your own approach even if your tool provides it, since you will then be independent of any tool.

The overall aim is to provide the easiest possible way of entering the test input without introducing unnecessary repetition or detail. Further support of this kind can be gained by using script pre-processing to convert or translate from a high-level language (4GL-like?) into the tool-specific language.

3.3 Script pre-processing

Script pre-processing is a term we use to describe any of a number of different script manipulation techniques that strive to make the process of writing and maintaining scripts easier and therefore less error prone. Pre-processing is one or more pre-compilation functions (where scripts have to be compiled before they can be executed by the test tool). Some testing tools, or rather their scripting languages, provide facilities for some types of manipulation though it may not be called script pre-processing. There are a number of script pre-processing functions that can benefit script writers including beautifier, static analysis, and general substitution. These are described in the following subsection.

3.3.1 Script pre-processing functions

An important aspect of any pre-processing is that it is tool supported, that is, it is more or less automated. It may be necessary for the script writer to invoke a specific tool or utility to perform a pre-processing function. Ideally, the test execution tool will be able to run pre-processing functions automatically, but at the time of writing this was rarely the case.

3.3.1.1 Beautifier

A beautifier checks the layout and format of scripts and if necessary edits them to make them conform to some standard. Having all scripts conforming to a standard layout helps make them easier to read and understand for different people. If only one person were to write and maintain a set of scripts then there is not so much advantage in using a beautifier. However, it is unlikely that any scripts used over the lifetime of most software products will be written and maintained solely by one person. In any case, a beautifier can take over the cosmetic chores, leaving script editors to concentrate on the technical accuracy of their work.

For example, Figure 3.11 shows two versions of the same script segment. The first one is as a script writer might first produce it, and the second version is the result of it having been 'beautified.' This has inserted blank lines before each comment line and indented the instructions within each control construct.

3.3.1.2 Static analysis

Static analysis facilities take a more critical look at scripts or tables, checking for actual and possible scripting defects. Of course the testing tools themselves will find and report some script defects, for example a misspelled or incomplete instruction. However, they tend not to do any more than is really necessary and in any case they cannot assume any knowledge of the script semantics. A static analysis facility has as its only goal the detection of all the defects and anomalies it is able to find. For example, if Type "F1" appeared in a script rather than the correct version Type "{F1}", the effect would be that the characters 'F' and '1' would be entered rather than the F1 function key. A static analysis facility could highlight this as a potential problem whereas the test tool would not pick this up since the incorrect version is syntactically correct.

We are not aware of any commercial tools that perform static analysis on test automation scripts. However, the most useful static analysis functions are best provided by in-house tools since these can concentrate on the defects actually made by your script writers.

```
While CURRENT_RECORD <> LAST_RECORD
;   Invoke new client option.
Type "{F2}"
;   Wait for the data entry screen.
Wait "Maintenance" in "~CMAINT.EXE~CMDE~Client Maintenance V2.1 Data
Entry"
;   Enter client surname.
Type "{=.1}{Tab}"
;   Enter remainder of client details.
While CURRENT_FIELD <> LAST_FIELD
Type "{=.+}{Tab}"
EndWhile
; Confirm details OK and wait for completion.
Type "{F1}"
Wait "New client added successfully" in "~CMAINT.EXE~CMDE~Client
Maintenance V2.1 Data Entry"
EndWhile
```

```
While CURRENT_RECORD <> LAST_RECORD

    ;     Invoke new client option.
    Type "{F2}"

    ;     Wait for the data entry screen.
    Wait "Maintenance" in —
    "~CMAINT.EXE~CMDE~Client Maintenance V2.1 Data Entry"

    ;     Enter client surname.
    Type "{=.1}{Tab}"

    ;     Enter remainder of client details.
    While CURRENT_FIELD <> LAST_FIELD
        Type "{=.+}{Tab}"
    EndWhile

    ;     Confirm details OK and wait for completion.
    Type "{F1}"
    Wait "New client added successfully" in —
    "~CMAINT.EXE~CMDE~Client Maintenance V2.1 Data Entry"

EndWhile
```

Figure 3.11 The script segment at the top is as it might be produced by the scriptwriter, the one at the bottom is the same script segment having been 'beautified'.

3.3.1.3 General substitution

General substitution offers some big advantages though it is possible to go too far. The idea is to hide some of the complication and intricate detail of scripts by substituting simple but meaningful alternatives. Some scripting languages support substitutions to varying degrees and where there is such support we recommend it be used, wisely.

Two main purposes for substitution are to replace cryptic character sequences with more simple and meaningful ones, and to replace long and complicated sequences with more simple and meaningful ones.

For example, Figure 3.12 shows a short segment of script taken from the example in Figure 3.11 with two instructions highlighted in bold. These

```
;   Enter client surname.
    Type "{=.1}{Tab}"

    ;   Enter remainder of client details.
    While CURRENT_FIELD <> LAST_FIELD
        Type "{=.+}{Tab}"
    EndWhile
```

Figure 3.12 A script segment with two cryptic notations highlighted.

use a special notation {=.1} and {=.+} to read data from a data file. These mean 'take the first field from the current record' and 'take the next field from the current record,' respectively. However, this is not an obvious interpretation and the notations could easily be confused with each other or with other similar notations.

This is a good case for using a substitution. Figure 3.13 shows an improved version of our script segment. Here we have used the keyword FIRST_FIELD as a substitution for "{=.1}{Tab}" and NEXT_FIELD as a substitution for "{=.+}{Tab}". We believe these are more understandable and much less likely to be confused.

An example of a long and complicated text string being substituted for a short keyword is shown in Figure 3.14. This type of substitution is particularly useful when the string appears several times throughout a script. It is

```
; Enter client surname.
    Type FIRST_FIELD

    ; Enter remainder of client details.
    While CURRENT_FIELD <> LAST_FIELD
        Type NEXT_FIELD
    EndWhile
```

Figure 3.13 An improved version of the script segment shown in Figure 3.12 using more meaningful keywords in place of cryptic notations.

```
;   Wait for the data entry screen.
    Wait "Maintenance" in —
    "~CMAINT.EXE~CMDE~Client Maintenance V2.1 Data Entry"
```

```
;   Wait for the data entry screen.
    Wait "Maintenance" in MAINT_DE
```

Figure 3.14 An example of a long and complicated text string being substituted by a short keyword.

also most useful in cases where the string itself can change between different versions of the software under test. For example, in Figure 3.14 the string contains a version number V2.1, which could well change. It would be much more efficient to change just one occurrence of it (the definition of the keyword) rather than every occurrence of its use throughout a set of scripts.

3.3.1.4 Test-specific substitution

The idea of being able to perform automated substitutions in scripts can be exploited further. Take a script or set of scripts that perform a test case and that have the input data embedded in the script(s). Using substitution, we can easily generate another script (or set of scripts) that implement a slightly different test case, that is, one that uses different input data. This is perhaps most practical where it is only a few key inputs that need changing from one test case to another.

For example, if a test case specifies a date that is used during processing (such as in calculating an interest payment), generate another script by substituting a different date. Of course this can be done as many times as you wish. The important point to keep in mind, however, is not to maintain the generated scripts. Only ever maintain the original script and regenerate the others whenever they are required.

A problem with this approach can be the verification of the new test cases. Different input values imply different expected outcomes. It may be possible to substitute the expected output values or it may be sensible to generate additional test cases that are less sensitive (i.e. perform fewer comparisons between actual and expected outcomes). This approach is not a panacea but it may be helpful in some circumstances.

The idea of substituting text strings in scripts can be carried too far. Depending on how it is implemented just about anything in a script can be substituted though doing so is not generally recommended. We discuss this further in the following section.

3.3.1.5 Things to be careful of when using substitutions

Don't get carried away with unnecessary substitutions. There will be some that are clearly excellent candidates for pre-processing, but it is all too easy to find yourself substituting things which are no less difficult to remember or error prone to enter than the tool equivalent.

Remember that the tool recognizes only the processed version of the script. This means that all scripts need to be pre-processed before the test tool can use them. When you come to debug the script (and this will happen) by having the tool step through the script under your control one instruction at a time, the script you see is the tool version, not the more readable version. If you have adopted too many or too frivolous substitutions debugging the script may be similar to debugging the 3GL code generated by a 4GL; it will bear little resemblance to the original.

Also, when you debug keep in mind the fact that the defect could be in the definition of what is substituted rather than in the original script.

We wanted to make our scripts able to cope when new fields were added to any screen, without the need to change them. The tool we had did not allow us to directly access a field by name, but it could tell us the name of the field the cursor was in.

We were able to make the scripts do what we wanted by writing our own special script to search for the field we wanted. What we did was to tab around the whole screen until the cursor had returned to the place it started from. At each field, we checked its name.

If we couldn't find the field, then we would back out of that test and run the next test.

This meant that all of our scripts could cope when fields were moved or were in a different order, provided they were still on the same screen.

Moral: if your tool doesn't provide a facility you need, don't give up; use what the tool does provide to achieve your aim another way.

Source: Herb Isenberg, 'Flexible testing systems', *Dr Dobb's Journal*, June 1995, pp. 88–95.

3.3.1.6 Implementing pre-processing

All of the pre-processing functions we have described can be implemented using standard text manipulation tools (providing the scripts are held in text files). Describing in detail how these could work is beyond the scope of this book but one simple approach is described below. In some cases the implementation of a script pre-processor will be similar to that of the filters described in Chapter 4.

What is needed for substitutions is a substitution table that contains the definition of all of the shorthand terms we have used in our master scripts. For general definitions the substitution table should be made available to all of the scripts using the same conventions. You may have several different substitution tables, with a pre-processing pass for each relevant table.

One way to implement this is to use a non-interactive editor, and a command file to drive the editor; this is your pre-processor. This command file is run immediately before the scripts are compiled. Your command file may also contain the compilation instructions, if the tool permits compilation from the command line. Alternatively, if the tool you have allows you to call other command files, you can make use of that feature. At the time of writing this is a feature we have yet to see test tools provide, but one we would certainly encourage.

Summary

Scripting techniques are similar to programming techniques. Good programming produces software that is easy to maintain. Good scripting produces testware that is easy to maintain. The scripts need to be engineered, and the scripts are written in scripting languages which are programming languages.

Scripts contain data and instructions for the test tool, including synchronization, comparison information, where to read data from and where to store data, and control information, such as 'if' statements or loops. The simpler the script is, the less effort it will take to create it, but the more effort it will take to maintain it. So to minimize maintenance effort requires investing effort in script creation.

A good set of scripts will be well structured, rather than simply being one script per test. A good script will be annotated with comments, will perform a single task, will be well structured, understandable, documented, and likely to be reused. The way in which test cases are designed has an impact on the test scripts, but the structure of the scripts may be different from the structure of the tests.

Vendors sometimes describe the raw tool scripts as being 'easy to read' or 'self documenting.' What is important is that the script can be understood (not just the words able to be read) and that the documentation is meaningful.

We recommend that the documentation for each script is placed in the header of the script. This should include the name of the script, the author, the date it was created/edited, the purpose of the script, any parameters it requires or produces, any pre- and postconditions before it can be run, any other information that would help someone who is maintaining the script, and the history of all amendments made to the script.

We considered five scripting techniques. Each technique has its strengths and weaknesses, and is best used in particular situations. Table 3.3 shows a summary of the different scripting techniques.

Table 3.3 Summary of scripting techniques.

	Structured or unstructured?	Script contains	Script intelligence	Test cases defined by	Approach
Linear	Unstructured	Constants	None	Script	Prescriptive
Structured	Structured	Constants	Ifs and loops	Script	Prescriptive
Shared	Structured or unstructured	Constants and variables	Ifs and loops	Script	Prescriptive
Data-driven	Structured	Variables	Ifs, loops, and data reading	Script and data	Prescriptive
Keyword-driven	Structured	Variables and keywords	Ifs, loops, data reading, and keyword interpreter	Data	Descriptive

A linear script is what a recording produces. It is a quick way to get started and doesn't require programming knowledge to produce it. A linear script is useful for one-off repetitive actions, conversions, editing, or demonstrations. Linear scripts are not useful for long-term maintainable automation. They are inefficient, expensive to change and very vulnerable to minor software changes, and 'fragile' – easily broken by unexpected events occurring in a test. Test inputs and expected outcomes are 'hard-wired' into the script.

Structured scripting, like structured programming, uses control structures. 'If' statements increase robustness as they allow the test to do different things when something happens. Loops allow a script to perform many repeated actions. Calling other scripts helps to make scripts more modular. Structured scripts still contain 'hard-wired' test information. The script is now more complex but it is also more powerful.

Shared scripts are reused in more than one test case. This enables common actions to be in only one place rather than in every script. This means that maintenance effort is significantly reduced. It is worth making a shared script more robust because it will be used more often. Shared scripts can be application specific or application independent. Shared scripts still contain 'hard-wired' test information and tend to be specific to one part of the software under test, but there are more scripts to keep track of. In order to benefit from shared scripts, it is important to be disciplined and have a good configuration management system.

Data-driven scripts store the test inputs and expected outcomes in a data file that is then read by a more general control script. This enables new tests to be added much more easily, since it is only the data table that is updated. A more sophisticated data-driven approach may have columns in the data file relating to logical entities in the software being tested. Significant benefits can be gained in test automation using data-driven scripts. New tests can be added easily, and many more tests of a similar nature can be performed, and the script does not need to be changed when new tests are added. In addition, testers can concentrate on the tests without being distracted by the technical programming issues of scripting. The disadvantages of this approach are that the initial set-up does take a fair amount of effort, technical programmers are needed to implement the scripts, and it must be well managed. The scripts and the data tables need to be consistent.

The keyword-driven scripting technique takes the generalization into the realm of the application as well as the data. The keywords are stored in the data table, representing application functions. This method is descriptive rather than prescriptive; we say what the test should do rather than having to prescribe the detail that was necessary with the other scripting techniques. This additional level of sophistication also requires an additional implementation level, but now it actually gets simpler rather than more complex. The control scripts and the supporting scripts that interpret the keywords are now very generic, so there are fewer of them, and they are worth making very robust. All of the information about what to test is now contained in the data table, so the separation of test information from implementation is the greatest in this technique. Two implementations of the keyword-driven technique are described in Chapters 22–25.

Pre-processing can be applied to any scripts. This may include a beautifier, static analysis, general substitution, or test-specific substitutions

Automated comparison

4.1 Verification, comparison, and automation

4.1.1 Verification by comparison

Test **verification** is the process of checking whether or not the software has produced the correct outcome. This is achieved by performing one or more **comparisons** between an actual outcome of a test and the expected outcome of that test (i.e. the outcome when the software is performing correctly). Some tests require only a single comparison to verify their outcome while other tests may require several comparisons. For example, a test case that has entered new information into a database may require at least two comparisons, one to check that the information is displayed on the screen correctly and the other to check that the information is written to the database successfully.

There are several important decisions to be made when planning automated comparisons that have a significant impact on both the effectiveness and efficiency of your automated testing. The information you decide to compare and how much of it you compare affects the test cases' ability to detect defects, the implementation costs, and the maintenance costs. These are discussed in this section. Section 4.2 discusses what comparators can and cannot do. The two key types of comparison, dynamic and post-execution, are described in Sections 4.3 and 4.4. Simple and complex comparisons are described in Sections 4.5 and 4.6, and Section 4.7 discusses test sensitivity (to changes in the software being tested). Section 4.8 describes different types of outcome that can be compared: disk-based, screen-based, and others. Section 4.9 describes a technique of using what we call filters for constructing comparisons that are powerful and flexible, yet relatively simple to implement. We conclude the chapter with some guidelines for effective and efficient automated comparison.

4.1.2 Planned versus ad hoc comparisons

During manual testing it is possible for the human tester simply to look at what the software is producing and decide whether or not those outputs are correct based on an understanding of what the software should produce. In this case the comparison is between the actual outcome (for example, on the screen) and the expected outcome held in the tester's head (or the expected outcome determined by the tester from his or her understanding). Of course, what the tester understands may not always be correct but it is difficult to check this when verification is done so informally. (Systems that are developed using Rapid Application Development (RAD) techniques often have a high degree of informal verification, particularly for newly developed functionality.)

At the other end of the scale a planned and formal approach to verification would involve a comparison of specific outcomes carefully chosen to insure that the objectives of the test case are met. These would be compared against rigorously predicted expected outcomes. Once again, though, it cannot be guaranteed that the tester will always be able to predict the exact outcomes. However, this approach does make it easier to have other people check the predicted outcomes to help insure that they are correct.

The same is true for automated testing. It is better to have the verification details of each test case carefully thought out in advance so the automator can concentrate on how best to implement the automation without having to worry about the quality of the tests themselves. This is particularly important where the test case designer and the test automator are different people and the automator does not have the same business knowledge as the test case designer. It is possible to automate some specific comparisons, but it is not possible to automate a 'check the output is right' instruction!

Designing test cases in advance of automation creates a better opportunity to achieve a good balance between the many issues that affect the quality of both the tests and the automation itself. Unplanned automation can be beneficial, but planned automation is likely to be much more so.

4.1.3 Predicting outcomes versus verifying actual outcomes

When automating test cases, the expected outcomes have either to be prepared in advance or generated by capturing the actual outcomes of a test run. In the latter case the captured outcomes must be verified manually and saved as the expected outcomes for further runs of the automated tests. This is called reference testing. Which approach is the best in any particular situation depends on the following considerations:

1. The magnitude of the expected result. If the expected outcome is a single number or a short text string (such as an error message) then it can be prepared in advance quite easily. However, if it is a multi-page report containing much detailed information then it may be easier to manually verify the result of the first test run.

2. Whether or not the result can be predicted. There are situations in which it is not possible to predict an expected result such as when system tests are performed on 'live' data (e.g. stock market share prices), the details of which cannot be known in advance. This is more difficult to automate, though not impossible.

3. Availability of the software under test. The first set of actual results cannot be generated until the software is available so if we wait until then before implementing the automated tests, there may not be sufficient time left to automate as many of the test cases as we would like. Of course it will be possible to do some of the work in any case, particularly if the scripts are to be written manually (rather than recorded).

4. Quality of verification. Generally speaking, it is better to predict test outcomes in advance than it is to verify the first set of actual outcomes. This is because human beings tend to fall foul of the cognitive dissonance barrier; that is, we will see what we want to see rather than what is actually there. Thus, it is more likely that we will miss defects when verifying test outcomes than when planning them in advance.

4.1.4 Why compare automatically?

Comparison is arguably the most automatable task in software testing, and is often the most beneficial to automate. Comparing extensive lists of numbers, screen outputs, or data of any kind is not something that human testers do very well. It is easy to make a mistake, and we find it very boring, because it is a repetitive and detailed task. This makes it ideal for a computer to do (which will never become bored!). In fact, it is a good idea to use comparators to automate the comparison of the outcome of tests performed manually. This may be the best place to introduce tool support into the testing process.

Automated execution can and will generate a lot of outcomes. Usually these outcomes will need to be verified in some way, though not all tests will need detailed comparison of their outcomes. Volume tests, for example, may only need to check that the software is still running.

EXPERIENCE REPORT

A client had automated test input and execution, but not the comparison of test outcomes. When we visited, staff pointed out the three-foot (one-meter) high pile of printout in the corner, which were the test outputs that had been painstakingly checked by the testers. This manual verification took three or four days, and was also somewhat error prone. If it had been automated, it could probably have been completed in an hour or two.

Without automated comparison of outcomes, we will not have automated testing, even if we have automated execution. However, in some situations this is a very sensible thing to do. For example, if inputs are very detailed and tortuous, automating them will save a lot of time and errors, even if the output of the test is verified manually. (See Paul Herzlich's case study in Chapter 16.) If the correctness of a screen output is easy to see at a glance and the automation of that comparison is difficult, then automated execution and manual verification may be a good solution.

4.1.5 What should be compared?

Normally we think of checking what is output to the screen as each test case is performed, and sometimes this is all we think of checking. Of course, screen output is something that should be checked, but it may not be all that should be checked.

In addition to the visible output to the user, the software execution may have added, altered, or deleted data in a file or database. In order to verify that the test worked correctly, we may need to check that the correct changes occurred in the database. It is possible for a program to update the screen display but erroneously omit to save those updates in the database. If this were the situation and we only checked the screen display then our test case would not reveal this defect.

There are many other types of output that may need to be checked; for example, data sent to a printer, email messages, messages sent across networks to other machines and processes, signals sent to hardware devices, etc. It is common to find that manual testing does not always verify all of these effects either. However, because manual testing is known to be ad hoc and incomplete, this aspect is often just one more area of incompleteness. If tests are to be automated, we can take the opportunity to improve the quality of the testing by checking more things, particularly if checking can be automated.

4.1.6 Limitations of automated comparison

When testing is performed manually, the tester is likely to undertake many more individual checks on the validity of the outcome of tests than have been prescribed. Many of these may be done subconsciously, but even so they may highlight problems that even the most well-planned set of specific comparisons will miss. However, automated comparisons inevitably stick to exactly the same checks every time and these are likely to be a small subset of the comparisons actually performed by a human tester. Of course, it is possible for an automated test to check 'everything,' but it is rarely practical or desirable.

Automated comparisons can only ever be as good as the expected outcomes with which the actual outcomes are compared. If a defect exists in an expected outcome, automated comparison will hide, not highlight, the same defect in the actual outcome.

Furthermore, manual regression testing done manually is more flexible. Testers can vary comparisons undertaken each time the tests are performed based on their understanding of the changes that have been made. Automated testing is not so flexible. Once automated, the same comparisons are performed in precisely the same way every time. If any changes are required the test cases have to be updated, a maintenance cost that may not be acceptable.

Comparison is the means to verification and much of it can be automated. Although automation can only compare the actual outcome to an expected outcome, which is not necessarily the correct outcome, it is much faster and far more reliable than manual comparison of those things that are compared.

4.2 What do comparators do?

An automated comparison tool, normally referred to as a 'comparator,' is a computer program that detects differences between two sets of data. For test automation this data is usually the outcome of a test run and the expected outcome. The data may be displayed on a screen or held in files or databases, and can be in a variety of formats including standard text files. Where a comparator facility is built into a test execution tool the data is more likely to be screen images.

4.2.1 What can be compared?

The data that can be compared will depend on the capabilities of the comparator tool. Some commercial comparators have extensive capabilities for comparing several different data formats. With the simplest comparators you can compare only standard text files but with more sophisticated comparators you can compare more complex and specialized forms of data, including graphical formats and the content of databases.

4.2.2 What comparators can tell you

All comparators basically tell you whether or not the two sets of compared data are the same but many will also highlight the individual differences in some way. There is a variety of ways of highlighting differences across different comparators, and what is output by any one comparator can vary enormously, depending on what has been asked for.

During execution of a series of automated test cases, we only need to know whether or not there are any differences between the actual and expected data. This will enable the test execution automation tool, or us, to determine whether or not each test case passed.

After a test case has failed, we will have to investigate the cause of the failure. Now we need additional information from our comparator. It is often helpful to be told how many differences there are, where they occur, and exactly what the differences are. Ideally, this information will have been reported at the time each comparison was performed. (Examples of comparator outputs are given in Section 4.8.)

The more advanced comparators provide facilities to help you browse the differences; for example, an interactive capability that allows you to see portions of two compared files side by side (or one above the other). In this case the differences may be highlighted in some way, such as with bold type or a different color. Another variation displays only one file at a time but allows you to switch between the two files in rapid succession.

Where graphical images are being compared, some comparator tools are able to highlight the differences using various graphical manipulation techniques. For example, where two bitmap images are being compared it is possible to produce a third image that is the result of subtracting one image from the other, leaving the third image blank where the first two are identical.

These facilities make the task of analyzing differences much easier and quicker.

Some word processors provide useful facilities to compare two versions of text documents. While they probably do not make the best comparators for test automation purposes they may prove useful where differences in textual outputs occur, particularly if the people undertaking the analysis are more familiar with a word processor than a comparison tool.

Other information output by dedicated comparator tools may include the time and date the comparison was performed, how long it took, the version of the comparator tool used, etc. This is mostly used for auditing purposes to show that the tests were performed correctly.

4.2.3 What comparators cannot tell you

A comparator cannot tell you if a test has passed or failed (although that is how they are used). A comparator can only tell you if there are differences. We often infer a 'test passed' result when a comparison finds no unexpected differences and a 'test failed' result when it does. However, this is not necessarily correct. If the expected outcome is actually incorrect, then we will be inclined to say 'test passed' when the software being tested fails in exactly the same way!

It can be very difficult to insure that the golden version, containing the stored expected outcomes, is correct in every detail, and it may not be worth the effort. A golden version that is slightly tarnished can still save a lot of time if it is used within its limitations. It is important to remember that any golden version is not guaranteed to be perfect anyway since human beings are prone to make errors in either constructing it or verifying it the first time.

4.3.1 What it is

Dynamic comparison is the comparison that is performed while a test case is executing. Test execution tools normally include comparator features that are specifically designed for dynamic comparison. Dynamic comparison is perhaps the most popular because it is much better supported by commercial test execution tools, particularly those with capture/replay facilities.

Dynamic comparison is best used to check things as they appear on the screen in much the same way as a human tester would do. (Comparing other outputs after the test case has ended is known as post-execution comparison. This is described in Section 4.4.) This means that outputs to the screen during the running of a test case can be checked even if they are overwritten later by further outputs from the same test case. Outputs that are not visible on the screen can also be compared dynamically, such as GUI attributes.

4.3.2 Tool support and implementation

As we saw in Chapter 2, the dynamic comparison instructions must be inserted into the test script. These instructions tell the tool what is to be compared when, and what it is to be compared against.

Comparison instructions do not have to be inserted into a script manually. With most tools it is possible to suspend the recording of a test case so that the tool can be shown what to check at that point, saving the current version as the expected outcome.

In either case, the tool can be instructed to capture a particular part of a screen or window (or indeed the whole screen, though generally this is not recommended), and save the current instance of it as the expected result. The tool will automatically add instructions to the script that will, whenever the script is replayed, cause the tool to capture the same output and compare it with what has been saved as the expected outcome.

Where tools do not allow checks to be added while a script is being recorded, they may allow them to be inserted while the script is being replayed. The test is replayed in 'slow motion,' i.e. one step at a time. When a verification point is reached, the screen output is first verified as correct by the tester, and then if it is acceptable, the tool is instructed to capture the relevant output as the golden version. This means that two passes are necessary, the first to record the inputs, and the second to record the dynamic comparison instructions.

For tools that do not support either of these approaches it will be necessary for the test automator to edit the script. This will, of course, require some programming knowledge, since the tool script is written in a programming language. This is why we advise against using simple recording techniques (with or without dynamic comparison) for long-term test automation.

4.3.3 Test case intelligence

Dynamic comparison can be used to help program some intelligence into a test case, to make it act differently depending on the output as it occurs. For example, if an unexpected output occurs it may suggest that the test script has become out of step with the software under test, so the test case can be aborted rather than allowed to continue. Letting test cases continue when the expected outcome has not been achieved can be wasteful. Once a test script is out of step with the software, any further actions are unlikely to replicate the right conditions and may even corrupt data that is to be used by other test cases.

Adding intelligence to the test scripts in this way can also help to make the scripts more resilient. For example, if the software under test performs an action that cannot always be guaranteed to work first time (such as logging on to a remote machine over a busy network) then the script can be programmed to retry the action a number of times.

4.3.4 Increased complexity, higher maintenance costs

Dynamic comparison appears at first to provide compelling reasons for using it as much as possible, but there is a downside. Because dynamic comparison involves embedding further commands or instructions into the test scripts, it makes the test scripts more complex. So test cases that use many dynamic comparisons take more effort to create, are more difficult to write correctly (more errors are likely so more script debugging will be necessary), and will incur a higher maintenance cost.

A lot of seemingly trivial changes to the screen output can result in many unimportant differences being highlighted by dynamic comparisons. Although most test execution tools make it easy to update the expected outcomes in such situations, if a lot of comparisons are affected the updates can take considerable time and effort, and this is not the most interesting of work.

4.4 Post-execution comparison

4.4.1 What it is

Post-execution comparison is the comparison that is performed after a test case has run. It is mostly used to compare outputs other than those that have been sent to the screen, such as files that have been created and the updated content of a database.

4.4.2 Tool support

Test execution tools do not normally include support for this type of comparison directly; rather, a separate tool or tools are used. However, it is possible to design test cases such that other outcomes are displayed on the screen to enable the dynamic comparison facilities of the test execution tool to be used. However, if the information to be compared after the test case has completed amounts to more than a few screens-full, this approach is not very satisfactory.

EXPERIENCE REPORT

A client was evaluating a test execution tool to see how well it supported the testing process. The system under test was a mainframe application accessed via terminal emulation software running on PCs. Most of the test verification involved checking large output files at the end of each test case. The tool vendor (presumably to insure the sale) was putting quite a lot of effort into writing scripts that displayed the output files on the PC one page at a time where the dynamic comparison facilities of the tool were then used to compare each page with the expected result. Apart from being slow, the comparison was limited to a record size shorter than was used in the files and so could not be as accurate as was required.

We recommended that a more sensible approach would be to do post-execution comparison with a standard file comparator and using filters, and not try to use the test execution tool at all for the comparison of the file contents. This would result in an order of magnitude performance improvement in running the comparisons and would also achieve more accurate comparisons.

Because test execution tools generally do not support post-execution comparison as well as dynamic comparison, post-execution comparison often seems to be more work to automate.

At the time of writing, there were few commercial post-execution comparison tools on the market. Sometimes these tools are sold together with a test execution tool and may not be available separately. Where an appropriate tool does exist it may be well worth buying it. However, there is much that can be done using in-house tools and utilities to provide a comprehensive and yet easy to use set of comparison tools. One approach to this that has proved successful is described in detail in Section 4.9.

4.4.3 Order and structure of comparisons

Unlike dynamic comparison, where outputs have to be compared as they occur, with post-execution comparison it is possible to be more selective over the order and extent of comparisons performed. Rather than comparing all of the selected outcomes for any one test case we may prefer to divide them into two or more groups of comparisons such that we compare the second and subsequent groups only if the first group was successful.

For example, general results may be verified first, since if they have failed, there is no point in spending any time on detailed verification of those results. (The defects should be fixed first so that the general tests pass before the detailed results are checked.)

It may seem a strange idea to try to save time in automated checking because if a tool does it, it doesn't matter how long it takes. However, when a large number of automated test cases are in place or there are a large number of time-consuming complex comparisons, you may run out of time to run and verify all of the tests. It is better to plan ways to be selective at the start even if you initially always run all test cases and comparisons.

EXPERIENCE REPORT

During a conference presentation we had said that one difference between manual and automated testing is that with automated testing you can afford to run more regression tests as a final check on a system. Afterwards one delegate told us that his company's mainframe-based automated regression test suite took two weeks to run so whenever they needed to run a regression test pack overnight they still had a hard job selecting which test cases to run.

4.4.4 Active and passive post-execution comparison

Post-execution comparison can be done either actively or passively. If we simply look at whatever happens to be available after the test case has been executed, this is a passive approach. In our example test case of Chapter 2 the only thing available to us at the end is the edited document. All the information that was output to the screen has gone and so cannot be looked at. We could have used dynamic comparison to verify the screen outputs but we could also use active post-execution comparison.

If we intentionally save particular results that we are interested in during a test case, for the express purpose of comparing them afterwards, this is an active approach to post-execution comparison. In our example test case we could instruct the tool to capture portions of the screen output at particular times (e.g. error messages) and save them in one or more files. In this case the outputs we would capture for post-execution comparison would be the same as those we would choose to use for dynamic comparison.

This active approach to post-execution comparison offers only subtle benefits over dynamic comparison that may be valuable in some situations but not in others. The benefits are:

1. The actual outputs are saved. A more detailed record of the outcome of test cases will be retained, giving potentially useful information in the event of test case failure and perhaps to archive for future audits.

   Where a complex comparison is performed the actual and expected outcomes may differ in expected ways (so they would be deemed to match), so saving the actual outcome could be important. However, where a simple comparison is performed and no differences exist, the expected and actual outcomes are identical.

2. Comparison can be done offline. Comparison can be processing intensive and take considerable elapsed time. It may be useful to be able to run comparisons after all the test cases have been executed. The comparisons could be performed on a different machine from that used to execute the test cases, particularly useful where machine resources for testing are available only for a limited time.

3. Different comparators can be used. The sophistication of dynamic comparison is usually limited to the capabilities of the test tool. Post-execution comparison permits a much wider range of tools and techniques for performing more complex comparisons.

4. Other outputs can be saved. Not all captured information has to be compared. It can be useful to capture additional outcomes that are used only in the event of test case failure as an aid to analyzing the cause of the failure.

Note that 'simpler scripts' is not listed as a benefit. This is because the instructions required for dynamic comparison are being replaced by similar instructions to capture and save specific outputs. These are unlikely to be much different and will still require 'programming in' to the test script.

Although active post-execution comparison can be used in place of dynamic comparison, it is rarely done. Verifying outputs as they occur during a test case run is generally superior to verifying them at the end of a test case run since the test execution tool can be instructed to act differently depending on the results. For example, the script could abort a test case as soon as something goes wrong.

4.4.5 Implementing post-execution comparison

4.4.5.1 Integration of test execution and post-execution comparison

Implementing post-execution comparison is not as straightforward as it may at first appear. When an automated test case is performed we would like to be told whether or not it passed without us having to take any further action. However, when a test case requires one or more post-execution comparisons, it is usually a different tool that performs it. In this situation the test execution tool may not run the post-execution comparator(s) of its own accord so we will have to run the comparator(s) ourselves. Figure 4.1 shows this situation in terms of the manual and automated tasks necessary to complete a set of 'automated' test cases.

Figure 4.1 does not look much like efficient automated testing and indeed it is not. It would be nice if the test execution tool were responsible for running the comparator, but unless we tell it to do so, and tell it how to do so, it is not.

To make the test execution tool perform the post-execution comparisons we will have to specifically add the necessary instructions to the end of the test script. This can amount to a significant amount of work, particularly if there are a good number of separate comparisons to be performed.

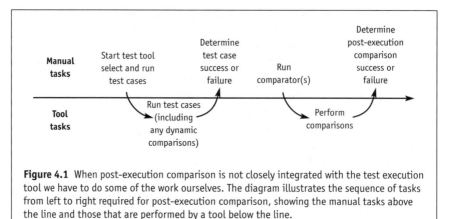

Figure 4.1 When post-execution comparison is not closely integrated with the test execution tool we have to do some of the work ourselves. The diagram illustrates the sequence of tasks from left to right required for post-execution comparison, showing the manual tasks above the line and those that are performed by a tool below the line.

Across a number of test cases we can reduce the amount of work by using shared scripts (see Chapter 3 for a description of scripting techniques). By carefully planning where the actual and expected outcomes will be stored such that they can be located easily and in a consistent manner across many test cases, the additional instructions in each test script can be further simplified. (See Chapter 5 for a discussion of these issues.)

Even when we have added the instructions to perform the post-execution comparison we may not have solved the whole problem. Figure 4.2 shows why. The test execution tool will probably be able to tell us that the test case ran successfully (or not) but it may not tell us anything about the results of the post-execution comparisons. Assessing the results of the post-execution comparison is then a manual task. We have to look in two places to determine the final status of the test case run: the execution tool's log or summary report and the output from the comparator tool(s).

We would like to be given one all-encompassing status for each test case – in other words, whether or not it was successful. However, enhancing a test

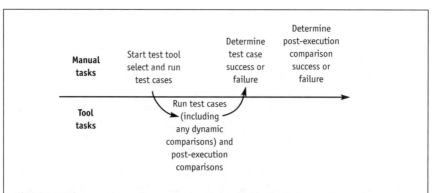

Figure 4.2 When post-execution comparison is invoked by the test execution tool we may still be left with the job of looking at the results of the test execution and, separately, the results of the post-execution comparison.

script so that it runs the post-execution comparisons is one thing; enhancing it so that it understands the results of the comparisons and returns one over-all test case status is another. This latter task may not be trivial but there is much to be gained by solving the problem in a way that all test cases can benefit from the solution.

4.4.5.2 Four ways to integrate execution and post-execution comparison

In an ideal world the interface between the test execution tool and the post-execution comparators would be seamless, but there is usually a gap that we have to fill ourselves. There are a variety of ways to overcome the problems of running the comparisons and assessing the final test case result. We shall now consider a few of them.

The models in Figure 4.3 depict four approaches to the implementation of post-execution comparison. These are not the only alternatives but are perhaps the most common and are the ones which we will now consider. Three of these show a 'harness' around the comparator. This is meant to imply something that is 'homegrown', not a part of any commercial test tool. What this does and the reasons for it will be made clearer later on but for now it is best considered as a means of filling in a gap left by the commercial testing tools.

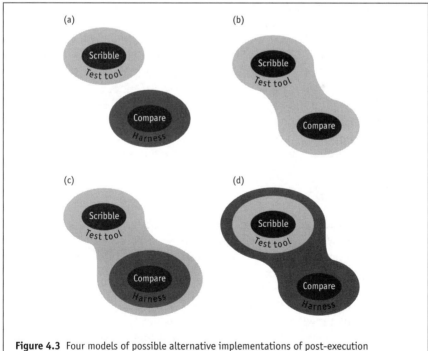

Figure 4.3 Four models of possible alternative implementations of post-execution comparison: (a) a separate harness (usually home-grown) runs the comparator after the test tool has executed the test cases; (b) the test tool runs the comparator; (c) the execution tool is used to provide a common interface to both the test execution and comparison processes; and (d) the harness provides a common interface to the two processes.

The first model uses the homegrown harness around the comparator but remains separate from the test execution tool and process. With this approach it is necessary for a tester to invoke the comparison process after the test execution process has completed (usually after all the test cases have been executed). While this eliminates the need for a human tester to repeatedly invoke the comparator, it is still a long way from an automated process. However, it is perhaps a good solution where there are benefits in running the post-execution comparison process at a completely separate time or on a different machine.

The second model is perhaps the best one in that both the execution and comparison processes are handled by the test tool, but in our experience this is more of a myth than a reality at the time of writing. In practice the post-execution comparison tool is not very well integrated with the execution tool, if at all. For a seamless integration it becomes necessary to build a harness around the comparator, which brings us on to the third model.

The third model provides a common interface to both the execution and comparison processes but relies on a harness to interact with the comparator.

The fourth model uses the test harness to provide a common interface by driving the testing tool itself. This has been the most common approach by successful large automation projects that we have seen. However, we believe that this may become less common as the commercial testing tools are now beginning to provide better overall support.

In each case the harness may be implemented either as a software program in its own right, as one or more command files (job files, batch files, shell scripts – whatever the terminology is for the environment you use), as shared test tool scripts, or a combination of two or more of these. Note that where some or all of the harness is implemented by tool scripts, in our view it does not mean that the tool is providing the necessary support. The fact that the test automator has to implement scripts to do a task means that the tool itself does not already provide appropriate support.

4.5 Simple comparison

Simple comparison (sometimes called dumb comparison) looks for an identical match between the actual and expected outcomes. Any and every difference will be found. Since a lot of testing can be automated using only simple comparisons, the benefits of simple comparisons should not be ignored. Because they are simple it is easy to specify them correctly so fewer mistakes are likely to be made, and it is easier for other people to understand exactly what is, and what is not, being compared. Usually much less work is involved in implementing and maintaining simple comparisons (compared with complex comparisons, described in Section 4.6).

There will be tests that have outcomes that can legitimately differ each time the test case is run. Simple comparison will cause these test cases to fail even though the differences can be safely ignored. If only a few test cases are prone to this problem then we can probably live with it. However, if many test cases are affected, the cost of having to trawl through each highlighted difference time and again just to confirm that they can be ignored can seriously impact the benefits of automation.

To avoid, or at least reduce, this cost we need a way of comparing outcomes that allows us to specify differences that are to be ignored. Fortunately this exists, and perhaps not surprisingly, we call it complex comparison.

4.6 Complex comparison

4.6.1 Why are complex comparisons needed?

Complex comparison (also known as intelligent comparison) enables us to compare actual and expected outcomes with known differences between them. A complex comparison will ignore certain types of difference (usually those that we expect to see or that are not important to us) and highlight others, providing we specify the comparison requirements correctly.

Perhaps the most common complex comparisons ignore dates and times that are usually expected to be different. Some commercial comparison tools have built into them knowledge of several different standard date and time formats which you can choose to enable or disable as your comparison requirements demand. Here are a few more examples of where complex comparisons are required:

- different unique identity code or number generated each time;
- output in a different order (new version of the software may sort on a different key);
- different values within an acceptable range (e.g. temperature sensing);
- different text formats (e.g. font, color, size).

EXPERIENCE REPORT

A client organization had formed a separate test automation team within a test department to automate system tests designed by the manual testers. The manual system testers by and large had a business background whereas the automation team had a technical background.

Test automation was not perceived as particularly successful and it turned out that one of the reasons for this was that the manual system testers disliked having to confirm that many of the differences found by the automated tests were simply different dates that were not of interest. Unfortunately, the automated testers did not realize that the system testers did not need or want to verify these differences, and the system testers did not realize that it was possible to make the comparison tool ignore such differences. The system testers never asked for an improved comparison process, and the test automators never thought to offer it.

4.6.2 Simple masking

Complex comparisons ignore specific differences by excluding from the comparison those parts of an output that are expected to differ. This is achieved in a variety of ways but most of them come down to specifying a field location or a particular pattern of characters. For example, the sales invoice shown in Figure 4.4 contains an invoice number and two dates that are expected to differ every time the test case is run.

A simple approach to masking involves ignoring complete records. In our invoice example we could make the comparator ignore the first two lines and the eleventh line of the invoice. While this would work for this particular output it would not work for other invoice outputs that contained a different number of items, causing the `Payment due` date to appear on a different line. Of course we could give the comparator a different set of instructions for other invoice outputs but then this involves us in a lot more work. What we really want is one set of comparator instructions that will work for all invoice outputs. One way to do this would be to ignore any line starting with `Payment due`.

A problem with this simple approach to masking is the fact that we are ignoring the whole record. In our example this works fine but it is unlikely to be acceptable in all cases. For example, if the `Payment due` statement included the total cost (`Payment of $5.50 due by 09-Jun-98`) we may wish to verify that the total is correct. Ignoring the whole line will preclude us from doing so.

An alternative approach is to specify the fields that are to be ignored. In our example we would instruct the comparator to ignore characters 19–26 on line 1, 7–15 on line 2, and 16–24 on line 11. The way in which these are specified will depend on the comparator tool used but may be something like the following:

```
IGNORE(1,19:26)
IGNORE(2,7:15)
IGNORE(11,16:24)
```

While this does mean we will be comparing the remaining parts of the lines, this approach does not overcome the problem of having to specify different

```
              Sales Invoice No. 03/11803
              Date: 26-May-98

              Code       Description      Price
              -----------------------------------
              CL/3       Chain link        2.00
              HK/1       Hook              3.50
              -----------------------------------
                                   Total: 5.50

              Payment due by 09-Jun-98
```

Figure 4.4 Example output of a simple invoice statement.

instructions for different invoices. Not only could the `Payment` due statement appear on a different line but if it includes the total cost the date field
could be positioned differently depending on the cost. For example:

```
Payment of $5.50 due by 09-Jun-98

Payment of $15.50 due by 09-Jun-98

Payment of $115.50 due by 09-Jun-98
```

4.6.3 Search technique for masking

Both of these problems can be overcome by using a search technique.
Rather than specifying a particular location, the idea is to specify a string of
characters that it is known will appear adjacent to the field to be ignored.
The following would work for our invoice example:

```
IGNORE_AFTER("Invoice No. ",8)

IGNORE_AFTER("Date: ",9)

IGNORE_AFTER("due by ",9)
```

Our `IGNORE_AFTER` function tells the comparator to ignore a specified
number of characters immediately following the specified string. This
approach is more flexible than those we have already described because it
will work for different invoices and in some cases will reduce the number of
instructions we have to give. Where there are a number of similar fields to
be ignored, it may be possible to use just a single instruction. For example,
if the `Payment` due statement appeared as `Payment due by date: 9-Jun-98` the same instruction could mask both dates if either the search
were case insensitive or we specified `IGNORE_AFTER("ate: ",9)`.

Using this search technique does help us to specify some reasonably
complex criteria but is not sufficient for all cases. For some outputs, it is
not always possible to specify an adjacent string either because there is not
one, or there are many of them. Consider the version of our invoice shown
in Figure 4.5.

This has an additional `Stock Id`, which always comprises four digits
followed by two upper-case letters but we shall say the actual values will be
different every time the test cases are run. None of the approaches we have

```
          Sales Invoice No. 03/11803
          Date: 26-May-98

          Code      Description     Stock Id   Price
          -----------------------------------------
          CL/3      Chain link       1743AF     2.00
          HK/1      Hook             8362JD     3.50
          -----------------------------------------
                                     Total:     5.50

          Payment due by 09-Jun-98
```

Figure 4.5 Simple invoice statement with the addition of a Stock Id.

described so far will handle this very well since they will all require a specific set of comparison instructions for each different invoice output.

4.6.4 Search technique using regular expressions

This problem is best handled by a more sophisticated search technique that looks for the fields themselves, rather than something adjacent. This technique uses a description of the fields to be ignored, called a **regular expression** or pattern. Regular expressions (sometimes abbreviated to 'regexp') describe a pattern of characters by treating particular characters in a special way. These special characters are known as metacharacters or wildcard characters. For example, a period character '.' is taken to mean any character and the question mark '?' is used to indicate an optional character. Different implementations of regular expressions sometimes use different metacharacters or they have different meanings; however, any commercial comparator that implements any form of regular expressions will of course document their implementation. A full description of regular expressions can be found in Friedl (1997).

In our invoice example we could use the regular expression [0–9]{4}[A–Z]{2} to specify each of the Stock Id numbers. Regular expressions often look rather complicated but they are surprisingly easy to understand once you understand the basic syntax. In our example [0–9] means any one of the digit characters 0 to 9 inclusive. {4} means match exactly four of the immediately previous characters (or character class, as in this case). So together [0–9]{4} means match a string of any four digits. Similarly, [A–Z]{2} means match a string of any two upper-case letters. Put the two together and we have a description of our Stock Id.

The regular expression does not have to be limited to the field to be ignored. In fact, it is often better to include in the expression a few literal characters that will appear adjacent to the fields to help insure that only the target fields are matched. For example, we could include a space character at the start and end of our regular expression: ' [0–9]{4}[A–Z]{2} '.

4.6.5 Implementing complex comparisons

There tends to be an assumption that the comparison of a test output has to be a single comparison. However, there is no rule that requires any comparison to be performed in only one pass. Using multiple passes gives you the opportunity to compare one aspect at a time. This approach is described in Section 4.9.

A commercial comparator may not be as good at performing complex comparisons as it is at performing simple comparisons. (Test tools are not immune from defects, and defects like to congregate in complex areas of software!)

The way in which commercial comparator tools implement the masking does vary. Some literally remove the masked fields before performing the comparison (this is done on a temporary copy of the outcomes rather than your originals). Others replace the field with some standard character to indicate that something has been ignored at that place. This works all right but can make failure analysis a little awkward when differences are highlighted, because the differences are shown using the edited version rather than your original and this can look quite different. Being able easily to relate any differences to the original content is important as it is both annoying and time wasting not to be able to locate the place quickly.

4.7 Test sensitivity

4.7.1 Sensitive and robust tests

At some point we have to decide what information needs to be compared in order to verify the outcome of each test case. How much should we compare and how often should we compare something? Should we try to compare as much as possible as often as possible, or take the opposite view and compare only a minimum right at the end of the test case?

We call this the 'sensitivity' of the test (technically, it is the sensitivity of the comparisons). If we compare as much information as possible, for example, comparing the whole screen after each step in a test case, then more or less any change in the output to the screen will cause a mismatch and the test case will fail. This is known as a **sensitive test** case. However, if we compare only a minimum of information, for example, comparing only the last message output to the screen at the end of a test case, then only if this message differs will a mismatch occur. Any other changes in the output to the screen will not cause the test case to fail. This is known as a **robust test** case.

When using dynamic comparison we have also to decide how often to perform a comparison during the test case. If we compare the outcome after every keystroke, we may be able to detect the instant something is not as expected, but our test cases are likely to take a very long time to complete and cause us a lot of difficulty in updating the expected outcomes when the software under test changes. On the other hand, if we only compare an occasional outcome, it may take us a long time to find out what went wrong when the test case fails.

Test sensitivity is affected not only by the amount of information compared but also by the way in which it is compared. For example, if a comparison ignores a date field in an output report file, this makes for a more robust comparison than if it looked for a particular pattern such as mm/dd/yyyy. Similarly, comparisons that compare only content and not the position of screen messages are more robust than comparisons that insist on the message appearing in exactly the same place every time. The difference is in the complexity of the comparison, which was discussed in Sections 4.5 and 4.6.

4.7.2 Trade-offs between sensitive and robust tests

Making the right choices is important since if we compare inappropriate or insufficient outcomes then the value of the test case will be reduced, if not lost altogether. If we compare too much information the cost of implementing and maintaining each automated test case may overwhelm the benefits it can bring.

Figure 4.6 highlights a number of different effects test case sensitivity can have. The diagram should not be taken too literally, as it is meant only to highlight possible differences between robust and sensitive tests.

The more sensitive a test case the more likely it will need some updating when the software under test changes. This may be a simple matter of updating the expected outcomes for the test case but there is a difference between doing this for one test case and doing it for 100 test cases (about 100 times as much work?).

Naturally, the more comparisons there are to perform, the more time it will take to prescribe them all correctly. Making it easy to implement both dynamic and post-execution comparisons can help reduce the implementation time and reduce the number of implementation errors made. Similarly, the more comparisons there are, the more work will be required to maintain the tests. Sensitive tests take more effort.

Many defects do not give themselves up lightly so we have to be on our guard all the time when testing, looking out for the unexpected. This is easier to do when we are testing manually than when we are implementing automated tests. When we implement a robust test we are effectively assuming where a defect will and will not show itself. The more robust our test cases, the more chance there is of a defect escaping our attention.

The more data there is available at the end of a failed test case, the easier it will be to analyze and debug. For example, if we know only that a post-execution comparison used to verify a new database entry failed,

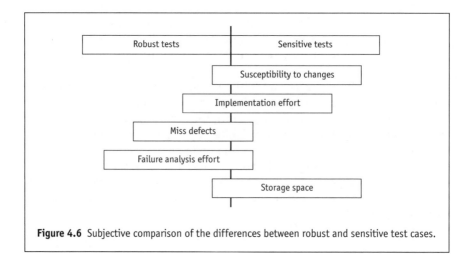

Figure 4.6 Subjective comparison of the differences between robust and sensitive test cases.

we can only guess why it failed until we investigate it further, possibly by re-running the test case manually. On the other hand, if we had performed a number of dynamic comparisons as the data was entered we might be able to determine where something had gone wrong without any additional investigation. Robust tests are, therefore, prone to more failure analysis effort.

Although storage space is not a particularly big issue for a lot of organizations, it may nevertheless be an important consideration. The more comparisons we specify for our automated tests the more storage space will be consumed by the expected and actual outcomes. Sometimes it is the number of outcomes that have to be uniquely identified and stored that causes hassle, rather than the amount of disk space consumed.

4.7.3 Redundancy

Too much sensitivity rather than a lack of it can adversely affect the failure analysis effort for a large number of automated test cases. If we run a set of sensitive test cases there is a good chance that a number of them will fail for the same reason. In this situation each of the failed test cases is highlighting the same defect. While we would wish to be told about such an unexpected difference we would not wish to have more than one test case telling us about it; a single test case failure per defect does very nicely. This is illustrated in Figure 4.7.

Of course if we run a set of test cases and several of them fail we will start to analyze each failed test case in turn. After we have looked at a few we may decide to stop there and re-run the test cases on a repaired version of the software. However, we have already wasted some time analyzing test case failures that did not tell us anything we did not already know.

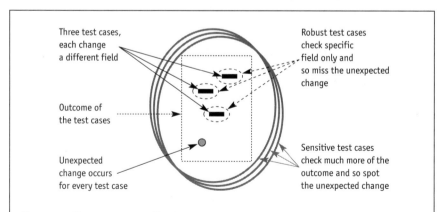

Figure 4.7 The consequence of having too many sensitive test cases is that more of them fail for the same reason, which often results in wasted effort analyzing the failed test cases.

4.7.4 Strategies for test sensitivity

So, which is best? As with many other aspects of testing, there is no absolutely correct answer to this question. Either extreme could be the right thing to do in different circumstances. This is one of the design decisions that you make when you design an automated test. In practice, we are unlikely to take either extreme but do something in between. However, the degree to which a test case is sensitive or robust is an important issue. We can recommend two possible strategies that you can adopt or adapt to your own situation.

Our first recommendation is to use sensitive comparison predominantly at a high level where test cases are run as a sanity check whenever a change is made to the software. A high-level **breadth test** or **roll-call** would be a standard regression test set that is run at the start of every test cycle. The idea is that we want these test cases to detect any unexpected changes anywhere in the system. These test cases should be predominantly sensitive so that they will pick up any change, no matter how small. Robust comparison should then be used predominantly at the more detailed levels where each test focuses on some specific aspect of the software under test. These tests are better designed to be robust, as there are usually a good many more of them with fewer differences (or more overlap) between them.

Our second recommendation is to consider designing sets of test cases such that one or two of them use sensitive comparison while the others use robust comparison. In this situation each set of test cases explores a different aspect of the software so within a set there is a lot of overlap in what they see of the software. If one or two test cases compare the peripheral information then there is little point in the other test cases within that set doing so again since one unexpected difference in the peripheral information may cause all test cases within the set to fail.

A good test automation strategy will plan a combination of sensitive and robust tests, taking advantage of the characteristics of each aspect (and many shades in between) to accomplish the objectives of each set of automated test cases in the most effective and efficient way.

4.8 Comparing different types of outcome

4.8.1 Disk-based outcomes

We include databases, files, and directories/folders in this disk-based category of outcomes.

4.8.1.1 Comparing text files

Text files are perhaps the easiest type of data to compare. Most simple comparators deal with text files (and only text files). In this section we look at an example comparison of two small text files, using the Scribble application that was introduced in Chapter 2.

Figure 4.8 shows the output from a simple comparator given two slightly different text files, countries1 and countries2. Comparators should be capable of detecting records that are different (have different, extra, or missing characters), records that have been added, and records that have

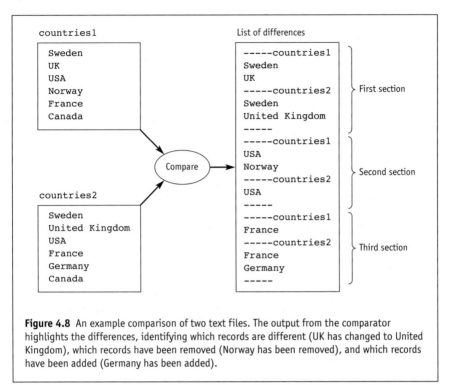

Figure 4.8 An example comparison of two text files. The output from the comparator highlights the differences, identifying which records are different (UK has changed to United Kingdom), which records have been removed (Norway has been removed), and which records have been added (Germany has been added).

been removed. The output from the comparator in Figure 4.8 shows us that each of these three differences occurs between the two files. The comparator identifies sections of the two files that are different and outputs the contents of the corresponding sections in pairs one after the other. How to interpret this output is explained further in Figure 4.9.

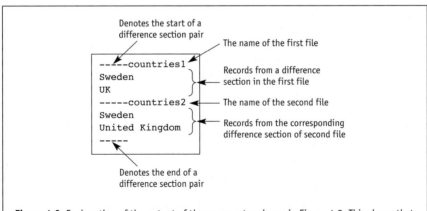

Figure 4.9 Explanation of the output of the comparator shown in Figure 4.8. This shows that the record following Sweden is 'UK' in the first file but 'United Kingdom' in the second. (Note that here Sweden is output to help you identify where the difference occurs.)

The format of comparator output varies from comparator to comparator, and many will allow you to specify different options. For example, in our case we have shown the comparator including the record 'Sweden' at the start of each difference section shown in Figure 4.9 despite the fact that it is the same in both files. This is done to help you recognize where the unmatched records (in this case there is only one unmatched record) occur in the two files. Depending on your comparator, it may be possible to specify that more of the preceding matched records are used in this way or that no matched records are copied to the output. Another option may allow one or more matched records following the unmatched records to be included in the output from the comparator. A sequence number added to each record is another common and useful feature.

4.8.1.2 Comparing non-textual forms of data

To compare anything other than standard text files usually requires a specialized comparator. Some test execution automation tool vendors can supply specialized comparators, for example to handle character-based screen images that use escape sequences and graphical characters or that are specifically designed to handle a variety of graphics data formats.

If an appropriate comparator cannot be found we recommend considering changing the format of the data into a textual form since this is usually much easier to compare. This is discussed further in the following section.

4.8.1.3 Comparing databases and binary files

Comparators that handle databases and/or binary files tend to be fairly specialized and concentrate on just one particular type of database or binary file format. However, this does not mean that your databases and binary files cannot be compared if you cannot find a suitable commercial comparator tool.

In most cases it is the information in the database or binary file that is of interest, rather than the database or binary file itself. This information can usually be converted into a textual form. For example, information in a database can be extracted and written to a text file, perhaps using a report generator. Data held in a binary file can be converted into a textual form if there is not already a textual equivalent. Converting the information into a textual form often makes it much easier to compare and allows a simple comparison tool to be used. Furthermore, you can be much more selective over what is compared and what is not compared. If the format of the resulting text file is under your control you can design it to make both comparison and difference analysis easy.

For example, consider a binary file that contains a description of a simple line drawing. The format of the file may comprise a header with a format like that shown below, followed by a number of vector records consisting of the starting and ending coordinates of each line in the drawing. (Note that the value for the 'Date last changed' field is expressed as the number of days since the base date of the software.)

Field Name	Size (bytes)	Content	Example
Format version	6	ASCII	'2.1'
Drawing type	1	Integer	1
Owner	14	ASCII	'M. Fewster'
Date last changed	2	Integer	3143
Number of vector records	2	Integer	24

As a means of examining binary data, it is common to produce a hexadecimal dump that shows the content of each word (where 'word' means a pair of bytes, or 16 bits of storage) as a hexadecimal number. A hexadecimal dump of a header record containing the example values shown above would look like this:

2E32 0031 0000 4D01 202E 4546 5357 4554 0052 0000 0C00 0046 0018

For comparison purposes, it would be much better to build a simple utility program that will convert this binary version into a textual equivalent like the following:

```
Format version            2.1

Drawing type              Schematic

Owner                     "M. Fewster"

Date last changed         10-Aug-89

Number of vector records  24
```

This is much easier to read and understand and much more useful in a comparison. Using one line for each field name and value will make analyzing any differences simple. For example, if the drawing type was found to be different we would see a difference report like the one shown below.

```
-----file1
Format version            2.1

Drawing type              Schematic

----file2
Format version            2.1

Drawing type              Draft

-----
```

Compare this with the difference report from a comparison of the two equivalent hexadecimal dumps shown below.

```
-----file1
2E32 0031 0000 4D01 202E 4546 5357 4554 0052 0000 0C00 0046 0018
----file2
2E32 0031 0000 4D02 202E 4546 5357 4554 0052 0000 0C00 0046 0018
-----
```

As you can see it is not particularly easy to spot the difference (it is the last digit of the fourth word reading from left to right), much less say what it means.

4.8.2 Screen-based outcomes

4.8.2.1 Character-based applications

If you are testing a character-based application, then all you have to worry about when comparing screen outputs is text and special graphics characters (an extended character set) and any display attributes such as bold, blinking, and reverse video. It is usually fairly straightforward to specify the location of the characters you want to compare since the screen is already an array of individual characters each addressed by a row and column number.

The masking here might be specified by including or excluding specific rows, columns, fields (a consecutive sequence of character positions), or blocks (rectangular areas encompassing more than one row). In each case the masked character positions need not be completely excluded from the comparison. For example, it is possible to specify that the display attributes be excluded while the actual text content is included, or vice versa.

4.8.2.2 GUI applications

Applications that have a GUI can display a much greater range of output styles than a character-based application. Most of these output styles have become the norm for the majority of users as applications have standardized on the use of items such as windows, icons, menu bars, dialog boxes, buttons, and check boxes, to name but a few.

Whatever is displayed, it is converted into a bitmap (unless it is already stored as one) before being sent to the screen. Bitmaps are a notoriously troublesome format to compare. For this reason they are best avoided wherever possible.

When checking screen output from a GUI application, it helps to know exactly what is being tested (in other words, we must know the test objectives). For example, if the outcome of a test is for a specific text message to appear on the screen, there could be at least three different test objectives:

1. To insure that the application software outputs the correct message. If the wrong message is output it is usually a problem with the application software.

2. To insure that the application software specifies the correct display attributes. For example, the message may be correct, but if the application requests it be displayed as black text on a black background it will not be particularly helpful.

3. To insure that the text string is displayed correctly (that is, the graphics software correctly formats the text string for display). Although the application may send the correct message and display attributes to the graphics software, the latter has to generate a bitmap that displays it correctly. Graphics software is not immune to defects.

Our approach to automating the comparison of these three objectives may be quite different. The text message usually starts off inside the software as a literal text string. By the time it reaches the screen it has been converted into a bitmap.

If the objective is to check for the correct message, then it is better to look at the text message while it is still a text string (and before it is converted into a bitmap). This is because problems can occur when trying to bit-match text:

- a different font is used;
- a different color is used;
- a word is now in bold or italics;
- the text is now 12 point instead of 11 point;
- the background on which the text is displayed is a different color or is now shaded;
- the box in which the message is written is a different shape, so the words wrap around in a different place;
- the box in which the text appears is in a different place on the screen.

In all of these examples, the content of the message is exactly the same as before, so the test of whether the right text is shown should show no differences at all, i.e. the test should pass. However, all of these examples (and many more) can cause a bitmap comparison to fail. When it fails the reason for the mismatch needs to be investigated and this takes time, but the point of automating comparison is usually to save time.

If the second objective applies (to check for correct display attributes) we would be better off capturing the display attributes as they are passed from the application software to the graphics software. This can be done by some tools but it may also be possible to have the application (or graphics software) report this information in a text form.

If the third objective applies (to insure the text is displayed correctly) then we must look at the bitmap sent to the screen.

This consideration of the test objectives applies equally to other types of output such as icons representing files and applications, check boxes representing the state of particular flags or switches, and a graphical scale representing a percentage of completion.

Some test execution tools are capable of capturing such information at this earlier stage, which is often referred to as the 'logical level' (the bitmap state is referred to as the 'physical level'). The ability of tools to capture information at the logical level will always depend on how the software has been implemented. If non-standard implementations have been used, some test execution tools may not be able to capture the information at the logical level. This is often the case where custom controls (graphical interactors) are used. We know of some organizations whose automated tests have been confined to that subset of their applications that only use standard graphical controls.

We recommend the use of different tests to compare different aspects of a GUI application. Specifically, we recommend testing the graphics software (which governs how information is represented on the screen) separately from the application software (which governs what information is displayed). To test graphics software, we should use a representative sample of data to exercise the many different aspects of the graphics software, such as different colors, text fonts, line widths, shapes, patterns, etc.). To test the application software, use a representative sample of data to exercise the many different aspects of the application. These two sets of data will usually be very different. Combining tests to exercise both pieces of software at the same time is likely to result in poor testing of one or other, or both of them. Furthermore, having more specific tests (which will be more robust) will make failure analysis easier and reduce the likelihood of having a large number of tests fail because of the same problem.

Of course, after these tests have been run successfully, it will be necessary to run some tests that check that the application software and the graphics software function correctly together. There will be fewer of these tests though.

4.8.2.3 Graphical images

Graphical images are made up of a fine array of dots called pixels. The more pixels that are used to create the image, the finer the image details appear; that is, the greater the spatial resolution of the image. Computers store graphical images as an array of bits called a bitmap in which one or more bits are used to represent each pixel in the image. The number of bits used per pixel (the bit-depth resolution) governs the maximum number of different colors that can be displayed. For example, if only one bit is used for each pixel only monochrome images are possible whereas with 24 bits per pixel millions of colors are possible.

When a graphical image has to be checked it is the bitmaps of the actual and expected images that are compared. Unfortunately, bitmap comparisons can be rather fraught. The bitmap needs to be only one single bit different for a mismatch to occur even though such a difference is unlikely to be noticeable to the human eye. Some bitmap comparators permit you to specify a tolerance with the aim of making the comparison ignore differences that would not be noticeable.

Most of the graphical images output by software applications are not permanently stored as bitmaps but in some other, usually more descriptive, form. The bitmap is generated when it is required. Since there are many different algorithms for generating bitmaps and even more implementations of those algorithms in commercial software the same result cannot be guaranteed across different software implementations, nor indeed across different versions of the same implementation. Thus, even if our software under test sends the same graphical description to some 'standard' bitmap creation software, we may not end up with exactly the same bitmap every time.

Another reason we can end up with very different bitmaps for what is essentially the same graphical image is that different screens can have different resolutions.

Another problem with bitmap images is their large size. The size of the bitmaps is calculated by multiplying the spatial resolution and the bit-depth resolution. A small toolbar button may take about 1 Kbyte while a full screen image may take somewhere in the range of 2–5 Mbytes. If each test case performs a number of bitmap comparisons the disk space requirements can soon become enormous. This is likely to have a considerable impact on the long-term maintenance costs of your automated tests.

The types of masking done for bitmapped images include ignoring a region of the screen or selecting a region (this is like the character screen but on a far finer grain). It may be possible to ignore a preset number of mismatched bits, or mismatches in certain areas, such as at the edges of images. It may also be possible for the bitmap comparator to ignore color.

4.8.3 Other types of outcome

4.8.3.1 Multimedia applications
Multimedia applications involve forms of test outcome that are not readily comparable; for example, sounds that are played, and video clips and animated pictures that are displayed. At the time of writing, no commercial tools known to the authors were capable of comparing video or sound though we anticipate that this is an area where improvements will be made. However, for now all is not lost.

It may be possible to enhance the application under test to give the tester access to a useful level of information. This is an aspect of testability that is discussed further in Chapter 9. For example, if the application can output information (preferably in text format) that records when a sound was played and the size of the file containing it, this may be sufficient to give confidence that things are OK, or at least have not gone horribly wrong.

Again it is important to consider the objective of the tests so you can automate at least a subset of them. For example, the human tester may listen to sounds to confirm that they are what they are labeled as, so that the one called 'lion roar' doesn't sound like a duck quacking. Once this link has been verified manually, the automated test could check that when the 'lion roar' sound is required, the software plays the sound clip that is labeled as 'lion roar.'

4.8.3.2 Communicating applications
Applications that have outcomes involving communication with other applications/processes or hardware devices (this includes embedded software) are likely to require a specialized testing tool or, more conveniently, a test harness in addition to a test execution automation tool. Such a test harness will be able to send messages to the software under test and/or receive messages from it. The test harness is most useful when it can read its instructions and output the messages it receives in a text format. Once again, this makes the automated comparison of the outcomes simple. The

test harness should also be able to record additional information such as the time when messages were received.

We have seen a few examples of such test harnesses and implemented one or two or our own. These have all been homegrown test harnesses, designed specifically for testing one particular application. However, it is always worth looking for any commercial tools that match your needs, as they are likely to offer much more functionality and be better supported.

4.9 Comparison filters

4.9.1 Practical approach to building your own post-execution comparison tools: a comparison process

There is not an abundance of comparator tools (used for post-execution comparison) available commercially, which appears to leave a gap in the market. While there is usually at least one simple file comparator tool with each operating system, they offer few, if any, pattern matching facilities to help us with complex comparisons.

However, in our experience there is little need for complex comparator tools as it is a relatively easy matter of using whatever simple comparator is available in conjunction with one or more other tools that are also readily available with most operating systems.

This section describes an approach to post-execution comparison of text files that uses whatever simple file comparator is available in conjunction with one or more other tools that manipulate the information to be compared. Before the comparison is made the data is edited using one or more **filters** to extract the data required and mask out expected differences. This creates what we call a **comparison process** – a series of one or more filters followed by a simple comparison. This process could probably be applied to non-text files though we have never done so. It is our preference to convert the outcomes into text first as this gives us the greatest flexibility and makes the whole process easier to implement, debug, and maintain.

EXPERIENCE REPORT

When we were developing the test automation tool described in Chapter 12, we realized that there were a number of fairly complex comparisons that would need to be made in order to automate test comparison. Being well into the idea of writing our own tools, we were keen to write a good comparator. We estimated that it would probably take around six months, but we would then have a very sophisticated comparison tool.

Unfortunately (as it seemed to us at the time), resources were scarce, so we were left with only simple and basic comparators. In order to try to automate some complex comparison even with our existing tools, we discovered the power of filters, which are actually a more flexible and better way to automate comparison.

Moral: make best use of the tools and utilities that you have available.

A filter is an editing or translating step that is performed on both an expected outcome file and the corresponding actual outcome file. More than one filtering task can be performed on any expected/actual test outcome before comparison. A comparison process using a single filter is shown in Figure 4.10.

Using filters before comparing the files means that the actual comparison can use a much simpler comparator tool.

Effectively, a filter removes the legitimate differences from the expected and actual outcomes, thereby ensuring that a simple comparison tool will highlight only unexpected differences; that is, the differences that we do wish to know about. The way in which the filters achieve this task is very much up to you but we recommend that masked fields be substituted by a literal text string that indicates the type of field that has been masked out. This will make failure analysis easier since the reported differences will still look something like the original.

Most commonly, therefore, a filter is a text editor with a predefined set of substitution instructions, though it is not restricted to just substitution. Data extraction is another useful task. Rather than comparing the whole file, an extraction filter is used to extract just those parts of the file that can be meaningfully compared, or perhaps that need comparing in a different way to the rest of the file. Sorting is another task that can be usefully performed by a filter (in this case the filter is usually a standard sort utility). Some filter tasks can be more specialized and would involve you in writing a small tool or utility to manipulate your outcome data in a particular way. We have found that regular expressions (which were described in Section 4.6.4) are an invaluable aid to implementing filters.

Undoubtedly there is an overlap between some of these filtering tasks and some of the post-processing tasks described in Chapter 6. However, we leave further discussion of this to that chapter.

4.9.3 Implementing a comparison process

In order to automate a comparison process, some form of 'glue' will be required to stick together the filters and comparison tool. This can be shell scripts (in UNIX parlance), batch files (MS-DOS parlance), command

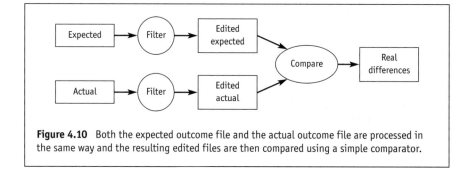

Figure 4.10 Both the expected outcome file and the actual outcome file are processed in the same way and the resulting edited files are then compared using a simple comparator.

procedures (VAX/VMS etc.), or a compiled programming language – in fact, anything that will allow you to create a simple comparison utility that, given the expected and actual outcomes, will pass them through the necessary filters and comparator and return an appropriate status (i.e. whether or not there are any differences).

The scripting language of a test execution automation tool could be used. This would provide a logical extension to the script that executes the test cases. The script that controls the test case execution could then invoke the post-execution comparison process script, or the comparison process could be implemented as a separate test case. This latter approach has the advantage of allowing the comparison process to be run independently of the test case execution if necessary. (It could therefore be run at a different time, on a different machine, and repeated as required.)

How well this approach works will depend on the capabilities of the tool's scripting language and your comparison requirements. If all is well, it will be possible to integrate the post-execution process into the test execution process.

Other approaches to implementing post-execution comparison processes use some other scripting or programming language. We recommend using an interpreted language (rather than a compiled language) because it lends itself more to prototyping, trying out one thing, changing it, and trying that. Batch files, command procedures, etc. are eminently suitable for this kind of job and we have found that many testers (including those without a technical background) already use them to implement their own handy utilities.

4.9.4 Advantages and disadvantages of filters

There are several advantages of implementing complex comparisons using filters rather than developing or buying sophisticated comparison tools. These are explained below.

1. Availability of text manipulation tools. There are many tools readily available for performing text substitution, extraction, sorting, and the like. The tools we have used most often are *sed, awk, grep,* and *egrep*. These and many other such tools originated in the UNIX environment but executables for many different hardware platforms, and the source code, are available (often free of charge) from several sources, including the Free Software Foundation.

    More recently we have found the programming language *Perl* (Practical Extraction and Reporting Language) to be a good substitute for those tools we have just mentioned. The scripting language *Tcl* has also been recommended to us though we have no experience of it. Actually, most any programming language for which there is support for regular expressions will do.

    Python is another suitable language, and there is a C library package for regular expressions.

2. Reuse. Once a filter has been implemented, it can be reused in many situations in addition to the one for which it was first developed. Indeed, the regular expressions themselves can be reused and we recommend doing so. Once a regular expression has been implemented and tested (for a date, for example) it should be documented and made available for reuse. There is no value in having different people implement their own regular expressions to achieve the same tasks.

3. More stringent comparison criteria. Because filters allow us to work on individual parts of an outcome at a time, we can produce more stringent comparison criteria than may otherwise be achieved by using a single complex comparison tool.

   For example, a commercial comparator may provide a means of ignoring a date field but this would ignore any date (presumably any valid date, though this is worth checking when you evaluate any candidate tools). We may wish to insure that the date falls within a certain range or is a specific date relative to the date on which the test case is executed, something we can easily achieve using our own comparison process employing filters.

4. Easier implementation and debugging. Since even the most complex of comparisons is divided into a number of discrete steps, each step can be implemented and tested separately. The series of steps can then be incrementally integrated, each being tested, achieving better confidence in the whole comparison process. Having a complex comparison process is one thing; having confidence that it works correctly is another. It is easy to spot a problem with a complex comparison if it highlights a difference that you intend it to ignore. However, it may not be possible to prove that it will not ignore differences that you intend it to find. So any approach that makes implementation and testing of the comparisons easier has to be welcome.

5. Simple comparison tools can perform complex comparisons. For the final comparison any simple comparison tool will usually suffice (such as the MS-DOS operating system file comparison tool *fc*, and the UNIX operating system *diff* utility). The filters enable a series of steps to build up progressively more complex building blocks for simple comparison.

   Other special-purpose in-house tools can also be developed where more specific comparisons are required, for example, comparing dates or times to insure one is later than another, or checking that a single value falls within a given tolerance. Such tools are relatively simple to build for anyone with reasonable programming skills.

There are a few disadvantages of filters. They generally require programming skills to implement them and they need to be tested and debugged before they can be used with confidence. If the format of the output being filtered changes, then the filter will also need to be changed. (This is similar to the effect of software changes on dynamic tests.) Finally, in common with other reusable items, they should be documented and managed so all those who need to use them can quickly find them and easily put them to good use.

4.9.5 Filter examples

Figure 4.11 shows how the expected and actual outcomes from a test would be changed by the application of a single filter that substitutes three fields: a job number, a date, and a time.

In this case the filter could be implemented using any one of a number of tools that support string substitutions using regular expressions. Three regular expressions are required, one for each type of field. These are shown in bold type within the following Perl script.

```perl
while (<>) {
    s/J[0-9]{5}/<Job No.>/g;
    s/[0-9]{2}-[A-Z][a-z]{2}-[0-9]{2}/<Date>/g;
    s/([01]?[1-9]|2[0-3]):[0-5][0-9]/<Time>/g;
    print;
}
```

This is the whole program to implement the required filter, coded in Perl. We are not expecting readers without experience of Perl to understand this, rather marvel at how little work is required to implement a useful filter. Note that different tools and languages have different implementations of regular expressions so these examples will not work for all tools. We have chosen to use a dialect of regular expressions implemented by Perl version 5.002 or later as this offers concise constructs.

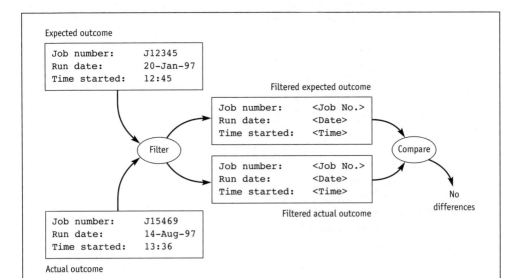

Figure 4.11 A comparison process using a single filter. The same filter is used for both the expected and actual outcomes and performs three substitutions. In this case we have chosen to use angle brackets <> to delimit text that replaces an ignored field. This will help us to distinguish the substituted text from the rest of the original outcome.

The regular expression given in the Perl script above that is attempting to match a date string is perhaps too simple. As it is, it will match an invalid date, e.g. 45-Abc-99 but would not match 6-Apr-99. While this may be sufficient for some outcomes, there may well be occasions when we need to be sure that only valid dates and times are ignored. The regular expression can be extended so that it matches only valid dates within a defined range.

4.9.6 Multiple filters in series

When there are many different comparison criteria for a particular test case outcome it is often better to literally dismantle the outcome into discrete pieces and then separately compare each of the pieces. This keeps the filters themselves simpler and makes the whole comparison process easier to understand, implement, and maintain.

For example, consider the directory listing shown in Figure 4.12, which is some test output showing files that have been created or changed by the test. We wish to compare this with the expected outcome (the directory listing generated by the first test run, which was verified manually). The purpose of doing this is to insure that all the same files are present and are of the same size, and that no extra files have appeared.

The two directory listings may contain different files or they may have different sizes but this is what we are checking for. However, the two listings may be in a different order and the dates and times will be different, so

```
Volume in drive F is UserDisk
Volume Serial Number is 2DF9-8752


Directory of F:\Mark\Doc

18/08/98  14:01          <DIR>          .
18/08/98  14:01          <DIR>          ..
19/05/98  16:34                    253 Actual.txt
17/08/98  17:05                234,677 dates.txt
16/06/98  22:27                    967 dir.dat
18/08/98  14:01                      0 dirnt.dat
17/08/98  11:21          <DIR>          Examples
17/08/98  16:55                 14,400 invdates.txt
17/08/98  13:11                     33 invdates2.txt
17/08/98  13:52                    430 numbers.txt
               10 File(s)         250,760 bytes

Directory of F:\Mark\Doc\Examples

17/08/98  11:21          <DIR>          .
17/08/98  11:21          <DIR>          ..
16/08/98  19:37                 26,317 date.txt
17/08/98  11:19                 16,764 time.txt
17/08/98  11:21                 63,760 dir.txt
                5 File(s)         106,841 bytes

         Total Files Listed:
               15 File(s)          357,610 bytes
                            584,860,160 bytes free
```

Figure 4.12 A directory listing to be compared using multiple filters.

we will have to cope with these differences but otherwise ignore them. A different disk may be used, so the volume label, serial number, and drive name can all legitimately differ. The other records in the files (directory names, file counts, etc.) are not relevant to the check we are performing and so can safely be ignored.

Of course, it would be better to generate a more suitable outcome in the first place (i.e. just a list of files with their sizes). However, we are using this directory listing as an example of an outcome that we cannot change since this will be true for many outcomes that you have to deal with.

Since our intent is merely to compare the list of filenames and sizes we can discard all the other information. This can be done with the following filter:

```
while (<>) {
    print if /^\d[^<]*$/;
}
```

This filter outputs (by means of the Perl print statement) all lines which match the regular expression delimited by the / characters. The first few characters in the regular expression, ^\d, match only lines that begin with a digit. This selects only the lines that start with a date, i.e. those that contain filenames and directory names. The next few characters of the regular expression, [^<]*$, match only those lines that do not have a < character. This selects only the filename records since it is the directory name records that contain a < character. The output is now as shown in Figure 4.13.

We are not interested in the dates and times, but only in the filenames and sizes, so the next filter should mask out these dates and times by either substitution or deletion. We have chosen deletion.

```
while (<>) {
    s/^.*:.. *//;
    print;
}
```

This filter deletes the date and time from each record by substituting them with nothing. The regular expression between the first two slashes matches the date and time and the space characters up to the file size. The first part

```
19/05/98   16:34                    253 Actual.txt
17/08/98   17:05                234,677 dates.txt
16/06/98   22:27                    967 dir.dat
18/08/98   14:01                      0 dirnt.dat
17/08/98   16:55                 14,400 invdates.txt
17/08/98   13:11                     33 invdates2.txt
17/08/98   13:52                    430 numbers.txt
16/08/98   19:37                 26,317 date.txt
17/08/98   11:19                 16,764 time.txt
17/08/98   11:21                 63,760 dir.txt
```

Figure 4.13 Output of filter 1: eliminate everything except filenames.

of the expression, `^.*:`, matches all the characters from the start of the record up to the colon. The next part of the expression, `.. *`, matches the first two characters immediately following the colon (which will be the minutes part of the time) and then any number of spaces. This has the effect of deleting everything that we are not interested in, i.e. the dates, times, and leading spaces before the file sizes. Our filter output now is shown in Figure 4.14.

If the filenames can appear in a different order we need to sort the two lists before comparing them. It would also be better to have the filename followed by the size. This is done with the following:

```
while (<>) {
    s/([^ ]*) (.*)/$2 $1/;
    print;
}
```

This filter swaps the filename and size fields using a substitution command. The first part of the regular expression, `([^ ]*)`, matches any number of non-spaces, which will be the size field. Putting this expression in parentheses means that it can be referred to later (as $1). The space character in the regular expression matches the space character separating the size and name fields. The last part of the expression, `(.*)`, matches the rest of the record (which will be the filename). Again, the parentheses mean that the filename can be referenced later (as $2). After the slash, the $2 $1 references the filename and size fields in reverse order, thereby exchanging their positions. Our third filter produces the output shown in Figure 4.15. This file is then sorted to produce the output shown in Figure 4.16.

Now comparing the two filtered file lists (using a simple comparator) will highlight missing and extra files, as well as files that have a different size. This is just what we wanted. Using a series of filters we have edited the test case outcome to remove those parts that could not be compared or are not relevant to the check we are performing.

Actually, although we have described this comparison process as a series of filters it is more likely that we would choose to implement it as just one or two filters. All the edits (extractions, deletions, and substitutions) can easily be performed by one filter. If it were implemented in Perl then it

```
253 Actual.txt
234,677 dates.txt
967 dir.dat
0 dirnt.dat
14,400 invdates.txt
33 invdates2.txt
430 numbers.txt
26,317 date.txt
16,764 time.txt
63,760 dir.txt
```

Figure 4.14 Output of filter 2: remove dates and times.

```
Actual.txt 253
dates.txt 234,677
dir.dat 967
dirnt.dat 0
invdates.txt 14,400
invdates2.txt 33
numbers.txt 430
date.txt 26,317
time.txt 16,764
dir.txt 63,760
```

Figure 4.15 Output of filter 3: swap filename and size fields.

```
Actual.txt 253
date.txt 26,317
dates.txt 234,677
dir.dat 967
dir.txt 63,760
dirnt.dat 0
invdates.txt 14,400
invdates2.txt 33
numbers.txt 430
time.txt 16,764
```

Figure 4.16 Output of filter 4: sort by filename.

could also undertake the sort for us, but if it were implemented by a text editor then it would be easier to use a second filter to perform the sort.

This is fine if the files are required to stay exactly the same size, but what if the file sizes can legitimately differ within a certain tolerance? A lot of people believe that this is not automatable and this situation puts an end to their attempt to automate comparisons, but it is fairly easy to automate a tolerant comparison.

As an example, let us say that the file sizes can differ by up to 10% of the expected outcome value. We will need to write a small program (about 20 statements) that is in effect a specialized comparator to do the job for us. This program will be much simpler than a normal comparator because the two lists of files can be guaranteed to have the same filenames in the same order. This is something we can arrange by only performing the file-size check after a successful file list comparison. If we had discovered that the file lists differed because of a missing or extra file, we would probably choose not to perform the file-size check (though we should report the fact that it has not been performed). This gives us two levels of checking the results, with the deeper level only being invoked if the higher-level comparison had passed. This approach to comparison is called Multi Level Verification, a component of Herb Isenberg's Flexible Test System (Isenberg, 1998).

We have now completed our comparison of the filenames and sizes. We could go on to look at a different aspect of the original outcome in order to apply some different comparison criteria. For example, we could extract just the directory name records, masking out the drive name if this can legitimately differ. What is then passed to the comparator is shown below.

```
Directory of <drive>:\Mark\Doc
Directory of <drive>:\Mark\Doc\Examples
```

This will highlight any differences in the directory names (ignoring any difference in the disk drive mnemonic). Breaking outcomes down into separate pieces like this can make it much easier to analyze any differences.

Note that there is another advantage of using multiple comparison processes to verify a particular outcome. When a particular comparison fails, it can produce its own message relevant to the type of comparison being performed. For example, we have used three comparison processes to verify the directory listing. Each comparison process can report a different message so we will be told if there was a missing or extra file in the list, if a file differed by more than 10% from its expected size, or if the directory name was different.

4.9.7 Standardizing comparisons

For any software system there is going to be a finite number of different comparison requirements. One of the aims of a pilot project implementing test automation should be to identify the most likely comparison requirements and implement standard regular expressions, filters, and comparison processes to deal with them. As other comparison criteria are recognized, tool support can be implemented (once) for each one and the tools reused wherever the comparisons are required.

Once the concept of standard comparisons is implemented, there need be only one person who has the necessary skills and knowledge to implement and maintain the comparisons. The automated test writers need then only reference the type or types of comparison required for each outcome. Just as the details of how a test is automated are not necessarily the concern of the tester (the person who designs the tests), the details of comparison processes are best 'hidden' from their end users (the test automators), particularly if they do not have a programming background. Their interface to post-execution comparison should be the utility that implements the comparison process. The details of how it works need not concern them

Adopting standard filters and regular expressions will reduce the amount of effort involved in automating complex comparisons of different outcomes. However, this should not prohibit the use of non-standard comparisons, as it is likely that some programs will have special requirements. These will require 'one-off' comparators, if they are worth producing. Don't forget that you still always have the option to compare manually, perhaps after some filtering to make it easier. This may be the most cost-effective solution in some cases.

4.9.8 Generating expected outcomes

It is not always possible to have a prepared expected outcome for every aspect of a test case. For example, if the expected result is that a particular output should be the date one week from today, the actual value will depend on the date the test case is executed. Ideally, we will be able to fool the software into thinking it is being run on some specific date rather than the actual date, so the expected outcome can be predicted. However, this ideal is not always possible.

If we are stuck with the actual date the test case is executed, we need to be able to generate the expected outcome independently from the software. This is something that can be done but is outside the scope of this chapter. We explain how this and a few other unpredictable outcomes can be verified in Chapter 6.

4.10 Comparison guidelines

Comparison of test outcomes is often the easiest of test tasks to automate and also one of the most beneficial. Here are some basic principles to follow that will insure that comparison is both effective and efficient.

4.10.1 Keep it simple

Computer people tend to think that every problem needs a computerized solution. It is better to let the comparator tool do the 80–90% of the simplest comparisons, even if we then do the other 10–20% manually. This may actually be the most efficient option. Comparisons that are as simple as possible are less likely to either generate false failures or to miss true differences.

Although some comparison tasks appear to need highly specific and complex comparison criteria, there is usually no need to perform all of the comparison in one go. By breaking down the comparison criteria into smaller, less complex ones, the whole comparison task can be undertaken by a number of separate or sequential processes comprising simple comparison and data processing, using the idea of the filter mechanisms.

4.10.2 Document the comparisons

It is important to insure that everyone using a comparison process understands exactly what is and what is not ignored. Sensible naming conventions for comparison process utilities will go a long way to avoid confusion and misunderstandings. However, a short description aimed at telling users of the comparison process what it does and does not do will help even more. Additionally, a separate paragraph aimed at maintainers will sometimes prove invaluable. This may be little more than an explanation of the implementation or a warning about the existence of a similar filter but it could save a lot of wasted time and effort in the future.

4.10.3 Standardize as much as possible

The more things are standardized, the easier it will be to automate comparisons (and other test activities). Standard filters and regular expressions will become building blocks that can be used to build other filters and comparison processes. This will reduce the amount of effort involved in automating comparisons.

4.10.4 Divide and conquer

Small comparisons that are limited in scope are easier to set up and less likely to go wrong. If each comparison pass focuses on one specific aspect to compare, a multi-pass strategy can apply different aspects in succession.

4.10.5 Keep efficiency in mind

Comparison can be processing intensive and take considerable elapsed time, particularly when a comparator capable of complex comparisons is being used. However, the reason some comparisons become complex is solely to deal with possible differences between significantly different versions of the software being tested, rather than probable differences between intermediate and bug fix versions. In cases like this it can be annoying, if not wasteful, to have to run a lot of complex comparisons.

Sometimes it may be possible to verify the outcomes of such test cases using simple comparisons (which will complete faster than complex comparisons). If the simple comparison fails it will then be necessary to perform the complex comparison but this may happen infrequently compared with the number of times that the test cases are performed. This dual comparison can be implemented easily in a single comparison process, so once done the automated test writer need not know anything of it, though he or she will hopefully appreciate the improved efficiency.

4.10.6 Avoid bitmap comparisons

The best advice is to avoid bitmap comparisons if at all possible. They are notoriously troublesome, and can greatly increase the amount of time needed for the analysis of the results of the comparison. A bitmap is also dependent on the hardware used to display an image. If you want to test the same software on different PCs, the bitmaps may completely fail to match when the images are clearly (to a human being) the same.

If you do need to do a bitmap comparison, restrict the area that you compare to the smallest possible part of the screen or image.

4.10.7 Aim for a good balance between sensitive and robust tests

The breadth tests, the ones that are always run every time anything changes, should be relatively few in number but predominantly sensitive to any changes. For example, the comparison may include an entire screen, masking out only the minimum information such as current date and time.

For **depth tests**, those tests that each explore a particular area or feature in detail but are generally only run when an area has been affected by a change, aim for robust tests. Avoid comparisons of entire screens. Be selective about what it is important to compare to meet the objectives of a given test. Restrict the comparison to individual fields or small regions.

Summary

In this chapter, we have looked at how verification of test results is done by comparison of actual outcomes to expected outcomes, a process that can be automated. Expected outcomes are ideally predicted in advance; otherwise actual outcomes become the reference set or golden version for future comparisons.

Comparators are software packages that can detect differences between two sets of data such as files. A comparator cannot actually tell you whether or not a test has passed; it can only tell you whether or not it found any differences. Comparators can compare text, graphical images, or formatted data. If complex forms of data are converted into text, then simpler comparators can be used.

Comparison can be done dynamically, while a test execution tool is running, or it can be done post-execution, as a separate step after a test has completed. Test execution tools offer support for dynamic comparison, but post-execution comparison should also be considered.

A sensitive test compares more and more often; a robust test compares more selectively. A good automated testing regime will have a good mix of sensitive and robust tests, to balance failure analysis effort with the ability of the tests to detect unexpected differences.

A simple comparison looks for identical matches between data sets. A complex comparison can cope with some differences that are not of interest, such as the date and time the test was run, or by masking out or selectively including specific areas or items. Complex comparisons can be implemented with special-purpose tools, or through the use of filters and a multi-pass post-execution strategy using simple comparators, as described in the examples.

Different types of outputs can be compared automatically, including disk-based and screen-based. In comparing screens, especially for GUIs, some comparisons are required at the physical (bitmap) level, but it is generally more effective and efficient to compare at the logical level.

Automated comparison should be kept simple, but is one of the most productive areas to automate. Design your own standards for automated comparison to be applied throughout your regime, keeping in mind the balance between simple and complex comparisons, ease of use, and efficiency.

CHAPTER FIVE

Testware architecture

5.1 What is testware architecture?

Testware is the term we use to describe all of the artifacts required for testing, including documentation, scripts, data, and expected outcomes, and all the artifacts generated by testing, including actual outcomes, difference reports, and summary reports. Architecture is the arrangement of all of these artifacts; that is, where they are stored and used, how they are grouped and referenced, and how they are changed and maintained.

Of course, some testware is specific to automated testing (such as the scripts) and some is specific to manual testing (such as the test procedures). However, much testware is common to both automated and manual testing (such as the test plans and test data). In this chapter we cover testware architecture specifically in relation to automated testing but the points we raise and the recommendations we make can be applied equally to manual testing. In fact we would recommend that the testware architecture be developed to cover all testware generically. It should make no difference whether the artifacts are related to manual or automated testing, unit or system testing, or functional or non-functional testing.

We begin this chapter by highlighting four key issues that we believe have to be addressed if long-term success in test automation is to be achieved. The chapter ends with an approach to testware architecture that we have found works well. It may not suit everyone, as different environments and systems proffer different problems that require different solutions. However, even if the general approach is not suitable for you, we believe that there may be some ideas that could prove useful if adopted or at least adapted.

5.1.1 Terminology

We use specific terms to describe different types of testware artifact. Figure 5.1 shows the relationship between these terms. Testware comprises all artifacts used and produced by testing. The artifacts used by testing we call the test materials, and these include the inputs, scripts, data, documentation (including specifications), and expected outcome. The artifacts produced by testing we call the Test Results. There are two types of Test Results, the products and the by-products of testing. The products are all the artifacts that make up the actual outcome whereas the by-products are those additional artifacts that may be generated to record other information about the test execution and end result, such as an audit trail and difference report.

5.2   Key issues to be resolved

5.2.1 Scale

Inevitably there are a large number of artifacts required for test automation. The example automated test case that we developed in Chapter 2 had the following three basic files:

- countries.scp, the test script;
- countries.dcm, the initial document to edit – our test data;
- countries2.dcm, the expected output for post-execution comparison.

These are the test materials for the test case. Once the test has been run, we might additionally have the following three files:

- countries2.dcm, the actual output;
- countries.dif, the difference report produced by the comparator;
- countries.log, the audit trail of what happened when the test ran.

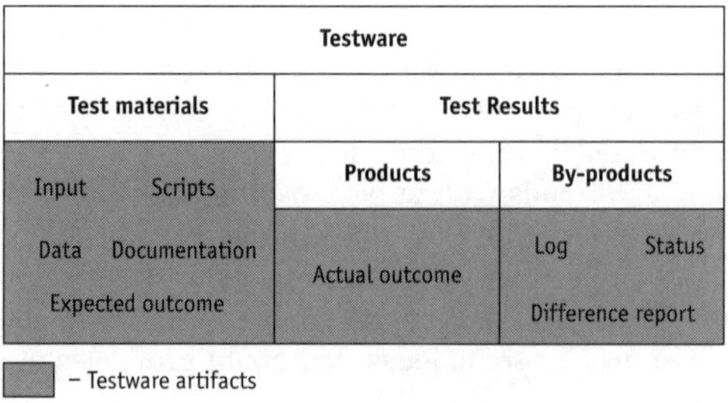

Figure 5.1 Hierarchy of the terms we use to describe the different types of testware artifact.

The actual output countries2.dcm is the product of the test case and the other two are by-products. Depending on the scripting approach and tool used we may also have the following files:

- ScribbleOpen.scp, a shared script;
- ScribbleSaveAs.scp, a shared script;
- compiled versions of each script.

Finally, there ought to be a specification associated with this and probably other test cases:

- test specification, documenting the design and implementation of the test case.

This gives us a possible total of twelve files, just for one test case. Of course, a second test case may be sharing some of these (particularly the test specification, the shared scripts, and the test data file countries.dcm). However, this still leaves us needing six new files for a second test case, and yet another six for a third test case.

Different environments, test tools, and test cases may require more or fewer files, but the point we are making is that for even a few tens of automated test cases there are likely to be several tens or perhaps a few hundred files. OK, not all of the information needs to be stored in separate files. For example, if a data-driven scripting approach is used, many different sets of input data may be contained in a single data file. There will be a limit to the amount of compression that can be done since the size of some individual files is likely to become unmanageable.

While there are only a few tens of automated test cases, and particularly when there are only one or two people dealing with them, more or less any testware architecture, structured or ad hoc, will be adequate. However, as soon as the number of test cases increases, say, tenfold or new people take on the responsibility for maintaining the automated tests, what was previously adequate will then become the root cause of many mistakes and inefficient automated testing.

EXPERIENCE REPORT

'We started using a test automation tool a couple of years ago but the person who used it has now left the company. We do not know how to develop new tests or maintain the existing ones.'

This experience report is typical of a number of organizations where test automation has been the responsibility or merely the special interest of one or two people. When they leave or move on to other projects their knowledge of the automated tests (what they do and how to use them) goes with them. All the effort they have put into automating tests and the experience they have gained is lost from the project. A common theme to most of these cases is the lack of organization of the testware. Which files go where, how they can be shared, and how to deal with old versions are all left to chance.

All the artifacts have to reside somewhere, and it is much better to decide where this should be at the start of an automation initiative, otherwise you will end up with as many different ways of organizing testware as you have testers. Yes, most people will do something sensible given the constraints of the test cases they are working on, but whatever it is, it is unlikely to be consistent with the approach taken by someone else. Test automation is difficult enough without having to decide repeatedly where to put which files every time a test is automated, or having to work out where to find the Test Results every time another test is run.

When one person starts to use tests automated by someone else, he or she will have to stop and find out where the scripts are, where test data is held, where the results are stored, and so on. This will, of course, take time and make automation that much less efficient.

We recommend that a concerted effort be made during the pilot project to identify the most appropriate testware architecture. This should help to insure that the needs of different types of automated test case and different testers are considered. Of course, this can be improved over time as new requirements and opportunities present themselves but it should mean that the improvements are building on a good foundation.

5.2.2 Reuse

To make real headway with test automation, reuse of scripts and data is essential. A good set of automated scripts will involve a lot of script reuse. As we explained in Chapter 3, the main reason for reuse is to eliminate duplication (e.g. for navigation), thereby speeding up implementation of new tests and saving on maintenance costs.

An intention to reuse scripts and data does not guarantee actual reuse. Much effort must be spent on developing reusable scripts and data but this effort is only worthwhile if the scripts and data are indeed reused. To be reused, different testers must be able to find these shared scripts and data, and be able to reference them easily without creating copies.

In our discussion of shared scripts in Section 3.2.3.4 we mentioned a limit for the amount of time (two minutes) someone would spend looking for a reusable script before deciding to implement their own version. We believe this is real. The ability to find out quickly whether or not a script exists to do a particular job is crucial to successful reuse, then being able to find the script quickly is likewise crucial. How quickly scripts can be found is governed by the testware architecture. If there is no consistency across all automated tests, it will be more difficult and error prone, encouraging automators to reinvent scripts rather than reuse them.

Even when reusable scripts can be found easily, reuse is still not guaranteed. The automator then has to be able to determine the script's suitability. (Strangely, some reusable scripts are not that reusable. Reuse is something that has to be designed into scripts.) How much effort will be required to determine a script's suitability for a specific purpose will largely depend on the quality of the script's documentation. This will also govern how easy it is to learn the details of how to use the script. These matters were discussed in Chapter 3.

It is better if different testers are able to use shared scripts and data without creating copies of them but by referencing them in some way. Creating a copy of a script is all right providing it is understood that the copy should not be edited (unless it is merely being used as a starting point for a different script). If copies are created there is a danger that these will be edited and then become an alternative version of a shared script. This will make maintenance of an automated Test Suite more difficult since whoever does the maintenance may not realize that a different version exists until the tests are run. Even then it may not be obvious what the problem is.

Clearly, some form of reusable script library is needed. The requirements for this can be clearly stated. For example, it must not take longer than two minutes for any tester to find any library script. Having found the required script, the tester must be able to determine exactly how to use it within some reasonable amount of time. We can expand on these requirements to take into account other aspects such as how easy it is to add new scripts to the library and how quickly an up-to-date catalog of all library scripts can be produced. (Specifying such requirements in a measurable way means that they can be tested; that is, we will be able to check that our implementation does indeed meet our requirements.)

The script library will require some implementation effort but, in our view, it should not require any significant management effort in the long term. That is, the testware architecture (more specifically at this point, the configuration management system for reusable scripts) should largely be a self-sustaining system.

5.2.3 Multiple versions

The real value of an automated Test Suite should be realized when a new version of the software is to be tested. However, before this is possible the automated tests themselves are likely to require some changes. Perhaps a script that controls the menu navigation or a script that deals with entering information into the system will have to be updated to reflect changes to the user interface. Perhaps the test input or test data may need updating to reflect functionality changes. When all the necessary changes have been made to the automated Test Suite, these tests can then be run on the new version of the software, but not on the old version. So should the original versions be kept? If they may be required to regression test emergency fixes for the old version of software then most certainly they should be kept. In any case, it is as well to keep old versions of tests so they are available to go back to should it become necessary, such as if changes to a software feature have to be withdrawn.

So, where should they be stored and how can they then be accessed? One approach would be to take a copy of all the automated testware, making clear which set of testware belongs to which version of software. This works for small numbers of automated tests and infrequent revisions of software but soon becomes inefficient, if not downright unmanageable, once we accumulate many tests or have to deal with frequent software revisions. The inefficiency comes about because we have two (or more) copies of every script and every data file, etc. If we find an original problem in one copy we may be compelled to correct it in every other copy.

This simple approach does not work well in situations where testing is done incrementally. That is, one part of the revised system is tested before another is ready. The automated tests have to cope with a hybrid of versions, old this, new that.

A more sophisticated approach to managing multiple versions of testware would be to have only multiple copies of those files that are changed. This will make the job of reconstructing any particular version of a test case more complex but will avoid having potentially huge numbers of duplicated files. For example, suppose there are three releases of the software currently in use: release A, the oldest release which all customers now have, release B, a later release to which some customers have upgraded, and release C, the newest release which is now being tested. Suppose also that the script for function Y is the same for all three releases, while the script for function X is different, and the data file differs only between two of the releases. Table 5.1 shows this situation.

Table 5.1 A possible situation in which different combinations of script and data file versions are used in each of three software releases.

	Release A	Release B	Release C
Function X script	V2.0	V2.1	V3.0
Function Y script	V1.0	V1.0	V1.0
Data files	V5.1	V5.1	V5.2

When we want to test the latest release (release C) of our testware, it will probably be relatively easy to find the appropriate testware since it is the latest version of everything. However, picking out all the appropriate versions of testware for software release B is not going to be so easy. In order for an automated test to run, it needs to have all of the right versions of testware. The tool will not stop and say, 'Excuse me, I don't think this is the latest version, I am about to fall down.'

Controlling multiple versions of tests will be a nightmare if it is not well managed. Of course, a good configuration management system should make the job simple but in our experience few organizations have a configuration management system, never mind a good one.

'Having fixed an urgent defect in an old version of software we thought it would only take a couple of hours to run the automated tests. One day later we decided to do most of the tests manually. We thought we had the versions of the scripts that corresponded to the old software, but we found that some had been lost when previous tests updated them but didn't save the old version. We also found that some data files were missing. We tried to reconstruct them, but that proved troublesome as well. In the end, we just had to do what manual testing we could in the time. This was very frustrating considering that we were supposed to have automated tests!'

5.2.4 Platform and environment independence

This fourth testware architecture issue applies only where the same software has to be tested across different environments or hardware platforms. Ideally, all tests would be platform independent such that the same files, scripts, etc. can be used on every platform or in every environment. In practice there will inevitably be some differences.

Some expected outcomes will likely be different. Due to the way a particular operating system implements a 'standard' package, different numerical results may result from the same calculation using the same input values. Different platforms may display things on the screen in a different order, in different colors or fonts, etc. Some of these differences are 'invisible' to the human tester, but can affect an automated test. This is one reason why the use of filters, described in Chapter 4, is useful.

Perhaps test set-up instructions will change for different environments, such as for different database management systems. If a test database needs to be set up and populated for a given test, the commands to create the database and even the way in which data is entered may be quite different from one proprietary database to another.

If the automated tests are required across different platforms, the testware architecture should provide a means of holding the necessary copies of platform-dependent information without requiring all the testware to be repeated.

5.3 An approach

5.3.1 Introduction

In the remainder of this chapter we describe an approach to testware architecture. This has been used as a starting point in a number of organizations to develop successful testware architectures. We offer it here to help readers who are looking for some guidelines and as a pragmatic way to explain ideas that may be of use. This approach may not suit everyone. Readers are encouraged to adapt this approach to their own situation or, at least, take away those ideas that appeal.

The approach described handles the four key issues explained in the first part of this chapter: scale, reuse, multiple versions, and platforms.

5.3.2 Basic concepts

We will consider the test materials first; that is, all the testware artifacts that are required before test execution can begin.

5.3.2.1 Test Sets

We divide the test materials into logical sets that we call **Test Sets**. Each Test Set contains one or more test cases. Normally Test Sets would contain a few tens of test cases but they may contain a few hundred or, at the other extreme, a single test case.

The decision as to how many test cases are put into one Test Set is not usually a difficult one. For example, we may put all the test cases for a single function or all the breadth test cases (regression tests) for a small application into a Test Set. There are no rules as such as to how test cases are to be divided among Test Sets, but sensibly there will be some logical rationale for the decision.

The basic concept of a Test Set is that it will contain all of the test materials associated with the test cases, including the scripts, data, expected outcome, and documentation. For example, a Test Set containing tests for the List function of our Scribble application is shown in Figure 5.2.

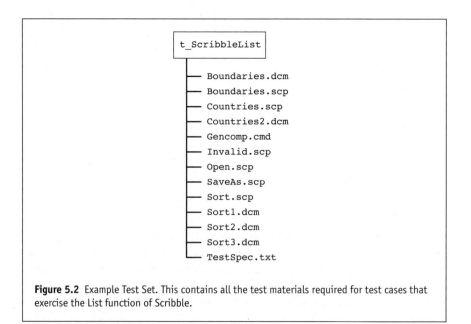

Figure 5.2 Example Test Set. This contains all the test materials required for test cases that exercise the List function of Scribble.

The Test Set is called t_ScribbleList. It contains the script Countries.scp, which implements the test case that we used in Chapter 2. The Scribble document Countries2.dcm is the expected outcome of this test case. The Test Set contains some other test cases. The Boundaries.scp script and the Scribble document Boundaries.dcm exercise boundaries such as minimum and maximum List lengths. The Invalid.scp script exercises invalid actions such as attempting to remove items from an empty List. There is no expected outcome file for this test, as this is verified by comparing error messages that appear dynamically when the test is run (so the expected outcome is contained within the script). The final test case exercises the List sorting feature. For this test case we have one script Sort.scp, but three expected outcome files, Sort1.dcm, Sort2.dcm, and Sort3.dcm. These may represent the outcome of three tests included in the test case of the List sorting feature.

The scripts Open.scp and SaveAs.scp are shared scripts that are used by all of the other scripts in this Test Set. The utility GenComp.cmd is a command file that provides a simple interface to a post-execution comparator and is used by several of the test cases in this Test Set. The test specification file TestSpec.txt documents the design and implementation of the test cases.

Other Test Sets would contain different test cases and, therefore, different scripts, data files, and expected outcomes.

5.3.2.2 Test Suite

Most likely when we need to run some tests we will wish to run more than the few that are contained in any one Test Set, so we can bring together two or more Test Sets to form what we call a Test Suite.

A **Test Suite** is simply a collection of Test Sets and therefore contains all the test materials required to run the test cases contained within the Test Sets. Normally this would be a collection of test cases to meet a given test objective, for example to test a bug or to undertake system testing of a range of products. There can be as many Test Suites as you like.

For example, Figure 5.3 shows a Test Suite of just two Test Sets. The objective of the test cases in this Test Suite is to verify a bug fix to the List function of Scribble.

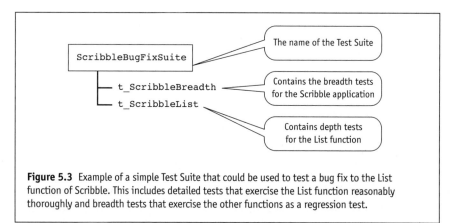

Figure 5.3 Example of a simple Test Suite that could be used to test a bug fix to the List function of Scribble. This includes detailed tests that exercise the List function reasonably thoroughly and breadth tests that exercise the other functions as a regression test.

5.3.2.3 Limitations of the basic concepts

These basic concepts of Test Sets and Test Suites are not sufficient in themselves to deal with the key issues described at the start of this chapter. While they give us a way of managing a potentially large number of different test cases and all the test materials associated with them, they do not tell us what to do about shared scripts and data, or about how to handle multiple versions.

For example, if the scripts Open.scp and SaveAs.scp were to be shared by test cases in both Test Sets of Figure 5.3, where should they go? If a copy were held in both Test Sets that would rather defeat the purpose of them being shared scripts. If they were held in one of the Test Sets but not the other, how would anyone know where to find them?

To overcome these and other limitations we need to introduce a few more concepts. We shall introduce the concept of Script Sets to hold scripts that are shared between different Test Sets. We will also introduce Data Sets and Utility Sets to hold data and utilities that are shared between different Test Sets. We use the term Testware Set to mean any of these different types of Set. Finally, we will introduce the Testware Library, a repository in which to store all of the Testware Sets. Not only does it store all the Testware Sets, but it also stores all versions of the Testware Sets.

These additional concepts are sufficient to enable us to handle the key issues of testware architecture.

5.3.3 Testware Sets

A **Testware Set** is a logical collection of testware artifacts (scripts, data files, etc.). They are the building blocks of our testware architecture. We describe four different types of Testware Set: Test Set, Script Set, Data Set, and Utility Set.

5.3.3.1 Test Sets

A **Test Set** defines one or more test cases. It comprises all the testware artifacts that are unique to the test cases defined by the Test Set. These could be any or all of the following:

- test scripts;
- expected outcomes;
- test data;
- test input;
- documentation files (e.g. test specifications);
- source files for utilities such as test drivers and specialized converters;
- executables of the utilities built from the source files.

All of the testware artifacts in any Test Set have one common attribute: that they are used *only* by the test cases defined by the Test Set in which they reside. For example, a script appearing in the Test Set t_ScribbleBreadth is not allowed to be used or referenced by tests or scripts in any other Test Set. This is a basic and important rule of our testware architecture. If it turns out that we would like to reuse a script held in a different Test Set, then we must move the script from its original Test Set and place it into a Script Set (Script Sets are described below).

Some example Test Sets are shown in Figure 5.4.

In Figure 5.4 the Test Set that defines test cases for exercising the List functionality of Scribble is shown as t_ScribbleList version 2. The prefix 't_' indicates that this is a Test Set and the version number '2' implies that there is an earlier version of this Test Set (i.e. one or more artifacts in it have been updated for some reason).

Note that the Test Set t_ScribbleList is different from the one shown in Figure 5.2. It no longer contains the shared scripts Open.scp and SaveAs.scp since they are shared by test cases in other Test Sets. (They will appear in a Script Set a little later on.) Similarly, the utility GenComp.cmd has been removed from this Test Set since it is used by test cases in other Test Sets. (It will appear later in a Utility Set.)

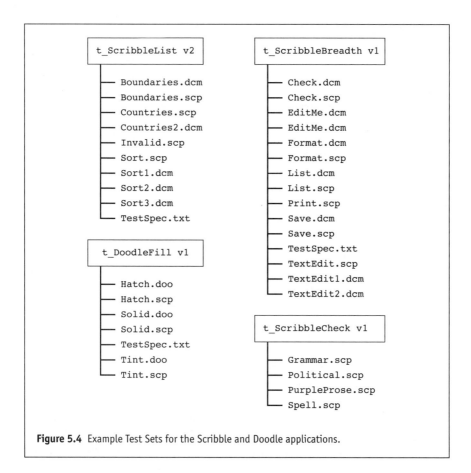

Figure 5.4 Example Test Sets for the Scribble and Doodle applications.

Figure 5.4 contains three other Test Sets. One is for testing the Checking functionality of Scribble (this is the 'professional' version of Scribble, not the simple one we saw in Chapter 2). This contains scripts that implement test cases that exercise the individual features that check for incorrect spelling, poor grammar, political correctness, and 'purple prose.' The fact that there are no .dcm documents suggests that these are all compared dynamically rather than post-execution. The t_ScribbleBreadth Test Set contains breadth tests for a range of Scribble functions. Something that is different with this Test Set is that there appear to be two copies of the Scribble document EditMe.dcm. These are two different versions; one is used as test data and the other is the expected outcome (the document having been edited in some way). The two versions will need to be stored separately in the physical implementation, as discussed in Section 5.3.7.

We also have included a Test Set for Doodle, our drawing package. This Test Set contains test cases for exercising the functionality of filling a drawing or shape with different kinds of pattern.

5.3.3.2 Script Sets

A **Script Set** comprises only scripts and documentation, and all the scripts in a Script Set are used by different test cases in more than one Test Set. The scripts can be any collection that can sensibly be held together (such as the navigation scripts for an application or a set of shared scripts offering logging functionality). The one common attribute of all the scripts held in any Script Set is that they are reusable. The fact that they are held in a Script Set implies that they are used by different test cases defined in two or more Test Sets.

The documentation is optional but highly recommended, particularly where the scripts themselves do not contain their own documentation (for users of the script, describing the script's purpose and use). Even when the scripts do contain their own documentation, it may be helpful to produce a single document that forms the catalog or user manual of all the scripts in the Script Set.

Some example Script Sets are shown in Figure 5.5.

In Figure 5.5, we have the shared scripts that were discussed in Chapter 3 and shown in Figure 3.5, i.e. the script to open a Scribble document, and the script to save a Scribble document under a new filename. These are also the shared scripts we had in our first version of the Scribble List Test Set shown in Figure 5.2.

Note that we have the same basic functionality for Doodle in the Script Set s_DoodleDocument (the 's_' meaning that this is in a Script Set). Although the two scripts have the same name in both Script Sets (Open.scp and SaveAs.scp) they are different scripts. They have the same name because they are dealing with similar functionality. They are different scripts because the functionality is implemented slightly differently in each of the applications. There is no danger of confusing them since they will always be held in their respective Script Sets, the names of which identify

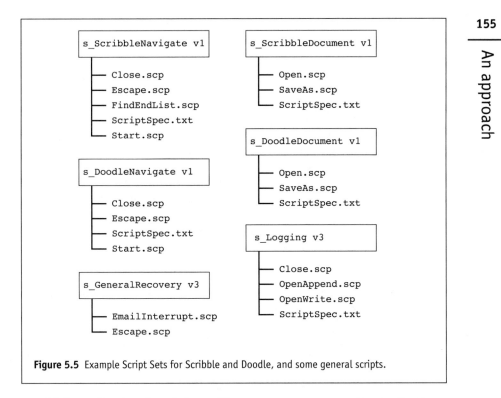

Figure 5.5 Example Script Sets for Scribble and Doodle, and some general scripts.

to which application they belong. The same comment applies to the three Escape.scp scripts that escape from Scribble, Doodle, and a general recovery routine, respectively. Note that the general recovery Escape script could be called by the Escape scripts of Scribble and Doodle.

The Script Set s_ScribbleNavigate deals with Scribble navigation, starting and closing the application, finding the end of a List, and escaping from Scribble altogether if something drastic goes wrong. The s_Logging Script Set contains scripts that provide standard functionality that allows each test case to record its progress in a test log. The scripts here provide the means to open and write (the first time), open and append for subsequent test events, and finally close the log file at the end of a test case.

5.3.3.3 Data Sets

A **Data Set** comprises only data files and documentation, and all the data files contained in a Data Set are used by different test cases in more than one Test Set. The data files can be any collection that can sensibly be held together (such as a collection of standard database entries or standard input data). As with Script Sets, the one common attribute of all the data files held in any Data Set is that they are reusable. Again, the fact that they are held in a Data Set implies that they are used by different test cases defined in two or more Test Sets.

The documentation is optional but highly recommended. Hopefully the data files themselves will contain information explaining what the data is, what it is used for, and any other salient points. However, this is not always possible since the format of the data file may allow it to contain only the necessary data. In these cases, one or more documents containing this information are best placed in the Data Set alongside the data files to which the information refers.

Example Data Sets are shown in Figure 5.6.

Figure 5.6 shows four Data Sets, two for Scribble and two for Doodle. The Data Set d_ScribbleTypical contains the input file countries.dcm that was used in our test from Chapter 2. It also contains another test for Scribble, where the List items are the titles of articles in a journal. The other Scribble Data Set contains four Scribble documents, one with a large list, one with a small list, one where the document itself is very large, and a small document. The Data Sets for Doodle show typical things to test and some extremes, such as large and complex doodles. We have used the suffix .doo to represent a Doodle document.

5.3.3.4 Utility Sets

A **Utility Set** comprises utilities (stubs, drivers, converters, comparators, etc.) that are used by test cases in more than one Test Set. The Utility Set contains both the source code and the executables, and any relevant documentation. As with the other types of Testware Set, the utilities can be any collection that can sensibly be held together (such as all the comparators dealing with a particular format of output). These utilities are reused by different test cases defined in two or more Test Sets.

Both source code and executables are held in the Utility Set since the latter is built from the former. Note that some utilities comprise neither source code nor executables as such. Command files, batch files, shell scripts, and the like are usually interpreted, meaning that the file itself (the 'source code') is also the executable. These also belong in a Utility Set if they are shared by different test cases defined in two or more Test Sets.

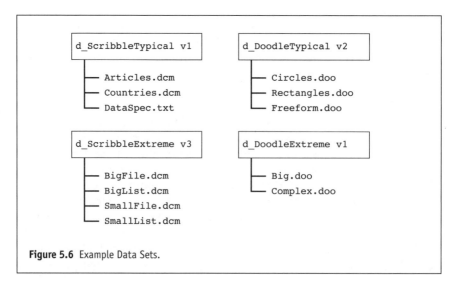

Figure 5.6 Example Data Sets.

Documentation associated with the utilities should be included in the Utility Set. User documentation, maintenance documentation, requirements, and functional and design specifications for the utilities, where appropriate, can all sit comfortably in a Utility Set.

Example Utility Sets are shown in Figure 5.7.

Figure 5.7 shows three example utility sets. u_GenericFilters (where the 'u_' indicates a utility set) contains generic filters. The first, DateReplace.cmd, is a command file (.cmd) that replaces any occurrence of a date with the text string <Date> (as described in Chapter 4). Similarly TimeReplace.cmd is a command file to replace any occurrence of a time with the text string <Time>.

The next three elements of this Utility Set are all related to converting US date formats to UK date formats (by exchanging the month and day fields). The .frm and .vbp files are compiled to create the executable .exe file.

We also have a Utility Set of filters specific to Scribble. The first command file, StripList.cmd, will strip out a List from a Scribble document, i.e. deleting any text not contained between the List Start and List End markers. The second command file, StripNonList.cmd, will remove Lists from Scribble documents, leaving only the text that is not within the List Start and List End markers.

The Utility Set u_GeneralCompare contains only one utility and an associated documentation file. This utility is a command file to implement general comparison instructions. It provides a simple interface to a standard comparator. For example, by assuming knowledge of our testware architecture it can convert a single filename into the two full pathnames of the expected outcome and actual outcome files to be compared, which it then passes on to the standard comparator. After the comparison has been performed, if no differences are found it may delete the difference report produced by the comparator and in any case exit with a status indicating the number of differences found.

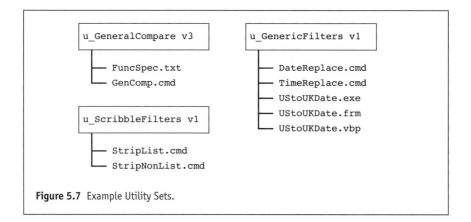

Figure 5.7 Example Utility Sets.

5.3.4 Test Suite

A Test Suite is a self-contained environment from which all the selected test cases are run. A Test Suite is simply a collection of Testware Sets. Test Suites may contain as many Testware Sets as are required.

An example Test Suite is shown in Figure 5.8. This shows a Test Suite called ScribbleBugFixSuite that contains all those test cases we wish to run on a version of Scribble that contains a bug fix to the List function. This Test Suite happens to contain one of each type of Testware Set that we have described, and it includes the test case of Scribble from Chapter 2. We have seen all of these Testware Sets before in the various examples in this chapter.

There must be at least one Test Set (since it is only Test Sets that contain test cases) and there need not be any other type of Testware Set (if there are no shared scripts, data files, or utilities). Note that a Test Suite may comprise one Test Set and one or more Script, Data, and Utility Sets, even though there are no other Test Sets in the Test Suite with which to share these shared artifacts. The other Test Sets do exist; that is why the artifacts are 'shared' (i.e. in Testware Sets of their own). For example, if we removed the t_ScribbleList Test Set from the Test Suite shown in Figure 5.8 we may not be able remove anything else. The Data, Script, and Utility Sets are used by both Test Sets (and others not in this Test Suite) and have to be there even if only one Test Set is present.

It is not necessary to run all of the test cases in a Test Set. For example, if we only want to run the test case from Chapter 2, we need the t_ScribbleList Test Set that contains it, but we will ignore all of the other test cases that the Test Set contains.

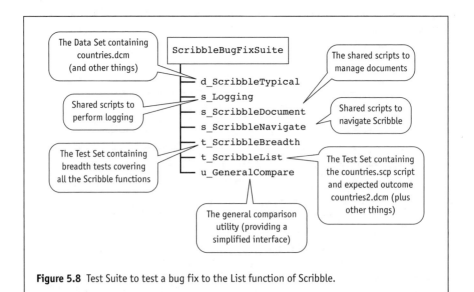

Figure 5.8 Test Suite to test a bug fix to the List function of Scribble.

5.3.5.1 Example Testware Library, Test Suites, and Testware Sets

The **Testware Library** is a repository of the master versions of all Testware Sets. This stores all test materials (test data, scripts, documentation, etc.) long term. These materials have to be copied to be run. In our implementation, they can be searched and read from the library but they cannot be used (i.e. tests cannot be executed) from within the Testware Library.

Figure 5.9 gives an example showing the relationship between the Testware Library, Test Suites, and Testware Sets. In our architecture there is only ever one Testware Library. In this example the Testware Library contains test materials for all automated (and manual) tests of Scribble. In practice, the Testware Library will also contain all the testware for tests associated with other applications but we have not shown these in this figure. Some of the Testware Sets in the Testware Library have more than one version, implying that something in them has been changed at some time so a new version was created.

Figure 5.9 shows two Test Suites, one that is being used to test a bug fix version of Scribble and another that is being used to test enhancements in a new version of Scribble. The bug fix Test Suite is using a small subset of all the testware since it is required only to test a bug fix to one area of functionality (the List functionality in this case) and perform some regression

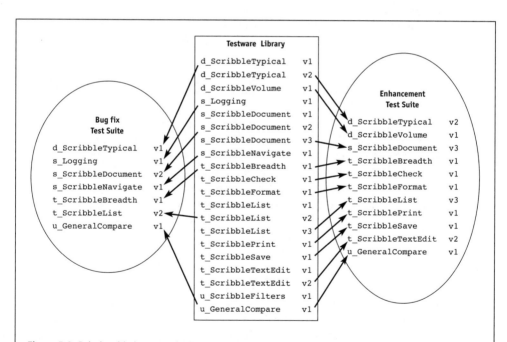

Figure 5.9 Relationship between the Testware Library, Test Suites, and Testware Sets. This Testware Library contains some of the testware used in testing our Scribble application. (Note that this is for a much more functionally rich version of Scribble than we have described in previous chapters.)

testing across the rest of the application. The enhancement Test Suite is using the latest versions of most of the Testware Sets to test new functions and features as well as regression testing the unchanged functions.

Whenever any of the test materials in the Testware Library are to be used (to perform testing) they have to be copied. (In your own implementation you may decide it is better to allow people to use the test materials directly from the Testware Library. This is very much an environment-specific issue – it works well one way in some environments but not in others, and vice versa.) The required Testware Sets are copied into a structure that we call the Test Suite.

5.3.5.2 Accessing the Testware Library

It is important that the task of copying Testware Sets from the Testware Library is as simple as possible. By this we mean as quick as possible and as foolproof as possible. If the task takes a long time, people may become reluctant to undertake it or may simply not have sufficient time to do it. When evaluating any particular architecture for testware, we like to consider what someone will have to do in a hurry. We imagine a severe defect has been reported and fixed, and the fixed software has to be sent out the same night. Because there are automated tests most people will expect that the tests can be run 'at the touch of a button.' However, some of the tests you need have been updated for testing a new version of software, so the original versions have to be retrieved and run within a couple of hours. If it is going to take a couple of hours to locate and copy the required tests from the Testware Library there is something wrong.

The mechanism for copying Testware Sets from the Testware Library should make it impossible to transfer an incomplete set of Testware Sets. If it does not, you can guarantee that it will happen, and probably when you can least afford such a mistake. For example, in creating the bug fix Test Suite shown in Figure 5.9, it should not be possible to copy the two Test Sets t_ScribbleBreadth and t_ScribbleList without the Script Set s_ScribbleDocument and the Data Set d_ScribbleTypical. If this were done, most if not all of the tests would fail. For such a small collection of tests the consequences of this may not be too terrible. However, when it is a large collection of tests that have to be run overnight, the consequences of just one data file being omitted might be to cause most of the tests to fail, leaving the software largely untested.

If the testware architecture is designed with this in mind a few simple tools can be used to insure that all the testware for the tests requested has been copied. For example, if all of the Testware Sets required for a test suite to be run were listed in a text file, this could form a checklist that could be used to copy them automatically into the appropriate Test Suite. Since this list can be generated automatically, for example by searching each script to identify any other scripts and data files required and adding them to the checklist, the whole checking and copying process can be automated.

5.3.5.3 Configuration management

There are two alternative ways of managing the configuration of the testware. The method that we favor is for the Testware Sets to be stored in the Testware Library as **configuration items** (that is, having a version number). The individual testware artifacts that make up the content of each type of set do not have their own version numbers. The effect of this is that whenever anything in the Testware Set is changed, a new version of the Testware Set is created containing the changed artifacts and the unchanged artifacts.

A baseline is something that has a version number but comprises a number of configuration items, each version of a baseline being built from specific versions of the configuration items. In Figure 5.10, our baseline is a Test Suite, made up of the Testware Sets, which are the configuration items.

An alternative way of managing the testware configuration would be for the individual testware artifacts to have their own version number. In this case, whenever anything in a Testware Set is changed, only those artifacts that change have new versions. The lowest level of the diagram would then become the configuration items, with version numbers. The Testware Sets then become baselines instead of configuration items. The Test Suite remains as a baseline but is a baseline comprising other baselines (rather than configuration items directly). A new version of the Testware Set baseline will then comprise those artifacts that have not changed and the new versions of those that have changed. This alternative way of managing the configuration may be better in some situations (particularly where a good configuration management system is in place).

More than one version of a Testware Set may coexist in the Testware Library but only one version of a Testware Set can be held in a Test Suite.

5.3.5.4 Controlling testware updates

Controlling modifications to the testware artifacts is clearly an important issue. Within our testware architecture we have established a framework in which testers can update testware artifacts, thereby creating new versions of

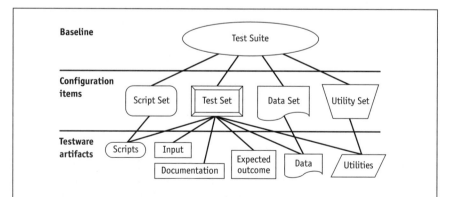

Figure 5.10 The relationship of the testware artifacts at the lowest level, organized into Testware Sets (the configuration items) and a Test Suite (the baseline) comprising a number of Testware Sets.

configuration items. However, we have not prevented two or more people attempting to change the same configuration item at the same time. If there is a good configuration management system in place then this will already be catered for in some way. If not, it is possible to avoid most conflicts if people follow a few simple rules.

If there is an existing source code control system it may be sufficient for controlling the testware. This has the advantage of using a known system, so minimizes learning time. Develop utilities to automate configuration management tasks, particularly if they are error prone or tedious to do manually.

We suggest that the mechanisms for accessing the Testware Library allow people to record whether or not they intend changing any Testware Sets. If any other people have already taken copies of these, they can be informed (automatically by email perhaps). Conversely, when someone tries to record their intent to update a Testware Set that is already marked for an update, they will be told who is currently editing it.

Keep the system as simple as possible to make it easy to access the testware, and test the system in all the different ways it will be used. For example, select a subset of test cases for an old version of software and run them under two different environments. If this can be done successfully, quickly, and with little manual intervention then you probably have things about right.

5.3.6 Test Results

So far we have described a testware architecture that deals with the test materials – that is, all the testware we need to run test cases. We have not said anything about the artifacts that are generated by testing. These we refer to as the **Test Results**, and they include the actual outcomes, difference reports, and test tool log.

The Test Result artifacts are different from the other testware artifacts. The Test Result artifacts are produced by test case execution whereas the other testware artifacts are used by the test cases. Test Results are produced each time a test case executes. A test case may be executed many times, reusing the same test materials each time, but is likely to produce different Test Results.

Another difference between Test Results and test materials is that the Test Results are generally 'write-once' and then 'read-only.' It would not be a good idea for Test Results to be editable if we want to have accurate records of our testing! The pre-execution testware (the test materials), on the other hand, need to be editable, and indeed need to be under configuration control so that changes to the testware can be tracked over time. Test Results, once generated, should never be changed. It may be necessary to retain some Test Results, most likely the results from the last run of each test case before the software is released. This is perhaps best done under the control of a configuration management system so they are associated with the correct versions of testware and software.

5.3.6.1 Test execution products and by-products

There are two different types of test result artifacts. The purpose of executing a test is generally to produce some outcome, which is then compared to the expected outcome. So the test outcome can be thought of as the 'product' of the test execution process.

However, a test case also produces some 'by-products', such as the test difference reports and the test tool log. These test by-products are very important since they comprise an audit trail that can tell us when a test was run, the version of software it exercised, the test status (whether the test passed or failed), and so on.

5.3.6.2 Should the Test Results be kept?

When a test case fails, we are probably most interested in the differences between the actual and expected outcome. The test by-products are also useful to know about, but if the test fails, it will most likely need to be run again. So unless we are saving the history of all test cases ever executed, we may 'throw away' most of the by-product testware and keep only the actual outcome and difference report. This is just one possible view. We actually recommend keeping everything in the event of test case failure since you cannot always tell in advance exactly what you will need when analyzing a test case failure. After all, it is easier to delete something than it is to recreate it.

When a test passes, we are no longer interested in the difference report (because by definition there are no differences – this is what constitutes a test pass). We are also no longer interested in the actual outcome (unless all actual outcomes need to be kept for legal reasons) because this is not likely to tell us anything that we do not already have in another form. Because there are no unexpected differences, we can safely discard the actual outcome and the difference report. We may need to keep at least some of the other by-products, the test log for example, if this is required to provide evidence of the testing carried out. Otherwise all test results can be deleted.

5.3.6.3 Logical structure

The logical structure of the Test Results is shown in Figure 5.11. The whole set of test result artifacts for a single run of the test cases in a Test Suite can be grouped according to the Test Sets in which the associated test cases reside. Note that there will only be Test Results for those test cases that have been run.

5.3.7 Physical implementation

Our description of the Testware Sets and Test Suite has been confined to a logical view of them. That is, we have described the relationship between the various artifacts but have not specifically stated how these relationships might be implemented. Of course any one implementation is unlikely to suit everyone but the one that we favor makes extensive use of a hierarchy of

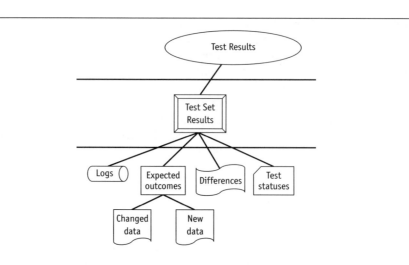

Figure 5.11 The hierarchical relationship of the testware result artifacts. At the lowest level the test result artifacts belong to a particular Test Set (they are the products and by-products of the execution of the test cases defined by the Test Set). These 'sets' of test results then make up all of the results produced by the Test Suite. Thus, the Test Results level in this figure corresponds to the Test Suite level.

directories (folders). We do not necessarily expect readers to implement verbatim the structure we describe, but rather adapt it to better suit their own needs.

5.3.7.1 *Testware Set Directories*

We strictly maintain the same physical structure for every Testware Set regardless of where it is located (in the Testware Library or in a Test Suite). This is to facilitate the use of standard utilities for performing a range of useful tasks and avoids any restructuring of the Testware Sets as they are copied from one place to another.

We propose a basic physical structure of a Testware Set Directory as shown in Figure 5.12. The whole Testware Set is held in a directory (folder) that contains a series of subdirectories, one for each category of testware. The same subdirectory names are used consistently throughout all Testware Sets. This hierarchical structure of directories makes them very easy to copy and move about. In most environments it is possible to copy or move a directory hierarchy (sometimes this is referred to as a directory tree) with a single command or user interaction (such as 'drag and drop'). This is not the only way that the testware in the Testware Sets could be organized physically, but this implementation has worked well in a number of organizations.

We are basically taking the logical files of a Testware Set (for example t_ScribbleBreadth v1, a Test Set in Figure 5.4) and arranging them into various physical subdirectories based on the type of file (this is shown in Figure 5.14). So all of the expected results from the Test Set would be put into a subdirectory called Expected, for example.

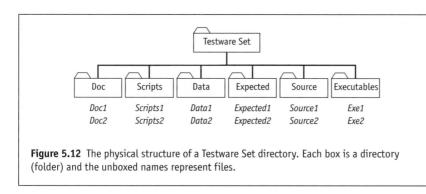

Figure 5.12 The physical structure of a Testware Set directory. Each box is a directory (folder) and the unboxed names represent files.

Note that not every lower-level subdirectory would be present for all Testware Set Directories. A Test Set Directory could contain all of the subdirectories shown in Figure 5.12; a Data Set Directory would not contain script, source, or utility subdirectories, a Utility Set Directory would not contain scripts, data, or expected results, and a Script Set Directory would contain only scripts and documentation.

Figure 5.13 shows an example of the physical structure of each type of Testware Set. The Test Set t_ScribbleList contains one document (the test specification), which goes into the document subdirectory 'Doc.' The four scripts go into the Scripts subdirectory, and five expected outcome files (in this case all are Scribble documents) go into the Expected subdirectory. There are no data files in this Test Set (t_ScribbleList) as these test cases use shared data files, which are held in the separate Data Set d_ScribbleTypical. There are no utilities in this Test Set, as they are held in the Utility Set u_GeneralCompare. Therefore the Test Set subdirectory only contains the Doc, Script and Expected subdirectories; the other subdirectories are omitted.

Figure 5.13 also shows an example physical implementation of a Script Set, s_ScribbleDocument, which contains a documentation subdirectory (Doc) and a script subdirectory (Scripts), but no other subdirectories.

Similarly, the physical implementation of the Data Set contains a documentation subdirectory (Doc) and a data subdirectory (Data).

The Utility Set is implemented by three subdirectories, including one for documentation (Doc). The Utility Set includes two source files UStoUKDate.frm and UStoUKDate.vbp. These are used to build the executable image UStoUKDate.exe. In our test automation regime the executable image is not held in the Testware Library but is generated from the source after the Utility Set has been copied into a Test Suite. This is a task that can be undertaken as a Test Suite or Testware Set pre-processing task (see Chapter 6).

The subdirectory for all the executables (Utilities) includes the compiled program (.exe suffix) and two command files (.cmd suffix) which are interpreted rather than compiled. This means that we have all executable utilities in one subdirectory.

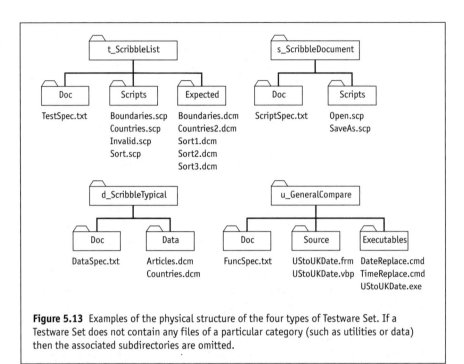

Figure 5.13 Examples of the physical structure of the four types of Testware Set. If a Testware Set does not contain any files of a particular category (such as utilities or data) then the associated subdirectories are omitted.

5.3.7.2 Test Suites

A Test Suite is also a directory hierarchy in that all of the Testware Set Directories are held in the one directory that is the Test Suite. The name of the top-level directory should reflect the purpose of the Test Suite. Figure 5.14 shows the physical implementation of our Scribble bug fix Test Suite.

If you compare the physical structure of the Test Set t_ScribbleBreadth shown in Figure 5.14 with the logical Test Set of the same name shown in Figure 5.4, you will see that the files have now been put into the subdirectory reflecting the type of file. This also shows how the two files of the same name (EditMe.dcm) are physically separated. One of these files is data, so is in the Data subdirectory; the other is expected output, so is in the Expected subdirectory.

Just as the hierarchical structure of directories for each Testware Set makes them very easy to copy and move about, the same is true for the Test Suite – it is just bigger.

5.3.7.3 Test Results

In our scheme for testware architecture we keep the test results separate from the Test Suite (i.e. the test materials) and hold them in their own hierarchy of directories. The top-level directory can be given any name you choose but is best given a name that relates it to the relevant Test Suite. Figure 5.15 shows the physical structure of the Test Results produced from a run of the Scribble bug fix Test Suite.

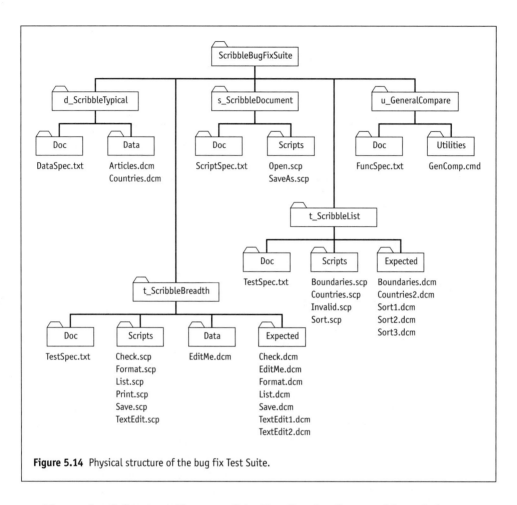

Figure 5.14 Physical structure of the bug fix Test Suite.

The top-level directory (the root of the Test Results directory hierarchy) contains a subdirectory for each Test Set in the Test Suite. The names of the subdirectories are the same as those used in the Test Suite, and these in turn contain one subdirectory for each test case in the Test Suite. Each test case subdirectory contains all of the results for that test case.

Note that our test cases each have a name rather than a number; for example, the Test Set t_ScribbleBreadth comprises six test cases, Check, Format, List, Save, Print, and TextEdit. It is perhaps more conventional to refer to test cases as Test1, Test2 and so on, but such a naming convention does not tell us anything about the test cases, so we have chosen names that reflect their purpose. (The name of the Test Set tells us that these are breadth tests for the Scribble application. The test case names tell us which feature they are breadth tests of.)

The content of each test case subdirectory depends entirely on the test case itself. In our example of Figure 5.15 each automated test case has been designed to create a log file (Log.txt) that contains an audit trail of the test case execution. This may contain messages output by instructions in the

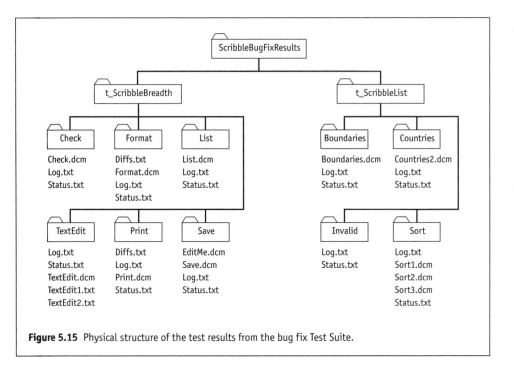

Figure 5.15 Physical structure of the test results from the bug fix Test Suite.

test scripts and output by the test tool itself. They also have a status file (Status.txt) that contains a single keyword describing the status of the test case (typically PASSED or FAILED but see Chapter 9 for a discussion of other possible statuses). A difference report (Diffs.txt) exists only if any unexpected differences were found. In this example, there are two difference reports, one in the results of the 'Format' test case and the other in the results of the 'Print' test case. (In our regime difference reports contain a list of the differences found by all of the comparisons performed – this saves having to open more than one file to view the differences.) Most of the other files in the test results hierarchy are Scribble documents output by the tests.

In our test automation regime the test automation vehicle is responsible for creating the subdirectory structure below the results tree root directory. When a test case in a Test Set is executed the corresponding test case subdirectory in the results hierarchy is created. If the subdirectory already exists then everything in it is deleted. This policy insures that we cannot end up with a situation where there is a mixture of results from different test runs in the same directory. If the results from a previous test run are required to be kept then a new test result hierarchy can be used for the new test run, or the old test results can be archived before the test is run. The Test Set result directory is created when the first test case in that Test Suite is run.

5.3.7.4 Naming conventions

Every good testware architecture implementation will have a sensible naming convention for just about everything. Scripts, data files, expected outcomes, documentation, and even the test cases themselves are candidates for sensible naming conventions. The need for some convention is fairly obvious. Imagine a relatively small collection of, say, 100 automated tests. This could easily involve anything between 500 and 1000 files. If these were all given random names (such as Mark, Barbara, Franky, and Bobby) it would be rather difficult to isolate a particular script or data file.

One convention could be to name all scripts with a prefix of 'script' and all data files with a prefix of 'data', for example script1, script2, script3, data1, data2, data3, etc. This will help us distinguish between scripts and data files but is not much help beyond that. Often filenames have extensions that indicate the type of file so we need not repeat this information.

In our view the goals of a good naming convention are for it to be useful and meaningful without being repetitive or unnecessarily cryptic. The pieces of information we may like to be able to glean from the name of a file (or the name of anything else, e.g. directories or folders, databases, and even test cases) are the type and purpose of its content, and with what it is associated. Not only do we have the file's name but also the name of the directory (or folder) where it resides. In our example test architecture we have adopted the following convention for Testware Sets:

The name of a Testware Set starts with a single lower-case letter indicating the type of the Testware Set (s for Script Set, d for Data Set, t for Test Set, and u for Utility Set) and an underscore character follows this. The rest of the name comprises one or more words or abbreviations, each starting with an upper-case letter. Testware Sets associated with a specific application have the application name as the first word. Any other words should indicate the function or action exercised by the test cases or supported by the testware.

For example, the Script Set called s_ScribbleDocument contains two scripts: Open.scp and SaveAs.scp. Knowing that Open.scp belongs to the Script Set s_ScribbleDocument should suggest to us that it probably has something to do with opening documents in the Scribble application.

5.3.7.5 Platform and environment dependencies

All the hardware platform or environment-specific versions of a testware artifact are kept together. This should not be confused with different versions of testware artifacts for the same hardware platform or environment that belong in different versions of the same Testware Set. For example, suppose that the expected outcomes in the Test Set t_ScribbleList were hardware platform specific. (Although this is not actually the case, we will assume it is just for the purpose of this example.) Figure 5.16 shows how this might be structured.

Having all the hardware platform or environment-specific versions in the same Testware Set is both convenient and sensible. When it comes to accessing the expected outcomes for a specific platform there are two

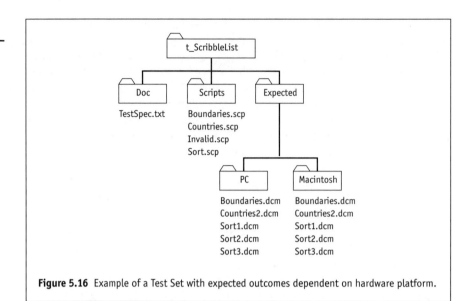

Figure 5.16 Example of a Test Set with expected outcomes dependent on hardware platform.

schemes that work well. We can use a pre-processing task for the Test Suite to identify the appropriate version and copy all of the appropriate artifacts up one directory level into the Expected directory. A post-processing task may then be used to remove this copy at the end of testing. Alternatively, all the references to artifacts that can be platform-specific can be edited by a pre-processing task.

Note that it will not be necessary to make any such distinction in the test results structure since a different instance of the test results directory hierarchy should be used for each different hardware platform or environment.

5.3.7.6 Scaling up

The physical structure we have described for Test Sets works well for relatively small numbers of test cases but the situation becomes difficult when we end up with many artifacts (say several tens) in one subdirectory within a Test Set. To overcome this we reorganize the Test Set.

Rather than considering all of the test cases in a Test Set as one group, we now divide them into separate groups within the Test Set. This need not entail segregating scripts and data files, although this is a possibility. Figure 5.17 shows a different physical structure for the Scribble breadth tests Test Set.

This structure does away with the Expected outcome subdirectory and replaces it with a subdirectory for each group of test cases. In this case we now have a group of test cases for each function in Scribble rather than a single breadth test case for each function. The same idea can be applied to the scripts and data though care must be taken to handle those scripts and data files that are shared across test cases in different groups (but not shared by test cases in other Test Sets).

In the example of Figure 5.17 we have included a set of test case definition files in the Doc subdirectory. The purpose of these is to draw together

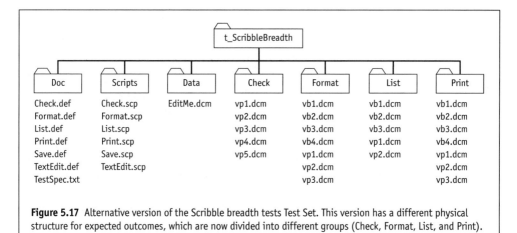

Figure 5.17 Alternative version of the Scribble breadth tests Test Set. This version has a different physical structure for expected outcomes, which are now divided into different groups (Check, Format, List, and Print).

in one place all the relevant information on the test cases in the Test Set. This becomes more important the more test cases there are but is something we would recommend in any case. These are discussed further in the next subsection.

5.3.7.7 Defining test cases and traceability

As we have seen, the physical implementation of a test case often comprises many different types of testware artifact but is not guaranteed to contain any particular one. For example, keyword-driven test cases do not have scripts uniquely associated with them. Test cases implemented by linear scripts need not have test data files associated with them and, similarly, if the expected outcome is held in the script, there need not be any separate expected outcome files.

Given this rather flexible situation how is it that we can identify what test cases there are in a Test Set? If the implementation of the test cases is understood it may not be difficult. For example, if we know that a data-driven approach is being used, we may find a separate data file for each group of test cases. If we do not know the approach taken then it will not be so easy.

This is an important consideration. Remember the experience report at the start of this chapter: 'We do not know how to develop new tests or maintain the existing ones.' This situation may have arisen because it is not understood what needs to be found (script, data file, something else?), never mind where to find it. Even if our testware architecture is well structured and consistent, it could prove to be flawed if the test cases themselves cannot be identified in a straightforward and consistent manner. As will be explained in Chapter 6, there is a big difference between automated tests and automated testing. The latter requires many more tasks to be automated (such as set-up and clear-up). In order to do this we are likely to require some utilities that are capable of finding test cases and identifying all the relevant testware associated with each one.

We recommend defining test cases specifically in a text file. This will enable us to bring together into one place all relevant information on the test cases in a Test Set.

Figure 5.18 shows an example of a **test case definition file** for the group of breadth test cases dealing with the check functionality of Scribble. The layout of the file is such that a utility could perform a text search on the file to identify things such as what test cases exist and what testware they use.

The 'TEST MATERIALS' section lists all the files that make up test materials for the test case. Similarly, the 'TEST RESULTS' section lists all the test result files that should exist at the end of the test. The keywords at the start of each of these records ('SCRIPT', 'DATA,' and 'SCRIB_DOC') indicate the type of file. In this example the data file resides outside of the Test Set. It is possible to identify exactly where within the Test Suite the shared data file will be (since it remains in its own Data Set) but we cannot predict where the Test Suite itself will be located. Thus we have used the keyword '@TESTSUITE,' where the '@' tells us that this will need

```
;                        Test Case Definition File
;                        -------------------------
; FILENAME: Check.txt
; AUTHOR:   A. Tester
; DATE:     January 1999
;
; TEST SET:   t_ScribbleBreadth
; TEST GROUP: Check
;
; TEST OBJECTIVE: Breadth tests for check functions
;                 of Scribble
;
;-------------------------------------------------------------
; AMENDMENTS:
; <id> <name> <date> <what & why>
;-------------------------------------------------------------
; TESTNAME: vp1
; PURPOSE:  Exercise valid equivalence partitions
;
; TEST MATERIALS:
SCRIPT Check.scp
DATA   @TESTSUITE\d_ScribbleTypical\Data\Countries.dcm
;
; TEST RESULTS:
SCRIB_DOC  vp1.dcm
;
;-------------------------------------------------------------
; TESTNAME: vp2
; PURPOSE:  Exercise valid equivalence partitions
;
; TEST MATERIALS:
SCRIPT Check.scp
DATA   @TESTSUITE\d_ScribbleTypical\Data\Countries.dcm
;
; TEST RESULTS:
SCRIB_DOC  vp2.dcm
```

Figure 5.18 Example test case definition file. This defines test cases that exercise the check functions of Scribble (only the first two test cases are shown).

substituting for a real pathname. This can be done whenever required by the utilities that need to know it since if they are already looking at this file they must know where the Test Suite is.

A different layout could be used to reduce the overlap between different test cases. For example, if the same data file is used for all test cases in the group, rather than defining it specifically for each test case, this could be put into a special section that defines test materials that are common to all of the test cases in the group.

There are many more ideas that can be applied to test case definition files to make them more succinct and to support further automation of testing activities (such as pre- and post-processing activities). However, many of these may be implementation- and environment-specific so we will not cover them in this book. Besides, there are a lot of ideas that we do not know about ourselves!

5.3.8 Interface with test tools

Having a Test Suite containing all the test cases we wish to run is all well and good, but we have to make the test tool understand what test cases exist, where they are, and how to run them. The way in which this is achieved will vary greatly depending on the test tool to be used. For example, some tools require all the scripts (or rather, the compiled versions of the scripts) to be in a single directory or to be inserted into a special type of indexed file. Other tools can work with scripts distributed across different directories.

Another key interface issue is the actual definition of a test case. Some tools identify test cases by direct correlation with scripts while others require you to specify test cases independently of the scripts. In either case we have found it useful to hold some information on each test case in a text file, as discussed in the previous section. This may only be the test name (or number), its purpose, and a list of scripts and data files that implement it. This provides a single point from which any information about a test case can be found. It also provides the information that some test tools require. In our view, this information is best kept in a text file in a tool-independent form within the testware architecture (i.e. in the Test Sets) and, therefore, under configuration management.

The question then is how to copy this information into the test tool. This may be a simple case of presenting the tool with the text file in a particular format, or it may involve automating the process of data entry using the tool itself. Whatever approach you need to take, you must automate it.

All of the tasks associated with the interface between the Test Suite and the test tool (such as copying scripts and loading test definitions into the test tool) can be undertaken as Test Suite or Test Set pre-processing tasks (see Chapter 6).

5.4 Might this be overkill?

The testware architecture that we have described in this chapter may at first seem like taking a sledgehammer to crack a nut. In fairness, if you do not have many test files, this approach will take more effort than the time it will save you. However, if your test automation efforts are successful they will grow, and the number of files you need to control will also grow very quickly. The examples we have shown are of necessity small scale. In practice we would expect to see tens of test cases (even a few hundred) in most Test Sets. We would also expect to see many more test cases for each feature of the Scribble application.

The benefits of being able to easily isolate a subset of testware, whether for copying test cases from one environment to another or for working on updates, should not be underestimated. Flexibility in the ways testware can be handled is a key to long-term success in test automation.

If you do not put a suitable architecture into place at the start of the test automation initiative, it will take much more effort to undo any initial organization, particularly if it has already become unwieldy. If you start with this architecture and make it part of your test automation standards from the beginning, it will be accepted as 'the way to do automation.'

Summary

Testware architecture is the arrangement of the artifacts required for testing and test automation.

The implementation of your own testware architecture will depend on the ultimate scale of your automation. It will affect how you reuse testware such as scripts and data, how you keep track of multiple versions, and how you test on different platforms and environments. One consistent approach means greater reuse and more flexibility, and should be evolved from the start, rather than letting numerous different and incompatible schemes emerge.

Our scheme groups test cases into structures that we call Test Sets. These contain all the artifacts (such as data, scripts, and expected outcome) required to run the test cases. A Test Suite is then a collection of Test Sets containing all the test cases required to meet some objective, such as bug fix testing or regression testing. Any test data or scripts that are shared between test cases that are grouped into different Test Sets are stored in separate structures that we call Data Sets and Script Sets, respectively. Similarly, any shared utilities (such as drivers, stubs, and special comparators) are held in Utility Sets. Master versions of all these different types of set (collectively known as Testware Sets) are held in a Testware Library.

The Testware Library must be under configuration management to insure that the testware artifacts can be easily accessed and all changes are controlled.

Test Results are organized in a separate structure that is parallel to the structure of the Test Suite. Test Results are generated each time a test is run. The product of the execution is the actual outcome; the by-products of the execution include test logs, difference reports, test status reports, etc.

We implement the testware architecture in a directory structure. Each Testware Set has its own directory (folder) and this contains a subdirectory for each type of testware artifact that exists in the Testware Set. A Test Suite Directory reflects the purpose of the Test Suite, and contains as subdirectories all of the relevant Testware Sets. Test Results are held in parallel directories. A sensible naming convention is important.

To aid traceability of tests to their physical implementations, we recommend that the details of test cases are described in text files, so that these can be searched by utilities. Ultimately, the test cases need to be run by the test execution tool; any restructuring of testware (such as copying scripts into the tool's own script library) should also be automated.

The approach described in this chapter has worked well in many organizations that have extensive test automation. Although it may appear to be 'overkill' now, you will have serious problems later if you do not address these issues at the start.

CHAPTER SIX

Automating pre- and post-processing

6.1 What are pre- and post-processing?

6.1.1 Pre-processing

For most test cases there are prerequisites that must be in place before execution can begin. These should be defined as part of each test case and implemented for each test case before it is performed. For example, the tests may need a database that contains some specific customer records or a particular directory must contain certain files with specific information in them.

For some test cases the prerequisites need be set up only once, as they are not changed by the actions of the test case. Others, though, do need restoring each time the test case is executed as the prerequisites are changed during the test case's execution.

Any tasks associated with setting up and restoring these test prerequisites are what we refer to as **pre-processing,** since it is processing that must be done before test execution can start.

6.1.2 Post-processing

Immediately after a test case has been executed the test result artifacts, comprising the products (actual outcome) and by-products (e.g. tool log file) of test execution, may be scattered far and wide. We will have to do something with these artifacts either to assess the success or otherwise of the test case, or by way of a housekeeping chore.

Some of these test result artifacts we can simply delete (such as a difference report that says no differences were found) while others we may need to keep (such as an output file that is found to be different from the expected output). The artifacts to be kept may have to be moved to a common location for ease of analysis or simply to prevent them from being altered or destroyed by subsequent tests.

These are some examples of what we refer to as **post-processing**, since they are tasks performed after an automated test has been executed.

6.1.3 Why use these terms?

The terms pre- and post-processing are a convenient way of describing a big chunk of testing work that crops up time and again. Although the tasks that make up this work are often seen as disparate and independent there is plenty of commonality to warrant them being considered together. Consider the following characteristics of pre- and post-processing tasks:

1. There are lots of them. Potentially there are a lot of pre- and post-processing tasks to perform and some of them (those associated with test cases) have to be performed every time a test case is run. This usually amounts to a significant amount of work.

2. They come in packs. Often there are several pre- and post-processing tasks to be performed at any one time. For example, it may be necessary to copy not just one file but several files, or compile many scripts.

3. Many of them are the same. There may be only a few different types of pre- and post-processing activities since many tests on a particular system will require a similar physical set-up. Much of the variation in preconditions between test cases comes in the data values being used. For example, most test cases for a system that relies on information in a database will require the database to be there and loaded with data but each test case may require different data.

4. They can be automated easily. These tasks can be achieved with a simple instruction or command since they are usually simple functions (such as 'copy a file'). More complex functions can be reduced to a simple command by implementing them in a command file.

The first of these characteristics implies that there is much to be gained by automating pre- and post-processing tasks and the second characteristic means that they can be automated as groups of tasks rather than having to be automated individually. The third characteristic implies that once one task has been automated then so have many others, and, finally, the fourth characteristic suggests that it is possible to use a single mechanism to automate all pre- and post-processing tasks. That is, once the means of automating pre- and post-processing is in place, new test cases have only to describe the pre- and processing tasks, not prescribe the details of implementation.

6.1.4 Why automate pre- and post-processing?

Pre- and post-processing tasks cry out to be automated. Performing these chores manually is both error prone and time consuming.

If we want to have automated testing, as opposed to merely having some automated tests, then the pre- and post-processing tasks that surround test execution must also be automated. We do not have automated testing if a tester has to be involved at regular intervals during a series of tests simply to restore data, etc. We cannot have unattended overnight or weekend testing if manual intervention is necessary.

Figure 6.1 shows the series of tasks necessary to perform a number of test cases and how having automated tests is different to having automated testing. A key difference is in the automation of the pre- and post-processing tasks.

There is a difference in the sequence of the tasks shown in Figure 6.1. If tests are run manually, the analysis of results is usually done immediately after the comparison of actual outcome to expected outcome. The tester will spend time analyzing why there are differences, and whether it is the software that is wrong or the test itself. With automated testing, all analysis of differences is postponed until after the tests have run. If the test suite ran overnight, for example, the tester will spend time in the morning looking at the failed test results and analyzing whether the software or the test is wrong, or whether some other factor disturbed the automated test, causing it to fail. This can take a significant amount of time, and it is important that this effort is planned for.

In the rest of this chapter, we will look in more detail at the pre- and post-processing tasks, and how to automate them.

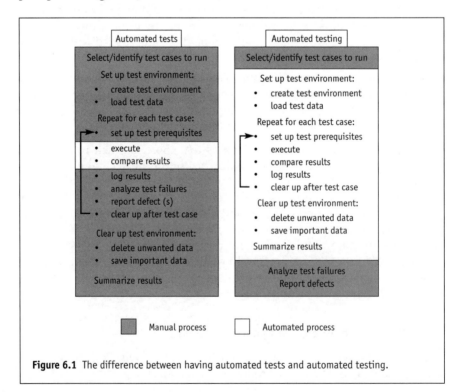

Figure 6.1 The difference between having automated tests and automated testing.

On occasions we have seen test specifications that require the manual tester to prepare the test data as part of the test case. This usually involves entering data into the system or changing some existing data using the system much as an end user would do. This may be acceptable if it is only a few test cases that are designed this way but it becomes rather inefficient when applied to lots of test cases.

The rationale for this approach to test case design is either that it exercises the other parts of the system (those parts used to enter or change the data) or it is the only way to achieve the required data state. The former rationale is seriously flawed. If the other parts of the system need exercising then specific test cases should be designed to do just that. Relying on an arbitrary collection of test cases to do so when they have quite different objectives is not good practice. The second rationale is merely flawed. Ninety-nine times out of a hundred it is possible to save the required data state and restore it whenever the test case is to be executed. Even if this requires a purpose-built utility the savings that can be made in time and effort far outweigh the cost of the utility.

In general, we recommend that test cases not be designed such that they require long or complex interactive set-up sequences. This is because the required data state can be saved after it is created the first time and then restored each time the test case is run. The tasks of saving and restoring data are straightforward pre- and post-processing tasks that can be automated far more easily (and maintained with much less effort) than interactive sequences.

A disadvantage of this approach is that it is likely to require larger amounts of test data. However, it will not always be necessary, or indeed sensible, to save the data required for every single test case. Often, a set of test cases will share the same basic data but require only a small change for each one. In such situations common sense must prevail.

6.2 Pre- and post-processing

6.2.1 Pre-processing tasks

There are a variety of tasks that can be described as pre-processing. We have found it helpful to consider the four basic types that are described below. Which category a particular task falls into is not important (indeed some tasks fit comfortably in more than one): they are used here merely to help explain the variety of tasks that can be thought of as pre-processing tasks.

1. Create. Tasks aimed at constructing the correct preconditions for the tests such as building a database and populating it with the data required by the tests. While some preconditions require certain data to exist, others may require certain data not to exist. In this latter situation pre-processing tasks may involve removing unwanted records from a database or removing files from a directory.

2. Check. It may not be possible to automate all of the set-up tasks (for example, freeing up sufficient disk space) but it still may be possible to check that specific preconditions are met; for example, checking that files that must exist do, and that files that must not exist do not. Other examples include environment checks such as the operating system version, checking that the local area network is operational, and checking that there is a write enabled disk in the floppy drive.

3. Reorganize. This is similar to some of the 'Create' tasks described above but specifically concerns copying or moving files from one place to another. For example, when a test involves changing a data file we may need to copy that data file from where it is held into our working area (or from the Test Suite to the Test Results hierarchy, structures that are explained in Chapter 5). This will insure that the master copy of the data file is not destroyed by the test.

4. Convert. It is not always convenient or desirable to hold test data in the format in which it will be required by the tests. For example, large files are better stored in a compressed format, and for maintenance purposes non-text formats (such as databases and spreadsheet documents) may be better held in a text format where one exists. (One rationale for this is to make the test data platform independent. Other rationales are explained in Chapter 7). The conversion into the required format is a pre-processing task.

If any of these pre-processing tasks fail, the test case should be aborted immediately, rather than waste time running a test case that is destined to fail for reasons that are already known.

6.2.2 Post-processing tasks

As with pre-processing, there are a variety of tasks that can be described as post-processing. Again, we have found it helpful to consider the four basic types that are described below, although category assignment is not important. The categories are used to help explain the variety of tasks that can be thought of as post-processing tasks.

1. Delete. Tasks aimed at clearing up after a test has executed, for example deleting files and database records, are typical post-processing tasks. Some test cases generate a lot of output even though only a little of it is used for comparison purposes. For example, a test case may capture a lot of screen images as a detailed record of what went on during execution. If the test case fails they can be used to help determine the cause of failure without having to re-run the test case. If the test case passes then they can be safely deleted.

2. Check. Part of the expected outcome of a test case may be that a particular file does not exist (either because it has been deleted by the test case or because it is not supposed to be created). Similarly, a postcondition of a test case may be that certain files do exist. These checks can be automated and come under our banner of post-processing.

3. Reorganize. Although similar to the 'Delete' tasks described above, this specifically concerns copying or moving files. It is not always possible to have all of the test results created in one specific place and yet it is desirable since doing so makes test failure analysis much easier. This is a simple matter of copying or moving each of the artifacts to this one place.

4. Convert. Sometimes the formats of the outcomes that we wish to compare or otherwise analyze are not suited to the task. For example, it is easier to analyze database data if it is copied into a formatted report file. Not only can we concentrate on the relevant subset of data but also we can usually choose the format in which it is presented. Another example where this type of post-processing is useful is in converting data from a platform-dependent format into a platform-independent format or at least into the format in which the expected outcome is held.

We have specifically not counted comparison among the post-processing tasks. This is because it is usually a fairly major activity in its own right. However, it may be convenient to think of it as a post-processing task simply because it is possible to implement it in that way.

If any post-processing task fails it should cause the test case itself to fail regardless of its outcome. This is a fail-safe policy. A post-processing task could fail because a file that it was meant to move or delete had not been created (so the test case outcome is not as expected). In this case the post-processing task has failed because the test case itself failed to produce the expected outcome.

However, a post-processing task could fail because the disk to which it was meant to move a result file did not have sufficient free space. This may occur quite independently from the test case, which could have been successful in all other respects. If the file that could not be moved was to be compared after the move then the comparison cannot be performed so this too should cause the test case to fail. If the move operation was part of a final clear-up operation then it may seem unfair to fail the test case but we prefer to do so. We will then be sure that if a test case passes, it really has passed within the limitations of its design and implementation.

It would be sensible to report the cause of the test case failure in the log file (or wherever else is appropriate). Post-processing tasks are specific so it will not be difficult to come up with a meaningful message (such as 'Post-processing task failed to move file *filename* because of insufficient disk space on drive *drive name*').

6.2.3 Pre- and post-processing at different stages

Pre- and post-processing tasks are most likely to occur immediately before and after each test case is executed, every time it is executed. There are, however, other times when tasks are performed that can be conveniently considered as pre- and post-processing tasks for more than a single test case. In our test automation regime we consider two other stages when pre- and post-processing tasks are useful. These are associated with the Test

Suite and the Testware Sets. Pre- and post-processing for a Test Suite would typically be performed when the Test Suite is first created and at the end of testing, and other pre- and post-processing may need to be done for Testware Sets.

An example where we have pre- and post-processing at Test Suite and test case level is when a database is used in a series of tests (Figure 6.2). We may need to create the database to hold customer records to be used by all the test cases in a Test Suite. The database then needs to be populated with customer records before any of the test cases can be run. If the test cases alter these records, it may be necessary to restore the original records at the start of each test case. Thus, we can say that in this situation we need to restore the database every time a test case is run, but we need only create the database once. Creating the database is a pre-processing task associated with the Test Suite since it is done just once when the Test Suite is created. Restoring the database is a pre-processing task associated with each test case and is repeated each time that a test case is run.

Similarly, after each test case has been run we may need to perform some post-processing tasks like running a report generator to extract data from the database. These post-processing tasks are associated with the test cases. After the whole series of test cases has been run successfully we may need to clear up by deleting the database, which is a post-processing task associated with the Test Suite.

The pre- and post-processing tasks associated with each test case may well be different. That is, the pre- and post-processing done for one test case may well be unique to that test case. Similarly, other test cases may have their own pre- and post-processing tasks. The same situation applies to the other levels; the details of the pre- and post-processing tasks are likely to vary from one Testware Set to another and from one Test Suite to another.

Having said that, there may also be many pre- and post-processing tasks that are common to all test cases in a Test Set. In this situation it usually will be possible to share the same utilities to perform the tasks. It will

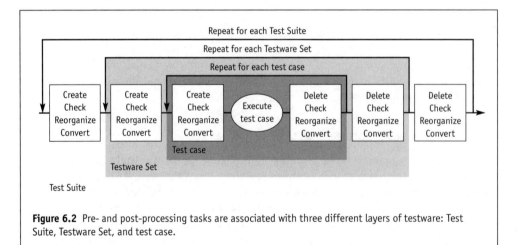

Figure 6.2 Pre- and post-processing tasks are associated with three different layers of testware: Test Suite, Testware Set, and test case.

not be possible to share the same processes (i.e. perform the pre-processing task once for all test cases) since it is a necessary part of each test case.

Other example Test Suite and Testware Set pre- and post-processing tasks include compiling scripts and copying the compiled versions to a common place where the test execution tool can access them, performing static analysis (see Chapter 3 for a discussion about static analysis on scripts), compiling the source code of utilities to create the executable images, and generating a summary report of the status of all test cases.

Whenever any updates are made to an existing Test Suite it may be necessary to repeat some or all of the pre-processing tasks associated with the Test Suite and the Testware Sets affected by the updates.

6.3 What should happen after test case execution?

6.3.1 After normal completion

After normal completion of a test case, i.e. when all the actual outcomes match the expected outcomes, all of the actual outcome files can be deleted. There is little point in keeping them if they are known to be the same as the expected results. This seems at first a strange thing to do: we have gone to all the trouble of assembling and executing our automated tests, and now we immediately throw away the very outputs that we took so much trouble to generate! However, we need not delete any of the status information from the test – this will be kept as a record of the test having been done. So the test status and test log would be filed away in a safe place. Alternatively, once a summary report is generated detailing the status of every test case, then all the by-products of test execution (the log file, etc.) can also be deleted.

What we can delete straight away is the actual outcomes, which we have just determined to be the same as the expected outcomes. So we now have two similar, if not identical, copies. This takes twice as much storage space as one copy would take, so it is wasteful to keep both. We certainly don't want to throw away our expected outcomes, so it is the actual outcomes that we can now safely delete.

The exception to this is where a Quality Management System (QMS) or industry regulations require that all test results be kept. Sometimes only the results of the final run of all tests need be kept, rather than the results of all the runs of every test. Also, it may be appropriate to change the QMS as test automation offers a better way of recording the testing that has been undertaken and the results achieved.

6.3.2 After abnormal termination

After abnormal termination of a test case, i.e. where any part of a test case fails, or where a test case does not run to completion, we want to keep everything. In this case, the more information that is available to help with analysis the better. When you are trying to find out why a test did not pass, often the first thing that the developer who is fixing the problem wants to do is to re-run the test. The reason for this is that there may not be enough information to actually find out in detail what went wrong. Hence the more information we can supply with a failed test case, the more efficient the debugging process can be.

We can even take this a step further, and design our tests so that they create more output than is actually used in the comparison of the test, just in case the test case fails. This additional output may then be deleted as part of the test case post-processing if the test case passes. If the test case fails, then this additional data serves to help the failure analysis and possibly the debugging effort.

You don't need to analyze the failure data immediately. For example, you could capture the state of a database after an abnormal termination (for later analysis) and return the database to a known sane state to allow subsequent test cases to run. The known sane state may be the expected result of the failed test case. If a subsequent test case then destroys the data, this is not a problem if the right data and the right amount of data have been captured at this point.

6.4 Implementation issues

6.4.1 Example test case

To illustrate alternative approaches to implementing pre- and post-processing we will use an example test case. The one we have chosen to use is an enhanced version of a test case used to exercise the *Save* function of Scribble and belongs to the Test Set t_ScribbleBreadth. This was first shown in the examples given in Chapter 5. This test case has a number of preconditions that can be put into place by pre-processing tasks and a couple of postconditions that can similarly be dealt with by post-processing tasks.

The preconditions are that some specific files should exist in the working directory (i.e. default directory or folder) and a particular version of a configuration setting file (Scribble.ini) for the Scribble application must reside in the same place as the Scribble application itself. The pre-processing tasks required to achieve these preconditions are shown in Figure 6.3.

The pre-processing tasks are as follows:

- copy data files EditMe.dcm, NoRead.dcm, and NoWrite.dcm from the Test Set (Data subdirectory) to the results directory;

- set 'no read access' permission on file NoRead.dcm and 'no write access' permission on file NoWrite.dcm;

- copy the shared data file countries.dcm from its Data Set to the results directory;

- rename the current configuration settings file Scribble.ini for the Scribble application to Saved.ini;

- copy the file Test1.ini from the Test Set to the Scribble directory (where the application is held), and rename it to Scribble.ini so it becomes the new configuration settings file.

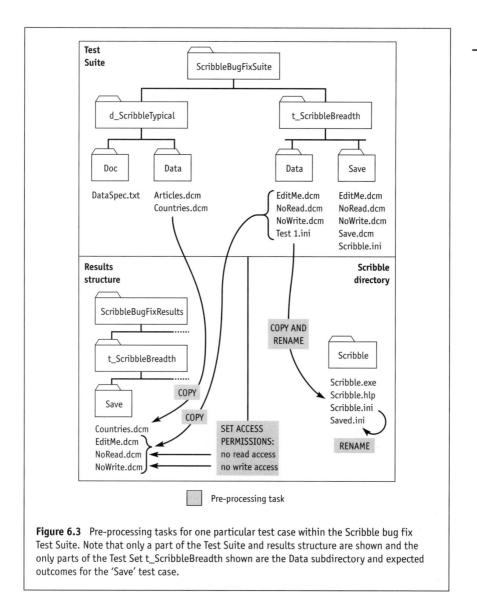

Figure 6.3 Pre-processing tasks for one particular test case within the Scribble bug fix Test Suite. Note that only a part of the Test Suite and results structure are shown and the only parts of the Test Set t_ScribbleBreadth shown are the Data subdirectory and expected outcomes for the 'Save' test case.

Note that the Test Suite and Test Set shown in Figure 6.3 are not complete; we have shown only the details that are relevant to the example test case.

Once the test case has been executed, there are a couple of post-processing tasks to perform. These are shown in Figure 6.4 and are as follows:

- delete the files NoRead.dcm and NoWrite.dcm from the results directory;
- move the configuration settings file from the Scribble directory into the results directory;
- rename the saved Scribble configuration settings file Saved.ini to Scribble.ini.

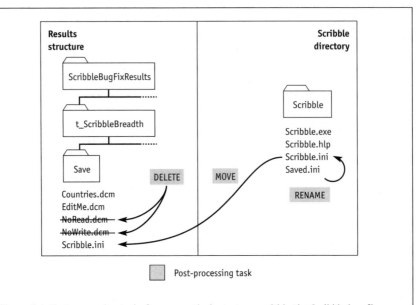

Figure 6.4 Post-processing tasks for one particular test case within the Scribble bug fix Test Suite.

6.4.2 Scripts

Pre- and post-processing tasks can be implemented in scripts so that they are performed directly by the test execution tool. Given that many of the tasks are similar, this can be done most efficiently using shared scripts. For example, one shared script may provide a standard file copy function. The test script would pass to the shared script the name of the file to be copied and the shared script would then be able to determine the full pathnames of the source and destination file (since it can have built into it a knowledge of the testware architecture).

This approach is clearly suitable when there is a script for each test case. Figure 6.5 shows two scripts, one of these (SaveTest1.scp) implements the 'Save' test case itself and the other performs the pre-processing before calling the other script to run the test case, and then performs the post-processing.

The pre- and post-processing is implemented by separate shared scripts that each perform a common processing task. The CopyFile script has built into it knowledge of the testware architecture. When it is passed a simple filename it knows to find this file in the Data subdirectory of the Test Set to which the test case belongs. If it is passed a pathname (i.e. filename with directory names such as is given for countries.dcm in the example script of Figure 6.5) then it will use it directly. Where a pathname contains a variable name (such as @TESTSUITE and @SCRIBBLE in the example) it will replace it with the appropriate pathname. The CopyFile script also knows

Save1.scp

```
; Pre-processing

Call CopyFile ("EditMe.dcm")
Call CopyFile ("NoRead.dcm")
Call CopyFile ("NoWrite.dcm")
Call CopyFile ("@TESTSUITE\d_ScribbleTypical\Data\Countries.dcm")

Call SetAccess(NOREAD, "NoRead.dcm")
Call SetAccess(NOWRITE, "NoWrite.dcm")

Call Rename("@SCRIBBLE\Scribble.ini""@SCRIBBLE\Saved.ini")
Call CopyTo("Test1.ini","@SCRIBBLE\Scribble.ini")

; Execute test case.
Call SaveTest1()

; Post-processing.

Call MoveFile("@SCRIBBLE\Scribble.ini")
Call RenameFile("@SCRIBBLE\Saved.ini""@SCRIBBLE\Scribble.ini")

Call DeleteFile("NoRead.dcm")
Call DeleteFile("NoWrite.dcm")
```

Figure 6.5 Example control script implementing pre- and post-processing with the aid of shared scripts to perform individual tasks. The test case itself is implemented by the SaveTest1 script that is called by this script.

that the destination for any file it is given to copy is the results directory of the current test case. Thus, we are able to use a very simple interface to achieve a common pre-processing task.

The CopyTo script differs in functionality from the CopyFile script in that it has to be given a destination pathname. This is used to copy files to destinations other than the results directory. The MoveFile script always moves files to the results directory, and the SetAccess and DeleteFile scripts assume the pathname is that of the results directory when given only a filename.

The reason for these simple interfaces is that it makes it easier to specify pre- and post-processing tasks, thereby reducing the chances for error. Furthermore, these shared scripts can have built into them additional checking to insure that specific errors are not made. For example, we would not want a pre-processing task moving a file out of the Test Suite (since it will not be there the next time the test case is executed) so the MoveFile script would not accept a pathname that matches the Test Suite pathname.

6.4.3 Use of command files

As shown above, pre- and post-processing tasks can be implemented in scripts so that they are performed directly by the test execution tool. However, we recommend that an alternative approach be considered.

Most pre- and post-processing tasks can be implemented using some form of command file (command procedure, shell script, or batch file, to give a few alternative names). There are a few compelling reasons for this:

1. Command languages are generally more suited to the pre- and post-processing tasks than the execution tool's scripting language.

2. Usually, more people are familiar with the command language, since these commands are used for basic functions such as copying and moving files (manual testers may already write their own command files to make things easier for themselves).

3. Command files can be run by anyone at any time independently of other testing tasks and without any special skills or knowledge of the test execution tool.

4. Command files can be used to automate the pre- and post-processing tasks of manual testing.

The fourth point is worth expanding. Test automation is usually taken to mean automation of test execution, but there is nothing wrong with automating testing tasks other than test execution. Pre- and post-processing tasks are ideal candidates for automation even if the execution is performed manually. This is a good way to make a positive and immediate impact on manual testing.

Some testers do this anyway but the command files do not become an official part of the tests, which is a shame. Encourage testers to use such command files and to share them. The use of command files can speed up manual testing a little and help avoid some of those annoying typing errors.

With a little ingenuity it may be possible to develop a few generic command files that are data driven, allowing testers to specify automated pre- and post-processing tasks without having to implement the automation. These may be able to perform perhaps 80% of the pre- and post-processing tasks. This will require consistency of testware architecture, as described in Chapter 5.

The command files would probably offer the same functionality as described for the shared scripts in the previous section. If this were done we would still need to invoke the command files. This can be done from the script, so rather than calling shared scripts, the test script would invoke the shared command files. Alternatively, a command file could implement each test case. This would call the shared command files to perform the pre- and post-processing and invoke the test execution tool to execute the test case itself.

6.4.4 Data-driven approach

Where a data-driven scripting approach is used the pre- and post-processing instructions may also be held as entries in a data file. Each shared script that performs a pre- or post-processing task would then read its input data from the data file.

While this may work, the keyword-driven approach seems much more suited to pre- and post-processing tasks.

Where a keyword-driven scripting approach is used the pre- and post-processing tasks can easily be implemented as keywords. The shared scripts we have already discussed in Section 6.4.2 will implement these keywords.

6.4.6 Using a test case definition file

Continuing our strategy of defining the test cases in a text file (as described in Chapter 5 and shown in Figure 5.18), we recommend including with the test case definition a description of the pre- and post-processing tasks. This will give us a complete picture of the test case and can be used to drive the automation of the tasks.

For example, the definition of our example test case in a test case definition file may look like that given in Figure 6.6.

The 'TEST MATERIALS' section contains the files required for the test to run. The 'PRE-PROCESSING' section lists all the pre-processing actions

```
;------------------------------------------------------------
;   TESTNAME: save1
;   PURPOSE:  Exercise valid equivalence partitions

;   TEST MATERIALS
SCRIPT          Save.scp
DATA            EditMe.dcm
DATA            NoRead.dcm
DATA            NoWrite.dcm
DATA            @TESTSUITE\d_ScribbleTypical\Data\Countries.dcm

;   PRE-PROCESSING
CopyFile        EditMe.dcm
CopyFile        NoRead.dcm
CopyFile        NoWrite.dcm
CopyFile        @TESTSUITE\d_ScribbleTypical\Data\Countries.dcm
SetAccess       NOREAD NoRead.dcm
SetAccess       NOWRITE NoWrite.dcm
Rename          @SCRIBBLE\Scribble.ini @SCRIBBLE\Saved.ini
CopyTo          Test1.ini @SCRIBBLE\Scribble.ini

;   POST-PROCESSING
MoveFile        @SCRIBBLE\Scribble.ini
RenameFile      @SCRIBBLE\Saved.ini @SCRIBBLE\Scribble.ini
DeleteFile      NoRead.dcm
DeleteFile      NoWrite.dcm

;   TEST RESULTS
SCRIB_DOC       Countries.dcm
SCRIB_DOC       EditMe.dcm
TEXT_FILE       Scribble.ini
```

Figure 6.6 Example section of a test case definition file. This defines one of the Save function breadth tests for Scribble. The pre-processing task copies the data file EditMe.dcm from the Test Suite to the results directory, where it will be changed by the test case.

that must be carried out before the test case can be executed. In this example we have used the same idea for a simple interface to each pre- and post-processing task, where each task is able to assume knowledge of our testware architecture. Similarly the 'POST-PROCESSING' section lists all the post-processing actions that must be carried out after the test case has been executed. The 'TEST RESULTS' section lists the files that are the actual output of the test, i.e. the names of the files that should be created, modified, or checked as part of the test.

Summary

Pre-processing is any processing that is carried out before a set of tests is executed, i.e. setting up or restoring any prerequisites that must be in place before a test can run. Post-processing is processing that is carried out after a set of tests is executed. There are often a lot of these types of tasks, and they tend to come in packs where many are the same. It is relatively straightforward to automate such tasks; indeed, if pre- and post-processing tasks are not automated, then all we will have are some automated tests (requiring manual intervention to set up and clear down) rather than automated testing.

Typical tasks performed in pre-processing include creating (files, databases, or data), checking that certain conditions are met (e.g. sufficient disk space), reorganizing files (to protect master copies), and converting data. Typical tasks performed in post-processing include deleting (files, databases, test result products, or by-products), checking (e.g. that files exist), reorganizing (e.g. moving Test Results to the results structure of the testware architecture), or converting outcomes into a form that can be more easily processed or viewed.

Pre- and post-processing tasks may be related to a single test case, to a set of tests in a Testware Set, or to all of the tests in a Test Suite.

After normal completion of a test, actual outcomes and intermediate results can be deleted, since we have a record of the test having passed. After abnormal termination all files and data should be kept as they may prove useful in analyzing the causes of defects.

An example was given showing how pre-and post-processing could be implemented using shared scripts or command files, and how the pre- and post-processing details can be documented in a test case definition file.

CHAPTER SEVEN

Building maintainable tests

This book is all about ways of increasing the maintainability of automated testware. The structure of the scripts, as described in Chapter 3, has a significant impact on maintainability, as does script annotation. The way in which the test data is organized is also a significant factor, as described in Chapter 5. However, there are a lot of other contributors to the maintenance effort which, if left unchecked, will almost certainly impair your test automation efforts, if not destroy them altogether.

This chapter covers specific maintainability issues that are not covered elsewhere in the book.

7.1 Problems in maintaining automated tests

New versions of software imply a need for new tests for the new functionality, and often changes to existing tests where existing functionality has changed. Furthermore, as the system changes some tests will become redundant, either because the functionality they test has been removed or because new tests have superseded their purpose. All of this contributes to the maintenance costs.

Software maintenance is a standard part of any software life cycle but often little thought is given to the maintenance of the tests. A Test Suite comprising test documentation, test data, and expected outcomes is a valuable resource that ought to be regarded as equally important as the software it exercises.

Maintenance costs are more significant for automated testing than for manual testing because the manual tester is able to implement changes 'on the fly.' For automated tests all the detail has to be specified in one way or another; nothing can be left for the tool to decide at runtime simply because the tool has no intelligence. For example, a software system for a commercial organization may record client names and addresses. Some tests will involve adding new clients to the database. If the system is changed to include the telephone number for each client the tests will need to be changed to either add a telephone number or skip over that new field in some way. A manual tester faced with the instruction 'Add details of a new client' will enter the details of an imaginary client; it will make no difference when the new system asks for a telephone number. In this case it is not necessary to change the test. In an automated testing environment, the testing tool will need to be told beforehand what the telephone number is to be or how to skip over the field. Otherwise when the test is executed, the test will become out of step with the software and will therefore fail.

7.2 Attributes of test maintenance

Some attributes that affect test maintenance are presented below. Each of these is explained from two points of view. The first point of view is what appears to be a 'good idea' on the surface but does not take into account any effect on maintenance costs. This shallow view is encouraged by initial enthusiasm for test automation and a desire to push on with it. The second point of view looks at the potential problems caused by the attribute. A third section under each attribute looks at possible solutions to reduce the maintenance problems. The solutions offered are not necessarily the best in every situation and are certainly not the only solutions. They are offered as something to start with and a source of ideas.

7.2.1 Number of test cases

Good idea? With each testing effort we add more and more tests to the Test Suite. New tests will be required for the new functionality and to check bug fixes. Additional tests can be added to increase test coverage in specific areas. There will also be a host of other tests that various people will deem a 'good thing' to put into the Test Suite. After all, it doesn't take so long to add these test cases to the Test Suite and it costs nothing to run them.

Problem The more tests there are in the Test Suite the more tests there will be to maintain. The more tests there are to maintain the more time and effort will be spent on maintenance. The effort involved in maintenance should not be overlooked, although it often is. Maintenance tasks include updating test scripts to reflect changes in the interface of the application they test, updating test data to conform to new formats and layouts, updating the expected outcomes or comparison instructions or both, and analyzing and correcting the cause of test failures that occur because the test is out of date with the software.

Each new test case that is added to an automated Test Suite does not in itself add much to the overall maintenance cost, typically only a few minutes at most. However, if the total number of test cases in the Test Suite grows by tens, hundreds, or even thousands, then the cumulative increase in maintenance effort will be significant if not severe. Also, the likelihood of redundancy and test duplication will increase. As testers come and go from the test team the automated Test Suite will continue to grow. It will soon reach the point where nobody can know all of the automated test cases so many will be maintained and executed just because they are there, regardless of whether or not they still contribute anything.

Solution Clearly one solution is not to let the Test Suite become too big, but what is *too* big? There is a balance to be made between the benefit of adding another test and the cost of maintaining it in the long term. Unfortunately this is not something that we can easily measure. It would not make much sense to put an arbitrary limit on the number of automated tests although this would avoid an ever-increasing maintenance cost. Such a solution may encourage a qualitative comparison between existing automated tests and (potential) new ones, leading to an improved quality Test Suite. However, it is more likely to have the opposite effect. Once the limit on the number of tests has been reached, many opportunities to add 'good' tests will be lost because of the effort required to prove them better than existing ones.

A compromise has to be reached. On the one hand it is not desirable to let the number of tests increase unchecked and on the other it is not desirable to limit the maximum Test Suite size. Before adding any test someone must ask what it will contribute to the Test Suite as a whole, both in its defect finding capability and its likely maintenance cost. Asking this question will achieve two things. First, it will help insure that tests are not added for the sake of adding them regardless of any other issues, and second, it will insure that the cost of maintaining the test is at least considered.

Another solution is to undertake periodic weeding. Before every major release or every two to three months (whatever makes sense in your environment) have someone (or a small team) go through the automated Test Suite specifically looking for 'deadwood.' In other words, check for test cases that have been duplicated or superseded, test cases that are no longer relevant for one reason or another, and any test case that costs more to maintain than the value it provides.

7.2.2 Quantity of test data

Good idea? Use lots of data in the tests to help insure thorough testing. With automation the number of data files and the size of the data files can be increased dramatically to provide a much wider range of input combinations, giving more thorough testing.

Problem The more test data there is the more maintenance effort is needed – not only updating test data to reflect new structures, formats, and layouts, but also the task of managing the data takes more effort. Tasks such as backup and transferring data from machine to machine or network to network take longer the more data there is. If test data has to be transferred between isolated machines or networks (it is common for testing groups to be isolated) it will be necessary to copy it twice.

Large amounts of test data also have an adverse impact on test failure analysis and debugging effort. The more data there is to go through, the longer it will take to locate and fix a defect.

Solution It may be possible to limit the total amount of disk space used by individual test cases or, more likely, for logical subsets of test cases. Test cases will then have to be designed specifically to keep within a specified amount of disk space. However, there is a balance to be made between the effort involved in optimizing the amount of data used and the final maintenance costs of large amounts of data. (We have heard it said that Pascal wrote a very long letter to a friend and at the end of it wrote, 'Sorry this is such a long letter but I did not have time to write a shorter one.' So it is with our test data – if only we could spend a little more time planning it we could achieve the same tests with less data.)

Experience has shown us that installing some means of ensuring that test designers and test builders make an attempt to reduce disk space use works well. For example, make submission of test cases into some form of configuration management system a formal completion criterion. The management system can automatically check the amount of disk space used and reject any that exceed the limit. This approach can eliminate much of the wasted space and will help to generate a culture that does not naturally assume vast amounts of test data will be acceptable or a 'good thing.'

7.2.3 Format of test data

Good idea? Use any format of data applicable to the system under test as test input and test output. This includes databases and file formats known only to the system under test. Using the data formats read and written by the software under test saves time converting before and after each test case and keeps it simple.

Problem The more specialized the format of data used, the more likely it is that specialized tool support will be needed to update the tests. Where changes occur to the structure and format of input and output data, the test data have to be updated. If tools exist to 'edit' special formats then this work is at least possible if not automatable. However, if the tools do not exist the test data has to be regenerated, and in some cases (such as copies of 'real' data) this may not be possible.

Solution Text format data is often the most flexible and easily manipulated. It is also portable across different hardware platforms and system configurations. Where it is possible to store test data and results in a text format (such as ASCII) this should be done. The time taken to convert data and the extra 'complexity' of tests is often much more acceptable than the cost of maintaining specialized formats. Test data in this form can easily be converted, either by editing the text data or by creating a special conversion process. The beauty of the latter method is that all the data can be updated automatically once the conversion process has been developed.

For example, word processors often store the documents they generate in a binary format. A suite of automated tests for such a word processor may well contain a large number of documents as starting points for various test cases. For the purposes of the test cases the documents must be of the format understood by the current version of the word processor. Thus, whenever a new version of the word processor involving document format changes has to be tested, all of the test documents have to be updated. While this may be easy to do, it nevertheless has to be done – it is a maintenance cost. This could be avoided if the test documents were held in some neutral format. The job of converting the documents into the latest document format can be implemented as part of the test set-up (or better still, Test Suite set-up). Now, whenever the document format changes only the document converting program has to be updated and all the existing test cases will remain unaffected by the change in document format.

7.2.4 Time to run test cases

Good idea? Test cases can be as long as you want since they are executed by computers that will not become bored or be distracted. Running long test cases in which the initial set-up and clear-up functions are performed only once is much more efficient than running many more shorter tests since the set-up and clear-up functions have to be repeated many more times.

Problem Often a test case which takes a long time to execute performs many varied and different things. In essence, it is a lot of tests all rolled into one. The intuitive savings gained by avoiding multiple set-up and clear-up actions are vastly outweighed by the inherent inefficiency of a long test case. When something goes wrong the test case has to be repeated at least up to the point of failure, usually a good number of times, to analyze the cause of the failure, debug it, and verify the fix. Failures that occur early on in a long test case may well hide others. These later failures cannot be found until the first one has been fixed. Thus the test case has to undergo further rounds of analysis and debugging.

Solution The aim must be to keep functional test cases as short and as focused as possible (within reason).

As an example, consider a test case that takes 30 minutes to run to completion. Say it fails after 5 minutes the first time it is executed, the defect is found and fixed, and the test case re-run. This time it fails after 10 minutes and again the defect is found and fixed, and the test case re-run. The third time it fails after 15 minutes. So far the test case has been running for a total of 30 minutes ($5 + 10 + 15 = 30$) and has given three pieces of information (namely the three failures) and yet has still only run halfway through. This is the 'nested defect' syndrome, in which defects are effectively stacked up and each can only be seen when the one above it has been removed.

Now if this same test case were split into ten 3-minute test cases, in 30 minutes the whole lot could be run and there would be ten pieces of information; some test cases may have passed, some would have failed. The chances are that the three defects found before would have been found this time along with a few others. Furthermore, any failure can be investigated quickly since it will take no more than 3 minutes to re-run the test case to the point of failure.

7.2.5 Debug-ability of test cases

Good idea? The only information required from an automated test run is a list of the test cases that have passed or failed. The job of the testing tool is to run the tests, verify the results, and report each test case as either 'passed' or 'failed.'

Problem When a test fails, how will I know what went wrong? If the only information provided by the automated test is that 'it failed,' someone has to investigate the cause of the failure. Failure analysis and debugging can be considerably more difficult for an automated test case than they usually are for one run manually. This is because the manual testers may have a good idea as to what caused a failure since they undertook the actions that led up to it. Furthermore, they are in an ideal situation in which they can experiment to try to pinpoint the problem a little more precisely. This then helps the developer tasked with fixing the defect.

Automated test cases, on the other hand, can only tell what they have been 'programmed' to tell at the time they were designed and built (which is typically 'passed' or 'failed,' or maybe a simple statement indicating that an actual outcome does not match the expected outcome). Thus it takes more effort to analyze failures of automated test cases than it does manual ones. The person doing the debugging may be tasked to 'fix the defect that causes test case number 37 to fail.' In a manual testing environment the same person may well be given a meaningful description of the defect along with some insights as to its cause.

Solution Test cases must be designed with debugging in mind by asking 'What would I like to know when this test fails?' The answer to this question will be system specific, and best answered by experienced defect fixers. Much will depend on the 'test-ability' of the software under test in that the information someone might 'like to know' may not be available from the system while a test case is running. Tools can also help, by making it easy to re-run test cases in a different context, such as under the control of a debugger.

7.2.6 Interdependencies between tests

Good idea? String together a lot of tests such that the outcome from one test case becomes the input to the next. This enables a lot of comprehensive testing to be undertaken by a series of short test cases.

Problem Clearly if one test case fails to produce correct output, all of the test cases following it will not even start correctly (sometimes referred to as the 'domino effect'). This is a special form of 'long test cases' described in Section 7.2.4.

Solution Stringing short test cases together is a powerful and useful technique, which would be greatly missed if it were to be 'banned' outright. However, it must be used with discretion because of the potentially disastrous consequences when things start to go wrong. We recommend a cautious approach to start with. Try a few short strings of test cases first to see how well they work, then expand the number and length as your needs and their effectiveness and efficiency dictate.

In some instances it may be possible to use 'snapshots' to restart a chain of test cases after one has failed, for example using the expected outcome of a test case rather than the actual outcome. However, in practice this could be very difficult to organize and may require more effort than it merits.

7.2.7 Naming conventions

Good idea? Don't bother with a naming convention as it will slow down automators and may even inhibit creativity. Let each person name scripts, files, etc., as they like.

Problem A free-for-all on naming scripts and files is fine while you have only a few test cases and only one or two people ever go near them. However, as the number of test cases increases and/or different people become involved, the situation will soon become chaotic. There will be no consistency across test cases implemented by different people, making it harder to find scripts and files that they wish to use and thereby encouraging less reuse and more duplication.

Solution Adopt some naming conventions right at the start (do not wait until it becomes a real problem). The sooner people learn the conventions the easier it will become to find scripts and files, and to name new ones. This will also lead to fewer mistakes being made. Another part of the solution is to organize the test items using a hierarchy, as described in Chapter 5.

7.2.8 Test complexity

Good idea? Now we have a tool we can implement test cases that are too complex to perform manually. Because tools enable us to test more intricate things, we can specify each aspect precisely, building up large and complex test cases.

Problem The more complex anything is, the harder it is to understand, and the more time will be needed to understand what is going on. Test cases are not just written once and never read again. When the test case is maintained, someone will need to understand it very well, even for small changes, so they can be sure their changes will not have any adverse affects. Another problem here is the tendency for technical people to become carried away with the technology. Some aspects of software systems can be difficult to automate and will require a clever and complex solution. We have seen instances where very complex test cases have been implemented only because they could be done, not because the test cases themselves provided any real benefit.

Solution There may be some test cases that have to be complex due to the nature of the software under test. However, these should be kept to a minimum. A heavy reliance on a lot of complex test cases could be dangerous as the maintenance cost can soon wipe out any savings they offered.

When choosing test cases to automate, always compare how much effort it will take to automate and maintain those test cases, with the effort likely to be saved over a reasonable period of time (one or two years). If a test case is likely to be executed only a few times, but costs a lot to automate, it may not be worth automating it.

7.2.9 Test documentation

Good idea? No documentation is needed for test cases; after all, it's only the tool that will read them. In any case, our test scripts are 'self documenting.' The tool vendor said so.

Problem This is like saying we don't need any documentation for software because it's only the computer that will execute it. We should know by now that this is not the case, and the problem of dealing with undocumented or poorly documented systems wastes inordinate amounts of time and money in our industry.

Solution The documentation for the test cases must be at the right level and useful. There should be overall documentation giving an overview of the test items as well as annotations in each script to say what the script is doing. It is the quality of the documentation, not its quantity, that is important.

7.2.10 Other attributes

There are many other attributes that can affect test maintenance though many of them will be specific to certain environments, systems, and types of testing. Different subsets of these attributes will apply to different organizations, depending on their environment, their way of working, and their approach to test automation.

7.3 The conspiracy

It appears to us that there is a conspiracy at work. Considering the following points, it is easy to see why so many organizations fall foul of a large maintenance burden.

7.3.1 Tools help you do the wrong thing

Most tools help people to implement automated test cases quickly and with minimal effort. Unfortunately this 'minimal effort' approach does not encourage much thought about maintenance issues and so these are left until it is too late. Some tool vendors do put useful information in their documentation about things to avoid and good things to do but who reads it? Often documentation is read only as a last resort and even then it is in an attempt to find out how to do a specific task, not necessarily to research the best way of doing it.

7.3.2 Easy approaches result in higher maintenance costs

Automating testing is like writing software – it is easy to create something that looks good on the surface but beneath the surface it is something of a tangled mess that is best left alone. Most development groups we know have a few pieces of source code that are known 'black spots.' Often these are monolithic code modules or horrendously complex modules with inadequate documentation. So it is with automated tests. Some test cases become known trouble spots, worth avoiding at almost any cost. Such things are neither easy to enhance nor easy to maintain. Often they have served their initial purpose but they are too costly to maintain.

7.3.3 Initial enthusiasm

A typical approach to testing is 'throw as much as you can at the software in the time available.' Automation means you can 'throw' an awful lot more and the novelty of having a tool to use encourages people to create tests quickly and with little thought about long-term consequences. Once the initial enthusiasm has worn off a lot of damage has already been done and the rework of the automated tests has to start if long-term benefits are to be realized.

7.3.4 Return on investment

It seems to be the case that the largest gains from test automation are to be made with that little bit of extra effort applied at the end – a case of the 20/80 rule in which the first 80% of effort gives 20% of the benefits and the last 20% of effort gives 80% of the benefits. If the last 20% of effort is not put in, most of the benefit of test automation will not be realized.

7.4 Strategy and tactics

7.4.1 Strategy

As has been explained there are many things that can be done to reduce the maintenance costs. However, no single solution is likely to have sufficient impact to make the maintenance problems diminish significantly. It will be necessary to adopt a strategy that encompasses many different solutions that together will deliver the benefits.

The basic strategy, then, is to identify those attributes most likely to have the largest impact on test maintenance in your environment and do something to reduce the impact of each one. Start by trying to find out where the effort goes in test maintenance and ask the people involved for ideas on how to reduce it. There are no right and wrong answers for what you should do; the important thing is that you do something that is targeted at each of your chosen attributes. Furthermore, you must measure what is done and the effects it has as best you can so future decisions can be informed ones. Chapter 8 discusses the measurement of test automation attributes in more detail.

7.4.2 Tactics

Here are some possible tactics for implementing a strategy for minimizing automated test maintenance costs.

1. Define preferred values and standards. Decide on maximum values for those attributes that can be readily measured. Make these known either as 'preferred' maximum values or, better still, standards that can be relaxed where reasonably justified and approved.

   For example, allow a maximum of 2 Mbytes of disk space to be used by any set of test cases (of course, 'set' would need to be well defined and may be a set of test cases associated with a single function or a typical unit of work for one person). Any limit may seem arbitrary but try to set it reasonably low (0.5 Mbytes or 200 Kbytes may be more appropriate) and if there are a lot of requests to exceed it then it can be raised; it is more difficult to reduce a limit, however. The disk space used should include everything required to be stored unique to that set of test cases, such as input data, expected outcomes, documentation, etc. The extent to which this is possible will depend on the organization of the Test Suite.

2. Provide tool support. Some attributes can easily be measured (such as disk space use and test execution time), particularly where appropriate tools are available. When tool support is possible it should be provided since without it some jobs will not be done regardless of how easy they may be. The tools required will usually be simple utilities that any keen software engineer can produce in an hour or two (though don't forget to build a few tests for the tools themselves). If a tool needs much more effort it is probably too complicated.

   Such tools are essential where standards or 'preferred' limits are used. In one case where a disk space limit of 5 Mbytes was imposed the tool proved to be the only way to make it work. Testers were required to submit their test sets into the source code control system used by the developers; it was a simple matter to program the system to accept those test sets that did not exceed this limit or that were approved to exceed it.

3. Automate updates. Updates to test data should be expected and antici-pated. Whenever updates are going to be required on a large scale, make every effort to automate these. Sometimes the best way of doing this is by using the capture/replay functionality of a test execution automation tool. Where test data is held in text format a simple command file feeding instructions to a text editor is very effective. However it is done, it will require uniformity and consistency of the test case definition and imple-mentation throughout the test suite. Files need to be organized and located in the same way from test case to test case. This need for unifor-mity alone should be sufficient justification for the adoption of standards.

4. Schedule periodic weeding. To keep duplication and redundancy to a minimum, schedule periodic weeding. It doesn't have to be done very often and it doesn't have to take very long but it must be done. Unless it is scheduled well in advance it is likely to be forgotten. If when the time comes for weeding there is little enthusiasm for it, take another look at the costs of test maintenance; they may provide sufficient incentive.

   Test documentation that is accurate and concise is perhaps one of the best aids to weeding test suites. A good approach is to involve the whole test team. In this way you can increase the team's knowledge of what tests there are and what they do. It will also reduce the elapsed time for the job and encourage a good team spirit, thereby keeping motivation and productivity high.

5. Maintenance utilities. Maintenance of the automated test cases will become an increasing overhead (the more test cases there are, the more maintenance effort will be required) that is necessary to keep the test cases up-to-date with the latest versions of the software. It is important to provide some form of tool support for this activity, particularly as any one software change may cause similar amendments to be made throughout a potentially large number of test scripts, test data files, etc. We have found a combination of search and edit utilities generally useful, particularly those that support regular expressions. (These were described in Chapter 4 for use in comparison filters.)

Summary

Because software needs to be maintained, the corresponding tests also need to be maintained to keep in step with the software changes. Maintenance costs are usually more significant for automated test cases than for manual test cases.

It is easy to make decisions about test automation which seem a good idea at first, but which prove to have significant problems later on. This chapter looked at aspects not covered elsewhere in this book:

- the number of test cases should not grow unchecked; each added test case should uniquely contribute value to the Test Suite;

- the quantity of test data should be controlled;

- test data should be in the most flexible format that is as independent as possible from future changes to the software under test;

- the time to run a test case should be minimized;

- test cases should be designed for ease of debugging;

- test cases should be as independent as possible;

- naming conventions should be adopted early on and used in conjunction with an effective testware organization strategy;

- test cases should be as simple as possible;

- test cases must be documented concisely but accurately.

Tools help you do most easily the wrong thing with regard to maintenance. The best strategy is to identify and combat those attributes of the automated testware that contribute most to your maintenance costs. Define test automation standards and enforce them where practical, and provide tool support and maintenance utilities wherever possible.

Don't forget to undertake periodic 'weeding' of your whole automated test suite.

CHAPTER EIGHT

Metrics

8.1 Why measure testing and test automation?

Why measure anything? Take for example your own automobile. Most people have measured the miles per gallon or kilometers per liter that their automobile achieves, at least at some point; a few people measure it regularly. There are a number of good reasons to do it, such as:

- to decide whether the automobile was a good investment;
- to evaluate choices, compare alternatives, and monitor improvement;
- to have early warning of problems, and to make predictions;
- to benchmark against a standard or in competition.

All of these apply not only to fuel consumption for an automobile, but also to testing and test automation. Although this book is about test automation, in this chapter on metrics we cannot ignore metrics for testing as well as looking at metrics for test automation. If you are only going to measure one thing, a measure of the testing process is more important than a measure of the automation process. A poor automated testing process, no matter how well automated, will give you less benefit than a good manual testing process. A good manual testing regime is a firm foundation on which to build test automation. We now consider the reasons to measure listed above as they might apply to testing and to test automation.

8.1.1 Return on investment

Return on investment (ROI) may be calculated for two reasons: before you invest in something (such as improved testing or purchasing a tool), to estimate how much you might gain, and after the proposed change has been implemented to see how much you have actually gained. The first is using measurement for prediction and the second is using it for assessment. (Fenton and Lawrence-Pfleeger, 1997).

8.1.1.1 *Return on investment from improved testing*

The following example shows how ROI can be calculated for an investment in improving testing practices (without automation).

Suppose that the current testing process costs $10 000 per year, and finds around 70% of the defects that would otherwise be found within the first six months of live use. (This measure is the Defect Detection Percentage (DDP), which is described in Section 8.4.1.1.) Assume that the cost to fix a defect in testing is $100, and the cost to fix a defect after release is $1000. (These are conservatively realistic approximations for a medium-sized organization at the time of writing. Use your own figures if you have them to do this calculation for your organization.)

A certain number of defects will have been inserted during the development of the system. For this example, suppose this is around 1000 in a typical system or major enhancement. With an assumed DDP of 70%, this means that approximately 700 defects will be found in testing, leaving 300 to be found after release.

We are considering investing an additional $10 000 in improving the testing process. This may involve, for example, training in testing techniques and improved documentation, which we think will enable us to improve our DDP from 70% to 90%. Would this be a worthwhile investment? We can calculate the ROI in one year as shown in Table 8.1.

Note that if the number of defects being inserted (1000 in the example) is reduced by an order of magnitude (to 100), say by implementing inspection of all development and test documentation, then the ROI calculation will give a different ROI. With only 100 defects inserted, the $10 000 investment in improved testing is still beneficial, but the ROI works out at only

Table 8.1 Simple ROI calculation for an improved testing process.

	Current process	Improved process
Cost of testing	$10 000	$20 000
DDP	70%	90%
Defects found in test	700	900
Cost to fix in test ($100 each)	$70 000	$90 000
Defects found after release	300	100
Cost to fix after release ($1000 each)	$300 000	$100 000
Total cost (testing plus fixing costs in test and after release)	$380 000	$210 000
Benefit of improved testing process		$170 000
Investment in improved testing		$10 000
ROI (saving/investment)		17 times (1700%)

80% in the first year. (This is still a very worthwhile return on investment.) If our DDP had improved from 70% to only 80%, this would still give a ROI of 800%.

8.1.1.2 Return on investment from test automation

Investing in a testing tool is a major investment for most organizations, and it is important to know whether that investment was worthwhile and is providing value for money, just as you would want to know whether the automobile you bought was a good buy.

A simple model for calculating the ROI in a testing tool is shown in Table 8.2. We need to compare the cost of running a given set of tests manually with the cost of running the same tests automatically, including the cost of the tool itself and the cost of automating the tests. If the total cost of automated testing is less than the total cost of performing the same tests manually, then the investment in automation is giving a payback, assuming that the benefits are equal. The benefits could include the number of tests run, coverage achieved, customer satisfaction, or whatever is relevant for your situation.

The costs of testing would include people's time, hardware, and software resources. In the example they are assumed to be included in the test design costs. The costs for automated testing would also include the cost of the tool, training in its use, and any additional hardware or software required. These are assumed to be included in the tool cost in the table.

For this simple example, we have assumed that the cost to execute a full cycle of tests is significantly less than that of executing those tests manually ($1000 versus $5000). Although this will eventually be true (if the principles in this book are followed), it will not be true for the first automated cycle. However, we will use a simple model to illustrate the basic principle. Chapter 10 discusses how to build a more realistic business case for a tool by taking this factor into account.

Table 8.2 Simple ROI calculation for test automation.

	Manual testing	Automated testing
Cost to design test cases	$6000	$6000
Cost of tool		$5000
Cost to implement automation of test cases		$11000
Total cost of automation		$16000
Cost to execute a full cycle of test cases (tester effort)	$5000	$1000
Number of cycles per release	3	3
Cost of testing per release	$21000	$9000
Savings per release		$12000
Releases per year	4	4
Benefit per year		$48000
Savings per year (benefit − investment in automation)		$32000
ROI (savings / investment)		200%

This simple model is not the only one that could apply. For example, the automated testing may not actually be costing any less, but if it enables a product to reach the market sooner, giving the company a competitive edge, it is still a good investment even though it is more expensive.

One measurement that is not likely to show a ROI from automation is the number of defects found by the testing (although this is very important for ROI from testing). Manual tests are better at finding defects than automated tests. Even in a highly automated testing regime, the majority of the defects are found when the tests are designed and run for the first time (manually) rather than when they are automated. Bach (1997) estimates that 85% of defects are found by manual testing. A think tank of test automation experts agreed that 60–80% of defects are found during test development (Kaner, 1997). However, this does not mean that automation is not beneficial. The true value of automated tests is often in providing confidence rather than finding new defects.

Unless you measure the costs and benefits of testing and test automation, you cannot know whether your investment is worthwhile from a business perspective.

8.1.2 Evaluate choices, compare alternatives, monitor improvement

There are many choices in testing and test automation. For example, in testing, you need to decide what testing techniques should be used, what levels of independence there should be, how detailed formal defect reporting should be, etc. For test automation, how much or how little should be compared to verify that a test has passed or failed? If the automated tests are found to have missed too many unexpected side effects of changes in the software, then it may be that insufficient comparison is being done, or the balance between sensitive and robust comparison is too biased towards robustness (see Chapter 4). There are also many choices to be made in designing the scripting method (see Chapter 3) and in data organization (see Chapter 5).

Without measurement, you cannot determine whether or not a given choice was a good one. Change is not the same as improvement. Making a change may seem like a good idea, and you may even have a 'gut feel' that this change has helped. But without objective measurements, you may be fooling yourself and could actually be making things worse.

8.1.3 Early warning of problems and prediction

If you regularly monitor aspects of your testing and test automation, you will be warned of an impending problem earlier rather than later, hopefully in time to do something about it. (If your automobile's fuel economy halved in a short time, you should probably worry about your engine.)

In testing, if your Defect Detection Percentage, DDP (see Section 8.4.1.1), falls by a significant amount, it probably indicates a problem in your testing process. Perhaps a new technique is less effective than an established technique, or perhaps new untrained testers are now designing the test cases.

In test automation, if you monitor the amount of time spent in maintaining automated tests, an increase in this time may indicate that the structure of the tests should be changed to make maintenance easier in the future.

Knowing the typical effort for test maintenance for different types of change, the number of automated tests likely to be affected, and the number of software changes expected in the next year will enable you to predict how much effort should be planned for test maintenance and test execution.

8.1.4 Benchmark against a standard or in competition

Suppose someone says to you: 'My testing or test automation regime is better than yours.' How can you tell whether this is just an idle boast or represents something you could learn from?

Suppose someone says: 'We automated more tests than you did, so we must be better.' The number of tests automated is one measure, but it is certainly not the only one, and (in common with most measures) is misleading if taken in isolation. Your regime may be less mature, so you would not expect to have automated as many tests. You may be following a careful plan to automate only the most important tests, but invest the time in automating them well. In six months' time, your regime might have successfully re-run all of the tests you have automated, while your friend's larger Test Set has been abandoned.

There are standard benchmark figures for the fuel economy of every manufactured automobile. Unfortunately, at the time of writing, benchmark figures do not yet exist for test automation. However, such figures did not exist for automobiles when they were as new as test automation is now.

8.2 What can we measure?

8.2.1 Gilb's Law

We subscribe to Gilb's Law: anything can be made measurable in some way, which is superior to not measuring it at all (Gilb, 1988).

Note that this does not say that anything can be made measurable in a perfect or even adequate way, simply in a way that is better than no measurement.

The measurements of testing and test automation that we propose are not intended to be a complete set or a totally authoritative answer, but are intended to give you some ideas about what may be useful.

8.2.2 Examples of what could be measured

Software has many attributes that can be measured fairly easily, such as:

- size (in lines of code);
- function points;

- bytes of object code;
- number of decisions ('if,' 'while,' 'case' statements, etc.);
- build cost (time or effort to write the software);
- number of defects found in testing and in use;
- number of developers.

Testing also has attributes that can be measured fairly easily, such as:

- the number of tests in a Test Suite;
- the number of tests planned, run, and passed;
- the cost (effort or time) spent on testing activities;
- the number of defects found in testing and in use;
- coverage.

Note that the number of defects found is an attribute of both software and testing. In the terminology of Fenton and Lawrence-Pfleeger (1997), it is an internal direct measure of the testing process and an external indirect measure of the attribute of software quality (although there are many other factors that affect software quality).

As discussed in Chapter 1, the automation of tests is different to testing. Therefore there are also attributes of test automation that can be measured fairly easily, such as:

- the number of automation scripts;
- the number of tests automated;
- the time to run the automated tests;
- time or effort to maintain the tests;
- the number of test failures caused by a defect.

8.2.3 Useful measures

Bill Hetzel (1993) defines a useful measure as one that supports effective analysis and decision making, and that can be obtained relatively easily.

How easy is it to obtain measures for fuel economy for an automobile? An exact measure could be obtained by seeing precisely how far the vehicle could travel on a measured amount of fuel. A rough idea can be calculated much more easily, by dividing the distance traveled from one fill-up to the next by the amount of fuel needed to fill the tank. Because it takes much less effort to measure it, this rough measure is more useful even though it is less accurate.

Is fuel economy a useful measure for an automobile? Not if you want to know whether it will fit into your garage! Then the useful measures are height, length, and width. Whether a given measure is useful or not depends on what you want to know, i.e. your objectives. This is why it is essential to know your objectives in order to choose what measures you should analyze.

8.3.1 Objectives for testing

Testing can have many different objectives, which will determine how the testing process is organized. If the objective is to find as many defects as possible, then the testing may be directed towards more complex areas of the software or to the areas which previously had the most defects. If the objective is to give confidence for end users, the tests may be directed towards the main business scenarios that will be encountered most often in real use.

Different organizations will have different objectives for testing; the same organization will have different objectives for testing different areas, or different levels of testing for the same area. For example, an organization that develops safety-critical software will have more stringent defect detection objectives than an organization developing games. Objectives will also vary over time. In a highly competitive market, elapsed time may be critical to success, but in a few years, if market share has been established, the quality of the product may be more important. The testing should be directed towards the most appropriate objectives at any given time.

8.3.2 Objectives for test automation

Many organizations have spent a great deal of money on test automation. In a survey of test tool users,[1] we asked what benefits test automation had provided. This was the response:

14%	no benefit at all
18%	little benefit
41%	some benefit
27%	significant benefit

Some organizations have been very successful in automating testing. Typically they are able to do far more testing more reliably than could ever be achieved with manual testing alone. However, many organizations have not been successful in automating testing, and the money spent on investigating tools and on trying to use them has all been wasted. Still other organizations have had some benefit, but not as much as they had hoped.

It would be very useful to know what metrics could be used to predict success or failure in test automation, and be able to measure them. This would make it possible to set goals for test automation, measure progress toward them, and monitor the results of corrective actions if the process began to go off track. It is a long-term aim of the authors to be able to

---

[1] This four-page written survey was completed by around 100 people in 1997, half from the USA and half from Europe. They were mainly attendees at testing conferences and events. Results from subsequent surveys may be found on the authors' web site at www.grove.co.uk.

establish industry benchmarks for test automation, but this ideal is still well in the future at the time of writing.

One thing is clear, however: attributes of test automation must be measured in order to be compared.

What are typical objectives for test automation? Figure 8.1 shows the results from our survey. For each objective listed, we show the number of respondents who had that objective as one of the goals of their automation effort, and the number of respondents who had actually achieved that objective (the shorter line in each case).

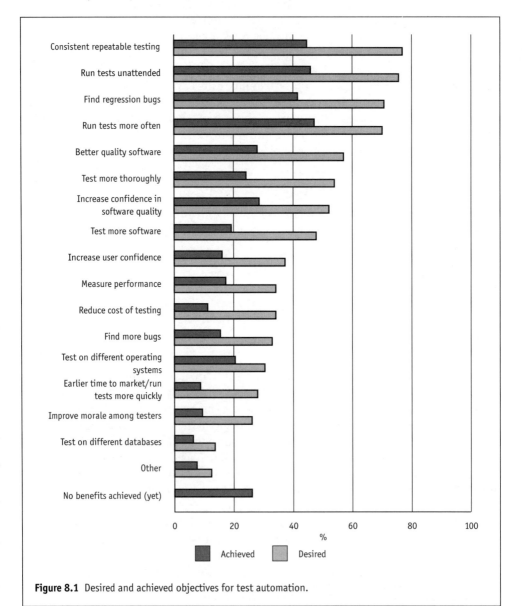

Figure 8.1 Desired and achieved objectives for test automation.

This survey indicated that many organizations did not fully achieve all of their objectives for test automation. The reason for this may be that expectations for test automation were unrealistically high, or that achieving real benefits was more difficult than people realized when they started.

There are a number of attributes that can be measured for test automation, which are discussed in Section 8.5. These measures should help you to find a way to assess whether your own test automation regime is meeting your own objectives. In order to do that, you must first know what your objectives are.

8.3.3 Achievable objectives

Just as a good measure is one that is useful, a good objective is one that is achievable. A test automation regime will not exist in a vacuum, but will be constrained by factors that may make some objectives too difficult to achieve in a reasonable time.

For example, running the tests unattended may be a desirable objective in theory. To achieve this, the automated tests may need to be designed to recover from unexpected events, and this will take time and effort. This may detract from other aspects of automation that also take time and effort, for example, script development, which may be more beneficial.

A good regime will meet its objectives within its constraints.

8.4 Attributes of software testing

Although the focus of this book is on test automation, we cannot ignore measures for testing, since a regime that automates poor tests will be of little benefit regardless of how well the regime is implemented. In this section we discuss measurements of test effectiveness and test thoroughness.

8.4.1 Measuring test effectiveness

The measure of the effectiveness of any process should be related to the objectives of that process. The main objectives of testing are to establish confidence and to find defects. This subsection describes some measures for test effectiveness. This is not an exhaustive list of possible measures of effectiveness, and these measures may not suit you, but it should give you some ideas to think about.

8.4.1.1 Defect Detection Percentage (DDP)

Definition Whenever a piece of software is written, **defects** are inserted during development. The more effective the testing is in finding those defects, the fewer will escape into operation. For example, if 100 defects have been built into the software, and our testing only finds 50, then its DDP is 50%. If we had found 80 defects, we would have a DDP of 80%; if we had found only 35, our DDP would only have been 35%. Thus it is the escapes, those defects that escaped detection, which determine the quality of the detection process. Although we may never know the complete total of defects inserted, this measure is a very useful one, both for monitoring the testing process and for predicting future effort.

The basic definition of the **Defect Detection Percentage** is the number of defects found by testing, divided by the total known defects. Note that the total known defects consists of the number of defects found by (this) testing plus the total number of defects found afterwards. The scope of the testing represented in this definition may be a test phase such as system testing or beta testing, testing for a specific functional area, testing of a given project, or any other testing aspect which it is useful to monitor.

$$DDP = \frac{\text{defects found by testing}}{\text{total known defects}}$$

The total known defects found so far is a number that can only increase as time goes on, so the DDP computed will always go down over time. If initial estimates of DDP are too high, measuring it will help to control optimism (the software industry's disease).

Although we will only know the 'real' value after the product is retired (and we may not know of all defects even then), this should not stop us learning something useful from the information we do have available now. Incomplete information can still be very useful, especially to compare to similar situations (with similar incompleteness).

DDP for successive test stages is discussed below. Note that this definition is exactly parallel to the definition of inspection effectiveness (Gilb and Graham, 1993). The authors have previously erroneously regarded the DDP measure as synonymous with 'test effectiveness.' Thanks to Bill Hetzel for helping us to see the difference.

It is important that estimates are made for DDP and also for the number of defects expected (as shown below); otherwise there is often an unconscious assumption of 100% DDP and 0 defects.

Knowing your DDP can help you to monitor changes to your testing process to see whether or not they are improvements.

How to measure DDP: integration testing example Suppose we want to know how effective integration testing is. We make an initial estimate that the DDP is 80%, as shown in Figure 8.2.

When the integration tests are run, suppose a total of 56 defects is found. This now gives an estimate of 70 for the total number of defects to be found, since 56 is 80% of 70.

Suppose that system testing now finds another 14 integration defects, bringing the total to 70. At this point we have not proved that our initial DDP estimate was wrong, so we *could* conclude that we have now found all the defects. However, it would be more sensible to worry a little at this point.

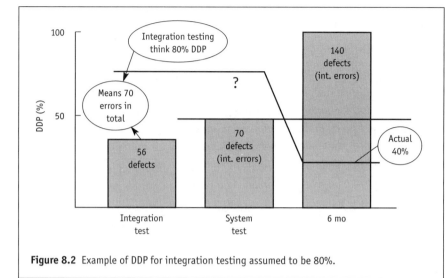

Figure 8.2 Example of DDP for integration testing assumed to be 80%.

Suppose that after six months of operation we have found a total of 140 defects that should have been found in integration testing. We now know with certainty that our 80% DDP figure was wrong; in fact 56 out of a total of 140 is 40%, and this figure may decrease further over the next few months.

DDP at different test stages or application areas DDP can be measured at different stages of software development and for different types of testing.

- Unit testing. Because testing at this stage is usually fairly informal, the best option is for each individual developer to track his or her own DDP, as a way to improve personal professionalism, as recommended by Humphreys (1997).

- Link, integration, or system testing. The point at which software is turned over to a more formal process is normally the earliest practical point to measure DDP.

- Different application areas, such as functional areas, major subsystems, or commercial products. The DDP would not be the same over all groups, as they may have different test objectives, but over time this can help the test manager to plan the best value testing within limited constraints.

- DDP of early defect detection activities such as early test design and reviews or inspections. Early test design (the V-model, as described in Chapter 1) can find defects when they are much cheaper to fix, as can reviews and inspections. Knowing the DDP of these early activities as well as the test execution DDP can help the test manager to find the most cost effective mix of defect detection activities.

At the end of 1996, we carried out a health check of testing practices at a major UK insurance company. One of the strengths of this organization was that it collected extensive metrics, although it had not previously tracked its DDP. We were able to calculate that the DDP of the system testing group was just under 70% for the most recent release, based on the company's figures.

Over the next six months, various changes were implemented in the company's testing practices. First, entry criteria were established and agreed with development so that System Testing would not waste time testing software that was not yet ready to test. However, these entry criteria were not just applied at entry to System Testing, but were informally tested on the software as early as it was possible to do so, based on a more cooperative approach with the development teams.

Another change was the streamlining of the System Testing and the User Acceptance Testing to foster more cooperation and less duplication of tests, allowing more tests to be run.

As a result of these improvements, System Testing DDP, as measured to the first month of operation, rose to over 90%. The recognition that the testers received at the semi-annual management review meeting was very rewarding!

Source: Mandie Chandler, 1997.

Options for analyzing DDP Several options can be chosen when calculating DDP. The simplest way to calculate it is to use the number of defects or severe defects found by testing and those found afterwards. Most organizations already have this information in some form, so an initial calculation can be done immediately.

At the other extreme, very detailed analysis could be carried out on every defect found both in testing and afterwards, to determine exactly what type of defect it is, where it was inserted, and what testing stage should have found it. This will enable a very accurate (and expensive) DDP figure to be calculated for each testing stage. For example, if you found a defect in live operation that could have been found in integration testing, without analyzing it you may count it 'against' system testing instead. This is less accurate, but does it really matter? Performing detailed defect analysis will take time, and it is important to make sure that it is really worth spending time achieving this additional accuracy.

If you do not do the additional analysis, your measures will not be as precise, but you will still have some idea without having to invest any additional time. It is generally far more useful to have simple measures taken consistently over time than to spend a lot of time refining a measure to a very detailed level.

The following are some choices for measuring DDP:

● Defect severity rather than number of defects. Record DDP separately for different severity levels, only for the most severe, or using a weighting system.

- Different types of defects in different test stages. If the additional analysis effort is worth investing, categorizing each defect for the stage where it should have been found will give a more accurate measure. However, accuracy is less important than tracking differences in the DDP over time.

- Successive releases. In maintenance or in Rapid Application Development (RAD), an existing system is changed at frequent intervals. This raises a number of questions for measuring DDP, such as whether defects found in a new release should be counted against the previous release or the new one. The simplest DDP measure is a cumulative one, which will show trends even if it is not completely accurate. An advantage of measuring DDP is that it can show whether your testing process is improving over time.

- 'New' defects. Should the DDP count include new defects introduced by fixes, defects that were not looked for earlier, defects that were 'nested,' i.e. not visible until another defect was fixed, or latent defects only found when the software is used in a novel way? Again, the choice here is balancing accuracy (at increased analysis cost) with more basic information that can be very useful at low analysis cost.

Some pitfalls and other aspects in measuring DDP We have found that there is generally some resistance to the DDP measure when it is first introduced, despite it being a very simple measure to implement. Below are some aspects, questions, limitations, and pitfalls that may occur to you about the DDP measure.

- Existence of at least one fault. If no defects are found in testing or afterwards, then DDP would divide by zero and be invalid. However, if this happens, just award yourself a DDP of 100%, since you did find all available defects (but don't be too smug – it may never happen again).

- Later stages affect apparent effectiveness. If the testing at a later stage is poor, it will make the DDP of earlier stages appear better than it really is, i.e. be overestimated (at least until the true number of defects becomes evident later).

- No bugs reported does not mean that no bugs exist! If users are very unhappy with the software, they may not report any faults at all because the task of reporting so many is too daunting.

- We will never have complete information. When introducing this measure at a conference recently, one of the delegates remarked: 'Well, of course we can never know all of the defects, so this measure wouldn't be of any use.' We disagree: just because we cannot know everything does not mean we should be satisfied with nothing, when an approximation is easily available and very useful.

- DDP is an 'after the fact' measure. This is true – you can only find out what the DDP is after some time has elapsed with the software in use. DDP does not replace measures of testing that can be taken during the testing process. DDP helps to validate those immediate measures. It also characterizes the test process and enables you to learn from your own history. For example, if high DDP were usually associated with high code coverage, this would indicate that code coverage might be a good predictor of this aspect of test effectiveness.

- The DDP measure is highly dependent on the amount of testing and the amount of operational usage. For example, a product that is poorly tested but never actually used may appear to have been well tested, since no defects were reported from the non-existent operational use.

Exercise

Table 8.3 shows a calculation that was done incorrectly by a client who did not yet fully understand the definition of DDP. The stages of testing listed were sequential, with one stage finishing before the next one started (at least for the purposes of this exercise.) What is wrong with this calculation? Which percentage figures are correct, if any? What should the DDP be at each stage?

Table 8.3 Erroneous calculation of DDP.

Stage of testing	Number of defects	Incorrect calculation	DDP
Module and integration	299	75%	
Development testing	40	10%	
Release testing	19	5%	
User acceptance test	10	2.5%	
Pilot	9	2.5%	
Live use (1 month)	20	5%	

The answer is given in the appendix on p. 553.

8.4.1.2 Defect Fix Percentage (DFP)

In his book, *Applied Software Measurement*, Capers Jones (1991) assesses 'defect removal efficiency.' This implies that defects are fixed as well as found, so debugging is included as well as testing. This is therefore a different measure of test effectiveness to DDP, as shown in Figure 8.3. However, we feel that the measure he calls 'efficiency' is actually an effectiveness measure, not an efficiency measure. We prefer to call it **Defect Fix Percentage** (DFP) or Debug Effectiveness. Marnie Hutcheson (1995) refers to this same measure as Performance of the Test Effort.

Debugging is not a test activity; it is a development activity. However, measuring the DFP is also important for total quality.

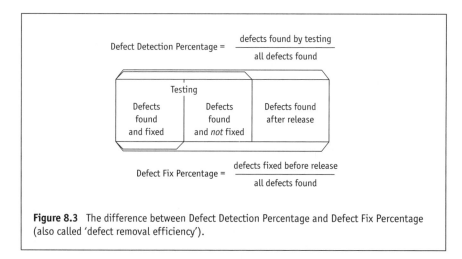

Figure 8.3 The difference between Defect Detection Percentage and Defect Fix Percentage (also called 'defect removal efficiency').

8.4.1.3 Confidence-related measure of test effectiveness

The measures of test effectiveness discussed so far are all related to the number of defects found by testing, and are most useful when there are a lot of defects to deal with. If the software quality is very high, so that there are very few if any defects to deal with, then the defect-based measures are less useful. But it is still important to know whether the testing that has been done was effective. Running tests that do not find defects is not a waste of time (provided they are good quality tests). They provide confidence that the software has reached some standard of quality. How can this confidence be measured?

One way is simply to take a consensus of people's opinions, and merge them into a numerical score which represents confidence. For example, if five people were asked to rate four areas of the system on a scale of 0 (no confidence) to 10 (complete confidence), the confidence measure could be computed as shown in Table 8.4.

This gives us an average confidence rating for each of the four functional areas of the system. The number in brackets after the average score indicates how widely opinions varied. For the first functional area, the average is 8.2, but the individual scores varied only by 2 (from 7 to 9).

Table 8.4 A confidence rating table.

Area	Person					Average
	A	B	C	D	E	
Functional area 1	9	8	8	7	9	8.2 (2)
Functional area 2	6	5	4	7	5	5.4 (3)
Functional area 3	0	2	4	1	6	2.6 (6)
Functional area 4	9	10	3	9	10	8.2 (7)

However, the fourth functional area, with the same average score of 8.2, had a much wider diversity of opinions, from 3 to 10, giving a difference of 7.

This confidence measure is based on what may be very subjective opinions. This can be useful, but it may also be useful to have some objective way of assessing how confident we should be, rather than how confident we feel. Measures of test thoroughness, particularly coverage measures, provide this.

8.4.2 Measuring test thoroughness

8.4.2.1 The value of tests that have not found defects

The thoroughness of testing is one way in which to assess the quality of testing. A test effort that is more thorough is likely also to be more effective.

Myers' (1979) definition of a good test is one that finds a defect. This is very helpful in educating people to perform defect-centric and negative testing rather than just demonstrating correctness. However, taking this definition too literally can lead to the misconception that tests that do not find defects are worthless – this is not true.

There is a detailed and rigorous science of reliability growth models that also support the value of testing that does not find defects. For example, Bev Littlewood found that a system that has been tested operationally for n hours without failure has a probability of surviving the next n hours without failure (Fenton and Lawrence-Pfleeger, 1997).

Measuring how thorough the testing has been gives a partial indication of the quality of the testing (without regard to the quality of the software being tested). A more thorough test is not always better than a less thorough test; it depends on the test objective. If the objective of a test is just to see if a function is still present and able to be called, then one test case is sufficient. However, if the objective of a test is to investigate the detailed functionality of a module, then even hundreds of test cases may not be thorough enough.

8.4.2.2 Subjective assessment of thoroughness

It is possible to try to assess thoroughness subjectively; this may be partly what goes into the confidence measure described in Section 8.4.1.3. If a group of knowledgeable experts has reviewed the tests and considers them to be sufficiently thorough, this will lead to confidence in the results of that testing.

This is not a very rigorous form of measurement, but it is probably better than not even thinking about thoroughness at all. This is also a subjective view of thoroughness, and not very scientific or reliable. It is also prone to being overly optimistic.

8.4.2.3 Objective assessment of thoroughness: test coverage measures

Coverage is an objective measure that is very useful in software testing. There are many different types of coverage that can be measured, some related to the structure of the software being tested, some related to lists of functions. The concept of coverage can be used at any level of testing, from unit testing to high-level system testing. However, commercial tools tend to support unit- or code-level test coverage.

The essence of a coverage measure is first to identify something that can be objectively counted (the coverage items), and then to assess the percentage of those coverage items that a given set of test cases has exercised.

Coverage items for code include:

- statements;
- decisions or branches (the outcome of an 'if' statement has two branches, 'true' and 'false');
- conditions (e.g. 'a < b');
- condition combinations (e.g. 'a < b AND c = d');
- data definition-use pairs.
- Linear Code Sequence and Jumps (LCSAJs);
- module calls.

Coverage items for a system-level test may include screens, menu items, user scenarios, functions, business rules, etc.

A set of test cases that covers or exercises all of the identified coverage items (whatever they are) is thorough; a set of test cases that leaves some coverage items uncovered is less thorough. Because this measure is objective and algorithmic, it can be automated (at least for many code-level measures), and there are tools on the market that measure coverage.

However, coverage is not the same as thoroughness – each coverage item is only one aspect of thoroughness. For example, there may be hundreds of data combinations that will cause an 'if' statement to take the 'false' branch. To achieve 100% branch coverage of this branch, only one test is needed. Of course exercising all branches is more thorough than leaving some branches unexercised, but just exercising a branch once is not necessarily thorough enough testing – it depends on your objectives.

8.5 Attributes of test automation

Which attributes of test automation should be measured? In this section we give some examples of measurable attributes. There may be other attributes that we have not listed which are important for you, or some of the ones we list here may not be useful for you. The important thing is to know what your objectives are and to measure attributes that are related to those objectives.

When choosing what attributes to measure, don't bite off more than you can chew, i.e. don't try to use all possible attributes you can think of. Choose three or four that will give you the most useful information about whether or not you are achieving your objectives.

8.5.1 Maintainability

An automation regime that is highly maintainable is one where it is easy to keep the tests in step with the software. It is a fact of life that software will change; for most organizations it is important that the effort of updating the automated tests should not be too great, or the entire test automation effort will be abandoned in favor of cheaper manual testing. 'Small changes in a program have made magnetic trash out of many carefully built comparison files' (Kaner *et al.*, 1993, p. 195).

How can maintainability be measured? Possible scales of measurement include:

- average elapsed time (clock hours) or effort (work hours) per test to update tests;
- how often software changes occur.

This is probably a sufficient level of detail to measure maintainability for most test automators. However, it would be possible to measure maintainability in more detail by considering different types of software changes, such as:

- Changes to the screen layout or the user interface. This type of change is very unsettling to immature regimes and tools.
- Changes to business rules. Not all aspects of a test may be affected. For example, a change of interest rate may affect outputs but not inputs.
- Changes to the format of a file or database.
- Changes to the content of a report.
- Changes in a communication protocol.
- Simple changes in functionality. A simple or minor change to functionality should not have a significant effect on existing automated tests.
- Major changes in functionality. A major change to the software would be expected to have a significant effect on existing automated tests.

It is important to make the tests easiest to update for the most frequent types of software change.

8.5.2 Efficiency

Efficiency is related to cost. The dictionary defines efficient as 'functioning or producing effectively and with the least waste of effort'. Efficiency is generally one of the main reasons why people want to automate testing, to be able to perform their tests with less effort, or in a shorter time. Early automation efforts are likely to be less efficient than manual testing, but a mature automation regime should be more efficient than manual testing.

In order to measure test automation efficiency, we need to know about the cost of the automation effort. The cost of automating includes the salary and overhead cost of the people and the time and effort they spend in various activities related to test automation. It also includes the cost of hardware, software, and other physical resources needed to perform the automated tests.

The simplest measure is the cost of automated testing as a whole, which can then be monitored over time. Automated testing is composed of a number of different activities, which could be measured separately if more detail were required. Some activities, such as the design of new tests, would incur a similar cost whether the tests were executed manually or automatically. Other activities, such as test execution, will have a significantly different cost.

Figure 8.4 shows how some aspects of testing may change when automation is introduced. In manual testing, test execution takes most of the effort. If those tests are automated, the time taken for test execution should go down dramatically, but the cost of other activities may increase.

In Figure 8.4 we have illustrated what typically happens when a set of test cases is automated. The time taken for test execution is significantly less for the automated tests, compared to the manual testing. However, maintaining the tests themselves before they are run on a later version of the software may take more effort for automated tests than for tests performed manually. This is because the manual testers can often adjust the tests intuitively as they are executing them. The necessary changes to automated tests have to be specifically and precisely implemented.

Setting up the environment and test data for automated tests needs very careful planning, which can take a significant amount of time. If you are testing manually and find that a file is missing, you can fetch it. If the tool finds that a file is missing when it executes a test, the test will fail. Although the automated set-up itself should be very quick (once the set-up instructions have been debugged), the effort to implement automated set-up will be greater than for manual testing.

The clear-up activities will probably be more extensive with automated testing than for manual testing, mainly due to the larger number of files that

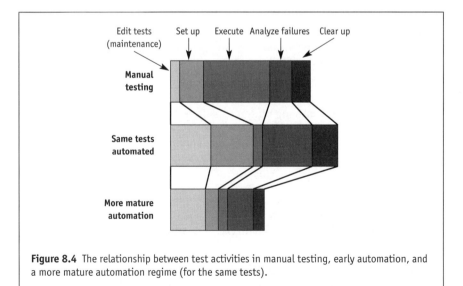

Figure 8.4 The relationship between test activities in manual testing, early automation, and a more mature automation regime (for the same tests).

are created. The automated clear-up instructions also need to be debugged or subsequent tests may be affected. As with automated set-up, more effort will be needed in the planning.

Analyzing failures often takes significantly longer with automated tests. If you are testing manually, you know exactly where you have been and what has happened before a failure, so it doesn't take long to find out what is wrong.

Figure 8.4 shows how trying to justify savings based only on test execution may be misleading, if the other test activities are not taken into account.

The bottom example in Figure 8.4 shows what a more mature automation regime may look like, if the advice in this book is followed. This should be your aim, but you can only tell whether or not you have achieved a good regime if you measure it.

How can efficiency be measured? Possible scales of measurement include:

- elapsed time (clock hours) to perform certain tasks (see list below);
- effort (work hours) to perform certain tasks (see list below);
- the number of times a test element is used. For example, if 100 tests use the same navigation script, then the script is used 100 times;
- the percentage of test scripts that are used at least x times.

The tasks to be monitored (by time and/or effort) could include:

- adding a set of new automated test cases;
- setting up a set of automated test cases ready to execute;
- clearing up after a set of automated test cases has been executed;
- selecting or invoking a subset of test cases to be run;
- the automated execution of a set of test cases;
- involvement or monitoring required while a set of automated tests is executed. For many situations this should be zero, but there are instances when automated tests are still worth running even if human intervention is required;
- ascertaining the test results. This includes determining the status of a set of test cases, and knowing which tests failed and why;
- debugging the automated tests.

8.5.3 Reliability

The reliability of an automated testing regime is related to its ability to give accurate and repeatable results.

How can reliability be measured? Possible scales of measurement include:

- the percentage of tests that fail because of defects in the tests themselves, either test design defects or test automation defects;

- the number of additional test cycles or iterations required because of defects in the tests;
- the number of false negatives, where the test is recorded as failed but the actual outcome is correct. This could be due to incorrect expected results for example;
- the number of false positives, where the test is recorded as passed, but is later found to contain a defect not picked up by the test. This could be due to incorrect expected results, incorrect comparison, or the comparison incorrectly specified or implemented.

8.5.4 Flexibility

The flexibility of an automated testing regime is related to the extent to which it allows you to work with different subsets of tests. For example, a more flexible regime will allow test cases to be combined in many different ways for different test objectives.

How can flexibility be measured? Possible scales of measurement include:

- the time to test an emergency fix on an old release. For example, a regime that allows this in two hours is more flexible than one that takes two days;
- the time taken to identify a set of test cases for a specific purpose, for example all the tests that failed last time;
- the number of selection criteria that can be used to identify a subset of test cases;
- time or effort needed to restore a test case that has been archived.

8.5.5 Usability

There may be different usability requirements of an automated testing regime for different types of users. For example, a regime may be designed for use by software engineers with certain technical skills, and may need to be easy for those engineers to use. That same regime may not be usable by non-technical people. So usability must be considered in terms of the intended users of the regime.

Possible scales of measurement for usability include:

- the time taken to add, say, ten new test cases of a similar type to an existing regime;
- the time or effort required to ascertain the results of running a set of automated test cases, e.g. how many passed and failed (this could also be a measure of efficiency);
- the training time needed for a user of the automation regime to become confident and productive. This may apply in different ways to the testers who design or execute the tests and to the test automators who build the tests;

- the time or effort needed to discount defects that are of no interest for a particular set of automated tests, for example a minor defect which is not going to be fixed until some future release;
- how well the users of the regime like it, their perceptions of how easy it is for them to use it. This could be measured by a survey of the test automation users.

8.5.6 Robustness

The robustness of an automated testing regime is how useful the automated tests are for unstable or rapidly changing software. A regime that is more robust will be able to cope with more changes or with a wider variety of changes to the software. It will require few or no changes to the automated tests, and will be able to provide useful information even when there are a lot of defects in the software.

Possible scales of measurement for robustness include:

- the number of tests which fail because of a single software defect. A more robust regime will have fewer tests failing rather than the 'domino effect,' in which many tests fail for the same reason;
- how frequently an automated test 'trips up,' i.e. failures due to unexpected events, or the number or percentage of automated tests which fail for the same unexpected event, or the number or percentage of automated tests which fail due to unexpected events compared to the number of unique defects found by that set of tests. An unexpected event may be a communication line being disconnected, mail arriving, etc.;
- the mean time to trip-up, i.e. the average elapsed time from the start of a test until an unexpected event causes it to fail;
- the time taken to investigate the causes of unexpected events that result in the test tripping up.

8.5.7 Portability

The portability of an automated testing regime is related to its ability to run in different environments.

Possible scales of measurement of portability include:

- the time or effort needed to make a set of automated tests run successfully in a new environment (e.g. different database or management system) or on a new hardware platform;
- the time or effort needed to make a set of automated tests run using a different test tool;
- the number of different environments in which the automated tests will run.

The measurement profile for one organization may be quite different from that of another organization. For example, consider the six test automation attributes of maintainability, flexibility, reliability, robustness, usability, and portability.

Three different regimes are measured against these six attributes. Each attribute is scored along the spokes of the diagram, with the better values being farthest from the center. These are shown in Figures 8.5–8.7.

So which of these is the best?

'Which is best?' is the wrong question, as we do not know what the objectives are for these three organizations. For dynamically changing software with frequent releases on many platforms, the most important attribute will be ease of maintenance of the tests. If the software runs on different platforms, portability is also very important. In this case, it may

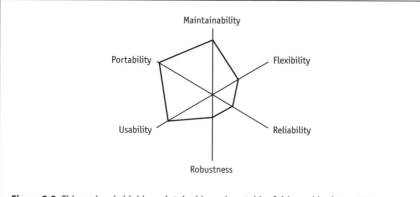

Figure 8.5 This regime is highly maintainable and portable, fairly usable, but not very robust, reliable, or flexible.

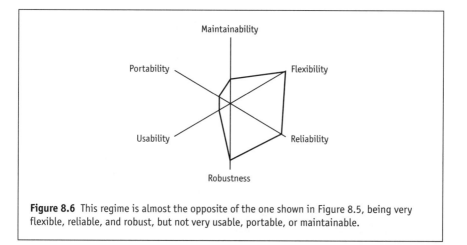

Figure 8.6 This regime is almost the opposite of the one shown in Figure 8.5, being very flexible, reliable, and robust, but not very usable, portable, or maintainable.

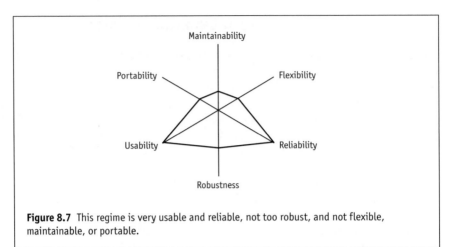

Figure 8.7 This regime is very usable and reliable, not too robust, and not flexible, maintainable, or portable.

not matter too much if the tests are not very reliable or robust, as the time saved in being able to test quickly gives the organization a competitive advantage. It may also be that occasional manual intervention is perfectly acceptable in the automated tests. If these are the objectives, then a good regime for that organization is the one shown in Figure 8.5.

An organization with a large number of highly technical tests, where the software is very stable with minor changes from time to time and runs on only one platform would benefit most from the regime in Figure 8.6.

The regime shown in Figure 8.7 may represent a fairly new automation regime, using only capture replay. This may be perfectly acceptable in the first few months of test automation, but would not be a good profile after two or three years.

Knowing your objectives is important in order to answer the question 'What is best?' for your own situation at the current time.

Trying to set your objectives may well highlight the fact that the objectives are not very well understood and may not be directly measurable at all. The ensuing discussion can be very useful in gaining a common understanding of what your goals for test automation should be.

8.7 Should I really measure all these?

No! This chapter is intended to give you some ideas for what might be important for you to measure. Choose only three or four measures that will enable you to monitor your testing and test automation regime against your most important objectives. Monitor these for a few months and see what you can learn from them. Don't be afraid to change the things you measure if they aren't telling you useful information.

A sample 'starter kit' of measures may include:

● The DDP for serious defects by the testing done for a release, measured three and six months after release.

- Average time to automate a test case or a set of related test cases. This will enable you to plan the continuing automation effort, and to tell whether changes you make to your regime are helping to speed up the automation process.

- Total effort spent on maintaining automated tests, perhaps expressed as an average per test. This will enable you to predict automation effort based on the number of new tests to be automated. This will also give you early warning of problems so that you can take corrective action in changing the automation standards. For example, after a few hundred scripts have been captured, navigation changes may be taking 50% of the automation maintenance effort. If you change to a data-driven script, this may go down to, say, 10%.

- Some measure of benefit, such as the number of tests run, or the number of cycles or iterations completed. For example, suppose that the previous manual testing had three cycles in two weeks (test – debug – retest – debug – retest) but with only 10% of tests run more than once. For the automated testing, there may have been six test cycles in two weeks, but every test was run each time. This gives two quantified benefits: if the same testing had been done manually, it would have taken four weeks rather than two, so twice as many test cycles were completed. A second benefit is that nine times more tests were repeated each time (100% of tests instead of 10%).

Summary

Testing and test automation can and should be measured. Anything can be made measurable in some way that is better than not measuring it at all. In order to be useful, a measure must be related to objectives and be relatively easy to measure.

Two measures for the quality of testing were described. Test effectiveness can be related to defects found, defects fixed, or confidence gained. The Defect Detection Percentage is the percentage of defects detected by a testing process, compared to the total including those found afterwards. This is a useful measure that is relatively easy to obtain in most organizations. Test thoroughness can be assessed by measuring test coverage.

There are a number of quality attributes for a test automation regime:

- maintainability (the ease of updating the testware when software changes);
- efficiency (related to cost);
- reliability (whether the regime gives accurate and repeatable results);
- flexibility (to run subsets of tests);
- usability (by different types of users, testers, or test automators);
- robustness (ability to cope with unexpected events without tripping up);
- portability (ability to run tests on different environments).

It is important to measure your test automation regime (as well as the quality of the testing process). It is only through measurement that you will be able to monitor and control your test automation and be able to optimize it for your own situation. However, it is important to be realistic: measure what is achievable, addresses your objectives, and is useful.

Other issues

In this chapter, we deal with various miscellaneous points that need to be addressed but do not come under the other chapter headings.

9.1 Which tests should be automated (first)?

9.1.1 Is it worth it?

If we have a set of tests for a particular system, some will be automatable, and some will not. Of those which are automatable, you need to decide what tests you want to automate. You will not be able to automate all at once, even of the ones that could be automated.

There may be some tests which it simply will never pay to automate – it would take longer to automate them than the time taken to run them manually the total number of times they would ever be run. For example, if a test takes 10 minutes to run manually, and is normally run once a month, this is a total of 120 minutes a year, or 2 hours. If it would take 10 hours to automate this 10-minute test, the same test would have to be run every month for 5 years before the automation of that test had paid for itself.

There may be other reasons to automate a test. For example, if our 10-minute test above was very tricky to type in, and the tester normally had to try it five or six times before getting it right, then automation would pay for itself within a year. But it might be a good one to automate simply for the 'hassle factor,' i.e. the testers get really annoyed at having to run it, even though it doesn't really take that much time.

9.1.2 Types of tests to be executed

Many different types of tests are typically executed in testing an application. Some types of test are very amenable to tool support; others are not.

9.1.2.1 Function

Testing the functionality of the software, i.e. what the software actually does, is a prime target for testing, both manual and automated.

Functionality tests are often the most straightforward of tests, where something is done or typed on the screen, and the results are clearly visible on the screen. This type of test is fairly easy to automate.

9.1.2.2 Performance

Testing the performance of the system may involve measuring response times under various loadings of normal or abnormal system 'traffic.' This type of test is notoriously difficult to do manually, especially when you want to repeat a test that was performed earlier. If you want to simulate the system conditions with 200 users active, for example, it may be difficult or impossible to find 200 volunteers, even assuming you have the equipment for them to use. Reproducing exactly what even one user did previously is not possible if you want to repeat exact timing intervals. This type of testing is a good candidate for automation.

However, a performance test is not the same as a function test. When you are testing performance, you don't care what all the individual outcomes of all the transactions are. A performance test passes, not on whether it gives correct output, but on whether the system ran quickly enough to cope with the traffic (even if it gave all the wrong results).

9.1.2.3 Non-functional qualities

Systems that perform their functions correctly, even if they do so within performance criteria, still may not be successful. Systems must meet other non-functional qualities as well as performance, such as maintainability, portability, testability, usability etc. if they are to have a long and useful life. Tests should also be designed to test for these non-functional quality attributes. Gilb (1988) gives a technique for designing this type of test.

Some non-functional tests are appropriate to be automated; others, such as taking a survey of users' opinions about how they like the new interface, are not. Usability tests often require manual verification, for example, to see if the colors are displayed correctly. An automated test could verify that something was displayed as color number 462, but would not be able to tell whether color 462 as displayed on this terminal looked revolting.

9.1.3 What to automate first?

So what tests should you automate first? Note that you don't have to automate everything in order to get significant benefits from test automation. If 10% of the tests are run 90% of the time, automating them alone may be worth doing. There are factors that you could take into account when deciding what to automate, including:

- most important tests;
- a set of breadth tests (sample each system area overall);

- tests for the most important functions;
- tests that are easiest to automate;
- tests that will give the quickest payback;
- tests that are run the most often.

Often the approach taken is to try to automate all of the tests in a given set of tests. Overall it may well be better to automate a subset of the tests for each program but have more programs with automated tests.

We recommend that the automated tests be required to include in their documentation an indication of the relative importance of each of the tests. Some tests are more important than others, and they are the ones that should be run every time something changes. Other tests may only need running whenever a particular function changes. Automating the important tests first across many programs will more quickly yield an automated Test Suite with greater potential for payback.

Example

The first tests within a given set are the 'field validation' tests which check that invalid entries in each input field are handled correctly. This is time consuming and painful to do manually, but generally has to be done only twice (once to find the errors, and a second time to confirm they have been fixed). Should they be automated or not?

There are a number of factors to consider in answering the question of what to automate first, and what is appropriate for one organization may be totally wrong for another. For example, it may take a long time to automate these tests if the software is relatively unstable, since too many other errors would be encountered while trying to test the field validation. This would seem to indicate that this is not a good set to automate.

On the other hand, if the field validation changed fairly often, while the underlying processing remained stable, it may take very little effort to edit an automated set of tests for field validation. If there are only a few fields that are volatile and the rest are stable, then the validation of the stable fields could be automated, leaving the varying validation to be done manually. In this case, the stable field validation is a good set to automate.

As a general rule of thumb, automating a breadth test of core functionality is probably a better set to automate early, as these tests are probably more important to end users.

9.1.4 Do not automate too much too soon

One of the most common mistakes is to try to automate too much early on. It is tempting to try to show rapid progress by automating as much as possible as quickly as possible, but this is not a good idea. It takes time for the best ways of doing things to be proven in practice. If you automate too many tests initially, you may have created a big problem for yourself when you discover a better way to organize the tests, for example.

9.1.5 Go for 'quick wins'

Try to identify those areas where automation of tests can have the largest impact most quickly. This need not be large-scale efforts. In fact, it is better to do something on a small scale that helps to overcome some frustration that many people experience.

For example, automating performance or soak tests or tests of client/server communication may be fairly easy to set up, and will implement tests that would be difficult if not impossible to do manually.

9.2 Selecting which tests to run when

9.2.1 How to select subsets of tests

Sometimes we may want to run all of the automated tests at once. For example, if we want to confirm that all tests still pass after a last-minute fix, we may set the tests to run overnight or over a weekend.

However, we most often would want to be selective about which tests to run. Even with automation, running a lot of tests may take a long time.

It is rare that we would wish to execute all the tests in one go. Most of the time we will want to select a subset, which may be based on several different selection criteria.

Here are some examples of the different types of selection that we may wish to make:

- An individual test. We may need simply to reproduce a single test in isolation, possibly to help isolate a fault. Of course a single test could be run manually, but sometimes the software behaves differently under manual testing and the defect may not appear unless it can be run automatically, if it is due to slight differences in timing, for example.

- A range of tests. We may wish to run a set of tests that perform a complete business function, for example opening an account, adding and withdrawing from it, and closing it, or we may wish to open a series of different accounts.

- By level. We may want to re-run the unit tests for a module that has just been changed. We may wish to run the integration tests if we have installed an upgrade to a third-party product, or we may want to run only the acceptance tests to check overall system integrity.

- Tests specific to a subsystem. If major enhancements have been done, we may want to test that area separately, but may not run any other tests now.

- By type of test. It could be very useful to be able to run all of the performance tests or stress/volume tests, for example if new network software has just been installed. It could also be useful to be able to run a breadth test, or selected depth tests, or all the bug fix tests.

- Based on length of time to run. If there is limited time available, you may want to select the shortest tests to run, since a long test would be more likely to be thrown off the system before it had completed.

- Run only the tests that have not yet been run in the current test cycle.

- Failed tests only. This is a very useful subset to run. When a number of defects have been found by a set of tests, they would typically go back to development for fixing. If a new version of the software with all of these defects supposedly fixed is then supplied, the first thing you need to do is to confirm that by re-running all of the tests that failed last time.

These are example criteria for selecting what tests to run. There may be others that are more appropriate for your own situation. Other examples may include all of Sarah's tests, or the database team's tests, or the client-supplied tests.

9.2.2 Implementing a 'test selector'

In setting up your regime, you need to plan for the Test Sets you will want to be able to run at once. For each such Test Set, choose an appropriate unique keyword that can be stored somewhere that associates it with that Test Set. For example, create a test file for each Test Set and in it maintain a list of these keywords appropriate for this test. When you define your standard information about each Test Set, allow a field (or two) for these attributes. You can then perform a simple search to identify all of the Test Sets with any individual attribute, which can then be run as a subset of the total number of tests.

Note that this approach probably is not practical at the individual test level, because of the complex interdependencies that may exist between tests.

Table 9.1 is an example of what such a test file might contain.

Table 9.1 Example test file.

Test or Test Set number	ID	Type 1	Type 2	Owner	Time	Status
1	OP3.1	Breadth	Order processing	DRG	00:00:30	P
2	OP3.2	Depth	Order processing	DRG	00:02:15	F
3	OP3.3	Perf	Order processing	MF	01:40:00	P
4	IV5.2	Breadth	Invoicing	BH	00:00:55	P
5	IV5.3	Depth	Invoicing	BH	00:03:10	F
6	IV5.4	Depth	Invoicing	DRG	00:00:45	P
7	IV7.1	Perf	Invoicing	HVW	00:30:00	P

The following test groups could be run from this example test file:

Breadth tests:	1 and 4
Order processing tests:	1–3
Invoicing tests:	4–7
DRG's tests:	1, 2, and 6
Performance tests:	3 and 7
Tests that failed last time:	2 and 5
Short tests (<1 min each):	1, 4 and 6

You need to have the same standard header for all of your tests in order for this to work, so this would be part of your own regime.

9.3   Order of test execution

9.3.1 The test analysis burden

Suppose you have a suite of 1000 tests that are run overnight. When you come in the next morning, you find that 20% of them have failed, 200 tests. What do you do next?

You would probably begin looking at the failed tests one by one to find out what was the cause of each failure. It may take some time to analyze each test. If it only takes 10 minutes per test to identify the fault, this analysis time will take 2000 minutes, 33.3 hours, i.e. over 4 working days. This is a significant amount of time to have to invest, especially when the tests were run overnight.

It may be that as you analyze the tests, you discover that the test you are looking at now has actually failed for exactly the same reason that another test failed. You may in fact find that a large number of failures were caused by the same defect. It is very unlikely that you will have 200 unique defects revealed by your 200 failed tests. But you do not know that until you have analyzed all of the tests.

Even if you can quickly recognize the same defect in another failed test, you still need to spend a minute or two on each test, so your analysis time is still likely to be a day (2 minutes on 200 tests = 400 minutes = 6.7 hours).

In manual testing, the test analysis is done in parallel with the test execution. In automated testing, all of the analysis activity now becomes post-execution, and therefore becomes much more visible. In addition, automation should be enabling us to execute more tests, so there may be many more test failures to analyze. The danger is that the analysis time remains proportional to execution time, whereas in a good automated regime, there should be proportionally less analysis and more execution, as shown in Figure 9.1.

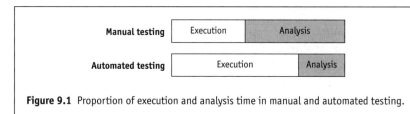

| Manual testing | Execution | Analysis |
| Automated testing | Execution | Analysis |

Figure 9.1 Proportion of execution and analysis time in manual and automated testing.

9.3.2 A logical hierarchy to minimize analysis time

What can be done to minimize this analysis time? If the tests are organized into a logical hierarchy, the failure analysis time can be considerably shortened.

Suppose the tests are organized as shown in Figure 9.2.

The first subset, at the top level, would contain the most general tests or breadth tests, and would normally be expected to pass. The lower levels of subsets would contain the more investigative tests, the depth tests, the tests that are probing more for errors.

If any tests in the first subset failed, don't analyze any failures at the lower levels until all or most of the failures at the top level are fixed or at least thoroughly understood. If the top-level tests are likely to fail, such as the first time they are run, it may not be worth even running the lower-level tests, provided that they can easily be excluded. But even if they are run, don't waste analysis effort if you are not likely to gain useful information. Finding that all of the tests in the second and third subsets failed for exactly the same defect which failed the tests in the first subset is not good use of your time.

9.3.3 Other requirements for running tests

In addition to grouping tests for execution there may be requirements for running tests at specific times or on specific machines. Some examples are given below.

- Run all selected tests now. If you are setting a Test Suite to run overnight, you might get the tests started just before you go home.

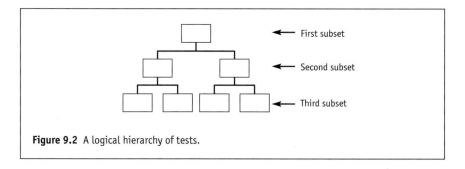

First subset

Second subset

Third subset

Figure 9.2 A logical hierarchy of tests.

- Schedule the selected tests to run later. You may need to start your tests after the normal overnight processing has finished, so you might want to set the tests to start at a specific time, e.g. 2:00 a.m., or when they have detected that the other processing has completed.

- Target a specific machine or group of machines. You may need to run a set of tests on a particular configuration which exists only on one machine, or under some constraints that are set up on a specific set of machines.

Your regime should enable you to do what you need to do in order to run the tests you want to run when you want to run them. You can probably make use of your standard operating system scheduling facilities to kick off the tests at particular times.

9.3.4 Distributing tests

If you are testing over a network, you may need to distribute the tests to be run to a number of different machines. For example, your central server may be the test controller, which would assign the next test in the queue to be run to any client that is now ready to run a test. If there are some tests that can only run on specific configurations in the network, this information needs to be stored where it is accessible to the test controller, so that an NT test does not get sent to a Windows machine, for example.

If information about all tests, including their required environment, is held centrally along with information about the machines available for running the tests, the distributed test scheduling can be automated.

9.4 Test status

9.4.1 Pass or Fail

The purpose of a test is to investigate whether or not the software does what it should. The **test specification** contains the specific inputs and data for each test, and also contains what the outcome of each test should be, the expected outcome. If the actual outcome of a test matches the expected outcome, then the **test status** is passed. (Actually what we really mean is not that the *test* has passed, but that this version of the *software* has passed this version of the test.)

In the example shown in Figure 9.3, we have Run 1 where the software is correct, so the actual outcome matches the expected outcome. Because there are no differences found by the tool, it gives this test a status of Pass.

In Run 2, the software now has a defect (*). This results in some errors in the outcome. When the comparison is made to the expected outcome, there are differences. Therefore the tool assigns the test status as Fail.

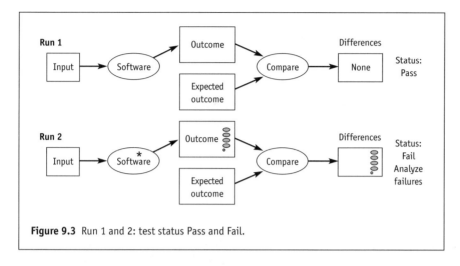

Figure 9.3 Run 1 and 2: test status Pass and Fail.

9.4.2 The tool cannot judge Pass or Fail

An automated test can compare a given expected outcome with the actual outcome produced by the software, but the tool itself cannot tell you whether the software has passed or failed – it can only tell you whether it has matched or not matched. This is an important distinction to remember for test automation.

For example, if your expected outcome is incorrect, a manual tester may well notice this and declare the software to be correct even when the actual outcome does not match the erroneous expected outcome. A tool will never do this.

Most people assume that Pass and Fail are the only two statuses for the software with respect to a given test. However, with test automation, there is a need for some additional statuses.

9.4.3 Known unfixed defect

Suppose a set of tests has failed, but the defect that caused them all to fail is not a serious one, and there is no urgency to fix it just yet. We now have a known unfixed defect in the software. For example, suppose that the word count in Scribble is out by 1, so if there are 143 words, it only counts 142. This one defect may fail half a dozen tests, where the word count is one of the things checked for different paragraphs.

The next time we run the automated tests on that software, if the defect has not been fixed, we will get failures again. It is quite likely that they are the same failures, but we will not know this until we have analyzed them all. As we have already seen, the failure analysis time can be significant. Yet we are not interested in any of the failures due to this known defect.

This is not a serious problem if you only have a few tests. But if you have hundreds or thousands of tests, having to spend time analyzing failures that you then find are not of interest is not only wasteful but very frustrating.

The analysis of the failures shown above will take time. But it has already failed in exactly the same way before, and we are not interested in this now.

9.4.4 Possible solutions

9.4.4.1 Ignore all failures of previously failed tests?

We could simply ignore all of these failures. Whenever a test is run that failed before, we would not spend any time in failure analysis for this test.

But why was the test run at all? It may have been easier to run it and ignore the results than to eliminate this test from the current set – then ignoring the results is a good solution.

We may have run the test again because the software has been changed in some other way even though our known defect has not yet been fixed. Now we do want to look at the results. But the fact that we have 100 spurious results to sift through to find perhaps one interesting result is not a good use of our time, and we may well get so bored that we miss the interesting result we were looking for.

9.4.4.2 Pretend that the failed results are OK?

Another alternative is to call the failed results the new expected results. This will have the benefit of eliminating them as failures next time. Now when we run the tests, we may get only two or three failures and they are things that we are interested in. This is shown in Figure 9.4 (Run 3).

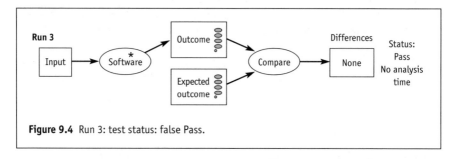

Figure 9.4 Run 3: test status: false Pass.

There is a significant danger here. As long as we remember that we have altered the expected outcomes to be intentionally wrong, we can go back and reinstate the real expected outcomes after the minor defect is fixed. However, human nature being what it is, this can be forgotten.

9.4.5 Test status: Expected Failure

9.4.5.1 An alternative expected outcome

What we actually need is a test status that says:

It's not right yet.

I am not at the moment interested in anything different from last time.

I don't want to forget about the real expected results.

This test status we call an '**expected fail**.' The fact that it is labeled a test failure means that we cannot forget that we have changed it. The fact that it is an expected outcome means that we can save ourselves from wasting time in analyzing failures we are not interested in.

When the test is run, we compare to the expected failure outcome instead of the true expected outcome.

We may keep the true expected outcome, storing it somewhere, if it is particularly difficult to analyze this test manually. Otherwise we will replace the expected outcome with the expected fail outcome.

In Run 4, shown in Figure 9.5, the defect has not been fixed yet. We do want to re-run this test, possibly because it is easier to keep this test in a suite to be run than it would be to exclude this test specifically. We are not interested in the same failures as last time.

We therefore compare the actual outcome to the expected fail outcome. Because there are no differences, we do not need to spend any time in analysis. We still know that this test is not yet passed, because the test status is Expected Fail, not Pass. This has solved the problem in a very neat way.

9.4.6 Test status: Unknown

9.4.6.1 Defect fixed

Suppose that the original defect has been fixed. We could now restore the original true expected outcome before we run the test again, if we had saved it somewhere. This would result in a Pass status. But what happens if we don't restore the true expected outcome yet, but run the test on the corrected software with the expected fail outcome?

Now there are no defects in the software, so the actual outcome is correct. However, we are comparing the actual outcome to the expected fail outcome. This means that the tool will find differences, and they will need to be analyzed. This is shown in Figure 9.6.

This is exactly what we want at this point. We now know we have to investigate a change, so this will prompt us to replace the expected fail outcome with the true expected outcome, so we have not forgotten.

What should the status be for this test? We can't say that the test has passed until we perform the comparison of the actual outcome with the true expected outcome rather than with the expected fail outcome. We know it is not an expected fail, because there are differences, and an

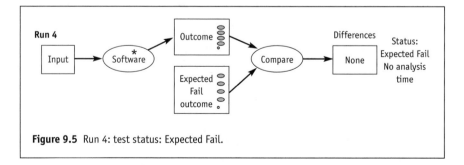

Figure 9.5 Run 4: test status: Expected Fail.

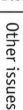

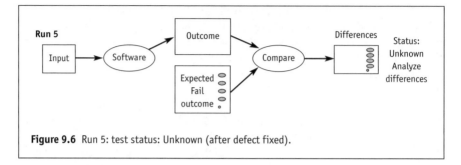

Figure 9.6 Run 5: test status: Unknown (after defect fixed).

expected fail has no differences to the expected fail outcome. We could call it Fail, but that could be misleading since it may be that the software is now correct, and calling that a failure seems rather unfair! We therefore introduce a fourth test status: **Unknown**. If the test status is unknown, we do need to analyze the differences, but we may then be able to assign a status of Pass or Fail after this analysis.

9.4.6.2 Software changed but original defect not yet fixed

What happens if the software has been changed in some other way with our original defect not fixed yet? Suppose this results in one additional new faulty outcome in the test. This is shown in Run 6 in Figure 9.7 by a second defect (*) in the software. If we compare the test outcome to the expected fail outcome, we will have a difference, but it will only be one that we are interested in. We only have to analyze one difference so we have saved time. (This is assuming that the defects don't interact with each other; if they do, you will need to spend time analyzing the failures.) This situation is not a Pass and not an Expected Fail. It might be a Fail (as in this example), but we do not know this yet, so this test status is also Unknown.

9.4.6.3 Missing expected outcome

If the expected outcome to compare to does not exist or cannot be found by the test tool, it is not possible to compare anything. If you cannot compare against something, you cannot say whether there were any differences and therefore cannot say whether the test has passed, failed or is an expected fail. The test status in this situation is also Unknown.

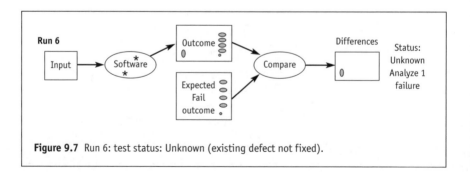

Figure 9.7 Run 6: test status: Unknown (existing defect not fixed).

Once the original defect has been fixed, and the software is now correct, we need to restore the test status to Pass, by restoring a correct version of the expected outcome instead of the expected fail version. There are two ways to restore the true expected outcome. The first is to restore the original expected outcome. Now when we run the test, there are no differences so the test has passed. This is shown by Run 7 in Figure 9.8.

You may be able to automate the restoration of the true expected outcome. Any time you are comparing to an expected fail outcome and there are differences, run the comparison again using the true expected outcome. If there are no differences now, as in Run 7, then you have saved yourself even more time, by automatically confirming that the software is now correct, and assigning a Pass status to the test.

The other way, if the true expected outcome was not saved, is to analyze the actual outcome and check if it is now correct. This is shown in Figure 9.9 (Run 8).

If the actual outcome of the test is now correct, this version of the outcome will now be 'promoted' to become the expected outcome for the next time this test is run. It is very important that the actual outcome is checked extremely carefully, since all future executions of this test will now be compared against it, and will depend on its correctness. If this step is rushed, and you end up comparing against incorrect expected outcomes, you can waste a lot of time.

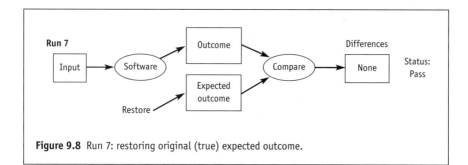

Figure 9.8 Run 7: restoring original (true) expected outcome.

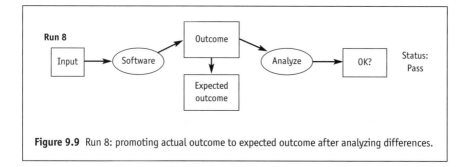

Figure 9.9 Run 8: promoting actual outcome to expected outcome after analyzing differences.

9.4.7 Summary of test statuses

We can now define what we mean by the four test statuses:

Fail:	When differences are found to (true) expected outcome
Pass:	When no differences are found to (true) expected outcome
Expected fail:	When no differences are found to the expected fail outcome
Unknown:	Any other situation

Table 9.2 summarizes what test status should be assigned in what circumstances.

Table 9.2 Summary of test status.

Compare to	No differences found	Differences found
(true) Expected outcome	Pass	Fail
Expected fail outcome	Expected Fail	Unknown
Don't know/missing	Unknown	Unknown

9.4.8 More detailed failure status

The four status values outlined above will help to make test automation more efficient by saving analysis time. There may be other ways in which even more time can be saved by having more detailed information about the failures that are of most interest, if this information is easily accessible to the testing tool or to your regime. Some examples are given below.

If a test cannot run to completion, there are no or incomplete outcomes to compare. We cannot assign any of the usual test statuses. Normally we would need to spend time analyzing why the tests did not complete. If we can automatically report on some of the following circumstances, we may be able to realize immediately that the relevant tests simply need to be re-run:

- environmental failure, such as the network going down in the middle of a test;
- initial set-up is wrong, such as files needed for the test are missing;
- the software to be tested is missing or is the wrong version;
- no comparison can be done because there are no expected outcomes to compare with;
- extraneous files exist that should have been deleted before the test began;
- something times out, for example if a printer is not switched on and the test is trying to print something;
- the disk is full.

If any of these (or others that cause problems in your environment) can be detected by your regime, it can save you a lot of time.

The benefit of a more detailed test failure status is that it more accurately reflects the quality of the test environment. Otherwise it appears to reflect badly on the quality of the software, which may be unfair.

9.5 Designing software for (automated) testability

The effort needed to test can be significant. But testing software that has not been designed to be easy to test is considerably more difficult than it need be. For example, if the system builds up a complex set of data, validating user entries and cross-checking values, before sending the entire Data Set to a database or to some other system, it may be useful to be able to check that Data Set just before it is sent. This is because it may be far more difficult to check all of the data by retrieving it from the various parts of the database after it has been sent. Having access to these intermediate results can be very useful in testing, both in manual testing and in automated testing. If defects are found, the analysis time is considerably shorter for our example if you know whether the defect was introduced before the data was sent or after.

Access to intermediate results is often referred to as inserting 'test hooks' into the software. The number of such test hooks and their granularity determine how testable the software is. It is also useful to be able to specify the amount of information available by any test hook. For some tests only a minimum of information may be needed; if a large amount of information available is the only choice, then the test will be inefficient.

The application being tested can also be enhanced in order to facilitate automated testing. For example, if the application includes a 'test mode' of operation, where inputs are taken from a file rather than from the screen, the application can test itself from tests set up in its own test file.

The best way to build in testability is to think about how the application will be tested while it is being designed and written. Thinking about what should be tested and how it could be tested will result in better quality designs and software, and will help developers when they come to debug the software.

9.6 Synchronization

Synchronization of the automated tests with the software being tested can be a major problem for test automation, although it is not necessarily a problem for everyone.

The problem is that a test execution tool can fire inputs to the software under test at a much more rapid rate than a human user could ever run tests. When the human tester interacts with a user interface, the tester keeps in step with the software. For example, the tester may request that a file be opened. He or she will not try to type in the data for that file until the window has appeared on the screen.

When the test is automated, however, the tool does not realize that it has to wait for something to happen (window open on screen and has focus) unless it has been explicitly told about it.

The tool may or may not be able to synchronize with specific system events. If it cannot identify the event, it can be told to wait for a specified amount of time, but this may not be enough in some cases, causing the test to get out of step.

It may come as a surprise that having strange filenames or not being able to find a file created by a test may be due to synchronization problems. However, if the test asks for the *Save As* menu option, and does not synchronize with it, perhaps the first three characters sent as the filename will be lost. This will give a strange filename, and the next test will not be able to find the file that should have been created by this test.

If an entire set of characters is missed, the application will finally arrive at the state in which it is expecting characters, and will stay there until it gets some. If the next test inputs are a selection of options, these may be invalid if the application expects text, so these are also ignored. The automated test can soon be completely unrelated to what it is supposed to be doing.

9.7 Monitoring progress of automated tests

When a suite of automated tests is run, for example overnight, you don't want to have to spend a lot of time the next morning sifting through files to find out what the overall results are. Some tools may make it very easy to produce a management level report about the tests; use this if it is helpful.

It is important to automate the production of some meaningful report, but this need not be a complex technical task. Just a simple text file can be produced by searching the tool output files and compiling some simple numbers.

The format of the report could either be on screen, updated at regular intervals or even dynamically as the tests are run, or it could be a printed report. Keep it to a single page in any case.

EXPERIENCE REPORT

When we first started running the automated Test Suites overnight, we wrote the results on the whiteboard outside the test lab every morning. We soon noticed that the managers would frequently come down to read the whiteboard to find out how the testing was going. Although it was nice to see them, it was rather time consuming for them. We developed a reporting tool which automatically collected the information that we normally wrote on the whiteboard, and emailed it to the managers and other interested parties every morning. This was always the last step of the overnight run.

We recommend that you produce a report containing the following information:

- the number of tests selected to run;
- the number of tests actually run;
- the number of tests that passed;
- the number of tests that failed;
- the number of expected failures;
- the number of incomplete tests;
- for each failed or incomplete test, an explanation of the failure (see below);
- resource constraints (machine availability, disk space, etc.);
- the elapsed time so far and estimated to completion.

Reasons for failure could include the following:

- set-up failed, <message>;
- execution failed, message logged: <message>;
- expected output file missing: <filename>;
- differences found in output file: <filename>.

Reasons for expected failure would simply be the defect number and its priority, and a brief description of the defect.

Clearly the reporting tool must know where to look for certain information, and it must be able to determine how many tests were expected to run, how many failed, etc. The reporting tool must be able to extract error messages from log files and determine in which files differences were found.

The more information that the set-up and clear-up utilities provide, the better the reporting overall. Investigate the use of your own system's generic utilities, as these can give fairly thorough error messages. For example, if it is known that a test requires a lot of disk space in order to run successfully, the set-up could perform a check to insure that sufficient space exists, and if not, fail the test without running it. An error message would be given to explain the reason for the failure.

By having regular reports monitoring the progress of the automated tests, the manager can use trends to predict the amount of development or test effort needed, the test resources required, etc. over the next weeks or months. For example, if a lot of tests are failing, that may indicate a need for more development effort to fix defects. If a lot of tests are not running to completion because of network outages, the network may need attention.

For example, the use of S-curves to show the number of tests run and the number passed is shown in Figure 9.10 (Hutcheson, 1995).

Another useful aspect to monitor is the availability of the test system. Graham Thomas (1997) suggests the example graph covering five days, as shown in Figure 9.11.

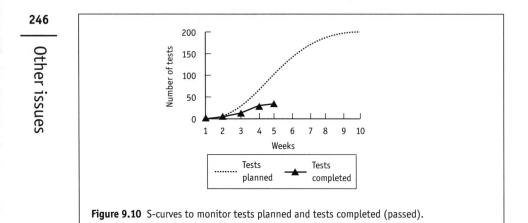

Figure 9.10 S-curves to monitor tests planned and tests completed (passed).

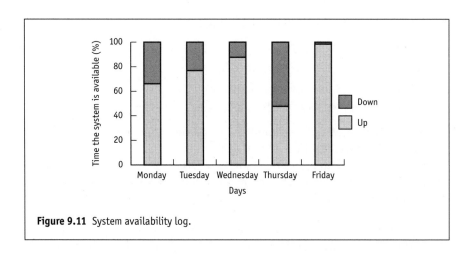

Figure 9.11 System availability log.

9.8 Tailoring your own regime around your tools

All commercial testing tools are designed to be used in a wide variety of environments and situations. It is not possible for the tool vendors to produce a tool that suits every organization. It is inevitable, then, that some 'tailoring' of a tool is desirable. This applies both to the 'front-end' and the 'back-end' of the automation. The report generator discussed above is an example of a back-end development.

A simple front-end should be developed to provide a user interface that is independent of the automation tool used. This can make the task of selecting and running tests much more straightforward and will remove the need for special skills. See Hans Buwalda's Action Words for a good example of this approach, in Chapter 22.

The type of interface program we are recommending can be implemented using a language like Visual Basic in a matter of days (perhaps hours). The specification is simple: display a list of the tests available, allow the user to select one or more (or all) of them, and when instructed by the user (clicking the *execute* button) send the relevant instructions to the automation tool to execute each of the selected tests.

The interface program must be able to determine what tests exist directly from where the tests are held on disk. Improved versions of the program would extract further information about each test, such as its purpose, the expected run time and the results from the last time it was run.

Further development of such a front-end will enable it to take on more of the set-up and clear-up tasks and possibly even the creation of a test environment. For this to happen the set-up and clear-up activities will have to be performed by generic command procedures that are data driven. Thus, the tester will specify 'what' tasks are to be performed and not 'how' they are to be performed. This will be much more efficient as specifying new automated tests will require less effort.

Summary

You can't automate all tests at once, so you need to decide which tests to automate first, and which tests are best always performed manually. This is based on the number of times a test might be run, the importance of the tests, or other factors. Go for 'quick wins' and don't try to automate too much too soon.

We may need to select a subset of automated tests to be run, for example, a specific test, a range of tests, or a type of test, or all the tests that failed last time. This can be implemented using a 'test selector.'

Test analysis can take an inordinate amount of time in automated testing. A logical hierarchy can minimize the time spent in analysis.

Test status is not just Pass or Fail. Expected Fail status minimizes test analysis time while 'remembering' about a minor unfixed defect, for example. A further test status is Unknown, which is used when an expected fail defect is fixed or when expected results are missing.

Software should be designed for testability. For example inserting 'test hooks' into the code enables intermediate results to be assessed.

Synchronization of test inputs with the software under test can be a serious problem for some but not all test automation efforts.

The progress of the automated tests should be monitored with progress reports sent to managers and other interested parties. This monitoring should be automated.

You will need to do some tailoring around any commercial tool.

Choosing a tool to automate testing

10.1 Introduction to Chapters 10 and 11

10.1.1 The tool selection and implementation process

Chapters 10 and 11 cover the tool selection and implementation process. This process is shown in full in Figure 10.1. This chapter covers the left-hand side of the diagram; the right-hand side is covered by Chapter 11.

The tool selection process evaluates and selects a tool that is appropriate for your organization from the many that are available on the market. The tool implementation process then insures that the selected tool is used throughout the organization in an effective way.

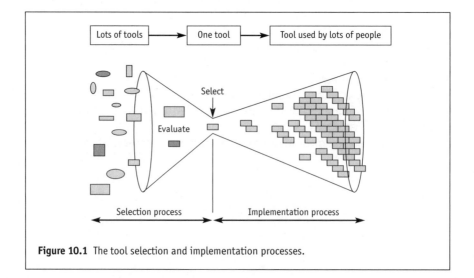

Figure 10.1 The tool selection and implementation processes.

10.1.2 Is this process applicable to choosing any type of tool?

249

If you are in charge of the selection of a tool to be used by dozens or hundreds of people within your organization, then you will need to approach the tool selection process in a formal and detailed way. If you are looking for a tool to try on an experimental basis with only two or three people, then your tool selection process will be on a much smaller scale, less detailed and less formal. However in both cases, the stages of the process will be the same. You will probably use all of the ideas in these chapters for a more formal evaluation; an informal evaluation may simply pick up some useful tips by reading these chapters. We have written this chapter for a medium-sized organization. See Chapter 15 for a good example evaluation.

This material is included in this book because many of the people who are charged with selecting testing tools have not done a formal selection before. There are books and courses that cover the topic of general tool selection and implementation processes in greater depth, including IEEE standards 1209 (IEEE, 1992) and 1348 (IEEE, 1995).

10.2 Where to start in selecting tools: your requirements, not the tool market

If you want to automate testing and do not yet have a testing tool, you will need to investigate what commercial tools may be suitable for you. However, looking at the tool market is not the place to start. It is important to start by evaluating your requirements. This will insure that you make the best decision within an appropriate amount of time.

The ultimate aim of the tool selection process is to identify a tool that will enable you to automate testing in your organization. The way in which the tool is selected is very important in achieving this goal.

If you choose the wrong tool, it may not do what you need or expect it to do. There may be significant technical difficulties in making the tool work in your environment. The initial users of the tool may find it difficult to use, slowing them down so much that they give up altogether. Situations like these will at best set back your test automation efforts, and may sabotage them for some time.

EXPERIENCE REPORT

When we evaluated the [test management] product, the lack of some functionality seemed like a minor problem. However, now that we have implemented it, we have found some big 'holes' in the tool's functionality, and some of the functions cannot be used as we had intended.

Source: Frode Utvik, Avenir a.s., Norway.

Another pitfall in tool selection is to choose the tool in the wrong way. Even if the tool is quite suitable from a technical perspective, if the right people do not 'buy-in' to the selection process, they will be reluctant to use the tool once it has been acquired. For example, some people may think that a different tool would be better. If they are not part of the decision-making process, they will resist using the 'wrong' (from their point of view) tool. This is why it is important to have a team of people involved in choosing the tool, and to address all of the non-technical issues as well as the technical ones.

10.3 The tool selection project

10.3.1 Importance and priority

Choosing a test automation tool is a project in its own right, and must be funded, resourced, and staffed adequately. It should never be a large project, though it will be a larger project in a larger organization.

The tool selection project for a medium-sized organization will typically take from four to six person-weeks of effort, and may involve three to ten people.

> **EXPERIENCE REPORT**
>
> We heard about one large organization whose tool selection project lasted for more than six months, involving three people full time. The cost of the 18 months of effort would probably have paid for two or three tools to have been acquired and experimented with and then thrown away. Also no progress towards test automation was made during the elapsed six months.

The tool selection project needs to be given adequate priority, not only from the project's manager, but also from the other people involved. This will affect the schedules and resourcing of 'normal' projects. This is one reason why a tool solution should not be sought if you are already under time pressure for your development and/or testing projects!

Figure 10.2 gives an overview of the tool selection process. This is the left-hand side of the diagram in Figure 10.1.

10.4 The tool selection team

There is a need for a team of people to make the tool selection decision. If only one person makes the decision, it is much more difficult to achieve a broad user base for the tool within the organization in the implementation phase. The amount of time required from the team members need not be too great, perhaps three to five days each, spread out over a month to six weeks. More time would be needed from the leader of this team.

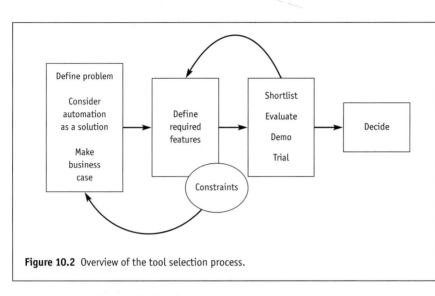

Figure 10.2 Overview of the tool selection process.

10.4.1 The tool selection team leader

One person should be put in charge of managing the tool selection and evaluation process. This individual should be someone with management skills or potential, and the ability to build a team of people from different areas of the organization. This person should ideally be someone who has a broad view of the organization and who is well respected.

The tool selection and evaluation team leader may be the tool 'champion,' the person in the implementation phase who is most enthusiastic about selling test automation within the organization, and the focal point for test automation practices.

10.4.2 The other tool selection team members

The team should include representatives from each area of the organization that may want to automate its own testing. This may involve people from several projects, departments, or locations. As this is an important decision that may affect the efficiency and productivity of the whole organization, the team members should be knowledgeable about their own areas of the organization and capable of making an objective evaluation that can be justified to their colleagues.

The team should also include a variety of skills representing the different roles or jobs of the target users for the tool. This would include end users who want to automate acceptance testing, test specialists who want to automate system testing, and developers who want to automate unit or integration testing. It would also include the potential test automators, the people with software development expertise who will be responsible for building the automated testware according to the principles described earlier in this book. The tool selection team may also include a test manager, internal test consultant or test coordinator, or a project manager.

The tool selection team will become a network of communication with the rest of the organization, both to find out what is required in each area and to help to promote good test automation practice and 'sell' the use of the tool once it has been acquired.

Some or all of the tool selection team members may also go on to become the implementation team, but not necessarily.

10.5 Identifying your requirements

There will be a number of requirements for your testing tool. Some requirements will be related to the testing problems you currently have that you hope will be solved, or rather eased, by a testing tool. Other requirements include the technical and non-technical constraints on tool selection. These tool requirements must be identified first, so that there is something to evaluate the candidate tools against.

EXPERIENCE REPORT: DON'T FALL IN LOVE WITH A TOOL!

The organization was under fairly strict budget constraints, so there were not that many tools to choose from, and the staff didn't think it was worth elaborating their requirements in detail or doing a thorough search of the market. They were on the brink of signing the order for the cheapest of the tools that they had found, when one of the people happened to attend an exhibition where a tool was being demonstrated which was of the category they wanted. This tool was very sophisticated; it drew pretty colored pictures and was very easy to use. In short, our hero just fell in love with this new tool. He then found out that it would have cost over five times more than his budget and twelve times more than his selected tool. He did try to increase his budget, but that didn't succeed. But because he had been so 'taken' with the new tool, he couldn't bear to go back to the first one, so they ended up with no tool.

Eventually, many months later, they revisited the tool issue and ultimately ended up buying yet another tool (which was within budget but four times more than the first tool), which they have found to be useful. The selection process would have been better had they identified usability issues as a requirement initially.

10.5.1 What are the problems to be solved?

The starting point for tool selection is identifying what problem or problems need to be solved, where a tool might provide a solution. Specifying the problems insures that everyone sees them the same way and they can be used as the basis for specifying test automation success criteria. Some examples of problems are:

- manual testing problems (e.g. too time consuming, boring, error prone);
- no time for regression testing when small changes are made to the software;

- set-up of test data or test cases is error prone;
- inadequate test documentation;
- don't know how much of the software has been tested;
- testing is ineffective.

Not all of these problems are best solved by test automation, although automation can address all of them to some extent. Rank your problems by importance or current cost to your organization. You will get the greatest benefit from addressing your worst problems.

10.5.2 Exploring different solutions

Let us look at each of the problems listed above in turn, and consider different solutions, not just tool-based solutions. It is important to consider alternative non-tool solutions to be able to assess whether the tools would actually give better value. There is often a great rush of enthusiasm for any automated solution (the 'silver bullet' syndrome) without regard for alternative (and sometimes cheaper) solutions. This will lead to disillusionment when the tool solution does not solve all of your problems completely.

Each solution considered should be assessed for the impact it will have on the problem and its cost. The best value comes from implementing high-impact low-cost solutions. (A formal way to do impact analysis is found in Gilb (1988).)

This section is intended to stimulate you to think about alternatives. In many cases a testing tool will help, but not necessarily, and there may be other solutions that may be even more effective in your current situation. Don't just leap to the conclusion that 'a tool must be the answer,' or you may find that it isn't.

10.5.2.1 Manual testing problems

Manual tests are often labor intensive, time consuming, inconsistent, boring, and lengthy, and comparison of test results is tedious and error prone. At first glance, these problems look ideal for test automation, and indeed that may be true. However, it is not necessarily the only solution to these problems.

The first question to ask is whether these manual tests actually give value for money. If they are too lengthy, weeding out ineffective or redundant tests could shorten them. This may enable them to be run manually within a shorter time frame.

If the tests take too much elapsed time to run manually, perhaps recruiting more testers would help. If the tests are very labor intensive, perhaps they could be redesigned to require less effort per test, so the manual testing would be more productive. For example, a test may require testers to sit at different machines in different rooms. If all of the test machines were moved into one room, one tester may be able to oversee two or more machines at the same time.

If the test input or comparison of results is error prone, perhaps the test procedures are unclear. Have the testers been trained in how to input, execute, and analyze the tests correctly? Are they aware of the importance of the correctness of test results?

Comparison of test results is probably one of the best uses of a computer. Most test execution tools include some comparison facilities. However, most operating systems also have comparison utilities that can be used to good effect, whether or not you have a comparison tool. The use of filters, described in Chapter 4, shows how complex comparisons can be done using simple comparison utilities.

If executing the current tests is boring, this probably does indicate a need for tool support of some kind. Things which people find boring are often done better by a computer.

10.5.2.2 No time for regression testing

Automated test execution is a good way to achieve thorough regression testing. Once the automated regime has been set up (using the principles described elsewhere in this book), regression tests can be run in far less time than when they are run manually.

However, it is worth asking why there is insufficient time for regression testing. If there are numerous late changes to the software, perhaps this should be better controlled so that there is time to do regression testing even manually. Perhaps better discipline in change control would mean that the regression tests are not invalidated by small, inessential changes to the software.

10.5.2.3 Set up of test data or tests

Setting up test data or test cases is repetitive and 'mechanical'; the testers find it boring and make too many 'simple' errors. This problem is a good candidate for a test execution tool.

On the other hand, why are test cases and test data being set up in this way? It may be better to organize the test data into pre-packaged sets which could be called upon when needed, rather than setting them up every time, particularly if this is an error-prone process.

10.5.2.4 Inadequate test documentation

Test documentation serves different purposes. Test plans contain management information about the testing process as it should be carried out. Test scripts contain information about the detail of tests to be run, such as what the inputs and test data are. Test reports contain information about the progress of tests that have been run.

An area where test execution tools can help overcome documentation problems is where inadequate records are kept of what tests have been executed. If careful records are not kept, tests may be repeated or omitted, or you will not know whether or not tests have been run. The test log does provide an audit trail (although it may not necessarily be easy to find the information you want from the raw logs produced by the tool).

An area where test management tools can help is in organizing the information about the tests and providing traceability of tests to requirements and to the software. Some test management tools are concerned with the management of the tests rather than the management of the testing process.

Other test management tools do help to support the management of the testing process. Project management tools can also be used to keep track of management-level information about testing, although there may be problems in catering for activities that are repeated more than once, such as test execution.

However, simply using a tool to document information about tests or the testing process will not help if the information being documented is not well organized. If your current test documentation is unwieldy, the form and content of that documentation should be addressed. Perhaps there is no clear separation of test conditions from the test cases. The reporting of what tests have been done could perhaps be improved by having a list of tests in a word processor table or spreadsheet, with the date of the execution of the test being recorded more faithfully than at present. Assigning one person to be the test 'bloodhound' to track down what tests have and have not been run may well overcome this problem at minimal cost. Improving the quality of manual documentation may be quicker, cheaper, and more effective than introducing a new test tool.

10.5.2.5 Don't know how much of the software has been tested

A test execution tool, if the reporting is well organized, will give you information about whether a defined set of tests has run or not, but this does not actually tell you how thoroughly you have exercised the software.

Test coverage tools can give you information about what percentage of various 'coverage items' have been exercised by a given set of tests. But coverage tools are not generally bundled with test execution tools at the time of writing, although some vendors offer suites of tools that include both execution and coverage tools.

Coverage can also be measured manually, although this is best done at a high level. For example, if you simply list the total number of business rules, screens, or menu items in the system, you can check manually whether all of the things listed have been covered by a set of tests, and devise new tests to extend the coverage if necessary.

10.5.2.6 Testing is not effective

Defects found in testing should have been found earlier; defects found by users should have been found in testing, i.e. testing is not effective enough at finding defects. There are some circumstances where this problem can be addressed by test automation tools. For example, if the reason defects are slipping through the net is that there is insufficient time to run all the planned tests manually, then a tool may well help.

However, if the tests themselves are ineffective, i.e. not directed at those defects that the users find, then no matter how you run them (automated or manual), the tests will not find those defects. It is the quality of the tests that determines how good they are at finding defects. Automating tests has no impact whatsoever on the quality of the tests themselves; automation affects efficiency.

EXPERIENCE REPORT

Peter Oakley from Lloyds Bank Registrars gave a presentation describing the bank's experiences in automating testing with a commercial test execution tool. (It took them 16 months before they achieved payback for their investment, but at least they measured it, so they knew what it was!) The title of the talk was 'Why won't my tool find the bugs?' and his concluding statement was that tools don't find bugs, the tests do. (See Peter Oakley's case study in Chapter 15.)

Source: Peter Oakley, Unicom seminar, October 4, 1995.

There are some types of tool (not test execution tools) that will help to find some types of defect. Static analysis tools will detect some types of defect before the tests are run, such as dead code, infinite loops, and data items stored but not used or used before they were initialized. Dynamic analysis tools detect memory leaks and some other resource problems, and can help to find these defects in the code while tests are being run or even during operation.

The best way to make the tests more effective is to use testing techniques that are 'defect-centric,' aimed at finding defects. The proper use of testing techniques can easily double the effectiveness of tests in finding defects. There are several books that cover testing techniques to greater or lesser degrees. A bibliography is maintained on the authors' web site.

Software inspection is a powerful defect detection and removal (and defect prevention) technique which can be applied not only to code but to any written document, and has been shown to be the most effective of all review processes. (Inspection can find up to 80% of existing defects in a single pass, 95% or more in multiple passes.) More information on the inspection process can be found in Gilb and Graham (1993).

10.5.3 Timing of the tool selection

Having considered your current testing problems and concluded that a testing tool would be an appropriate solution (perhaps in addition to some others), the next step in tool selection is to consider whether or not this is the right time. There is a right and a wrong time to try to choose a testing tool. If the time is not right, even the best tool in the world, chosen in the best way, is unlikely to succeed.

An automated solution often 'looks better' and may be easier to authorize expenditure for than addressing the more fundamental problems of the testing process itself. It is important to realize that the tool will not correct a poor process without additional attention being paid to it. It is possible to improve testing practices alongside implementing the tool, but it does require conscious effort.

The right time is:

- when there are no major organizational upheavals or panics in progress;
- when one person has responsibility for choosing and implementing the tool(s);
- when people are dissatisfied with the current state of testing practice;
- when there is commitment from top management to authorize and support the tooling-up effort.

If one or more of these conditions do not apply to your organization it does not mean that you should not attempt to introduce test automation. It merely implies that doing so may be somewhat more difficult.

10.5.4 How much help should the tool be?

Once you have identified a problem for which tool support is a viable solution, how will you be able to tell whether any tool you buy has actually helped? Depending on your circumstances, you should set measurable goals as the success criteria for the tool. Setting measurable criteria is not difficult to do, at least to obtain a broad general idea of costs. A general idea is all that is necessary to know whether the tool will be cost justified. For example, if the length of time taken to run tests manually is the problem, how long does it currently take to run a set of tests manually? What is a reasonable length of time to run them once the test automation regime has been set up?

A realistic measurable criterion for a test execution tool might be set out as follows:

Manual execution of test cases currently takes 4 person-weeks.

After three months of using the tool, 50–60% of these test cases should be automated, reducing the execution time for all the tests to 2–2.5 person-weeks.

After 12 months we aim to have 80% of the test cases automated, with the equivalent Test Suite being run in 4 person-days.

When looking at the measurable benefits it is best to be fairly conservative about what could be accomplished. When a tool is used for the first time it always takes much longer than when people are experienced in using it, so the learning curve must be taken into account. It is important to set realistic goals, and not to expect miracles.

If you find that people argue about the numbers that you have used, ask them to supply you with more accurate figures to give a better quality evaluation. Do not spend a great deal of time 'polishing' your estimates. The tool evaluation process should be only as long as is needed to come to a decision, and no longer. Your estimates should reflect this granularity.

10.5.5 How much is this help worth? Making the business case

Some organizations will require a business case to justify the purchase of a tool. If so, this section will help you prepare one. If a business case is not required, it can still be useful at least to think about the issues described here. However, do not spend a great deal of time preparing something that is not going to be used.

A business case quantifies what the 'help' provided by a tool is worth, so that you can tell if you can afford to buy a tool, and whether you achieve any cost–benefit when you do.

One of the simplest ways to quantify the benefits is to measure the saving of time and multiply that by approximate staff costs. For example:

If regression tests which normally take 4 person-weeks manually can be done in 2 person-weeks, we will save 2 person-weeks of effort whenever those tests are run.

If they are run once a quarter, we will save 8 person-weeks a year.

If they are run once a month, we will save 24 person-weeks a year.

If a person-week is costed at, say, $2000, we will save $16 000 if they are run once a quarter or $48 000 if they are run once a month.

There will also be other benefits, which may be difficult if not impossible to quantify but which should also be mentioned. The risk of an embarrassing public release may be reduced, for example, but it may not be possible to put a monetary value on this. Morale among the testers may improve, which will likely result in an increase in productivity, but it may not be possible or desirable to separate this from the productivity increase from using the tool. There may be some things that are not even possible to do manually, which will not be discovered until the tool has been in use for a while. These unanticipated benefits cannot be quantified because no one realizes them yet.

By the way, the time that you save will not translate directly into reduction of staffing for testing, but will enable your testers to be more productive. In our experience organizations do not reduce the number of testing staff following a successful implementation of test execution automation; rather, they enjoy the benefits of being able to perform far more tests more often.

The business case could contain the following information.

- Cost of current manual testing. This could be done per test cycle, or for the testing done in a fixed time period (say, per quarter or per year). These numbers do not need to be very accurate; we are only looking for approximate costs. Determine what the future costs of manual testing would be in, say, two or three years' time. This may include tests on more software or on more platforms, for example.

- Coverage of current manual testing. How much of the software is currently not tested, especially due to limitations which test automation could overcome?

- Cost of defects not found by current testing in the past year. This could be calculated by multiplying the number of defects found by users (missed by testing) by an average cost, for example $1500 per defect. (In our experience this is a very conservative figure and therefore a good one to use until you can determine a more accurate one of your own.)

- Cost of the first tool use. This would include tool purchase or initial leasing cost, training in the use of the tool, additional hardware, and software. It may be a good idea to include additional time for the learning curve; for example, analyzing test results will probably take longer the first few times. This cost would also include time needed to set up a workable automation regime. Automating a test for the first time normally takes at least four times longer than running the same test manually. This should also be taken into account.

- Cost of subsequent use of the tool. This is where the benefits would be seen, where more tests could be run for example. However, there are also costs associated with continuing use, such as license fees, and effort to maintain tests and to improve the automation regime.

- A calculation of the breakeven point, taking the costs and benefits into account.

The business case should also include the assumptions that were made in constructing it. This may include assumptions about testing in general, such as what test activities need to be done, the number of tests expected to fail, number of test iterations (tests re-run after fixes), new functionality to be tested, etc. There may also be assumptions about the test automation such as time taken to add verification, time for test maintenance, and setting up standards for the testing regime.

An example business case summary is shown in Figure 10.3. More details of our forms for choosing tools can be found on our web site.

If anyone wants to argue with your figures, welcome their input. The more accurate your figures are, the more confidence you will have in your business case. Don't let anyone say they 'don't like your figures' or they 'don't think they are right' without them supplying you with better figures. If they can't, then your figures are the best you have, so they are OK. In any case, they don't have to be perfect, only good enough to justify a decision.

Make sure that your business case is conservative. If you make extravagant claims for savings, it will be very difficult to achieve them. Make realistic claims to set a realistic level of expectation. You then give yourself the space to exceed your initial benefits, which will make your test automation effort look even better.

Business case for tool _____

Prepared by _____ Date: _____

Costs	Without tool		With tool	
	Test cycle 1	Test cycle 2	Test cycle 1	Test cycle 2
Test cycle	$10 000	$15 000	$17 650	$6500
Tool			$20 150	
Evaluate			$8 200	
Implement			$15 000	
Other	none	none	none	license per cycle: $500
Totals	$10 000	$15 000	$61 000	$7000
Breakeven			Cycle 7, 14 months	
		Savings: Year 1	($11 000)	
		Savings: Year 2	$37 000	
		Savings: Year 3	$85 000	

Assumptions
1. One cycle every two months, six per year.
2. License fee 15% of purchase cost for second and subsequent years.
3. All tests will be re-run after last fix for second and subsequent cycles.
4. Failure estimates assume:
   (i) one third of new tests will fail each time they are run;
   (ii) previously failed tests are re-run;
   (iii) four test runs will be necessary;
   (iv) 10% of old tests will fail.
5. Cycle 2 for both manual and tool-supported testing represents an estimated typical 'snapshot' in one year's time.
6. 25% increase in new functionality to test over the year (new tests to write).

Figure 10.3 Example one-page business case for implementing a test execution automation tool.

10.6 Identifying your constraints

Having established what your testing problems are, and having established that this would be a good time to introduce a test automation tool, only now are you ready to begin looking at the tool market. (In practice, you will undoubtedly have seen some tools, perhaps at an exhibition, or may even have had a demonstration or two. But that is just to give a taste for the type of tool support available.)

There will be a number of factors that will constrain your choice of tool. If you can identify them right at the beginning, you can save yourself a lot of wasted time and effort investigating tools that will be rejected anyway.

Testing tools are software packages and therefore will be specific to particular hardware, software, or operating systems. You would not want to spend any time considering a tool that runs only on a UNIX platform when you have a Windows environment and no possibility of acquiring or using anything else.

You may want to acquire additional hardware or software along with the tool. This is sometimes more of a psychological barrier than a technical or economic one. In your tool selection process, especially if there are not many for your 'home' environment, it is worth considering tools based on a separate environment, even though this will add to the purchase price (see Section 10.6.2).

However, you may need to acquire extra hardware or software even for a tool that runs on your own current environment, for example extra disk space to store test scripts, or a specialized comparator tool to help verify test outcomes.

Make sure that you find out exactly what each tool requires in terms of hardware and software versions. For example, you would not want to discover at installation that you needed to have an operating system upgrade or additional memory before the tool can work. Have you considered security aspects? Do you need a separate language compiler for the test scripts?

10.6.2 Should the tool be co-resident with the software under test?

Most people look for a tool that will run on the environment in which they are currently developing or maintaining software, but that is not the only possibility. Many tools can work in a 'host–target' formation, where the tool runs on one environment and the system under test is on another environment. Consider the future direction of your organization for hardware and software, and plan the test tools for the long term, not just for what you have now.

If the tool resides on the same platform as the system under test, the advantages are:

- no additional hardware will be needed (though this is not always the case even when co-resident);
- integration with your applications will be easier and better (e.g. synchronization with the tests).

If the tool resides on a separate platform or environment, the advantages are:

- it is non-intrusive and will not affect the performance of the system under test;
- the tests are independent of the application environment;
- it does not use system resources (disk space, CPU time).

10.6.3 Commercial supplier constraints

The company that you buy the tool from may be an important factor for you in the future. If you have problems with the tool, you will want them to be sorted out quickly and competently. If you want the best from the tool, you will want to take advantage of the tool vendor's expertise. You may want to influence the future development of the tool. A good relationship with your vendor can help you to progress your test automation in the direction you want it to go.

Here are some factors that you should take into consideration in evaluating the tool vendor's organization.

- Is the supplier a bona fide company? The commercial details of the supplier can be checked in various testing tool reports or the normal commercial channels for such information.

- How mature are the company and the product? If the company is well established this gives confidence, but if the product has not changed significantly in recent years, it may be rather out of date. Some organizations will feel that they need to buy products from the vendor who sets the trend in the marketplace. Others will be wary of new product companies.

- Is there adequate technical support? How would the vendor respond to major or minor problems? Does the vendor run a help desk? What hours is help available? (If your vendor is on the opposite side of the world, there will be no overlap of its working day with yours!) What training courses are provided? How responsive is the vendor to requests for information?

- How many other organizations have purchased this tool? How many are using the tool well and achieving benefits? You may not want to be the first commercial user of a new tool. Can you talk to any other tool users? Is there a user group? If so, when does it meet and who controls it? Will the vendor provide reference sites for you to talk to?

- What is the tool's history? Was it developed to support good internal testing practices, to meet a specific client need, or as a speculative product? How many releases have there been to date, and how often is the tool updated? How many open faults are there currently reported in the tool itself?

Your relationship with the tool vendor starts during the selection and evaluation process. If there are problems with the vendor now (when they want your money), there are likely to be more serious problems later!

EXPERIENCE REPORT

'We are currently using a test management product from a market leader in the testing tools industry, but we are now evaluating for a new tool for test management. There are two reasons for this. One is that the cost for 50 users is very expensive for us. The other reason is problems with the vendor. They are very arrogant yet have little product knowledge and no service attitude at all!'

10.6.4 Cost constraints

Cost is often the most stringent and most visible constraint on tool selection. But the purchase price of the tool may be only a fraction of the total cost of fully implementing the tool. Of course there must be guidelines, but it is also important not to be too rigidly bound by what may be a fairly arbitrary number.

Cost factors include:

- purchase or lease price (one-off, annual, or other anniversary renewal);
- cost basis (per seat, per computer, etc.);
- cost of training in the use of the tool (from the tool vendor);
- any additional hardware needed (e.g. PCs, additional disk space or memory);
- any additional software needed (e.g. updates to operating systems or netware);
- support costs (maintenance agreements);
- any additional start-up costs (e.g. consultancy to insure the tool is used in the best way);
- internal costs (for tool maintenance, establishing your own regime, implementing the tool within your own organization, etc.).

Note that the internal costs will be far more significant in the long term than all of the others, as discussed further in Chapter 11.

10.6.5 Political constraints

Political factors may well override all of the other constraints and requirements. For example, you may be required to buy the same tool that your parent company uses. There may be a restriction against buying anything other than a tool supported in your own country. Your boss's boss may have a brother who works for a tool vendor. It is frustrating to tool selectors to discover these factors late on in the selection process, so make inquiries now.

Don't underestimate the role of political factors. Although we like to think that tool purchase decisions are always based on rational technical factors, decisions are often based on emotional and irrational factors.

> **EXPERIENCE REPORT**
>
> We spent a week working with a large financial institution to help them in their tool selection. The selection process was performed very well, with the relevant people being included in the evaluations. Two shortlisted vendors (X and Y) were called in to give demonstrations, and the team made their decision to go for X. When the final budget went for approval from the highest levels, they were then told that in fact another branch of the company already had a company-wide license for Y! The political factor inquiry in this case did not go to a high enough level in the organization.

Identifying your constraints

10.6.6 Quality constraints

What are the required quality characteristics of the tool? This may include both functional and non-functional aspects. Here are some suggestions you might like to consider.

- How many users can use the tool at once? Can test scripts be shared?

- What skill level is required to use the tool effectively? How long does it take to become proficient? What programming skills are needed to write test scripts?

- What is the quality of the documentation supplied with the tool (paper or online)? How thorough is it? How usable is it? Are there 'quick reference guides,' for example?

- What about the help line, web site, or other support for the tool itself from the vendor?

- What is the frequency of failures during realistic use?

- Can it corrupt any of your data?

- What overheads are caused by the tool (how much time or resource does the tool itself use)?

- Can the tool integrate with other tools you are already using (e.g. configuration management and project management tools)?

We have found it very useful to apply a technique, known as the quality attribute technique, developed by Tom Gilb for specifying and testing non-functional qualities. An example of the use of Gilb's Quality Attribute Table for the evaluation of test execution tools is given in Table 10.1. Note that you will need to put your own numbers in the 'Must do' and 'Planned' levels to reflect your own requirements. The table is intended to show the types of non-functional attributes that can be expressed in this way, based on a real example.

The 'DM' in Table 10.1 is an abbreviation for 'Defect Measure'. This is defined as defects multiplied by a weighting factor reflecting their severity, so a single defect would count as one, five, or nine units of Defect Measure. The 'DM rate' is Defect Measure realized by one hour of test effort. Further details of the use of the quality attribute technique can be found in Gilb (1988).

Note that the 'Must do' level for reliability in Table 10.1 does not mean that at least one defect must be found – it means that one defect is the maximum that is acceptable.

EXPERIENCE REPORT: QUALITY OF THE TOOL

We discovered that the tool itself had a bug that would have given the wrong results for 84% of our Year 2000 tests. The tool would have said that the tests passed, when in fact they had failed.

Source: David Slacke

Table 10.1 Quantified evaluation criteria for a test execution tool.

Attribute	Test	Scale	Must do	Plan	Comment
Ease of use	Average time for at least three different people to complete the following tasks:				
	Invoke tool, select and start a sample of 10 tests	Minutes	3	1	Must be an assorted subset of tests
	Record 5 minute test case with three dynamic comparisons	Minutes	20	10	Use three different comparisons at different points within the test case
	Obtain summary statistics from run of set of test cases	Minutes	3	1	Should involve at least 100 test cases
Documentation usefulness	Time to learn how to perform four basic tasks (add a new test, add dynamic verification, execute test, analyze results)	Minutes	40	20	Use at least three people and take the average time
Reliability (of the tool)	Number of defects found weighted by severity	Defect Measure (DM rate)	1.0	0.1	Severe = 9 Moderate = 5 Minor = 1
	Number of critical defects found in evaluation	Number	1	0	
Availability	Time tool is available for effective use during evaluation	Percentage of total time in use	90%	100%	Evaluation period not less than 20 work hours

Table 10.1 Continued

Attribute	Test	Scale	Must do	Plan	Comment
Support service	Assessment by evaluation team grading on a scale of 1 (unacceptable) to 5 (excellent) (Intermediate grades are: poor; fair; good)	Average grade	3 (Fair)	4 (Good)	
Usefulness	Percentage of typical regression test cases which it is estimated can be automated within a reasonable time	Percentage of test cases	3 months: 10% 12 months: 50%	3 months: 20% 12 months: 70%	Consensus of all people involved in evaluation
Disk use	Count of working files created in using the tool	Number of extra files for each test	7	3	
	Largest amount of extra disk space used at any time during the execution of a set of tests	Factor of disk space used by manual tests	5 times more	2 times more	

Tom Gilb's quality attribute template was used to define the non-functional requirements for a test coverage tool. There were many arguments about what the numbers should have been, but it provided a useful thinking tool for specifying the expectations from the tool.

We defined performance of the test coverage tool in two ways: the time to instrument the code as a factor of the source code compile time, and the time to run the test using the instrumented code as a factor of normal (automated) test run time. The tools that were evaluated actually failed because their performance for test running was outside the 'Must do' level. We had set a planned level of twice as long to run, and a 'Must do' level of ten times longer to run. It actually took fourteen times longer to run the tests with the instrumented code than with the original software.

Source: Mark Fewster, Racal-Redac, 1991.

10.7 Build or buy?

After you have evaluated the commercial market, you may find that there are no tools that meet your requirements within your constraints. It is worth considering whether it might be better to build your own (or wait for the market to catch up with you).

If you build your own tool:

- it will be most suitable for your own needs;
- you may be able to compensate in the tool itself for a lack of testability in the software under test;
- the tool may be able to assume knowledge of your own applications, thereby reducing the work necessary to implement automated tests;
- it will probably not be very well supported in terms of documentation, help, and training;
- it may suffer from 'image' problems ('something developed by Joe in the next office can't possibly be as good as the tool described in this glossy color brochure from a tool vendor');
- the user interface may leave something to be desired (a tool developed by technical people often considers ease of use to be unimportant).

If you buy a commercially available tool:

- it will probably be considerably cheaper to achieve a given level of features and quality (such as usability) than the cost of developing the tool yourself (the cost of commercial tool development is spread over a large number of users; you have to bear all of that cost yourself if you develop your own);

- it should be well supported in terms of documentation, help, training, etc.;
- it is often seen as 'sexy' – something people want to be involved with;
- you will not entirely avoid building your own even if your basic engine is a commercial tool; you will still need to build support for your test automation regime.

If you do build your own, do not attempt to produce a tool on the same scale as the commercial tools. Remember in most cases they have been under development for many years, funded by numerous users in many organizations. Build the smallest and simplest tools that will give you immediate and real benefit. You might start by building some filters to use with your existing comparison tools, for example. You could collect information about any existing tools or utilities that different people or groups in your organization have already developed to meet some need within their own scope; these starting points can often be developed at minimal cost to give more general benefits to the organization.

10.8 Identifying what is available on the market

10.8.1 Feature evaluation

If you buy, the next step is to familiarize yourself with the general capabilities of the test automation tools available in the commercial marketplace.

Which features are the most important ones to meet your needs and objectives in your current situation? For example, if you need to synchronize with a database or a network, the tool should be able to detect the relevant signals so that the tests will stay in step with the application being tested.

Make a list of the features, and classify them into categories. Some are suggested below; use whatever categories are most useful to you. As a minimum, have categories for mandatory and not mandatory.

10.8.1.1 Mandatory
The mandatory features together with your constraints are used to rule out any tool that does not fulfill your essential conditions.

Make sure that the things you list as mandatory really are only the essential minimum required to solve your problem. The tool you choose will not have only these features, but without these features you could not use it at all.

10.8.1.2 Desirable
The desirable features are used to discriminate among those tools that fulfill all the essential conditions. You may want to divide this category into highly desirable and desirable.

10.8.1.3 Don't care
The 'don't care' category is used for features that are not of interest to you.

10.8.1.4 Features will change from one category to another
Note that your feature list will change as you progress in evaluating tools. You will almost certainly discover new features that you think are desirable as you go through the evaluation process. The tool vendors are sure to point out features they can supply but which you did not specifically request.

Other tool users may recommend a feature as essential because of their experience, which you may not have thought was so important. For example, you may not consider the importance of being able to update your test scripts automatically when the user interface changes because you are concentrating on the use of the execution tool for capturing tests the first time. However, this may be a significant running cost for using the testing tool in the future.

It is also possible that a feature that you thought was desirable is not required owing to the way other features are implemented.

10.8.1.5 Types of features
Some tool features are either present or absent, for example, whether the tool records mouse clicks. The evaluation of this type of feature is straightforward. If the feature is a mandatory requirement, then any tool that does not have this feature is eliminated from further consideration.

Other features may be present to a degree, or the tool may offer support for one of your requirements but only partially, for example, non-functional attributes such as ease of use. Some tools may be easier for non-technical people to use, but tedious for the technical test automator to use.

Evaluating this kind of feature is not as straightforward, as there may need to be a value judgment on some scale. The DESMET project, an ESPRIT (European strategic programme for research and development in information technology) method for rigorous method and tool selection, suggested a seven-point scale, given below in a slightly modified form.

---

5   has the greatest effect or fully supports the requirement;
4   very strong support but not fully complete;
3   strong support, probably adequate;
2   some support, but leaves a lot to be desired;
1   very little support, may be survivable;
0   no support whatever for this feature;
−1 this tool actually makes it more difficult to meet a requirement, or makes things worse.

More information on the DESMET methodology can be found in Kitchenham (1996) and Kitchenham *et al.* (1997).

Identifying what is available on the market

10.8.2 Producing the long list

How can you be sure you have investigated all of the tools that are commercially available? There are a large number of tools that provide support for testing, and the marketplace is constantly changing. If you do not cast your net wide enough, you may miss a tool that could be just what you need. The place to start is with 'information about the information,' i.e. lists of current testing tools.

There are several sources of information for currently available testing tools. The authors' web site has information about current sources of information, including publications and web sites.

Some of these sources may just be contact details for vendors, with no information about what the tools do. Others may have summary information about what each tool does, so you can at least eliminate the ones you are not interested in. Still others may contain evaluations of the tools themselves, with comments on how well they do what they do.

Your long list will contain all potentially suitable tools, i.e. all those which meet both your constraints and your mandatory features.

10.8.3 Constructing the shortlist

If there are more than three or four tools now in your long list, use your list of desirable features to eliminate some, so that you are left with a shortlist of two to four tools.

If your long list contains only one tool, you may wish to go ahead and evaluate that one for suitability. After all, you only need one tool in the end.

If your long list is empty, you will need to either relax your constraints and/or mandatory features list and try again, or consider building your own tool (see Section 10.7), or you may decide not to opt for tool support at this time.

If you want to try to find more tools, here are some possible sources:

- internal 'informal' tools or utilities;
- ask the vendors of your other software or hardware products;
- ask the vendors of testing tools which are almost suitable (for example if a tool does not yet run on your platform, ask whether the vendor has plans to port it soon);
- investigate whether you could use a tool if you ran it in a different environment than the one you had thought;
- check the testing features of other software development tools, such as CASE (Computer-Aided Software Engineering) tools;
- attend a testing conference or event with a tools exhibition;
- look for tools sourced from a country other than your own.

The end result of this part of the evaluation process is to have a list of two or three tools that all look suitable on paper for your requirements. Having several tools means that you should have a choice and can therefore better meet your needs, both for tool functions and features and for non-functional aspects of the tools.

10.9.1 Feature comparison

10.9.1.1 Collect current information about the tools

Contact the vendors of the shortlisted tools and arrange to have information sent (if you have not done this already). Study the information and compare features. Request further information from the vendors if the literature sent does not explain the tool function clearly enough.

If you are looking at three tools, X, Y, and Z, you may find a feature in X that is not in Y or Z. Ask the other vendors about this feature. They may have a different way of solving the same problem that would be suitable.

It can be very interesting to ask each vendor why their product is better than the competition. Pay close attention to what they don't say, as well as gaining ideas from what they do say.

Your function and feature list will be evolving at this point, depending on the information you are gathering and the greater understanding of what the tools can do. This should help you to decide between the tools.

A list of questions to ask the vendors is given in Table 10.2.

Table 10.2 Questions to ask tool vendors.

1. What does this tool do? What are the benefits of using this tool?

2. How can this tool solve my problems? Which of my current problems can and can't this tool help with? (You need to know what your own problems are.)

3. Will you demonstrate your tool using our tests on our site? What environment is needed to run this tool (version numbers of operating systems, RAM, network configuration, etc.)? How much disk space does it use?

4. What does this tool not do? What future enhancements are planned for the tool? (Note that this also indicates current limitations of the tool.) What influence do tool users have on future development of the tool?

5. Can tests be re-run in debug mode within the tool? Can the tests be run as a background task, so I can do other work while it is running the tests (if this matters)?

6. What is the market share of this tool? How do you define market share? (Every vendor will have a different definition, which makes their tool look best.)

7. Why is this tool better than other similar tools?

8. What proportion of tools sold are providing real benefits to the organizations which bought them? For those that have not succeeded, why haven't they? What will I have to do to be sure to succeed with this tool?

9. What support is available – training, consultancy, help desk, Service Level Agreement for resolution of problems, technical expertise in our area? What effort is needed in-house by us to support the tool?

10. What test planning standards, test processes, test structuring scheme, etc. need to be in place to gain real benefits from using this tool? (Ask if the vendor has read this book.)

11. What features are included to ease the learning curve for the tool?

12. How do other sites usually work with the tool?

13. Is there a user group? If so, can I attend the next meeting?

14. Can you give me the names of reference sites, and can I meet with at least two users who are achieving real benefits using this tool?

15. How many versions have been released in the past year? How is release management handled? Do you release a defect list with the product?

16. How many known defects are there in the tool currently? (If they say none, be wary!)

17. What are your QA and test processes? What testing is done on the tool itself? (What does the vendor know about testing in general?) Is the tool used to test itself? (This doesn't necessarily mean a lot.)

18. What kind of tailoring/customization is possible for this tool? What extensions, add-ons, and in-house routines have other users built? (This may indicate tool drawbacks or additional work that you will need to do to achieve the best benefit from the tool.)

19. How does this tool integrate with other tools, e.g. other testing tools, project management tools, configuration management tools, etc.? Ask specifically about tools you already have.

20. How long will it take to achieve real payback from this tool? Can you give me case histories of financial benefits from other users? (This is surprisingly difficult – not many users actually track it. Make sure you plan to!) Can you help me estimate how much effort will be involved in implementing this tool in my organization?

Thanks for contributions from Paul Herzlich, Peter Oakley, Peter Herriott and Matthew Flack.

10.9.1.2 Consult tool evaluation reports

This is the time to consult one or more of the publications that have evaluated testing tools, if the ones you are interested in are covered in such reports. These reports are often perceived as being very expensive. However, the cost of the report should be compared to the cost of someone's time in performing similar evaluations, and the cost of choosing the wrong tool because you did not know about something that was covered in published material. (Don't forget to allow time to read the report!)

10.9.1.3 Contact reference sites

Ask the shortlisted vendors to give you the names of a couple of their existing customers as references, preferably using the same hardware and software that you have. If there are user groups for any of the tools, contact them and attend one of their meetings if possible.

Contact the reference sites from each shortlisted vendor and ask them some questions about the tool. An example list is shown in Table 10.3.

Remember that the reference sites supplied by the vendor will be their best customers, and so they will likely be very happy with the tool. The user group is a better source of reference sites as you will find a better cross-section of experience with the tool. But those who have had the least success with this tool may not attend the user group either. You may be able to find people with both positive and negative experience of the tool by attending a special interest group in testing or a testing conference.

The reference site's situation will be different to yours, so the benefits or problems that they have had may not be the same as the ones that are important to you. However, the experience of someone else who bought a tool for similar reasons to yours is invaluable and well worth pursuing. Most people are very pleased to spare a couple of hours to talk about their experience with someone outside their company who is interested in what they have done.

Many vendors are aware that a tool does not always add up to a total solution and are keen to present it as part of a more comprehensive offering, often including consultancy and training beyond just their product. They usually understand the issues covered in this chapter and the next, because bad selection and bad implementation of their tools gives them a bad reputation. Because the vendors should have good experience in gaining the best from their tools, their solutions may enhance the tools significantly and are worth serious examination. Not all vendors may have this enlightened view, and it is always worth bearing in mind that the vendor is ultimately trying to persuade you to buy the product.

At any point in the selection and tool evaluation process it may become clear which tool will be the best choice. When this happens, any further activity may not influence the choice of tool but may still be useful in assessing in more detail how well the chosen tool will work in practice. It will either detect a catastrophic mismatch between the selected tool and your own environment, or will give you more confidence that you have selected a workable tool.

Table 10.3 Questions to ask other tool users.

---

1. How long have you been using this tool? Are you basically happy with it?

2. How many copies/licenses do you have? How many users can be supported? What hardware and software platforms are you using?

3. How did you evaluate and decide on this tool? Which other tools did you consider when purchasing this tool?

4. How does the tool perform? Are there any bottlenecks?

5. What is your impression of the vendor (commercial professionalism, ongoing level of support, documentation, and training)?

6. How many users actually use the tool? If the tool is not widely used, why not? (For example, technical problems with the tool, lack of management support to go through the learning curve, problems maintaining test scripts when software changes, resistance, lack of training, too much time pressure, etc.)

If the tool is currently 'shelfware,' i.e. not used, skip to question 18.

7. How much space does the tool-related test data take up, and how is this controlled? (This can be a hidden cost.)

8. Does the tool perform your entire set of tests or are there pre- and post-test activities that have to be performed manually? (If so, why?)

9. How easy is it to interpret the results of the automated tests?

10. What is your assessment of the quality of your own internal testing practices prior to acquiring the tool? How did the use of the tool affect the quality of the testing?

11. Were there any non-technical problems in your organization through introducing the tool, and how were they overcome?

12. Is the tool now integrated into your work processes and standard procedures? If so, how much effort and how much time did this take?

13. Were there any other benefits or problems in using the tool, which were not anticipated?

14. Do you feel the tool gives you value for money?

15. Have you saved any money by using this tool? Can you quantify the savings or improvements?

16. How long did it take you to achieve real benefits? What are the critical factors for achieving payback?

17. What improvements are needed in the tool? Is the vendor responsive to requested enhancements?

18. What were your objectives or success criteria when buying the tool? (For example, run more tests, more consistent regression tests, improvement in meeting release deadlines, improved productivity, capacity planning, performance assessment.)

19. Have your objectives been achieved? Were they the right objectives? If not, what should they have been?

20. If you were doing it over again now, would you still purchase this tool? What would you do differently?

Thanks to Peter Oakley for additional ideas.

10.9.2 In-house demonstrations

The advice in this section assumes that your shortlisted tools are not of the shrinkwrapped off-the-shelf variety. If you are going for this type of tool, you will need to do your own demonstration, since the vendors will not visit you to demonstrate the tool. The advice for what and how to demonstrate will still apply, but you will need to do more work if you are going to be as thorough.

If you do involve the vendors in the type of demonstrations we outline below, you need to gain their support for this process. Explain clearly what you expect from them in advance.

10.9.2.1 *Pre-supply tests to vendor*

Before contacting the vendor to arrange for them to visit you to do a tool demonstration, some preparatory work will help to make your assessment of the competing tools more efficient and unbiased. Prepare two test cases for tool demonstration:

- one of a normal 'mainstream' test case;
- one of a worst-case 'nightmare' case (or something more complex than normal).

Rehearse the tests manually, in order to discover any defects in the test cases themselves.

It is important that the tools be set up and used on your premises, using your own configuration, and we recommend this, if at all possible, for the demonstration. We have had clients report to us that they found this single step to be extremely valuable, when they discovered that their prime candidate tool simply would not run in their environment! Of course, the vendor may be able to put it right but this takes time, and it is better to know about it before you sign on the dotted line, not after.

> **EXPERIENCE REPORT**
>
> The three shortlisted tools seemed to have sorted themselves into order before the demonstrations. Tool X definitely looked like the one to have. However, when the vendor came, they could not make tool X run at all on the current environment. We ended up with tool Y (which was also suitable though it didn't have all of the things we would have liked).

Invite the vendors of all shortlisted tools to give demonstrations within a short time frame, for example on Monday, Wednesday, and Friday of the same week. This will make sure that your memory of a previous tool is still fresh when you see a different one.

Give vendors both of your test cases in advance, to be used in their demo. If they cannot cope with your two cases in their demo, there probably is not much hope of their tool being suitable. However, be prepared to be flexible about your prepared test cases. The tool may be able to solve your underlying problem in a different way than you had pictured. If your test cases are too rigid, you may eliminate a tool that would actually be suitable for you.

Find out what facilities the vendors require and make sure they are available. Prepare a list of questions (technical and commercial) to ask on the demo day. Allow time to write up your reactions to each of the tools immediately after each demonstration.

Prepare evaluation forms or checklists for:

- general vendor relationship (responsiveness, flexibility, technical knowledge);
- tool performance on your test cases. Set measurable objectives, such as time to run a test case on your own (first solo flight), time to run a reasonable set of test cases, or time to find an answer to a question in the documentation;
- typical test cases that you wish to automate.

10.9.2.2 Additional test on the day

Prepare one additional test case that is not supplied in advance to the vendor. After they have shown you what the tool can do with your other two test cases, see how easy it is to put this other one into the tool from 'cold.' This test case should be neither too easy nor too complex, but somewhere in the middle. This is illustrated in Figure 10.4.

10.9.2.3 Tool demonstrations from each vendor: on the day

Provide facilities for the vendor's presentation and demonstration. Listen to the presentation and ask the questions you had prepared. Observe what happens when the vendor sets up the tool in your environment. Perform the additional test and script maintenance test (see Section 18.9.3).

Ask (and note) any more questions that occur to you. Note any additional features or functions that you had not realized this tool provided. Note any features or functions that you thought it did provide but does not, or not in the form you had thought.

Try to keep all demonstrations the same as far as possible. It is easy for the last one to incorporate improvements learned during the other demonstrations, but this is not fair to the first one.

Thank and dismiss the vendor and then write up your observations and reactions to this tool.

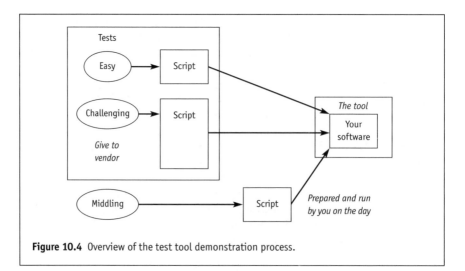

Figure 10.4 Overview of the test tool demonstration process.

10.9.2.4 Post-demonstration analysis

Ask the vendor you saw first any questions that occurred to you when watching a later vendor's presentation or demonstration. This will give the fairest comparison between the tools.

Assess tool performance against measurable criteria defined earlier, taking any special circumstances into account. Compare features and functions offered by competing tools. Compare non-functional attributes, such as usability. Compare the commercial attributes of vendor companies. You might want to test the technical support by ringing the vendor's help line and asking a technical question or two (you may need to gain the permission of the tool vendor for doing this).

10.9.3 Test of script maintenance

One other important aspect to investigate is how easy it will be to maintain the test scripts. This is an important investigation both for vendor in-house demonstrations and for shrinkwrapped tools.

Prepare an altered version of the software being tested. Make changes to it in line with what typically happens from release to release of your system. For example, if screen layouts usually change, then change the screen layout. If new fields are added, add a new field, and perhaps delete a field or move a field to a different screen.

Now replay one of your test cases through the new version of the software, to see how the tool copes.

Next edit the scripts until they run successfully. Note how easy or difficult this is, how error prone it is, how much editing is necessary, etc. Remember that you will ultimately adjust your approach to implementing automated test cases to minimize this type of effort, as described in the rest of this book. Some tools may be less susceptible to your most frequent types of software change than others, which will make the basic script editing easier. This is illustrated in Figure 10.5.

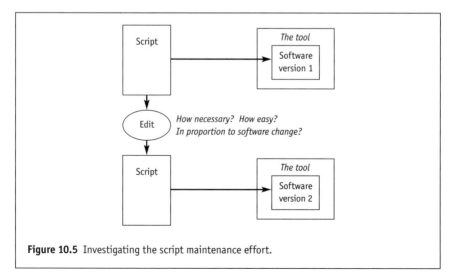

Figure 10.5 Investigating the script maintenance effort.

If a clear winner is now obvious, select the winning tool. Otherwise select two tools for a final competitive trial. Inform the non-selected vendors of your decision and give the reason for their elimination.

10.9.4 Competitive trial

An in-house competitive trial will give you a clearer idea of how the tool will work out in your own situation. This does involve additional effort, and is probably more appropriate for larger organizations where the tool chosen will eventually be used by a large number of people.

Many tool vendors will allow short-term use of the tool under an evaluation license, particularly for tools that are complex and represent a major investment. Such licenses will be for a limited period of time, and the evaluation team must plan and prepare for that evaluation accordingly.

EXPERIENCE REPORT

'We acquired an evaluation license for one month for our top candidate tools. However, the people who really ought to have been evaluating it were tied up in higher-priority activities. They kept thinking they would be free very soon, but a month is not very long and our time was up before we had a chance for all but a very cursory look at the tool. Effectively, our evaluation license was wasted.'

(Note that you may be able to obtain a free extension to the evaluation license, but don't count on it.)

The preparation for the trial period includes selecting or designing a set of test cases to be used by the tools in the trial. Measurable success criteria for the evaluated tools should be planned in advance, for example, length of time to record a test case (perhaps expressed as a multiple of the time taken to run the test case manually – see Chapter 8), and the number of discrepancies found in comparison (real, extraneous, and any missed). Attending a training course for each tool will help to insure that they will be used in the right way during the evaluation period.

When you perform the competitive trial evaluation, install each tool and run your chosen test cases. Insure that all mandatory requirements are met. Use the discriminatory factors and the ranked list of features and functions to give an objective score to each tool. Measure the success criteria and estimate the potential savings.

Finally, analyze the results of the trial. Compare the features and functions offered by the tools. Compare the non-functional attributes, especially usability, and general 'gut feel.' Compare the commercial attributes of vendor companies, and experience in tool installation and support during the trial. Compare other users' experiences in using the tool, from reference sites. A tool that looks impressive at a one-day demonstration may not be the best tool at the end of the trial.

Assess any additional tool features that were not evaluated in this trial, but that are likely to be required at a later date. This may influence your choice of tool, especially if there is more than one tool that is suitable in all other respects.

10.10 Making the decision

10.10.1 Assess against the business case

Having spent a considerable amount of effort in assessing the candidate tool(s), the evaluation report would normally recommend the purchase of the tool that best meets the requirements and constraints of the organization.

Before making this recommendation, assess the business case: will the potential savings from this tool give a good return on investment, including purchase/lease price, training costs, and ongoing internal tool costs? The likely benefits need to be clearly communicated, so that expectations for the benefits are realistic. Deciding not to go ahead with purchasing any of the tools investigated could be the best economic decision at this time; do not be afraid to make it if a tool is not justified.

10.10.2 When to stop evaluating

If there is only one clear candidate tool, you could stop evaluating as soon as this became obvious. However, it may be better to continue with the evaluation process until all of the people involved are happy with the final decision. Otherwise there may be problems later on if some people believe the evaluation was not done thoroughly enough (see Figure 10.6).

If a clear-cut winner is still not obvious, then you are likely to be equally successful with any of your shortlisted tools. Commercial factors such as the status of the tool supplier, the flexibility of licensing arrangements, or the company most willing to be flexible on some other aspect of

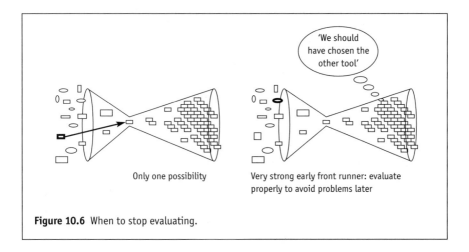

Only one possibility

Very strong early front runner: evaluate properly to avoid problems later

'We should have chosen the other tool'

Figure 10.6 When to stop evaluating.

the purchase may now become the deciding factor. If the commercial factors have not swayed the decision to a particular vendor, then further agonizing over the choice will not be profitable. If the technical and other issues cannot make the decision, then trust intuitive feelings about the people involved. Or you could always just flip a coin! (See Figure 10.7.)

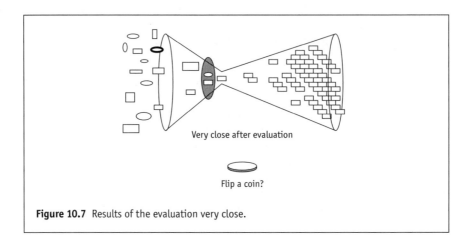

Very close after evaluation

Flip a coin?

Figure 10.7 Results of the evaluation very close.

10.10.3 Completing the evaluation and selection process

Inform the winning vendor, and let them know what your organization's purchasing procedure is. For example, if a management meeting has to approve the expenditure and purchase orders have to be raised, it may be several weeks or even months before you can begin using the tool.

It is also an important courtesy to inform the loser(s), and to let them know why you have decided on another tool.

You should prepare a short written report on your evaluation, including your criteria for selection and the scores of each of the evaluated tools. Be as brief as possible, but do include sufficient information so that anyone who was not involved in the selection process can see what happened.

The selection and evaluation process should be limited in time, but once the winning tool has been identified, the more significant process of implementing the tool within the organization can start being planned. This is the subject of the next chapter.

Summary

Choosing which tool to buy is a project in its own right. It requires a team of people (not full time) and a team leader (ideally full time) to guide the selection process in a medium-sized organization.

The place to start is to identify the current problems in testing, and to evaluate different solutions, including the purchase of test automation tools. The cost justification for the tool should be written up as a business case.

Organizational constraints on tool purchase must also be identified, such as environment, cost, quality, commercial, and political factors. Any tools that meet the requirements will go into the initial long list for consideration.

A list of features that are mandatory, desirable, or optional is prepared, and available tools are compared to this list. The feature analysis will help to eliminate the less suitable tools to form a shortlist of perhaps three candidate tools.

The shortlisted tools are compared with each other in more detail. Evaluation reports and reference sites give an idea of other people's experiences using the tools. If appropriate, in-house demonstrations are organized with each vendor. The tools should be tested with realistic test cases, and the maintenance of the test cases when the software changes should also be investigated. If needed, a competitive trial of the top two tools is then carried out.

The decision to purchase should be based on a business case for a realistic anticipated cost–benefit ratio.

CHAPTER ELEVEN

Implementing tools within the organization

11.1 What could go wrong?

We begin this chapter with a test automation horror story. It is Robert Glass's report on a keynote presentation given by Linda Hayes.

EXPERIENCE REPORT: TESTING AUTOMATION – A HORROR STORY

This story started on a real high note. The evaluation team that chose the tool to try out won a corporate excellence award. The company involved bought 82 copies of the tool, then another 20 later during what Hayes called the 'honeymoon' period.

And the honeymoon was truly a honeymoon. Using the test tool to perform capture/playback of old test data to re-run the test cases, the company cut tasks that had taken 8 hours down to 1.5 hours.

But very quickly, things started coming unravelled. As the application of the tool broadened to new PC applications, there was confusion – capture/playback is ineffective if there is nothing yet to capture. Furthermore, internal competition began. A newly formed user group dissolved in standardization attempts – '80 people invented 80 different approaches.' At the end of this period, Hayes said, we 'woke up with this hangover called maintenance.'

What had gone wrong? Even back at the beginning, Hayes said, when the evaluation team was winning its excellence award, a severe mistake was made. The chief goal for tool selection had been 'ease of use.' But ease of use did not equate to good functionality. It was too easy to misuse the tool, and there were things it simply couldn't do very well.

Another problem had arisen because of the decentralized nature of the testing organizations. Different users of the tool had used it in different ways (that's why the standardization effort was such a nightmare).

Source: Robert Glass, in *The Software Practitioner*, 1416 Sare Road, Bloomington, IN 47401 USA. Used with permission.

What should have been done differently? According to Hayes, at least these things:

- more comprehensive selection criteria should have been used;
- centralization of use of the tool was essential, in order to standardize on ways of using the tool;
- assigned roles and responsibilities were essential to any centralization effort;
- a small-scale pilot study should have been conducted to further understand the value of the tool.

The real bottom line, from Hayes' point of view? 'You can't automate a process that's not yet defined.'

11.2 Importance of managing the implementation process

Once a tool has been chosen, the real work starts. Although it is important to choose carefully, success in the tool's use is by no means guaranteed, as is illustrated in the Experience Report. This chapter covers the critical implementation factors in ensuring that the potential benefits from the purchased tool are actually achieved.

As in Chapter 10, we are aiming this chapter at medium to large organizations, which should follow these steps more formally. However, if you are in a small organization, it is important to consider who will perform the roles, and how the implementation will be planned. Even though the whole process will be more informal, the steps described still need to be followed in order to increase your chances of succeeding with test automation.

11.2.1 Tools tend towards shelfware

There are many organizations that have successfully chosen and purchased a test execution tool but around half of those organizations have not achieved any benefit from their investment because their tools have ended up not being used, i.e. on the shelf or '**shelfware**.'

At various events, we have asked the audience for a show of hands for their current status with testing tools. Here are some results:

February 1995, 150 attendees at the British Computer Society's Specialist Interest Group in Software Testing (BCS SIGIST) in London:
50% had shelfware

May 1997, 1250 attendees at the Software Testing Analysis and Review (STAR97) conference in San Jose, California:
45% had shelfware

350 attendees at the International Conference on Testing Computer Software in Washington DC:

45% had shelfware in 1997

40% had shelfware in 1998

(See our web site for more recent surveys.)

Testing tools are not alone in this. Do you remember the late 1980s when CASE tools were really 'hot'? Whatever happened to them?

After one year:

70% of CASE tools and techniques were never used

25% were used only by one group

5% were widely used but generally not to capacity

Less than 25% of organizations were using CASE. Single organizations were not using 80–90% of the CASE tool packages they had purchased (Kemerer, 1992).

11.2.2 The tool implementation process

If the process of tool selection is one of gradually narrowing down the choices, the implementation process is the reverse: it is a process of gradually widening the tool's acceptance, use, and benefits, as illustrated in Figure 11.1.

The cost of purchasing or leasing a tool is a minor cost compared with the cost of the internal effort needed to implement it. This includes 'selling' the tool internally, providing support and training, and building the infrastructure to support the ongoing test automation regime.

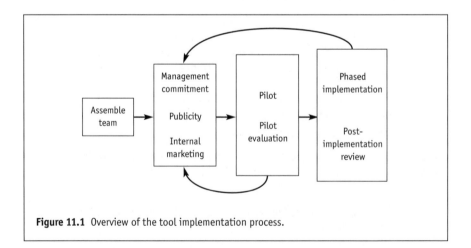

Figure 11.1 Overview of the tool implementation process.

11.2.3 Change management

The important thing to remember is that when you introduce a testing tool into an organization, this will change the way people work. People generally do not like change, but there are ways to make the process of change easier for everyone involved.

The process described in this chapter is adapted for test automation tools, but is based on the principles of the management of change. Books and courses are available that go more deeply into this topic in its own right. If you are the change agent within your organization, it is worth investigating these in more depth.

11.3 Roles in the implementation/change process

The following roles are important to consider in any organization. In a small organization, one person may actually play all roles (although there is then a danger of automation being abandoned if that person leaves). In larger organizations, some of the roles may be full time.

11.3.1 Tool 'champion'

In every successful implementation of test automation that we have seen, there is one person who is the focal point for the introduction of the tool. This person is a very enthusiastic believer in test automation, and has a clear vision of the benefits that test automation can bring to the company. This person could also be called an evangelist; he or she tends to try to convert everyone to the cause.

The champion will likely have been the driving force behind the tool evaluation and selection effort. He or she will not need to be highly technical, although should have a good basic understanding of the technical problems likely to be encountered. The champion must also work well with people, and be diplomatic and patient.

Changing the way people work takes a long time and is not easy. It can be a rather thankless task at times, so it also helps if the champion doesn't mind others taking the credit for the changes that he or she suggested. You know you have succeeded as a champion when your boss says, 'I've just had an idea ...,' and your reply is 'Oh, that's a good idea' although it is one of your own and you have been pushing it for ages!

Having a good champion does not guarantee a successful implementation, but not having a champion probably guarantees an unsuccessful one.

11.3.2 Change agent

The change agent is the person who plans and manages the process of change within the organization. This may be the same person as the champion, or in a larger organization it may be a separate person.

The change agent is in charge of the day-to-day progress of the tool uptake while it is being phased into the working practices of the organization. The change agent's task is to plan what changes will happen to whom and when, and to lead people through these changes. The change agent's job may or may not be full time.

There is much very useful advice in Barbara Bouldin's book, *Agents of Change* (1989). Although this book was written for the introduction of CASE tools, the method is directly applicable to the introduction of testing tools.

The qualities needed by the change agent (adapted from Bouldin) are:

- recent and extensive experience in testing;
- progressive rather than reactionary personality;
- practical and business orientation, as well as technical background;
- highly developed analytical skills.

11.3.3 Management sponsor or 'angel'

It is critical that the change initiative has the support of top management in order to succeed. It helps if there is a very senior person who visibly supports the champion and change agent, and makes it known that test automation is something that meets with his or her approval. The sponsor could also be the champion.

11.3.4 Tool custodian

The tool custodian may be the same person as the change agent and/or champion, but is more likely to be a separate role. He or she is responsible for technical tool support, implementing upgrades from the vendor, and providing internal help or consultancy in the use of the tool.

This person would also be in charge of implementing any of the additional interfaces to the purchased tool, such as the interpreters for Action Words as described by Hans Buwalda in Chapter 22.

The tool custodian would also be the likely owner of the standards for the way in which the tool is to be used. These standards would be developed as part of the implementation project.

11.3.5 The implementation team

The team that selected the tool may also be the team that helps to implement it. Ideally it would include representatives from the different parts of the organization that would be expected to use the tool. In particular, it should include end users if the tool will be used for user acceptance testing.

The team will meet regularly (perhaps one day a month) over a period of months or years. It has two tasks, an inward-facing and an outward-facing one.

11.3.5.1 Information gathering

The team's inward-facing task is to gather information from their own part of the organization. They should find out what people need, want, and expect from the test automation tool, and feed this information back to the rest of the implementation team and the change agent. This will be used to guide the implementation process and to insure that important needs are addressed. This is discussed further in Section 11.5.6.

11.3.5.2 Dissemination of information and support

The outward-facing task for each team member is to act as a mini change agent within his or her own area. They need to keep people informed about what is happening, help to raise enthusiasm while tempering unrealistic expectations, and help to solve problems which arise when the tools begin to be used in earnest within their groups.

The implementation team may also play the role of internal consultants in test automation. It will be useful to capitalize on this and have them provide support for improving testing practices as well by looking for opportunities to improve test effectiveness. This will slightly increase the scope of their work, but may give dramatic payback if current testing practice is weak.

EXPERIENCE REPORT

We have recently implemented an automated test tool, and in hindsight should have planned the implementation with these roles in mind. Although we are currently only a small testing team, I can see that unless we elect a 'tool custodian' soon, our tool could end up becoming shelfware.

Source: Melanie Smith, Gartmore Investment Management plc

11.4 Management commitment

11.4.1 Importance for success

If a tool has been selected and purchased, then there already is a level of management commitment to tool support for software testing. But the commitment needed from top management is not just a one-off agreement to purchase the tool, but needs to be continual throughout the implementation process, especially when things get difficult.

In order to gain initial management commitment, the champion or change agent will present the business case for the selected tool, summarize the tool selection and evaluation results, and give realistic estimates and plans for the tool implementation process.

The change agent must have adequate support from management in at least two ways: first, visible backing from high-level managers; and second, adequate time, funding, and resourcing (this may mean adversely impacting other projects in the short term). Having visible backing without adequate support is classic 'lip service' and is the way to end up with shelfware.

11.4.2 Realistic expectations

Managers also need to realize that the first thing that happens when a tool is used for the first time is that productivity goes down, even though the tool is intended ultimately to increase productivity. Adequate time (i.e. months rather than weeks) must be allowed for learning and 'teething problems,' otherwise the tool will be abandoned at its point of least benefit and greatest cost.

In our industry there is a tendency to latch on to each new initiative as a 'silver bullet' which will solve all our problems. But no technology can solve all problems, and testing tools will not solve all testing problems either. The tools can bring significant benefits, but not without some hard work.

In selling the idea of test automation, the champion does need to generate enough enthusiasm so that management will be willing to invest in it. However, if the picture painted is unrealistically optimistic, the benefits will not be achieved. The champion must find a good balance point between achievable and saleable benefits.

You will be seen in a better light if you are successful in achieving a lower target than if you fail to achieve a more ambitious target.

11.5 Preparation

11.5.1 Publicity

Once you have the management commitment, both verbal and financial (which may just be time allowed to work on the implementation), the change agent needs to begin putting in place a continuing and highly visible publicity machine. All those who will eventually be affected need to be informed about the changes that will be coming their way.

Most people seriously underestimate the amount of publicity that is needed for successful implementation. People are not convinced by one presentation, and even if they are, they don't stay convinced over time. Your role as change agent is to provide a constant drip-feed of publicity about the tool, who is using it, success stories, and problems overcome.

The larger the organization, the more publicity is needed.

11.5.2 Raising initial interest

The first step is simply to raise interest in the new tool, for example by giving internal demonstrations, or just going and talking to people about it. This initial blitz may last for weeks before anything else happens, but it lets people know that something will be coming.

Once the managing director had bought in to the idea of test automation, we wanted to tell all the software engineers what was planned. First we asked if we could assemble everyone in the dining room during working hours, but that was not allowed. So how could we persuade around 100 software engineers to attend an out-of-hours presentation on software testing? The answer was to hold the event one evening in the local pub, and to supply free beer, chicken, and fries. Over 80 of the engineers came. Testing had never been so popular!

Source: Mark Fewster, Racal Redac, 1991 (see Chapter 12).

11.5.3 Continuing publicity

The most important publicity is from the earliest real use of the tool, for example from the pilot project (see below). The benefits gained on a small scale should be widely publicized to increase the desire and motivation to use the tool. 'Testimonials,' particularly from converted skeptics, are often more effective than statistics.

It is also important to give relevant bad news to keep expectations at a realistic level. As the implementation project proceeds it is possible you will discover that some of the planned uses of the tool are not practical or will not work as expected. Be sure to let others know ahead of time so they will not be disappointed.

Throughout the implementation project, it is important to continue to give a constant supply of information about the test automation efforts. There is no substitute for regular communication with the people you want to influence. This may be a mixture of special events such as demonstrations, publications such as a test automation newsletter, announcements that appear when people first switch on their machines, competitions with silly prizes, or whatever works in your organization.

Publicity is an activity that is constant throughout the implementation. Although we do not specifically return to the topic, you will need to keep returning to publicity activities.

11.5.4 Test your demonstrations

It is also important to make sure that when you do organize a demonstration, you have carefully tested it beforehand, or you will very quickly lose all credibility and this will endanger the whole test automation initiative.

During a visit to a client, a 'demonstration' of the automated tests was not particularly successful since it took a number of attempts to run the tests (some wrong files had been used in the first instance). This did not give a good impression to those watching this demonstration.

11.5.5 Using an evaluation license to confirm suitability

Most people think that the main purpose of an evaluation license is to evaluate a tool. However, if you have made your decision, either with or without using an evaluation license, it can be well worthwhile to use the evaluation license to investigate how your own organization would be able to use the tool (as opposed to evaluating the tool itself).

EXPERIENCE REPORT

Alison Tipper reported about using the evaluation license as the first step of their implementation of their selected tool. They found that there was significant benefit from using the evaluation license time to explore how they might use the tool. This prepared people for more effective take-up of the tool when it was implemented 'for real,' as they had overcome a number of teething problems already.

Source: Alison Tipper, presentation at EuroSTAR93.

11.5.6 Internal market research

In parallel with the publicity drive, the change agent and the change management team need to do a significant amount of internal market research, talking to the people who are the targeted users of the tool. Find out how the different individuals currently organize their testing and how they would want to use the tool, and whether it can meet their needs, either as it is or with some adjustments. The lines of communication set up by interviewing potential tool users can also be used to address the worries and fears about using the tool that contribute to people's resistance to change.

11.6 Pilot project

11.6.1 Why do a pilot?

'If you don't know what you're doing, don't do it on a large scale' (Gilb, 1988, p.11).

It is best to try out the tool on a small pilot project first. This insures that any problems encountered in its use are ironed out when only a small number of people are using it. It also enables you to see how the tool will affect the way you do your testing, and gives you some idea about how you may need to modify your existing procedures or standards to make best use of the tool.

The pilot project should start by defining a business case for the use of the tool on this project, with measurable success factors. For example, you may want to reduce the time to run regression tests from a week to a day. Actually, applying the 'don't be overly optimistic' rule, it may be better to set a target such as reducing the time for 20% of the tests by a factor of 50%. This may result in a five-day regression test taking four and a half days, but might be a much easier target to hit. The pilot project should be neither too long nor too short, say between two and four months. Subsequent phases of the pilot project could extend this time beyond four months but each phase should have measurable objectives. If the pilot drags on too long without producing tangible results it will cast doubt on the viability of test automation. Small benefits gained quickly are much better than larger benefits that are a long time coming, and they are also less risky.

EXPERIENCE REPORT

In a small organization, there is more emphasis on the pilot and less on marketing the concept. There's more cooperation between testers and developers in an effort to make it somewhat of a 'development' effort. I've found by doing this that the developers begin to 'get into it' and start to identify other areas of development (i.e. unit or early integration test) where automation can be used.

Source: Kerry Zallar.

11.6.2 Assess the changes to your testing processes

The use of the testing tool will change your testing procedures in ways that you will probably not expect. To understand this effect, consider the following analogy of purchasing a domestic appliance:

Suppose you decided that washing dishes was taking up too much time. After considering other alternatives, such as hiring someone to help with the housework, you decided that the answer was to buy a dishwasher.

You made a list of the essential and desirable features of the dishwasher, and started comparing the different offerings against this list. You asked some of your friends about dishwashers, and through their experience became convinced that you needed to add 'quiet operation' to the list of features.

Eventually you purchased and installed a particular machine which best met your requirements.

Now, three weeks later, you find that the dishwasher has altered your household routine. On the one hand, it had the desired effect and reduced the activities associated with washing dishes from 40 minutes to 15 minutes after each meal. However, you now find that you spend about 10 minutes unloading the dishwasher every morning. Previously, you put dishes away as you washed them, so this is effectively an extra job to do.

Furthermore, you no longer have as much social time chatting with your partner while washing up after a meal, so you feel that you have lost something of value along with gaining the extra time.

In short, the dishwasher changed your domestic routine in ways that you did not expect.

The implementation of a new testing tool will also have effects that are not anticipated. For example, using a test execution tool may make debugging more difficult; previously, when testing manually, you knew where you were when something went wrong, which would help you to find the bug. Using the tool, you only know afterwards that something went wrong, and you then have to spend time recreating the context of the bug before you can find it. So there is an extra job to do which you did not have to do before.

You may find that you lose some value in the testing process through the use of the tool as well. For example, when running tests manually testers often think of other things to test while they are supposed to be following a script. They could either divert from the script or make a note of new tests to add, but the inspiration for the new tests was a by-product of running the planned tests. Having a tool run the tests guarantees no diversion from the script, but does not yield any new tests.

You need to make sure that the negative effects of the tool, anticipated or not, real or perceived, do not outweigh the realized benefits of test automation.

11.6.3 Set up and trial your automated regime

The pilot project is the place to experiment and to discover how to build automated Test Suites that will be sufficiently easy to maintain in real situations, using the principles described in this book. Once your script structure, data organization, naming conventions, etc. have been seen to work well in the pilot, they can be rolled out to a wider set of tool users.

11.6.4 Evaluation of results from pilot

After the pilot project is completed, the results should be compared to the business case for this project. If the objectives have been met, then the tool has been successful on a small scale and can safely be scaled up. The lessons learned on the pilot project will help to make sure that the next project can gain even greater benefits.

If the objectives have not been met, then either the tool is not suitable or it is not yet being used in a suitable way (assuming that the objectives were not overly optimistic). Determine why the pilot was not successful, and decide the next steps to take. Do not attempt to use the tool on a wider scale if you cannot explain why it has not succeeded on a small scale. The overheads for start-up may be much more significant on a small scale, for example, and may not have been adequately taken into account in the initial business case. It is best to proceed fairly cautiously in scaling up, and to increase tool use incrementally by one project group at a time.

For example, the pilot project in its later stages may want to use some of the metrics described in Chapter 8 to monitor the benefits. If test creation time seems to be a problem in early attempts to automate, the pilot can try to shorten this time, while keeping the test maintenance costs or time under control.

11.7.1 Importance of planning

Assuming the pilot project was successful, the use of the tool in the rest of the organization can now be planned. This is a major activity in any organization, and without careful planning, it will not be successful. It is also important that the plans react to any problems encountered, so they need to be flexible.

The following are the tasks to be done in the roll-out period:

- publicize the success of the pilot project as widely as possible;
- modify company policies and strategies to take test automation into account;
- insure that project managers take note of test automation issues in project plans, quality plans, and test plans;
- continue to build a good infrastructure for your regime;
- aim to make it easier to use the tool than to test manually;
- schedule when different groups will get involved in test automation;
- monitor test automation efficiency;
- train both direct and indirect users of the test automation.

The change agent and change management team can act as internal consultants to the new tool users, and can perform a very useful role in coordinating the growing body of knowledge about the use of the tool within the organization.

11.7.2 Provision of training in tool use

It is very important to follow through on the tool investment by insuring that adequate training is given in its use. A tool that is not being used properly will not give the benefits that could be realized.

Every tool user should be trained in the way that is appropriate for them. For those who will use the tool directly, this usually means the training given by the vendor of the tool.

There may be scope for a brief introductory course to start with, followed by more detail after a few months of use, with regular technical updates and expert tips at, say, six-monthly intervals after that. The cost of training is paid back many times by expert use of the tool, and this is what gives the real payback from the tool investment. Attendance at tool user groups can also be very useful to pick up new tips for better use of the tool.

Once your own regime is in place, the training for users of test automation may consist exclusively of how to use the additional procedures, routines, spreadsheets, etc. which you have set up to interface to the tools themselves. This latter training you must design (and probably present) yourselves, since it is based on your own way of doing things, that is, your test automation regime.

You might ask: 'Why not just send a couple of people on the vendor's course – surely we don't need to send everyone who will use the tool?' It is not fair to expect those sent on the course to 'train the others,' unless this is a very explicit task. People do not learn new skills by osmosis, sitting next to someone who has been trained!

If you do wish to use second-hand internal training instead of vendor training, then your internal trainers will need a level of expertise in the tool similar to the vendor's trainers, which only comes with plenty of experience.

They will also need to be excellent presenters, which is not always true of technical people. They will need time to put together an internal course; this typically takes many times the course time (e.g. 10–25 hours of preparation per course hour for good quality course material). During this time, they will not be doing any testing.

This approach may be a viable proposition for very large organizations, but if properly costed out, vendor training is generally much cheaper. Most vendors will be able to do on-site training, an option worth exploring.

11.7.3 Monitoring test automation efficiency

Test automation can only be a real benefit if the effort saved in using automation significantly outweighs the effort put into using it. To insure real success with any automation project the effort put in and the effort saved must be measured. (See Chapter 8 for ideas on key factors to monitor.)

11.8 Special problems in implementing testing tools

11.8.1 Interfaces to other tools and systems

The implementation of development tools tends to be planned when it should be, at the start of a project. Unfortunately, this is not always the case for testing tools. This presents some additional problems.

The testing tools may need to work with or interface to other tools that are already in place, such as configuration management, development tools, or project management tools.

The testing tools will also have to interface to the software under test. There can be significant problems in synchronizing tests with the software, which may or may not be easy to overcome.

11.8.2 Time for the learning curve

The learning time for a testing tool seems to be more critical from a psychological point of view than the same learning time for a development tool. Although a week of training near the end of a project takes the same amount of time as a week of training at the beginning of a project, somehow it seems longer. Actually this is one of the many reasons why a test automation tool should never be introduced to a critical project that is running late.

In one afternoon we saved a client a significant amount of money (around 4 person-weeks of work by vendor consultants) as well as clinching the sale of the tool to the client, by resolving a misunderstanding on each side.

The client already had existing tests in a word processor in a standard format. These were able to be automatically translated into tool scripts. This was good.

When the tool scripts were run, there was a synchronization problem between the test execution tool and the software under test, which had been developed using a 4GL. When the tool replayed the test inputs, the software saw the first input, processed it, and then hung up waiting for the second input. However, the tool had already sent all of the inputs by the time the software was ready for the second input.

The 4GL company came up with a solution: add an 'end of processing' trigger to send a signal to the screen (think of it as writing a message saying 'I am ready now'), which the test tool could then pick up and read. The tool vendor assured the client that this would work, and referred to the synchronization as an 'arbitrary wait,' meaning wait for an arbitrary message. After sorting out some teething troubles, this did indeed work. All of the test scripts would now need to have the 'wait' statements added.

However, the client's misunderstanding was that an 'arbitrary wait' meant a wait for x seconds. (This is the way the term had been used by other vendors.) Since they wanted to use this tool to measure performance while the tests were being run, this did not seem a viable solution to them.

Meantime, the vendor's misunderstanding was in thinking that the 'wait' statements were required to be added automatically as part of the translation process from the word processed test scripts into the tool scripts. This task was not trivial, and was estimated to take around 4 person-weeks of vendor consultants' time, with no guarantee that it would actually work correctly in all cases.

Both of these misunderstandings were resolved (by asking 'stupid questions,' a technique we commend to all consultants). The client was quite happy to insert the wait statements into the word-processed scripts manually, thus saving the 4 weeks of effort. The sale was insured when they realized they could still measure performance, since the waits were not for an arbitrary length of time, but for the ready signal.

11.8.3 In a maintenance environment

It is in maintenance that the greatest benefits can be gained from test automation, by automating regression tests that can then be run every time the system is changed. However, if your starting point is a completely manual test environment, where should you start to automate?

Benefits can be achieved by automating only a small proportion of the tests – for example, your current regression test bottlenecks or those tests which are the most tedious or error prone to run manually, the bug fixes, or just the most critical core business functions.

You do not need to automate everything – in fact, you cannot. Aim for a gradual build-up of tests over time, with the tests being automated giving the greatest benefit for the least effort.

Over time, you will become better and better at building automated tests, particularly in a maintenance environment. This should lead to a cycle of continuous improvement in your test automation regime.

11.9 People issues

11.9.1 Dangers of not managing people issues

Managing change is all about people issues, for it is the way people work that is being changed. A good manager will be sensitive to these issues, but often technical people are not aware of the effects a technical change can have on people emotionally and psychologically.

If you go about trying to change the way people work in the wrong way, you may engender suspicion about the value of the change, and resistance to the change. Resistance is a natural part of the process of change, but if it is not handled well, it can lead to resentment or even sabotage of the change effort. An attitude of 'We tried that once and we're certainly not going to try it again' can make any future change attempts much more difficult.

EXPERIENCE REPORT

There is a cultural change required in order to get a tool adopted by the developers and testers. We don't really have time for the cultural change, and the additional tools don't fit into the development budgets. There are also additional hardware requirements for these tools, and that's sometimes enough to kill their usage. The testers can't administer these tools alone, so they need to steal time from the developers – time that's just not available, at any price.

Most projects are agreeing to use a capture playback tool to build up a set of regression tests, but when it comes to actually getting the scripts into a state where we can replay them, we run out of time. Actually, by the time we get through running and debugging a test case, there's little time to get it into an automated script at all, let alone debug the automated scripts. So the tools are not free (even after you have paid for them).

Source: Norm Goodkin, president, Quality Matrix International, Inc.

11.9.2 The change equation

This is a psychological equation, not a mathematical one. We first encountered it at church (where it applies equally well).

Change only occurs when three things are greater than the fourth.

$$f\,(a,\,b,\,c) > z$$

where a is dissatisfaction with the current state, b is a shared vision of the future, and c is concrete knowledge about the steps to get from a to b. These three things taken together must be greater than z, the psychological or emotional cost to the individual of changing the way they work.

This equation explains many things about the change process. There are some people who will jump on any bandwagon that comes along – they have a very low threshold of change, and are easily dissatisfied with the status quo.

At the other extreme are people who say 'I've done it like this for 30 years and I'm not about to do it any differently, no matter what.' These people have a very high threshold of change and will be very resistant to any new ideas.

11.9.3 How to persuade people to change the way they work

It is very difficult to change someone's psychological personality, i.e. to alter the value of z in the above equation.

However, the way to encourage people to change the way they work is to concentrate on the other three things (a, b, and c). Make them more dissatisfied with the current way testing is done ('You mean you're still doing all that testing by hand?'). Give them a fuller vision of the way things could be in the future ('Come and see what we've been able to do in the pilot, and see if some of this might be of interest to you'). Explain the first easy step toward a complete change ('Let us help you automate a few key tests for you to try on the next project').

This is probably the most important thing you can do: to give them more detailed information about the steps they need to take from where they are now to where you want them to be in the future. People don't like taking large steps into the dark, but if you illuminate the way, they can usually be convinced to take a small step forward. Note this is one reason why you need to plan the implementation, so that you have these steps mapped out in advance!

11.9.4 Successful change breeds further change

Once people begin to change the way they work, change breeds further change, provided the experience is a good one. Once they have taken the first step and found that it was beneficial, they will be more willing to take the next step, i.e. their threshold of change will be lower.

For example, if someone currently spends too much time in some tedious and error-prone task, such as populating a database before a test can be run, you could set up the test automation tool to do just this one job for them. In the first instance you may need to do it for them if they are not confident to do it themselves. In any case, they will need your support ('hold their hand') as they have their first experience of using the tool. If you can insure that this experience is both pleasant and beneficial for them, you probably have a convert, who will go on to use the tool in all of the ways it could provide benefits for them.

11.9.5 Categories of changeableness

Your best friends in your change effort are not the 5% of people who will immediately rally to your cause, because when the next bandwagon comes along, they will immediately dump you and go onto the next one.

You should concentrate first on the 'early adopters.' This is around 15% of the people, who will take a bit of convincing, but are prepared to change if it looks like it could bring benefits. This may include highly respected opinion leaders. These would be the people involved in the pilot project.

If there is someone who is very skeptical, and makes no secret about it, it is worth spending some time with him or her. If you can convert a skeptic to your cause, he or she may well become one of your most enthusiastic supporters. It is generally more convincing to other people when a known skeptic now supports test automation. The early majority (around 30–35%) will be the people targeted for the first roll-out of the phased implementation, followed by the late majority (30–35%). Of course, the decision about who is involved when is not determined simply by their willingness to change – project groups are likely to contain all types. However, look for a project with people who would be more rather than less willing to change, especially at first.

Eventually everyone will probably change, although there is also a class called 'laggards' (10–15%) who will be very resistant to change. This group can be very frustrating to the change agent. Resist the temptation to take them on as a challenge, particularly early on; you are better to ignore them. They will eventually fall into line or may even leave.

EXPERIENCE REPORT

When test automation was being rolled out, there was one manager who would have nothing to do with it. Partly through political factors and personal antagonism to the change agent, he did not 'buy in' to the idea of test automation, but was adamant that manual testing was better for them. Various rational reasons were given for this decision, which the change agent was not able to refute, at least not to this manager's satisfaction.

Three years later, when all of the rest of the company had automated testing, which was working very efficiently, saving significant effort, and giving better quality software, this manager was eventually forced to conform, and his group then automated their tests. By this time, it was probably considerably easier for them, since the regime was already established in the rest of the company, but they had wasted a lot of time testing manually in those three years.

11.10.1 The implementation 'iceberg'

The significance of the tool implementation process is shown in the iceberg diagram of Figure 11.2. If you have read this far in this chapter, you will realize that buying a test execution tool is only the first step towards test automation, and is probably the easiest part of the job. The half of organizations that fail at test automation run aground on the part of the iceberg that is not immediately visible. The job of implementing the tool involves three important elements: the infrastructure or automated testing regime (which this book describes), an internal selling job (done by the tool champion), and continuing support, both from management and from the implementation team.

The cost of a tool is more than the cost of the tool! The purchase price is a small percentage of what you will have to pay in terms of internal effort in order to succeed.

11.10.2 Evaluating the tool implementation

Remember that business case that was prepared when the tool was originally selected? Once the tool has been rolled out to a reasonable number of users, the business case should be revisited to see whether or not you have achieved your objectives.

It is likely that there will be some aspects that have not turned out as well as you had hoped, but you may have realized other benefits that are very valuable.

You should re-evaluate the use of the tool in the light of what has happened, and set new goals for continuing automation. If you have not done so already, you should put some means in place to measure your automation regime, as described in Chapter 8.

11.10.3 When does it end?

Never. You should now enter a cycle of continuous analysis and improvement of your automation regime that will never stop. If you do not pay

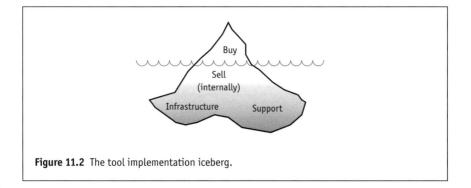

Figure 11.2 The tool implementation iceberg.

continuous attention to your automation regime, it will decay over time. The work that needs to be done should be minimized, and your automation regime should give you value for time spent on it. The measurements you use should help you to achieve those goals.

Summary

Successful tool selection is no guarantee of successful implementation of that tool within the organization: 40–50% of organizations have test tools that are 'shelfware,' i.e. not used.

Implementing a test execution tool is a 'management of change' process that gradually widens the tool's acceptance and use within the organization. There are a number of roles to be played in implementing a tool, not necessarily by separate individuals. The tool 'champion' is the enthusiastic evangelist for the tool. The change agent is in charge of the day-to-day changes to the way people work. The angel or sponsor gives high-level support. The tool custodian is in charge of the technical aspects of the tool such as implementing new versions from the vendor and building the automated regime and testware. The implementation team is drawn from all of those who are expected to use the tool. They are a means of communication about tool requirements and about how best to use the tool.

The first step of the implementation process is to prepare for it. This requires management commitment, both visible and material. It is important that management expectations are set at realistic levels. The next step is internal publicity (usually much more than is realized) and internal market research (by the implementation team).

It is a very good idea to implement a new tool first of all on a small-scale pilot project. Set quantified objectives and evaluate your results against the pilot's business case. If the results are good, then the tool can be rolled out on a wider scale.

It is critically important to be aware of 'people' issues. This is one reason why a lot of tool implementations fail.

Evaluate tool use against original and continuing quantified goals, and continue to improve.

PART TWO

Test automation case studies and guest chapters

Introduction: case studies and guest chapters

Why these chapters are included in this book

In Part 1 we have discussed test automation and outlined how to organize and structure the testware for an efficient maintainable regime.

It is always interesting to know what other people's experiences are. Our collection of contributions reflect people we know who have had both good and bad experiences and are willing to share their hard-won knowledge.

The case studies represent experiences over more than ten years, but often the problems encountered and lessons learned are the same. Some of the problems encountered by the authors may have been avoided if this book had been available to them at the time. Our aim is that you will be able to minimize the problems you encounter and overcome them more easily, through the experiences and advice contained in both parts of this book.

Some of the authors in Part 2 use different terminology than we have defined in Part 1 and the Glossary, but this will be explained in the chapter.

In this part of the book, specific tools are mentioned by many of the authors. This is not intended to imply any approval or otherwise of these tools or of the tools that have not been mentioned. The particular tool used is not really relevant to the lessons learned in these case studies. The same lessons need to be learned with every tool.

The table on pp. 303–304 gives summary details of all of the chapters in Part 2. Below we give a brief description of each chapter.

Historical case histories: chapters 12 and 13

The first two chapters in Part 2 are the oldest, both dating from 1988, and both with tools developed internally. (The commercial testing tool market was in its infancy at that time.)

Chapter 12 relates Mark Fewster's experience in developing automated testing, where the principles outlined in Part 1 of this book were initially

Chapter	Author	Dates	Tool	Platform	Main message
12	Mark Fewster, Keiron Marsden	1988–91, 1998/9 update	Homegrown Autotest	> Nine platforms	Outright success story, proved to stand the test of time
13	Marnie Hutcheson	1988–92	Home grown Gremlin	Prodigy online service	Methods more important than tools
14	Clive Bates	1992–97	SQA TeamTest	Windows, PC workstations	Importance of planning
15	Peter Oakley	1989–96	DEC DTM and V-Test	VAX VMS	Tool selection, good metrics, payback in 16 months
16	Paul Herzlich	1993–98	WinRunner	Client/ server, Windows	Tool selection, dynamic technically challenging environment
17	Simon Mills	1994–98	Automator QA (QARun), Lotus 123, SPSS	PC DOS and Windows	Test design for monthly varying data
18	Steve Allott	1995–98	SQA TeamTest	Windows, three databases	Practical lessons learned over three generations of automation
19	Ståle Amland	1995–97	Not specified	PC, IBM server	Failure stories: lessons learned
20	Bob Bartlett, Susan Windsor	Not specified	Not specified, could be any	PCs	Automation is worth doing even in unexpected situations
21	Lloyd Roden	1996–99	QARun	Windows	Good automation, attention to people issues and architecture

Chapter	Author	Dates	Tool	Platform	Main message
22	Hans Buwalda	1994–99	Any	Any	The Action Word method, keyword-driven level
23	Iris Pinkster	1996–98	WinRunner	AS/400, PCs, ATMs	Success using Action Words
24	Graham Dwyer, Graham Freeburn	1995–99 any	RadSTAR plus test execution tool	Any	Tool-supported keyword-driven level using tables
25	Jim Thomson	1997–98	RadSTAR plus another not specified	OS/2, NT, mainframe	RadSTAR method met stringent requirements for automation
26	Linda Hayes	1995	Any	Any	Much useful advice reprinted from her *Handbook of Test Automation*
27	Chip Groder	Early 1990s, restarted 1996	QA Partner, XRunner	GUIs	Good automation for GUIs, technical detail and advice
28	Angela Smale	1988–99	Many	Microsoft	Variety of types of test automation with strengths and weaknesses

developed. These ideas have been proved in practice over the intervening years; this is now one of the most successful and long-running automations that we know of. The first part of this chapter describes the story of how test automation was developed at the company from 1988 to 1991. The second part of the chapter describes the current state of automation at the company and was supplied by Keiron Marsden, who has been involved in the use and further development of this regime.

Chapter 13 describes a tool that went through phases of use followed by disuse. The main underlying problem was that having a good testing process is more important than automation. This led to the development of Marnie Hutcheson's MITs (Most Important Tests) test management method. The lessons learned are still applicable today.

This set of case histories represents contributions from those known to us who have had useful experience in test automation that they are willing to share.

Chapter 14 by Clive Bates describes both bad and good experiences in automating testing at a UK bank. Their first experience was not a success, as the tool became shelfware. However, they did eventually succeed using the same tool. A major key to success is good planning.

Chapter 15 describes Peter Oakley's experiences at a financial institution in the UK. Like the previous chapter this is a 'failure first, success later' story, but in this case a different tool was used for the second attempt. A rigorous selection process was carried out for the second tool, including a detailed business case for expected benefits. One of the features of this chapter is the detailed metrics kept about the costs and savings from the test automation.

Chapter 16 describes Paul Herzlich's experience testing one of the first electronic stock exchanges. Testing was very important but also difficult, due to the dynamic nature of the application, both in the data it handled and in rapidly responding to changes in this specialized marketplace. An efficient test regime was planned from the start, so this is definitely a success story. Paul quantifies the benefits over the first 18 months.

Chapter 17 is from the UK insurance industry. The testing was outsourced to Simon Mills' company, which drew up tests based on standard quotes. These were designed for automation independent of any specific tool, and have been running successfully for four years. The distinction between the role of the tester and the automation technician is illustrated with an interesting story.

In Chapter 18, the software product is a sales and marketing support system, made of standard and customer-tailored components, on multiple platforms using different database engines. This chapter by Steve Allott describes three attempts at automation, with increasing maturity each time, but also with significant problems.

Failure stories can be more interesting than success stories, and are often easier to relate to. However, the stories in Chapter 19 are not complete failures, just as many of the success stories in other chapters are not complete successes. Ståle Amland describes two projects where test automation was attempted using two different tools. The reasons for the problems are outlined together with advice for how to avoid them.

Chapter 20 describes the automation of tests that initially seemed a very unlikely candidate for automation. Bob Bartlett and Susan Windsor work for a testing services supplier, and were asked by their client, a bank, to help select a software package. A good testing approach proved its worth at all stages, and the same automation strategy was eventually used by both the supplier and the customer (the bank).

Chapter 21 by Lloyd Roden outlines the successful implementation of test automation for human resource management software by an independent testing team, with a useful summary of the key points from each stage.

Advanced methods and associated case studies: chapters 22–25

The next four chapters are in two sets of two. Chapters 22 and 24 describe what we consider to be good examples of implementing keyword-driven scripting, and Chapters 23 and 25 are case studies of people using each of the techniques.

In Chapter 22 Hans Buwalda describes the Action Words technique, which provides a way to separate the tests from the automation of those tests. The test clusters are kept in spreadsheets and contain the action words to be performed and the data to be used in the test. Navigation Scripts interpret the Action Words and implement the actions in a specific tool language. An example is given to explain how the method works. Chapter 23 by Iris Pinkster is a case study using the Action Word method.

Chapter 24 describes an approach using spreadsheet tables to store Window definitions, test steps (navigation), and business object scenarios, supported by their proprietary tool. Chapter 25 is a case study by Jim Thomson. An early attempt to automate testing had failed, and a second attempt was not satisfactory either. The approach described in the previous chapter was then found and it provided what was needed for their third and successful attempt. The chapter includes examples of a number of useful metrics to monitor the progress of testing.

Advice: chapters 26–28

The final three guest chapters of the book are more in the nature of useful advice rather than straight case studies, although all three are based on extensive experience in test automation.

Chapter 26 is a reproduction of extensive extracts from Linda Hayes' useful booklet *The Automated Testing Handbook*. We have selected the parts that most complement the material in the rest of this book.

Chapter 27 by Chip Groder gives useful and detailed advice for testing GUI systems. There is information about how to estimate costs and savings for automation, test planning and design, how to structure test cases, a detailed example, and a checklist.

Chapter 28 by Angela Smale describes her experience at Microsoft since 1988 using different types of test execution automation tools. Sometimes a certain approach proves very useful in unusual situations. She also argues for an element of randomization in automated tests, and concludes with a top ten list for successful automation.

Conclusion

All of the chapters in Part 2 have a useful message to those who are attempting to do what the authors have done. Take the advice offered in Chapter 19: 'If you want to automate your testing, listen to people with experience before you start!'

CHAPTER TWELVE

Racal-Redac case history

Mark Fewster and Keiron Marsden

12.1 Introduction

This case study describes the project where some of the techniques described in this book were initially developed. Mark Fewster worked as a developer, development manager, and test automation manager at Racal-Redac for ten years. He was responsible for the automation of testing – managing the teams that provided the test tools, test data, and methods. He began automating testing in 1988.

The first part of this chapter is derived from a conference presentation and paper written by the co-authors of this book. It was originally presented at the International Conference on Testing Computer Software in 1991. The paper was later published in the *Journal for Software Testing Verification and Reliability*.

As you will see, starting test automation was not an easy task. However, the techniques described in this book have proved themselves in this organization. We are grateful to Keiron Marsden for providing the updated information about test automation as it is practiced now, over seven years after the initial story was written.

12.2 Background

12.2.1 The company and the products

Racal-Redac at the time was a part of the Racal Electronics Group and one of the top five vendors of electronic design automation software. The company's product range included a family of products called Visula. This comprised over 120 programs, with 2.5 million lines of non-comment code statements, and was ported to all leading industry workstation hardware platforms. The main programs were graphical, user interaction being both keyboard- and mouse-driven.

12.2.2 Original testing activities

The software engineers who developed or modified a piece of software performed their own tests. Subsequently, the software was handed over to the Product Assurance Group, a team of about 10 engineers (called application engineers) who were skilled in the use of the product. There the product would undergo three distinct testing phases: *evaluation, integration testing,* and *system testing.* Evaluation involved assessing the software from the product user's point of view. Integration testing ensured that all the required programs were present and that they were compatible. System testing involved a more thorough approach – simulating the environment and the use that customers made of the software.

12.2.3 The problems with manual testing

Integration and system testing were performed manually and were repeated for each platform. In 1989 these activities typically consumed 38 person-weeks of effort for every software release on every platform. In that year, Visula was delivered on four platforms, and there was a nine-month delay between delivery on the first and the last; much of this delay was attributable to the manual testing bottleneck. Furthermore, as Visula grew in size and complexity, each release required more testing. If support for an increasing number of platforms were to continue (nine had been planned for 1991), a more efficient method of testing would be required.

As Visula had been supported on a progressively larger number of platforms, it is not meaningful to compare the total test effort release on release. The graph of Figure 12.1 shows the average effort per platform for a series of releases of Visula, and takes into account not only the manual test effort but also the evaluation effort and administrative overheads.

Because the tests were performed manually (and often from a vague test specification), they usually found a number of generic bugs (bugs present on all platforms) in the second and subsequent platforms, thereby proving that the tests were effectively random, being performed differently each time they were carried out.

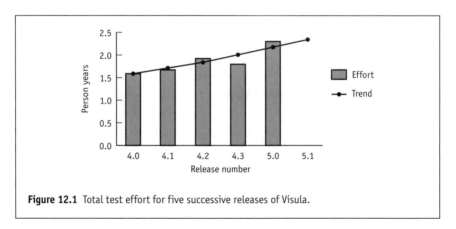

Figure 12.1 Total test effort for five successive releases of Visula.

12.3.1 Multi-solution strategy

The requirement was to reduce the cost of testing without reducing the test coverage. In addition to test automation other solutions were implemented in parallel: the use of an outside consultant, training in testing techniques, and better deployment of testing staff. While these are not the main subject of this case history, they are outlined below as each had an impact on the test automation solution.

12.3.2 Test automation tools

A decision had to be made between buying a tool and developing one in-house. Buying a tool would mean that implementation of automated tests could be started immediately, but it might be found that the tools did not suit all our needs. Developing a tool in-house would use up precious development resources, not only in implementation, but also in maintenance. We did have a little experience of automated testing, albeit on a very small scale. (Two development groups had used UNIX shell scripts to 'automate' certain unit tests. These were based on a common script – an attempt at a generic script – but each had been customized to meet the specific needs of specific sets of test cases.)

A brief market survey of commercially available testing tools did not reveal any that addressed our particular needs. It has to be said that the survey was not very thorough. At that time, we were not aware of any available catalogs of testing tools. Furthermore, there was a strong belief that developing some basic test tools would be straightforward. The decision was made to develop all the required tools in-house.

The functionality of the tools is discussed in Section 12.4.1.

12.3.3 Outside consultancy

An outside consultant was used during the planning stage of system testing automation. The purpose of this was to check that our chosen solution overlooked neither a better solution, nor potential problems. The least that was hoped for was a 'warm feeling' that we were on a good track. This we achieved, and we also obtained some valuable advice.

12.3.4 Training in testing techniques

Changing the approach to testing provided an ideal opportunity to invest in training and improve on the techniques being used. Myers (1979) provided the initial inspiration and a training course provided the follow-up. The effectiveness of the training course was measured by recording the number of software defects found by five application engineers over the same time period just before and just after the training. After the training they found four times as many defects as they had found before the training. However, some of the defects were considered low priority so we weighted them according to priority, 9 points for a high priority defect, 5 for a medium priority, and 1 point for a low priority. The testing performed with the benefit of the training proved to be three times as effective and gave a sevenfold payback for the cost of the training over a one-month period.

This paved they way for a series of tailored courses to train all our application engineers and most of our software engineers (over 80 people in all). Testing techniques such as equivalence partitioning and boundary value analysis were taught. Additional follow-up, support, and encouragement in the use of testing techniques to all the engineers who had been trained proved worthwhile to ensure a good and consistent use of the techniques.

12.3.5 Better deployment of testing staff

The primary task of the company's application engineers was to evaluate new software from the product user's point of view. However, it is wasteful to tell the software engineers, after the fact, that it wasn't a good idea to develop a piece of software. It is much better to tell them not to develop the software in the first place. This was thought to be best achieved by moving the application engineers into the development groups to work alongside the software engineers. Also, assigning to the development groups their own application engineers meant that the group managers had direct control over the products for which they were responsible.

12.4 Integration test automation

12.4.1 Tool function

The automatic test harness tool (called Autotest) controls a series of test cases on different programs and software units in Visula.

Each test is defined by its input data, instructions on how to run the test, and the expected output data. The tool requires that the programs to be tested are capable of being driven solely from data held in files. Fortunately, most of our programs did have this capability. The testing process is depicted in Figure 12.2. The comparison process is performed by different programs depending on the format of the data to be compared. Some formats require only simple comparison such that every difference between the two files is reported. More complex comparison programs are required for files that contain legitimate differences.

Expected output data is not prespecified manually. Instead a reference testing approach is used in which the initial test output is manually verified, and then serves as a reference point for automatic comparison of all further runs.

A test report is generated giving the status of each test run. This also contains details of the versions of software, the machine used, the elapsed times, etc.

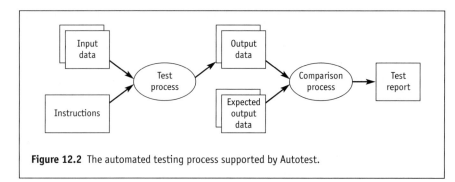

Figure 12.2 The automated testing process supported by Autotest.

12.4.2 Development effort

The test harness tool and a few 'standard' comparison tools were developed in just under a year with nearly 4 person-years effort. Much use was made of prototypes before the detailed requirements could be confirmed. Towards the end of this development period, the Product Assurance Group under-took the automation of the integration tests. This was completed using about 9 person-months of effort. Not all of the required tests could be auto-mated. It was still necessary to perform some of them manually because the programs being tested did not facilitate access to their internal data struc-tures. Often, the final result data was insufficient to indicate that the test had worked.

12.4.3 First use of Autotest

The automated integration tests were used, for the first time, to perform a complete integration test of the Visula 5.0 release. The manual tests took 2 person-weeks, and the automated tests 1 person-week. The automated tests could actually be run in about 10 hours, but a lack of comparison tools meant that manual effort was required to verify some of the results.

Without automation, integration testing took 10 person-weeks on every platform. With automation, this had been reduced to 3 person-weeks. Further reductions were possible with more automated comparisons.

12.5 System test automation

12.5.1 The new goal

Having made a significant impact on integration testing, the next step was to automate system testing. However, this was a much larger undertaking: 28 person-weeks of manual tests had to be condensed into tests that could be run automatically.

Unfortunately, not all the manual testing was supported by detailed test specifications. Some areas of functionality, when system tested, would be 'exercised' by the application engineers as they saw fit. There was also little official test data. Manual testing relied on each application engineer either knowing where a suitable Data Set could be found or generating it on the spot. In addition, most of the data was platform specific as there was no mechanism for transferring certain types of data between platforms.

This situation was not as bad as it sounds, since many of the engineers had been involved with testing for some time, and knew just where to find test data that had been used previously. However, this did mean that it was necessary not only to automate the tests, but also to define what had to be automated. This complication made it imperative that the application engineers be involved in the test automation.

Taking a somewhat cautious approach, a proposal was put forward for a project, requiring about 3 person-years effort, to reduce the system test effort by 80%. However, convincing the Managing Director that it was still necessary to perform 20% of the testing manually proved too difficult. He called for 100% test automation!

12.5.2 Development effort

The test data development was split into two phases, which were referred to as breadth test and depth test development phases. The first phase, or 'breadth testing,' aimed at insuring that all programs were exercised in some way. The intention was not so much to find defects, as to demonstrate that each program did do at least some things correctly. The second phase, or 'depth testing,' aimed at improving the test coverage (i.e. functional coverage) of the more critical areas in the software; essentially increasing the depth of testing for a subset of the programs.

For breadth testing, the application engineers predominantly implemented a subset of the manual tests: those that they believed to be best for the job. No test plans or test specifications were written. It was necessary to complete this initial Test Set as quickly as possible so that a more rigorous approach to testing could be used for the most critical areas in the software.

For depth testing, test specifications were produced. These insured that good use was made of test case design methodologies such as equivalence partitioning and boundary value analysis, in which the engineers had been trained.

We decided to combine the automated integration tests with those being developed for system testing. With manual testing, passing the integration tests was, in effect, the entry criterion for starting system testing. For automated testing, there seemed little value in retaining the two sets separately, since either could be run in a matter of hours, rather than weeks. Problems in locating the integration test data several months after it had last been used highlighted the need for formal control. It was clear that control standards and procedures had to be introduced. Fortunately we were able to use our source code control system to mechanize much of what was required.

Another notable problem was that much of the task of validating the results from integration testing had been performed manually, so that the tests themselves needed further work. (By then a richer set of comparators was available which facilitated automation of test result validation.)

12.5.3.1 *Programs not designed for testability*

From the very start of the test automation program, poor testability of many programs was a constant source of trouble. The development groups often proved unwilling, or unable, to make changes that would enable better testing of their applications. Fortunately, the decision to develop the test tools in-house prevented a lot of anguish. It was sometimes possible to implement a temporary workaround by building into the test tool some knowledge of the program to be tested. This temporarily contravened our tool development policy, which demanded that the tools be generic – a policy that has made it easy to maintain the test tools because of their independence from the programs they test.

Few of the programs had been designed with automatic testing in mind. During the two and a half years of this story, many improvements were made to them, but there was still more that could be done. What we learned through this experience meant that we could design facilities into new programs that made it possible to test automatically most of their important aspects.

12.5.3.2 *Cross-platform differences*

Despite designing the test data to be 'portable,' it came as something of a surprise to find just how different the test results were on different hardware platforms. It was always known that binary files would be of little use as test result data because they could not be compared across platforms. (It is necessary to compare the Test Results from one platform with the expected result data from a different platform since it is neither desirable nor practicable to store the expected result data for all of the platforms.) However, we were not prepared for the subtle differences in the ASCII files that were generated by the same tests on different platforms. Most of the differences could be handled intelligently with existing comparators, but it did take effort that was not planned. The most difficult of these differences to cope with involved graphical output data, such as the order in which items were drawn.

Strictly speaking, many of the unexpected differences were defects in the programs being tested. However, as they had no net effects, and certainly none on the end user, they were regarded as acceptable differences. Whether to fix a bug or make the comparator ignore the difference is not an entirely objective judgment. For us it depended primarily on the effort involved in each particular case.

12.5.3.3 *Debug information*

When the automated testing of the applications started in earnest, debugging the failed test cases soon became a time-consuming task. Large tests were inefficient because the software engineer often had to re-run each failed test case a number of times with monitoring tools, and then had to wait until the test reached the point of failure, before starting work on tracing the fault.

The debugging activity also suffered under test automation because the software engineers had to do more work to identify the problem. Prior to automation, application engineers identified a fault and then experimented with different input data or actions to try to pinpoint it. They then presented their findings to the software engineer. With automated tests, the software engineers were left to fathom out why the test case had failed (this often required an understanding of what the test case was trying to achieve) and then pinpoint the fault themselves. This problem was made worse by early versions of the tool, which had been designed specifically for finding defects, and not for helping with debugging. A number of test tool enhancements were identified and implemented to ease this problem in later versions.

12.5.3.4 Platform architecture

Differences in the various hardware platform architectures caused some problems. The most obvious of these differences is the processor speed. The test tool has the ability to abort a test case that either 'hangs' or runs into an infinite loop. This is achieved by declaring the test case's expected run time as part of the test definition. The run time of a test case can vary tenfold across different platforms, so that either a test case can be aborted prematurely, or machine time can be wasted in waiting for the test tool to abort a test case that 'died' some hours earlier.

12.5.4 Non-technical problems

12.5.4.1 Too much change too soon

We undertook too much change too soon. Perhaps the most significant change, apart from the test automation itself, was the reorganization that resulted in the application engineers being moved into the development groups. Had they been left in their own group, fewer people would have become involved at a time when teething problems were still being sorted out, and these problems could have been dealt with more efficiently, and with much less anguish.

The reorganization also meant that some software engineers were required to do testing that had previously been performed by application engineers. This met with resistance – resistance to testing, and to the tool. The problem was partly addressed by the test training program – one engineer said of the course: 'Beforehand, I thought "Oh, no! Not a testing course!" but I was pleasantly surprised with how enjoyable testing now seems.'

Other problems arose from a change in software-version release. When we started system test automation, it was planned to use Visula 5.0 for all but the two platforms that had already been tested manually. The completion of the automated tests was to coincide with the completion of the software ports to the remaining platforms. However, it was decided to supersede Visula 5.0 with Visula 5.1. Once Visula 5.0 system test automation had been completed, it was necessary to add further tests for the new and changed functionality in Visula 5.1. This became the responsibility of the development groups (since these now included the application engineers), and so involved a good many more people in the first attempt to automate testing than was desirable.

12.5.4.2 Implied automation of development testing

The original goal, that of attaining 100% test automation, was widely publicized, but not qualified sufficiently well. There was an implication that development testing (unit or module testing, performed by the development staff) was to be automated. The result of this was that some software engineers took a quick look at the test tools, saw one or more problems, and then backed away. Resources were not available for introducing them all to the tool in a more helpful way. (Note that all developers eventually did use the tool, as described in Section 12.8.)

12.5.4.3 Teething problems caused delays

Because of the number of people involved with automated testing in the first few weeks of its introduction, the number of problems and difficulties that people encountered with the new approach to testing seemed enormous. Most of the problems were fairly simple to correct, but the task of communicating the solution to everyone involved proved difficult. The tool became a good excuse for everybody's problems. Many problems blamed on the test tool were found to have nothing to do with it. 'Autotesting' had taken on a very general meaning – any problems encountered while Autotesting could be blamed on Autotest itself! Most managers failed to see through this, and they still believe Autotest caused their projects to run behind schedule and over budget.

12.6 The results achieved

12.6.1 Test effort per product release

For the first major release of Visula to undergo automated testing, the average effort per platform was about 48% of what would have been expected with manual testing. This average was falling; at the time of writing, the software had not yet been ported to all the platforms.

As a result of all the teething problems, the first platform showed no real gains (96% of the testing effort that would have been expected with manual testing). Subsequent platforms have used 60%, 50%, and 35% of projected manual effort. The testing effort on the ninth platform was anticipated to be around 20%. Figure 12.3 depicts the average testing effort thus far, compared with previous software version releases.

It turns out that no further reduction is likely, even if the ultimate goal of 100% automation is achieved. This is because the software that is being tested contains defects. The first pass of testing usually finds a good few defects and once these are fixed the second pass finds more. It is this repetition of testing that keeps the test effort high. It does, however, have one advantage – any small improvement to test automation is repaid several times over.

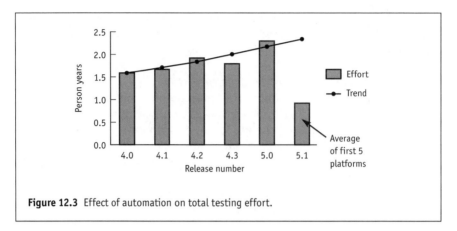

Figure 12.3 Effect of automation on total testing effort.

In terms of the original goal of 100% automated testing, the results are also good. A total of 8 person-weeks of manual testing is being planned for each of the remaining platforms. It is thought that this could be reduced to 4 person-weeks if the software were to contain fewer defects at the start of testing. So 79% test automation has actually been achieved, though, in theory at least, it could be as much as 89%.

12.6.2 Lessons learned

12.6.2.1 Need management commitment
This is very important, but it has to be planned. In retrospect, test automation was not explained well enough to our managers. There was an initial 'sales campaign' which explained to all the technical staff the aims and the benefits of test automation. On its own, this was not enough. We should have repeatedly asked for their views in order to check their understanding. It was all too easy to assume that they would see and understand the problems as we did. There would have been benefits from reading a book on the management of change such as Bouldin (1989) if only it had been known of at the time.

12.6.2.2 Makes debug effort more visible
For the first time, testing of a major product release was suspended to await the arrival of bug-fixed software from the development groups. Never before had the testers caught up with the developers. The testing and debugging activities have become more distinct.

12.6.2.3 Need to design for testability
There is no substitute for the freedom to choose what, and when, data is recorded during a test case. Not only does this make testing more precise and meaningful, but also it eases considerably the task of tracing faults. Many of our test cases have had to 'make do' with whatever was offered by the programs. This situation has led to difficulties in finding out why test

cases failed, and has made debugging much harder. For example, certain of the interactive programs can be driven by ASCII command files. If a command fails, the program gives no reason despite the fact that it 'knows' – at the time, there was no way of extracting this information from the program during a test run.

Again, certain tests check that particular commands are executed correctly. To do this, they extract from the program under test the state of its data structures before and after the command is executed. Often, it is not possible to be selective about the details that are output – it is 'all or nothing.' This creates unnecessarily large amounts of data that take more time to generate and compare; it also uses more disk space, makes debugging more difficult, and adds nothing to the value of the test.

12.6.2.4 Need training in testing techniques

The training proved successful, not only in encouraging new techniques, but also in changing people's attitudes towards testing. There is also much to learn about designing tests for automation, some of which will be general, and some program specific.

Certain of the problems might have been overcome by providing training in the use of the test tools. While such training was available, the take-up was small. More emphasis should have been placed on its benefits. Unfortunately, at the time, we didn't realize them ourselves!

12.6.2.5 Tests should be short

At the start of the system test automation, there was concern about the overheads associated with a large number of small tests. It was known that long tests (tests that take hours to run) were not desirable, but it was thought that a lot of short tests would incur unacceptable overheads (principally for run-up and run-down times of programs under test, and result comparison times).

It is now clear that a test case which runs for more than a few minutes has greater potential for wasting time than several shorter ones. There are several reasons for this. First, because of the different platform architectures, the test case time-out period is usually much larger than is necessary. This can lead to several hours being wasted on only a handful of aborted test cases. Second, long test cases have the potential to find many defects, but usually only one at a time, and the test cases have to be re-run after each fix. Third, the time spent debugging after failure of a long test case can be several times that for a short one.

12.6.2.6 Control cost of maintaining test data

Much of the automated test effort has been spent reworking the test data. The unexpected differences in test results from different platforms forced us, for a time, to employ platform-specific test Data Sets. Merging the different versions took several person-weeks, but was necessary to prevent the expected maintenance effort being repeated for each platform.

12.6.2.7 Test-stopping bugs stop tests!

This seems obvious, but the impact of it was not clear to us before testing commenced. The danger of leaving code untested when a test case aborts before completion is all too real. To minimize the number of such occurrences, test cases must be short, and failed test cases thoroughly investigated.

The fixing of some of the defects that caused test cases to abort before completion took on a high priority, even though they may not have affected the end user. When a decision was taken not to fix a defect, there was then the choice of abandoning the test case (and risking leaving software untested), changing the test case so that it could resume (if this were possible), or reverting to manual mode for that test case.

12.6.3 Benefits achieved

12.6.3.1 Test effort per platform halved

The average test effort per platform was halved even for the first four platforms. While the first platform required only 4% less effort than would have been expected for manual testing, the subsequent platforms have improved on this significantly. The fourth platform achieved a 65% reduction.

12.6.3.2 Consistency of regression testing

The repeatability of the automated tests is reassuring. A start has now been made on automating tests for bug fixes; this should guarantee that defects found in one product release never appear again (something that did not happen often, but was very embarrassing when it did).

12.6.3.3 Less dependence on application expertise

Less experienced application engineers and software engineers have been able to assist with testing that had previously been the domain of experienced application engineers. This has allowed better use to be made of valuable skills.

12.6.3.4 Bug fixes fully regression tested

Bug-fixed releases have been more rigorously regression tested than would have been practical with manual testing. The technique has uncovered further defects (caused by the bug fixes) which otherwise would have reached our customers.

12.6.3.5 Improved time to market

Visula has been delivered on more hardware platforms in a shorter period of time than has ever been achieved before. Also, a new hardware model is now being supported. This would not have been possible for weeks, if not months, without automated testing. Before automation, we delivered four platforms in nine months; after automation we delivered nine platforms in four months.

12.6.3.6 *Improved cross-platform quality*

The consistency of regression testing has given greater confidence in the different platform releases; what works, works on all platforms.

12.6.4 The payback

Over the two and a half years since the start of the test automation project, five person-years were spent on developing and maintaining the test tools, and a further five person-years on developing the test data. Significant benefits were first noticed only at the beginning of 1991, but by the end of the first quarter, about three person-years of manual testing effort had been saved. By the time Visula 5.1 is released on nine platforms, it is expected that the breakeven point will have been reached. Beyond that, person-years of manual testing effort should be being 'saved' every three or four months.

The graph of Figure 12.4 depicts the cumulative effort used in developing the test tools and the test data. The 'savings' line represents the actual and estimated benefit of the test automation program. Work on the project started in July 1988, and it was predicted that the breakeven point (considering major releases of Visula only) would occur around July 1991. (In 1993, Mark Thompson reported at the STAR conference that test automation was saving the company £350 000 ($500 000) per year.)

12.7 Summary of the case history up to 1991

Manual testing had become a bottleneck in the product life cycle and was becoming increasingly costly. Furthermore, the requirement to support more hardware platforms was likely to accelerate the cost. Automated testing was chosen as the principal solution.

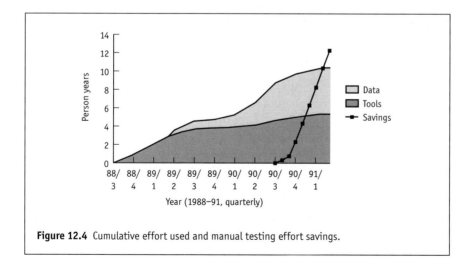

Figure 12.4 Cumulative effort used and manual testing effort savings.

A brief market survey of commercially available testing tools did not reveal anything suitable. With a strong belief that developing some basic test tools would be straightforward, the decision was made to develop the tools in-house.

A trial of the test tools was successful, and so encouraged an aggressive target of 100% automated testing. Many problems were encountered, both technical and non-technical, but significant benefits were realized. We achieved the automation of 79% of the testing, and were able to deliver our products to the market much earlier. Tests are now repeatable and consistent across all platforms.

The ten person-years of effort spent in developing the tools and test data will have been matched by the savings gained through the reduction in test effort in about July 1991. From then on, savings of person-years of manual test effort should be realized every three to four months.

12.8 What happened next?

The story so far represents the birth pangs of the automated testing regime at Racal-Redac. In the years since this part of the story ended, what has happened at this company? Keiron Marsden has provided the following information on where they are at the time of writing (1999).

'Testing is at the heart of our quality system. Test automation makes it economic enough to be worthwhile.'

Source: Keiron Marsden, Visula CAD/CAM Product Development Manager.

12.8.1 History since 1991

The company is now called Zuken-Redac and has moved to Bristol, UK. The Quality Assurance (QA) and Support functions have been combined because the people who have been involved in QA in the past have the knowledge needed to support, and those who have been involved in support in the past know what to look for when assessing the quality of new releases.

Market share for the Visula product range is still the highest worldwide. There are no products that have been discontinued since 1993, so all existing products continue to be supported. In addition a number of new products have been added, and more functionality has gone into each new release of the existing products. Test automation has been a significant factor in enabling the company to become far more efficient to meet marketplace challenges in a dynamic industry sector.

The company has also achieved ISO 9001 certification for maintenance and enhancements. Zuken-Redac now has a formal release procedure that depends on automated testing at every stage. We have thousands of automated tests, and this is still growing. There is as much testware as software.

The aim is for any full regression suite to run in 12 hours, although the largest, the CAD system, currently takes a little longer.

For example, a sample Test Suite run recently for a component of the CAD system produced the following statistics:

1201	Pass
15	Expected Fail
7	Unknown
56	Fail
7	not run
Total: 1286 tests	

12.8.2 Technical advances in Autotest

There have been some technical advances in the tool itself after its initial development. Autotest can now cope more easily with programs that require messages to be sent to communicate with them. It can automatically re-run all failed tests at the end of a set of tests, to overcome problems of unexpected events such as network failures.

A very interesting technical development is the use of Autotest together with a specially written demonstration tool (called Dramatix) to semi-automate manual tests. Autotest is used to set up the test environment, i.e. make sure the correct version of software and data files are there, initialize test data, etc. The software being tested is then invoked but control is handed to Dramatix, which displays the test script for the manual test. The manual tester then performs the operations (which are not practical to automate because of the visual nature of the verification), such as checking whether objects can be moved around while preserving all connections. The tester then records Pass or Fail status in Dramatix. At the end of the test, Autotest performs any clear-up, and collects the Pass/Fail information to process in the standard way.

There have also been some minor enhancements over the years, for example to make the integration into the release procedures more efficient. Now a single command to the configuration management system will copy the source code, perform the build, and run the automated tests.

12.8.3 Technical problems

There are still a couple of technical problems being encountered. One is that around 1% of the expected outcomes are actually incorrect. These are discovered over time and corrected when they are found, but there are probably still some incorrect expected outcomes in the Test Suites.

There is also a domino effect that happens at times. If 10 test cases fail, and a fix is supposed to correct this, the new software may actually fail 90 tests. This can be disheartening.

Some manual testing is still needed. For example, the function key layouts are different for different platforms. This means that they must be tested manually, at least once. If the x-events are stored from the manual test, they can be replayed to repeat the test when changes are made, provided the function key layout is not affected by the change.

12.8.4 Changes and benefits

The most striking benefit is the level of quality of the products which is guaranteed by being able to run such a large set of tests so often. All fixes, patches, and changes are fully regression tested, not just once but at every milestone. The tests can all be re-run after the 'last' fix so that the software sent out to customers is known to be of very high quality. Automated testing is indeed at the heart of the quality system.

The greatest impact from a management perspective is that time estimated for any work now always includes time to run a full regression test. Previously, estimates for development had been given by (optimistic?) developers, who did not tend to remember to include the time taken for adequate testing. For example, they may have included time to test a new feature, but may not have included regression tests or maintenance of existing tests. This led to being 'caught out' at the end of development, with time having to be extended. For example, if ten weeks were estimated for a development project, no one could accurately predict how long the testing would take or even how many tests should be run. Thus development work was not as predictable as it should have been.

The biggest single change in the culture is that end dates can now be predicted with very good accuracy. This means that the planning can be done with confidence, and the whole process is much better managed. Of course, the process is not perfect, so there is occasionally a small slippage, but on the whole, things are far more predictable. An example of this was when a contractor recently finished his contract, they were able to reallocate work and know what the impact would be five months in the future. Previously it was considered pretty good to see an impact a few weeks ahead. Without the automated test system, it would be difficult to predict with this accuracy and so far into the future.

Another significant benefit of the automated testing regime was when we moved to Windows NT. This has a completely different architecture to the UNIX platforms supported so far. The automated testing helped enormously; in fact, it probably would not have been possible to port to NT without it. We moved 95% of the product line to NT, and existing tests were run where possible. The porting work is now done in development before QA sees it. When the final QA of the platform was done, very few defects were found in the programs that had undergone automated testing. The defects that were found were mainly in the unique features of NT, for example pipe communication between processors.

Another benefit comes when there are a lot of minor changes for customers. It is all too easy to overlook minor changes when you are dealing with a great number of things. Autotest is a great way to find out if you've remembered them all.

We have made use of filters in complex comparisons. For example, when a picture is redrawn, it must look the same to the user regardless of the order of drawing of the elements. The tool may find differences in the order of the draw instructions, but we can sort the order before doing a comparison. This feature was not actually a recent innovation, but has been improved over time. We also found it useful to build in some rounding error tolerance when moving to a 64-bit platform (Alpha).

It is our policy to re-run all tests for any patch, no matter how minor. This has been very useful. In the past year, a number of defects have been found that were introduced by a fix. This is the worst thing from the customer's point of view; they report one defect only to have it replaced by another.

Another problem that we used to have is worth mentioning. What used to happen was that many important customers tended to find a significant defect in the first week of using a new release. This didn't happen every time, but it was very embarrassing when it did. What we do now is to give an early release to a few selected customers worldwide. These are generally the customers who asked for a particular function that is included in the release. This early release is not a beta test; everything has gone through exactly the same quality system, so the quality is as good as we can achieve without having real users. The early adopters can then check out the release to see if they are happy, and of course they do also find some defects in the first few weeks. These defects would then be fixed with patches for each customer. All the patches are fully regression tested. After three months, a general consolidation release, incorporating all of these patches, goes out to all customers. This general release would also have been completely regression tested from program level through to system level. The majority of customers only receive the general release, but it is now higher quality than we used to be able to produce for a general release. So we have not compromised on quality, we have extended it; not only are all of the automated tests performed, but the problems that would only show up in real use are also found early, with the most serious ones being encountered first. This gives greater reliability to our customers; any defects that are found after general release are found later and are more minor.

The post-release defect density for the areas that are automatically tested is now much lower than it used to be, plus the defects that are found tend to be less serious.

When new enhancements are being developed, having such a large Test Suite is a great aid in stabilizing the software. We can be confident that if a new enhancement passes all the automated tests, then it will be OK. The reason for this is the high coverage that the tests achieve.

A final point here is related to our organizational maturity. ISO 9001 requires us to perform defect root cause analysis. In the early days, most of the root causes tended to be that functionality wasn't tested. Now we are identifying things earlier in the life cycle, such as problems with omissions in specifications. The problems that do slip through the net tend to be where the procedures were not followed properly, or where insufficient testing was done.

12.8.5 The current culture

The quality system has a number of benchmarks or milestones:

A1: Development Test Complete. Early in development, the product tests will have been planned and the test plans reviewed. The A1 automated tests test each product and all changes, including tests with printers and peripherals if relevant (e.g. for driver programs) and tests on all platforms. Any defects found in running the tests go back to development to fix. The support group looks at the product from a user perspective after all of the automated tests have been run. When the developers are happy about the individual products, the A1 milestone is achieved.

P2: Product Test Complete. A number of software products are combined to form a release, which is tested by QA engineers running real-user tests (manually). Any customer patches are also tested, and all previous critical defects are re-tested to insure that they are still fixed in this release. Every product must work with every other product. Some informal integration testing may be done in development before P2, e.g. to generate files in a layout editor to be handled by the route editor. If the second program cannot read the format produced by the first program, then at least it has been found early. When QA are happy about the integrated products, milestone P2 is achieved.

S4: Final System Test and Integration Test Complete. All tests are run on all platforms before being put on the distribution media to be sent out to customers. A 'gold CD' of the system is produced after milestone S4 has been reached. This milestone is signed off by every manager and approved by QA. S4 is the last point at which any tests are run: any changes after this require a complete re-run of all of the S4 tests.

S5: Early Adopters Release. A few copies are made and distributed to sales and support offices for local training and testing, and to the early adopters. Any patches are recorded.

S6: General Release. This is where the bulk media duplication (sourced externally) of the new gold CD has been completed, before distribution to all customers. This normally comes around three months after the Early Adopters Release. Note that S4, S5, and S6 are all identical software: a CD cut at S5 is indistiguishable from one cut externally at S5; it is not a separate or different release.

There is a much better relationship between the quality department and the software developers than there used to be. Both parties are more assertive and less aggressive. QA now know they have a right to expect software of an adequate level of quality. Developers know that they have a right to be helped by QA to produce quality software. Those parts of the organization with the lowest standards (and the least test automation) are the parts that currently have the greatest conflict with QA.

When changes are requested to the software, the impact on the automated Test Suites is now a serious influence on whether or not that change will be approved. For example, a requested customer enhancement might take only a few weeks to develop but it might take months to test. It may be more expensive to change a user interface than to add a new feature. This is because the user interface would need to be changed in many existing test cases, while adding a new feature would result mainly in new tests being added, and fewer changes to existing test cases.

Because test estimates are always included in any development estimate, these also include the test maintenance impact. So there may have been features that were not developed because the effort to test was too great. One example is that the redevelopment of the user interface to the PCB products has probably been delayed because of the impact of the proposed changes on the tests, which had many person-years invested in them. We would like to be able to work at a scripting level that is closer to the changes the users have made, rather than being concerned with what buttons they pressed.

Company policy is now that all software engineers write automated tests for all platforms. Every fix requires a set of automated tests for all platforms before it is accepted. In the early days of test automation there was great resistance from developers, not only in the use of the tool, but also in perceiving that testing should be part of their job. Now it is an accepted part of the culture that developers must write tests for any software that they develop. The advertisements for new staff mention test automation as a key feature of the job.

References

BOULDIN, BARBARA (1989) *Agents of Change: Managing the Introduction of Automated Tools*. Prentice Hall, Englewood Cliff, NJ.

MYERS, GLENFORD (1979) *The Art of Software Testing*. Wiley, New York.

CHAPTER THIRTEEN

The evolution of an automated software test system

Marnie Hutcheson

13.1 Introduction

This case study is a rare breed: it admits to less than total success, at least at first. The reasons why a good tool fell into disuse (twice), and the ultimate lessons learned make fascinating reading for anyone who wants to automate testing successfully.

This case study was originally written in 1992, and describes Marnie Hutcheson's experiences at Prodigy, where she was working at the time. She has developed the excellent test management method MITs (Most Important Tests) partly as a result of her experiences described in this case study.

She now runs two companies, Prosys and Ideva, the former involved in test consultancy, and the latter in internet and intranet development and training. Her book *Software Testing Method and Metrics* will be published by McGraw-Hill. This chapter was originally published in the proceedings of the Ninth International Conference on Testing Computer Software (ITEA and ASQC).

The tool described in this chapter no longer exists. The application which it tested, an on-line shopping system, was superseded by internet technology. However, the lessons learned are still relevant.

13.2 Background

Prodigy Services Company developed a wide variety of software that was required to run on many diverse platforms. Consequently many types of software and hardware test tools were used to test the PRODIGY service.

The Gremlin Automated Test System began in 1988 as a set of PC-based test script automation tools used primarily to test applications on the PRODIGY service. It was eventually developed to automate many testing tasks in addition to capture replay and it has been used to test many types of software across the Prodigy network. Many changes have been implemented, both in the test system and in our thinking.

Possibly the most important lesson learned in this process is that it takes a lot more than test tools to make test automation succeed. There must be some reliable method for using the tools to insure the quality of the testing that is done.

13.3 Gremlin 1

13.3.1 Features

The first financial application on the PRODIGY service took a year to develop and a year to test. Management wanted the next four financial applications completed and online in 16 months. The schedule called for considerable overlap in the implementation and testing of the applications.

Gremlin 1, a script automation test system, was developed in six months in order to allow testers to meet the schedule. The toolset utilized existing internal capture replay and image capture technology where possible.

The system functioned as a non-intrusive operator emulator, running on the same machine as the application being tested, and allowed users to:

- capture keystrokes and screen images;
- build suites from captured key trace scripts;
- re-run Test Suites and capture test images;
- compare test images to master images and write a report (showing the number of mismatched pixels).

Additionally, an image viewer was developed which allowed the user to view first the captured master image, then the captured test image, and finally the test image superimposed on the master image. The superimposition image highlighted the differences between the master and test images and blanked out the areas that matched.

13.3.2 Gremlin 1 achievements

The financial applications test groups were able to automate 80% of their testing with the Gremlin system. Gremlin was given to the client financial institutions, and in many cases they used it in both the system test effort and the user acceptance test effort. Automated testing reduced the system test cycle for a financial application at Prodigy Services Company to one month. The entire test cycle, for Prodigy and the financial client, was reduced to less than three months.

Not only was the testing of the new financial applications completed on time, it was possible for the tester to perform regression testing while engaged in other work. It was also possible to use the Gremlin system to monitor the health of the existing applications on the live PRODIGY service.

13.3.3 The rise and fall of Gremlin 1

Gremlin 1 was made generally available to Prodigy employees and Prodigy's clients in March 1989. Within eight months of its introduction, the automated test system had 56 registered internal users and 15 external users. The usership was split almost equally between development groups, the Systems and Application Test (S&AT) group, and various non-technical groups performing user acceptance testing.

However, 18 months later it was discovered that fewer than 20 of the 71 registered Gremlin 1 users were still using the system in their testing. Most of the active users were in the S&AT group. Even the development group for which the system had initially been developed was no longer using the system to test financial applications. The ex-users had not replaced the Gremlin system with other automation tools; they had apparently just stopped using test automation. The usage is shown in Figure 13.1.

13.3.4 Causes for the decline in use of Gremlin 1

A survey was taken of the users and ex-users of Gremlin 1. The reasons for the decline in use fell into two distinct groups: those related to testing in general, and those related to tool functions.

13.3.4.1 General testing problems
Many of those surveyed were concerned about general testing issues, such as:

- Where do I start?
- How do I design my test scripts?
- How do I know what to test?
- How do I know when I have tested enough?

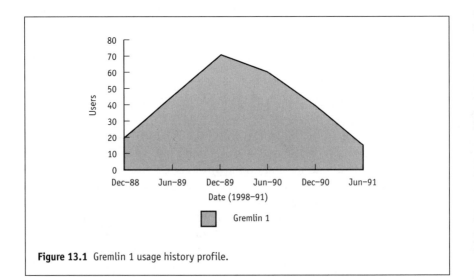

Figure 13.1 Gremlin 1 usage history profile.

The tools were not expected to supply answers to these questions, yet these were the problems which people were struggling with. This was something of a surprise, and clearly showed the need for some kind of education or class to teach software testing as a discipline. We did not yet realize the true significance of this finding.

13.3.4.2 System/tool deficiencies

There were also a number of technical problems identified in Gremlin 1. This is not surprising for the first release of what was at the time very new technology. (In 1988/9 the commercial testing tool market was only just getting started.)

The following deficiencies were highlighted by the survey:

- Interface problems. Gremlin 1 was text-based rather than a mouse-driven graphical user interface. Users had to type in many hard-to-remember filenames with paths. If they made a mistake, they had to start that operation again at the beginning.

- Can't drive my application. Gremlin could only drive key traces through the user interface of the PRODIGY system.

- Validation. Gremlin 1 only did screen image comparison, and didn't allow masking out areas of the screen, or the comparison of files or messages.

- Environment. Set-up and clear-up had to be done manually. For example, if a certain file had to be in a certain directory at the start of each script, the tester would have to place it there manually before the automated test could be run, and similarly for clear-up tasks. Not only were these types of operations time consuming, they were also difficult to document and were easily overlooked. An entire run of a Test Suite could be wasted if the correct environment was not in place.

- Test scripts hard to edit. Testers had to know what each keystroke and mouse movement did before they could edit a key trace. The scripts required correct syntax and case in both mnemonics and commands. Any edited script then had to be tested and debugged.

- Key traces hard to include in test documentation. Testers had to format and manually copy key trace scripts in order to include them in their documents.

- Test scripts quickly outdated. Many elements were 'hard-coded' into the scripts, for example menu option numbers, which gave them a short life expectancy. This promoted the view that key traces were 'disposable' and not worth documenting or maintaining. Consequently testers were continually retyping key traces instead of replaying them.

- What does this key trace test? Typically, no one but the tester who created a key trace had enough confidence in its validity to use it. Even if descriptive 'comments' were edited into a key trace, they couldn't easily be reproduced in any documentation.

- What does this key trace need to run? There was no mechanism for recording or managing physical environment requirements, making it impossible to say for sure if it had tested what it was supposed to test.
- No conditional logic in key traces. Our initial scripting language did not include an 'if' construct, so if a test failed, little automated recovery was possible.

None of these problems will come as a surprise to anyone who has used the earliest commercial capture replay tools. The conclusion seemed clear, however: we needed a better tool.

13.4 Gremlin 2.0: a step beyond capture replay

Gremlin 2.0, a prototype, was introduced in October 1990. It provided a platform approach to testing rather than the isolated tool approach. The system provided a number of automated services in addition to capture replay.

13.4.1 Gremlin 2.0 features

13.4.1.1 All new interface
All the tools featured a mouse-driveable, graphical user interface with online help. With the new interface, the user was able to select operations and filenames. The need to remember long filenames and path names or arcane commands was virtually eliminated.

13.4.1.2 Script macros
Script macros were implemented to solve the problems associated with the short life of key traces. A script macro is actually a title that represents a key trace segment. The title is inserted in the script instead of the key trace segment. At runtime the macro title is expanded into the set of keystrokes that it represents. An example is given below.

```
Macro Title: Log On
Macro Text:
 <COMMENT LOG ON to PRODIGY service>
 ABCD01A<TAB>PWORD<ENTER>
 <COMMENT Take snapshot of result>
 <SNAPSHOT:>
```

A sample test script using macros is shown below:

```
<COMMENT TESTSCRIPT NAME TEST01>
<COMMENT: Script logs on to the PRODIGY service, jumps to
Tester's Paradise, views Mini TV, and logs off>
{MACRO: LOG ON}
<ENTER> TESTER'S PARADISE <ENTER>
```

```
<COMMENT: Snapshot of Tester's Main Menu>
<SNAPSHOT:>
<COMMENT: Pick menu option 3: Mini TV>
3<ENTER>
<COMMENT Snapshot of Mini TV>
<SNAPSHOT:>
{MACRO: LOG OFF}
```

13.4.1.3 Import of a specialized script editor
Prodigy chose an external script editor with the key trace script language built in. The user could type script language mnemonics and commands directly into the script. The user could also create and embed script macros in the key trace. It actually became faster and easier to create a script using the editor than to capture it online.

13.4.1.4 Automated document generation
A document generator was developed that would produce a coverage analysis matrix for suites, results reports, and error listings. The system allowed the tester to build the outline for a document and embed ASCII text files. Once the outline was built, the Gremlin 2.0 documentation facility could generate the entire test plan.

13.4.2 New training provided

13.4.2.1 Automated Validation and Verification Tools workshop
This class was a hands-on workshop where testers became familiar with the Gremlin 2.0 system tools. The students developed test scripts and suites, conducted automated suite runs, and learned to interpret test results using the new tools.

13.4.2.2 Software Testing Methods and Metrics workshop
This class was first developed to serve the needs of non-technical personnel. The class placed heavy emphasis on use of evaluation techniques and professional standards in software testing.

The original syllabus included:

- test term definitions;
- introduction to software testing metrics;
- introduction to McCabe's Cyclomatic Complexity;
- function coverage and test coverage analysis for test design;
- criticality analysis for test paths and data;
- documentation: test plans, status, and results reports.

The demand for the workshop was high among technical personnel as well and the syllabus was greatly expanded in 1991.

13.4.3 Gremlin 2.0 beta test results

One systems development group that had used Gremlin 1 to shorten their package test cycle from 10 weeks to 7 weeks in a project we will call D9.1 acted as the beta test site for Gremlin 2.0.

Using Gremlin 2.0, they were able to further reduce the test cycle from seven weeks to three weeks in their release D10.0. Much of the additional productivity gains were due to the new Gremlin Document Generator, which they used to generate their package test plan and all their results reports. Building on the test scripts and test plan from the first automated test cycle, they were able to run more test cases and find more errors than ever before. This is shown in Figure 13.2.

13.4.4 New system didn't attract users

The results of the beta test effort were used to promote the new Gremlin system. The Gremlin 2.0 system was presented to groups of developers and testers at Prodigy. Even though many of the user requirements had been addressed and new automation functions had been added, only a few users were recruited. The two most common arguments expressed by prospective users were:

- I don't have time to perform the special pre-test tasks necessary to set up for an automated test effort.
- It's faster to rekey the script I need than to find the key trace and assemble an automated Test Suite.

While it was difficult even to get people to attend demonstrations of the new Gremlin test system, the Methods and Metrics workshop was well attended whenever it was offered. After completing the Methods and Metrics class, testers were decidedly more interested in the test system.

13.5 Finding the real problem

Ironically, it was the fact that more people were interested in attending the Methods and Metrics workshop classes than the tool demonstrations which finally provided some clues to the underlying problems, as shown in Figure 13.3.

Testers wanted tools that they could use to solve their immediate problems. They needed objective, defensible ways to size their testing efforts, design their test scripts, publish their assumptions, and demonstrate clearly what they had and had not accomplished. The workshop gave them solutions for these problems; the test system did not.

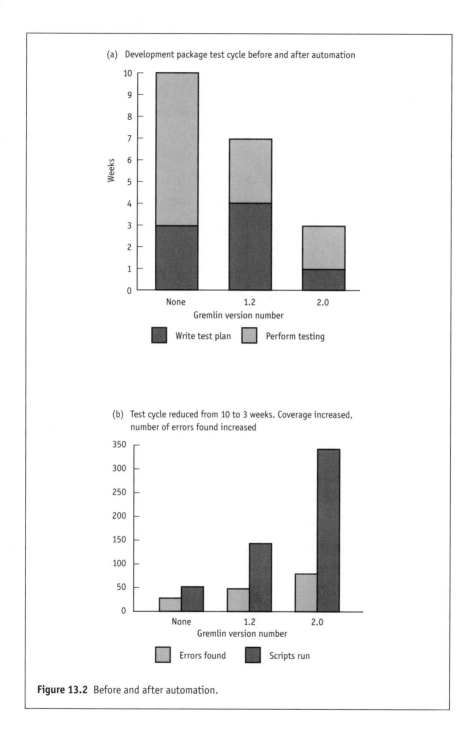

Figure 13.2 Before and after automation.

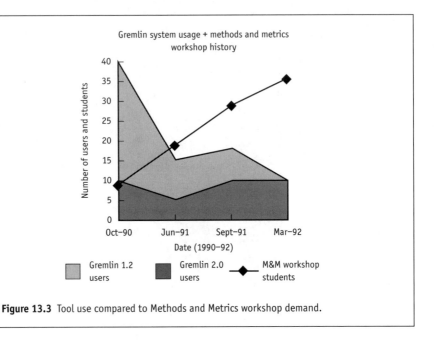

Figure 13.3 Tool use compared to Methods and Metrics workshop demand.

13.5.1 Faulty underlying assumptions

13.5.1.1 If the tools are good enough, people will use them

It had been assumed initially that the tools fell into disuse because they were just not good enough. The solution seemed to be to provide better tools. The better tools that the testers asked for were provided, but that did not result in the testers automating their testing.

13.5.1.2 Test automation will just 'happen'

It was assumed that since almost everyone agreed that test automation was a better way, it would become the preferred way of testing without any special promotion, education, or support. Test automation did not just happen.

13.5.2 It takes time to automate

13.5.2.1 Pre-testing tasks are critical

A first-time test automation effort requires a significant investment in analysis, planning, test design, and script creation before any code is ever tested. Once this set-up work has been completed, testing is accomplished quickly. Subsequent releases of the code can usually be tested with only some minor adjustments or maintenance on the existing test plan and test scripts.

If the initial work is not done, if key traces are not created, then there is virtually no benefit to test script automation. The real benefit of script replay automation occurs during regression test efforts, and it can only occur if there are scripts to replay.

13.5.2.2 Test design must start well before code turnover

The information available to testers before the code was turned over, such as traditional design documentation, was not usually suitable for detailed test script design from the perspective of the user interface. The established development process rarely provided any opportunity for the testers to begin to analyze the application or start to create test scripts until they had actually received the software from development.

After the code turnover, the script development time which is required to set-up for the automated test effort was not usually available. Testers were regularly forced to abandon automation plans and simply grind through scripts manually in order to meet exit deadlines. At best, they might be able to use the capture replay tools to capture what they could of the manual test effort for possible automated reuse. This environment was not conducive to creating durable, reusable automated scripts.

13.5.2.3 Key traces were viewed as disposable

Testers were not eager to invest time in maintaining key traces when they believed that they would be quickly outdated. Captured key traces came to be viewed as 'disposable.' Consequently, there were few durable automated Test Suites created for regression test efforts.

13.5.2.4 Effect of delayed release from development

When a project came to test from development several weeks behind schedule, test end dates were not allowed to slip accordingly. There seemed to be a feeling that somehow test automation would allow testers to make up the lost time.

13.5.3 People issues

13.5.3.1 Increasing staffing levels made it worse

This situation was actually exacerbated if more personnel were added to a test effort in an effort to make deadlines. Typically the extra personnel assigned to testing were knowledgeable system users but not trained testers. If the trained testers could not provide formal test scripts along with concise instructions, the testing that took place was an ad hoc user acceptance test effort rather than a focused test effort. Ad hoc testing is the least productive test method for finding errors.

However productive this type of test effort might have been, only rarely was any of this testing captured as key traces by the temporary testers. As a result, none of the testing could be reused in subsequent automated regression test efforts.

13.5.3.2 When personnel moved, automation was lost

When trained personnel, testers, and/or managers left a project, automation was lost. The key trace scripts were largely undocumented and therefore had no credibility with the new staff.

It was accepted practice that a new tester would create his or her own test plan and scripts to test new releases of existing applications. So, existing test plans and test scripts were often abandoned.

13.5.4 Tools did not support formal methods or metrics

13.5.4.1 What was tested?

The test system did not support any structured analysis method, nor did it require or maintain any type of test coverage data. Since no function coverage analysis was conducted, test coverage could only be 'assumed' to be adequate.

The Gremlin 2.0 toolset provided no support for task enumeration (planning), sizing information, or complexity analysis. Testers who had attended the Methods and Metrics workshop were using formal methods and metrics and began to ask for tools to support them.

13.5.4.2 What happened when testing took place?

When the Gremlin 2.0 system was used extensively, large amounts of results data were generated. Testers in the D9.1 project carried clipboards from test machine to test machine gathering results data. All this data had to be compiled and tallied by hand.

The need for results tracking and cumulative reporting was recognized. Cumulative results needed to be maintained by the system.

13.5.5 Gremlin 2.3: the marriage of methods and tools

Extensive redesign of the capture replay tools hadn't solved the problems. What had been asked was, 'What is wrong with the test tools?' The question that needed to be answered was, 'What is it about the process that keeps us from succeeding in our efforts to sustain test automation?' It was becoming clear that software testing methods and metrics had to become an integral part of the test tools. This became the formula for the implementation of Gremlin 2.3.

13.6 Lessons learned

13.6.1 Lessons learned: methods and metrics must come first

The problems experienced at Prodigy were not unique or unusual. The methods and metrics taught in the Methods and Metrics workshop were shown to be more valuable to many testers than the test automation tools.

Without the systematic application of formal testing methods, testers have no objective ways to analyze or size the test effort. Without measuring the software there is no way to demonstrate what has and has not been accomplished in a test effort. There is no objective way to estimate the risks associated with promoting a new piece of software into the production environment.

From the beginning, the testers attending the Methods and Metrics workshops made it abundantly clear that they were being overwhelmed by the software test efforts they were trying to carry out. Their immediate needs were for some way to make the magnitude of the problem clear to management. They needed to be able to measure the size of a project so they could make realistic estimates of the time and resources required to complete their tasks. They needed ways to describe what they were testing, justify their assumptions, and determine adequacy criteria. When the tools support and automate the test methods and metrics, only then does the job become do-able.

This led to the development of the MITs (Most Important Tests) method. MITs is a formal way of inventorying, prioritizing, and tracking tests.

Testing must be measured so that testers can demonstrate what they have accomplished, and so that management can make well-informed decisions about how much testing is enough, as well as about the risks associated with more or less test coverage in a test effort. The tools must help measure the software, or at the very least, help keep track of the measurements.

Using these metrics it is possible to give a more precise answer to the question:

What did you test?	
Without metrics	With metrics
I tested *it*.	I tested 60% (141 out of 236) of the paths (picked by rank, as the most important paths) and 80% (4 out of 5) of the Data Sets in the software, for a total of 53% (624 out of 1180) overall coverage.

13.6.2 Lessons learned about tool support

As we discovered at the time, capture replay is only a small part of the toolset required to automate software testing. Other testing tasks that need to be automated include documentation, environmental controls, function tracking, complexity analysis, test script and key trace generation, and test validation.

13.6.2.1 Make the best way the easiest way
Software testers know the importance of measuring software but the size of the task can be overwhelming. Gremlin 2.3 provided a test platform that automates much of the measuring and counting for the tester.

The test tools platform is the ideal site from which to impose testing standards and institutionalize metrics with a minimum of pain and no perceived 'extra work.' For example, the tester rarely has to mount a concerted documentation effort for scripts, because the test platform documents most activities automatically as the scripts are created and used. Coverage analysis is achieved in the same way.

The goal is to make the test system as indispensable to testing as the integrated development platform is to code generation.

The tools must automate the analysis process so that testers will know the answers to the following questions:

- What does this script test?
- What scripts should be run to test this function?
- What functions are being tested in this Test Suite?
- What functions are not being tested in this Test Suite?

The tools must also support cumulative results reporting. When cumulative results are available, statistical analysis can be performed. The tools should store results for all the runs of a suite from the time it is initialized. For instance, test data should answer the question, 'How many releases of code are required to correct an error?'

This statistical information has been very valuable in evaluating risk and identifying trends. In the D10.0 test effort, the cumulative test results showed that 12% of all sessions were failing due to an apparently random fatal error. Human testers had not reported the error because it occurred only rarely to any individual. The Gremlin system accumulated data from the equivalent of 36 testers and the cumulative data showed the true impact of the failure.

13.6.2.2 Test platform must be integrated and flexible

The toolset should be presented collectively as an integrated testing platform, not a collection of individual tools. The user should not have to deal with command line arguments and programs that terminate in the operating system, possibly leaving them wondering what to do next. The system must guide the user through the processes in the testing cycle.

The user should never have to rekey data. It is not helpful to have a toolset that cannot share data. The design analysis tool must feed the test script generator. The functions verified by the test scripts must be contained in a function inventory. The document generator must be able to access and utilize function inventories, test scripts, and the reports generated by testing.

The tools must also support manual testing. Even if a script cannot be automated, all of the other automated services of the test platform (except replay) will apply. Function coverage analysis, results reporting, set-up and clean-up instructions, and automated validation, etc. will operate as they do when the script is automated.

13.6.2.3 Scripts must be intelligent

A script must know what it tests. Each script must carry the list of functions, from testable function inventories, that it tests. This includes manual test scripts.

Scripts must know what physical environment they require in order to run and what set-up and clean-up operations must be performed to insure script validity. Again, this includes manual test scripts.

13.6.2.4 *Documentation must be automated*
The system must be able to produce printed status reports from the internal test results reports.

The system must be able to generate test plans and turnover documents which include:

- embedded text documents;
- results reports;
- complete function inventory and project listings;
- coverage analysis reports;
- complete Test Suite listings, including the complete listing of each script in the suite.

13.6.3 Lessons learned: organizational issues

13.6.3.1 *There must be a commitment to support test automation*
In order to make test automation work, and to keep it working, both testers and management have to be willing and able to make changes in the established development process.

Testers must be willing to learn new methods, measure their work, and commit to creating and maintaining high quality, reusable test scripts.

Management must be willing to make time for tester education and to recognize the importance and value of their testing resources.

13.6.3.2 *The role of management*
One of the issues identified in the failure of the original tools was that management had not been actively recruited to support automated testing. Since everyone assumed test automation would happen of its own accord, little emphasis was placed on engaging management in the loop. While nearly everyone viewed test automation as desirable, management was often unable to insure the set-up and maintenance time required for a focused automated test effort.

An education effort was mounted in 1990 and as a result not only did several first-line managers become supporters, but support and commitment began coming from higher levels as well.

There were many benefits to Gremlin 2.3's automation in addition to the speedy execution of test scripts. When software testing was being measured, testers had a much easier time communicating their problems to management.

Using the new tools, testers can provide measured answers to the following questions:

- How big is the project?
- How long will it take to test it all?
- How much can we test given the time and resources we have?
- What are we not going to test?
- When have we tested enough?
- How many errors are expected to be found?

Once these questions are answered, management has several options and is in a position to make informed choices.

13.6.3.3 Finding the time to automate testing

The reality of commercial software development is that testers must be ready to test when they receive the code from the developers.

Virtually all the current software development models advocate the involvement of the testers during the design and development phases of the project. Prodigy has always encouraged this early tester involvement as well. But there had been no satisfactory method for communicating design and implementation details that was both clear and reliable.

The problem is that maintaining formal detailed documentation, design specifications, and test plans is too cumbersome and time consuming for use in an environment where development can complete and discard six or seven prototypes in a day and testers may be expected to test seven versions in a week.

Since there was no mechanism for conducting and documenting a meaningful developer–tester dialog, the results of early tester involvement were often disappointing. Testers were not normally able to gain a sufficiently detailed description of the software function to size the effort, let alone begin detailed planning.

13.6.3.4 Reuse testing resources

Test scripts and test plans cannot become 'disposable'. They are as durable as source code and design documentation. What would be the reaction to a developer who insisted on rewriting every program that had an error or every program that came from some other developer?

Ideally, test scripts and key traces should accompany code through the entire project life cycle. Each group in the project life cycle should be able to add to or refine the repository of available test scripts.

The test base benefits greatly from the diverse perspectives and priorities of the contributing testers. In this way the test repository grows along with the system, becoming the best defense against the ever-growing complexity of the software.

13.6.3.5 Use test data statistics

Collect and analyze quantified information (metrics) about the testing. Once testers can perform statistical analysis on their testing, they can greatly lessen their dependence on expert testers and allow for more automated test script generation. The statistics will allow companies to answer questions such as:

- How much did this application cost to design, develop, and test?
- Statistically, which modules have the most problems? The fewest problems?
- Where should the test efforts be concentrated?
- How much testing should be done in order to have a comfort level with the finished product?

Supplying testers with tools alone does not insure that test automation will take place. Several things are necessary to sustain test automation:

1. methods are more important than tools;
2. there are many testing tasks that must be automated besides test script capture and replay;
3. the test tools must support a structured test methodology and automate the measuring of software;
4. greater value must be placed on test resources. If test scripts are not maintained for reuse there is little value in script replay automation;
5. management has a key role to play in enabling automation. They must insure that testers receive the education that they need to succeed and that the development cycle is adjusted to accommodate the pre-testing tasks required by automated test efforts. Management must also expect software measurements and cumulative results reports from testers.

The benefits of good testing practice together with test automation are significant:

1. test efforts can be reduced dramatically, from 30% to 50%;
2. the quality of software testing can be greatly improved through the use of structured test methods and software metrics;
3. through the use of measurements, project sizing and scheduling estimates can be greatly improved.

Test automation is a part of the product development life cycle, a complex dynamic process spanning years. The end is not in sight. Continuing support and commitment must be provided if software test automation efforts are to succeed. The most important thing that we learned was that testing is much more important than automation. Without good testing methods and metrics, test automation may not succeed.

Acknowledgments

I would like to thank Mr L. Gary Nakashian, Mr David Mayberry, Mr Charles Barlow, Mr Edgar Hartmann, Ms Joan Rothman, Ms Beate Kim, Mr Eric Mink, Ms Minna Beissinger, and Mr Joseph Mueller, for all their help and support in the Gremlin 2 project. I would also like to thank my reviewers for their time and their well-considered comments.

CHAPTER FOURTEEN

Experiences with test automation

Clive Bates

14.1 Background

14.1.1 The company

This case study looks at the implementation of an automated testing tool for regression testing of a new product range for a major UK clearing bank. The software tested was an electronic banking portfolio sold to the bank's corporate customers for use on their office PC workstations. The product range provides users with information on their accounts electronically. As well as balance and transaction details, it also provides reconciliation, payment, and cash collection services. This system is therefore a major delivery platform for the bank's electronic banking products.

14.1.2 The software to be tested

The software under test is designed to operate under Microsoft Windows. The first release of the electronic banking application was launched in 1992. For the bank, this was the first time a customer-focused development had been undertaken on any Windows-based application, and it therefore presented us with new challenges. Furthermore, as the product is aimed at external customers rather than internal clients, we had problems in covering all the operating systems and configurations that each customer could have. This was further exacerbated as the design of the products was such that there were different versions for use as standalone or as networked products. As previous experience from the team had been restricted to the different versions of DOS, a new approach for testing on Windows had to be adopted.

Due to the nature of the product, there were a number of other mainframe systems and interfaces that also needed to be tested, but this case study concentrates specifically on how we tested the PC elements.

At the time of the first development, it was felt that automated testing needed to be considered, and accordingly suppliers provided demonstrations of the different products available on the market at the time. Wonderful claims were made by all the companies invited to present their product. It focused our minds on the ultimate solution of switching the test tool on before going home, then coming in the next day to review how good the testing had been. In other words, it demonstrated an ideal opportunity for improvement in the quality of life for the testers with thorough automated testing.

14.1.3 Tool selection and initial failure

The biggest factor we had to consider at the time of tool selection was who the operators or users of the testing tool were to be. Eventually, the staff identified were not from a technical background, but were business oriented people who had no programming skills. With this key factor in mind, identifying the right testing tool for us was a fairly easy task, as we were looking for a product that had straightforward record and playback facility, but with the opportunity to tweak the functions by someone with programming skills if necessary. This should be able to give us the best of both worlds as we matured the process.

Accordingly, SQA TeamTest was selected and purchased early in 1992. The identified tool users went on initial training courses and learned how to use the product. However, once back at work, it soon became apparent that the preparation time needed before scripts could even be recorded was much greater than originally expected. As a result, the project simply ran out of time to set the testing tool up properly. Therefore the more familiar manual testing was invoked, and the test tool quickly became shelfware.

At the time all the blame went on the test tool for being too complicated, etc. whereas in reality not enough time had been allocated to implement it properly. Clearly this scenario is the most common reason why implementing a tool fails. Not enough time is allowed for the preparation, probably because it is regarded as a short-term overhead rather than appreciating that a longer-term view would result in a better quality test automation effort.

14.2 Planning, preparation, and eventual success

14.2.1 My new role

Once the first development was completed and tested, the next releases were already planned with aggressive dates. It was felt that a separate testing team needed to be established specifically to handle the amount of regression testing that would need to be undertaken. At that point I was asked to set up the team with specific responsibility for the regression testing side. This was a task that had always been looked at as even more troublesome than user acceptance testing because it was more repetitive and less interesting than other forms of testing.

14.2.2 Restarting with the test tool

I started by brushing off the dust from our shelfware test tool and set about getting it upgraded and bringing it into use. I drew up some high-level plans to cover the activities needed and obtained the buy-in from senior people to those activities. In some areas it was harder than others, but this was due in part to the fact that testing as an activity was never considered during the whole life cycle of a project, but more usually a few weeks or so before testing began. So there was also an education process that I had to manage in raising the awareness of the overall testing discipline.

Initially I had one person who was trained by the tool vendor, so we could start with planning properly. Our initial objective was to load up scripts from the first product that had already gone live. The manual test scripts for that release were reviewed and filtered down to the key ones that could be loaded onto the test tool. We found that on average we could condense ten manual scripts into one automated script. This was a bonus and meant that we had to do less recording of scripts than we expected.

14.2.3 The importance of planning and preparation

It is at this early point that the planning work is essential. There isn't anything very much to show for effort expended, but it is one of the most important steps. It is like anything where a neat or clean finish is required – the preparation can make or break the end result. The key message here is to make sure enough time is given to planning and structuring tests in such a way that they follow a logical sequence and hierarchy.

There needs to be recognition before this point by the sponsors that this effort needs to be put in, and they should not expect payback too quickly. In getting this buy-in from the sponsors you need to keep them informed of progress: 'No pain no gain.'

I make no apology for focusing here on the planning, because it is the area where it is easy to underestimate the effort involved. In our case it took us nine months from starting with raw software and the tool to being able to run a full regression test on our first product. In hindsight, and learning from mistakes, that time could probably have been brought down to approximately three months. However, this timescale does very much depend on the complexity of the system being automated and the skills of the staff involved.

14.2.4 Organization and motivation

The team was organized around a single System Expert, who is basically the one person in charge of the workflow and detailed knowledge of the testing tool we use. This person operates as the in-house troubleshooter and single contact point to the vendors in case of questions, upgrades, etc. By having this structure, the testers can be self-sufficient to a degree in resolving their own problems as they arise. In addition to the testers, I also have a technical support team to address the more detailed technical problems that may arise in hardware, LANs, communications, etc.

I believe that the necessary technical skills (which are varied) can be taught. In my area, the testers need to know the product they are testing, the operating systems it will run on, network configurations, hardware set-up, communications, and some programming skills. Different organizations will have different needs but these are the ones of value to us.

However, the team members need to have the right mindset towards testing if they are to fit in. They need to be keen, enthusiastic, interested in testing, a thinking person, and able to keep quality in mind, while striving to improve all the time.

Motivation has been well covered in many management books and all of the main principles apply. However, due to the repetitive nature of the testing work, it is important to insure that the testers see the value in what they do by having the respect of their colleagues. This is best achieved by raising the importance of the testing process in the projects and demonstrating its achievements. Furthermore, the value is best understood by seeing what the alternative would be if a testing tool and dedicated staff were not available.

14.2.5 Payback

Once the tool was loaded and ready to run, payback was achieved after the second project, even after nine months of preparation. In addition to the normal payback, it was clear during those projects that we were able to run the regression suite many more times than was possible manually. We were able to run a full regression test after every drop of software that we received weekly from the developers. This gave us a very good feel on the quality of builds, etc. and insured that any problems were found early on rather than at the end of the testing phase. This is a factor that needs to be borne in mind when looking at justifying using a testing tool.

14.2.6 Financial justification for test automation

Given the number of scripts loaded it is a simple sum to work out what it would take to run them manually and therefore what the alternative to automated testing would be.

In our case we have approximately 5000 conditions loaded. When you consider that one automated condition can cover many manual scripts, we have the equivalent of over 20 000 manual scripts loaded.

We estimated that each script would take approximately three minutes to run manually. If these were run seven hours a day, five days a week, it would take approximately $7^1/_2$ person-months of effort to fully regression test on one platform. The automated tool can run one full pass on one platform in three days. Need any more be said?

14.2.7 Platforms supported

In addition to the amount of regression testing for each platform, we have five platforms and four migration paths to test, i.e. nine passes of the software in total.

Fortunately, the tool we use supports a number of different platforms and operating systems. Once scripts are recorded on one platform they can be played back on any other that is supported, with no change needed. This to us is a major benefit.

14.3 Benefits of test automation

The key results seen from introducing automated testing can be split into a number of areas as outlined in the following subsections.

14.3.1 Reduce risks

Because you are always testing to the same known level you can be certain how well the software is being tested each time. This can be further improved by constantly increasing the level of coverage given by the scripts as part of the maintenance activity.

14.3.2 Fast

We can run through some 20 000 scripts in three days plus the allowance of one day for contingency. The one day is to cover various unforeseen events, such as the data or network, etc. not being 100% correct. This day's contingency allows time to get the problems rectified.

14.3.3 Cover more platforms

As the testing tool is portable, i.e. record on one platform, playback on many with no amendments, it makes the inclusion of additional platforms fairly straightforward.

14.3.4 Center of excellence

By having a stable team that concentrates on regression testing, you can build a team that has a great deal of expertise based on experience and training. This knowledge can then be used in future projects to give a greater level of guidance to the testing phase. This also encourages the involvement of the testers at the early requirements phase, to insure that all requirements are testable. This will help insure a better end product.

14.3.5 Better estimating

Because we now know how long it takes to undertake a full run of the regression tests for the software on one platform, it is a simple case of multiplying that up by the number of passes that will be required in a project.

14.3.6 Staff recruitment and morale

Certainly in the bank and quite possibly in other organizations, the role of testing is now seen much more as a possible career move, which was not envisaged only a few years ago. Previously there was a lot of stigma attached to testing that I am pleased to see is fast disappearing, and testers are now being given the recognition they deserve. As a result, there are people who now wish to concentrate in the discipline, and even for those who do not, it can be a good area to work in as part of an overall career progression. It is now considered valuable to have some formal training and/or period of work experience in testing. This also makes it easier to recruit new staff into the testing group.

14.3.7 Interest from other areas of the bank

With the success of our work, the word is spreading to other areas within the bank about what we have done and continue to do. As a result we can give advice about the process to follow and pitfalls to avoid. This reflects very much on the point earlier about the team being a center of excellence.

14.3.8 Volume testing

An unexpected spin-off from the use of the testing tool was that it enabled us to perform volume testing much more easily. We were able to undertake fairly simple programming of the testing tool to allow other tasks to be built in that are not directly recordable, but which can be used for volume testing. For example, we can record some payments and then go into the tool's code and build in loops for additional payments to be incrementally added. This saves an enormous amount of time recording individual scripts.

14.3.9 Year 2000 testing

Another example is the checking of specific dates for Year 2000 in the application to insure that it reports them correctly. Obviously with the speed that the tool plays back, rapid testing of new platforms and patches gives us a great advantage

14.4 Lessons learned

Although we achieved significant benefits from test automation, there were also some lessons that we learned along the way.

14.4.1 Training and consultancy

Proper training in the use of the tool selected is essential. In addition, we obtained five days' consultancy from the tool supplier to insure we kept on the right track. We were then able to request the consultant for the odd half day to review where we were up to and answer any specific questions we had. To me that was a very beneficial process and kept us heading in the right direction to use the tool to its full potential. I also attended Mark Fewster's test automation course (covering the principles described in this book).

14.4.2 Scripts

When loading up scripts onto the testing tool, they can be based on the manual scripts used in user acceptance testing and system testing. To assist in that process, the scripts should be written with the tool in mind, so it is easy to automate them, and reduce duplication. The actual recording of scripts is the easy part.

14.4.3 Data

Insure good quality static data is available to insure that the tool runs are consistent. If your data varies all the time, the tool will fail the tests and you will need to investigate whether it is a software or a data error. That can take a great deal of time and is not very productive. Enforce strict control and limit the use of the data to those who *need* to use it. As an aside, I know it is obvious, but insure backup of data and scripts is maintained. You do not want to remember this point when all the data has been lost due to a hard disk failure.

14.4.4 Set-up costs

Recognize that there will be set-up costs and insure that they are fully allowed for and are realistic. Too often, they are underestimated and the automation of scripts is suspended because it seems that no progress is being made and it is seen as a costly and benefit-free exercise. Make sure you do not fall into that same trap; appreciate that it can be expensive initially.

14.4.5 Learning curve

Depending on the tool you use, the learning curve for new staff coming in could be significant. I find it can take up to three months for a raw recruit to become a skilled member of the team. That is taking someone with the right mindset who is interested in testing, but does not have a working knowledge of the tool or may not even have seen it before. You will need to insure any project plans take that time lag into consideration.

14.4.6 Justification

As described above, our calculations justified our investment in test automation, but this is an area that always needs to be thought through carefully. Calculate when payback is expected, but make sure it is realistic. However, the results here can be impressive to even the worst skeptic.

Allow for ongoing maintenance of the automated tests. This is an area often neglected but is very important. An automated test and the test tool cannot be put on the shelf once testing has finished and pulled off some months later expecting everything to work. There are too many variables that could mean it fails on the first run. Therefore it is necessary to keep the tests up to date.

Constantly strive to improve the tests, and use the time to enhance existing scripts and add new dimensions. For example, you could work to make the system more robust: in our system, if a download is undertaken in the morning, a cut-off time for payments is not necessary. However, if the same download is undertaken later and a cut-off time is important, the tool needs to recognize this and function properly in either situation. This is achieved by building in an 'either/or' statement in the test script code for the testing tool.

14.4.8 Handling changes

Some change requests can be coded directly into the test tool at the test script program level. This will mean that when the test is run, the tool will be expecting the updated results. This could also be seen as an independent quality check that the developer has done the change correctly, as well as a check on the build.

14.5 The way forward

For the forthcoming period of time there are two major pieces of work that cannot be ignored: Year 2000 and EMU (Economic and Monetary Union, i.e. the European single currency). Without doubt we will be able to make good use of automated testing in these applications and continue with our program of projects. As I can see real value from the introduction of a testing tool, I would like to see its use expanded, and in the short term want to link the testing tool to a coverage tool. This will help us see what code is and is not being exercised by our tests, and will allow us to make it even more effective and efficient.

14.6 Summary

I have run through the main events that led to the introduction of our test tool, both our initial failure and our ultimate success. I have listed the benefits we achieved, along with some pointers that you may find of value in terms of lessons we learned along the way. Looking back, I am sure there are areas where we could have done things in a better way, but at the end of the day our initial objectives were met.

When looking to introduce automated testing, you need to be clear about what it can do and, more importantly, what it cannot do. Some of the basic items are listed below:

Automated testing is *not*:

- the quick cure;
- magic;
- just a press of the button – in the early days it needs preparation;
- learned and applied in days;
- able to drive outside hardware, for example external devices such as smart card readers, where manual input is also required in entering different cards and PIN numbers;
- able to check paper printouts. It can print to a printer but it cannot read what has printed out – but it can check the screen output.

Automated testing *is*:

- thorough – depending on the preparation that is put into it;
- fast – we run at 200 milliseconds between scripts;
- consistent and never becomes bored or tired;
- configurable to run outside office hours, that is evenings and weekends, with no need to have staff attending;
- capable of doing *anything* repetitive, including volume testing;
- easy to amend/update without having to always re-record the scripts;
- able to offer a great deal by coding in additional functions, for example volume testing to create data input;
- worth it!

© Clive Bates, OSC Consulting plc, 1998.

CHAPTER FIFTEEN

Automating system testing in a VMS environment

Peter Oakley

15.1 Background

15.1.1 The company

Lloyds Bank Registrars (LBR) maintains the Registers of Members for over 550 companies quoted on the London Stock Exchange. This is over 50% of the total number of quoted companies, and accounts for over 50% of the volume of daily trading. The work undertaken by LBR entails maintaining the names, addresses, and holdings of all shareholders, and running dividends, takeovers, rights issues, analyses, and other batch jobs for the companies (known as clients) for whom we act.

In the mid-1980s LBR took its IT in-house, away from the central Lloyds Bank IT department that had previously done the work for them. This was at the time when they were planning the replacement of their IBM batch system, which was becoming too slow and cumbersome to cope with the rapidly changing and growing share registration market.

15.1.2 Testing practice

As part of LBR's IT set-up, a System Testing team was formed from staff who had previously been end users of the IBM system, and had little or no formal IT training. As a result, testing was initially carried out almost as a user acceptance exercise, where each tester had their own constantly evolving test database against which they ran the program under test in a common testing environment.

Over time testing became more disciplined, with test plans being developed to make regression testing more consistent, and backups of the test databases were taken in order to have a static initial position so that testing was repeatable. With this foundation in place, and a large backlog of testing building up, a way of increasing the productivity of the testing team was required, and automating some of the testing appeared to be a way of accomplishing this. When I joined LBR in 1989 as a trained IT manager, I was given the task of managing the testing team and introducing automated testing.

15.1.3 The software to be tested

The development project under way at LBR at the time we introduced automated testing was a rewrite in VAX Basic language of the share registration system, making it online and real-time instead of overnight batch, and migrating the hardware from an IBM mainframe platform to a DEC VAX cluster.

The two main types of programs were two-phase (input and check) data capture programs to maintain the registers of members of the companies for whom we act as registrar, and background (though not necessarily overnight) batch programs to make bulk changes to the databases, to perform analyses, and to run dividends, corporate actions, etc.

All jobs were run from dumb terminals connected to the VAX cluster. There was no use of PCs.

The basic system initially required between 500 and 1000 program modules to enable the system to go live in 1989. However, new requirements very quickly pushed this up to around 3000 modules by 1991. Once the live date had been achieved in 1989, the scale of the extra programs to be written became apparent, and the push to improve productivity was started in earnest. The main thrust of this was the plan to automate as much testing as possible.

15.1.4 Our objective for test automation

The aim of the test automation task was to be able to perform more tests on more programs with the same number of staff and thereby find more errors more quickly. This should enable us to implement better quality code in the live environment more quickly than is possible by manual testing alone.

This case study details my experiences in attempting to achieve this objective.

15.2 The first attempt at automation

15.2.1 The tool: DTM

As all our development was on a Digital platform, it was logical to look first at the testing tool provided free with the Digital system software, known as Digital Test Manager (DTM).

The first step was for me to undergo a familiarization exercise, using small sample programs to investigate all the facilities available in DTM. I found the product to be workable, and the language simple enough to be

used by the testing team with their limited technical backgrounds. There were
pre- and post-processes to allow set-up of the test environment and pre-editing of the results before performing comparisons against the benchmarks.

15.2.2 Problems with interactive programs

Having understood the product, we selected a genuine screen-based interactive program under test and proceeded to record the tester conducting the tests from the test plan. The script for each test was stored separately. The program was returned to the developers for correction, and on its return we attempted to play back the recorded tests. This was fine so long as the correct result was returned from each keystroke. As soon as an unexpected result occurred the rest of the script became out of step with the program, producing some very undesirable results. The scripting language did not appear to have sufficient intelligence to allow us to overcome this problem, so any tests that did not run cleanly had to be abandoned.

Updating the script to allow for changes to the screen format (additional fields being the most common change) was not difficult, but as each test was stored separately they all had to be very carefully updated, ensuring that all occurrences of use of that screen were amended. This inevitably led to some errors that sent the program haywire again when it reached that point.

15.2.3 Problems with batch programs

When running batch programs that produced reports, the screen interface was relatively straightforward. The challenge here was checking the report contents. The DTM post-processor was intended to filter out dates from the headers, page numbers, and other items that would vary from run to run. As the programs were still in development, however, there were inevitably differences in the results from run to run. There was always a large number of differences reported from each re-run of the tests, and it was very difficult and time consuming to wade through the enormous printouts, working out which differences were from problems that had been corrected, which were from new problems, and which were acceptable differences that had not been filtered out.

15.2.4 Result: the tool was abandoned

Over time some of these problems were reduced, but never sufficiently to make consistent savings, and all too often using DTM took longer than manual testing. This led to total disillusionment among the testing team, not just with DTM but with the concept of automated testing. The scripts and result files were also starting to consume vast amounts of disk space, causing us to archive some data to tape, with all the attendant delays when we needed to restore those tests for a new release of the program.

As we were unable to make DTM work for us in the way we had intended, we abandoned its use. Our experience had, however, given us a good insight into what to look for in any automated testing tool that we would look to purchase in the future.

15.3 New tool selection and evaluation

15.3.1 Market search and selection of V-Test

When looking on the marketplace for an automated testing tool, we found a bewildering number that were suitable for PC developments, but very few that were suitable for a DEC VAX mainframe and dumb terminal environment. The final choice was between only three tools, and from presentations by each of the vendors we identified V-Test from Performance Software (later Cyrano) as the preferred tool, for the following reasons:

- the DEC VMS operating system was its prime market and the main focus of its enhancement efforts;
- the vendor had close links with DEC so kept up to date with changes to the hardware and system software;
- the price was reasonable;
- the vendor had a good customer base;
- there was seen to be commitment to support and enhance the product by a dedicated development team;
- some of the vendor's staff were obviously testing 'experts.'

We decided to undertake a six-week evaluation of the V-Test tool in-house.

15.3.2 Evaluation of V-Test

15.3.2.1 Evaluation criteria

The first step was to draw up an evaluation plan and set out success criteria that, if met, would allow me to recommend the purchase of V-Test.

The evaluation plan consisted of a description of the functionality to be tested, and details of the tests that would be performed to test each of these areas. The areas we evaluated were:

1   Performance monitor
    1.1   Response time for database inquiry
    1.2   Produce daily graph of response times
    1.3   Produce weekly graph of average response times

2   Test script generation
    2.1   Recording tests from the keyboard
    2.2   Using data files to input values on the screen
    2.3   Random number generation
    2.4   Manual script generation

3   Test script amendment
    3.1   Edit a script to change input values
    3.2   Add commands to cater for a new field on a screen

4   Comparator
    4.1   Comparing screen images
        4.1.1   Ignoring portions of the screen
        4.1.2   Comparing only specific positions on the screen
    4.2   Comparing files
        4.2.1   Ignoring fields within records
        4.2.2   Comparing files unique to this test
        4.2.3   Comparing common system files
    4.3   Comparing prints
        4.3.1   Comparing files with no page headers
        4.3.2   Ignoring page headings

5   Special requirements
    5.1   Transferring data generated by the system in one test to another test

6   Multiple pseudo-users (stress testing)

The success criteria that were defined were as follows:

- all functionality tests described above must work on our data;
- use of V-Test as a performance monitor does not degrade system performance;
- the set-up of test scripts and data, the running of those tests, and the interpretation of the results are to give significant personnel savings over the same exercise performed manually;
- modification of test scripts to cater for changes to screen layouts should be achievable within reasonable time scales.

15.3.2.2 Evaluation team

Due to the legacy of DTM, the staff who had been in System Testing at that time were skeptical of another automated testing tool, and we were concerned that this evaluation would not therefore be as objective as it should be. To overcome this, we carefully selected an experienced member of staff who was supportive of this initiative, and two newly employed students fresh from university who were keen to bring new technology to the team.

Along with myself, this small team received a training course from the vendor and a full set of the product documentation. An evaluation copy of the software was installed in a testing environment, and the team set about executing the tests defined in the evaluation plan, recording not only the results but also the time taken and their thoughts on ease of use, etc.

New tool selection and evaluation

15.3.2.3 Outcome of the evaluation

The evaluation team was very positive about the product, achieving all the required tests within the six-week period and needing very little help from the vendor, thus demonstrating the user-friendly nature of the tool and the effectiveness of the training and documentation.

V-Test was found to have the following benefits over DTM:

- the scripts could have logic instructions built into them to:
  - allow repetition of parts of the script with 'do loops'
  - detect messages indicating incorrect results and, via 'if then else' clauses, take alternative actions to allow the script to continue or close cleanly
  - call scripts from within scripts to allow a modular approach to be adopted, thus simplifying amendments and reducing the time taken to make them;
- masking areas of the screen that should not be compared was complex with DTM as the masking had to cover the entire test, whereas V-Test has screen-level masking automatically invoked every time that screen is compared;
- V-Test can compare screens, print files, and RMS files, whereas DTM can only compare screens.

V-Test passed virtually all the tests with flying colors. The only real exception was a minor graphics anomaly between screen formats in the results and benchmark files, and a problem with the fact that we use 25-line screen formats whereas V-Test expects 24. The latter was soon overcome by the vendor supplying a 25-line screen mapper.

15.4 Implementation of V-Test

15.4.1 Concerns

15.4.1.1 Performance monitoring

One of the features of V-Test is performance monitoring. It was envisaged that we might use this to monitor response times on the live system when using the software that we had tested. This information could be used to check conformance with Service Level Agreements.

If performance monitoring was enabled, V-Test could be used to break into other users' sessions. This was seen to be potentially useful if a tester left a V-Test session logged in which subsequently had a problem, as the V-Test coordinator could then break in to log them out.

The problem here was that we did not want people to be able to break into sessions on the live system. As performance monitoring was an unexpected bonus in V-Test, and the prime use was for testing, we decided to restrict V-Test to the test system, and find another tool to monitor the performance of the live system.

15.4.1.2 Security

V-Test can be installed as a closed system, where only the Administrator has access to anything and has to grant all required accesses to all required users specifically. Alternatively, it can be installed as an open system where everyone has access to everything unless the access is removed by the Administrator. As the tool was to be restricted to the test system, I decided to implement the open security, and close it down specifically where necessary. Not only was this quicker to implement, it also meant that people would not be hampered in their use of V-Test by security locks that were not really necessary and would simply be unlocked when discovered.

15.4.1.3 Staffing

As the development of scripts requires a programming aptitude, and as there were a limited number of staff in System Testing who were suitable, I decided to have a separate team of four to six keen young staff to develop and run the scripts and comparator programs, while the majority of the team would develop test plans, create test data, and check the output from the V-Test runs.

15.4.2 Proposed benefits and the business case for V-Test

The major factor that limited the effectiveness of our manual testing was the tight deadlines, which did not allow sufficient testing to take place before the program was required in live. The benefit that we were looking to achieve was therefore to have more testing done by the same number of staff, rather than the same amount by less. The method of measuring this was, however, the same – how many extra person-days would have been required to achieve manually the testing done by V-Test.

In order to get some baseline estimates I had to make some educated assumptions:

- that System Test test an average of 15 program iterations a week;
- that only one of these is on its first iteration;
- that an average program takes 5 person-days to test/re-test manually;
- that an average program will take 15 person-days to initially load to V-Test;
- that it will take on average 2 person-days to re-test a program using V-Test;
- there are 7 person-hours in a person-day

An average week would therefore entail 75 person-days of clerical work (15 programs at 5 days each). With V-Test this should be reduced to 43 person-days (1 program at 15 person-days and 14 at 2 person-days). Once all programs are loaded to V-Test, therefore, we would be able to undertake 32 more person-days testing each week, which is (assuming 40 working weeks a year) 1280 person-days a year.

The cost of the V-Test software for the first year equated to 322 person-days, and 58 person-days per year thereafter.

Depending on how quickly we got the tests for a program loaded to V-Test, it looked as if it could be possible to get V-Test to pay for itself in extra testing within the first year.

15.4.3 What was automated – and how

The planned approach to integrating V-Test into System Testing was to form a small team of two to three people who would write the scripts and comparator programs to enable two or three programs that had test plans and test data already in place to be loaded to V-Test.

After a month these tests should have been run, and the format of test plans and test data would be reviewed to identify ways that they could be improved for V-Test use.

A modular approach would be taken to building scripts, masks, and data files, so that over time a library could be built up that could be used to construct future tests. The script for each screen would be stored once only, and be called from a control program each time it was required, specifying the appropriate data file(s) to be used to fill each of the screen's fields.

A team of seven staff was established, three of them having been trained by the vendor. The others were trained through the product's tutorial.

15.4.3.1 *Choice of programs to automate*

As our system is fully integrated, most developments consist of building some new programs, and making changes to some existing common ones to allow for the new functionality. We therefore had to make the decision whether to automate all new programs, all existing programs, all programs involved in new developments (new and existing), or some other combination. As the greatest payback was to be gained from programs that were re-tested many times, I chose a general inquiry program that is often enhanced for new developments and requires a lot of testing due to its complexity.

We tried to continue the theme of loading tests for existing programs that were changed relatively frequently and had a long manual testing cycle. The problem we encountered was that many of the programs did not have comprehensive test plans, and generating these as part of the exercise of loading them to V-Test distorted our figures and made the time spent difficult to justify. Loading programs to V-Test without test plans proved equally fruitless as only the author knew what the tests were for, so they soon fell into disuse.

We therefore tended towards loading the tests for new programs to V-Test, ensuring that comprehensive test plans were developed for all new programs.

15.4.3.2 Some surprising benefits

We found some programs where full automation was not practical, but on further investigation there were predictable processes regularly repeated during the manual testing cycle, and we used the tool to automate these.

There was an occasion when we had two large files of cash values that should have matched, but had different totals. We used the comparator feature of the tool to extract and compare the relevant fields from these two files. Within moments we had not only found the cause of the totals difference, but had also found a number of compensating errors that would not have been spotted if the prints of the files had been manually searched for the amount of the difference.

15.4.3.3 Out with the old . . .

After about six months' use of the product, we were relatively happy with the format of the scripts and test data. We began to have some difficulties in updating the earlier scripts that had not been developed in this way, so had to spend some time rewriting these in the new regime in order to keep them current and usable.

15.4.4 Technical problems

15.4.4.1 Testing environment and common files

The main problem, apart from some glitches with the tool which were fixed by the vendor, was to do with the testing environment. The Share Registration System has a number of common files which are updated by a great many programs, as well as files that are specific either to one client or even one job. When testing programs using V-Test, we generally have a test client for each tester, or each program. This enables us to reset the client- and job-specific files to their initial values at the beginning of each test. The only way we could do this with common files was to set up a separate environment for each set of tests, which included all common files that were updated by the program, or that needed to be set to specific values in order for the tests to run cleanly. Many of the test plans did not specify all the common files that the program used, so we would suffer failures due to conflicts in common files.

Unless the test plan or program specification was specific about the common files that the program updated, the only way to avoid the problem was to set up a copy of the entire environment, or keep adding files each time the tests fell over. As a compromise we set up a standard environment that included the files that were most commonly used, and added any others that were identified for the program.

15.4.4.2 Comparison problems: don't ignore too much

With V-Test there is the facility to ignore various things when comparing results to benchmarks, in order to avoid being advised of differences you don't care about. This includes some dates and times, page headings, the case of a font, etc.

One problem we had to be very careful not to fall foul of was ignoring these items altogether. It is fine ignoring the date on a page header because you know it will be different from the benchmark, but someone has to check that the date produced – though different – is correct. Similarly, V-Test can strip out page headings on a report and compare a continuous file of data to avoid the complications of page throws happening in different places, but the print must then be examined by hand to insure that the page headings are correct.

15.4.4.3 Building our regime

Overcoming capture replay Our initial view of automation was capture replay of the tests previously carried out manually. This required all data and environment set-up work to be performed clerically beforehand, as well as any clean-up work afterwards.

We soon learned to build V-Test scripts to perform the set-up and clean-up jobs, either by recording the manual process or, more commonly, writing the scripts directly.

After building the tests for a few programs in this manner, it became clear that it would be more efficient to set up the test data in files that could be called in by the script. This would make the script modular, calling the data for each screen each time it was entered within the test. This approach gave a much quicker start to the testing, since it was able to be prepared before the program was delivered. It could also run automatically on the first release instead of requiring a tester to run through the program manually in order to create the scripts.

Script structuring After building tests for several programs in the above manner, we found further commonality between the scripts. We have four basic types of programs to test:

- online input
- online checking
- batch job input
- batch job release.

A common script was built for each of these program types, each one called by a parent script that was unique to the program under test. In order to get the common scripts to work, we had to be able to pull in data related to the specific program under test by a common call from the script. This was achieved by moving away from the idea of having a data file for each field on a screen to having a table with a common interface, but variable contents, in which the columns represented tests, and the rows represented the input fields for all the screens in that test.

One of the major benefits of this approach was that the specific script writing required for each program was reduced to a minimum, and the testers who were not proficient in V-Test were easily able to create the tables of test data.

It was also possible to use expressions in the tables, such as 'today's date,' rather than static data in order to make the test dynamic and able to be run on any day without the need to set a special date on the system.

15.4.5 Non-technical problems

15.4.5.1 The legacy of skepticism

Despite the promising start with V-Test there were still a number of people with painful memories of DTM who were very skeptical and took delight in every problem that appeared.

I found the way to convince these people of the value of V-Test was to involve them in a project where V-Test was already being used successfully, and where they would have to use it if they were to work effectively within the team. The use of new people in the initial team was a way of overcoming the inertia, but if not handled properly could result in a feeling on both sides that the V-Test team was an elitist group, and this could make experienced staff even more resistant to change.

15.4.5.2 The use of students on the team

In order to have a motivated and technically able team working on V-Test, I decided that apart from one or two key permanent staff, the people best suited to work in this area were the students we employed for their 12 months' work experience during their degree.

The only problem with this was that these people were new to LBR as well as V-Test, so had a very steep learning curve to overcome before they became productive. Despite this the decision proved very successful until the year was up and all the experience walked out the door, leaving us to train a new batch of students – although we did benefit from their new ideas.

15.4.6 Benefits achieved

During the early days of using V-Test, the time taken to load a program to V-Test varied between 0.4 times (for a very long manual test) and 8 times (for a very short manual test) as long as a manual test cycle. Once we had settled on the latest script format we found this settled down to a more consistent twice as long to load as to test manually, but there were some programs where loading to V-Test took considerably less time, so a saving was made on the first cycle.

After four months of use we had 22 programs loaded to V-Test. Twenty iterations had been run by V-Test, doing the equivalent of 6 person-months of work in 9 days.

Below is a summary of the actual values as at the end of 1992 after 5 months' use of V-Test, compared to the estimates used to justify the purchase of the tool.

	Estimate	Actual
Initial cost of product for first year	322 person-days	446 person-days
Average number of programs V-Tested per week	15	1.5
Average time to test a program clerically	5 person-days	5.8 person-days
Average time to create V-Test scripts for a program	15 person-days	10.3 person-days
Average time to complete a V-Test re-run	2 person-days	0.8 person-days
Weekly savings over manual testing	32 person-days	−2 person-days

Apart from the first two figures, it can be seen that the other estimates were on the cautious side. When the number of programs loaded to V-Test is sufficiently high for us to reach the 15 per week estimate, the savings will be around 87 person-days – much higher than estimated.

The personnel savings shown above are of course only part of the picture as far as cost recovery is concerned. Our initial aim was to recover the license costs (446 person-days in the first year). This was achieved within 8 months of the product's installation, thanks to a number of re-tests of large, frequently amended programs.

As a result of this success we were able to justify investment in PCs to replace the dumb terminals we had been using for script development at a cost equivalent of 143 person-days. This cost was recovered the following month.

Having recovered all capital costs in 9 months, we then looked at the revenue costs, including the time spent on developing, enhancing, and running scripts, checking the benchmarks, and the overheads for these staff. The overheads incurred up until this time were recovered by the end of the next (10th) month, after which we fairly rapidly started recovering the scripting costs.

During this time we continued to load more programs to V-Test, so continued to incur more revenue costs. The next year's license fees also had to be paid after the 12th month. After 16 months we had finally made savings equivalent to everything we had spent (equivalent to 1343 person-days).

Throughout the rest of 1993 and until August 1994 we continued to make true savings which amounted to the equivalent of 364 person-days (Figure 15.1). To achieve this, V-Test had to do a total of 2148 person-days of testing, which is 1056 person-days more than we would have been able to achieve if we had used the same staff on manual testing over the 25 months of using V-Test (Figure 15.2).

Figure 15.1 shows the cost of software, hardware, and personnel, all expressed in person-days, compared to the person-days that would have been required to achieve the work done by V-test. Figure 15.2 shows the same work done by V-Test, compared to just the personnel from the previous graph, to show how much more work was achieved with V-Test.

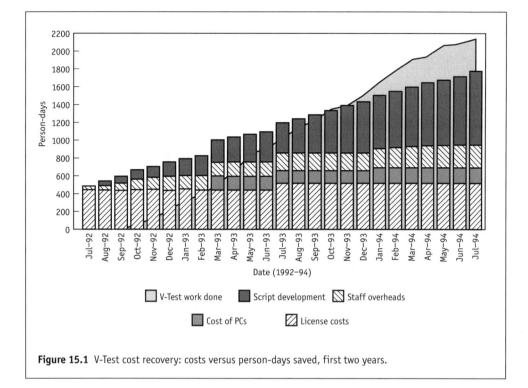

Figure 15.1 V-Test cost recovery: costs versus person-days saved, first two years.

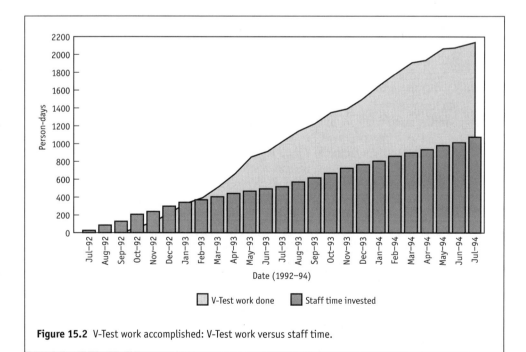

Figure 15.2 V-Test work accomplished: V-Test work versus staff time.

15.4.7 Demise of automation

Despite the very promising start made by V-Test as demonstrated here, there came a time during 1995 when the pressures to deliver software to a fixed deadline for the major project under way at that time became too great to allow time for programs to be loaded to V-Test in the manner that had been adopted during the first three years. This was partly because the test plans, which are so essential to good test automation, were long-winded and took some time to construct in the format in use at the time. Also, the code being delivered was of poor quality, resulting in tests not completing, and large amounts of differences between the results and benchmarks of those that did run.

We still had only a small V-Test team who had to write and run these tests, so with the number of testers growing and a lot of releases of the programs, a delay between receiving the code and getting the tests run automatically began to frustrate the testers. Attempts were made to simplify the format of the test plans, but the perceived failure of the V-Test team to deliver the goods had set a negative mentality in place again and after a couple more months of trying, V-Test was abandoned for the major project under way at that time. People were moved off the V-Test team to do manual testing, with the result that virtually all V-Test work stopped for the next 12 months.

15.4.8 Resurrection plans

We are happy that the method we have adopted for developing V-Test scripts is a good one; it is simple and efficient, but it relies on good test plans.

The first step, therefore, will be to create a new template for test plans that is much simpler than the previous verbose document, and is specifically geared to automated testing.

Where possible the testing team will work with the Business Analysis team to develop test cases in order to insure that all scenarios are covered in the specification, and test cases documented at that stage.

The second step will be to install the newest version of V-Test, which has a Windows front-end to make it more attractive to a wider number of staff. As this will entail setting up directories on the PCs to be used by Windows, it will also give us the opportunity to review and document the file management issues surrounding testing as a whole, not just the automated parts.

Step three involves a change in the test client databases that are to be used. In the past each tester or project has had its own test client with varying degrees of coverage of live conditions. When space is at a premium on the test system, and a program is not currently in testing, these clients tend to get deleted, so when the test is due to be re-run it cannot be, as the database has gone. To avoid this we have developed a common test client database that contains as many live conditions as we are able to identify. It will only be necessary to store one backup of this client, which can then be renamed and used for each program under test. As the test client is enhanced to take in newly discovered conditions, a copy of the version last used by each and every test must be retained, so that a change in the program that requires re-testing can still use the original benchmarks as it is still able to use the same version of the client.

Finally, we will find a method for deciding which types of programs can have some of their testing automated, which parts can be automated, and what the best method is for achieving that automation. An example of this is database set-up at the beginning of a test, and clean-up at the end. V-Test is not the best tool to use for this, as we cannot use the table of data and general script principle to achieve it, so we will look at using VMS command files instead.

With this groundwork in place, we will revert to our original plan of automating existing programs that have a long test cycle but change relatively frequently. Once we have completed sufficient of these programs to have a groundswell of experience and approval among the permanent staff, we will look to move into automating new program testing, with a better attitude and much firmer guidelines than we had in the past.

15.5 Conclusion

15.5.1 Lessons learned

15.5.1.1 Staffing

It is a good idea to include appropriately educated new young staff into a new automated testing area. They have fresh ideas and are not hampered by preconceived notions of how testing has been done in the past. They have also been exposed to the latest ideas and techniques.

It is not a good idea to have *only* new young staff in such an area, as they have no knowledge of the business or the system that they are testing, so have a very steep learning curve to go through.

Where possible avoid using temporary staff in the automated testing area if it is going to be a discrete team, for obvious retraining reasons when they leave. We have also discovered that it is better not to have a separate area set aside to automate testing as this only creates barriers and makes the manual testers defensive of their role, and therefore hostile to automated testing. It is far better to involve everyone in some aspect of the automated side even though they will not all be suited to writing scripts.

15.5.1.2 What to automate first

When deciding on which programs to automate first, it is better to avoid those that are under time pressure. In order to be successful at automating the majority of program testing, a calm unpressured period needs to be set aside to develop the techniques, establish templates for documentation, and create any common scripts. Once everyone is happy with the process of automatically testing a program then it should be possible to introduce it for new programs in order to get the benefits that you were looking for in buying the tool in the first place.

15.5.1.3 Housekeeping

Automated testing will generate vast amounts of data. It is essential to be aware of exactly what is generated both by the program under test and by the tools, as it is possible to run a great many more tests in a much shorter timeframe once a test is automated.

Strict naming conventions and locations for all appropriate file types must be established and policed, and archiving/deletion philosophies established to insure that only essential data is kept, and can be readily located, and no essential data is deleted. (See also Chapter 5.)

15.5.1.4 Externalize data

As described in Chapter 3, it is a good idea to remove all test data from the scripts into files or tables. This makes it much easier to:

- add new tests – by adding data to the end of the file(s);
- segregate tests – by splitting the data files into subfiles for each test subject;
- modify tests – by changing the script once and either creating a new file of data or modifying the existing one(s);
- modularize scripts.

15.5.1.5 Modularize scripts

Take a leaf out of the developer's book and modularize script development as much as possible. This has the same advantage as in programming; that is, every time you use a common script, you save the effort of coding and testing it. Providing that the purpose of each module is clearly documented, it should also save the embarrassment of building a script that works, but does not achieve what is desired.

Use the right tool for the job

It is all too easy to select an 'automation tool' (in our case V-Test) and be tempted to try to use it for the total automation of all programs. Some tasks do not lend themselves to the tool, but can still be automated using other tools such as command files or PC functionality. There may also be some processes where it is more efficient to test manually, and we should not attempt to automate these.

15.5.2 Benefits achieved

Apart from standard program testing we found V-Test was useful for:

- comparison of specific areas of large print files;
- creation of test data;
- performing regular weekly housekeeping tasks;
- acting as an input clerk to create data in earlier runs of a suite in order to test a job that runs at the end.

Over 2 years, V-test has done 1056 person-days more testing than would have been possible manually, if the staff in the automated testing area had done manual testing instead of implementing V-Test scripts.

For those programs we did get loaded to V-Test, we were able to do full re-testing of each iteration of the program, so we picked up knock-on errors as well as insuring that the intended changes had been correctly implemented.

Automated testing of an electronic stock exchange

Paul Herzlich

16.1 Background

16.1.1 Stock markets in London

Tradepoint Stock Exchange is a secondary cash equities market in London, UK. It was founded in 1993 by a small group of former London Stock Exchange managers from technical and marketing backgrounds. The vision was to propel equities trading in London fully into the computer age. The result would be lower cost trading and better performance for the investor.

It took some two years to bring the market to life. There were difficult financial technical problems to solve, most notably the market rules for a fair, order-driven market and the arrangements surrounding the use of a central counterparty to all trades. At the same time, the electronic trading software had to be developed. A deal was made to buy the Vancouver Stock Exchange's VCT system, which Tradepoint further adapted to reflect UK market rules, also replacing the text market-access terminals with Windows-based clients. Throughout, the founders had to navigate the road carefully through the regulatory obstacles and to 'sell' a skeptical London financial services industry on joining the new exchange. Tradepoint was finally given approval to operate as a Recognized Investment Exchange and the market went live in September 1995.

16.1.2 Impact of new technology

At the time it went live, Tradepoint's technology was revolutionary for London. Tradepoint's competitor, the London Stock Exchange, operated a quote-driven market. Quotes from market makers were distributed electronically over a system called SEAQ. Trading and post-trade allocations to accounts involved telephones and faxes. The Tradepoint market and system were totally different. Instead of quotes, firm buy and sell orders are placed

in an order book, which is instantly visible to all members. A trade is
effected by clicking on an order in the book and confirming the intention to
trade. All the post-trade preparation for settlement is also fully electronic.

16.1.3 Market regulator concerns

Throughout Tradepoint's initial development, the financial services industry regulators were extremely concerned about the electronic nature of
the market and Tradepoint's ability to insure a level playing field for all
players in the market. 'Level playing field' translated into several key
technical issues:

- no user could be disadvantaged because of variable system performance;
- the system had to be available equally to all participants;
- the software had to be free of bugs which inhibited trading or caused
  mis-trades.

These would be requirements of almost any computer system. But in the
case of a fledgling electronic financial market, any fault could have a catastrophic effect on the stability of the market. It could lose the business
customers, cost unimaginable sums in rectifying a trading error, and ultimately lose the business its license as an exchange. Without that, there
would be no business.

No wonder, then, that the Tradepoint developers had a healthy respect
for testing from the outset.

16.2 The system and testing

16.2.1 Initial system development and testing

Even though the system was based on VCT, it was largely rewritten for
Tradepoint. To give an idea of the scope, there were about seven million
lines of source code originally. Forty-eight person-months went into the
rewrite leading up to live. The system's structure, which has not changed
substantially in the past couple of years, looks like the diagram in Figure
16.1 But the various products, particularly the workstations and central
trading system, have been continuously upgraded.

I joined Tradepoint as test manager five months after the market went
live. Already, by that time, the developers were readying the first release of
improvements. The test library consisted of about 1800 manual test cases of
a mainly functional test nature. They were run against the one platform that
was supported, with workstations on Windows 3.11. There were two types
of API server: one that connected to the trading system via X.25 communications and one that connected to a local 'demonstrator,' which simulated
the central trading system locally. There were three workstation applications. Manual testing took four person-weeks.

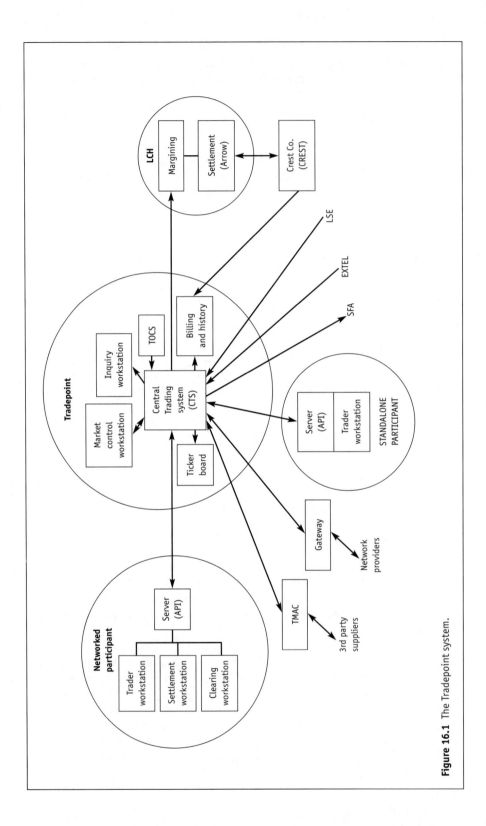

Figure 16.1 The Tradepoint system.

It was well understood from the outset that the system would undergo regular enhancements, for both business and technological reasons. As soon as the market went live, feedback from customers and marketing generated a steady stream of enhancement requests. On the technological side there was a need to port the workstations from Windows 3.11 to Windows 95, Windows NT 3.51, and Windows NT 4.0. There was also a need to evolve from MS Windows-specific DDE to Corba, in order to allow integration with UNIX-based products.

It was clear that the testing that went into the initial go-live release was not a one-off. Each new release would require testing of new features and regression testing of the rest. The regulatory obligations to keep an orderly, fair market running remained in force and the risk in deploying the new releases was, if anything, higher than the original development.

From the development manager's perspective, the test burden was set to grow and it threatened to become a drag on development. New functionality would automatically increase the number of test cases, and new platforms and servers were set to multiply the number of test cycles. The development manager was also aware that the quality of test execution, and the breadth and depth of testing, needed to be improved. It had been hard to insure consistency of test execution manually. There were areas of functionality that needed deeper, more thorough test cases, and there were whole areas of the system, such as performance, which needed a more systematic, repeatable approach.

With this in mind, we set out to automate functional and performance testing. Test automation held some promise of improving testing quality, while at the same time enabling us to get more from the test effort and do more in the elapsed time.

16.3 Test automation requirements

16.3.1 Our goals

Having automated Test Suites before, I knew we needed to analyze our requirements before choosing a tool. I focused on three central points:

- objectives of automation – we had to be clear what we wanted to achieve;
- development and test process – we needed to be sure that the process lent itself to being automated;
- scope of automation – to understand what capabilities the tool had to have.

Reducing testing resources, the testing budget, and the testing team were emphatically *not* objectives of test automation. The objective was to insure thorough regression testing, releasing resource to do deeper testing of critical features, concentrate on the new functionality, and test the performance impacts of new releases.

To cover the manual test library for the first release after going live took four person-weeks, in two elapsed weeks. The objective of automating was to insure that the proliferation of new platforms, new servers, and new workstations, along with the functional enhancements to the system, didn't simply multiply the elapsed time to test linearly.

16.3.2 Test team organization: independent teams abandoned

The development process was a RAD-like iterative process, timeboxed into three-month releases on average. The stages of testing are clearly defined. The programmers do unit testing; the testers do integration and system testing. Only system testing was to be targeted for automation. There was already a database in place for the management of changes and faults.

The test team was part of the development team. The development manager had followed the textbook on independent test teams during the initial development and had found it had a number of serious drawbacks, which he did not want to suffer any longer. With an independent test team, it took longer to report bugs, the quality of bug reporting was poor, and it took several iterations to fix bugs. Developers and testers did not understand each other's problems and all of these caused delays. Having independent testers, but within the development team, seemed a better solution. It insured that testers were involved early in the development of a release. We get previews of code – which helps in keeping scripts up-to-date, as well as in planning new tests.

The scope of the automated testing was therefore set to be the functional regression testing, which is performed by the test team as part of system testing. The intention was to automate in order to get repeatable test execution of the workstations. Using an 'outside-in' test strategy, the test cases entered via the workstation were designed to cover the workstations and the capabilities of the central system.

16.4 Test tool selection

16.4.1 Constraints

In addition to our requirements, the framework for selecting a tool consisted of two other elements:

- technical constraints
- practical considerations.

The technical constraints we had to take into account were the language we develop in (Visual C++), the third-party components (e.g. Farpoint Spreadsheet), and architectural features such as our networking, use of DDE, Corba, real-time messaging, etc.

The practical considerations included, first and foremost, what tools were available. There is little point in developing an idealized requirement for a tool that doesn't exist, unless you are prepared to argue that partially meeting your requirement is worthless, which is rarely the case. It was valuable to set our expectations based on what we could actually license, rather than to daydream about what might be ideal.

The other practical considerations were:

- Who will use the tool? The main distinction is whether it is technicians with programming experience or users without programming experience.

- What kind of testing will they do? Functional or non-functional? Unit, integration, system, or acceptance (with all the differences in test cases and scripts that those levels imply)?

- How long must the tests last? Are you building a test library or just trying to automate a one-off release? This will affect how biased the tool you select is towards capture replay versus script programming.

16.4.2 Things that I ignored

There were a raft of things I decided to take little notice of, that you are supposed to care about in tool selection, including:

- training
- support
- vendor viability
- price.

The reason is simply that the test tools market is too immature to let these things get in the way of choosing a technically capable tool that will do the job for you. They are icing on the cake. I include 'price' because there is not a vast difference in pricing, and because it is my observation that you get what you pay for, relatively speaking. Weak, immature tools are cheaper.

16.4.3 Stages of tool selection

16.4.3.1 The 'test drive'

In doing the selection, there were essentially three stages. First, I contacted vendors, talked to the salespeople, and looked at the technical literature. Then, I obtained evaluation copies, and did what I call a 'test drive'.

The test drive was aimed mainly at determining how accurately I could automate the various components of our application in our environment. There is huge diversity in the construction of Windows applications, and the test execution tools often respond very differently to any non-standard or complicated usages of Windows API calls, screen controls, and object classes. You get a pretty good idea of the overall capability of a tool during the test drive, but the real object of the exercise is to determine whether it will work with your specific application. You find that you can put up with a great deal of inconvenience if the user interface of the tool is slightly unfriendly in places, but there is nothing you can do if the underlying engine of the tool just won't replay tests and check results with your programs.

16.4.3.2 Vendor relationship

The next stage of the selection was to get the vendor's support people to resolve the technical queries raised by the test drive. Once again, I found that it is pointless to judge the technical support by things like the time it takes to get through to them on the telephone. The real judge of the technical support was whether they could solve the problem, and how long and how much effort it would take to enhance the tool, if this were the only way to resolve it. A technical support group might be slightly frustrating to deal with because they are rushed off their feet, but I can't mark them down for that, provided they solve the problem or answer the question. You don't have enough capable choices in test tools to engage in that kind of discrimination.

In addition to the list of things above that I ignored in selection, there are a few more things to ignore or downplay while performing the selection. Don't give a lot of credit for features that you don't need. Ignore all promises from salespeople or technical support people that anything is easy. Above all, don't give any credit at all to promises that a feature you need will be in the next release – unless you can test a well-advanced beta that proves it.

16.4.3.3 Technical issues

In our environment, there were a couple of technical issues that became the real 'make or break' differentiators among the products: how they dealt with dynamic results and embedded third-party OCXs.

The 'dynamic results' problem is this. In our test environment some data cannot be reset to exactly the same starting position for every test, unless you completely restart the test system before each test (or simulate that). It is not a practical approach. Instead, we end up with results that can only be predicted at the time that the test inputs are entered. The results cannot be reused from one test to the next. Next time, you will calculate a different answer. Most of the test execution tools give you mechanisms for checking things programmatically, avoiding the need to compare results stored from a previous test, but it was simplest to do this in WinRunner.

The problem with OCXs is that either a tool recognizes a particular OCX, and you can enter data and capture results, or it doesn't. If it doesn't, you cannot test that part of the application

16.4.3.4 Our choice: WinRunner

The final stage was to choose the tool. The candidates were QA Centre from what was then Direct Technology, TeamTest from SQA, AutoTester, QA Partner, and Mercury Interactive's WinRunner.

We chose WinRunner because it supported 16-bit and 32-bit using the same scripts. It also gave us the ability to deal with our dynamic results and to test our third-party components. Using WinRunner's text recognition, we were able to program input and capture routines for all OCXs that we used.

Price was not a determinant. QA Centre, which was our runner up, and WinRunner were the two most expensive tools.

Ease of use was also not a determinant. WinRunner was the most powerful of the lot, but version 3 had some pretty unhelpful features in the user interface. That improved enormously by the time we took delivery of the product, which had moved up to version 4.

16.5 Implementation

16.5.1 Where to start?

There are some experiences from our early days of implementing WinRunner that are worth relating. It took about four weeks to get familiar with the tool completely and start configuring a test environment for data and scripts. During this period, we decided on naming standards and directory structures. We developed our own routines for test logging and a few other utilities for common functions. We captured 'maps' of the windows of our applications.

We then ran into a 'where to start' conundrum. Should we develop a series of easy, low-value scripts or harder, high-value ones? You get valuable experience from the easy ones, like a logon script, but the results are not worth much. Automating the order entry of bids and offers was much more valuable, but was a much harder point at which to start. Virtually everything in the market system turns on the entry of orders, so this is where the functionality is the richest, most critical, and riskiest. We decided to get on with the order entry.

Regardless where you start, you immediately have to solve the basic problems of automated test execution. We developed techniques (and common routines where possible) for trapping errors, synchronizing between the test script and the application, and custom checking of results.

16.5.2 Choices in implementing a data-driven approach

Key architectural issues had to be solved for order entry, too. We were trying to build a permanent library of repeatable tests. Common functions like order entry are repeated over and over – it is insane to engineer the tests without some form of common script routines. Typically, you want such routines to be data driven. So you prepare a generic script to do order entry, and you drive it through different test cases by feeding it different data inputs. For example, there are many combinations of Stock, Size, Price, and Order Type for us to test. Each order entry test might take the form:

```
Order (<stock>, <size>, <price>, <order type>)
```

A script might consist of a list of such 'calls' to an order entry test routine. In most discussions of data-driven testing, the values of the parameters would be expected to come from a spreadsheet. I considered this and asked why. Why put rows of data in a spreadsheet separately from the script? If it is for users, I can see why. They are not likely to be able to modify the script. But for technical testers, I saw no advantage. The maintenance of the calls in the script is identical to the maintenance of the rows in the spreadsheet. The advantage of maintaining the calls in the script is that you don't have two things to maintain, and you don't have to create a routine for reading in the spreadsheet values at runtime. The script is no less data-driven, but you avoid the overhead of having to store and locate dispersed elements and to maintain your test suite with different tools.

16.5.3 Script architecture evolution

There are other, perhaps surprising, architectural issues to grapple with, like 'what is a test?' Deciding how much should go into one script was not simple or evident. The relationship between manual and automated tests was not a simple one-for-one conversion.

Within a script it became necessary to distinguish between a failure of a test action, and an error that was part of the lead up to (or follow on from) a test action. More infrastructure – error handling routines, reporting, recovery routines – was developed as a common element of all test scripts and the whole test library became clearer. Could we have designed it in advance? In retrospect, the early scripts were like prototypes. Since we started there have been two complete overhauls of the infrastructure to refine it in line with what we learned.

16.6 Maturity and maintenance

16.6.1 Script maintenance

Much play is given to the workload involved in maintaining scripts. Indeed there is work to do, but it is not as onerous for us as one would predict. We don't automate the testing of new features until the release following their first release. We take a view on changes. When the test team gets early copies of changed software, they decide whether to upgrade the scripts immediately, or to test manually this time and automate afterwards, for the next release. This approach is another example where automated testing rightfully does not replace manual testing.

Application changes are not the only source of script maintenance. As we refine the infrastructure and learn new techniques, we have retrofitted them to old scripts. Usually this is to reduce the level of checking or improve test execution speed.

As the number of products, platforms, and servers increased, so did the size of the test team. This introduced a new script maintenance problem: concurrent changes to scripts, particularly for the common routines. When we recognized that we had all the problems of ordinary program development, we adopted source code management techniques. All the scripts were put under the control of Microsoft SourceSafe. I don't believe this would have been possible with any of the other test execution tools we evaluated.

WinRunner is often mocked by its competitors for its extensive use of directories in the file system. It is this very feature that allowed us to place our test scripts under version control so easily.

16.6.2 Relationship of manual to automated tests

Another problem that has increased over time has been the mapping of manual scripts to the automated versions. We have continued to maintain manual scripts so that it is always possible to choose to test manually. It is not a contingency measure, but rather more one of documentation. It also allows us to check the quality of automated testing by re-testing an area manually from time to time.

We also maintain the manual scripts in support of a technique I call 'input only' or 'semi-automated' testing. For some test cases the results are too hard to check automatically, and you would spend a disproportionate effort to program an automated script. Nevertheless, you can save yourself the trouble of keying in the input. You get the advantages of speed and accuracy in repeatable test data entry, and avoid a boring task. You then check the results manually.

16.7 Our results

16.7.1 Size of our testware

After 18 months the test script library contained 50 000 lines of code, of which 21 000 were common routines. Of 1900 test cases, 725 were automated. A further 400 test cases were deemed unautomatable (at any reasonable cost). The initial set of test cases took three hours per case on average to develop, for a total effort of one and a half person-years. At the end of the 18 months, it was taking experienced test developers about two hours per test case on average.

All scripts and test results were under the management of Microsoft SourceSafe. The SourceSafe library occupied 45 Mbytes centrally and 12.5 Mbytes for each tester. There were three people testing, of whom only two did automated testing.

16.7.2 Objectives achieved

You may be horrified by the effort expended, which is not trivial. But considering the growth of the application, the automation has achieved its objectives. To compare our testing effort over time, I developed what I call my *magic number*. In the beginning, recall that we had one platform, two server types, and three Windows 3.11 server/platform-specific workstations, which gave me a 'magic number' of six, calculated as follows:

1 platform × 2 server types × 3 server/platform-specific products = magic number of 6

The manual testing took four person-weeks in two elapsed weeks, so we had:

---

20 days divided by magic number of 6 = 3.33 days per magic unit

---

After 18 months, there were three platforms, and three server types, and three server/platform products, one of which had a second variant. So the magic number was 27, plus a bit for the variant. In fact, because some combinations were not deployable, the real magic number was 18. Testing took six person-weeks per release, over three elapsed weeks, so we now had:

---

30 days divided by magic number of 18 = 1.66 days per magic unit

---

Roughly speaking, the automation halved the effort and elapsed time to test. The application grew but release times were maintained. Also, this allowed the test team to develop the performance tests (which were automated using a tool written in-house) and to do the Year 2000 test. Over the 18-month period nine releases were tested, and the pace of development will continue at a similar rate for years to come. The value of the automation is certain.

16.7.3 Some paybacks of automation are in the process of automating

Improved efficiency was an important achievement, but not the ultimate objective. What about the quality of testing? By the end of the 18-month period, the application was being tested more thoroughly and fewer errors surfaced in live running. It is now typical to discover zero or one error after a release goes live, and no error has ever caused an interruption to the market or any form of mis-trade.

But was it the automated test that caught the errors before release? No, not really. Over the period only a few errors were ever caught by an automated test. They were mainly to do with differences between the central trading system and the demonstration simulator. Less than a handful of regression errors were caught.

However, dozens of bugs in the applications were found while writing the test scripts.

Automated testing yields big gains in productivity; *automating testing* improves your efficiency at finding bugs.

CHAPTER SEVENTEEN

Insurance quotation systems tested automatically every month

Simon Mills

This case study deals with a test automation project, from the reasons for its inception, through some of the critical milestones, to the present day, some four years after its beginnings.

17.1 Background: the UK insurance industry

In the UK there are many ways by which individuals and businesses can obtain various types of insurance, so that on paying an annual premium they may have financial support in the time of a disaster. In the case of automobile insurance, there is a legal requirement to have some form of recognized insurance.

The most common way in which insurance is obtained is by an individual approaching an insurance broker, or agent, who will offer a selection of insurance 'products' from different insurance companies. The job of the insurance broker or agent is to locate the most competitively priced premium for the client. The broker collects many details about the client and about the situation he or she wishes to insure (e.g. home, business, automobile, boat, etc.), to search for appropriate alternatives. All brokers have access to the products of hundreds of insurers, who themselves often offer many different insurance products. All insurers have varying 'underwriting cultures,' meaning that they will accept certain kinds of risk in preference to others. Certain insurers will offer products to attract various target groups, such as lady drivers.

Insurers maintain very accurate records about what is more likely to result in a claim. This may be certain types of vehicles, parts of the country, age groups, and many other factors. On the basis of these details, as collected by a broker, any given insurer will have a view toward a risk. It is critical to the insurers that their requirements are adhered to in order to minimize their risk.

During the 1980s a number of PC-based quotation systems became available, which made the selection of competitive and appropriate insurance products much easier for the brokers. There are approximately 20 such systems in the UK covering personal lines of insurance. These systems were written by third-party software providers who were entirely independent of the insurance companies.

Having input all of the details into the system, the broker is presented with a series of quotations. For the insurance product selected, the broker would have a series of proposal forms and other documents (specific to that product), which would be completed by the individual. The broker would collect a premium and the individual would then be insured. The broker would send the proposal to the selected insurance company.

In the past, this final step was done on paper. However, in the mid-1990s, the quotation systems enabled the proposals to be sent electronically over a wide area 'value added' network, using Electronic Data Interchange (EDI).

Up to this point in time, insurance companies had taken little or no notice of the quotation systems, but the emergence of EDI technology presented a whole new arena for selling products, and one where administrative effort was minimized. The major insurance companies, of which there were eight to ten at the time, all joined the race to have quoted products being transacted by this new EDI technology.

As time progressed, these quotation systems became used more regularly. For example, one system grew from being used by tens of brokers to having nearly 2000 users. At the same time, the number of products and insurers represented on the quotation systems was increasing, from 78 to 298 in five years for one quotation system. Certain insurers have seen their annual premium income from this source grow from less than 1% to over 25% of their annual new automobile insurance business; that is nearly 10 000 new policies per month. This electronic trading rapidly became a business force to be reckoned with.

Unfortunately, when the amount of business presented was small, the insurers had paid little or no attention to the quality of the decisions being taken on their behalf. All of a sudden, they had a large job on their hands to bring the quality under control.

This change in technology had a significant effect on the insurance business. One particular insurance company decided to use 'textbook' system testing as the necessary discipline to progress the business in this new area. This is the story of that company and our involvement with them. Many testing issues as well as automation issues needed to be addressed in order to meet this new challenge.

17.2 The brief, or how I became involved

The first meeting was between the tester (me) and representatives from a major UK insurance company: one from the marketing department and several business managers. This company had several products for vehicle insurance, which were accessed by a dozen or so quotation systems, used by thousands of insurance brokers.

The marketing representative explained that the company wished to improve the volume of sales generated through the quotation systems. In order to do this, they would have to provide lower rates, better discounts, and, by far the most important, a 'guarantee.' The guarantee would be the marketing equivalent of the Holy Grail; every premium quoted would be stood by, even if in error.

This idea was not well received by the business managers, who were insurance underwriters. It was only the business managers who could authorize this Holy Grail, since they were responsible for all costs and discounts, and ultimately for insuring the company remained in profit.

However, the experience of the business managers with the quotation systems was almost entirely negative. Of course, they had only ever been involved in the erroneous quotations that had been accepted by a client, generally because they were priced well below anyone else in the market, and often with business unacceptable to the company at any price. Their assessment of the quotation systems was therefore highly subjective and mostly expressed in non-technical (and unprintable) forms of words.

Enter the tester, on the invitation of the marketing department, an unusual association in itself. The marketeers thought that the subjective assertions of the business managers could be turned into measured assessments from which reasoned judgments could be made, based on an objective view of the quotation systems as a whole. This would involve extensive testing of the quotation systems using this company's insurance products. Specialist testers were required, because previous attempts to test thoroughly had failed due to the sheer volume of testing required.

It was agreed that we would design tests, execute them, devise strategies for correction of problems, and re-test after they had been fixed. Most importantly, we would produce a way of presenting the findings to the business managers, hoping one day to sway their opinions.

17.3 Why automation?

The reason to embark upon an automated approach from the outset was influenced by two basic factors. Although there were only two different products to test, they were represented across approximately 15 different quotation systems and were updated at least every month. There were known difficulties in the past, which had arisen following monthly releases, even when the insurer had not requested any changes to how their product should work.

It was obvious that we would be required to test each system every month for quite some time, during which we would hope to track the fixes we had suggested and prove that matters were becoming no worse. Our first job was to establish that the systems were performing correctly; then we could build the monthly regression tests.

17.4 Our testing strategy

Clearly, we could not test all of the quotation systems straight away, so we chose to concentrate upon one system, as a model. We would then work our way through the other systems after we had confidence that our test plan was good. We started with the system producing the most business, the one that was used by the majority of insurance brokers.

We knew that we were going to have to set up a series of test quotes based upon the underwriting rules for each insurance product and apply them to the system under test, as if they were real input. These tests would have to reflect the many rules that are applied by underwriters when they determine whether or not to accept a particular risk and, when they do, what they will charge for an annual premium.

The two products we were to test were quite different from one another but were to be treated in exactly the same way by each quotation system. So, our test strategy became insurance product based.

Before commencing serious work on the first system, we had to know something about how the various other systems behaved, as our test strategy was going to involve us in setting up a number of test conditions that would have to be applied to each system. Could this be done?

There was not a lot on our side. The systems all looked different, ran on a variety of PC platforms (DOS, UNIX, XENIX, TRIPOS, etc.), and asked 50–100 questions in different ways. At least the questions were roughly the same!

The answers, on the other hand, had to be delivered in a variety of differing ways. Name and address were no problem; after all, there are only so many ways of expressing them. However, other issues were less straightforward. For example, there are three types of vehicle insurance cover to chose from: Comprehensive, Third Party Fire & Theft, and Third Party Only. If the test demands that Third Party Only is to be selected, in one system the users select *item 3* on a drop-down list, in another they enter *O Enter,* and in yet another *TPO Enter,* and so on. We were looking at interesting times ahead.

These various questions asked have two fundamental results for a given insurer's product, when they are input to a quotation system:

1. Placement in one of 20 areas, 20 vehicle groups, 15 age groups, 3 cover types, and a group for age, value of vehicle, and so on. From these groups, the basic premium can be calculated from tables.

2. Placement in a risk category, based on questions about the proposer's accident history, previous claims, convictions, period driving, occupation, health, etc. The proposer may be unacceptable to this particular insurance contract or may require to have adjustments made to the premium, by way of loadings or discounts.

For our product-based strategy this allowed us to concentrate on the types of rules and the kinds of treatment they dictated. We devised a Test Category structure, and we also established the concept of a Standard Quote.

The testing effort was broken down into both simple and combined Test Categories, which would determine the tests for particular elements of the product. For example, Category 05 – Age of Vehicle would carry tests for just this element and *strictly* no other. This category list therefore became the detail behind the test strategy.

The Standard Quote was to be a proposer whose profile would result in an acceptable quote but which would not attract any special attention from the labyrinth of validation going on. He was a 39-year-old museum curator, with a Fiat 126 BIS, with a full driving license for 17 years, no claims, accidents, or convictions, and not the merest hint of any physical infirmities in the last 10 generations.

The Standard Quote concept allowed us to 'swap in' only the characteristics required for a particular test, and to correctly predict what our outcome would be, for example if our museum curator were 78 years old or had a bad claims history.

Our second Standard Quote was based on two drivers (partners). Our museum curator gained a 39-year-old museum-curating wife!

Our next task was to work out how many tests there should be within each category of test for each insurance product. Then the tests had to be run and analyzed.

17.5 Selecting a test automation tool

We were making strides in terms of the strategy we were aiming to employ but we had yet to firmly decide how all of these tests were to be applied, manually or using a test execution tool. Just before reaching for a copy of the *CAST Report* (Graham and Herzlich, 1995), which I can assure you we did, we took stock of our situation. We had done this type of thing before. (My company, Ingenuity Unlimited, is a specialist testing company providing testing contractors and testing services to UK businesses.)

These were our requirements, which we took into consideration first:

1. We were going to keep our test case requirements outside of any test tool environment. We were not going to lock ourselves in to any particular CAST tool vendor's methodology.

2. (Of equal priority to 1.) We were going to run each test system as though it came from an insurance broker, as far as possible. Then we would know we were emulating the native environment of the system under test. I feel that this is a pivotal element to any testing process. Any 'unnatural' test must have some impact on the credibility of the test itself.

3. Because of point 2, we were going to have a number of different machines, due to the variety of platforms we would have to accommodate when eventually testing across all systems.

4. Although all the current quotation systems were character-based, we would probably end up having to test GUI systems.

5. The normal operating circumstances at an insurance broker's office usually involved some form of 'network,' even if it was simply three terminals connected serially to the UNIX 'main machine.'

We had previously gained some experience of Automator QA but had a look at the opposition anyway. The strengths we were seeking were robustness and track record, together with pertinent, timely, and informed technical support. Direct Technology (now Compuware) offered all of these. We therefore settled upon Automator QA but purely as a means of applying our test cases by automation. Our test scripts and actual results, as obtained from our automated runs, would be held in files entirely of our design and under our control.

We had a test strategy, a DOS-based system to test, a testing tool, and a plan for how we were going to forge ahead, but there was not a test script in sight. It was time to get started.

17.6 Some decisions about our test automation plans

We had several decisions to make about our test automation; all of them stood us in good stead, as matters turned out.

We hoped to run Automator QA resident on the same machine as our DOS-based test systems. On the other platforms, we would substitute a dumb terminal with a PC (running Automator QA and a suitable terminal emulator), and the system under test would not know the difference.

Our chosen tool was feature-rich and quite able to assist us in handling all matters related to test data generation, test data maintenance, results handling, and comparison. However, as with any broad-spectrum tool, there are often better ways of doing certain jobs and we had experience of a few. We were also about to embark upon a huge amount of regular testing which, once under way, simply had to produce results month on month for a long time. We were not prepared to load all aspects of our testing into one basket.

The next decision we made was based on some past experience and partly, I must admit, because we were limited by the number of people who could work on this project. We decided to separate the disciplines of testing technician and automation technician. There were two of us – it could work.

Immediately, we set about defining the roles of the two disciplines, which proved important.

17.6.1 The tester's job

The tester's responsibility is for the tests themselves. He or she is responsible for the quality of the tests and the effectiveness of the testing. The tasks are:

1. Define what is to be tested by producing test plans and test scripts, which would contain a number of Test Quotes.

2. Create the test scripts, execute them manually, analyze the test outcomes, and prove that each test has merit. This manual 'proof' was to hold a great benefit later in the process.

3. Supply the data required for each automated test run in a form suitable for and dictated by the automation technician.

4. Define the expected outcome for each test case; this would be a financial sum and/or a message or messages.

5. Supply the expected outcome in a form to be compared with the actual results.

6. Execute and preside over the results of the later comparison between expected and actual outcomes.

17.6.2 The automation technician's job

The automation technician's responsibility is for the efficiency of the testing. He or she creates the automated process by which the manual operation of keying in of input data is replaced. The basic tasks were expected to be:

1. Produce a 'map' of each system to be tested.

2. Produce a script to apply each Test Quote as supplied by the tester.

3. Write a script to reliably collect the outcome from a final screen and write it to a file of actual results.

4. Produce an audit trail of some type, to indicate that what the tester dictated should be input had been reliably applied.

5. Become expert at running the automation tool without 'tripping up' the system under test or the terminal emulator. We had gained enough experience to realize the importance, and relative specialism, of good memory management. We use QEMM™, and we always have the latest version on account of the fact that each version appears to assist in finding a few more useful bytes for the automation tool to use.

These two disciplines meant that the tester would remain very close to the 'user,' and would present test cases for review by a business manager. The automation technician was going to be far away from the business perspective and deeply involved in making highly technical things happen – nearer to a developer mentality. By and large we still maintain the same separation of disciplines on a day to day basis as this works very well in practice.

It is worth pointing out that much of the scripting and the languages that are encountered among the different automated testing tools require skill in programming coupled with great discipline in the manner with which they are used. The writer has experimented by using pure programming skills as a way of preventing good test planners from becoming bogged down in the technicalities of automation scripting, but the developer versus tester divide always shows its head and takes quite a degree of managing. This mixture is found to work when a focus is maintained on the reason for using automation – it is to reliably and regularly execute the tests as demanded by the tester.

17.7 The test plan

We analyzed the insurance products and created a comprehensive list of Test Categories encompassing all of the facets of each product's decision making. One test plan would be written for each category – this was considered satisfactory to cover each facet of the products.

This was going to be a long job and we were eager to prove some automation. Category 01 – Simple Premium Accuracy was as good a place as any to start.

What other tools did we use? Our test planning tool was already a hit from the past – Lotus 123, now with multiple worksheets. Our test case generator? No such luck, no silver bullets here. When we got to Claims, Accidents, and Convictions on one of the systems to be tested there would be over five million permutations to decide from. Anyhow, we were purists – the test case generator was to be a human being. The final selection of tests, of the order of 1200 for Convictions alone, was based upon a pure analysis of permutations coupled with much input from an expert in this field of insurance, as provided by our client. By this means, we insured a user focus, but kept control of the number of potential tests.

While the mapping and some trial scripting were pressing ahead, the Category 01 test plan became an embryo. Several worksheets were set out in a format to be adopted for every test plan. The test plan contained the following information:

1. Development notes. The scope of what was to be tested and what was to be disregarded were all noted here, signed and dated.
2. History notes. Who did what to this test plan, and when.
3. Shared information. Lookup tables, etc., as supplied with the product information and some of our own designing.
4. Test data: The big one – see below.
5. Export for test system. To be populated with the data to be exported for the automation run, and to be repeated for each test system, for example *C* for Comprehensive or *item 3* for Third Party Only.
6. Expected results. A résumé sheet with expected results set out ready for export to the comparison tool.

At last, Test Case No. 01/10001, the first one (Category 01/Test 1), was about to be written out. For premium accuracy we had to set up our Standard Quote and then create areas 1 through 20, vehicle groups 1 through 20, and all of these permutations for each of three types of insurance cover. Lotus 123 has always been a magnificent tool for drafting out all of this information.

Our lookup tables contained all the information for the test. The leftmost column described the test condition, the next column contained the postal (zip) code for the selected area, then we had various details describing the vehicle (we had chosen one for each rating group).

The next set of columns collected the rating factors for each permutation, ending with a premium calculation and our expected outcome. Having finally created test case 1 and checked the calculation as being accurate to the penny, 'copy down' came as such a relief. At this point we were grateful for the printer that could print onto double-size paper!

Our test data worksheet was capable of being presented to a business manager as the means of describing the tests that would be performed in this category, all 20 × 20 × 3 of them. Already we had created, albeit limited in terms of test coverage, a list of scheduled and reasoned tests. The client had never done this to this extent before.

Our test data worksheet described in literal but understandable terms 'I want area 1, vehicle group 1, cover type comprehensive.' It then showed the data that had to find its way into the quote system and reasoned out exactly what the expected result should be. The quote-specific information then had to be mapped into the 'Export for Test System 1' worksheet, in order to appear in a form understandable by the system under test and the automation. This mapping task is very straightforward, and yet another good use of a spreadsheet.

The automation was ready, so we fed it the input file and ended up with a result for each case. The automated run was complete long before the manual execution and so we compared the actual results with the expected. One of them was wrong. After some perseverance, a good number of the manually executed results were available and they didn't agree with either the test plan or the automated results.

We had all permutations to consider. The result of the analysis? The automation had flaws, the test plan had calculation errors, and the system under test had its fair share of 'undocumented program features' (bugs) also.

The worst thing had happened. Our automation and the methods used to drive it had created an unreliable set of test results much quicker than ten humans could do working flat out. We returned to traditional methods. Tests were scheduled carefully, reviewed, and checked by us and, when necessary, the business managers. They were executed manually and the results reconciled *before* any automated run results were taken seriously. Only when we *know* that the only differences are due to errors in the system under test do we go with automated test results.

An exact match of a set of results from an automated run, compared against a fully reconciled set of manual results, allows only limited trust to be placed in the automation results, whether there are faults in the system under test or not. It is easy, unless your procedures allow for it, to place too much trust in an unproven automated process.

In that first run the audit trail highlighted miskeying on the part of the automation scripts. It also pinpointed where it occurred and assisted with rapid debugging of the automation scripts.

Gradually, we built each test plan and executed it manually, dealt with the errors in the systems, and followed up with the automation.

17.8 Some additional issues we encountered

We used a statistical package, SPSS®, to perform the comparison of results. It enabled the building of straightforward scripts, which pulled together the expected results and actual results files, performed the comparison, and produced a report sorted by magnitude of error. These reports formed the basis for detailed viewing of malfunctions.

Many of the test plans have information that varies from year to year or month to month, not an uncommon circumstance. We anticipated this and spent much time in seeking ways to reduce the maintenance of test plans. Many of the tests were based around events with implied dates. For example, a test may require a driver aged 19 years and 11 months. As the test would be run every month, the date of birth would have to be altered every time the test case was used.

As we had many thousands of similar circumstances to consider, together with the likelihood of rating table changes and such like, the spreadsheets containing the test plans and the lookup tables were built with a variety of mechanisms that would allow for updating from a Master Shared Information spreadsheet. Without this facility (yet another virtue of the humble spreadsheet), the maintaining of such test plans would be a logistical nightmare and would be open to all types of clerical error.

With up to 90 categories and of the order of 30 000 test cases per insurance product, maintenance is a serious issue.

Our early experiments included an attempt to justify the use of automation. We timed all manually input runs and compared them against the automated equivalent. A single test quote took a well-practiced operator, on average, 1 minute 50 seconds. This effort was found to be impossible to sustain for long periods while maintaining any dependable accuracy. In automation, 30 000 test quotes could be input at a rate of one test per 11 seconds without tiredness or inaccuracy. The difference is truly astounding, the accuracy impossible to equal in a manageable way.

At least once a month, we have to produce a set of files to be collected by the automation procedures when they run. These files contain the test data, adjusted where necessary, following any test plan maintenance (there will be many dates that need to step on one month, if nothing else). To cater for this we have built automated procedures which 'make ready' all of the automation input files upon receiving a request from the tester to produce an automated run. This request is made after any test plan maintenance.

17.9 A telling tale: tester versus automator

On one occasion we put the tester versus automation technician issue to the test, with interesting results.

One category of test was seeking to prove that premium loads were being correctly applied for higher-value vehicles. A flat additional sum of money was to be applied for each extra £5000 (approximately $7500) in value over a threshold of £25 000 (approximately $37 500) and up to a limit of £75 000 (approximately $112 500), beyond which insurance should be refused for the product.

The automation technician built a script with a parameter table, using a test case generator method.

The tester built a formal test plan creating a boundary test from the threshold across each breakpoint and some mid-range points up to the limit, where a refusal to insure was expected. The values tested were therefore £24 999, £25 000, £25 001, then £29 999 and £30 001 and so on up to £75 001 (not forgetting a £100 000 test!).

The tester created a 'lean and mean' set of about 32 test cases, giving reasonable coverage from which to detect errors. The automation technician caused around 1600 test cases to be generated, at values starting from the threshold of £25 000 at £30 intervals, thereby missing the threshold boundary, missing many of the intervening boundaries, and stopping at the limit; hence the 'over limit' refusal was also missed.

Why did the automation technician do it this way? We concluded after much analysis, 'because he could.' This is most definitely a cautionary tale and cements our ideology that you do not replace the tester with automation, you augment the process by building the ability to readily re-apply proven tests in a manner that is both quick and accurate.

17.10 Summary

There were many stages where, if we had not been seasoned testers with some automation experience, some of the hurdles we faced would have been enough for us to give up.

As it is, several years have passed since Test 01/10001 was written and the vehicle insurance testing is still being run every month. Now, for a number of insurance companies, we run tests containing around 30 000 test cases per product on 14 quote systems. The number of products has increased and we test between 6 and 16 products depending upon the quote system.

In addition to private vehicle insurance, we also test commercial vehicle products, together with the hugely more complex household insurance and commercial products currently being traded by these electronic quote systems.

As we anticipated, we are now testing certain products on both character-based and GUI quotation systems. This has caused the need to use an additional testing tool but the test cases and the method of supplying the automation technician with input files remain the same, vindication for our earlier decision to keep our test plans in an environment totally within our control.

The Holy Grail changed hands, for our original clients, once the performance of the systems was corrected and proven stable, following many months of repeated tests in certain cases. The level of reliable testing performed for that client alone, in the time frame in which it had to be completed, could not have been conducted by wholly manual means.

As this is being written, I am heavily involved in making use of what has been learned to provide reliable repeated application of tests in many types of circumstance. The early lessons alluded to above are constantly acting as a reminder of how to cope with a variety of automation issues.

Acknowledgments

I would like to thank the Commercial Union Assurance Co., and particularly Urszula Kardasinska, Alan Dilley, and Neil McGovern, for their initial faith and subsequent support and commitment. Without them this significant automation effort would never have been given the opportunity to flourish.

Three generations of test automation at ISS

Steve Allott

18.1 Introduction

Automation is both desirable and possible but there are many pitfalls along the road to success. Rather than learn the hard way, by trial and error, we hope that our experience and history will help you in automating testing in your organization. This chapter describes my experience as a test manager over three generations of test automation development.

I was inspired by this quotation from George Santayna: 'he who does not study history is doomed to repeat it.' As a rookie programmer for ITT back in 1976 I remember quite clearly setting out the tests for my own PL/1 programs painstakingly on paper tape! Little did I realize that, more than twenty years later, the disciplined training I had as a programmer would be invaluable as I wrestled with the very latest CAST (computer aided software testing) tools.

18.2 The software under test

The company, Integrated Sales Systems (ISS), designs, builds, and maintains large-scale sales and marketing automation systems. Our flagship product, Oxygen, is a sophisticated client/server application that provides essential management information for the sales and marketing organizations of large financial and pharmaceutical companies.

Oxygen runs on several different flavors of the Windows operating systems (e.g. Windows 95, Windows 98, NT4) and supports a variety of relational databases (e.g. Oracle, Sybase) depending upon the customer's requirements. Oxygen has a component-based architecture and is delivered with many additional components, some configured in-house and others built by third-party companies. The 'core product' contains the common functionality for all variants of our products; different customers have individualized or standard front-ends to the core product. The product is positioned to implement the latest technology as soon as it is available, and often serves as a beta test site for new versions of operating system and development software.

18.3 First generation

18.3.1 What was our initial reason to automate?

The decision to try out test automation was made for a number of reasons:

- we thought it would save time and speed up the testing;
- repetitive testing of our application was dull – in the early days there was no independent test team, therefore the project team had to do all of the testing;
- because it was there – i.e. the tools existed and looked a lot of fun.

18.3.2 Tool selection

A decision was taken at the end of 1995 to purchase five licenses for SQA TeamTest. This comprised the automated test execution tool SQA Robot and the defect tracking and test management tool SQA Manager. We chose these tools primarily for their integration with each other, and their support for testing GUIs on Windows. SQA TeamTest was also reasonably priced and the supplier (Systems FX, later Cyrano) offered good training and consultancy to help us get started. We did not feel at the time that it was worth doing a formal evaluation of the tool.

18.3.3 From capture replay to scripts

As with most companies, the first tentative attempts at automating tests relied on using the capture replay component of the automated testing tool. This was unsuccessful and was eventually abandoned. It has been our experience that companies have to go through this stage of capture replay to see 'if it will work for them.' There is a valuable learning experience from this exercise, but it can take a long time. In our first generation, we went through this stage but also moved on enough to see where we could go next.

Within our customer delivery area, developers use tools to design and configure the GUI portion of the Oxygen application for individual customers. Common functionality often exists in many parts of the system, and needs to be tested in each part and for each customer. We started by capturing these repetitive tests and also the regression tests for updates to common functionality.

The basic commands captured in the test script were then modified to make the scripts more generic, using SQA Basic (the scripting language supplied with SQA Robot). Dan Reid designed and wrote a series of high-level functions that enabled complex test activities to be done in a single command. For example, a function with two parameters (screen name and wait time) replaced several test tool script commands (navigate to a particular screen, check if it is there, if not wait for it to appear and give it the focus, etc.)

These high-level functions are much easier to understand, as the complexity of the scripting language is hidden from the developer of the test. Dan also used Excel spreadsheets to hold screen names, wait times, and other parameters to drive the tests. The spreadsheets also held the specific data input for each test case.

Dan's work inadvertently started us towards the development of a 'meta-language,' i.e. our own test automation language that simply called low-level SQA Basic functions to perform the tasks required. As we built more functions the meta-language effectively grew into another architectural layer between the tester and the application, as shown in Table 18.1. The tester would write the script, which contained meta-language statements that either accessed the tool, or went directly to the application program interface.

We realized that if the meta-language were fully developed we would have a powerful automated testing infrastructure. Other products could replace the tool-specific layer, if necessary, and testers did not need to know the specific details of each individual automated tool. In fact, we had discovered some of the scripting techniques described in Chapter 3.

Table 18.1 The layers of interaction between the human tester and the Oxygen application.

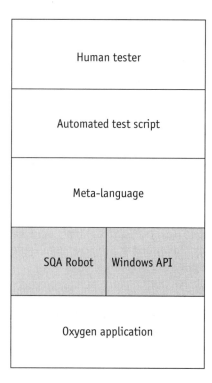

We stopped short of actually developing this meta-language due to time constraints – we wanted to get something working for the current release, and also we wanted to focus on testing our software rather than building test tools. However, we had made some progress and had automated some tests.

18.3.4 Costs and benefits of our first generation

License costs for our tool were approximately £2800 per seat and we had five seats. After the initial experimentation Dan probably spent around 3–4 weeks developing his ideas. So the tool costs were £14 000 (around $21 000), and the development time roughly £5000 ($7500).

The main benefit was in taking a tool that no one liked and was difficult to use, and showing how it could be made usable. Our application is very flexible and configurable; every screen, profile, and field can be determined by the underlying database. Each customer has a totally different version of the product. Manual testing therefore could be very tedious as similar tests (e.g. on date fields) would potentially have to be repeated on many different systems. Automating tests by using simple capture replay at the GUI level was obviously a step backwards in technology with our computer-generated approach to application development. Add to this the need to test on multiple environments and you see that manual testing is virtually impossible if complete coverage is required.

It was debatable whether or not Dan's time would have been better spent just writing more test scripts rather than trying to get the tool to work in our environment. However, he did demonstrate that it would be worth pursuing these ideas further.

18.3.5 Problems with our first generation approach

18.3.5.1 Automated test tool issues

1. The automated test tool was difficult to apply to test the core product (common functions).

2. There were a number of problems with the automated test tool, many of which were overcome by workarounds in SQA Basic.

3. The tool vendor cannot be expected to know your application in detail, and so specific problems that we found were often difficult for them to track down. We found that we needed to strip out the application-specific parts of the test to create a script that failed at a simpler and more basic level. Then the vendor had a better chance of fixing the problem.

18.3.5.2 General issue

We found that gaining acceptance of the automated testing technology was an uphill struggle. Developers liked the idea of automated testing, but tended to shy away from the tool for two reasons: the learning curve on SQA Robot and the seemingly unsophisticated user interface.

1. You need programming expertise to develop the test automation infrastructure.

2. You need a champion (as with any kind of change) who can manage the increasingly high expectations that project managers and developers have of the test automation technology.

3. The automated test tool technology always lags behind the development capabilities, at least for our leading-edge applications. However, this should not be used as an excuse to blame the tool vendor and suspend the test automation effort.

18.4 Second generation

18.4.1 Why did we continue with test automation?

Despite the problems encountered in our first generation, management decided (July 1997) that it was important to continue on the path of automated testing for two main reasons:

1. Our product had become more sophisticated, which led to a higher test resource requirement.

2. With the transition to Windows 95 we were in a legacy situation and now had twelve environments to support (four different databases and three flavors of operating systems).

The challenge for us was to build an automated test tool infrastructure based on the knowledge we had accumulated in the previous two years.

18.4.2 What we did this time

A small test team (three people) was formed, and a new release of TeamTest was acquired. Iain Ollerenshaw, a computer science student from the University of St Andrews, joined the team as part of his work experience. Iain adopted a data-driven approach to scripting. We chose a Microsoft Excel spreadsheet as the mechanism for storing the test input data, but we could easily have used parameter or variable assignments within the header files of the scripts. The spreadsheet approach provides more flexibility in that non-programmers can read, sort, and otherwise modify the test data. The scripts were coded directly in SQA Basic without using the capture replay facility to generate the scripts.

To put this approach into practice we started all over again but this time did not try to automate everything. We limited the scope to simple navigation and basic record creation tests. Often this is referred to as a breadth test, but we call it a smoke test. This means that we are trying to prove that the application and database build was good on a variety of test environments. Be warned that sometimes a smoke test has to go quite deep within the code to prove that the build was OK. Until the smoke test ran successfully, we knew that it was not worthwhile to commence manual testing on that build.

The tool supplier (Cyrano) provided some initial on-site training in July 1997. We followed this up with a full day workshop where the team experimented with the tool and immediately put into practice what they had learned. During the initial training Cyrano made some very useful suggestions, which helped us with our design. One of these was that it is important to have a good structure to the tests and a sensible naming convention for all of the automated test procedures. We were fortunate in that we were able to align our testware naming conventions with those used by application developers.

18.4.3 Our naming convention

Each major application component or functional area can be described by a two-character code. The application is too functionally rich to show everything but some examples are given in Table 18.2.

Table 18.2 The application naming convention.

Code	Component	Description
DY	Diary	Standard calendar functionality to record appointments
MT	Meetings	Allows schedule and planning of meetings, approvals, etc.
EV	Events	Records events such as sales calls, visits, letters sent, telephone calls, etc.
QY	Query	Allows query on many different database fields
CP	Campaign management	Campaign management module

Each component has a main GUI screen (called a profile) and several other profiles, depending upon the complexity of the particular component. Our test procedures were created in a three-tier hierarchy as follows:

- Main test procedure
- Test activity
- Test functionality

We created one main test procedure for each component. Each of these test procedures could be run on its own and would eventually fully test the component by calling one or more test activity procedures. We identified four possible test activities:

- Navigation
- Creation

- Editing
- Deletion

Each test activity procedure would in turn call one or more individual test procedures that ran a test for a specific area of the component's functionality.

We have used the example of the diary functionality to illustrate our naming convention in detail, as shown in Table 18.3.

Table 18.3 The testing naming convention.

Test procedure name	Type	Description
DY	Main	Main test procedure for the diary component
DYN	Activity	Navigation test procedure for the diary
DYC	Activity	Creation test procedure for the diary
DYE	Activity	Edit test procedure for the diary
DYD	Activity	Deletion test procedure for the diary
DYCWK	Test	Tests that create diary items in 'week to a page' mode; specific tests were called DYCWK01, DYCWK02, etc.
DYC1D	Test	Tests that create diary items in 'day to a page' mode

18.4.4 Our new regime

The tool allows you to create new shell scripts in order to create a particular mix of the individual test procedures. This works fine but was very tedious to use when several rapid changes were required. We built a very simple front-end using Microsoft Visual Basic that allowed us to pick and choose specific tests that we required in a particular run.

A common test procedure read in the test input data from the spreadsheet to a global array that could be accessed by all subsequent test scripts. This was done for performance and programming efficiency reasons.

When, for example, the diary create test procedure was executed, it read its input data values from the diary create test input spreadsheet. There would be one row in the spreadsheet for each diary item we wished to create. Each column in the spreadsheet would represent a particular data field on the appropriate 'create diary item' profile; for example, date, time, item type, summary text, and so on. We also had a column in the spreadsheet to indicate whether or not the data was valid (i.e. success would mean that the application should correctly create the diary item record in the database) or invalid (i.e. we expect an application error dialog box to pop up). The tests were sensitive to the valid/invalid column in the spreadsheet and would take the appropriate action.

Note that we also had another 'application configuration' spreadsheet that held the 'meta-data' to describe various aspects of the configuration to the tests. This would include, for example, path names, locations of results directories and log files, and locations of specific test scripts.

In our opinion, there are three types of test data:

1. the meta-data to configure and run the automated Test Suite;
2. the test data itself: inputs and expected outputs for each test case;
3. the test database: a populated baseline on top of which the tests will be run.

One thing that we soon learned was the importance of being able to get back to a baseline situation. For example, having created several diary items with one test procedure, we would then run a test that deleted them all. This allowed the diary create test to be run again under its original circumstances. We knew that ideally we should have rolled back the whole database but this was not practical at the time as several testers were sharing this test environment.

The test suite that Iain built was run daily for about four weeks on a number of different test environments. The primary purpose was not, as you might expect, to find bugs, but to demonstrate confidence in the daily builds of the Oxygen application.

18.4.5 Costs and benefits of our second generation

Iain spent almost six weeks developing and running the automated smoke tests. The tool cost was the maintenance contract with the vendor for around £2000 ($3000). Iain's time would have been around £7500 ($11 250).

This new approach proved to be effective in both achieving and proving the stability of our application. This in turn allowed us to concentrate our main effort on manually testing the new functionality. The automated Test Suite did find some new bugs, although this was not its primary benefit.

There was a psychological effect that we started to see here. If developers knew that their software was going to be run through automated test software by another developer, they might put in an extra effort to make sure it would not fall over. Without Iain's smoke tests we would have potentially wasted several person-weeks of effort in just proving the stability of the builds.

As a result of developing our automated smoke tests on this latest release of software and demonstrating their value to others within the company we changed people's attitudes towards this technology. We anticipated that we would be able to do more next time as a result of this success.

18.4.6.1 Automated test tool issues

1. It was difficult to get object properties into script variables.

2. Handling of unexpected windows could be improved.

3. Our application toolbar was treated as a single object by the tool and so we could not click on any toolbar buttons and had to rely on menu selections and accelerator keys.

4. Identifying certain objects on the screen was difficult with the version of the tool that we had.

5. Using mouse clicks to drive tests was unreliable so we tended to favor access using menu options, accelerator keys, and tabbing to the appropriate fields. This was troublesome at times; for example, when there were accelerator key clashes or when there was no alternative to the mouse operation.

6. Sometimes, but not always, the automated Test Suite stopped at a 'menu select' operation. We avoided the problem by using a short delay prior to the menu select command in the test script.

18.4.6.2 General issues

1. Differences in performance between Oracle and Sybase versions of our application on different platforms meant that when the tests were moved from one database to the other, slight modifications had to be made to any delays or wait state events in the tests.

2. Our application sometimes set the tabbing order to tab to protected fields, i.e. read-only fields. This meant that to enter data in a field following the read-only field we had to tab twice to access it; if this feature is changed then the test will require modification.

3. Application changes that the test team were not aware of caused some confusion, for example when the main menu item called 'system' was changed to the more widely used and recognized 'file,' and also when the main menu caption name was changed. Both examples caused the automated Test Suite to fail. This was not a technical problem, it was a communication problem. The developers were unaware at the time that their seemingly minor changes would affect the automated Test Suites.

4. If an automated test found a minor bug, we could never guarantee that it would be fixed before the next automated test run. We needed to keep the test in the suite so that when these minor bugs were fixed we would have a complete set of tests. Until the bug was fixed, however, we would get a failure report on our test log when we ran this Test Suite. (See Chapter 9 for a discussion of Expected Fail as a way around this problem.)

5. During development of the automated Test Suite we used a version control system to keep track of different versions of the test scripts. The test tool did not support a similar feature for its test procedures.

6. We had bugs in some of the automated test scripts. We soon realized that we needed to set up a test environment to test new versions of the test scripts and associated Excel spreadsheets.

7. We had still not gained acceptance by our developers of the automated test technology. This is unsurprising given the number of problems we had with the tool.

18.4.7 Lessons learned from our second generation

1. We found a few bugs with the tool, which were minor from our perspective, but the fact that they were found automatically impressed the other managers.

2. We realized that it is a lot more difficult than we thought at first to build an automated testing infrastructure.

3. We also learned to be careful not to oversell the technology. When our managers see the application starting up on its own and running through a sequence of 'tests' they can form an impression that it is doing a lot more than it really is. This has to be carefully managed so that they continue to support the project but give adequate time to do a proper job.

4. Once we had developed the tests, they had to be 'released' along with the application software and installed on the target test environments. When we found bugs in our test scripts we had a dilemma: where do we re-test the fixes to the test scripts? How and when do we apply version control?

18.5 Third generation

18.5.1 Designing a new infrastructure

By now the company had grown to a size where it was appropriate to establish a larger independent test team (6–8 people). A new recruit to the test team, Anthony McAlister, worked almost full time on test automation from January through March 1998. He was able to build on the work done by Dan and Iain, and successfully ran the original automated tests as a regression suite on our 3.3.1 release. Also, a bug fix release (3.3.2) was tested using these automated tests. It is notable that Anthony had no formal training as a tester until he joined ISS but he was experienced with Windows 95 and was a recent computer science graduate.

However, Anthony experienced several problems in getting to grips with automated test technology, and it turned out that the tests were still not robust enough for the new 32-bit version of Oxygen (known as release 4.0). Therefore we decided that a fresh look at the problem was needed, and so the third generation approach was born. We enlisted the help of Grove Consultants (Mark Fewster) in a design review of our proposed third generation test automation infrastructure.

Mark suggested that the directory structure for the test infrastructure should map that of the development environment. He also participated in a design review of the new automated testing infrastructure and Test Suite. The basic approach was that we would design and program each of the automated test scripts that we required using SQA Basic or Visual Basic as appropriate. The code would be as generic as possible.

Richard Hind, our senior test engineer on the team, proposed that we break down the application functionality into just three types of test activity. Furthermore, he suggested that each of these test activities be further subdivided into test automation levels according to the degree of complexity involved in developing the test script.

18.5.1.1 Characteristics of Level 1

A Level 1 test exercises the simplest aspect of the functionality of a particular module. It has the following characteristics:

- it is usually straightforward to test manually;
- it is easy to automate;
- the automated test is likely to work;
- it is unlikely to find a new bug.

18.5.1.2 Characteristics of Level 2

Level 2 tests explore all aspects of a particular module except those that require interfaces to other components. Level 2 tests have the following characteristics:

- it is possible but time consuming to test manually;
- it looks easy to automate, but doesn't always turn out so;
- the automated test is likely to have bugs;
- it sometimes finds a bug.

18.5.1.3 Characteristics of Level 3

These tests exercise the deepest level of functionality in a module, including those that interface to other components. They have the following characteristics:

- difficult if not impossible to test manually;
- hard to automate;
- unlikely to run succe ssfully, repeatedly;
- very likely to find a bug.

18.5.2 Estimating the effort involved

For each major component or functional area of the application we identified which levels were appropriate for each of the three test activities. This matrix, shown in Table 18.4, then provided us with the basis of an estimating tool for the test automation project. Level 1 tests we estimated would take approximately a half day of effort. Level 2 tests would take two to three days, and Level 3 tests would take a week.

Table 18.4 The test automation estimation matrix.

Functionality	Level 1	Level 2	Level 3
Naviation			
Edit			
Query			

Simply selecting a menu and clicking *OK* was the easiest form of navigation and could be considered Level 1. Navigating several profiles deep and then clicking on the right mouse button to pull up another menu might be Level 2. Trying to navigate to areas of the system provided by dynamic context-sensitive menus would be Level 3. A similar exercise was carried out for edit and query test activities. Note that edit includes creating database records, modifying them, and deleting them.

During the estimating phase, we realized that it was not practical to automate everything as we would have to spend too much time and effort to realize a good payback. However, if we settled for regression capability and 'proof of build' then we could quickly automate using Level 1 tests. A compromise was reached and we built all of the Level 1 tests, some Level 2 tests, and a few Level 3 tests.

18.5.3 Building the infrastructure

During implementation of the third generation approach, Anthony converted many of the old test procedures into SQA Basic scripts. However, he still experienced several problems with the scripting language and discovered some more limitations of SQA Robot. Therefore, since SQA Robot will allow more than one scripting language, we eventually decided to use Microsoft Visual Basic (VB) to continue development of our automated test infrastructure.

18.5.3.1 Scope – included

We built VB code to perform the following general functions:

- send keys (e.g. Alt-F, but not Ctrl-Alt-Del yet);
- interrogate menu structures (using resource files);
- send messages to Windows 95 or NT (click button, etc.);
- ODBC (open database connectivity);
- log results to a window/file.

These functions were kept together in a single VB module (general.bas). We then constructed additional VB modules for navigation (navutil.bas), data creation (create.bas), and editing/query (edit.bas), as well as extending our simple VB front-end, which allows selection/execution of the tests.

18.5.3.2 Scope – excluded

When running an automated test procedure, SQA Robot automatically logs bugs into the defect tracking system, SQA Manager. This was a useful feature of the tool. However, we chose not to develop this interface in our tool. Experience had shown that investigation and analysis were required prior to determining if the issue was truly a defect. Therefore we saw limited benefit from this feature. For example, the problem might be with the automated test script or the test data, or some combination of the two, rather than with the application. If we had logged a bug every time an automated test script failed we would have alienated developers from the technology.

18.5.3.3 The tests

The design of our automated test infrastructure allowed us to build the following tests of our application:

- simple navigation within the application;
- exercise all combinations of menus;
- creation and subsequent modification of basic records;
- ability to query the database.

The software uses comma-separated values (CSV) files as input for each test case and initiates SQL queries to determine whether the records have been successfully added to the database. Note that SQA Robot could have performed an equivalent function. However, we could not implement this because of ODBC clashes between the SQA repository and our application database (both used Sybase SQL Anywhere).

We focused on tests directed at our primary application functionality and excluded (for the moment) testing interfaces to external and third-party software (e.g. mail, mail merge, communications, reporting, OLE interfaces).

18.5.4 Costs and benefits of our third generation

We estimate that we've spent about three person-months on our third generation efforts, costing around £15 000 ($22 500). Benefits have been substantial in terms of proving the daily software builds and proving the test automation infrastructure. A few new bugs were found by the tool.

There is often debate in the testing industry as to whether or not all of the development effort for automated testing is worthwhile. Some experts suggest that we would be better off spending the time building more manual tests. However, with modern GUI-based client/server applications running on several operating system platforms on different databases, we believe there is no real alternative to test automation. The payback is not a true financial saving, rather it is a payback in terms of improved quality, quicker time to market, and more satisfied customers.

18.5.5 Problems with our third generation approach

18.5.5.1 Automated test tool issues

1. The automated test tool did not keep up with the application development technology. We feel that this would have happened whatever tool we had used; for obvious reasons, the tool technology is always likely to lag behind. Specific examples are:

   - It could not properly handle 32-bit application menu structures, especially those that are dynamically generated such as context-sensitive menus.
   - There were various new Windows controls (treeview, toolbar) that it did not recognize and for which it provided no workaround.
   - It found some of our application modal dialog boxes difficult to identify, especially when several (without captions) were presented in sequence.

2. Sometimes we could not trust the data written back to the log file. We had situations where tests had failed but they were logged as having passed. We were never able to properly explain this.

3. Sometimes tests would stop and the tool would hang for no apparent reason. The tool appeared to have a personality of its own and was somewhat temperamental. You really needed to get a feel for how it worked and coax it into action where necessary. Anyone who has used an automated test tool will understand exactly what we mean!

4. There was no 'fuzzy logic' at all in the tool; everything had to be programmed down to the last upper-case letter. Although there was a feature of wildcarding in the script language, if you wanted to select the *File* menu you had to set the case correctly. Compare this to a human tester, who would have no problem if the manual script asked him or her to choose the *file* menu (in lower case) and not the *File* menu.

5. The tool was not good at conditional processing. For example, a database query may present you with an additional modal dialog (to enable you to restrict the search) if you attempt to select too many records.

Manual testers will obviously react correctly even if they have never seen this additional dialog before. The automated test script did have conditional logic to process this dialog if it appeared. The problem seemed to be that when it did appear, the window appeared too quickly for the tool to be able to identify it correctly and the test subsequently failed. As a workaround we configured our database to insure that the window always appeared or never appeared so that the test could be written without the conditional logic.

6. The tool used a SQL database and accessed this via ODBC. So does our application. Therefore we could not use SQL utilities to interrogate or modify the database while we were running the tool.

7. We used PVCS to control the application code versions. The way we had structured our test repositories, everyone had to run the same automated tests. The tool did not support version control. We could have structured our tests as two projects, one for the new version and one for the old, but we would have needed manual version control.

8. Unexpected events were not handled very well. When testing, you know that error windows will appear – they're unexpected yet anticipated, as generally one of the reasons for running the tests is to make the system fail and generate the error window. Your test tool logic should be able to cope with this. However, an unanticipated unexpected event sometimes happens, such as a debug window appearing or a message from the system administrator. The tool did not handle this concept at all well. All that the tool could do was to send an escape key or other single character to any unexpected window or dialog box.

18.5.5.2 General issues

1. Again, managing the expectations of others was important as we were not making as much progress as we would have liked.

2. We should have allocated more time to this test automation effort and run it as a project on its own, rather than try to fit it in as part of the test effort for the 4.0 release.

18.5.6 Lessons learned from the third generation

1. Test automation needs to be funded and managed as a proper internal development project.

2. Failing to properly define requirements and skipping the design stage can lead to abandonment of the technology.

3. There will be a maintenance cost of the infrastructure we have built.

4. Automated test technology is not yet mature and the champion needs to be aware of this and plan accordingly. Quick wins, incremental improvements, and demonstrations to management are all ways to gradually gain acceptance of test automation.

5. Our new automated testware is very portable. No installation is required – we just ship a vb.exe wherever it is required. There are no significant training requirements (other than in test design, of course).

6. We now have much tighter integration between our Visual Basic automated toolset and our Oxygen application.

7. Developing our own Test Suite using VB has made us more aware of timing issues and we have to try to make our testware behave more as a human tester would. With the tool we would often just fire off a command to the application and expect it to cope.

8. We were able to abandon test hooks in the application. The tool needed them but since we develop tests and code together we are always aware of what the application is doing or about to do and so there seems to be little point in building test hooks as the testers are much closer to the developers.

18.6 Three generations: a summary

18.6.1 Characteristics of our three generations

Table 18.5 shows the characteristics of our three generations from 1995 to mid-1998. Note that it is not only the development environment that changes; the testware has its own life cycle too!

Table 18.5 A summary of our three generations.

	First generation	Second generation	Third generation
Application code	16 bit, pre-3.0	16 bit, 3.2/3.3	32 bit, 4.0
Controls			Treeview Toolbar
Operating systems	Windows 3.11 Windows NT	Windows NT4 Windows 95	Windows 95 Windows OSR2 Windows NT4 Windows 98
Web browser	N/A	IE3	IE4
Databases	Sybase SQL Anywhere	Sybase SQL Anywhere Oracle Personal Oracle	Sybase SQL Anywhere Oracle Personal Oracle
SQA Robot	4.0	5.1	6.1
Defect database	Paradox	SQL Anywhere	SQL Anywhere
Automation approach	Capture replay	SQA Basic Data driven Spreadsheets	Visual Basic Data driven Resource files
Costs: Tool Costs: Time	£14 000 ($21 000) £5000 ($7500)	£2000 ($3000) £7500 ($11 250)	£15 000 ($22 500)

We would like to be able to design our tests so that after a successful single-environment manual run, all other platforms and environments will be tested automatically. To accomplish this we need to enhance our test automation infrastructure so that it can run on different operating systems and support several database variants without any fundamental changes.

We will have three layers to our test infrastructure:

1. Infrastructure layer. General functions (must be platform independent).
2. Application utilities. Navutil, Create, Edit – application specific.
3. Test Suite. Scripts and spreadsheets to implement the test cases.

We had realized that as well as the automated test scripts themselves, there is a lot of code needed behind the scenes to make this all run in an efficient manner. This includes:

- a front-end to enable 'pick and mix' selection of tests;
- a mechanism for logging errors;
- version control;
- a scheduling mechanism to enable unattended testing.

The Test Suite will be structured around application functionality which will call various utility scripts in the application layer. For example, Meetings, Campaigns, Diary will call the appropriate lower-level utilities (navutil, create, etc.), which will themselves call the general functions to push buttons, click on windows, etc.).

In our opinion the technology of test automation must be integrated with the methods used for test planning and design of the manual tests. These have primarily been paper based and include, for example, test plans, test specifications, and checklists. Automated tests will never totally replace manual tests. However, the management of these test assets should be via a database solution rather than based on paper documents.

We envisage a strategy whereby bug system, coverage tool, manual and automated tests, and the results will all be linked together by either home-grown or bought-in third-party test asset management software.

We continue to move forward with test automation. Our products are expected to run on an increasing diversity of operating systems and databases. Furthermore, as we incorporate third-party components into our product we will have to test more communications links and interfaces.

18.6.3 Recommendations

1. The champion must keep going at all times when introducing automated testing. The champion has to accept that change management does not happen only once but at every stage of the tool's use. The champion also has to be prepared to handle setbacks and overcome

doubts caused by them. The champion must continue to sell the ideas and benefits of automated testing at all times and manage other people's expectations carefully.

2. Make sure the rest of your testing process is reasonably mature before you start to automate.

3. Before you buy an automated test tool first consider your requirements.

4. Evaluate a test tool in your own environment. Do not rely on the sales pitch or vendor demonstrations. Use an evaluation copy on a real project.

Consider carefully where in the project life cycle and test process you will use test automation: at unit test, integration test, or system test stages? For regression or performance testing? We have found that the best use of test automation is where we want to prove that a new application build will run on a variety of test environments. This actually saves a great deal of manual testing effort and allows the team to find the deeper, more serious bugs. Although this is not yet true regression testing, it is headed in the right direction. More importantly, it builds confidence in the concepts of automated testing.

Design your tests before you automate them. Remember that bugs are found by the tests, not by the tool, and that sometimes the act of attempting to build the test finds a bug.

18.6.4 So is this a success story?

We have certainly gained much by automating testing. We are able to test basic fundamental things very easily, but we certainly have not automated all of our testing. At least now we realize the limitations of test automation and can use it where it will be of most benefit to us.

We are now working more closely with our developers to define requirements for future test automation projects. First, we will attempt to port the current technology and test scripts to version 4.1 of Oxygen. Second, if this is successful, we will design and build a complete regression test pack for the Oxygen application. Rather than treat automation as part of a software release activity, both of these projects will have a separate project manager and be funded and managed exactly as any other internal project.

However, every advance we have made seems to have generated more and deeper problems. We seem to have done 'the right things,' yet we still encounter many technical problems, perhaps due to being overambitious when trying to automate all components of our leading-edge application software.

Although we started off intending to use a commercial tool, we have moved almost completely away from that to our own hand-crafted automation using Visual Basic as our test tool scripting language.

Test automation has had a checkered history at ISS. It is still not fully accepted by the developers, and management has yet to see tangible benefits.

However, our level of test process maturity has improved such that we are ready to face new challenges in our fourth generation.

Acknowledgments

Thanks to Annette Giardina for reviewing this chapter, and to Dan Reid, Iain Ollerenshaw, Richard Hind, and Anthony McAlister for their significant contributions to test automation at ISS.

Thanks to Andrew Myers, Technical Director at ISS, for his support and encouragement.

Steve Allott is now a senior consultant at Imago^{QA} Ltd.

Test automation failures: lessons to be learned

Ståle Amland

19.1 Introduction

This chapter is based on experiences from two test projects where auto-mated testing was a significant component. The experience from automated testing in these two projects is based on testing from systems testing (ST) and user acceptance testing (AT). Unit testing (as part of development) and integration testing (before systems testing) were part of both projects but automated testing was not used.

The use of test tools can serve several purposes, but in this chapter I limit the discussion of test tools to tools used for automating test execution. The purpose of using a tool for test automation could be to save time and/or money (i.e. better use of resources) or simply to improve the quality of the testing by documenting the test execution more thoroughly and thereby creating an audit trail of the test execution.

The two projects had different approaches to test automation, but nei-ther was successful in its use of test automation, even though substantial effort was put into the automated test regime. Unfortunately, I have seen the same mistakes that we made being repeated in several other projects, so there are lessons to be learned from our experience.

This chapter tries to point out what we did wrong in our attempt to automate the test execution and why – and hopefully give some recommen-dations on how others can avoid the same problems.

19.2 The projects

19.2.1 Project A

The first project (Project A) was testing of the server part of a retail banking system. All tests were executed using a test bed on a PC running an IBM mainframe terminal emulator. The project was a traditional 'waterfall' project, and the test phase was approximately 6 months of calendar time and included approximately 3000 person-days in 1995–96.

This project used test automation as part of ST. Prior to ST, unit testing had been executed as part of development, and all modules had been through integration testing.

Project A did not build detailed test documentation. All tests were based on test procedures, which included 'what to test' but not 'how to test,' i.e. the test procedure would say 'test a future date,' *not* 'insert 12/20/99 in the Posting Date field.' Also, the test procedures did not detail what combinations of fields needed to be tested for each transaction. This required the tester to be very familiar with the system, i.e. product specialists were used as testers rather than professional testers.

The testers used a capture playback tool to record the test as part of their ordinary manual testing. After they were satisfied with the test they would hand over the documentation to QC and the recorded test scripts were handed to the automation team. The automation team would take care of all archiving and filing and prepare the scripts for playback. If they identified some elements missing, they would go back to the tester, who would have to record the missing parts.

For the testers the test tool served two purposes:

1. to record all tests for audit trail and 'manual playback';
2. to record test scripts to be transformed into automated test scripts by the automation team. These scripts would later be used for automated regression testing.

The automated regression testing was originally planned to include 100% of all transactions. However, it became very cumbersome to prepare and execute, as I explain later in Section 19.3.2.

At the end of the project about 15% of all transactions had been tested using test automation. To achieve this, 25% of all available testing resources had been used in test automation, and only 2.5% of all faults were detected through automated regression testing.

19.2.2 Project B

The second project (Project B, 1997) was a home banking GUI application developed using the Rapid Application Development (RAD) method. The application tested was the client part of the system and included approximately 100 windows. The total system included over 15 mainframe systems, 5 hardware platforms, 4 suppliers, and 2 Windows versions. The project also included 25 developers for 6 months and 25 testers for 3 months. Of the 25-person test team, 8 used most of their time on test management and 2 focused on test automation.

This project used test automation as part of end user acceptance testing. Sample end users were brought in and trained in test techniques and methodology, how to build test documentation, and how to use the application.

The project had a large amount of structured test documentation (i.e. test case specification documents developed by the end users), and used the administration part of the test tool to maintain the test documentation and the test plan.

The test cases included input and output for a single function (e.g. one instance of a window or one calculation). The test data was either included in the test case or the test case would reference a separate test data document. To test one user operation in the system a sequence of test cases was required. The sequences were documented in test design specification documents.

The test automation was based on record and playback, where again the recording was done based on the manual test case specifications and test design specifications.

Even though some consultants said that 'this is the best structured test regime I have seen,' the test automation regime did not work efficiently. A disproportionate amount of effort was put into the automated testing for the benefits obtained.

19.3 Problems

19.3.1 Test tool problems

Two different test tools were used for Projects A and B. Later, I saw similar problems to what was experienced in these projects in other projects using different tools.

One of the problems we encountered was that the test tool did not support the development tool being used. This caused several problems, but the main problem was that the tool would not recognize the elements of the screens (e.g. radio buttons) as objects, so we had to rely on relative positioning at the pixel level to identify what is on the screen. If one tester then resized a window after the tests had been automated the first time, all of those tests would fail in the next regression. This was one of the major problems in both projects.

It is obvious that different tools have different benefits and problems, but if you do automation 'wrong,' selecting the 'right' tool will not save you.

19.3.2 The testers and their problems

The testers in both projects faced several problems. It was a conflict for the product people now being used as testers to concentrate on both testing the system (manually) and recording the tests for later automated regression testing.

Testing the server transactions sometimes included several steps to build test data to be used later in the test. For example, one function would add a record to the database that would be used by the next function to be tested. This type of function, whose only purpose was to build test data to be used by the function actually being tested, was called a 'build data transaction.' Very often these 'build data transactions' had already been tested, so recording them for audit trail purposes was therefore not necessary. However, to be able to convert the recorded scripts into an automatic regression test, all 'build data transactions' must be able to be replayed, and therefore do need to be recorded. Very often the product specialist forgot to record these data building transactions, and therefore recorded an incomplete test, making life miserable for the test automation specialists (and later again for the testers).

The tester had to keep track of his or her test data requirement to be able to test the function he or she was concentrating on at the moment, but also had to remember to record all these transactions to be able to do a playback later. This conflict of interest (i.e. having to concentrate on building a complete set of test data and also on recording for playback purpose) demotivated the testers and made them less productive as manual testers.

The main problem for the testers focusing on test automation in Project B (home banking) was the instability of the application when it came to user acceptance testing. This was a RAD project, and unfortunately, too many problems were detected during the user testing and too many major changes were implemented in the application. All these major changes caused severe problems to the attempts to automate any testing. The reason for this is that the automated testing was based on recording of the tests of one version of the software. Those tests were played back automatically when the next release was received. If a field had moved or some text had changed, this would then be reported as a difference (and a potential error). Because of the number of these types of changes in every release (which was done on a weekly basis), the maintenance of the Test Suite became a big problem.

19.3.3 Test environment problems

The main test environment problem in Project A (the retail banking server) was the data interference between testers. The application utilized a complex database, and a lot of basic test data had to be established before executing more complex functions. There was a hierarchy of functions, and they had to be executed in the right order.

Unfortunately, very often test data built by one tester's 'build data transactions' would be left on the system and another tester would reuse the same data (i.e. he or she would not record the build transaction because it was already there). Then when the test data was no longer there during replay (regression testing), this very often caused a problem because it was complicated to identify exactly the sequence of transactions that should have been executed.

Another basic problem with record and playback in database environments was the 'unique key' problem. This problem will occur when you record a function adding a record to the database. During playback you will again try to add the same record, which of course will be rejected because of unique key features in the database (i.e. most databases will automatically prevent you from adding records with the same key). Test automation tools now have several techniques to overcome this problem. We tried to resolve the problem by restoring the database each Monday morning to an initial state. The problem with this is that you will interrupt ongoing testing at the end of the week, and the testers might have to start all over again.

A third problem with the test environment was the test bed on the PC. For Project A, this was based on a mainframe terminal emulator running on the test PC. Unfortunately the test tools would not recognize anything except relative positioning on the screen. If any of the testers resized their windows, the test could not be played back on any other PC.

Project B also suffered from the same problem. The home banking application was written in Visual C and Visual Basic, but the tool would not recognize the objects without a specific DLL (supplied by the tool vendor) included in the code during development (compilation). However, since the development was outsourced, the supplier would not take the risk of including this DLL, which he did not know and could not control.

19.3.4 Timing and volume of the test automation

By timing and volume problems, I mean that we tried to do too much test automation in too short a time. We did not do any selection process on what areas would benefit from automating and what areas we should stay away from and therefore test manually.

Therefore, the recording processes done by testers, who were also responsible for manual testing, became very hectic, which again meant that we lost too much information in the recording process. This missing information had later to be recorded during the maintenance and playback stage, which would again slow down the testing process (keeping in mind the problems related to building basic data functions and unique keys).

The test script maintenance process (for automated test scripts) also became a bigger task than we had planned for. The work related to filing and archiving, updating the test scripts, and trying to do playback became massive. This is why we only automated the testing of 15% of the functions in Project A.

Our ambitious original objective, to automate 100% of the functions, became very demotivating. During the project it became obvious that the 100% mark could not be reached. However, there were from the beginning no prioritization or guidelines to assist in selecting which transactions to automate and which to test manually. A simple risk analysis could probably have solved this issue.

Another issue that I would like to call a volume problem was the testers' lack of programming experience. If the testers could have assisted the test automation team with maintaining the test scripts they recorded, the number of scripts to maintain might have been manageable.

19.4.1 Test tools recommendation

The prerequisite is to evaluate whether the test tools you are investigating support your development and test environment and will cover all the production environments your application will be released on. After this, the most important thing when choosing a test tool is to evaluate the tool's ability to handle documentation, planning, tracking, and defect handling simultaneously from automated testing, semi-automated testing, and manual testing.

The reason for this is that in real life you will very often have a combination of these tests. Some tests can be automated completely, some automated tests will need manual intervention, and some tests you will definitely benefit from doing manually instead of trying to automate them. If your tool cannot handle these types of test in the same structure, you might end up with several defect logs and different sets of test documentation, and your configuration control will be very complicated.

One other element to take into consideration is the tool's ability to record and log the recording in an editable form and also record user inputs (separate from the test being executed). The reason for this is the most beneficial use of test tools that I have seen, where the recording is to be used as an audit trail and for documentation purposes. If the tool can display a window asking the user for the expected result prior to the user actually recording the test in execution, you will have a complete log of tests being executed with expected and actual results. This log can be used as input to QA or as input to a manual regression test.

In my opinion the other tool selection criteria, such as price and ease of use, are less important, since the investment in training will be substantial anyway.

19.4.2 The testers: recommendations

It is important to allow time for training. Tool suppliers indicated one day of training for a tester and one week of training to become an expert user. To some extent this is correct, but you will not benefit from a tester in a test automation project after one day of training. As with most things in life, on-the-job training is the best, and testers must have seen and tried some of the pitfalls and useful functions in a tool before they can be productive. So, allow the amount of training recommended by the supplier (or a little less, if they try to squeeze money out of you), and plan the first project to have below average performance.

The test process should also allow for a combination of manual testing and automated testing, but usually test automation is so complicated that the project will benefit from having dedicated testers for test automation. They can receive proper training, and can also ignore the conflict between being able to execute a test and being able to record a test for replay.

Instead, they can record for building automated test scripts, and concentrate on building an automated Test Suite that can be maintained easily.

Testers executing manual tests can use the test tool to create documentation and manual regression tests. The test output should be readable but not necessarily replayable.

The tester working with automation will always benefit from programming skills. The reason is very simple: a script recorded during the test process is a small program. To be able to play back this 'program,' you will nearly always benefit from making the program more generic. This is like any other programming where you try to make reusable components. If the tester is lacking this knowledge he or she will not be able to support the automation team in building reusable component scripts.

19.4.3 Test environment: recommendations

To me it seems beneficial to integrate the automated test regime into development. The reason for this is that the development team often has to prepare the code for test automation anyway. Also, the test automation team must include people with development and programming knowledge to be effective.

The test environment for automated testing should be kept separate from the environment used for manual testing – unless you want to combine automation and manual testing. The reason to keep them separate is for the manual testing not to be limited by the rules set out by the test automation team. The benefits of manual testing are the ability to analyze the results of a test and make a decision about the next test based on the previous result. The tester might decide to follow a hunch, which might not be possible if the same test data is to be used by an automated Test Suite later.

Whether your test environments are separate or combined, expect the maintenance of the test environment to take time. In our server project including a mainframe database (Project A), the restore was done every Monday morning to set the initial state, i.e. the basic shared test data was loaded. The reload of the database with very limited data usually took two hours, but at the month end when the load on the machine was heavy, it would take six hours.

Another lesson learned is that it is very important to document basic shared test data (especially if you use a shared environment for manual and automated testing). The documentation is used for reference and for avoiding conflicts between testers. It is also useful to have a set of basic test data documented for each tester, which the individual testers can use as they like, but that will be restored to initial values as part of the database reload.

19.4.4 Timing and volume: recommendations

Clearly, given the problems we had with test automation, some areas would have been easier to automate than others. My recommendation is to start with some 'simple' functions to use as a pilot project to train the testers.

Given our problems as described earlier, a simple' function would be stable, i.e. changes to the design, code, or user interface would be very unlikely. Ideally, a simple function would also not include any database update to avoid any problems with unique keys. However, the latter is very hard to achieve.

Do not try to automate 100% the first time. Agree some procedures with the project management and customers on how to select functions for automation. Ideally those procedures should be defined in such a way that when your team has problems achieving the target automation level, the selection criteria should be tighter to limit the number of functions to be automated.

When you select functions to automate you should also focus on functions where you will really benefit from automation, e.g. functions that take a very long time to test manually but where it is possible to feed the data from a PC and save time. Everybody can see the benefit from saving time in testing.

19.5 Pilot project

We did have a pilot project for test automation, but unfortunately we did not know enough about automation when we planned the pilot. Therefore, the pilot did not discover the problems related to unique keys or to the number of tests being recorded.

The major benefit of the pilot was related to the training of the testers. During the pilot project we adjusted the training material.

However, if we had used experienced consultants during the planning phase and used their input to the pilot, I am sure the benefit from the pilot could have been substantially improved. Hopefully, we would have started working on the prioritization of functions as a criterion for automation at this stage, and could have avoided much frustration.

19.6 Epilogue

I still believe very much in automated testing, but I also know it is complicated and requires a lot of resources.

The projects I have been involved with have used tools successfully in areas other than automation. Tools used in planning, progress tracking, defect tracking, and documentation management have been extremely useful and productive. However, these areas are outside the scope of this chapter.

I do not believe that all projects will benefit from test automation, but I do think that a recording tool as part of the test documentation and audit trail is useful for most projects.

But if you want to automate your testing, listen to people with *experience* before you start!

© Ståle Amland, 1999.

CHAPTER TWENTY

An unexpected application of test automation

Bob Bartlett and Susan Windsor

20.1 Introduction and background

20.1.1 The client and the consultancy

This chapter is based upon a client case study where test automation was successfully used to support specific and complex business objectives and deliver testing efficiencies. However, it all started purely with a need for someone to independently test a software product; the client knew nothing about automated testing and cared even less.

The project was undertaken by SIM Group, which specializes in providing testing services to corporate clients using extensive practical experience in automated testing and other testing efficiencies to deliver cost-effective testing solutions.

The client in question is a major high street bank which, before this particular project, had been a client of SIM's for some two years. SIM was therefore already a known quantity in terms of its ability to deliver and there was a solid and successful working relationship in place.

20.1.2 This project

This particular project, however, was totally different from anything undertaken to date. It was initiated, resourced, and managed by a business product manager within the bank whereas all previous work had been undertaken directly for IT projects.

The bank wanted to migrate a special subset of its commercial customers, potentially up to 1000 of them, from a paper-based manual system to an automated computer system to handle their payment transactions. The decision was taken for the bank to provide them all with a software package to assist with this transition.

The majority of these commercial customers were small and therefore had very limited experience in using technology and were not likely to have any on-site technical support. It was therefore essential that the implementation and running of the software be exceedingly straightforward.

As this was a business-driven project, the bank wanted to source the software from products already available in the financial market and then to badge it as its own. This would require some modifications, of course, but the major focus for enhancements was for additional functions to facilitate easy installation and ongoing support of the software.

In addition, a comprehensive program of functional upgrades was also planned to follow on from the initial implementation of the software.

During this early marketing phase of this project, the need for efficient and effective testing was born.

Initially the business approached its own IT division to understand their view about the testing support needed for the project. They in turn suggested that the real need was for an independent testing organization to provide a service directly to the project. SIM met with the product manager to understand more about the requirements, and this led to what became an interesting and exciting testing project where our own ingenuity and skills could add real value.

20.1.3 Understanding the bank's objectives

The bank's product manager was an extremely talented, intelligent, and vibrant individual whose business vision motivated all around him. He fully recognized the business risks to the bank involved in taking on another company's software product. SIM's first meeting with the product manager started us working together to identify how testing skills could add value to the project by helping to manage those business risks on behalf of the bank.

The following represents the agreed objectives for independent testing:

- to review the invitation to tender to insure that there were sufficient questions to validate the technical base of the software;
- to enhance the selection process by reviewing how efficiently the software could be tested and providing some metrics to assist with decision making;
- to undertake some product selection tests on the shortlisted software applications to validate the information gathered to date;
- to define and undertake the user acceptance testing on behalf of the bank;
- to focus additional testing effort on areas supporting ease of use and installation;
- to insure that the overall project timescales were met because the business case depended upon a specific time slot.

In addition to all of the above, we wanted to review how automated testing might be able to enhance the project. This was a purely natural and instinctive thing for us to do as we always seek ways to improve efficiency in testing. It was not at this time driven by any project or client need.

20.1.4 Background to the project

The interesting thing about this project was that it did not start out as a project that was begging for an automated solution to the system that was to be tested. In fact, the contrary was true in this case. At the outset, it was anticipated that the testing to be done would in fact be minimal because the customer had intended merely to re-badge an existing market-leading piece of software. In the early days of the project it seemed as if this was going to be a simple case of re-badging the software by changing the name of it, then performing a test that made sure it still worked!

The initial discussions with the customer identified the need for careful testing, as there was a strong need to make sure the software would work. The repercussion of problems from a legal and practical point of view made the customer very nervous, in fact. The main reason for this attitude stemmed from the scale of the roll-out of the package and the importance of it. The bank was anticipating supplying the package to about 1000 of its customers, and this was at least 10 times more than had ever used it before. These implementations would take place over a relatively short time period and therefore had to be nearly perfect to meet the requirements.

In addition to the scale of the implementation, the package was also going to be handling a large amount of fairly sensitive and critical financial transactions. While one could not call it a safety-critical or life-threatening application, it was nonetheless important from a financial point of view. If things did not work well regularly with this package, our customer could be held liable for a significant financial loss.

Based on the seriousness of the project and the criticality of testing, we were able to convince the customer that the only way to really make sure that testing was properly addressed was to have testing assistance and guidance available at every stage of the project. While all testers say this all of the time, it is rare to convince people that this is necessary. Our customer never questioned the importance of testing, as I believe they were very worried that the worst nightmare of all would be for the software to go wrong with their name on it!

20.2 Helping the bank make its product selection

20.2.1 Phase 1: the ITT

The first stage of the project involved drawing up an Invitation to Tender (ITT), and, yes, we were called upon to contribute to this process. It was a real pleasure to be involved at this stage and to ask questions that we felt were important to evaluate. The following areas were covered in our suggestions for information to be provided by prospective suppliers:

- design of graphical interface and technology used;
- industry compatibility of development environment used;
- technical flexibility of delivered product;
- multiple platform support delivered;
- ease to test – and applicability for automation;
- delivery of product and fixes – and how these are tested;
- technical innovation employed;
- testing methods used by developer.

I am happy to say that all of the above areas were included in the ITT. Interestingly, we do not think that any potential suppliers realized why the questions were being asked, because all of the responses to the above points told us little more about the testing requirement and need. In fact, looking back on it, I think the potential suppliers were trying to outdo each other by minimizing the importance of the questions as often their responses were 'To be supplied later.'

The few that did attempt to answer the questions and supply further information were only really supplying platitudes that they hoped would make their product look bigger and more flexible than their competitors. In fact, this strategy could only work against them, because that would then tell us that the product was more difficult to test.

20.2.2 More questions for the shortlisted suppliers

As the information gathered from the ITT did not tell us what we needed, we then tried to think of a strategy that would give us the information in some other way. Luckily, the customer decided to submit a further request to the shortlisted suppliers, and this was our second opportunity to get more detail about the testing job that lay ahead. Therefore, when our customer put together a list of documentation they now wanted to see, we were very pleased to add to their list the following:

- functional specification of the software product;
- an example of a project plan and test plan for a recent set of enhancements;
- sample statistics showing the volumes of faults found during system testing;
- sample statistics showing the volumes of faults found during one-year live running;
- support desk procedures to manage and resolve customer issues;
- a diagram showing the technical architecture of the product;
- a description of any development tools, languages, testing tools, database products, and reporting tools the product used or contained.

This list was actually quite simple to supply for us, because it is in fact the same list that we ask customers to supply to us when we are doing a Testing

HealthCheck. The Testing HealthCheck includes an analysis of the above for one or more systems, and we have found this the best way to really see how things are being tested and to measure effectiveness. By asking potential suppliers to supply this information, we would then be able to perform a mini HealthCheck on each of them independently and remotely.

20.2.3 Phase 2: using testing to make the product selection

The next step of the project was what is popularly referred to as a 'Beauty Parade.' Each of five potential suppliers were invited to present in person their proposals and supply all documentation requested. This process was performed over a period of two days, and those in attendance were the customer and SIM Group. By attending the presentations, we could collect the documentation we requested as well as ask qualifying questions of the documentation. We were also allowed to ask further questions at the end of each presentation.

This worked quite well, and in addition to collecting the information we requested, it allowed us to establish valuable contacts with each supplier for further discussions and follow-up questions.

The most interesting thing that emerged during these presentations was the discussions about testing that we had with our customer's representatives at the presentation. Each question we asked about testing and each response we received was noted by our customer, and when we had the private debriefing sessions afterwards all of the questions and answers were recalled and discussed. Everyone wanted to know why on earth we were asking these questions about testing, and what on earth the answers really meant.

20.2.4 Developing the test strategy

The discussions that followed these debriefing sessions were really very valuable, and by the end of the last presentation, everyone was talking about testing and what was needed for testing. This allowed us to formulate a high-level testing plan with the following stages:

1. product acceptance testing
2. customer variation testing
3. performance testing
4. beta testing.

This resulted in a testing strategy being produced that covered (among other things):

1. risks for the project
2. stages of testing
3. types of testing required at each stage
4. verification and validation techniques at each stage
5. testing resource requirements for each stage.

The customer then took our analysis of each of the five companies that were proposing systems and used this in their evaluation of the five proposals. Eventually the five proposals were reduced to two contenders, and we were asked to assist again.

At this stage of the project, the two best systems and companies had been identified. As part of the final evaluation we were asked if we could offer any help in deciding between the two. We proposed that we perform the first stage of the testing strategy for each supplier, that is the product acceptance test. Using the supplied documentation from each supplier, we formulated testing plans that would cover all of the main functionality and features of each product.

We then visited each site and executed our test plan against the version of the product that related to the documentation we had already received. At each visit, we asked to have access to a 'clean' PC where we could install and test the system. Our customer provided us with test data and operational scenarios to use during the test as well.

When the product acceptance tests were completed, we documented the results of the tests and any problems encountered and delivered this to our customer. Therefore, at this point we had completed stage one of a four-stage testing strategy.

We then constructed product selection tests for the shortlisted software products based on the information gained from the documentation and supplier presentations. These were consolidated into a similar set of tests for each product so that our customer had an equivalent level of information on each one. Our findings were presented to our customer as input to the final software selection.

At the end of this phase of the project, we had a reasonably good understanding of the type of companies we were dealing with and a good feeling about the systems involved. Most importantly, we had a good basis for test planning from the strategy work we had done 'informally' with the rest of the customer's team.

The test strategy was now formally agreed as:

1. product acceptance testing
2. customer variation testing
3. performance testing
4. beta testing.

20.2.5 The waiting phase

At this point, there followed what seemed like an endless period of in-activity. In fact, our customer was negotiating commercial and operational arrangements with the final two potential suppliers. These discussions took place over an extended period of time, and involved numerous iterative meetings examining information from both parties that discussed potential arrangements.

From a testing point of view, there was nothing more that could be done during this time. Occasionally we could supply clarifying information, but no further preparation or planning could proceed until a decision had been made.

20.3 Doing the testing

20.3.1 A new twist from the supplier

Once the final supplier had been chosen, we were then ready to resume test planning and preparation. We were already thinking of the role automated testing would play in the whole process and had identified what sort of testing we wanted to automate and what parts of the system we wanted to build automated testing functions for.

We were in contact with the supplier, and were receiving more information from him as well as updates and new releases of the software as it evolved. We had outlined the testing strategy to the supplier and he was in basic agreement with this. The supplier was very happy that someone was caring so much about the testing work and was pleased we would all be working together to produce a quality product. It was clear to him that our test approach and strategy were well structured and would offer great value on the project overall. However, he was very aware that the testing we were planning to do was more on the implementation side and in the best interests of our customer.

Then, unexpectedly, the supplier telephoned us to find out if he could buy some consultancy from us to help him improve his testing methods and efficiencies. This was a big surprise, and we of course tried to help him out. He clearly saw an opportunity to improve his own testing and take advantage of our presence to improve his own methods and efficiency. As we would be very involved in the product and the project it seemed logical to him that we may as well help him while we were at it.

Although we had quite a lot of information on the product, we decided that a formal HealthCheck would be the best way to start this process, and we scheduled and conducted a Testing HealthCheck straight away. The HealthCheck report was delivered by way of a presentation to the supplier's management team. After considerable discussion, they accepted all of our observations and recommendations. A meeting was scheduled to discuss the implementation of the recommendations.

Implementing recommendations from a HealthCheck is always difficult, not so much in terms of accepting that the actions raised have to be done, but it is hard to figure out where to start and in what sequence things should be done. Great sensitivity to immediate problems and available resources is very important. Finally, the size and the scale of the problem have to be considered.

In the end, we identified five different initiatives that would be started to improve testing. This would allow an achievable target to be set and immediate actions put in place to make progress on improvements. We were asked to submit a proposal to cover two of the initiatives: automated testing and staff professionalism. Our proposal was accepted and we began a project to build an automated test system for the product that our client would be using (and that we would subsequently be testing).

20.3.2 All the pieces come together

So now we had two assignments on the same project. This was an interesting situation and an unusual one, to say the least. We reviewed the strategy and plans again and came up with a modified strategy that could be mapped onto the entire project. The project now looked something like the diagram shown in Figure 20.1. A more detailed explanation of each phase of testing now follows:

- System testing is the end of the base development process and includes functional testing, end to end testing, documentation testing, and negative testing. Test plans are constructed from specifications and are likely to be executed for multiple builds of the system.

- Product acceptance test is a full run-through of the product with a minimal set of test cases and simulates a user acceptance test. All business scenarios are tested, and testing includes all error messages and dialog prompts. This test will be run more than once, and is likely to be run with different builds of the application.

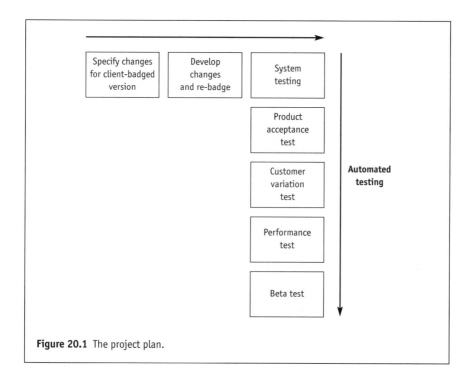

Figure 20.1 The project plan.

- Customer variation test is a test that uses actual customer configurations of each unique customer group. Customer groups are analyzed and defined from existing information on all 1000 customers. This test will test the product in the circumstances that all customers plan to use it.

- Beta test is a controlled release of the product that basically tests the production of the media, installation, and support. Some varying of technical configurations will be tested as well.

20.4 Automated testing

20.4.1 Developing the test system

The approach and methods used in automation of testing were the same as those used by most projects with the SIM Group:

1. analyzed the testing requirements;
2. did a survey of the application from a technical and functional point of view;
3. designed a full test system;
4. performed a proof of concept on the application;
5. developed and proved an automated test system.

The automated test system came together fairly quickly, and within a few days we had a basic automated test system that could navigate around the whole application and perform all of the data entry and data modification processes within the system. Input data and expected results to be used for this part of the automated system were held in spreadsheets and picked up dynamically as the tests were running.

The second stage of the automated test system was a facility to test all of the error messages in the system, and using the navigation functions from the first step we had this working in a few days. About 90% of the error messages were covered with this test and once again the instructions to navigate to a part of the application, perform a test, and check the error message were held in spreadsheets. Once a test was complete, the automated test system would navigate back to a common starting point of the system ready for the next test.

The third (and final) step in automation was performing the tests for all the business scenarios. As this stage involved more intricate navigation and results checking it took slightly longer, but in the end was completed on schedule and performed the testing and results checking required.

In total, the fully automated test system was designed, developed, and proved in a period of four weeks. Documentation of the test system was produced within this period, as well as an automated means to convert all of the documentation to HTML for access by a browser.

Two different builds of the test system were made available during the development of the automated test system. This enabled:

1. the immediate use of the test system for a partial regression test;
2. confidence that the test system could easily be updated without delay for application change;
3. making the test system more robust for application instability.

20.4.2 Using the test system

As there were four primary phases of testing to be accomplished, the test system was used in each phase. This of course was a planned feature of the test system; by designing it the way we did, we were able to achieve gains and benefits in each phase of testing. We normally find that each phase of testing has a different slant on defining testing conditions, and often a different type of test environment – but each phase is fundamentally testing the same things. By designing the test system with each of the other three phases of testing in mind, we were able to optimize the reuse of the test system.

Each phase of testing set up and maintained its own tables of test conditions, test data, and testing results. This allowed for the varying needs of the different phases of testing – but used the same test system.

1. System testing. Tables set up for this phase of testing were developed by test analysts who were working with the software developers. Test conditions were defined that produced a high coverage of testing, and each test condition was designed for its coverage benefit. Several different sets of tables were developed to be used during the development and system testing process.

2. Product acceptance testing. The tables set up for this phase of testing were split into two instances. There was one set of tables for positive testing and a second set of tables for negative testing. Each set served its own purpose of testing. In general, the positive tests were single-instance tests with simple conditions that when run would prove the application was performing as specified.

3. Customer variation testing. As this phase of testing was based on different customer profiles, there were individual sets of tables for each customer profile. This allowed for easy administration of test conditions, test runs, and test results. It also helped to prioritize tests.

4. Performance testing. The requirements for performance testing demanded an individual set of test data for each iteration of a test. Therefore, several thousand test conditions were needed to drive the needs of the performance test. Obtaining this high volume of test data instances was satisfied by an automated test data generation method we commonly use to create volume data.

The work to set up the various tables and confirm their accuracy was mostly performed by business analysts and current users of the system. These people had no technical background and were comfortable with techniques needed to populate and manage tables of data.

Due to the commonly seen pressures of the time available to test, the customer variation tests and the performance tests were conducted in parallel. This was easily achieved with the test system and encouraged the best use of the test assets available.

20.5 The results

20.5.1 The testing phases: what really happened?

In the real world, the way projects are planned is not always the way projects actually go. This project was no exception. Although things more or less followed the structure that had been anticipated, there were a few surprises that the testers had to respond to.

The development process was very iterative, in that the full set of requirements and specifications for development was finalized on a piecemeal basis and worked on by iteratively making development changes to a base system. This resulted in several builds of the application being produced that were getting closer and closer to the final product each time. This effectively produced builds that were incrementally different to the last, but still not the full product as required.

Testing in this environment was somewhat frustrating, but with the automated test system built, testing was actually quite easy and fast. It took approximately one day to perform a full functional test on the product and raise any faults or problems that had been found. This was quite a remarkable achievement, as previously it often took a full week to fully test the product.

Once it became known that testing was being performed so quickly, two very obvious things began to occur:

1. new builds were made available daily instead of weekly;
2. development (program) testing became less and less.

Looking at each phase, this is how the testing went:

1. System testing was performed every day by the development and system testing team. The system would be built at least once per day, and the automated test system would be run with selected sets of tables containing different testing conditions.
2. Product acceptance testing was performed approximately 12 times; each time the test took about one day with a saving of four days. The overall saving was about 48 days, but in reality testing would not have been done so frequently if manual testing had been performed for the product acceptance test. Manual testing would have elongated the whole iterative cycle of development and testing.

3. Customer variation testing. About halfway through the product acceptance testing iterations, the application became stable enough for the
customer variation testing. The customer variation testing was then performed over a period of one week, in parallel to further iterations of the
product acceptance test. Errors were raised and immediately fed back.
After the final build passed the product acceptance test, a second full
customer variation test was performed. Customer variation testing
occupied no elapsed time on the critical path of the project.

4. Performance testing was also executed in parallel to the product acceptance test.

5. Beta testing was conducted as planned, and any fixes were re-tested by
running a full functional regression test on the product using the automated test system built.

20.5.2 Benefits

Given that the prime reason for independent testing was to insure that the
business and technical risks were understood and contained, the major benefit to the bank was that the approach worked and there were no adverse
repercussions at all from the launch of the product.

The testing perspective injected into the supplier selection process
resulted in the selection of a package with a known level of complexity for
testing. This allowed SIM to complete a Strategy for Testing and Test Plans
while the final commercial negotiations were taking place between the
bank and the software supplier.

The interesting development of SIM working directly with the software
supplier allowed for a very trusting and flexible working relationship to
develop between developers and testers. This really paid off when we were
all working together to meet tight deadlines as defects have to be diagnosed
accurately and resolved quickly.

The software was enhanced using a prototyping approach with multiple
reviews with the bank to insure that the final implementation of the functional requirements would meet the 'ease of use' objective. As the software
evolved, so did the definition of the test cases for systems testing, which
meant that testing could be undertaken alongside development.

The automated test system was designed and developed using SIM's
own methodology. This meant that the scripts were robust, easy to maintain, had flexibility in the data components, and could therefore easily be
used for each new release of the software. The scope of testing that was
automated grew alongside the development so that by the time system testing was completed, a full set of regression tests was in place.

Once the project was completed, these automated tests were used frequently to validate new configurations and new releases of software for a
fraction of the time and effort it would have taken to conduct such a high
degree of testing manually. This clearly reduced the cost of ongoing testing
and also insured that a known level of quality was being delivered to the
bank's customers.

Having completed the systems testing, this detailed knowledge allowed SIM to undertake the acceptance testing with a clear focus on the business functionality with no duplicated testing effort.

This innovative three-way working relationship between the software house, the bank, and SIM worked extremely well. The software house improved its own testing processes and skills and was able to successfully undertake automated testing itself on future releases. The bank was confident in the quality of the software and was able to plan accurately for the level of support required during the implementation phase. SIM delivered a high quality of independent testing to another customer, which resulted in an excellent reference for future business.

As the project progressed, many changes to the timescales and business plans took place outside of the direct control of the project team. The trust that built up in this three-way team allowed for a flexible approach to be taken to meet these ever-changing needs effectively. Working together with this true partnership meant that the project completed on time, to schedule, and within budget.

Once the project was completed and the first customers started to use the software successfully, the product manager was asked how he felt the bank's objectives had been met. He confirmed that he would have no hesitation at all in repeating the process for any other software package being brought into the bank.

This chapter is gratefully received from SIM Group Ltd, who have consistently made significant differences to projects over the years through the use of automated testing.

CHAPTER TWENTY-ONE

Implementing test automation in an Independent Test Unit

Lloyd Roden

21.1 Introduction and background

21.1.1 The company

Peterborough Software develops, markets, and supports computerized human resource management, financial, and distribution systems, and offers a service ranging from bureau, consultancy, education, and training to installation assistance and ongoing support. Its solutions operate on most major hardware environments, whether open systems, mainframe, mini, or PC. It now has a global distribution of products in over 40 countries worldwide and employs more than 500 staff, 40% of whom are dedicated to research and development, and customer support.

The company has the largest human resource customer base in the UK, consisting of 1600 organizations, which includes 73 of *The Times* Top 100 companies. In addition, Peterborough Software has successful operations in France, the Netherlands, Australia, Singapore, New Zealand, and Hong Kong.

21.1.2 The case study and the test tool

We have been using test execution tools at Peterborough Software for the past eight years. This particular case study is as a result of the work we have done since 1996 in evaluating and using QARun, Compuware's 32-bit test execution tool, on our new product PSenterprise.

This case study unfolds into six distinct areas:

- Evaluation
- Implementation
- Deployment

- Usage
- Problems
- Benefits.

Each section describes the processes we went through and key decisions made. I have also included a subsection in each summarizing the salient points.

I was responsible for the Independent Test Unit (ITU) at Peterborough Software, which has been in operation since December 1996. This is where this case study begins.

21.2 The evaluation process

21.2.1 Our requirements

Our new product, PSenterprise, uses the latest architecture in software engineering, namely 32-bit, ODBC, three-tier, client/server technology. Having been involved in software testing for over ten years, I had already gained an appreciation of the benefits of using test automation.

To complement our new product we needed a testing tool that interfaced well, but at the time of evaluation it seemed that very few products were available. We did not, however, consult the *CAST Report*, which in hindsight would have assisted in this process. Visual Test and QARun were the two tools we evaluated.

The development department had already purchased and was using Visual Test. This meant that there was immense pressure for us to conform and inherit this tool within the ITU.

I decided that a requirements list was needed to help with the evaluation process. The list is shown in Table 21.1.

21.2.2 Relationship with the tool vendor

We also wanted to build relationships with the tool vendor, and the requirements shown in Table 21.2 were important to us at Peterborough Software.

We invited Compuware to demonstrate QARun on our own software. This was a challenge to them but must be a prerequisite in the evaluation process. A rule of thumb is that one should not become easily impressed with demonstrations given by tool vendors. Remember that they have mastered the demonstration and this will work every time! The acid test is to see the product demonstrated on your own software.

We then asked Compuware for an evaluation copy of QARun, so that we could compare both tools at our leisure. Once we had decided on the two tools the actual evaluation process took very little time – probably less than one week.

Table 21.1 Requirements for tool evaluation.

Requirement	Reason
Easy to use	This was top of the list. The tool had to be easy to use for the team, who were good testers but not programmers; it was therefore vital that the tool did not require too much technical expertise
	Also, having a tool that was easy to use meant that the testers would enjoy using it and the benefits would be seen sooner rather than later.
Reliable	Close second was reliability. We had previously experienced a tool that proved unreliable and it soon became shelfware
Good features embedded in the product	By 'good features' I mean anything that would help the testers perform their job effectively and efficiently. A good point to make here is that vendors are usually very quick to boast of their 'prize' features. Make a list of these when you are looking at all the tools so that you can compare and evaluate which would be most useful to you
A comprehensive scripting language	Yes, the tool had to be easy to use, but I was aware that this requirement would be superseded by the need for a comprehensive scripting language as soon as the testers became competent
Regular maintenance/ upgrades	I needed to know how often upgrades would be received as this showed the level of commitment to enhancing the product, as well as fixing issues that would be found

Table 21.2 Vendor requirements.

Requirement	Reason
The tool had to be developed in line with our own product	It was imperative that the tool was compatible with our own software now, but more importantly, in the future. Developing scripts and tests using the tool is a large investment and we needed to be convinced that the investment was long term
Good customer support	This requirement is a little like having insurance. We were going to find problems with using the tool, but we needed to be reassured that customer support would handle our issues with efficiency and urgency
Tool training	Comprehensive training was also a requirement – training which was flexible, but also in stages (beginners, intermediate, and advanced)

21.2.3 The business case

Having decided on QARun as our preferred test execution tool, I had to present a strong business case to convince senior management to spend more for our preferred tool. It is worth noting at this point that there is sometimes flexibility when it comes to price negotiation with the tool vendors.

The business case itself took into account factors such as benefits to us as a department: ease of use, important key features in the product, and help desk support. It also took into account benefits to us as a company: greater productivity within the team, the tool being used rather than becoming shelfware, and past business with Compuware.

21.2.4 Key issues to note in the evaluation process

- Produce a requirement list and prioritize which is most important;
- inform each of the vendors that there are others in the evaluation process;
- invite the vendor to demonstrate their tool on your own software;
- don't spend too long evaluating the tools;
- once you have decided on the preferred tool, produce a good business case and present it to senior management.

21.3 The implementation phase

21.3.1 First step: three copies

Having presented the business case and convinced senior management that this was the right way to go, I needed to insure that the tool was successfully implemented.

We had agreed to purchase three copies of QARun initially. This was an important first step – to minimize the initial costs and maximize initial benefits. It was important for us not to be over-ambitious in the early stages (to walk before we sprinted!). This philosophy is one I would advocate if you want to see the project succeed.

21.3.2 Training

Training in the tool is important and the timing is vital. My team consisted of three people, all of whom would be using QARun. To get maximum benefit from the course, we had implemented the tool four weeks before the course was due to take place. This gave us sufficient time to try things out and jot down any questions we had. We also asked Compuware to run the course in-house and on our software.

The problem I have found with 'standard courses' is that you learn about how to use the tool on a demo application. The enthusiasm wanes when you try applying what you have learnt back in the office. The bespoke in-house course may cost a little more but, in my opinion, it is worth every penny.

At this stage we had implemented three copies of QARun within the ITU. Development/Product Assurance were still using Visual Test. Although it is not necessarily a bad thing for a company to use more than one test tool, it is in my opinion not advantageous as we 'water down' the knowledge base. I wanted us to be 'singing off the same hymn sheet' for the benefit of PSenterprise and ultimately for the benefit of the company.

My goal was to adopt QARun as the company test tool. This was achieved by showing the potential of the tool to the rest of the project team.

21.3.4 Key issues to note in the implementation phase

- Start small to maximize benefits and minimize initial costs. Think about purchasing two or three copies of the tool initially;

- think about how you are going to train your staff in the use of the tool. Timing of this is essential – insure that the staff will be using the tool as soon as the training has finished, otherwise they will soon forget what they have learnt;

- try to have the training performed on your own software; this way it will be more relevant;

- once implemented, show the tool to others in the project team. It is important that the whole project team buy into the tool.

21.4 The deployment of the tool

21.4.1 Standards and naming conventions

It was important for us to deploy QARun correctly. We had made mistakes in the past in releasing the tools to too many people, too soon. We needed to put together sensible standards and naming conventions that could be easily understood, but more importantly that were proven to be usable and flexible.

Having only purchased three copies of the tool initially, it was easy to contain the deployment of this tool. Two of us worked on the naming conventions and standards and a draft version was implemented within the team in a matter of a few days. Ownership of these standards and naming conventions remained with one person in the team and that person became the recognized expert in the use of QARun within the company. Some examples of the standards and naming conventions we adopted are shown in Table 21.3.

Table 21.3 Standards and naming conventions.

Topic	*Standards and naming conventions*
QARun database	1. Central QARun database to be used at all times and this is to be stored on the common server for ease of maintenance and backup
	2. The database must be compacted once a week by the ITU
	3. On receiving a major release of PSenterprise, both QARun and associated data must be copied and archived as version x.x
Test data files	1. Test data files must be created in Microsoft Excel so that they can be easily maintained and can incorporate any comments for documenting purposes. • one Excel (xls) file for each driver script • each xls file will have multiple sheets to group the test data logically
	2. Excel files to be stored on the central server within folder called itu\data\xls
	3. Save each sheet in the xls file as a csv file which is used to drive the QARun scripts and store these on the central server within folder called itu\data\csv • the name of the xls sheet and its csv file should be the same • delete the comment lines
	4. Copy the relevant csv files to c:\program files\compuware\data when you need to use them
Naming conventions	1. Script names: ABCCCCCCCCCC, where A is T for test script, D for driver script; B is Y for Payroll, R for Personnel, and A for AMS; and CCCCCCCCCC is a meaningful name to describe the script, e.g. 'TYEleDef' for Payroll element definition
	2. Checks must have a meaningful name which describes the check, e.g. 'PD 48 GP1-0001 Payslip History Elements,' which checks the Elements tab on the Payslip History window for employee GP1-0001's period 48 payslip
	3. Events must have a meaningful name which describes the event, e.g. 'Formula Hypertext window exists'

In my opinion, it is essential to have someone within the company who is the recognized expert in the use of the testing tool – a champion. In my own team, this person has not only helped others, but has also insured standards and naming conventions are adhered to. I am also of the opinion that 'best practice' must be adopted and I was encouraged, having attended the 'Effective Test Automation' course run by Mark Fewster, that we were heading in the right direction.

21.4.3 The word began to spread

It was not long before other testers within the company wanted to see how we had used QARun and what benefits we had gained. I was soon asked to demonstrate the power and versatility of QARun to others in the project team. The outcome is that Peterborough Software has adopted QARun as its standard test execution tool.

Having already established the foundations in standards, naming conventions, and generic scripts, and by presenting key sessions on how we had used the tool, it was then easy to roll out QARun to the rest of the company. We have to date deployed 19 copies of QARun and it is currently being used with determination and enthusiasm on all our product range.

The use of an Access database as a central repository for scripts, object map entries, and checks provides a 'portable' testing tool which encourages the sharing of ideas, scripts, and knowledge.

21.4.4 Key issues to note in the deployment of the tool

- Deploy the tool when you are ready. Releasing the tool prematurely will lead to uncontrolled scripting and bad practices being adopted. Once this happens it is then difficult to regain control;
- set aside time at the beginning in order to produce naming conventions and standards for the tool use;
- assign a key person responsible for the implementation and policing of these standards.

21.5 How QARun has been used

The philosophy I adopt in all walks of life is based upon the KISS principle – Keep It Simple, Stupid. This philosophy has never let me down, and in testing terms this translates to breadth first, depth last.

21.5.1 Breadth tests

These tests are designed to test the breadth of our application. At this stage we are not concerned with detailed tests, but want a series of tests that provide maximum impact in the shortest possible time. These tests are usually very easy to automate. Examples of these tests are shown in Table 21.4.

Table 21.4 Example breadth tests.

Script	Description	Purpose
Dialog scripts	Script will open all menu dialogs within a given application and will perform a basic 'text' check before closing Time to run, approximately 5 minutes per application No data input	Tests all menu dialogs for each release Diagnoses any changes to the screens Used on different configurations (i.e. Windows 95, Windows 98, Windows NT)
Solo script	Script enters minimum data required to process a new starter, runs payroll and absence processes, and performs a number of key checks Time to run, approximately 20 minutes per application Minimum of data input	Test of 'key' processes within the applications Checks employee-based screens Used on different configurations (i.e. Windows 95, Windows 98, Windows NT) and on different databases (SQL, Oracle, and AS400)

I cannot emphasize enough the importance of these breadth tests. They are relatively easy and quick to produce and they provide you with sufficient confidence to continue with the depth tests and other manual tests.

Just by way of an example, our product has a number of applications, namely payroll, personnel, absence management, and recruitment. Each of these has its own dialog regression script. These took, on average, half a day to produce and would run in five minutes. Having four PCs available, I can be assured that all application windows would open and I would know whether any changes had been made to the actual windows. This is an excellent first test for any new release.

The solo script would put the minimum of data into the system to be able to run the batch processes connected to the application and would check all employee-based screens. More work was involved in producing these scripts due to the data entry aspect. On average, a solo script would take about 3 days to produce and it would execute in 20 minutes.

These solo scripts added to the dialog scripts, when run, provide me with enough confidence in the system to move to the next stage of regression benchmarks – the depth tests.

I have also found these breadth tests (solos and dialogs) useful for testing other aspects that may affect our application, such as machine upgrades, operating system upgrades (NT version 4 to NT version 5), and database upgrades (SQL version 6.5 to SQL version 7.0). Bugs can then be found quickly and efficiently.

By way of examples as to the usefulness of these scripts:

- it was our payroll solo script that found a problem when we upgraded from SQL version 6.5 to SQL version 7.0;

- it was the dialog scripts that found discrepancies between Windows 95 and Windows 98 clients.

21.5.2 Depth tests

These tests are designed to 'drill down' into the system, testing various features and attributes of the system. At Peterborough Software we call these regression benchmarks 'scenario tests.' Some examples are shown in Table 21.5.

Table 21.5 Example depth tests.

Script	Description	Purpose
Scenario Tests	These scripts test a particular scenario. The size of this scenario is variable, as is the time it takes to run; some of these scenarios are fully automated and some have manual intervention	1. Tests various test cases within each application
		2. Builds further confidence in the system
	Time to run varies between 1 hour and 2 days	3. Used on different databases (SQL, Oracle, and AS400)
	Lots of data input	

The time taken in initially setting up the scenario tests was in fact longer than anticipated. Past experience had shown that scripting usually took four times longer than manual tests and I had always used this ratio (4 : 1) to determine whether it was worthwhile automating the tests.

This time the ratio initially was probably closer to 10 : 1. The reason for this is that we took the decision to produce scripts that were data driven rather than coding the data into the scripts. The result is that initial set-up time takes longer but the benefits are as follows:

- scripts are easier to maintain;
- scripts can be copied and used as templates for similar style windows;
- more tests can be run without changing the scripts. This can be achieved by changing the data;
- while initial set-up times are longer, the net effect is one of long-term gain.

A point for managers reading this – please allow your testers sufficient time to build generic, low-maintenance, data-driven scripts. The long-term benefits far outweigh the short-term costs.

21.5.3 Other tests

Having spent the time developing these scripts, we decided to make more use of what we had and build further benchmarks relatively easily. By reusing scripts but increasing the volume of data we were able to build a performance benchmark, and by looping the solo script we were able to build a robustness benchmark. These are shown in Table 21.6.

Figure 21.1 shows example results of robustness testing. The tests ran for a period of 8 hours and were repeated on a P60 and a P166 machine, both with 32 Mbytes of RAM.

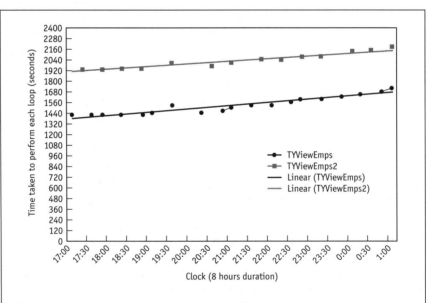

Figure 21.1 Results of robustness tests for the payroll system.

Table 21.6 Examples of other tests.

Script	Description	Purpose
Performance scripts	Performance scripts have been developed from existing scripts, but the amount of data has increased substantially Copying data in Excel is very easy, therefore increasing the employee data from 1 to 10 000 means that the solo script can become a volume script in an instant Time to run varies depending on the amount of data	1. Ability to generate large volumes to test database performance 2. Used on different databases (SQL, Oracle, and AS400) for comparison
Robustness scripts	Looping part of the solo script means that we can perform the same test over long periods of time to check the robustness of the system Also, by using QARun's clock checks we can time transactions on various specification PCs and can determine the degradation. This is vital for us so that we can advise customers what response times to expect on different PCs (Figure 21.1 is the result of such a test)	1. Check for memory leaks 2. Check the difference in response times on different specification PCs

Figure 21.1 shows that there is a steady linear degradation over the 8-hour period, which does indicate a slight memory leak. The other observation which interested me was that there appeared to be an improvement in response times of up to 30% when using a P166 machine when compared to a P60 machine.

The above information was achieved relatively easily using existing scripts with clock checks built in.

21.5.4 Key issues to note in the use of the tool

- Start with simple scripts that cover the whole system quickly – breadth tests;
- build upon the breadth tests to produce your depth tests;
- use test data files to drive your scripts. This makes the scripts easy to maintain and more versatile;
- think about how existing scripts can be used to run tests such as performance and robustness.

21.6 Problems we have experienced

So far I have painted a very positive picture of how we have evaluated, implemented, and used QARun within Peterborough Software. And it is a success story. But it hasn't been free from frustrations and headaches. This section looks at some of the problems we have encountered during the past two years – this section will keep your feet firmly on the ground.

21.6.1 Running of scripts

Most of us have the perfect picture in our minds, that we can run a script overnight with very few problems. We start the script, put our coats on, and expect the script to have finished perfectly the next morning. While in theory this is possible, my experience has shown that in reality it is unlikely. I would estimate that less than 40% of automated tests run without some form of manual intervention.

There are a number of reasons for this, but the point I would make is not to become overly optimistic but to persevere in trying to make the scripts more robust.

21.6.2 Maintenance of scripts and data

Don't be fooled by the tool vendors: there is a large overhead in maintaining your scripts and test data. Plan this into your project schedules. The problem here is when you don't plan for this activity. Obviously the amount of maintenance is dependent on the nature of the changes. However, this is not linear – a small change (such as a new ocx file) can have a large effect on your scripts.

By way of an example of this nonlinear effect, our own developers changed from using Visual Basic version 4 to version 5. This gave the developers more flexibility in developing the software, but gave us testers a headache because we had to change the controls within our testing tool so that our scripts could run against the new system.

A note must be made here for both testers and developers – we must work closer together, to understand how the system is being developed and how we are proposing to use the testing tool. This attitude promotes a good working relationship and testability in our software.

21.6.3 Maintenance of the tool

When purchasing the tool, two options were available: buy the tool with or without the maintenance agreement. I would always advocate taking the maintenance agreement option as you will encounter problems with the tool that will hopefully be fixed in subsequent releases. Also the tool vendors will hopefully be enhancing the tool for your benefit.

However, be aware that upgrading the tool takes time and needs to be planned. It might also mean that new problems arise which were not expected. We ourselves had problems with one such upgrade to the database, which did cost us time in resolving the issues with Compuware.

21.6.4 Bugs in the tool

At times we have found problems with QARun. Time has been spent determining whether the problem is with our software or the tool. Most of the bugs found have indeed been fixed by Compuware in subsequent releases, which is a further endorsement of taking out the maintenance agreement. However, there have been times when problems found could not be recreated – these have been the most frustrating, as they have been very real problems to us.

21.6.5 Configuration management of scripts and data

The more people there are involved in scripting and running of the tests, the greater the likelihood of problems occurring in version control. Even with strict change control, people will want to get their tests run as quickly as possible and will want to cut corners.

I had five people in my team and we shared a central QARun database. The benefits of this certainly outweigh the disadvantages. However, there have been times when changes made by one person have caused scripts not to run. Change control is not as good as it should be but is manageable with only five people. I could envisage serious problems if there were more people involved. It is worth pointing out at this stage that QARun does have version control built into the product, which makes it a little easier to manage.

21.6.6 Don't automate too soon

There is a distinct danger to try to automate tests before the software is ready. We have fallen prey to this. The result has been to code around 'buggy' software. It is far better to wait until the software is robust and reliable as this then leads to beneficial and positive scripting.

21.6.7 Key issues to note from problems we experienced

- Don't be too optimistic in running scripts overnight with no problems – this is a nice theory, but reality dictates otherwise;
- recognize and plan for the maintenance of your scripts. This is no easy task and could result in the test tool failing because of poor management. Remember that small changes could have substantial consequences in your scripts;
- don't automate too soon;

- it is advisable to take out the maintenance agreement, but be aware that the upgrade of the tool could take some time and present unexpected problems.

21.7 The benefits achieved in two years

This is a success story of how we have evaluated, implemented, deployed, and used QARun at Peterborough Software – despite some of the problems we have encountered along the way.

I guess the success should be measured by how Peterborough Software has responded to this tool. At the start we were given permission to purchase three copies of this tool for sole use within the Independent Test Team. QARun is now the company standard in test execution tools – Peterborough Software has 19 copies and it is being used on all our products. In this section, I outline the benefits that we have achieved.

21.7.1 More with less

The number one benefit has been the amount of tests that we can now run in the timescales given. The regression tests we now have would take us approximately four person-weeks to run manually (that is, if we were to key and check everything perfectly). During our last release, these same tests using QARun took two of us (using five PCs) only two days, so four person-days instead of four person-weeks, a five-fold improvement.

21.7.2 Improved testing

The test execution tool has given us more time – more time to develop better tests, more time to run ad hoc manual tests, and more time to think about what to test. All this has led to improved testing of the PSenterprise product, which has ultimately benefitted our customers.

We can also be assured that input and checks (using QARun) are accurate, which ultimately builds confidence.

21.7.3 Machine usage

Our PCs are usually running scripts unattended overnight, which is making the best use of the resources we have. By having two PCs per person, productivity increases as we are able to develop scripts on one while running regression scripts on the other.

21.7.4 Lack of regression in our product

The acid test for us, being in the software industry, is that our customers are satisfied with the quality of our products. Customers should also be confident when new product releases/upgrades are shipped to them. Automating our tests means that there is very little chance of product regression. The measurable benefit for us is fewer issues being raised by the customer.

21.7.5 Performance tests

I have already mentioned the ability to run performance tests relatively easily. Building a 10 000-employee database can be run over a weekend. Performing this manually would take considerably longer and would probably result in a lot of unhappy people!

21.7.6 Customer impact

I have been able to present the work of the ITU to Peterborough Software customers. The presentation has included the work that we have achieved with QARun. Without exception, all customers have been impressed with the work undertaken using the tool. The customer response has been encouraging, to say the least.

21.7.7 Testers being acknowledged in a skill

QARun brings with it a sophisticated scripting language (as do many of the test execution tools). Testers are encouraged to improve in this programming skill, making scripts structured, maintainable, easy to read, and efficient. This skill set is important for the tester building scripts as well as for the programmer building the system that is being tested.

21.7.8 Better morale within the team

'Running a manual test once is exciting, running a manual test twice is usually a necessity, running a manual test more than twice is boring' – a quotation from Lloyd Roden's testing handbook. We have to wake up to the fact that regression testing is boring if it is to be done manually. I have found that by introducing a test automation tool, the testers will get on and do the work they do best – creative testing. Someone once said that 'human beings were never created to repeat something more than once.' I'll say that again . . . .

21.8 Conclusion

It has been a privilege working for a company like Peterborough Software, which takes testing seriously. We have achieved a great deal in the past two years using QARun, but we must not rest on our laurels. There is so much more that can be achieved – with thought and training, and certainly in working with other companies with experience in test automation.

Lloyd Roden is now a consultant with Grove Consultants.

Testing with Action Words

Hans Buwalda[1]

22.1 Introduction

In this chapter I introduce a method of testing using automated tools with Action Words. The Action Word method started in 1994 and is now widely used in organizations in a growing number of countries, under the name TestFrame. Customers range from large banks to technical industries with embedded software. The method has been growing since its origin due to the contributions of many people. Although it is now well established, it is still subject to development as new possibilities are explored, new lessons are learned, and new ideas are incorporated.

22.1.1 Why the method was created

Why was the method created? Testing is one of the most difficult tasks in system development. A system developer can write down a formula in a design and the programmer can program it. The tester has to find concrete examples. The developer can work according to a predefined plan; the tester has to cope with somebody else's plan. The developer works with the structured understanding of the system to be built. In a stepwise fashion business demands will be translated into a working system. The tester has to look for the 'side paths,' those areas and combinations that the developer might have overlooked and where the pitfalls might be. Automated testing is even more difficult than manual testing. Apart from the hassle of testing one also has to set up extra automation efforts, resulting in one system testing another system. Still, test automation should be an attractive option

---

[1] Hans Buwalda works as a management consultant for CMG, a major European IT company. The Action Word method is part of TestFrame, CMG's standard method for structured testing.

because it opens the possibility of shortening the elapsed time, producing tangible results and saving boring work.

To address the challenges of automated testing the method with Action Words was developed. In this method tests are developed separately from their execution in the test tool. In this chapter I give an introduction to the method. The description is not complete but it should give enough information to make a start and to cope with the most common issues. I try to revisit the issues raised in the other chapters of this book and translate them to the Action Word method. The scope of TestFrame stretches beyond test automation; it also deals with techniques to produce tests and the way the test process can be organized. In this chapter I describe some of the main products of the method, but I focus on the way the test execution is automated.

22.1.2 Test execution

Executing a test on a system (which we will call the 'target system') means:

- performing actions on the system;
- checking results produced by that system by comparing them to expected results.

Both the actions and the checks involve test data, either input data or expected output data. In this chapter we deal with tests that are prepared in advance: described as a sequence of actions and checks before they are executed. In practice it might be a good idea to also make some room for 'intuitive tests,' sitting behind a machine and interacting with the system. The results will surprise you. Afterwards any newly found bugs can be translated into appropriate tests in the prepared collection.

In Chapter 3 different types of scripting techniques are described. In the Action Word method the focus is not on the test tool scripts to describe tests. Test tools are used intensively, but only to execute the tests, the area where test tools are usually very good. The tests themselves are described outside the test tool, in so-called test clusters. Usually spreadsheets are used to create and maintain the test clusters, but it is also possible (and done in some projects) to use word processors or database management systems to do so. Spreadsheets are favored because they are very flexible in handling test lines and expressing them in a readable way.

22.1.3 The Action Word method

In Figure 22.1 the main principles of the Action Word method are depicted. The tests are kept in the spreadsheet files, which we call 'test clusters.' In most cases the spreadsheet files are further divided into separate 'test sheets,' consisting of usually several hundred 'test lines' specifying the actions and the checks.

The test tool is programmed, using its script language, to interpret the test sheets line by line. In order to be read by the test tool the sheets are first exported to a tab-separated text file. In this format the rows of the

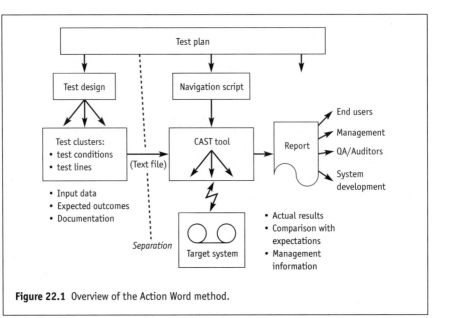

Figure 22.1 Overview of the Action Word method.

sheet are translated into text lines and the columns into fields within those lines, separated from each other by tabulation characters. This form is the most practical for the test tool to read and can be produced as a standard export format by most popular spreadsheet programs.

The test automation is regarded as a separate activity, apart from the test design. To interpret and execute the commands in the test cluster a special script is written, which is called the 'navigation script.' This navigation script is written in the script language of the test tool. Most test tools on the market have a script language powerful enough to have such a navigation script created. Sometimes navigation scripts are written in languages other than that of a test tool, for example in C when embedded software has to be tested.

After executing a test, a 'test report' is produced. The report is generated under the control of the navigation script; the built-in log facilities of the test tool are generally not used. The report contains general information about the test run, like the number of passed and failed checks, and detailed information about the execution of the individual test lines. There is a commonly used standard layout, but in some projects the level of detail, the contents, and the layout of the report are tailored to specific demands. It is also possible to let the navigation script produce more than one report, for example a summary for management and a detailed version for the tester. Another possibility is to connect the output directly to a system for problem management, in which the problems found in the test run can be managed further.

The method can be depicted as in Figure 22.2. The Action Words are strictly related to the business and not to the navigation in the interface of the target system. Action Words are typically 'enter client' instead of 'go to screen xyz.' It is not necessary or even desirable for the Action Words to

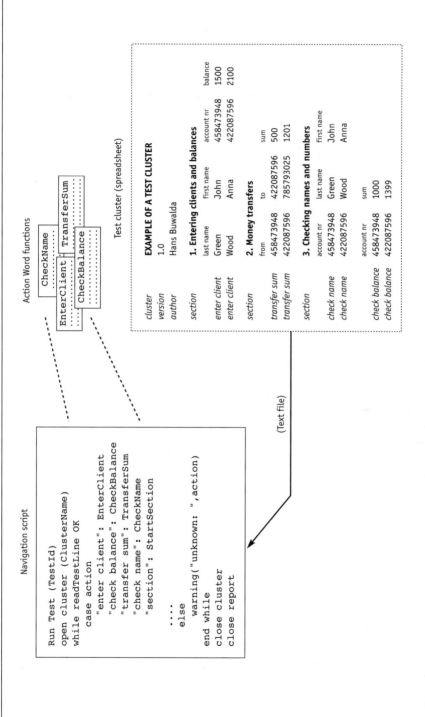

Figure 22.2 The relationship between a cluster, navigation script, and Action Word functions.

stick to the screens and the fields on them in the tested application. One Action Word might have input data in several screens and enter the fields in a different order, including default values for fields that were not specified with the Action Word. The strict separation between the tests and their navigation is an essential part of this method. In this way test clusters become readable for end users and are independent of changes in the system's interface. Only if the interface itself must be tested, one might describe a test in a test cluster specifying that if button x is pressed screen y should appear.

22.1.4 Reasons for using this method

The reasons to use the method differ from project to project, but the main ones are:

- reduced dependency on the specific details of the target system's interface: a change in that interface can usually be coped with by a change in an individual Action Word, in which case all the test lines starting with that Action Word will function properly again;

- better readability of the test specifications and the test reports: it is not necessary to have technical knowledge to understand what is tested and what the results are;

- better manageability of the test process: the test clusters are tangible products which can be created at an early stage of the project; also the tasks in a project can be clearly separated. The development and the execution of tests are separated. Also the system test can be separated from the acceptance test (by making separate clusters for them, still using the same Action Words);

- the motivation of testers increases: the routine tasks of executing tests are automated and results are clear and tangible.

In the following sections I go into more detail about the different aspects covered by the method.

22.2 Test clusters

One of the two major products in the method is the test cluster (the other is the navigation script). A test cluster is in essence a collection of test actions and checks, which on one hand comprises readable documentation of the tests, and on the other hand can be executed automatically by the test tool plus the navigation script.

A cluster consists of a set of one or more test sheets containing scenarios, with actions and checks expressed as test lines, each of them starting with an Action Word. In many projects the clusters contain only one sheet each, but if many tests are needed in a cluster, it is wise to split them into several sheets. In this way a better overview will be kept and individual runs will be not too long. A reasonable maximum for one sheet in a test cluster is around 500 test lines.

As mentioned previously, clusters are usually created and maintained in spreadsheets. The reason for that is that spreadsheets are well suited to manipulating lines and columns and also have the possibility of performing calculations. For example, it is easy to make copies of tests and vary them using formulas. Also it is a good idea to keep general data like a tax percentage in a separate cell at the top of the spreadsheet and make the appropriate test lines relate to it using formulas. If the percentage is changed, only one cell needs to be changed instead of editing several test lines in a cluster. Similar approaches are used for tests on the millennium changes and the euro currency conversion, which we do not treat in this chapter but which are important applications of the method.

22.2.1 Example application: Minibank

To illustrate the use of clusters we introduce a small demo application, called Minibank. This imaginary bank has only one purpose in life: being tested. The screens of Minibank are depicted in Figure 22.3. In the main screen an account number can be entered and Minibank will show the first and last name and the balance of the client, as long as it exists in its database. Minibank has a useful property: it throws away all of its data when it is stopped (it is only used for demonstrations). Every test run will therefore start with an empty database. After start-up it is possible to enter new clients with the 'relations' screen and to transfer money from one client to another, changing the balances of both clients.

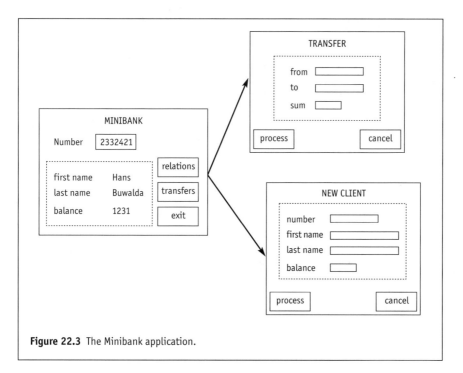

Figure 22.3 The Minibank application.

22.2.2 Cluster to test Minibank

The cluster to test our Minibank demo application is shown in Figure 22.4. We can see a number of test lines in the cluster:

- documentary lines, starting with words like 'cluster,' 'version,' 'author,' and 'section';
- test lines that input something, starting with 'enter client' and 'transfer';
- test lines that check something, in this example the ones starting with 'check name' and 'check balance'.

The documentary test lines have no impact on the test itself. They are, however, used in the production of a clear report and play an important role in the configuration and version management of the tests.

	A	B	C	D	E	F
1	cluster	**EXAMPLE OF A CLUSTER**				
2	version	1.0				
3	author	Hans Buwalda				
4	section	**1. Relation management**				
5		last name	initial name	account nr	balance	
6	enter client	Johnson	John	500103381	1500	
7	enter client	Juet	Marc	423137538	2100	
8	enter client	Savy	Anne	848656467	1700	
9	enter client	Puk	Piet	121003677	10	
10	section	**2. Transfers**				
11		from	to	sum		
12	transfer	500103381	423137538	500		
13	transfer	121003677	848656467	120		
14	section	**3. Checking names and balances**				
15		number	last name	initial name		
16	check name	500103381	Johnson	John		
17	check name	423137538	Juet	Marc		
18	check name	848656467	Savy	Anne		
19	check name	121003677	Puk	Piet		
20						
21		number	balance			
22	check balance	423137538	2600			
23	check balance	121003677	-110			
24						

Figure 22.4 Test cluster for the Minibank application.

There are also test lines that start with an empty cell. These test lines are ignored by the navigation. They are used to put headings above the columns with labels like 'account number' and 'last name'. Also the layout properties, i.e. different fonts and font sizes or different colors, are ignored in the test execution. These are only used for readability purposes.

The test lines starting with the Action Word 'enter client' (an Action Word may consist of more than one word) command the navigation script to enter a particular client. The navigation will activate the new customer screen (called a 'relation') by pressing the *relations* button on the main screen, enter the data in the relation's screen in the right order (which in this case is not the order in the cluster), and press the *process* button. The Action Word 'enter client' is used four times in this cluster. The actions executed by the navigation are always the same, but with different data for every test line.

The lines starting with 'transfer' will trigger the navigation to activate the 'transfer' screen by pressing the *transfers* button, entering data there, and pressing the *process* button.

The next block of actions consists of checks. It is checked whether the names that were entered before exist in the database. The lines start with 'check name'. The second field contains the number of the client to be checked. The following fields contain the expected values. They are compared by the navigation with the actual contents of the corresponding fields on the screen.

Finally the balances are checked. They are the initial balances plus or minus the sums that were transferred.

22.2.3 Unpredictable key data: keep and refer

In Figure 22.5 we see a variation of the cluster. Our imaginary Minibank application has undergone some 'maintenance' and in the new release the account numbers of new clients can no longer be entered explicitly. They are generated by the system, in a way that the tester cannot predict. Therefore another strategy is needed, which we call 'keep and refer'. Instead of the numbers of the new clients, 'place holders' are used, in the form of variables like 'john' and 'marc'. When used as &keep[john] and &keep[marc], the actual number appearing on the screen is kept. When used with & alone, like &john, this previously stored number is used. In this way we can still use key data like the account number to relate our test lines to each other without knowing what the actual values will be during the execution of the test.

22.2.4 Cluster execution report

In Figure 22.6 we see the report produced when the cluster is run. The report starts with general information about the test, then the test lines follow. If there are differences between the expected and the actual

	A	B	C	D	E	F
1	*cluster*	**EXAMPLE OF A CLUSTER**				
2	*version*	1.0				
3	*author*	Hans Buwalda				
4	*section*	**1. Relation management**				
5		last name	initial name	account nr	balance	
6	*enter client*	Johnson	John	&keep[john]	1500	
7	*enter client*	Juet	Marc	&keep[marc]	2100	
8	*enter client*	Savy	Anne	&keep[anne]	1700	
9	*enter client*	Puk	Piet	&keep[piet]	10	
10	*section*	**2. Transfers**				
11		from	to	sum		
12	*transfer*	&john	&marc	500		
13	*transfer*	&piet	&anne	120		
14	*section*	**3. Checking names and balances**				
15		number	last name	initial name		
16	*check name*	&john	Johnson	John		
17	*check name*	&marc	Juet	Marc		
18	*check name*	&anne	Savy	Anne		
19	*check name*	&piet	Puck	Piet	* mistake in last name	
20						
21		number	balance			
22	*check balance*	&marc	2600			
23	*check balance*	&piet	-110			
24						

Figure 22.5 New version of the cluster with implicit account numbers.

outcomes these are shown as 'fails.' In this case the tester has made an error in the test. Instead of testing on 'Puk,' the name 'Puck' is tested, resulting in a failure message in the report.

At the end of the report a summary is produced, showing general statistics such as the number of passed and failed checks. If there are failed checks, the lines where the fails occurred are shown.

22.3 The navigation

The second major component of the method is the navigation script. As we saw in Figure 22.2, it works like an interpreter, reading the test lines of the test cluster one by one and interpreting them based on the action specified in the first field. Figure 22.2 shows how Action Words like 'enter client' and 'check balance' are mapped onto functions like *EnterClient* and *CheckBalance*.

```
==========================================================
```

TestFrame report

cluster name	: **Example of a cluster**
cluster version	: 1.0
cluster author	: Hans Buwalda
cluster file	: c:\testframe\clusters\minibank.txt
script name	: TestFrame Navigation Script for Dephi
script version	: 1.0
script release date	: October 1998
run date and time	: 14-11-98 15:47:14

```
==========================================================
```

SECTION 1 – Relation management

1 (6):	enter client	Johnson	John	&keep john	1500
2 (7):	enter client	Juet	Marc	&keep marc	2100
3 (8):	enter client	Savy	Anne	&keep anne	1700
4 (9):	enter client	Puk	Piet	&keep piet	10

SECTION 2 – Transfers

5 (12):	transfer	89345591	15242252	500
6 (13):	transfer	45673874	86318245	120

SECTION 3 – Checking names and balances

7 (16):	check name	89345591	Johnson	John	
			Johnson	John	
8 (17):	check name	15242252	Juet	Marc	
			Juet	Marc	
9 (18):	check name	86318245	Savy	Anne	
			Savy	Anne	
10 (19):	check name	45673874	Puck	Piet	* mistake in name
FAILED			Puk	Piet	
11 (22):	check balance	15242252	2600		
			2600		
12 (23):	check balance	45673874	−110		
			−110		

```
==========================================================
```

end of cluster	: EXAMPLE OF A CLUSTER
finished at	: 14-11-98 15:47:19
time used	: 6
time used	: 6
number of cluster lines	: 23
number of test lines	: 12
number of checks	: 10
number passed	: 9
number failed	: 1
percentage passed	: 90%

failed at report lines:
10

```
==========================================================
```

Figure 22.6 The cluster report.

The actual functions could look like Figure 22.7. The arguments in the spreadsheet are in an array of strings called 'arg.' Typically arg[1] will be the Action Word itself, while arg[2], arg[3], etc. contain the data fields. In this case the fields on the screen are GUI objects with logical names like 'number' and 'balance,' which can be recognized by the test tool. This is not always the case. Sometimes more cryptic identifications like '@2' or '#132' can be found in a navigation script, depending on the particular interface/test tool combination.

The first routine, *EnterClient*, deals with entering a new client in Minibank. First it pushes the *relations* button on the main screen. It waits for the *New Client* screen to appear, then it enters the data of the new client, as specified in the cluster. Finally it presses the *process* button and waits for the main screen. Note that we have entered the customer's first name (arg[4]) first, in the order that the fields appear on the screen in Figure 22.3, even though the cluster shown in Figure 22.4 has the last name listed first (arg[3]).

The second routine does a check. In Minibank client data can be retrieved directly on the main screen by entering an account number. The Action Word routine does that and then checks the balance field using the third field in the test line as the expected value.

The routines listed here are relatively simple, dealing with screens with only a few text fields and buttons. In practice GUIs are usually much more complex. To execute an Action Word, several screens might be involved populated with objects of all classes, such as list boxes, buttons, and grids. Also the actual layout of a screen can be dependent on conditions in other screens. So Action Word implementations will be more complicated than shown here, but the main principles are the same: one function deals with all occurrences of the Action Word, using the varying data, input, or expected results, as arguments.

```
EnterClient
PushButton "Relations"              * push the 'Relations' button
WaitWindow "Enter New Client"       * wait for the entry window
EnterEdit "Number", arg[2]          * enter the values in the edit fields
EnterEdit "Firstname", arg[4]       * arg[2] etc. are coming from the cluster
EnterEdit "Lastname", arg[3]
EnterEdit "Balance", arg[5]
PushButton "Process"                * will bring us back on the main screen
WaitWindow "Minibank Demonstration Program"
```

```
CheckBalance
* we don't have to go to another screen,
* so there is no PushButton statement here
EnterEdit "Number", arg[2]    * enter the account number
CheckEdit "Balance", arg[3]   * check the displayed balance
```

Figure 22.7 Navigation scripts.

22.3.1 Implementation of the navigation

The navigation is implemented as a layered structure with three main layers:

- the engine
- the interface layer
- the Action Words.

The engine contains the basic coding of the navigation script. It depends only on the test tool and can be the same for all projects for which that test tool is used. The engine reads the test lines from the cluster, splits them up into separate arguments, and calls the navigation function for the Action Word listed in the first field of the test line. It also administers the test results, produces the report, and handles special constructions like the 'keep and refer' mechanism described above. For different test tools different engines are used, although all of them are based on one design, the 'engine model.'

The interface layer contains the supporting routines to deal with an interface. This can be one of the many GUIs available, but there are also interface layers to deal with mainframe or mini computer oriented terminal emulators, batch testing, or TCP/IP message protocols.

Based on the engine and the interface layer the actual Action Words can be implemented. They are related to the system which is being tested. For a mortgage system there will be different Action Words than for a stock exchange system. It is even possible that for one set of Action Words two different implementations are made. An example is a terminal oriented system that is being converted to a GUI. The system will still implement the same business functionality, so a large part of the clusters and Action Words can be the same for both versions of the system. However, the navigation is different, addressing a terminal emulator and a GUI.

22.4 The test development life cycle

The test clusters and navigation are embedded in a TestFrame test life cycle. Figure 22.8 shows the main steps in this life cycle. This section discusses some of the products in this life cycle.

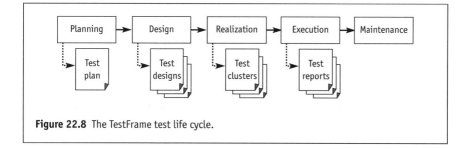

Figure 22.8 The TestFrame test life cycle.

22.4.1 The test plan

The test plan deals with the scope and the organization of the tests. The test plan is created before the start of the test development. When the test development is part of a system development project the test plan is typically made together with or directly after the general plan of approach. It can even be a part of this general plan of approach. It is important that realistic test planning is considered in relation to the planning of the main project. It should never be treated as a sideline. The total test effort will usually take 30% or more of the total effort and several tests are critical path activities, where they will take time and resources.

A good test plan should at least contain the following points:

- scope of the tests to be developed and performed
- organization and procedures
- planning and costs
- risk analysis of the test project.

The scope of the tests states the 'mission' for the testers. It describes which aspects of the system need to be tested and which do not. Typical tests might be program tests, system tests, and functional acceptance tests. But a performance test might also be necessary, or a platform test may be needed to check that the new system does not obstruct existing ones. All of these tests are candidates for test automation. Other tests might be implemented as a combination of automated and manual handling, for example a test for the correctness of the user manual of a new system.

The organization and procedures part of the test plan describes who is responsible for which tests. It also contains procedures about when a system will be accepted for the next phase and by whom. For example a system might be taken into production even if there are known errors, as long as those errors are non-fatal and the user management formally agrees. Also the functional acceptance tests may be developed by a separate group consisting of user representatives, business specialists, and professional test developers, and the resulting clusters may need to be approved by auditors as well.

The planning and costs can be estimated in the test plan in several ways. There are metrics based on the number of screens or the number of function points. The exact figure depends very much on the particular project. Typical estimates are 2–3 hours per function point for the creation of clusters and navigation scripts, but this can be much higher or lower.

When comparing costs with manual testing it is necessary to focus on the costs of the navigator and compare those with the costs of doing the tests by hand. The costs of preparing the test clusters and interpreting the test results can be regarded as more or less identical in both cases: it is even possible to execute tests described in test clusters manually instead of automatically.

Example

A complex system with 150 screens took 5 person-months for the creation of navigation scripts for about 25 000 test lines in total. To do the tests by hand would take about 5 person-months as well, estimating 2 minutes per test line, including the reporting of test results. So in this case the test automation breaks even with manual testing in the first run. After every repetition of the test run, theoretically another 5 person-months are won, compared to manual execution of the test. Of course in practice such tests would not be repeated that many times if they had to be done manually.

Besides costs, there are also a number of risks to be aware of. In our experience the following main risk areas are the most important:

- Incomplete or incorrect use of the method. When important basic principles like separation of data and navigation are not addressed properly the results can easily be disappointing;
- Underestimation of the effort needed to interpret the test results. For example, the actual behavior of a system can be different than expected in the test and it takes time to find out if this is a mistake in the system or in the test specification;
- Improper organization of the test maintenance. Maintaining the test might not be much work because of the separation between test clusters and navigation, but someone has to do it, and needs the files to do it with and the knowledge of how to do it;
- Political problems. For example, when a project is not meeting its planned deadline, problems between the development team and the test team can easily occur;
- Technical problems. Some GUIs are very difficult to access for the test tool. Retrieving values from the screen can be especially difficult, or even impossible.

22.4.2 The test design

After the test plan has described what is going to be tested, the test design will describe what tests will be developed. The tests are not described in detail yet; the main focus is to identify the test clusters that have to be developed. Typical items for the test design are:

- division of tests into test clusters
- the test environment.

22.4.2.1 Division of tests into test clusters

The most important result of the test design is a division of the tests into test clusters. Once this process has been done the further test development can be managed well. There are a number of criteria that can be used for the division:

- the business functions
- the system parts
- the kind of test
- the test techniques used to establish the test.

The most commonly used criteria for dividing the tests are the business functions that are supported by the system. For example, in a system with clients and orders it is a good idea to separate the test cases for the client administration function from the ones dealing with the order handling. Those test clusters can then be assessed by different departments of the user organization.

The system parts are important, especially when not all parts of the system are delivered at the same time. Also it is important not to mix tests for the interface of a system with those for the business functionality. For example a test for the tab order of the fields or an input check should be in another test cluster than a test of the correct monthly payment of a mortgage. Mixing such tests makes them difficult to read for those who have to use or review them.

If there are different kinds of tests involved, for example system tests and user acceptance tests, these should be documented in separate test clusters to reflect the task separation that is usually desired between such tests. These clusters can however often use the same Action Words and navigation scripts.

Apart from business test cases there might be test cases prepared by formal techniques like graph theory or decision tables. Their focus can be quite different, and it is therefore wise to keep them separated from each other in different test clusters as well.

22.4.2.2 The test environment
To be able to run the tests a suitable test environment is essential. In most organizations, it is essential to establish the need for such an environment well in advance, to have it available when it is needed. A test environment must be separated from other environments, for example those in use for development, production, or training.

It might even be a good idea to have more than one environment for a particular test. This way several tests can be run together without interfering with each other. If that is not possible it is a good idea to make a logical separation in the design of the clusters; for example, let each cluster work with different client names or product ranges.

Another important instrument for creating test environments is the 'zero cluster.' A zero cluster contains input lines that initialize the database with basic data. The other clusters can use this initial data. For every new release of the target system, the zero clusters are run once and the database is kept for further use by the clusters. Ideally every cluster gets a fresh copy of this initial database before being executed, an action being performed by the navigation script. If this is not possible care must be taken that the clusters use the basic data but do not change them, so if a new client is entered in a cluster it should also be deleted in that same cluster.

22.5 Applicability for other types of tests

22.5.1 Testing batch systems

Apart from online systems, batch systems can also be tested using clusters. The test clusters for a batch system are identical to those for an online system. The difference is in the way the navigation works. The navigation process is shown for a small example in Figure 22.9. The input data (in this case the transfer from Jones to Williams) is put into the batch input file(s) by the navigation script. The navigation script also generates a 'delayed checks' cluster (as a tab-separated text file). The delayed checks cluster contains test lines with Action Words. In the example it contains the checks for Jones and Williams. The Action Word used is 'd check balance,' where 'd' stands for 'delayed.' When the navigation script is ready with the input files it starts up the batch process and waits until it is ready. Then it starts interpreting the delayed checks cluster. The checks specified there will be carried out on the batch output file, in this case containing new balances for Jones and Williams.

22.5.2 Performance and load testing

A special application of this method is for testing performance. In these tests the focus is on the behavior of a system under a specified load. Figures that are measured are typically response times and the usage of system components. Those values can be compared to specified demands. This can be done in the test cluster introducing Action Words like 'check response 10,' meaning that a time of 10 seconds is the maximum allowed for the system to respond since the latest system entry. The test fails if the actual time exceeds 10 seconds, in which case the actual time is reported.

Similar solutions are applicable for load generation. A typical form is 'generate load 10 order-entry,' meaning that a cluster 'order-entry' should be executed simulating 10 simultaneous users. This can be done on physical machines or as processes in a multitasking environment. The action word 'generate load' does not do much more than starting the 10 processes.

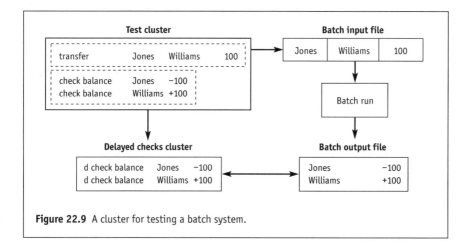

Figure 22.9 A cluster for testing a batch system.

Within the cluster 'order-entry' other performance issues are specified with proper Action Words, for instance measuring response times and synchronization with other processes.

22.6 Templates: meta-clusters

22.6.1 Using Action Words to make Action Words

For testing of large systems with many screens, resulting in many Action Words, some variations are developed to speed up the process of creating the necessary navigation. One example is the 'template' mechanism. In this mechanism an Action Word can be specified as a 'template' in an auxiliary cluster, which is sometimes called a 'meta-cluster.' In this cluster new Action Words are defined by a number of lines starting with 'define action word,' behind which are the new Action Word and its arguments. Then some test lines follow with reference to the arguments using '&.' The definition ends with 'end action word.' Every time the new Action Word is used, the engine interprets the lines belonging to it. The new Action Word can in turn be used as the basis for further new Action Words. In this way the process of making Action Words can be speeded up and in some cases it can even be done by the testers instead of a specialized navigator.

22.6.2 Example: Orderit

Let us look at an example. Suppose we have an (imaginary) order entry system, which we call Orderit. In Orderit data can be entered about customers, products, and orders. The screens allow for numerous details, but these details are not commonly used and for most tests are superfluous. In Figure 22.10 the order screen is depicted. It contains multiple fields for special situations, such as details about the delivery.

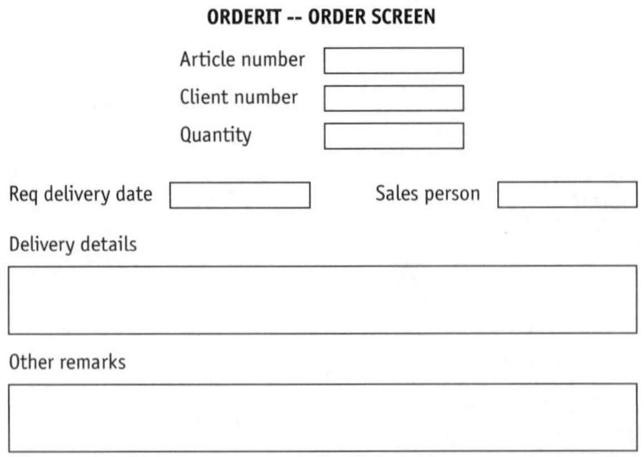

Figure 22.10 The 'Orderit' screen.

In Figure 22.11, a meta-cluster is shown with definitions of some Action Words using templates. A special Action Word, 'define action word,' is used. This Action Word takes all lines up to 'end action word' and stores them as a definition of the new Action Word. In the first case an Action Word 'standard order' is defined. This Action Word enters an order with only a limited number of specific fields. Those fields are specified as parameters with the new Action Word, in this case 'client,' 'article,' and 'quantity.' For the other fields on the screen, 'required delivery date,' 'sales person,' 'delivery details,' and 'other remarks,' default values are entered. In Figure 22.12 the new Action Words are used. The line contains actual values for the parameters 'client,' 'article,' and 'quantity.'

On encountering the Action Word 'standard order,' the navigation will execute the line defined in the template, with the '&' expressions substituted by real values. So the test action that is performed on the target system will be:

```
enter order  Williams  tea-saucer  20  asap  John  no details
no remarks
```

define action word	parameter 1	parameter 2	parameter 3				
standard order	client	article	quantity				
	client	article	quantity	deliv	sales	details	remarks
enter order	&client	&article	&quantity	asap	John	no details	no remarks
end action word							
define action word	parameter 1						
order something	quantity						
	client	article	quantity				
standard order	Jones	tea-cup	&quantity				
end action word							
define action word	parameter 1	parameter 2					
order tea-set	client	quantity					
	client	article	quantity				
standard order	&client	tea-cup	&6*quantity				
standard order	&client	tea-saucer	&6*quantity				
standard order	&client	tea-pot	&quantity				
end action word							

Figure 22.11 A meta-cluster for the Orderit system.

	Client nr	art nr	qty
standard order	Williams	tea-saucer	20
	qty		
order something	35		
	client nr	qty	
order tea-set	Jones	12	

Figure 22.12 A cluster using the new Action Words defined by the meta-cluster.

The other examples are similar. The Action Word 'order something' only needs a quantity and uses the earlier defined Action Word 'standard order' with the client and the article also set at standard values. In the last example, 'order tea-set,' one new Action Word is defined as several underlying actions. One tea-set is defined as consisting of six cups, six saucers, and one pot. So the line:

```
order tea-set      Jones   12
```

will be translated as:

```
standard order     Jones   tea-cup      72
standard order     Jones   tea-saucer   72
standard order     Jones   tea-pot      12
```

Using templates, complicated underlying actions can be mapped onto new Action Words by the analyst, without the need for additional navigation scripts.

22.7 Summary

In this chapter a method has been described for automated testing of systems using Action Words. The design of the tests is strictly separated from the development of the navigation script that automates their execution. This chapter has only given a first introduction to the method. There are many aspects to deal with in the actual implementation of the method. It is therefore recommended to start on a small scale and, if possible, let experienced people help. It is important to note that the method, although potentially useful, is not a magic wand. Testing is a complex activity that should never be underestimated, with or without the method outlined here.

Regression testing at ABN AMRO Bank Development International

Iris Pinkster

23.1 Background

23.1.1 Introduction

This case study describes the development and automation of tests for software developed at ABN AMRO Bank Development International, using the test methodology called TestFrame developed by CMG in the Netherlands. This method includes test automation using the Action Words technique developed by Hans Buwalda and described in Chapter 22. The application of the TestFrame method started with the regression test.

To set the scope of this case study, the ABN AMRO Bank organization, and within this the Development International (DI) directorate, is described in brief. At DI, the Platform Test Group is responsible for the Platform Acceptance Test (PAT), for which an automated regression test has been created as described later in this section.

In Section 23.2 we give a brief history of testing at DI and the problems involved. In Section 23.3 we describe our pilot project to investigate the TestFrame approach.

Section 23.4 describes the project team and the project itself. This includes the status of the project at the time of writing (October 1998).

Thanks to the success of the project a few spin-offs occurred; these are described in Section 23.5. The chapter is concluded with a few notes concerning the future.

23.1.2 ABN AMRO Bank organization and main product

This case study is concerned with the automated regression test within DI, a department within the complete ABN AMRO Directorate General IT.

One of the responsibilities of the DI department is the development of amendments and enhancements to its main product, an applications platform called International Standard Application Platform (ISAP). This platform is used in branches all over the world, and is able to support most of the main business lines of the bank, such as transaction processing. This system also supports ISAP-implementation activities and system support.

ISAP is meant to be implemented in most of the countries of the 'International Network,' the term used for all countries and branches, outside the Netherlands, where ABN AMRO Bank is active. In October 1998, ISAP was live in 47 countries. The software for the system is distributed in consecutive releases.

The ISAP platform includes:

1. SCORE (System CORE), an AS/400 application and centrally registered database file;

2. standard tables and parameters;

3. satellites, e.g. integrated and non-integrated AS/400 applications, PC applications, and various types of support tools;

4. standard security mechanisms.

Figure 23.1 illustrates the applications belonging to ISAP and the relationships between them. ISAP consists of AS/400 applications and many interfaces and PC applications. The initial scope of the automated regression test was focused on the AS/400 applications. The PC applications can be added to the automated regression test later.

23.1.3 ABN AMRO Bank test cycle

The first phase in the test cycle is the Unit Test (UT). The objective of the UT is to test whether there are differences between the specified modules and their realizations.

Next the Unit Integration Test (UIT) is performed, in which the cooperation between the various modules is tested.

The third step in the ABN AMRO Bank test cycle consists of the System Test (ST), in which the amendments created for one control release are tested as a whole. A control release is a set of changes to menu options and related programs within one functional area. These changes are presented to the test as one lot.

The next step is the Functional Acceptance Test (FAT). The objective of the FAT phase is to test the amendments created for a functional area. The test cases used are set up from the user's point of view.

The main objective of this chapter, the Platform Acceptance Test (PAT), is primarily aimed at verifying that all applications of ISAP are still functioning well together. Part of the PAT is executed by performing a regression test.

In the last phase, the Exploitation Acceptance Test (EAT), the objectives are to carry out the operations acceptance test and to test the installation procedure in a production environment.

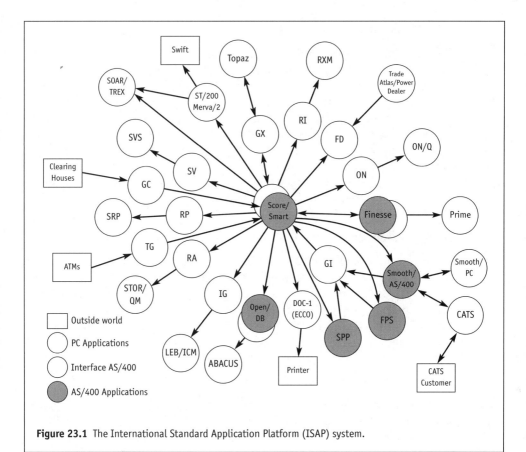

Figure 23.1 The International Standard Application Platform (ISAP) system.

23.2 Problems with conventional testing

Before we began using TestFrame for the regression test, a few problems were encountered. These problems can be divided into three areas: new release, technical infrastructure, and large scope projects. The problems in each of these areas are described below.

23.2.1 New release

Before the roll-out of a new release of ISAP, an acceptance test has to be conducted. With this acceptance test, two topics have to be secured:

1. that the *changed* functionality conforms to the *new* specifications;
2. that the *unchanged* functionality still conforms to the *original* specifications.

Testing the changed functionality can be executed using conventional (manual) testing. Testing the unchanged functionality (regression), however, is in practice not possible or takes up a number of key resources for a long period.

23.2.2 Technical infrastructure

For technical infrastructure problems, for example a new release of the operating system, there is a similar problem: the complete application should be tested. It must be proved that the functionality of the unchanged processes is not affected.

The impact of technical infrastructure projects on ISAP is difficult to determine. In general it is stated that there is no impact on user applications. To prove this, it is necessary to set up a test project where the whole application is tested. In practice, this is not possible. A limited number of test cases are executed and when no strange events occur, a pilot implementation is started with the new technical infrastructure.

23.2.3 Large scope projects

Sometimes the scope of tests performed in a project is not limited to a part of a functional area, for example Year 2000 and euro projects. In these cases, problems turn out to be similar to the ones found in new releases and infrastructural projects. All parts of ISAP must be representatively tested in order to prove the correctness of the result. In these cases limited tests are not enough.

23.2.4 Potential solutions

Workable solutions for these problems were not available in the past. The solutions that were tried resulted in projects with an excessive lead time. This resulted in a large trespass on the time of experts involved in the tests. Besides these resource requirements, this process resulted in applications not being tested thoroughly enough.

A theoretical solution would be to develop and maintain a representative test for the complete application. This test could then be used as a starting point for the testing of the three areas mentioned above: new release, technical infrastructure, and large scope projects.

This approach has been tried out many times and has two main pitfalls if using conventional manual testing:

- it is very difficult and time consuming, and it has proven to be impossible to create such a test and maintain it in such a way that it is useful for testing new software releases. The testware is outdated before its development is finished;
- the added value of the test is limited because of human errors (input errors and inconsistent result checking).

To try to overcome these problems a pilot with the TestFrame approach was started in March 1996. (At that time TestFrame was called CMG:CAST. The name was changed to TestFrame in mid-1998, but to keep uniformity and not cause any confusion the term TestFrame is used throughout this chapter.)

As a pilot project, an automated regression test was created for one functional area. Within this pilot the TestFrame approach was customized to the ABN AMRO DI situation to develop a regression test in the AS/400 ISAP environment. This working procedure was also documented to obtain a standard procedure. Using this customized working procedure an automated regression test was made for the pilot functional area.

The objective of the pilot project was to determine whether the problems of the conventional (manual) way of testing, mentioned in Section 23.2, could be solved using TestFrame; in other words, whether it was possible to create a regression test consisting of representative test cases for the whole ISAP platform, which can be maintained towards new releases. The pilot ended successfully and the results have been taken into production. This means that the automated test is now used every time the software of this functional area is tested.

The evaluation of the pilot project resulted in the following features to overcome the main problems of conventional (manual) testing described above:

- because the test data and the test navigation are physically separated, the accessibility has improved, so we now have the possibility of maintaining the regression test for new software releases;
- the engine and low-level Action Words which were developed specially for the AS/400 platform require practically no maintenance. Using these two basic layers, the high-level Action Words that are necessary for the automated execution can be created and maintained with limited effort;
- the test data (test cases) are registered in Excel spreadsheets. Using the Excel functionality and layout in a standardized way, the test cases are very easily accessible and maintainable;
- the output expectations are also registered with the test cases in the Excel spreadsheet. The expected output is automatically checked against the actual results during the execution of the test. The results are presented in reports;
- a working procedure has been defined which requires very limited effort by functional experts to create and maintain the regression test. This relieves these experts from their time consuming involvement during the test process.

Furthermore, the results of this pilot project offer opportunities and benefits stemming from the availability of a basic regression test for the ISAP platform, which can be used to:

- test the regression during the acceptance of new releases;
- test the impact of technical infrastructure projects;
- serve as a basic test set for the acceptance of large scope projects like Year 2000 and euro.

This will result in a significant quality improvement of the acceptance test as well as less dependency on the scarce staff able to define representative test cases.

As a result of this successful pilot, a new project was started on March 1, 1997 to develop an automated regression test for the most critical processes of 12 selected functional areas within ISAP.

23.4 Regression test project

During the pilot project we found that the average number of person-days to develop the regression test for one menu option was 1.5 days. This includes debugging of the developed testware and updating the documentation. More specifically, per menu option, one day is required to set up the test cases and another half day is needed to develop automated test scripts.

Based on these experiences in the pilot project, we estimated that the effort required to develop an automated regression test for the whole of ISAP would be approximately 20 person-years. This calculation was based on the average time required for building a regression test for one menu option and then multiplying that with the total number of menu options in ISAP. In this project one menu option results in one Action Word. In practice a regression test will not be necessary for all menu options. The number of menu options covered by the automated regression test is stated below.

For the selection of the functional areas covered in the automated regression test the following criteria were applied: the application must run on the AS/400 platform and the functional area must be critical in an operational environment. This resulted in 12 functional areas.

Within the regression test the classification of clusters is in accordance with the classification of functional areas. If necessary a certain area can contain more than one cluster. In the case of ABN AMRO Bank DI it resulted in 31 clusters.

23.4.1 The project team

In the pilot project a skill mix of two cluster developers to one navigator proved to be suitable. The project team started with nine staff members (extended from six staff members in the pilot). At its maximum, the project team consisted of 20 staff members developing the testware, separated into two teams, each focusing on different functional areas.

At the time of writing five staff members remain to implement the automated regression test within ABN AMRO Bank DI. These five staff members are responsible for the education of members of the maintenance groups. The members of these maintenance groups are responsible for the development and maintenance of the ISAP software belonging to their group. Furthermore, in every maintenance group a test infrastructure must be introduced: a test tool (WinRunner in the ABN AMRO Bank case) must be installed, extra tools that have been developed must now be implemented for every maintenance group, a test PC must be installed, etc. The members of the maintenance groups should review the existing test cases to see whether they are still up to date. All of these actions should be coached by the five remaining staff members. The intention is that the maintenance groups should eventually be able to develop and maintain their own testware.

23.4.2 Organization of tests

The 31 clusters covering the 12 functional areas can be divided among 6 maintenance groups. To give an idea of what testware is developed within the regression test project, Table 23.1 gives a summary of how the 31 clusters are divided among the maintenance groups, and Table 23.2 shows the total number of menu options per maintenance group over their clusters, the number of menu options covered, and the coverage per maintenance group.

At the time of writing, the total average coverage over all maintenance groups was 19%. When the regression test is fully realized to conform to the specifications, up to 25% of all processes within the ISAP will be covered

Table 23.1 Maintenance groups and number of clusters.

Maintenance group	Number of clusters
Core score	10
MACCS (transaction services)	12
Treasury	2
Reporting	4
Finesse (securities)	2
Operation services	1
Total	**31**

Table 23.2 Maintenance groups and menu options covered.

Maintenance group	Number of menu options	Number of menu options covered	Percentage covered
Core score	262	102	40
MACCS (transaction services)	1022	138	14
Treasury	222	40	18
Reporting	179	28	15
Finesse	215	62	29
Operation services	141	34	24
Grand total	**2041**	**404**	**19**

by the regression test, which is currently considered to be a representative coverage of the ISAP.

The exact time saving between conventional testing and automated testing is difficult to calculate, because there is no reference. Testing used to be performed on an ad hoc basis. With the introduction of TestFrame for the regression test, a structured way to set up test cases was provided. Furthermore, it was the first time a test with such a broad scope could be developed and maintained. This contributed to the quality of the software. Bugs were detected not only during the test phase but also during development. This resulted in fewer bugs being distributed to the branches.

23.5 Spin-offs

A few spin-offs occurred from developing and using the automated regression test:

1. With the reuse of Action Words developed for the automated regression test, it was possible to create a stable test environment. This environment is called the clean environment: clean means there are no transactions in the environment. Existing transactions can cause many problems and dependencies in the test environment. Now we can fill the environment with the information we need for our test without bothering about eventual existing information or eventual links. These could affect the test results. With this clean environment a stable test environment could be set up for the first time. At first the environment was only used for the automated regression test, but at the time of writing, it was also being used in other areas of DI.

2. The execution of the euro integration test. This test is performed on the same AS/400 platform as the automated regression test. This means that a lot of Action Words could be reused after a few amendments had been made for the euro software. The regression test clusters that are in production were used for the baseline test of the euro ISAP acceptance test. Action Words are reused to build dedicated euro clusters. Note that the euro project is supported in such a manner that without the existing basis of the regression test it would not have been possible to create a complete test with an acceptable effort.

3. The execution of the automated part of the Year 2000 test. The CAST regression tests are to a high degree reused for the acceptance of the updated software for the Year 2000 project. Besides reusing existing clusters, additional dedicated test cases for the Year 2000 projects have been developed based on the risk analysis for the test. Also, facilities have been created to support 'time traveling' with the clean environment and other Year 2000 required features.

4. Another spin-off from the TestFrame regression test project is the pilot project 'Automated Table Changes with CAST.' The ISAP platform contains tables. The parameters, used to define a platform, are stored in

these tables. The way these parameters are set defines the usage of the platform. Requirements of users cause the tables to change. Automated table changes were executed on the South Africa production environment in the weekend of May 23 and 24, 1998 using TestFrame. The implementation time was reduced by 38% in comparison to implementing by hand. The South Africa branch approved all the changes made and suggested automated table updates for future batch table changes.

23.6 Future

At the time of writing, the final scope of the project 'Development of an automated regression test for the ISAP using the TestFrame approach' has not been fixed. Because of successes with the automated regression test, support was also given to the euro and Year 2000 projects. Even a stable test environment was created within the project.

The intended result has always been to have a representative regression test for the complete ISAP. In this context representative stands for a coverage of all branch-critical processes, to be decided by the owners of the functional areas (this currently stands at 25%).

We are currently implementing the regression test into the current ABN AMRO Bank DI organization.

After this implementation the maintenance groups will:

- maintain the part of the regression test that is currently in production;
- finish tests under construction;
- start developing new tests, regarding their own scope.

In this way the regression test can grow to a further coverage.

DI is negotiating over covering the FAT test with TestFrame. For these FAT tests many of the Action Words developed for the regression test could be reused. In the more distant future it could be possible for TestFrame to cover other tests in the ABN AMRO Bank test cycle.

23.7 Summary

Within ABN AMRO Bank DI an automated regression test was developed for the critical processes in 12 functional areas using TestFrame. The major advantage is that it is the first time such a broad regression test could be set up and maintained with relatively little effort. This resulted in reliable software every time a new release was rolled out.

Furthermore, the development of the automated regression test resulted in the use of TestFrame in other areas than the Platform Acceptance Test, because it showed that it is relatively easy to reuse testware that is already developed.

Business Object Scenarios: a fifth-generation approach to automated testing

Graham Dwyer and Graham Freeburn[1]

24.1 Introduction

Automation of testing can provide considerable benefits when it is used effectively and the scale of the benefits is directly proportional to the ease of reuse of existing test assets or 'testware' (a generic term for all the material associated with a set of test cases). Like the software development process that it mirrors, the testware development process can be seen as a succession of generations, becoming increasingly sophisticated over the course of time.

The aim of this chapter is to provide information for test analysts and those involved in the automation of testing with a view to explaining why business objects should be used for test automation, when they should be used, and what should be done to achieve maximum benefits.

In this chapter we describe:

- the five generations of testware development;
- window-centric Scenarios;
- Business Object Scenarios;
- mixing Business Object Scenarios with existing tests;
- reuse versus repeatability.

24.2 The five generations of testware development

The testware development process is a succession of generations, becoming increasingly sophisticated, and working at a higher level of abstraction,

---

[1] The tool which is described in this chapter was initially developed by John Rouse and John Paseman, while they were working for IMI Systems Inc. The Business Object model was initially developed by Graham Dwyer and further developed by him and Graham Freeburn.

over the course of time. The five generations are shown in Table 24.1, and described in detail below.

Table 24.1 The five generations of test automation.

Generation	Description
First	Capture replay only – automated testing 'out of the box'
Second	Capture replay plus scripting, increased capability but with significant technical overhead
Third	Data driven – scripting with window-centric test data held separately
Fourth	Framework (Gerrard, 1998) and data driven – intelligent framework engine with window-centric test data held separately
Fifth	Framework and data driven – intelligent framework engine with both window-centric and business object test data held separately

Most organizations are capable of progressing through these naturally – the major variation is length of time in each 'generation' and the effort expended in moving forward.

24.2.1 First generation

Tools as sold by the vendors account for the majority of these. They look good but intervention is required in terms of either re-recording or editing as soon as anything vaguely complex is attempted. Results comparison is possible for screen-based data only.

24.2.2 Second generation

Capture replay is usually, but not always, still used. It is now primarily a means to create basic scripts that are then heavily tailored or restructured. Results comparison now includes limited support for data other than screen-based data. Second generation implementations start to show the real power of testing tools but often require significant technical experience and support. They may extend to the use of separate test data but still rely on scripting.

24.2.3 Third generation

Test data is held separately and is window-centric, i.e. a library will contain all the different scenarios of data to be entered against a specific screen or window. There is limited validation by scenarios. Access to test data is via a hierarchy of scripts built for specific applications. Capture replay may be used as input to the script-building process but more use is now made of driver scripts. Results comparison is still primarily for screen-based data only.

24.2.4 Fourth generation

Scripting is replaced by an intelligent framework 'engine.' Test data is held separately and is window-centric, i.e. a library will now contain all the different scenarios of data to be entered or validated against a specific screen or window. Results comparison for screen-based data and other media are fully supported. Capture replay is only used initially in checking what the testing tool can 'see' in an environment.

24.2.5 Fifth generation

The intelligent framework 'engine' now supports separately held test data that is either window-centric or related to specific business objects such as policies, accounts, orders, etc. Results comparison for screen-based data and other media is fully supported. Checking what the testing tool can 'see' in an environment is now done using the 'learning' functionality of the testing tools rather than capture replay.

24.3 RadSTAR

RadSTAR is a model-based, automated software testing approach initially developed in the USA by IMI Systems Inc. It is a combination of a test planning methodology and an automated engine which executes the planned test cases. One of its main characteristics is that by combining *planning and test design* with *execution* it embodies a 'design and replay' approach to test automation (Pettichord, 1996). It has three main elements:

- the application model
- the test designs (comprising Scenario Libraries and the Navigations)
- an automated engine.

The traditional implementation of RadSTAR implements Window-centric Scenario Libraries and fits into the fourth generation in the above model.

The application model describes each screen and each user interface element in the application being tested. The Scenario Libraries contain all the test data and the expected results for each window or screen in the application, each window scenario being the set of data for a single window in a given test.

The Navigations represent the tests themselves; they simply list each step to be performed. They are called 'Navigations' because each test step plays a window scenario on the current application window, which then navigates to the next window in the test. One of the great strengths of RadSTAR is that the Navigations can contain many kinds of test step as well as window scenarios. For example, a Navigation can contain steps to control batch programs which initialize the test environment.

The methodology component of RadSTAR underpins all of these by defining the procedures for test planning and design, together with guidelines for the use of the relevant testing tool and automated engine.

24.4 Window-centric Scenario Libraries

Each application window is modeled in a table called a Window Definition that lists a logical name for each user interface element (control) in the window. The Scenario Library has a column for each control, and the column names match the control names in the related Window Definition. When a scenario from the Scenario Library is used in a test, the sequence of control names in the Window Definition determines the sequence in which the scenario data are played on the window. With reference to the matching Window Definition, extra columns in the Scenario Library are ignored and missing columns are treated as errors.

With this type of Scenario Library, the Navigation only needs to specify the window name and the key to the scenario required. This means that the same scenarios can be reused in many different Navigations but a particular scenario is always played on the same application window. A window-centric scenario is shown in the example in Figure 24.1.

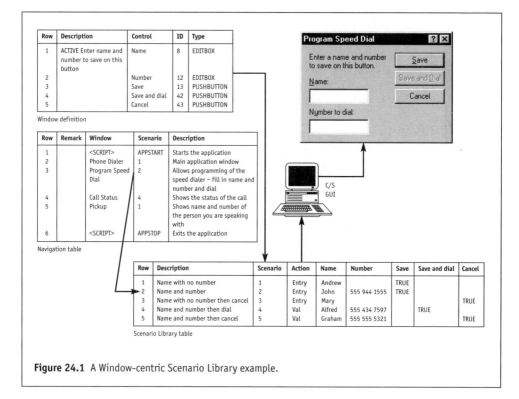

Figure 24.1 A Window-centric Scenario Library example.

24.5 Business Object Scenarios

Significant benefits are achieved in moving from a second- to a third-generation approach to the use of testing tools. However, it comes as no surprise that users soon express a requirement to have Scenario Libraries structured the same way as their business data and independent of any specific user interface. For example, they may wish to structure the scenarios as 'Business Objects' (clients, policies, etc.).

With the Business Object Scenario Libraries, you still model each window of whatever interface you are using to do the tests, even though this may not be the 'final' user interface. A Business Object Scenario Library will also typically have many more columns than any particular window because there will be a column for all data elements relating to that Business Object, whereas a window usually contains subsets of data from one or more Business Objects.

A scenario can still be reused in many Navigations but it can also be reused in many different application windows. This makes the test data independent of both the tests and the application.

The structure of a Business Object Scenario Library is different from the traditional Scenario Library in that a particular scenario can be used, at different times, for both data entry and data validation. There is a column for each data element relating to the Business Object. An example of a Business Object Scenario Library is shown in Figure 24.2.

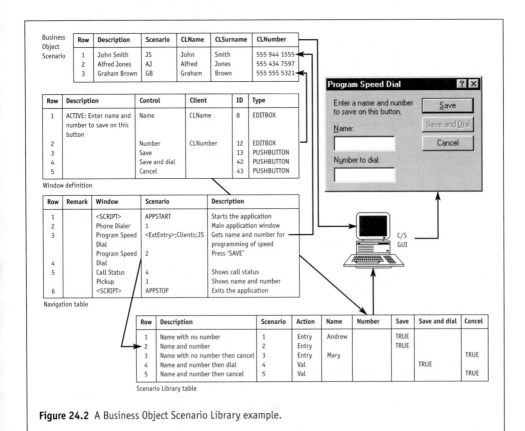

Figure 24.2 A Business Object Scenario Library example.

24.6 Mixing Business Object Scenarios with existing tests

RadSTAR now has support to allow test analysts to freely mix original (window-centric) Scenarios with Business Object Scenarios in a Navigation. With an original Scenario the test analyst specifies the window name in the 'Window' column and the key to the scenario in the 'Scenario' column.

With a Business Object Scenario the test analyst specifies the window name in the 'Window' column as before. In the 'Scenario' column the analyst places a scenario specification. A scenario specification begins with a keyword (enclosed in angle brackets) to indicate that the scenario is in an external table (a Business Object Scenario Library) and the type of scenario:

<ExtEntry>   an entry scenario
<ExtVal>   a validation scenario
<ExtWrite>   a write scenario to save result data to a table

The keyword is followed by the name of the table, the scenario key, and other information. In the simplest case, the scenario specification would look like this:

<ExtEntry>;Clients;AC12345

This would play an entry scenario on the current window using data from Business Object Scenario Library, Clients, with a key in the 'Scenario' column of AC12345.

24.7 Reuse versus repeatability

In discussing improvements to the reuse of testware it is important to differentiate between *reuse* and *repeatability*.

24.7.1 Reuse

Reuse is essential if the full benefits of automated testing are to be realized. By 'reuse' we mean the ability to make use of the design and data relating to a specific set of testware on more than one occasion. But people cannot reuse what they don't know about. Testware must be documented accurately and completely. It should also be maintained in an architecture where it is easily found.

In our experience the following two factors influence the amount of reuse that is achieved to the greatest extent:

- People. The single most difficult thing to overcome is the reluctance of people to adopt reuse because it has traditionally always been easier to ignore any existing tests than to make use of them.

- Relevance of data. Testware is often constructed using a particular set of data as a 'baseline.' When the baseline changes, as it inevitably will do, then the testware must be updated to stay in step.

To insure maximum reuse is made of the testware the following principles should be adopted:

- the reuse of testware must be a fundamental part of the development process;
- producing fully automated, repeatable testware is the goal;
- testware must be maintainable, e.g. easy to find and update, logically categorized;
- testware must be built which is easily rolled forward to keep it up to date;
- a system for effective and efficient management of testware objects must be in place.

24.7.2 Repeatability

Repeatability is a function of an automated Test Suite and it relates to the ability of that set of tests to be re-executed on two or more occasions. A fundamental factor in determining repeatability is the extent that the Test Suite can recover automatically in the event of errors occurring (Kaner, 1997).

The more mature a suite of tests is, the more likely that repeatability has been incorporated. One of the best scales for the maturity of a Test Suite is that proposed by Mark Fewster and Paul Herzlich (1994). Their model for Test Suite maturity is as follows:

- *Infant*: not very automated, needs babysitting.
- *Adolescent*: can leave unattended for an evening, but doesn't really behave itself.
- *Mature*: can leave for the weekend, can look after itself.

But also in many real-life cases:

- *Dead of neglect*: at any age, but often young.

24.8 Conclusion

When automated testing is achieved using a fifth generation approach, such as Business Object Scenario Libraries, then organizations are in a good position to build better testware directly from their business data using database extract tools.

We have implemented this approach using our proprietary approach, RadSTAR. This tool-supported approach enables the test team to concentrate on the business and the application under test without being distracted by the technology. There is no need for complicated scripting or re-recording sessions and there is more time to discover business data and processes which reveal bugs in the software.

Additionally, in a client/server system with a layered architecture, business tests can be created that can be used to test each layer independently and separately from any particular user interface. Such Business Object Scenario Libraries will also be reuseable when you come to build tests for user interfaces.

References

FEWSTER, MARK AND HERZLICH, PAUL (1994) How mature is your automated test suite? *QCCs Focus on Testing,* March.

GERRARD, PAUL (1998) Automated testing: past, present and future, paper presented at EuroStar '98, Munich.

KANER, CEM (1997) Improving the maintainability of automated test suites, paper presented at Quality Week '97.

PETTICHORD, BRET (1996) Success with test automation, in *Proceedings of the Ninth International Quality Week.* Software Research, San Francisco, California. Available at http://www.io.com/~wazmo/succpap.htm

A test automation journey

Jim Thomson

25.1 Introduction

My company is the Financial Services division of the Abbey National group and we have grown from inception in 1992 to be one of the major players by pursuing aggressive growth targets set centrally for each division by Group Management.

We are 'release driven.' What I mean by that is to insure we meet those targets we may release more than 50 products a year – an average of one per week. Some are major developments, others enhancements or updates to existing offerings, and then there are the changes required to comply with legislation. Whichever way you look at it, that's a considerable, ongoing testing effort and thus we have a requirement to insure that our testing is as thorough and efficient as possible.

The aim of this chapter is to provide you with details of our experiences of automated testing – both good and bad. It mentions our earlier attempts, why we made the decision to adopt RadSTAR, and experiences we have had using this approach.

25.2 First steps

25.2.1 Previous experience of attempted test automation

As part of a periodic review of our delivery process we looked very hard at testing procedures and methods, and heard again about the potential benefits of automating our regression testing.

The standard benefits are well documented elsewhere but, for me, are consistency, increasing the working day by running tests 'out of hours,' test 'audit trails,' and maximizing use of scarce business resource. However, I also believed that test automation had another benefit and, if accomplished in a way that was understood and endorsed by business-level users, could deliver tangible business benefit, which in turn would be a key element in securing its wider acceptance.

I said 'heard again' because autotesting had been attempted previously in-house but had been abandoned as unwieldy – which, according to my thesaurus has the synonyms bulky, cumbersome, awkward, and unmanageable. Therefore, any new undertaking had to be comparatively simple and straightforward but powerful.

25.2.2 The next attempt: new tool and support from tool experts

So, we tried again. We looked at the market and carefully selected a new tool that would support our varied platforms, OS/2, NT, and mainframe 3270 applications. It had a data table facility, which would greatly simplify script maintenance when the underlying testbed was updated, and also promised a pseudo-English scripting language which allowed us to build the tests before the application was complete.

For our pilot project we enlisted the help of experts in the tool to profit from their expertise and previous experience in getting the best from it across various scenarios. We carefully mapped out what we wanted to achieve, namely an organized but less technical means to automate tests, and we also knew to avoid record and replay. We worked with and took advice from the experts and this time we were successful. Or were we?

Well, yes – the tests ran and did what was specified – but then again no, because when the euphoria died down and I examined what we had it was unacceptable.

25.2.3 Experience of an ad hoc automated test process (the 'bad')

This was our experience:

- it had taken longer than planned, for several reasons;
- not all scripts were of good quality – they reflected the scripter;
- scripts were unusable as documentation – they were really programs, not scripts;
- programs were 'more complex than the application';[1]
- programmer-type skillset and mindset were required;
- only partially reusable test assets were created.

25.2.4 What we really wanted

So, it was back to the drawing board. But my ideas of what we should be getting out of autotesting now were driven by the concept of standardizing

---

[1] Quotation from the package vendor whose application we had used in the pilot when we demonstrated the results to encourage them to provide autotests with new releases.

the test build and execution, making it simpler and easier to use. If we could do that we didn't need to train programmers in yet another language – we could use the current business testers *and* we would get buy-in from them because they would understand what the tests were doing.

It was natural for business people to be suspicious of automated tests. Although they could follow what was happening on screen during a test it would be unacceptable to require them to sit and watch what was happening. What would be the point in automating the tests? Real benefit would be delivered when they could read the scripts/programs to confirm that the tests were doing exactly what they had specified and what they themselves would have done.

My goal therefore was a form of language, a pseudo-code that the tests could be easily constructed in and which the business could comprehend. I came up with a wish list as shown in Table 25.1.

Table 25.1 Wishlist for test automation.

Simple but powerful 'language'
Suitable as cross-discipline documentation
Compatible with current toolset
Use data tables or similar approach
Manageable – so it had to be measurable
Higher percentage of reusable test assets

25.2.5 Is this achievable?

I thought I knew what automated testing should be and started to search for a way to realize it. At this point I didn't really know my chances of success; I didn't know if my target was achievable. However, I read the books, visited the web sites, and attended a course or two, and at conferences I found that my experiences were not unique. I also found support for my 'wish list' and I knew then that I was on the right track because that support came from the right quarters.

In particular, a paper by Cem Kaner (1997) gave the following advice:

- reset expectations about timing and benefits;
- use a data-driven architecture;
- use a framework-based architecture;
- recognize staffing realities;
- consider complementary automation.

Now, all of these points are excellent and are fully explained in the paper but what particularly intrigued me about Cem Kaner's advice was the use of what he termed a 'framework-based architecture.' This, he defined, was a means of isolating the application under test from the test scripts by providing a set of functions in a shared function library – I couldn't have put it better myself!

A set of commonly used routines, executed by using a simple pseudo-code command, would certainly reduce the amount of work needed to build autotests. This would increase the reusability of script-type test assets *and* reduce the technicalities of test development.

Another way to put it is to emphasize the need for a process to be put in place and proven before any tools are selected: automate bad testing and it's still bad testing. Now that is exactly what had not been done in our autotesting pilot – I had expected the process to flow from, or be a by-product of, the project.

There's a similar theme in the advice from these sages, and to me both are, broadly speaking, delivering the same message, albeit to different levels. That is, you must lay a foundation before building your automated tests. There can be a temptation to just 'automate away' and hope that everything else will somehow take care of itself; well it didn't for me and it won't for you.

The key point is that to increase the chance of success with automated testing you must appreciate the need for a support structure. So, I adapted my wish list so that any new approach absolutely must have an explicit structure as the foundation. My requirements now became as shown in Table 25.2.

Table 25.2 How to build an automated testing foundation.

Construct a set of macros using the current test tool language

Use these macros to build a framework from which tests can be constructed

Use data tables to reduce data maintenance overhead

Enhance the test reporting to produce metrics base data

I knew that it would take several person-months to construct but I was also certain that it would be better to take the time and to insure that we got it right first time. We couldn't afford to degrade our testing performance but similarly we couldn't afford to stand still in the financial services market, plus our Year 2000 project was beginning to express an interest in automated testing. At one point there seemed to be a ready-made solution in that the test execution tool company had a successful offering which could help. However, it wasn't available outside the United States. I took this as another positive sign that we were now on the right track and made greater efforts to research the market and eventually heard of a product called RadSTAR.

But would it give us the support structure we needed? What did it offer?

25.3 An off-the-shelf automated test foundation: RadSTAR

25.3.1 What did this approach offer?

There were five characteristics that were key to achieving our wish list and requirements.

1. Framework driven. RadSTAR is built around a common function library which removes the requirement to write ad hoc code for standard business process operations.

2. Data driven. The application under test, the test process itself, and the test data are held in data tables.

3. Cross-discipline documentation. My idea of a pseudo-code understood by business-level users has been implemented and held in the previously mentioned data tables, which state explicitly the key to be depressed or the button to be clicked. This, along with the field or control names and the test data to be used, clearly communicates what the test will do.

4. Assisted management. In addition to the standard test logs and reports produced by the tool, each test executed via RadSTAR generates an information file that forms the basis of our metrics suite and allows us to measure our performance and demonstrate the benefits achieved.

5. Supported current test tool. RadSTAR supports several of the most popular test execution tools, and does not hinder tool use; instead the implementation of the framework approach delivers complex functionality beyond the expertise required of most test builders.

25.3.2 Would this meet our needs?

Could this tool and approach give us the foundation that we had determined was essential? There was a standard process, a method to follow, and the same method was used irrespective of the platform. This was very important because the Year 2000 project required us to test on mainframe and several client/server environments. The use of data tables removed the requirement that each test builder had to have programming skills – it complemented the test tool.

But for me the biggest benefit was that it also seemed to offer something along the lines of my cross-discipline pseudo-code in that the test plan was written in a form that the business could follow too: the data tables. These same test plans controlled test execution; there was no translation stage where a business requirement could be misinterpreted. This would allow us to take our autotest methodology to the business users and get their support for its use.

We brought it in for a trial and it proved useful almost immediately when we were able to reuse tests that had been developed for the trial in an emergency situation 'live' test. We then were asked to consider the use of a specialized mainframe-only tool and proved that our test execution tool together with RadSTAR could deliver more functional and regression testing benefit, plus we had the ability to test on the client/server environment.

We adopted RadSTAR and use it in our test automation infrastructure – in fact, it's central to it.

25.4 How we have implemented automated testing using RadSTAR

25.4.1 RadSTAR at the center of an automated testing infrastructure

Figure 25.1 shows the framework or infrastructure of our current automated testing. We now have five core elements to our infrastructure and RadSTAR could be thought of as the 'glue' which keeps it all together. The other four elements are described below.

1. Business process maps and functional test scenarios. We documented our critical business processes traditionally and then used the RadSTAR method to specify our functional test scenarios, which then drive the test execution tool. As stated previously, no translation is required – what the business sees is what drives the test.

2. Test asset management. Test asset management must be recognized as essential to successful automated testing. We have generated more than 25 000 test assets in 18 months. You can use a manual method or there are several tools. I believe it is probably best not to attempt it manually. We have constructed links between the RadSTAR technology and our test asset manager to build on their respective strengths and get the best out of both.

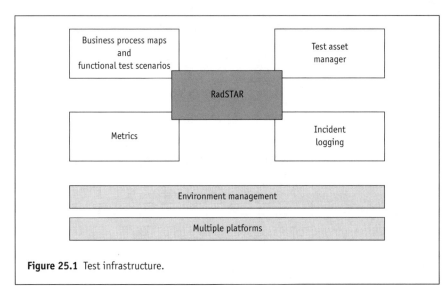

Figure 25.1 Test infrastructure.

3. Incident logging. A defect in a test is immediately logged in our tracking system, where it is monitored until resolution.

4. Metrics. It is well worth remembering that 'in order to manage we're required to measure.' We must therefore make use of metrics. Inputs to our reporting suite are:

    - incident logs
    - RadSTAR journal reports
    - time recording.

    Each RadSTAR test generates a report file containing among other data the name of the test, start and end times, and a result flag, i.e. passed or failed. We allocate a standard time allowance to build a test. We take these factors outside RadSTAR to generate performance graphs and charts, as shown below.

25.4.2 Sample reports (data from our Year 2000 project)

The following reports were generated from our automated testing infrastructure.

Figure 25.2 shows the defects raised by category. Typical of the issues associated with a Year 2000 project, most of the problems are linked to management of the 15 date-related environments and the sheer number of programs that must be amended.

Figure 25.3 shows the defects by date tested. The dates listed in the key are shown left to right in the graph (with 09/09/99 at the left and 01/02/01 at the right).The purpose of collating this data is to identify which of the millennium dates will cause most problems and give us a basis for contingency plans.

Based on current data the first day of processing in the new millennium will be bad – but not as bad as the first leap year date! This diagram will help us to communicate why we believe this will be the case and help us to insure that we have sufficient resources on site when required.

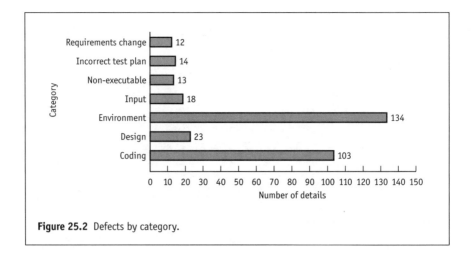

Figure 25.2 Defects by category.

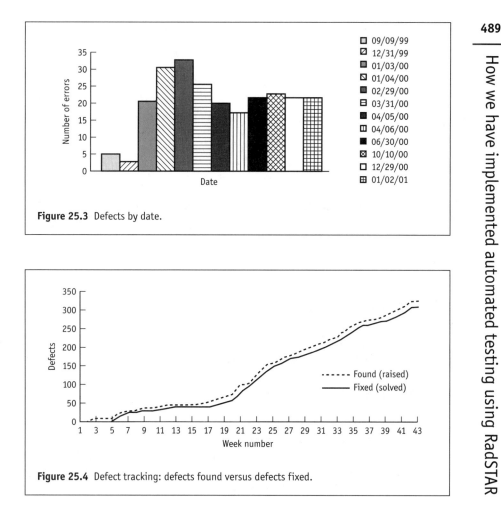

Figure 25.3 Defects by date.

Figure 25.4 Defect tracking: defects found versus defects fixed.

Two reports are of interest for defect tracking. Figure 25.4 shows the found versus fixed graph. A glance at this report is enough to determine the performance of our bug resolution team. The fact that the number of bugs is increasing only reflects the increasing number of tests carried out. If the lines begin to diverge the problems are beginning to go unsolved and we need to identify and remedy the causes.

Figure 25.5 shows the defects fixed and re-tested. The bars show the number of defects 'raised to solved' (on the left) and 'solved to closed' (on the right) grouped by the time taken to solve. Around half are simple defects and consequently are solved and re-tested in less than half a day. However, the more difficult problems are evenly spread up to about ten days. The two 'rogue' bars on the right actually reveal errors in our reporting – it's real data, those were real screw-ups. So we've not included them in our calculations, to give us an average of just under a couple of days to re-test.

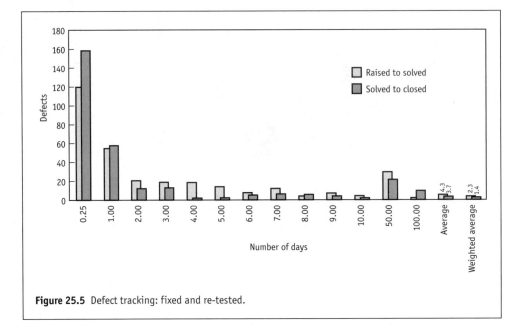

Figure 25.5 Defect tracking: fixed and re-tested.

There are two reports showing weekly progress. Figure 25.6 shows the report that is the centerpiece of my weekly progress report. It's a good general snapshot of how the autotesting is proceeding.

'Test case executions' (top line) is the one I look for first. Once again, a quick glance shows me that we're keeping busy. Then I look at 'Passed' (next line down), which shows me how successful the tests were.

'Failed' (lowest line) is the bad news, the failures. But as long as it remains very close to the x axis there's no need to panic. Although you'll see that I have panicked at least twice – in weeks 32 and 36. One was a problem with the 'baseline' test environment and the other was incorrect specification of business logic. Personally I like this graph; everyone can understand it immediately and it gives me most of the information I need, and as long as the number of tests executed is around 400 per week, we're doing well.

Figure 25.7 shows the other weekly progress report: the number of screens processed per week. This report is more spectacular; it shows that we regularly run through more than 5000 screens to test our business processes. This, for me, puts automated testing way ahead of manual testing. For a team of six testers on a five-day week this is 165 screens tested each day. When you consider the accompanying detailed reports and metrics, that throughput cannot be matched by manual testing.

The 'extra' consideration of the detailed execution reports is one that can sometimes be ignored by dedicated manual testers. If you're faced with this enlist the auditors' help – they are typically very pro autotesting and tend to have influence.

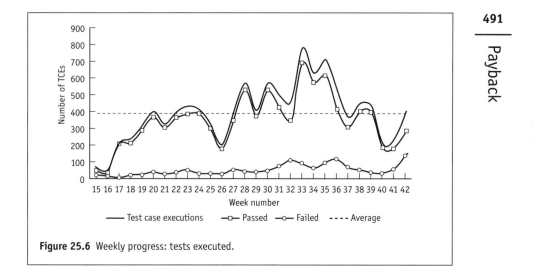

Figure 25.6 Weekly progress: tests executed.

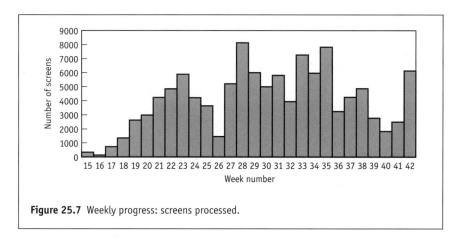

Figure 25.7 Weekly progress: screens processed.

25.5 Payback

25.5.1 Our numbers

A summary of our benefits achieved is shown in Table 25.3. Over 2000 tests in total have been built by the six people in my team. On average there are ten screens per test and the high percentage of reuse has kept the number of test cases required lower than expected. These cases cover six different platforms.

25.5.2 Are we there yet?

I have likened my experiences to a journey and the purpose of a jouney is usually to arrive at a destination, thereby completing it. Perhaps that analogy is not entirely accurate because I have not arrived at testing nirvana

Table 25.3 Our actual numbers.

Number of people building and running tests	6
Number of platforms	6
Automated test cases created	2133
Test case executions to date	21 108
Average test executions per week	400
Number of screens tested to date	216 896
Cumulative savings on all testing effort	21 332 hours
Equivalent manual effort	1523 hours
Test efficiency	0.305 hours per test case execution
Test effectiveness (Defect Detection Percentage)	90.48%

and I don't expect to, ever. What we have achieved by using the RadSTAR methodology as the key component of our foundation are very worthwhile improvements in our test process.

- Across multiple environments we now have one standard method for test documentation and execution, results report, defect tracking, and resolution.
- We have an implementation of my pseudo-code idea which enables us to communicate more effectively with business representatives and makes training new resources easier, because it is intuitive – or perhaps that should be because it is obvious.
- The Testing Efficiency figures in the table demonstrate that manual testing methods cannot achieve the same level of consistency in test execution and quality in test reporting. Automated testing is several times quicker and not at the expense of testing effectiveness.

So, in answer to the question 'Are we there yet?' and sticking with the theme, I would say 'No, but we're going in the right direction and we have a map.'

Reference

KANER, CEM (1997) Improving the maintainability of automated test suites, paper presented at Quality Week '97.

CHAPTER TWENTY-SIX

Extracts from
The Automated Testing Handbook

Linda Hayes

26.1 Introduction to this chapter

This chapter contains extracts from a little booklet written by Linda Hayes and published in 1995 by the Software Testing Institute, based in Dallas, Texas (Web address: http://www.ondaweb.com/sti). This booklet gives an introduction to many of the topics covered in this book, and also contains some interesting angles and information about test automation that is complementary to the rest of our book. We have therefore selected portions of the *Handbook* to reproduce in this chapter.

Some of the ideas contained in this extract are covered elsewhere in this book (for example, metrics); others are not covered elsewhere (for example, who should be on the test team). At the end of the chapter, we detail the sections that we included and excluded from the original *Handbook*.

26.2 Introduction to the *Handbook*

Since software testing is a labor-intensive task, especially if done thoroughly, automation sounds instantly appealing. But, as with anything, there is a cost associated with getting the benefits. Automation isn't always a good idea, and sometimes manual testing is out of the question. The key is to know what the benefits and costs really are, then to make an informed decision about what is best for your circumstances.

26.2.1 Why automate?

Automated software tests provide three key benefits: repeatability, leverage, and accumulation.

Repeatability

Repeatability means that automated tests can be executed more than once, consistently each time. This leads to time savings as well as predictability. But in order to realize this benefit, the application must be stable enough that the same tests can be repeated without excessive maintenance.

Leverage

True leverage from automated tests comes not only from repeating a test that was captured while performed manually, but from executing tests that were never performed manually at all. For example, by generating test cases programmatically, you could yield thousands or more – when only hundreds might be possible with manual resources. Enjoying this benefit requires the proper test case and script design.

Accumulation

The third benefit, accumulation, is the most critical for the long term. It is a fact that applications change and gain complexity over their useful life. Constant modifications and enhancements are typical; rarely does the functionality decline or even freeze. Therefore, the number of tests which are needed for coverage is also constantly increasing. But, if the automated tests are not designed to be maintainable as the application changes, the test library will be fighting just to stay even. Therefore, it is critical to adopt an approach to test library design that supports maintainability over the life of the application. Accumulation is illustrated in Figure 26.1.

In this *Handbook* we will present practical advice on how to realize these benefits while keeping your expectations realistic and your management committed.

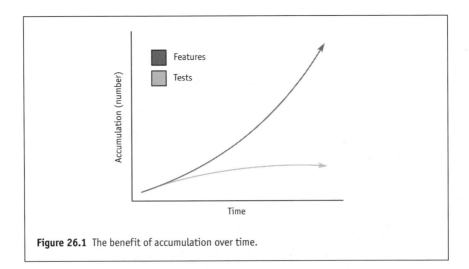

Figure 26.1 The benefit of accumulation over time.

The cornerstone of test automation is the premise that the expected application behavior is known. When this is not the case, it is usually better not to automate.

Unstable design

There are certain applications that are inherently unstable by design. For example, a weather-mapping system or one which relies on real-time data will not demonstrate sufficiently predictable results for automation. Applications whose data is not stable enough to produce consistent results are not good candidates for automation. The investment required to develop and maintain the automated tests will not be offset by the benefits, since repeatability will be doubtful.

Inexperienced testers

If the person(s) automating the tests are not sufficiently experienced with the application to know the expected behavior, automating their tests is also of doubtful value. Their tests may not accurately reflect the correct behavior, causing later confusion and wasted effort. Remember, an automated test is only as good as the person who created it.

Temporary testers

In other cases, the test team may be comprised primarily of personnel from other areas, such as users or consultants, who will not be involved over the long term. Because of the initial investment in training and the short payback period, it is probably not effective to automate with a temporary team.

Insufficient time, resources

If you don't have enough time or resources to get your testing done manually in the short term, don't expect a tool to help you. The initial investment for planning, training and implementation will take more time in the short term than the tool can save you. Get through the current crisis, then look at automation for the longer term.

26.2.3 How not to automate

Whatever you do, do not simply distribute a testing tool among your testers and expect them to automate the test process. Just as you would never automate accounting by giving a program compiler to the accounting department, neither should you attempt to automate testing by just turning a testing tool over to the test group.

Automation is more than test execution

Think of it this way. You are going to build an application that automates your testing, which is actually more than just running the tests. You need a complete process and environment for creating and documenting tests, managing and maintaining them, executing them and reporting the results, as well as managing the test environment. Just developing scores of individual tests does not comprise a strategic test automation system.

Duplication of effort

If you just hand an automation tool out to individual testers and command that they automate their tests, each one of them will address all of these issues – in their own unique and personal way, of course. Not only does this lead to tremendous duplication of effort, but it can cause outright conflict when the tests are combined, as they must and should be.

Need for a framework

Instead, you must approach the automation of testing just as you would the automation of any other type of application. You will need a plan, an overall framework, and an orderly division of the responsibilities. This framework should make the test environment efficient to develop, manage, and maintain.

Remember, test tools aren't magic – but, properly implemented, they can work wonders!

26.2.4 Setting realistic expectations

All too often, automated testing tools are expected to save the day by making up for too little time, resources, or expertise. Unfortunately, when these expectations are inevitably disappointed, automation or the tool itself gets a bad name. Before any effort can be deemed a success, realistic expectations must be set up front.

There are three important things to remember when setting expectations about test automation: one, an initial investment in planning, training and development must be made before any benefits are possible; two, the time savings come only when automated tests can be executed more than once and without undue maintenance requirements; three, no tool can compensate for the lack of expertise in the test process.

Test automation is strategic

If your test process is in crisis and management wants to throw money at a tool to fix it, don't fall for it. Test automation is a long-term, strategic solution, not a short-term fix.

Buying a test tool is like joining a health club: the only weight you have lost is in your wallet!

You must use the club, sweat it out and invest the time and effort before you can get the benefits.

Along the same lines, be wary about expecting outside consultants to solve your problems. Although consultants can save you time by bringing experience to bear, they are not in and of themselves a solution. Think of consultants as you would a personal trainer: they are there to guide you through your exercises, not to do them for you! Paying someone else to do your sit-ups for you will not flatten your stomach.

Here's a good rule of thumb to follow when setting expectations for a test tool. Calculate what your existing manual test iteration requires, then multiply it by ten, then add on the time scheduled for training and planning. This will approximate the time it will take to develop your test framework and build or capture your first set of tests. So, if it takes you two weeks to execute one iteration of tests manually, plan for twenty weeks after training and planning are complete to get through your first automated iteration. From there on out, though, you can cut your iteration in half or more. Naturally, these are only approximations and your results may be different. For intensive manual test processes of stable applications, you may see an even faster payback.

Not everything can be automated

But remember, you must still allow time for tasks that can't be automated – you will still need to gather test requirements, define test cases, maintain your test library, administer the test environment, and review and analyze the test results. On an ongoing basis you will also need time to add new test cases based on enhancements or defects, so that your coverage can constantly be improving.

Go slow

If you can't afford the time in the short term, then do your automation gradually. Target those areas where you will get the biggest payback first, then reinvest the time savings in additional areas until you get it all automated. Some progress is better than none!

Plan to keep staff

Don't plan to jettison the majority of your testing staff just because you have a tool. In most cases, you don't have enough permanent testers to begin with: automation can help the staff you have be more productive, but it can't work miracles. Granted, you may be able to reduce your dependence on temporary assistance from other departments or from contractors, but justifying testing tools based on minimal staffing requirements is risky.

Reinvest time savings

As your test automation starts to reap returns in the form of time savings, don't automatically start shaving the schedule. The odds are that there are other types of tests that you never had time for before, such as configuration and stress testing. If you can free up room in the schedule, look for ways to test at high volumes of users and transactions, or consider testing different platform configurations. Testing is never over!

When setting expectations, ask yourself this question: Am I satisfied with everything about our existing test process, except for the amount of time it takes to perform manually? If the answer is yes, then automation will probably deliver like a dream. But if the answer is no, then realize that while automation can offer great improvements, it is not a panacea for all quality and testing problems.

The most important thing to remember about setting expectations is that you will be measured by them.

If you promise management that a testing tool will cut your testing costs in half, yet you only succeed in saving a fourth, you will have failed! So take a more conservative approach: be up front about the initial investment that is required, and offer cautious estimates about future savings. In many cases, management can be satisfied with far less than you might be!

For example, even if you only break even between the cost to automate and the related savings in direct costs, if you can show increased test coverage then there will be a savings in indirect costs as a result of improved quality. In many companies, better quality is more important than fewer dollars.

26.2.5 Getting and keeping management commitment

There are three types of management commitment needed for successful test automation: money, time and resources. And it is just as important to keep commitment as it is to get it in the first place!

Commit money

Acquiring a test automation tool involves spending money for software, training and perhaps consulting. It is easier to get money allocated all at once instead of piece meal, so be careful not to buy the software first then decide later you need training or additional services. Although the tool itself may be advertised as 'easy to use,' this is different from 'easy to implement.' A hammer is easy to swing, but carpentry takes skill.

Do a pilot

Just because the money is allocated all at once, don't spend it that way! If this is your first time to automate, do a small pilot project to test your assumptions and prove the concept. Ideally, a pilot should involve a representative subset of your application and have a narrow enough scope that it can be completed in six months or less.

Take the time to carefully document the resource investment during the pilot as well as the benefits, as these results can be used to estimate a larger implementation. Since you can be sure you don't know what you don't know, it is better to learn your lessons on a small scale. You don't learn to drive on a freeway!

Commit time

All too often tools are purchased with the expectation that the acquisition itself achieves automation, so disappointment sets in when results aren't promptly forthcoming. It is essential to educate management about the amount of time it takes to realize the benefits, but be careful about estimating the required time based on marketing literature: every organization and application is different.

A six month pilot can establish a sound basis for projecting a full scale rollout.

When you ask for time, be clear about what will be accomplished and how it will be measured.

Commit resources

Remember that even though test automation saves resources in the long run, in the short term it will require more than a manual process. Make sure management understands this, or you may find yourself with a tool and no one to implement it.

Also be sure to commit the right type of resources. As further described in Section 26.4 (the Test Team), you will need a mix of skills that may or may not be part of your existing test group. Don't imagine that having a tool means you can get by with less skill or experience: the truth is exactly the opposite.

Track progress

Even though benefits most likely won't be realized for several months, it is important to show incremental progress on a regular basis – monthly at the least. Progress can be measured in a number of ways: team members trained on the tool, development of the test plan, test requirements identified, test cases created, test cases executed, defects uncovered, and so forth.

Identify the activities associated with your test plan, track them and report them to management regularly. Nothing is more disconcerting than to wait six months with no word at all, and if you run up against obstacles it is critical to let management know right away. Get bad news out as early as possible and good news out as soon as you can back it up.

Adjust as you go

If one of your assumptions changes, adjust the schedule and expectations accordingly and let management know right away. For example, if the application is not ready when expected, or if you lose resources, recast your original estimates and inform everyone concerned. Don't wait until you are going to be late to start explaining why. No one likes surprises!

In order for management to manage, they must know where things stand and what to expect. By letting them know up front what is needed, then keeping them informed every step of the way, you can get their commitment and keep it.

26.3 Fundamentals of test automation

With advanced tools and techniques accelerating both the development and complexity of new applications, test automation is the only real solution to keeping pace. Unfortunately, the success rate of test tools is low. Why?

Test process must be well-defined
A key reason is that you cannot automate a process that is not already well-defined. Because many testers are either new to the company, or are enlisted temporarily from the user community, the level of test expertise is often low. However, defining a complete test process is outside the scope of this handbook; entire books have been written about software testing (see *Software Testing Institute Resource Guide*). For our purposes, we will assume that you know what needs to be tested.

Testware is software
But even when the test process is reasonably well-defined, automation is still a challenge. The purpose of this handbook is to bridge the gap between what should be tested and how it should be automated. This begins by laying out certain fundamental principles that apply which must be understood before success is possible. All of these principles can be summarized in one basic premise: *testware is software!*

Test automation is two different disciplines
As odd as it sounds, test automation is really two different things. There is testing, which is one discipline, and automation, which is another. Automating software testing is no different than automating accounting or any other business function: in each case, a computer is being instructed to perform a task previously performed manually. Whether these instructions are stored in something called a script or a program, they both have all of the characteristics of source code. This is shown in Table 26.1.

Table 26.1 The difference between testing and automation.

Test	Automation
Application expertise	Development expertise
What to test	How to automate
Test cases	Test scripts

The fact that testware is software is the single most important concept to grasp! Once this premise is understood, others follow.

Context refers to the state of the application during test playback. Because an automated test is executing at the same time the application is, it is critical that they remain synchronized. Synchronization takes two forms: one, assuring that the application is in fact located at the point where the test expects to be, and two, assuring the test does not run ahead of the application while it is waiting or processing. We will cover the second type in Section 26.3.2.

Context controls results

Because tests are performing inputs and verifying outputs, it is imperative that the inputs be applied at the proper location in the application, and that the outputs appear where expected. Otherwise, the test will report an incorrect result. Also, when multiple tests run one after the other, the result from one test can affect the next. If one test begins at the main menu and ends at a sub-menu, the following test must either expect to begin at the sub-menu or risk failure. Similarly, if a test which expects to complete at the main menu instead fails and aborts within a window, the next test will most likely begin out of context.

The main menu approach

The simplest solution to beginning and ending context is to design all tests to begin and end at the same point in the application. This point must be one from which any area of the application can be accessed. In most cases, this will be the main menu or logon area. By designing every test so that it commences at this point and ends there, tests can be executed in any order without considering context.

Enabling error recovery

Adopting a standard starting and ending context also simplifies recovery from unexpected results. A test which fails can, after logging its error, call a common recovery function to return context to the proper location so that the next test can be executed. Granted, some applications are so complex that a single point of context may make each individual test too long; in these cases, you may adopt several, such as sub-menus or other intermediate points. But be aware that your recovery function will become more complex, as it must have sufficient logic to know which context is appropriate. Designing test suites, or combinations of tests, will also be more complex as consideration must be given to grouping tests which share common contexts. This is shown in Figure 26.2.

The key to context is to remember that your automated tests do not have the advantage that you have as a manual tester: they cannot make judgment calls about what to do next. Without consistency or logic to guide them, automated tests are susceptible to the slightest aberration. By proper test design, you can minimize the impact of one failed test on others, and simplify the considerations when combining tests into suites and cycles for execution.

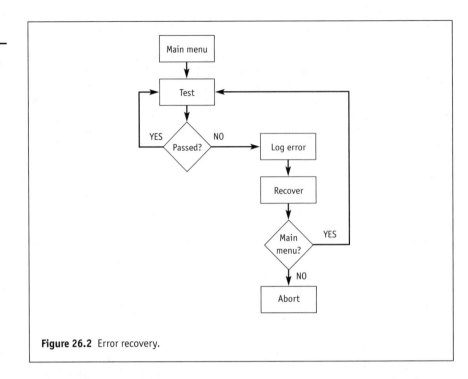

Figure 26.2 Error recovery.

26.3.2 Synchronization

Synchronization between the test and the application requires that they execute at the same rate. Because different conditions may exist at the time of playback than existed when the test was created, precise timing coincidence may not be possible. For example, if heavier system traffic increases processing time, the application may respond more slowly than it did previously. If the test does not have a means of compensating for fluctuating application speed, it may fail a test if the result does not appear in the time frame expected, or it may issue input when the application is not ready to receive it.

Synchronization is complicated when there are multiple platforms involved. Methods for synchronizing with a local application are different from those for synchronizing with a remote host or network server. But in any case, synchronization can affect the result of your automated tests and must be accounted for.

Global indicators

Some test tools compensate for local synchronization by waiting for the application to cease processing. In Windows applications, for example, this may take the form of waiting while the hourglass cursor is being displayed. In other cases, this may require that the tool check to see that all application activity has ceased. Unfortunately, neither method is infallible. Not all applications use the hourglass cursor consistently, and some conduct constant polling activities which never indicate a steady state. Verify your tool's synchronization ability against a subset of your application under varying circumstances before developing large volumes of tests that may later require rework.

Local indicators

Other tools automatically insert wait states between windows or even controls, causing the test script to suspend playback until the proper window or control is displayed. This method is more reliable, as it does not rely on global behavior that may not be consistent. However, this approach also requires that some form of timeout processing be available; otherwise, a failed response may cause playback to suspend indefinitely.

Remote indicators

When a remote host or network server is involved, there is yet another dimension of synchronization. For example, the local application may send a data request to the host; while it is waiting, the application is not 'busy,' thus risking the indication that it has completed its response or is ready for input. In this case, the tool may provide for protocol-specific drivers, such as IBM 3270 or 5250 emulation, which monitor the host status directly through HLLAPI (high level language application program interface). If your tool does not provide this, you may have to modify your scripts to detect application readiness through more specific means, such as waiting for data to appear.

Synchronization is one of the issues that is unique to automated testing. A person performing a manual test instinctively waits for the application to respond or become ready before proceeding ahead. With automated tests, you need techniques to make this decision so that they are consistent across a wide variety of situations.

26.3.3 Documentation

Documentation of the testware means that, in a crunch, the test library could be executed manually. This may take the form of extensive comments sprinkled throughout the test cases or scripts, or of narrative descriptions stored either within the tests or in separate documentation files. Based on the automation approach selected, the form and location of the documentation may vary.

Documentation means transferability

It may not be evident from reading an undocumented capture/playback script, for example, that a new window is expected to appear at a certain point; the script may simply indicate that a mouse click is performed at a certain location. Only the person who created the script will know what was expected; anyone else attempting to execute the script may not understand what went wrong if the window does not appear and subsequent actions are out of context. So, without adequate documentation, transferability from one tester to another is limited.

Mystery tests accumulate

Ironically, mystery tests tend to accumulate: if you don't know what a test script does or why, you will be reticent to delete it! This leads to large volumes of tests that aren't used, but nevertheless require storage, management and maintenance. Always provide enough documentation to tell what the test is expected to do.

More is better

Unlike some test library elements, the more documentation, the better! Assume as little knowledge as possible, and provide as much information as you can think of.

Document in context

The best documentation is inside the test itself, in the form of comments or description, so that it follows the test and explains it in context. Even during capture/playback recording, some test tools allow comments to be inserted. If this option is not available, then add documentation to test data files or even just on paper.

26.4 Test process and people

26.4.1 The test automation process

In an ideal world, testing would parallel the systems development life cycle for the application. This cycle is generally depicted as shown in Figure 26.3.

Unfortunately, not all test efforts commence at the earliest stage of the software development process. Depending on where your application is in the timeline, these activities may be compressed and slide to the right, but in general each of these steps must be completed.

26.4.2 The test team

But regardless of the approach you select, to automate your testing you will need to assemble a dedicated test team and obtain the assistance of other areas in the company. It is important to match the skills of the persons on your team with the responsibilities of their role. For example, the type and

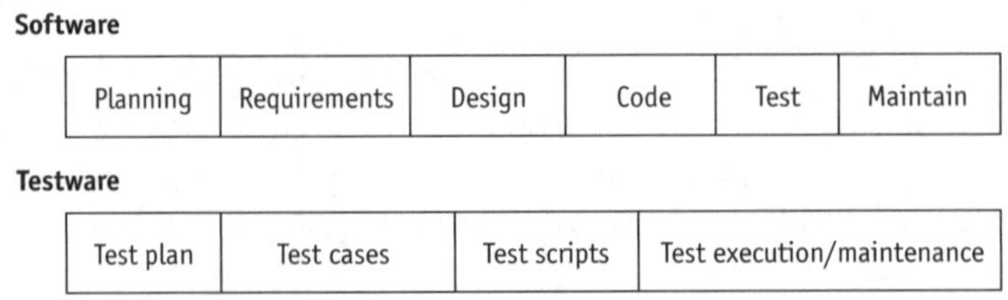

Software					
Planning	Requirements	Design	Code	Test	Maintain

Testware			
Test plan	Test cases	Test scripts	Test execution/maintenance

Figure 26.3 The software and testing life cycles.

level of skills will vary somewhat with the automation approach you adopt – developing test scripts is essentially a form of programming; for this role, a more technical background is needed.

You must also be sure that the person in each role has the requisite authority to carry out their responsibilities; for example, the team leader must have control over the workflow of the team members, and the test librarian must be able to enforce procedures for change and version control.

The suggested members of the test team are shown in Figure 26.4, and their respective responsibilities are described below.

Team Leader

The Team Leader is responsible for developing the Test Plan and managing the team members according to it, as well as coordinating with other areas to accomplish the test effort. The Team Leader must have the authority to assign duties and control the workflow of those who are dedicated to the test team.

Test Developers

Test Developers are experts in the application functionality, responsible for developing the test cases, executing them, analyzing and reporting the results. They should be trained on how to develop tests, whether as data records or as scripts, and use the test framework.

Script Developers

Script Developers are experts in the testing tool, ideally with technical programming experience. They are responsible for developing and maintaining the test framework and supporting scripts and publishing the Test Dictionary.

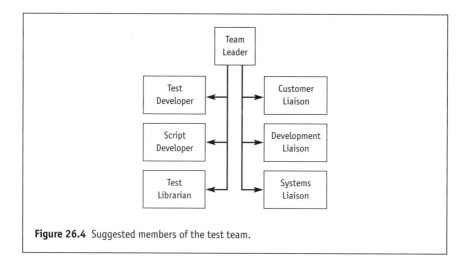

Figure 26.4 Suggested members of the test team.

Test Librarian

The Test Librarian is responsible for managing the configuration, change and version control for all elements of the test library. This includes defining and enforcing check in and check out procedures for all files and related documentation.

Customer Liaison

The Customer Liaison represents the user community of the application under test and is responsible for final approval of the test plan or any changes to it, and for working with the Test Developers to identify test cases and gather sample documents and data. Even though the Customer Liaison may not be a dedicated part of the testing organization, he or she must have dotted line responsibility to the Test Team to insure the acceptance criteria are communicated and met.

Development Liaison

The Development Liaison represents the programmers who will provide the application software for test and is responsible for delivering unit test cases and informing the Test Librarian of any changes to the application or its environment. Even though the Development Liaison may not be a dedicated part of the testing organization, he or she must have dotted line responsibility to the Test Team to insure the software is properly unit tested and delivered in a known state to the Test Team.

Systems Liaison

The Systems Liaison represents the system or network support group and database administrator, and is responsible for supporting the test environment to insure that the Test Team has access to the proper platform configuration and database for test execution. The Systems Liaison must also inform the Test Librarian of any changes to the test platform, configuration or database.

26.5 Test execution: analyzing results

Since an ideally automated test cycle does not depend on human intervention or supervision, the test execution process must thoroughly document results. This documentation must be sufficient to determine which tests passed or failed, what performance was, as well as provide additional information that may be needed to assist with diagnosis of failures.

At the conclusion of each test cycle, the test results – in the form of the execution, performance and error logs – must be analyzed. Automated testing may yield results which are not necessarily accurate or meaningful; for example, the execution log may report hundreds of errors, but a closer examination may reveal that an early, critical test failed which in turn jeopardized the integrity of the database for all subsequent tests.

Inaccurate results occur when the test results do not accurately reflect the state of the application. There are generally three types of inaccurate results: false failures, duplicate failures, and false successes.

False failure from test environment

A false failure is a test which fails for a reason other than an error or defect in the application. A test may fail because the state of the database is not as expected due to an earlier test, or because the test environment is not properly configured or set up, or because a different error has caused the test to lose context.

Or, a test which relies on bitmap comparisons may have been captured against one monitor resolution and executed against another.

False failure from application changes

Another type of false failure can occur if a new field or control is added, causing the script to get out of context and report failures for other fields or controls that are actually functional. Any of these situations will waste resources and skew test results, confusing the metrics which are used to manage the test process.

False failure from test errors

It is unfortunately true that the failure may also be the result of an error in the test itself. For example, there may be a missing test case record or an error in the script. Just as programmers may introduce one problem while fixing another, test cases and scripts are subject to error when modifications are made.

Duplicate failure

A duplicate failure is a failure which is attributable to the same cause as another failure. For example, if a window title is misspelled, this should be reported as only one error; however, depending on what the test is verifying, the name of the window might be compared multiple times. It is not accurate to report the same failure over and over, as this will skew test results.

For example, if a heavily-used transaction window has an error, this error may be reported for every transaction that is entered into it; so, if there are five hundred transactions, there will be five hundred errors reported. Once that error is fixed, the number of errors will drop by five hundred. Using these figures to measure application readiness or project the time for release is risky: it may appear that the application is seriously defective, but the errors are being corrected at an astronomical rate – neither of which is true.

False success from test defect

A false success occurs when a test fails to verify one or more aspects of the behavior, thus reporting that the test was successful when in fact it was not. This may happen for several reasons. One reason might be that the test itself has a defect, such as a logic path that drops processing through the test so that it bypasses certain steps. This type of false success can be identified by measurements such as elapsed time: if the test completes too quickly, for example, this might indicate that it did not execute properly.

False success from missed error

Another false success might occur if the test is looking for only a specific response, thus missing an incorrect response that indicates an error. For example, if the test expects an error to be reported with an error message in a certain area of the screen, and it instead appears elsewhere. Or, if an asynchronous error message appears, such as a broadcast message from the database or network, and the test is not looking for it. This type of false success may be avoided by building in standard tests such as a Monitor, that checks the status of the system at regular intervals.

26.5.2 Defect tracking

Once a test failure is determined to be in fact caused by an error in the application, it becomes a defect that must be reported to development for resolution. Each reported defect should be given a unique identifier and tracked as to the test case that revealed it, the date it was logged as a defect, the developer it was assigned to, and when it was actually fixed.

26.6 Test metrics

Metrics are simply measurements. Test metrics are those measurements from your test process that will help you determine where the application stands and when it will be ready for release. In an ideal world, you would measure your tests at every phase of the development cycle, thus gaining an objective and accurate view of how thorough your tests are and how closely the application complies with its requirements.

In the real world, you may not have the luxury of the time, tools or tests to give you totally thorough metrics. For example, documented test requirements may not exist, or the set of test cases necessary to achieve complete coverage may not be known in advance. In these cases, you must use what you have as effectively as possible.

Measure progress

The most important point to make about test metrics is that they are essential to measuring progress. Testing is a never-ending task, and if you don't have some means of establishing forward progress it is easy to get discouraged. Usually, testers don't have any indication of success, only of failure: they don't hear about the errors they catch, only the ones that make it into production. So, use metrics as a motivator. Even if you can't test everything, you can get comfort from the fact that you test more now than before!

Code coverage

Code coverage is a measurement of what percentage of the underlying application source code was executed during the test cycle. Notice that it does not tell you how much of the code passed the test – only how much was executed during the test. Thus, 100% code coverage does not tell you whether your application is 100% ready.

A source level tool is required to provide this metric, and often it requires that the code itself be instrumented, or modified, in order to capture the measurement. Because of this, programmers are usually the only ones equipped to capture this metric, and then only during their unit test phase.

Although helpful, code coverage is not an unerring indicator of test coverage. Just because the majority of code was executed during the test, it doesn't means that errors are unlikely. It only takes a single line – or character – of code to cause a problem. Also, code coverage only measures the code that exists: it can't measure the code that is missing.

When it is available, however, code coverage can be used to help you gauge how thorough your test cases are. If your coverage is low, analyze the areas which are not exercised to determine what types of tests need to be added.

Requirements coverage

Requirements coverage measures the percentage of the requirements that were tested. Again, like code coverage, this does not mean the requirements were met, only that they were tested. For this metric to be truly meaningful, you must keep track of the difference between simple coverage and successful coverage.

There are two prerequisites to this metric: one, that the requirements are known and documented, and two, that the tests are cross-referenced to the requirements. In many cases, the application requirements are not documented sufficiently for this metric to be taken or be meaningful. If they are documented, though, this measurement can tell you how much of the expected functionality has been tested.

Requirements satisfied

However, if you have taken care to associate requirements with your test cases, you may be able to measure the percentage of the requirements that were met – that is, the number that passed the test. Ultimately, this is a more meaningful measurement, since it tells you how close the application is to meeting its intended purpose.

Priority requirements

Because requirements can vary from critical to important to desirable, simple percentage coverage may not tell you enough. It is better to rate requirements by priority, or risk, then measure coverage at each level. For example, priority level 1 requirements might be those that must be met for the system to be operational, priority 2 those that must be met for the system to be acceptable, level 3 those that are necessary but not critical, level 4 those that are desirable, and level 5 those that are cosmetic.

In this scheme, 100% successful coverage of level 1 and 2 requirements would be more important than 90% coverage of all requirements; even missing a single level 1 could render the system unusable. If you are strapped for time and resources (and who isn't), it is well worth the extra time to rate your requirements so you can gauge your progress and the application's readiness in terms of the successful coverage of priority requirements, instead of investing precious resources in low priority testing.

Exit criteria

Successful requirements coverage is a useful exit criteria for the test process. The criteria for releasing the application into production, for example, could be successful coverage of all level 1 through 3 priority requirements. By measuring the percentage of requirements tested versus the number of discovered errors, you could extrapolate the number of remaining errors given the remaining number of requirements.

But as with all metrics, don't use them to kid yourself. If you have only defined one requirement, 100% coverage is not meaningful!

Test case coverage

Test case coverage measures how many test cases have been executed. Again, be sure to differentiate between how many passed and how many were simply executed. In order to capture this metric, you need to have an accurate count of how many test cases have been defined, and you must log each test case that is executed and whether it passed or failed.

Predicting time to release

Test case coverage is useful for tracking progress during a test cycle. By telling you how many of the test cases have been executed in a given amount of time, you can more accurately estimate how much time is needed to test the remainder. Further, by comparing the rate at which errors have been uncovered, you can also make a more educated guess about how many remain to be found.

As a simple example, if you have executed 50% of your test cases in one week, you might predict that you will need another week to finish the cycle. If you have found ten errors so far, you could also estimate that there are that many again waiting to be found. By figuring in the rate at which errors are being corrected (more on this below), you could also extrapolate how long it will take to turn around fixes and complete another test cycle.

Defect ratio

The defect ratio measures how many errors are found as a percentage of tests executed. Since an error in the test may not necessarily be the result of a defect in the application, this measurement may not be derived directly from your error log; instead, it should be taken only after an error is confirmed to be a defect.

If you are finding one defect out of every ten tests, your defect ratio is 10%. Although it does not necessarily indicate the severity of the errors, this metric can help you predict how many errors are left to find based on the number of tests remaining to be executed.

Fix rate

Instead of a percentage, the fix rate measures how long it takes for a reported defect to be fixed. But before you know if a defect is fixed, it must be incorporated into a new build and tested to confirm that the defect is in fact corrected.

For this metric to be meaningful, you have to take into account any delays that are built into the process. For example, it may only take two hours to correct an error, but if a new build is created only weekly and the test cycle performed only once every two weeks, it may appear as though it takes three weeks to fix a defect. Therefore, measure the fix rate from the time the defect is reported until the corresponding fix is introduced into the source library.

Recurrence ratio

If a code change that is purported to fix a defect does not, or introduces yet another defect, you have a recurrence. The recurrence ratio is that percentage of fixes that fail to correct the defect. This is important because although your developers may be able to demonstrate a very fast turnaround on fixes, if the recurrence ratio is high you are spinning your wheels.

This ratio is extremely useful for measuring the quality of your unit and integration test practices. A high recurrence ratio means your developers are not thoroughly testing their work. This inefficiency may be avoided to some degree by providing the programmer with the test case that revealed the defect, so that he or she can verify that the code change in fact fixes the problem before resubmitting it for another round of testing.

So temper your fix rate with the recurrence ratio. It is better to have a slower fix rate than a high recurrence ratio: defects that recur cost everyone time and effort.

Post-release defects

A post-release defect is a defect found after the application has been released. It is the most serious type of defect, since it not only reflects a weakness in the test process, it also may have caused mayhem in production. For this reason, it is important to know not just how many of these there are, but what their severity is and how they could have been prevented.

As discussed earlier, requirements should be prioritized to determine their criticality. Post-release defects should likewise be rated. A priority 1 defect – one which renders the system unusable – should naturally get more attention than a cosmetic defect. Thus, a simple numerical count is not as meaningful.

Defect prevention

Once a defect is identified and rated, the next question should be when and how it could have been prevented. Note that this question is not about assessing blame, it is about continuous process improvement. If you don't learn from your mistakes, you are bound to repeat them.

Determining when a defect could have been prevented refers to what phase of the development cycle it should have been identified in. For example, a crippling performance problem caused by inadequate hardware resources should probably have been revealed during the planning phase; a missing feature or function should have been raised during the requirements or design phases.

In some cases, the defect may arise from a known requirement but schedule pressures during the test phase may have prevented the appropriate test cases from being developed and executed.

Continuous improvement

Whatever the phase, learn from the problem and institute measures to improve it. For example, when pressure arises during a later cycle to release the product without a thorough test phase, the known impact of doing so in a previous cycle can be weighed against the cost of delay. A known risk is easier to evaluate than an unknown one.

As to how a defect could be prevented, there are a wide range of possibilities. Although the most obvious means of preventing it from being released into production is to test for it, that is really not what this is about. Preventing a defect means keeping it from coming into existence, not finding it afterwards. It is far more expensive to find a defect than to prevent one. Defect prevention is about the entire development cycle: how can you better develop high quality applications in the future?

By keeping track of post-release defects as well as their root causes, you can not only measure the efficacy of your development and test processes, but also improve them.

26.6.1 Management reporting

Although there are many sophisticated metrics for measuring the test process, management is usually interested in something very simple: when will the application be ready? If you can't answer this question, you run the risk that the application will be released arbitrarily, based on schedules, instead of based on readiness. Few organizations can make open-ended commitments about release dates.

Once management has invested time and money in test automation, they will also want to know what their return was. This return could take three forms: savings in money, time, and/or improved quality. By assuring that you have these measurements at your fingertips, you can increase the odds of keeping management committed to the test automation effort.

Estimated time to release

Although you can never precisely predict when or even if an application will be defect-free, you can make an educated guess based on what you do know. The best predictor of readiness for release is the requirements coverage as affected by the defect ratio, fix rate and recurrence ratio.

For example, if after four weeks you are 80% through with 100 test cases with a 20% defect ratio, a two day fix rate and a 5% recurrence ratio, you can estimate time to release as:

---

4 weeks = 80%   20% defects = 16
1 week = 20%   5% recurrence = 1
2 day fix rate = 34 days (At 5 days per week this is 7 weeks approx)
One final full regression test = 5 weeks
Total: 1 week + 7 weeks + 5 weeks = 13 weeks

Saving money

There are two kinds of savings from automated testing. The first is the productivity that comes from repeating manual tests. Even though you may not actually cut staff, you can get more done in less time. To measure this saving – the amount you would have spent to get the same level of test coverage – measure the time it takes to manually execute an average test, then automate that test and measure the time to execute it.

Divide the automated time into the manual test time. If it takes two hours to perform the test manually but it will playback in thirty minutes, you will get a productivity factor of 4. Next, execute a complete automated test cycle and measure the total elapsed time, then multiply that times the productivity factor. In this example, a twelve hour automated test cycle saves 48 hours of manual test time.

So, if you have four releases per year and three test iterations per release, you are saving (4 times 3 times 48 hours) 576 hours per year. Multiply that by your cost per man hour; if it's $50, then you are saving $28,800 per year.

Saving time

Getting the application into the market or back into production faster also saves the company time. In our above example, you are shaving 3.6 weeks off the release time (3 iterations times 48 hours/40 hours per week). This is almost a month of time savings for each release. If the reason for the release is to correct errors, that extra time could translate into significant productivity.

Higher quality

It is hard to measure the impact of higher quality: you can't really measure the amount of money you *aren't* spending. If you do a thorough job of testing and prevent defects from entering into production, you have saved money by not incurring downtime or overhead from the error.

Unfortunately, few companies know the cost to fix an error. The best way to tell if you are making progress is when the post-release defect rate declines.

Better coverage

Even if you can't tell exactly what it is saving the company, just measure the increasing number of test cases that are executed for each release. If you assume that more tests mean fewer errors in production, this expanded coverage has value.

26.6.2 Historical trends

In all of these metrics, it is very useful to keep historical records so that you can measure trends. This may be as simple as keeping the numbers in a spreadsheet and plotting them graphically. Remember to also keep the numbers that went into the metric: not just test case coverage, for example, but the total number of test cases defined as well as executed that went into the calculation.

The reason historical trends are important is that they highlight progress – or, perish the thought, regression. For example, the number of requirements and test cases which have been defined for an application should be growing steadily. This indicates that enhancements, as well as problems found in production, are being added as new requirements and test cases, insuring that your test library is keeping pace with the application. A declining recurrence ratio might indicate that programming practices or unit testing has improved.

Another reason to analyze historical trends is that you can analyze the impact of changes in the process. For example, instituting design reviews or code walkthroughs might not show immediate results, but later might be reflected as a reduced defect ratio.

Finally, remember that:

Quality is Everyone's Business

© Linda Hayes, 1995.

26.7 More information about the Handbook

If you are familiar with the original *Handbook*, or would like to know what is contained in the full *Handbook*, Table 26.2 shows the sections that we have included and excluded in this extract. The rationale for the parts excluded is outlined below.

From the Introduction, we have excluded the terminology section because we have defined our own terminology in this book.

Table 26.2 Sections included and excluded in this extract.

Section	Included	Excluded
Introduction	Why automate? When not to automate How not to automate Setting realistic expectations Getting and keeping management commitment	Terminology
Fundamentals of test automation	Context Synchronization Documentation	Maintainability Optimization Independence Modularity
The test framework		All
Test library management		All
Selecting a test automation approach		All
The test automation process	Introduction The test team	Test automation plan Planning the test cycle Test suite design Test cycle design
Test execution	Analyzing results	Test log Error log
Test metrics	All	
Management reporting	All	

In the Fundamentals section, we have selected three subsections, on Context, Synchronization, and Documentation. The other aspects, maintainability of testware, optimization (scaling up), independence of the tests, and modularity, are covered by the body of this book.

'The test framework' is the name given to the testware architecture, which is similar to the one described in Chapter 5 of this book.

'Test library management' covers configuration management topics, which are also covered in Chapter 5.

'Selecting a test automation approach' introduces three scripting models, which we describe in Chapter 3. Capture/playback is most similar to what we call linear scripting, but with elements of shared scripts. Variable capture/playback replaces constants with variables and so is similar to the data-driven scripting technique. Variable capture/variable playback is most similar to our keyword-driven scripting technique.

In the remaining sections, we have included the sections on the test team members, some useful ideas on inaccurate results and their causes, the summary set of metrics, and some final thoughts on reporting progress to management.

Thanks to Linda Hayes for permission to reproduce these sections of the *Test Automated Testing Handbook*.

CHAPTER TWENTY-SEVEN

Building maintainable GUI tests

Chip Groder

27.1 Introduction and background

As computer applications have become more and more sophisticated, equally sophisticated graphical user interfaces (GUIs) have been implemented, providing increased ease of use for the customer, and hopefully more profit for the vendor. Like any software, the GUI code must be tested. In the late 1980s, commercial GUI test tools became available that allowed engineers to write test scripts that manipulate the GUI in the same way that a human would use it.

Cadence Design Systems, Inc. is the largest provider of electronic design automation (EDA) software and services, and we were an early adopter of automated test tools. As newer versions of our EDA tools were produced with GUIs, we purchased automated GUI test tools and used them to write automated tests. Our rationale was typical of companies investing in test automation: since manual testing is expensive, we should put the effort into building automated tests so that we can run them repeatedly, then we can invest in testing the new features rather than retesting the old. During the early 1990s Cadence engineering and quality groups made substantial investments in building automated GUI Test Suites for a number of our products. Without exception, these tests were abandoned as soon as the next major release of the product entered the testing phase. In each case it was found that the effort required to modify the Test Suites to work with the new version of the product was far more than anticipated, to the point where it was deemed cheaper to throw out the existing tests and start over. While in hindsight this failure was due to the lack of an adequate methodology for designing and building GUI Test Suites, at the time the blame was heaped on the test tool, and the development and testing groups became very negative towards GUI test tools. GUI testing reverted to the state it was in before the test tools – manual testing done late in the development cycle.

In early 1996, we formed a group at Cadence whose charter was to procure, develop, and deploy test tools and the methodologies to use them effectively. One of the first tasks we tackled was to get automated GUI testing 'back on track.'

The methodology described in this chapter was developed over a four-year period by the author using best practices learned through experience, through conversations with the test tool vendors, and by talking to other professionals who had tackled the same problem at their companies. It sets forth a scheme to reduce test maintenance costs to as low a level as possible, even at the expense of higher initial test development costs. This methodology has been deployed throughout the software test organizations at Cadence Design Systems, and has been implemented at other companies with good results. It deals specifically with planning, designing, and building robust, maintainable automated GUI Test Suites.

27.1.1 Definitions

In this chapter we make use of the following terms:

AUT (Application Under Test). The application, product, subsystem, or component that is being tested.

GUI. An interface that provides a way of interacting with the computer by means of a graphical interface that organizes information in windows, and allows for keyboard and mouse input – in other words, the Windows, Motif, or Mac interface that we all know and love.

Test case. The smallest unit of a test. A test case is a subroutine that tests a single aspect (or function) of the application. A test case could also be a manual procedure, but it only tests one function of the AUT. The function can range in size from relatively simple, such as insuring that the *Apply* button performs the proper function in a dialog box, to very complex operations such as executing an entire ASIC design flow, utilizing several products to simulate real-world use.

Test program. An executable program that contains one or more test cases, usually ones that test a high-level feature of the application (e.g. searching for a given text string). The test program is the smallest executable test entity. In GUI testing, you will typically execute a test program that in turn executes many test cases that test a specific area of the application.

Test Suite. A collection of test programs. A Test Suite may test the entire application, or only one of its subsystems. Note that we generally use the term 'Test Suite' when talking about a collection of test cases. We use the term 'test program' only where we want to draw a distinction.

Why go to all that work? Why is GUI testing different from other forms of automated testing? Shouldn't an experienced test engineer be able to produce good GUI tests without having to embark on some specialized course of study?

The answer to these questions lies in the nature of GUIs and the way that they are developed and maintained.

1. The GUI tends to change more often than the underlying functionality that it invokes – as new features are added to the application, the interface is frequently reorganized to present the new data in a coherent way. This means that maintenance becomes more important, since it becomes *likely* that new versions will break existing GUI tests. In contrast, the underlying functionality tends to remain relatively static; features may be added and fixes made, but the external appearance tends to remain the same.

2. GUI code is complex – there are always a lot of ways to accomplish a given operation, which in turn means more things to test.

3. GUI test tools are themselves complex. Most GUI test tools on the market have their own scripting language that is as robust (and difficult to learn) as BASIC or C. GUI test tools run as a separate process from the AUT, which means that synchronizing the script execution speed with the speed of the AUT is required, a difficult job at times, requiring different techniques for different situations. GUI test tools also have to be able to manipulate and query the set of common GUI controls such as list boxes, push buttons, edit fields, and menus, resulting in a large number of runtime functions accessible to the script writer.

4. Modern GUI test tools provide a means to handle the common windows controls in an abstract manner, using semantics related to the function of the control (such as `button_press("OK"); `), but functions to deal with custom controls are very primitive, often requiring the use of x and y screen coordinates. Since most applications use some number of custom controls, the job of the test writer is made more difficult as the number of custom controls increases.

27.2 Cost drivers

The rationale for building automated tests is that although they are initially more expensive than the equivalent manual testing,[1] automated tests can be executed very cheaply and will thus result in cost savings with repeated runs over time. This frees scarce engineering resources to develop new tests rather than endlessly covering the same ground.

---

[1] The author is not aware of any formal studies that quantify the cost differences, but personal experience and conversations with others in the field suggest that automated tests are three to ten times more expensive to build than performing the same test manually, and usually closer to ten.

It is our experience that, when making the decision to invest in test automation, the cost of test maintenance is often minimized or is left entirely out of the equation. Test maintenance costs, as we will see, are the biggest single factor in the cost equation for automated testing. In our opinion, the failure to plan for maintenance and account for the costs is the single biggest reason for the failure of test automation projects.

If we look at the costs of manual testing, cost over the life of the product can be expressed in the following equation:

$$Cost = CostOfOneSession \times NumberOfSessionsPerRelease \times NumberOfReleases$$

Note that we've made some simplifying assumptions, namely that the cost of a single test session doesn't change from one session to the next, and that the number of testing sessions is constant from one release to the next. Now look at the equivalent equation for the life cycle costs of automated tests:

$$Cost = CostToBuild + (CostToRunOneSession \times NumberOfSessionsPerRelease +$$
$$MaintenanceCost \times NumberOfReleases)$$

In deriving the above equation, we took *CostOfOneSession* from the manual test equation and split it into three components: *CostToBuild*, *CostToRunOneSession*, and *MaintenanceCost*. Since automated tests are relatively cheap to run, *CostToRunOneSession* adds little to the total cost; the major costs are in building the Test Suite and updating it to track changes made to the AUT.

The important thing to recognize is that the cost to build the Test Suite is a one-time cost, and is additive to the total, whereas maintenance of the Test Suite happens each time the software is updated, and is therefore multiplicative. Thus the test maintenance costs have a much greater impact on the total cost of testing than the costs of building the tests in the first place. A successful automation strategy must seek to minimize the cost of maintenance even if it means raising the cost to build the tests. This is the overarching goal of the Cadence GUI test methodology.

27.2.1 A few words about record/playback

Some GUI test tool vendors promote a *record/playback* (also known as capture replay) methodology as the design center for using their tools. Building tests using record/playback involves invoking the test tool in 'recording mode' and then manipulating the application such that some useful action is performed. The test tool captures the actions and records them in a script, which can then be replayed to drive the application automatically.

These vendors promote record/playback as a low cost way to generate a lot of test code as well as being a very approachable method for new users. It is clear from the cost equations above that optimizing test creation is a good idea only if it does not increase the cost of maintenance. Schemes that optimize test creation at the expense of test maintenance will actually increase the life cycle costs rather than reduce them.

Unfortunately, record/playback is false economy. While it is possible for people with no coding experience to produce a lot of test code, that code has *none* of the attributes of properly engineered tests described in the next section. The use of record/playback as a design methodology was the reason that the test automation projects at Cadence failed in the early 1990s. *Every automated GUI testing effort prior to April 1996 had been abandoned due to maintainability issues with the test code.* The test tool was unfairly blamed for much of the problem, when the reality was that the record/playback development methodology was optimizing the wrong part of the cost equation.

That being said, the record feature of most modern GUI test tools is useful, but you should think of record/playback as the equivalent of the cut/paste feature of your favorite word processor. The record feature is a handy way to quickly capture sequences of keystrokes and mouse clicks and insert them into your code. You must accept the fact that, like cut/paste, you will have to go in and tweak the pasted code in order to integrate it properly into the test. When used in this manner, record/playback can be a timesaver, but remember that writing entire tests using record/playback is like trying to write this book using only cut/paste. It is highly unlikely that you will produce anything worthwhile.

27.2.2 Requirements for automated GUI tests

In our view, once you decide to build an automated GUI Test Suite, you have embarked on a software engineering project. Building automated GUI tests *is* software engineering, and requires the same skills and discipline as writing the AUT itself.

Since the GUI Test Suite is to be used across multiple product releases, it should satisfy some basic requirements:

- it must be *maintainable*, because the next release of the application under test will render some of the test cases obsolete, require modification of others, and require building new test cases for new functionality;
- it must be *modular*, because we can't afford the situation where a change to one part of the Test Suite causes tests to start failing in other areas;
- it must be *robust*, because we don't want a small change in the application to require a major change to the Test Suite;
- it must be *well documented*, since in most cases the engineer who built the Test Suite will not be the same one who has to update it for the next release;
- to the extent possible, it should be built of *reusable components*, because we don't want those who come after us to have to reinvent the wheel.

Corporate organizational structure may place requirements on the Test Suite design. Many larger development efforts have a Software Quality

Assurance (SQA) group that is organizationally separate from the product development group. In this model, the development group is usually responsible for performing unit testing and first-level integration testing on the software, and the SQA group is usually responsible for doing system-level testing. If GUI Test Suites are to be useful in this type of environment, the SQA group should be able to leverage work done by the development group, and vice versa. In fact, in many cases it is the SQA group that pioneers the use of GUI test tools for system test, and the development groups adopt them for unit test once they see the tools are being successfully used. In this situation, well-written tests and a common methodology are vital to insuring that the tests are transportable across organizational lines.

27.3 Test planning and design

Good test planning is the foundation of successful automated testing effort. Everyone knows that you must plan the testing effort, just as you must plan any other aspect of a software development project, but knowing is not doing. In the GUI testing space, it is tempting to skimp on the planning stage, since (i) testing is supposed to be easy (just record some scripts and play them back), (ii) the test code doesn't ship to customers, and (iii) 'we're a little behind schedule so we need to save some time.'

Rushing into the implementation phase without devoting time to planning and design is false economy; you will end up doing your planning and design work 'on the fly' as you implement the tests. The problem is that the quality of the planning and design will be much poorer than if you addressed them separately. It's like trying to build a house with no plans; if you manage to complete it, you probably won't end up with the house you set out to build, no matter how skillful a carpenter you may be. It is important to treat test planning as a separate intellectual exercise from building the tests:

- test planning and design is hard to do well;
- learning the test tool is harder than it looks;
- writing and debugging the test code is hard.

Don't try to do them all at once.

27.3.1 The dual purpose of test documentation

Good test documentation has to fulfill two functions: it must be a *communications vehicle* as well as a *blueprint for development*. We are more interested in the content than the format of the document(s). Some organizations produce a single document that contains all aspects of the test plan; others produce a test specification that addresses the high-level aspects and a more detailed test design document. In this chapter we use the latter convention. The test specification is to testing as the functional specification is to the application, and the test design document contains similar detail to the detailed design document for the application.

A test specification has to communicate a host of decisions concerning testing scope, schedule, test environment, staffing needs, and risks to management, SQA groups, development groups, and other organizations that need to know. In some circumstances, the test specifications may be given to customers or others outside the company. The value of a test specification lies in insuring that the testing effort is conducted in accordance with company policy and as a checklist to insure that all the necessary activities have been factored into the project and schedule. Most companies have developed their own test specification templates, and projects can 'fill in the blanks.' There are many good books on the subject of software testing, and any of them can provide you with a good template, or enough information so that you can build your own.

One good template is contained in IEEE Standard 829 – IEEE Standard for Test Documentation. Boris Beizer (1984) gives a different template:

Section A – General and Introductory
    A1 – Generalized verbiage and introduction to test plan documents.
    A2 – Glossary of terms used.
    A3 – Reference list to specifications, subsidiary specifications, design memoranda, correspondence, and so on.
    A4 – Test design standards and conventions.
    A5 – Test running order, procedures, summary sheets, and control sheets.
Section B – Test Data Base and Code
    B1 – General.
    B2 – Test data base documentation and cross-reference. One subsection for each variant data base.
    B3 – Support programs or code documentation for test generators, drivers, and load generators.
    B4 – Test configuration specification. Specification of hardware and software configurations needed for different tests.
    B5 – Test tools, hardware and software.
    B6 – Verification hardware and software.
    B7 – Miscellaneous support hardware and software used to generate and execute the tests.
Section C – The Actual Test Specifications.

The test design functions as a blueprint – a detailed description of exactly *what* will (and won't) be tested, and *how* each test case will be implemented. In its simplest form, this type of test plan can simply be a list of test cases with information such as the test name, the test purpose, the test method, and a short description of the pass/fail criteria. A test case design should contain at least the following elements:

- *Test name* or *test ID* – a unique identifier for the test.
- *Test purpose* – a one- or two-line description of what the test is supposed to accomplish.
- *Test method* – a description of the steps that the test will take. It is not necessary to go into great detail, but the steps should be clear enough so that a human could perform the test manually given the information provided.
- *Pass/fail criteria* – one or two lines describing how to tell if the test worked.

The following example illustrates the design for a test that checks for proper error handling when trying to save an empty buffer in the Windows Notepad application:

```
Testcase:  NP_SaveEmpty
Purpose:   Verify that trying to save an empty buffer causes an
           error
Method:    1) Insure that Notepad is up and running
           2) Use the File/New menu item to erase the text
              buffer
           3) Use the File/Save menu item to try to save the
              buffer
           4) Verify that an error message box appears
Pass/Fail: The test succeeds if an error message box appears.
```

Regardless of how you format the test documentation, it is important to take the test planning down to the level described above. This has several advantages:

1. It provides a basis for intelligent review of the test plan. Given that there is never enough time to do all the testing we'd like to do, the team must be able to make informed trade-offs based on a complete view of the tasks to be done. Our experience is that surprising facts always come to light at test design reviews, and the participants always leave the review feeling that real work has been accomplished.

2. It provides a basis for deciding what test cases to automate. Everyone starts a test automation project with the hopes that everything can be automated. While today's GUI test tools are generally mature and robust products, not everything can be automated. More importantly, not everything can be automated cost effectively. Some operations (e.g. printing) are best left as manual tests. Write the test design without consideration for whether or not the test can be automated. After the design has been reviewed and accepted, segregate out those tests that

can't or shouldn't be automated. Use the resulting collection of test cases as the basis for a manual testing checklist.

3. It provides the basis for the internal test case documentation. Test cases need to be well documented if they are to be maintainable. Once the test design has been reviewed and accepted, we put comment characters at the start of each line and use each as the header comments in the actual test code.

4. The GUI test design process finds bugs! This is perhaps the most surprising and powerful argument in favor of doing detailed test design. It is discussed in detail in the next section.

27.3.2 Finding bugs during the test design process

As we started writing very detailed GUI test designs we noticed a strange (but not unwelcome) side effect: we were discovering bugs in the application even before we started writing test code. After some reflection, we realized that the phenomenon was due to the way that today's GUIs are designed and implemented, coupled with the timing of the writing of the test design document.

The process used to build GUIs has undergone a significant change over the past few years. The advent of modern 'GUI builders' allows an engineer to build a working GUI very quickly and to make significant changes to the interface functionality in less than an hour. As a result, it is almost always true that there is a working GUI in existence at the point where detailed test plans are being developed, especially since the writing of the detailed test design is almost always delayed until the GUI 'stabilizes'.[2] The test designer almost always has the working GUI to use as a reference when writing the plan. It is natural, then, to use the application to verify the test steps required. You are doing a form of manual testing at the same time that you are writing the test design document! For new products, this is usually the first time anyone has systematically examined the user interface (UI), and given the complexity, it is not surprising that many defects are discovered.

This close coupling of manual testing and automated test design is the reason for the high level of defect detection, and is a powerful argument in favor of doing detailed design documents for automated GUI test projects. For GUI testing, the technique contradicts the accepted software engineering practice of writing test specifications and designs from the application's functional specification. It also contradicts the widely accepted view that 'if you commit to building an automated GUI Test Suite, don't expect it to pay off during the current release.' There is additional, political benefit to these

---

[2] I maintain that for the vast majority of commercial software developed today, 'the GUI is the specification.' Almost no one produces a detailed GUI specification beforehand, because for about the same amount of effort you can produce the actual interface, and modify it in minutes if need be.

techniques. If you are tasked with writing a test design, you get 'extra credit' for all the defects that you discover. On the other hand, if you are tasked with doing manual testing on the GUI, by documenting your actions in the format described above, you get 'extra credit' for producing a test automation document. This is an excellent way to make progress on automating tests even when the schedule is so tight that actually building the automated tests is not possible.

We have tracked the number of defects found during the design process, and have discovered that on average, we report one defect for every eight test cases designed. Table 27.1 shows the defect numbers for four GUI test automation projects in which the author participated.

Table 27.1 Metrics from four projects: test cases and defects found.

	Total test cases documented	Total defects reported[a]	Defects found during design	Defects found during execution[b]
Project A	77	7	5	2
Project B	50 (approx.)	13	11	2
Project C	107	12	12	0
Project D	186	30	27	3

[a] In all cases, the numbers represent 'real' defects, where the engineer responsible for the code agreed that there really was a problem that needed to be fixed.

[b] Not all of the planned test cases were implemented for projects C and D, so the numbers in this column may be a bit low. We believe that the number of bugs detected during execution will be much lower than the number found during the planning process.

As you can see, the overwhelming majority of defects were discovered during the test design phase. It is interesting to note that approximately half of the defects were what we call *testable* defects; that is, defects that were discovered as a result of designing a test case to specifically test for that condition. An example of this is a test designed to insure that alphabetic characters are not accepted in an edit field that is supposed to accept numeric input only. During the design of the test case it might be discovered that the edit field would accept alphanumeric characters, causing unpredictable results. Had the test been implemented and run, it would have detected the error and reported a failure. The other half of the defects reported were *incidental* in nature; that is, where a defect was discovered while designing a test case, but the test case was not designed to detect that particular error. An example of this type of defect is a spelling error in one of the labels in a dialog box. We were not designing a test to detect spelling errors, but we happened to pick up the error while looking at the window.

The defects reported range from trivial (misspelled words in a dialog box) to serious (an AUT crash). We have not kept metrics on the severity of the problems found, but we estimate that at least 10% of the problems found are serious.

Once the test specification and design are complete and the documents have been reviewed, it is time to start building the tests. Recall that the reason for putting all this effort into producing well-engineered Test Suites is to satisfy some fundamental requirements:

- they must be *maintainable*
- they must be *modular*
- they must be *robust*
- they must be well *documented*
- they should be built of *reusable components.*

It is possible to derive a set of attributes for tests that satisfy the above requirements, and design tests that possess these attributes.

27.4.1 A test case is independent

Each test case must take care of its own set-up, verification, and clean-up. During the set-up phase, the test case drives the application to a state where the actual test can then be performed. During the verification phase, the actual testing is performed, the results evaluated and a pass/fail status is determined. During the clean-up phase, the set-up is 'undone' and the application is returned to a known *base state,* ready for the next test.

If a test case were to rely on the results of a previous test case, a failure of the upstream test case would most likely cause a failure in the downstream test case. These cascading errors make it difficult to determine what application function was at fault. It also introduces an implied ordering of the test cases: if test case B is to be successful, then test case A must be executed before it. This ordering is rarely documented, and an innocent reordering of the test case execution in a subsequent test run can cause a long string of failures in a Test Suite that ran perfectly the previous day.

Test cases should be able to execute in any order. This allows a maintainer to pick and choose a subset of the total test cases to execute without having to worry about interdependencies between test cases. In practice, this is somewhat easier said than done. For applications whose functions modify a complex global state, such as an application that reads and writes to a database, beginning from 'ground-zero' for each test case would be far too expensive. In such instances, group the test cases together such that each of the groups relies on its own specific pre-existing state to conserve set-up time. Document the interdependencies carefully, so that future maintainers of the Test Suite will be aware of the dependencies.

27.4.2 A test case has a single purpose

A test case should only test one 'thing.' This keeps the test case code as short as possible and relatively simple, which makes it easy to understand, debug, and maintain. It also means that there are only two possible outcomes when the test case is executed: pass or fail. Test cases should always do sufficient checking to be able to return a pass/fail status. This makes it easy to determine the outcome of a test run, since no interpretation of the results is necessary.

Single-purpose test cases make it trivially easy to pinpoint the application function at fault in the event the test case fails. This implies that a Test Suite is comprised of many smaller test cases rather than fewer large ones.

27.4.3 A failed test case should not cause others to fail

If a test case fails due to an unexpected error, the application is by definition in an unknown state. The application is out of synch with what the test case is expecting. When such failures happen, a well-behaved test will log the failure and abort, and will do a best-effort attempt to reset the application to a known base state. The use of a generalized recovery procedure is covered in a later section.

The test tool should isolate test case failures such that an unexpected error in a test case doesn't cause the whole script to abort. All modern GUI test tools provide this functionality.

27.4.4 A test case is well documented

As mentioned previously, one of the advantages of writing a detailed test design is that you can take the test case description from the document, put comment characters at the beginning of each line, and use it for header comments in the test case code. Of course, you should also include in-line comments in the code to describe the logic. As a general rule, err on the side of writing too many comments, rather than too few.

Together, these attributes address all of the requirements listed above.

27.5   Encapsulated test set-up

If lots of small test cases are a good thing to have, and if each test case has to be independent of the others, how can we manage the complex set-up that is required? Won't that add a lot of code to the test case?

Encapsulated test set-up routines are a set of subroutines that allow a test case to drive the application to a state where the test can be performed, while drastically reducing the amount of duplicated code, with a corresponding improvement in the maintainability of the Test Suite. Consider an example where we want to test the functionality of a dialog for setting font information in a word processor. There may well be a large collection of tests that exercise the various options in the font dialog. If each of these tests is built using the record/playback paradigm, there will be a large amount of duplicate set-up code in the test cases, because each test has to load a text file, possibly select a region of text, and then bring up the font dialog. Now suppose the developer changes the mechanism by which the font dialog is invoked. All tests that use the old invocation mechanism will break, and the test maintainer will have to change every test case containing that code, a job that could take many hours. When encapsulated set-up routines are used, there will be only one subroutine that will contain the logic for the old invocation mechanism, and therefore only one routine that will have to be fixed. With encapsulated set-up routines, a job of hours is reduced to a few minutes.

The power of these set-up routines lies in the fact that they are arranged in a hierarchy. A test case simply makes a call to its designated set-up routine, and on return, the application will be in the expected state.[3] If an unrecoverable error occurs in the set-up code, the test case will abort.

The easiest way to understand encapsulated set-up is to view your application as a state machine, with each of the windows being one of the states. We'll illustrate by using part of the Windows Notepad application (with the old V3.1 interface) as an example. We start in the null state, as illustrated in Figure 27.1. When Notepad is first invoked, the main window appears and waits for you to do something. We can say the application is now in state main. If you then select the *File > Save As* menu item, the *Save As* dialog will appear and wait for input, and we can say the application is in state save_as. If we then click the *Network* button in the lower right corner of the *Save As* dialog, the *Network* dialog will appear, and we can say that the application is in state network. In addition, we can say that in order to get to state network, you must first be in state save_as, and in order to get to state save_as, you must first be in state main. We also know the specific set of actions that will drive the application from one state to the next. To get from the null state (Notepad not running) to main, we would simply start up Notepad by running C:\WINDOWS\NOTEPAD.EXE. To get from main to save_as, you pull down the *File* menu and pick the *Save As* menu item.

To implement the encapsulated set-up routines, write a set of subroutines, one for each state transition which drives the application from the parent state to the new state. For our Notepad example, we need three set-up routines. The first, which we'll call *MainSetup*, is responsible for invoking Notepad *if it is not already running*, which handles the transition from state null to state main. The second, *SaveAsSetup*, is responsible for bringing up the *Save As* dialog box, handling the transition from state main to state save_as. The third, *NetworkSetup*, handles the transition from state save_as to state network. The power of encapsulated set-up routines comes from the fact that, like the windows they invoke, the routines form a hierarchy. Among other things, this provides the ability to restart the application after a crash.

In Figure 27.2, we are executing a test case that tests some feature of the *Network* dialog. Obviously, in order to test that functionality, the *Network* dialog must be invoked. The first thing the test case code

[3] This concept is a generalization of QA Partner's *appstate* functionality.

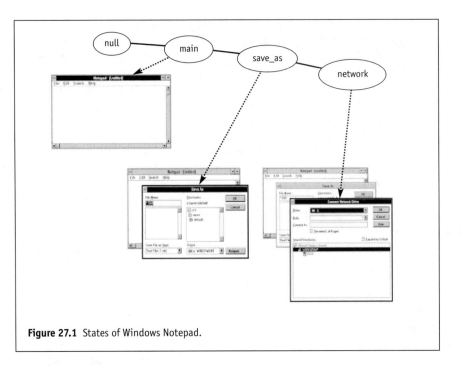

Figure 27.1 States of Windows Notepad.

(bottom right in Figure 27.2) does is to call its set-up routine, *NetworkSetup*. Because the application must be in state save_as before it can be in state network, the first thing *NetworkSetup* does is to call *SaveAsSetup*. Since Notepad must be in state main before it can be in state save_as, *SaveAsSetup* first calls *MainSetup*.

MainSetup first checks to see if Notepad is running. If it is not, *MainSetup* starts Notepad and then returns. If Notepad is running, *MainSetup* runs the *Recover* routine to insure that Notepad is in the base state. Recovery and base states are discussed in the next section.

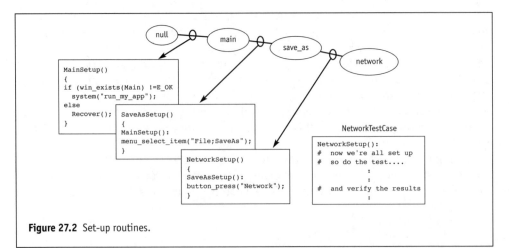

Figure 27.2 Set-up routines.

When *MainSetup* returns, control returns to the *SaveAsSetup* routine.
Notepad is now in state main. *SaveAsSetup* then uses the *File > Save As*
menu item to bring up the *Save As* dialog. The routine then returns, and
control is transferred back to the *NetworkSetup* routine. Notepad is now in
state save_as.

NetworkSetup now brings up the *Network* dialog by clicking the
Network button, then it returns, and control is transferred back to the test
case. Notepad is now in state network, which is where we need to be in
order to perform the test.

The power of encapsulated set-up can best be illustrated in the way a Test
Suite will recover from an application crash. Suppose there is a bug in
Notepad that causes it to crash during test case 12. The test tool will detect the
error and duly log it as a failure, but what happens to test case 13? Using
encapsulated set-up, test 13 will run normally. The set-up routine for test 13
will call its parent window's set-up routine, which will call *its* parent window's
set-up routine, and so on up the chain until finally *MainSetup* is called.
MainSetup will check to see if Notepad is in the right state and find that it
isn't running (because of the crash). *MainSetup* will restart Notepad, the set-
up will proceed normally, and test case 13 will pass or fail on its own merits.

27.5.1 Passing parameters to set-up routines

A set-up routine is just another subroutine as far as the test tool is concerned, and so you can pass parameters to it. This is most useful when a
dialog box contains property pages (also known as tab controls). You can
have a single set-up routine that brings up the dialog, and pass it a parameter that specifies which tab is to be activated.

27.5.2 Standardized error recovery

There are many things that can cause a test case to fail besides a bug in the
AUT. There could be a bug in the test code, an environmental error (e.g. no
disk space, network link down), a change made to the application, excessive machine load that causes timing errors, or a host of other reasons.

When an unexpected error occurs, the test case gets out of synch with
the state of the application. When this happens, we would like the test tool
to detect the fact that something is wrong and then:

1. log the fact that there is an error, including traceback information in the
   log so that we can tell where the error occurred;
2. abort the test case, since by definition, the application is in an unknown state;
3. attempt to get the application back to a known state so that subsequent
   test cases won't automatically fail. This may include restarting the
   application after a crash;
4. resume execution with the next test case.

All modern GUI test tools have built-in capability to detect an error, log it (with traceback information), and pick up again with the next test case. The problem that arises is that the application is now in an unknown state, and unless some action is taken to reset the AUT to a known state, subsequent test cases are likely to fail.

27.5.2.1 The base state

When thinking about error recovery, you must consider *where* you want to recover *to*. That place is known as the *base state* for the application. For the majority of applications, this state is where the application is running, is not minimized, has only its main window open, and is active. This corresponds to the normal state of the AUT immediately after it is started, state main in our Notepad example above.

This implies that there should be a routine that has the capability of examining the current state of the application and closing all windows except the main window. If such a routine can be designed, it can be run as required, and the application will be in the correct state and ready for the next test.

27.5.2.2 The recover routine

Recall that in our discussion of set-up routines, the *MainSetup* routine ran a routine called *Recover* if the application's main window existed (i.e. the application was running). Automatic recovery is run at this point to insure that the application is at the base state when the *MainSetup* routine exits, insuring that the subsequent set-up routines will work correctly.

The algorithm for an automatic recovery routine is as follows:

```
if the application's main window exists      // if the app didn't crash
  while the topmost window is not the main window
    close_the_window()                       // keep closing windows
till
                                             // we get to the main
window
```

The algorithm for closing an arbitrary application window is as follows:

```
close_the_window()
{
  send an ALT+F4 to the window
  if the window is still there             // if ALT+F4 didn't work
    if there is a File->Exit menu item
      use it to close the window
    else if there is a File->Quit menu item
      use it to close the window
    else if there is a File->Close menu item
      use it to close the window
    else if there is a Cancel button
      use it to close the window
    else if there is a Close button
      use it to close the window
```

```
    else if there is an Exit button
       use it to close the window
    else if there is a Quit button
       use it to close the window
    else if there is an enabled OK button
       use it to close the window
    else send an <ENTER> to the window    // try the default control
  if the window is still there            // nothing worked, give up
     log an error and exit
}
```

Note that this algorithm is not guaranteed to work in all cases. First, there is a finite list of actions that the algorithm will try. If the window is not dismissed by any of those actions, then the recovery action will fail. Note that if none of the actions dismisses the window, your window doesn't conform to accepted design guidelines, so you have a different problem on your hands.

Some people feel that this is imposing too much overhead, that too much work is being done, and that performance will be lousy as a result. While there certainly is additional overhead with this method, it is minimal, usually less than one second per test case. Remember also that while fast performance is certainly an issue for the application, it rarely is an issue for the Test Suite. Most people really don't care if the Test Suite takes 7 hours or 6 hours to run – the important thing is to test the application completely. The cost savings realized from increased maintainability and modularity of the Test Suite more than make up for the cost of the extra run time.

There *are* instances where this doesn't hold true. Whenever moving from one state to another is extremely expensive, you don't want to execute that state change for every test case. A good example is when performing some operation causes a connect to a database on a network server. This is typically expensive in that it may take many seconds to establish the link. In this situation, it makes sense to build a custom recovery module that only recovers to the state after the link was established, and use it for all tests that require the connection to the database. Note that your recovery code has to be clever enough to fall back to the base state if the network link fails for some reason.

27.5.3 GUI object mapping

Modern test tools are able to understand what is going on within the application's GUI by querying the GUI to determine the contents or state of objects on the screen. In order for the user's test script to be able to do this, it is necessary to distinguish between the objects and then to refer to them by some sort of ID.

It is possible to reference specific objects in more than one way, since there are various combinations of object attributes that can be used to uniquely identify an object. The *class* of an object (e.g. button, list box, menu item), its *title* or *label* (e.g. Cancel), and its *screen coordinates* are all ways of identifying objects in the GUI, as well as internal identifiers assigned by the GUI. Identification by title is a common and intuitive way to think about the ID, and most tools allow you to use this method for objects that have a title or label associated with them. For example, we would like to refer to the *Cancel* button as 'Cancel' in our test cases and have the test tool know which object we are referring to. This is straightforward and easy to understand, but not all objects have title text associated with them, and worse, the test tool often can't see custom objects because the tool can only know about the standard objects defined for the GUI. In this instance, the use of internal identifiers or screen coordinates will get the job done, but it is very prone to breakage, besides looking ugly. A classic example is when the developer decides that the *Cancel* buttons should really be named *Close.* The test maintainer is now faced with examining every test case and changing all occurrences of *Cancel* to *Close.*

By introducing a level of indirection into the object naming process, we can insulate the Test Suite from the impact of a whole class of changes to the GUI. We can associate a *logical name* with the attributes needed to uniquely identify the object. Using our example, we assign the object attribute 'Cancel' with the logical name *Cancel.* Then we use the logical name in the test case code. Later on, if the *Cancel* button is changed to *Close,* we simply modify the mapping to equate the logical name *Cancel* with the new attribute value 'Close,' and the code works as before. The actual implementation of this scheme is more complex than this, and many of the currently available GUI test tools support this feature.

GUI object mapping is a powerful way to make your Test Suite more maintainable, but it can cause problems during test development if your mapping files are not complete. You should view the GUI mapping files as the foundation of your Test Suite, and take pains to insure that all the objects are identified and that they have intuitive, consistent names before you start writing test code. If you don't, you'll pay for it later. In addition, if several test engineers are involved in building test cases, put the GUI mapping files under configuration management control early, as they will be 'high contention' files.

If you are using a tool that does not provide built-in support for GUI object mapping, you can fake it by defining a set of constants that map each GUI object to an attribute that identifies it. Constructing the mapping files is a tedious process, but the effort will pay off in reduced maintenance costs over the life of the Test Suite.

27.6 Putting it all together

The following is a brief checklist of the steps you should take to implement the methodology described here.

27.6.1 Test project planning

- Produce a test plan covering the high-level aspects of the test project;
- produce a test design document that will function as the blueprint for test case construction;
- hold formal review meetings, get approval on the design before you start writing test code. If you must start coding 'yesterday,' break the plan into several sections and review and implement by sections;
- keep track of the number of defects found during planning, and also how long it takes to write the plan (you will probably be surprised and pleased with the numbers).

27.6.2 Writing the tests

- Build the GUI object map first. Include all objects in all windows. Make a pass through the map, reviewing the logical names and making sure they are intuitive and consistent;
- design, build, and debug the encapsulated set-up routines. Use trivial test cases and a simple test program as a driver;
- build the individual test cases. Use the test plan as a source of header comments for each test case. Insure that each test case is clearly pass/fail in nature. Don't rely on the results of a previous test case as the set-up for another test case;
- put all test parameters (e.g. names of data files, test directory paths, names of temporary files, working directories) in one file so that you only have to go to one place to set up for different test environment configurations;
- err on the side of producing too much documentation, rather than not enough. Make it easy on those who have to maintain the code you write.

27.7 Summary

It is possible to build GUI Test Suites that are robust, maintainable, well documented, *and* cost effective.

It takes effort, discipline, and a consistent methodology, but when done correctly, the pay-offs are immediate and lasting. Cadence Design Systems has promoted and used this methodology for a few years now, and we have seen positive results. Adopting this (or any other) methodology takes effort, but it can be done, and with a little perseverance, you can be successful.

References

Beizer, Boris (1984) *Software System Testing and Quality Assurance.* Van Nostrand Reinhold, New York.

IEEE (1994) *IEEE Software Engineering Standards Collection.* IEEE Computer Society, New York.

Mercury Interactive Corp. (1996) *XRunner User's Guide V4.0.*

Segue Software Inc. (1996) *QA Partner User's Guide Release 4.*

CHAPTER TWENTY-EIGHT

Test automation experience at Microsoft

Angela Smale

28.1 History

Software testing was quite a young discipline when I started working as a software test engineer, back in 1988, and now many years later, it still has a long way to go in process maturity to catch up with software development and project management. A separate Testing Department in the software industry was not the norm in 1988 – there were some testers in development teams, their job being mostly ad hoc user interface (UI) or user-scenario testing (in other words, limited black-box testing). A systematic approach to software testing was not common. Even today, many companies do not have dedicated testing resources; the developers test their code themselves and then the project is delivered to their customers. I often interview developers who come from companies fortunate enough to have full-time test staff, but they believe that testers are non-technical people, who spend their time finding small UI bugs at the end of the project, missing many of the bigger issues.

This case study will give you a whirlwind tour of a decade of test experience on the leading edge of PC software technology, and will show you some shortcuts to a productive automated test environment for yourself. My experience spans applications, languages, databases, and operating systems, both English and localized versions. I have been through many phases of test automation, many times hoping to find a silver bullet, but one does not exist. Just like testing itself, automation is a continuous process; you can never say you're finished.

28.1.1 Career summary

My first testing experience was mostly manual, testing Swedish and Dutch versions of Microsoft DOS version 4.01. Besides the commands themselves, there was a UI portion, called DOS shell. UI testing was completely manual, checking through all the menu items, using written test cases. For the DOS commands themselves, we had some automation, in the form of DOS batch files, which helped to test some of the DOS commands and all their parameters.

After we released our localized DOS 4.01 versions in March 1989, I led the testing for Swedish, Dutch, and Finnish Microsoft PC Word5.0. Here we made exhaustive lists of all the menu items and options available in the product, and did manual testing. This testing was tedious and became boring at times when I found myself repeating the same actions over for the tenth time.

It was time to look at some tools to automate some of the testing. It would be nice to free the testers' time for writing new test cases for unusual error conditions, such as 'what happens if I'm editing an existing document on a disk, and the floppy disk is full when I try to save the changes I've made?' As Microsoft expanded into more European markets with more products, my team became responsible for testing all of the products, in up to thirteen languages. Over the next four and a half years, we used and evaluated many test tools, some of which were great timesavers and bug finders, and some of which did not work as well as anticipated.

In September 1993, I moved to Redmond, Washington, home of Microsoft's corporate headquarters. I was the test manager for FoxPro, a database development tool that uses X-Base as its programming language. It was time to expand my automation experience and put a full automation system in place for FoxPro testing. There were some API tests in place at the time, but no real automation strategy. Microsoft had bought Fox Software in August 1992, and the group was still learning to deal with the difference in culture and development processes. It was a good time to develop a test automation system from scratch.

After over two years as the test manager for FoxPro, I moved on to an entirely different type of product, internally known as the Information Highway PC, which ended up shipping as WebTV for Windows, in Microsoft Windows 98. This feature is initially only available in the US, due to the different TV signals between the US and other parts of the world. Each component of this system was unique and different from all the other components. This meant that an all-encompassing 'framework' would not work. So I hired some seasoned developers into my test group to develop specific test harnesses and simulators for each of the subsystems.

28.1.2 Preparing for automation

It takes several years to go from zero automation to where you feel you have a complete automation strategy. You will never be 'done.' One obstacle you could encounter early on is management resistance, particularly if your manager does not fully understand the importance of testing as an engineering discipline in his or her group. Managers like to see results, and when it comes to testing, those results are normally in the form of bug reports, followed by a shipping product. So unless you are extremely lucky, you will not be allowed to lower your bug find rate for six months while you get your automated tests ready. Is there a way around this? Yes there is. You must be willing to take small steps at a time, rather than giant strides.

To get initial buy-in, write a detailed test plan for your project, detailing what areas you will test, what you will automate, and what you will test manually. Get this document reviewed and approved by your manager, the development team, the marketing team, and any other functional teams with whom you have direct contact during the project lifecycle. Then, test the application as you write your tests – that way, you will be both reporting bugs and automating your tests at the same time, and management will not be so worried about the time you are spending on automation.

28.1.2.1 Automating applications testing

Applications testing can be subdivided into UI testing and functionality testing. Both are good candidates for automation. First, you need to decide where you will concentrate your automation efforts. If your application will be localized for many countries, then you should focus on tests that will find the common bugs across all the languages. If it is a single-language application, then your focus should be on tests that will test the functionality of the application, and can be reused for future versions of your application.

Application testing requires a standard test management system and tools, which can be used by every tester on your team. It must be easy for any tester to run the tests and view the results for any of the application's test areas. The tools can either be developed in-house by developers on your test team, or can be bought off-the-shelf from one of the many companies that supply test automation systems.

The decision on what tests to automate and your automation methodology should be independent of the tools you use. A test tool just helps you get your tests organized – you are the one who decides on the tests themselves – a tool cannot do the test strategy planning for you. Ease of use, reusability, and portability are the most important aspects of test automation for application testing.

28.1.2.2 Automating operating system testing

You need distinct automation tools for each operating system's subsystems. They are so different from each other. For WebTV for Windows we had network drivers to test by passing packets from end to end in a private network, insuring our drivers met the NDIS standards; we tested MPEG decoding by sending MPEG packets across a network; the broadcast data network was tested using a real VBI (Vertical Blanking Interval) encoder in a simulated environment; we tested the Electronic Program Guide UI using Visual Test, and we tested the underlying database by working with our external partners to send test data via satellite and local TV stations to us. We tested Conditional Access TV station security using specially developed access cards from our satellite TV partners and Test Suites we bought from one of their vendors – we were developing a system to work with advanced cryptographic security, without knowing the exact details of the crypto-graphic system.

In this type of environment, automation is very important, but is not as standardized as in any previous environment in which I worked. Each sub-system needs to be treated as a separate product under test, and then integrated as a whole with the rest of the system, with system-level tests to find the integration bugs. An example of an integration test for the WebTV for Windows is to log on to the TV program guide, update the TV listings, select a premium channel, e.g. HBO, and tune to it. If you have permissions for this channel, the channel should appear (confirmed via the presence of video signals to the PC), and if you have not got permissions, then a mes-sage should appear on the screen, saying something like 'to purchase this show, please call xxx-yyyy.'

28.1.3 Test management system

There were several test case management systems in Microsoft, but they managed either manual test cases or automated test cases, not both. I decided that my test team should develop our own test management system to manage both manual and automated tests in a FoxPro database. When it comes to running the tests, this system was what is known as a teacher–pupil system. A teacher–pupil system allows you to log many machines into the one server machine that manages the tests. The server machine is the 'teacher' and the other machines are the 'pupils.' The teacher knows which tests are to be run in the suite, and distributes them to each of the pupils. When a test is complete, the pupil sends the resulting test log back to the teacher, and requests another test. Each night, the testers log their computers in as pupils, and the test run is complete when they return in the morning.

The system contained the following abilities:

- author tests according to test case templates (testers could easily under-stand each other's tests, since everyone used the same format);
- upload tests into the system, or author them within the system;
- organize tests in a tree, as determined by the test area owner;
- execute a Test Suite against a specific product version, containing both manual and automated tests;
- automated tests would be sent to 'client' machines;
- manual tests would be emailed to the appropriate tester to run;
- the master machine would confirm the version and language of the client machine's installation before running tests;
- recover from failure – restart a machine if the product crashed under a test;
- testers could log in their PC as a test run client overnight;

- tests would log results to the master machine, and a report could be generated for each run – testers entered results of manual tests also;

- common functions were put into a common function library, which was called by all automated tests;

- historical data was easy to access;

- a summary report of test results could be emailed to the team or individual tester.

At a minimum, you must have a test case management system, which simply stores the tests for each test area. The tests should be under configuration management control, just like any development project. All of the above functionality is not required for a basic test case management system – we consolidated both a test case management system and a test harness into the one tool.

Once you have your basic test management infrastructure in place, you can decide on the additional tools you need to get your tests automated. The tools you choose will depend on your budget in terms of time and money, the type of project you are responsible for testing, and the test strategy you outlined in your test plan.

Over the next several pages, I will describe some of the testing tools used in my experience as a tester, some simple and some complex, with what I found to be their advantages and disadvantages.

28.2 Batch files

28.2.1 Theory of operation

Batch files were run overnight when we tested DOS and saved us a considerable amount of time. Many DOS commands have a variety of switches, and the batch files enabled us to test each of them. Verification of the test results was automated as much as possible, but still needed some manual verification of results. Testing *dir* was easy to verify via automation by piping the end results to a text file, and doing a file comparison to a file we knew to be correct. On the other hand, a command such as *format* needed to be run separately to the other tests (or we would lose the test results from the previous tests that night), and needed to be manually verified.

28.2.2 Advantages

- It was easy to write tests using batch files. The language was very simple and easy to learn;

- the DOS commands were always in English; only the verification portions of the tests were amended for each language;

- the tests were reusable on different machine configurations and languages;

- maintenance costs were low; DOS was not a rapidly changing environment;
- the tests could run unattended overnight, by using a test harness to drive the tests.

28.2.3 Disadvantages

- The batch files were great for testing only one product (DOS), and were not portable to other applications;
- UI testing (for example, the DOS shell) could not be automated using batch files, and required a different toolset.

28.2.4 Conclusion

Batch files were my first introduction to test automation. They worked great for the specific needs we had at the time, but the tests were project specific. We did not get as much economy of scale as with some other tools we later deployed.

28.3 Capture/playback tools

28.3.1 Theory of operation

The first third-party tool I looked at was a capture/playback UI automation tool, with its own scripting language. It sounded great – I thought that I could do my tests once, have the system record everything I did (both mouse movements and keystrokes), and then play them back again, and do an automatic comparison of the screenshots, and tell me the problems. It also had a simple scripting language, which was easy to learn.

28.3.2 Advantages

- Off-the-shelf test system, needed little time investment to use;
- it had a simple scripting language, which made it easy to understand and write scripts;
- the capture/playback technology required no prior programming experience – testers could develop tests in minutes;
- we could develop a large number of simple tests in a short time.

28.3.3 Disadvantages

- In DOS-based applications, the mouse cursor blinked on and off, and the tool would flag an error where the recorded image showed the cursor and the run image had it blinked off. (This was fixed in later releases of such tools);

- portability was an issue. We had to run the tests on the system with which we created them, due to different screen resolutions and color palettes;
- each time the product UI changed even by a single pixel, an accelerator key changed, or a menu item was added, the tests had to be recreated;
- the tests had to be recreated for each language we were testing, because translation changed the entire menu. There was no economy of scale;
- the tool only told us when there was a difference in the screenshots, so it assumed that everything in the comparison screenshot was final, and then reported 'errors' where there were differences found. In actuality, the screens were far from final when we were in our testing phase, so there were more false reports than actual bugs found.

28.3.4 Conclusion

The primary use of a capture/playback tool is for the final test pass, when one wants to make sure that nothing has inadvertently changed just before the software is as final. Other than that, using the tool in the early testing phases required so much maintenance that it was not worth the effort.

Always try to avoid screenshot comparisons when testing. Instead, try to come up with objective pass/fail criteria such that the test log reports a pass or a fail for each test. Log the test number, name, each task performed, each verification step performed, and the result of each step, as well as an overall pass or fail result for the test.

28.4 Scripting language

28.4.1 Theory of operation

If you decide that instead of purchasing ready-made tools, you will create your own, then at the very least, you need a scripting language. When automating the testing for FoxPro, we developed our own test scripting language. Why did we have a scripting language when we also had X-Base? The scripting language consisted of functions to traverse through the UI, send mouse and keyboard events to test the menus and dialogs, and log the results. FoxPro did not use standard Windows dialog boxes, so our development team added hooks to the dialog and controls, so that our automation could 'see' them, using our scripting language. Our tests did not rely on the positioning of screens, unlike capture/playback tools, and they worked across languages, screen resolutions, color schemes, and platforms. The way they worked was to ask the control itself for its position, and then we sent a mouse or keyboard event to an offset of that position.

For localization testing, some translation was needed for the menu item names. This translation was accomplished using a look-up table. The tester would specify a language when running the Test Suite, and the tests would look up the corresponding menu item in a table for that language.

In Microsoft, there is a standard glossary of menu names for every language, so that for a given language, the term is the same across many different products.

28.4.2 Advantages

- Versatility. The scripting language and product hooks made it easy to automate the way we wanted to automate. There were no complex workarounds needed to automate our test cases;
- the development team was involved in our testing efforts, and supported our needs for testability by providing the hooks into the product;
- our tests were usable cross-platform (Windows, Macintosh, UNIX, and DOS)
- our tests could be localized on-the-fly and used on all language versions without maintenance costs.

28.4.3 Disadvantages

- Creating our own scripting language took time and effort away from testing our product;
- it was product specific, and could not be used for any other application in the company;
- having a proprietary dialog manager made the task of test automation more difficult, requiring additional effort from the development team to support us.

28.4.4 Conclusion

Our goal was to use the same tests across multiple platforms and multiple languages, and all the third-party test tools were platform specific, and assumed your application used each platform's standard UI controls. Therefore, we needed a proprietary solution for our testing. It was worth the effort for us to go down this route, but if you have a standard application, then a commercially available tool with a scripting language should suffice.

28.5 Cosmetic dialog box testing

We needed a tool that was easy to maintain, and could be used across many languages, without having to continuously rewrite the tests. I started analyzing the bug reports, and the causes of the bugs. My analysis consistently demonstrated that, for localization, almost 80% of the bugs were due to cosmetic issues. This was a good example of the Pareto principle, also known as the 80/20 rule – 80% of the bugs were due to 20% of the causes. If we could automate the finding of even half of these 80%, then testing and reworking costs would be significantly reduced.

28.5.1 Theory of operation

Cosmetic dialog box testing

A test tool was developed to automate the cosmetic testing elements for dialog boxes. Each application test team could write their tests using any scripting tool or macro language that was capable of driving the application under test. These tests would simply go through the application and display each dialog box, then call the dialog box test tool, which would perform the tests listed below and log the results. Some of the common localization bugs were found using this tool, and it significantly reduced the amount of time to complete UI testing for each language.

This tool could:

- spell-check menu items and dialog box text;
- check for duplicate accelerator keys;
- check for text fit and truncation problems in controls;
- check dialog box size for 640 × 480 screen resolution;
- check alignment of dialog box controls, look for overlapping controls and spacing errors;
- check tab order of the controls;
- log all results;
- print a report diagrammatically showing the layout of each dialog box.

28.5.2 Advantages

- It found many cosmetic bugs;
- it was simple to write the tests: access a dialog, call the dialog test module, and have it log the results;
- reusable self-contained tests: the dialog test module was written once, and called many times in the Test Suite;
- the dialog test tool could be used for any application with dialog boxes that used the same dialog manager for dialog display;
- easy to maintain: need to add a test when testing each dialog? Add it to the dialog tester, and all tests are now updated;
- easy to move from one language to another: no screenshots to regenerate for each language;
- it ran unattended through the full Test Suite, which freed testers to do more complex testing tasks.

28.5.3 Disadvantages

- Maintenance of the tool itself took time and resources away from testing;
- to access the controls in the dialog box, the tool needed to be written to a specific dialog manager. So although it could be used for many applications, there were several applications that used all the standard

Windows dialogs and controls; several other applications shared their own 'standard' for controls, and other applications had their very own form of custom controls, not shared with any other application.

28.5.4 Conclusion

This is a perfect example of a reusable tool – it can be used across applications and across languages, and quickly finds cosmetic bugs. It is definitely a timesaver, and the advantages of such a tool can be demonstrated to management, to get buy-in for additional automation work.

28.6 Help testing tool

Help files often had a large number of errors in their internal links. The two main bug types were where a link took the user to a totally unrelated topic, and where there was inconsistency between the topic name on the originating page and that on the destination page.

28.6.1 Theory of operation

We developed a tool that would go through each of the help files looking for codes that indicated the following text was a link. The destination page was then found, and compared with the calling link. This tool reported on bugs where links were missing, links went to the wrong place, and where the link text and the destination page title were out of synch.

In addition to testing internal links, the tool could 'drive' the help file, such that all help topics could be viewed sequentially by the tester, missing none of them. The tester still had to view each page manually, to make sure that the appearance of the page looked good, and the text wrapped around graphic elements properly, and that it all fitted neatly into the page(s). The tedious work of testing each of the links, and knowing that each of them had been tested, was automated and cut the testing effort dramatically.

28.6.2 Advantages

- This tool automated one of the most tedious and boring aspects of testing;
- it used the raw source files (in rtf format) to test against, so bugs could be found and fixed, before the help files were even compiled;
- the tool reported on and found potential functionality problems that the help compiler did not report on;
- for localization testing, the tool provided a comprehensive list of all the differences between the English and the localized files; it verified that the localized project had the exact same source files and help topics, included in the same order. The functional content check insured that all the same browse numbers, links, bitmaps, and inclusions were present, as well as the number of keywords, and that topic titles corresponded to the original English files;

- this tool was self-contained, and could test the help source files for up to 55 common problems, and write a detailed report on all of its findings on each file;
- one manual test pass of the help files would take two weeks, and not find all the bugs; one automated test pass could run overnight, and find all of the functionality bugs;
- this tool could be used for any project that had help files, and for all languages;
- help authors and localizers could easily test their files, and fix their own bugs before sending them to testing;
- the help driver option displayed each of the help pages from the compiled help files, in both full-screen and quarter-screen mode, so the tester could verify the location of the help elements, and verify that word wrapping worked as expected when the help screen was reduced in size.

28.6.3 Disadvantages

- The tool needed full-time support for the first several months of use, as we were trying to get it adopted by all of Microsoft;
- the first version's UI did not give much user feedback – it was fairly basic, requiring the user to open a help project file and select the types of test to run, and then several hours later it produced the reports. Later versions had progress meters and more user feedback in the interface;
- it requires version control and testing itself. Tools to do automation must be tested themselves, as otherwise they could miss bugs, or falsely report bugs, or fail to complete a test run. The more complex the test tool, the more testing of the tool itself is required.

28.6.4 Conclusion

A universal tool, such as the help-testing tool, is an excellent automation tool. It has several clear advantages over generic scripting type tools. It is usable by those who create the source files, so it can find the bugs when they cost the least to fix. It is worldwide, being used on all languages of an application's help system. It requires little training to use, and can run unattended, and log all results. Such a project is large enough that it needs full management support, before you assign one of your few testers to the project for several months.

28.7 Tools to randomize test execution

Running the same automated tests in the same order for each run will find the same bugs each time they are run. To find new bugs with the same automated tests, some randomization needs to be introduced. At a minimum, a test tool can be run to help randomize the order in which the test cases are run. Also, when you develop your tests, you can write them with some randomization in them. For example, generate a random number between one and ten; if the number is less than three, then do action 1, else if the number is less than five, do action 2, etc.

Monkey testing is a method of finding bugs via a random sequence of path execution. There have been dumb monkeys and smart monkeys, and in FoxPro we used what we termed a data monkey to help find bugs. Dumb monkeys randomly hit keys, looking for a way to crash the product. A smart monkey normally uses state transition diagrams and probabilities to reflect more accurately a real user's usage of the product. Again, the primary aim is to find where the product hangs or crashes.

Our data monkey needed little maintenance. The monkey would pass various types and amounts of data to a variety of database operations, trying to corrupt the database to which it was writing. It was used to run database operations in random sequence, with randomly selected data, and to stress the system by adding thousands of tables, or hundreds of thousands of records.

28.7.1 Advantages

- Combined actions in random ways;
- varied tests with each run;
- simulated end-user usage better than traditional structured automation;
- found new bugs, whereas repeating structured tests found the same bugs;
- great for stress testing, which involved doing the same actions many times, looking for memory leaks, etc.;
- ran the system to failure, giving us a Mean Time To Failure (MTTF) measurement.

28.7.2 Disadvantages

- Required testers to reproduce the bug to report the problem to development, which was sometimes difficult to do due to the large number of random actions that ran prior to the system hang. The problems were rarely due to one or two tests being run – there was normally a long sequence of tests that led to the bug. We learned to log absolutely everything the tests did, to make the problems easier to track down and repeat;
- smart monkeys that used state transition diagrams required a lot of maintenance, particularly if used early in the project life cycle, when the application's feature set was still changing.

We found many bugs using different forms of random test execution, which either would never have been found before releasing the software to our customers, or would have only otherwise been found by testers performing ad hoc integration testing. True smart monkey testing involves a considerable amount of work upfront, and requires a lot of maintenance if menu options change. It is best used towards the end of the project as a final sanity check and to verify that MTTF is acceptable.

28.8 What should I automate first?

Decide which areas of which features the users will use 80% of the time or more. These are top priority for working correctly. The very first set of automated tests that I would encourage you to develop is the Build Verification Tests (BVTs). This is a suite of tests confirming that the basic functionality of a build is still intact, and that it's worthwhile for the testers to accept this build, and start reporting bugs against it. If the build fails this test, then the developer responsible for introducing the bug must fix it immediately and restart the build. The test team will only install and test a build after the build passes the BVT. The BVT should run for 1 to 2 hours, immediately after the build of the project completes, preferably overnight.

A further expansion of the BVT idea is the Developer Regression Test (DRT). This is a short suite of tests that runs for 10 to 20 minutes, on a private incremental build that the developer builds, just before checking in his or her changes to the source tree. This suite of tests covers the basic functionality of the product, and works to prevent developers from checking in changes to the code that break primary areas of functionality. The DRT can be a subset of the BVT, or a different set of tests that mirrors some of the BVT's goals. Alternatively, the DRT can be designed per feature, a different set for each developer – this is a much more costly approach, but the developer could assist in writing some of these tests.

28.8.1 Key points for developing automated tests

- Automate the most repetitive tasks;
- automate the tasks that have traditionally found the most bugs;
- architect the tests so you do not rewrite them for each language. This may be by translating the menu items on-the-fly using look-up tables, or using internal application hooks that are always in English, or by using the keyboard to navigate through the UI (e.g. go three menus across, two down);
- modularize your tests for easy maintainability, and reuse them on other projects;
- keep all your tests in a test case management database;
- architect the tests to run unattended.

28.8.2 Regression testing

The primary benefit of automation is to allow you time to use your creative abilities to come up with new ways to break the product under test. For automation to find many new bugs for you, you'll need to introduce some method of randomization in them. Most first-generation automated Test Suites repeat the same tasks in the same order each time they are run, seeing if areas have regressed in functionality and introduced some bugs.

Since automated tests are so good at determining if there have been regressions in functionality between builds, you should use this to your advantage. Look at the high severity bugs you found via manual testing, and write automated test cases for them. Bugs have a nasty habit of resurfacing when you least expect them, so having a bug regression Test Suite which you run before each milestone can give you confidence in the system, and catch any bugs that have crept back in. The bug regression suite should contain tests with the exact reproducible steps that found the original bug, and include several additional tests to test 'around' the bug.

28.8.3 Stress testing

Stress testing is one of my favorite areas for test automation. It is a clear example of an area that benefits from automation, and you get a return on your investment very quickly. In its simplest form, a stress test is any test that repeats a set of actions many times. The system is put through its paces under load conditions, to find where it fails.

In a multi-user environment, keep adding users to the system, and perform a common action. If your application uses a database, write tests that add, amend, and delete records continuously, and then look for a system crash, memory leaks, a corrupted database, or an extremely large database. As a first step, take the common actions in your application, and keep repeating them till the system fails. Adding some randomization to your tests will help you find more bugs – if adding users, add different types of users, with a variety of name lengths. How many days can your system stay functioning under such load?

Repeating the above tests manually is not feasible, so this is an example where automation provides you with more than just a mirror of your manual Test Suite. A monkey, as described earlier, is a perfect tool for stress testing. The most important thing to remember is to log everything as you proceed with your tests. You need to know what exactly was happening when your system failed. Did the system lock up with 20 simultaneous users, or 20 000 users? What types of users had been added during the test? For a system built assuming an average load of 200 users, the former is a far more serious issue than the latter.

The first tool I mentioned in this experience report is the test management system. The final and equally important tool I'd like to cover briefly is the bug tracking database. This database needs to track all of the bugs found in your application, which follow a life cycle of Active, then each gets Resolved, is re-tested to confirm the resolution, and is finally set to Closed. As the bug goes through its life cycle, it can be assigned to various team members. What has a bug-tracking database got to do with automation? It can actually be a very valuable tool for your automation efforts.

First, as I mention above, you can automate bug regression testing. You can also go to previous versions of your product, and write test cases that would find the most important bugs, if they were to resurface.

A bug database can help you determine the effectiveness of your automation efforts. When entering the bug report, you should have a field for 'how found.' An example of some options would be ad hoc, automation, test case development, manual test case, regression testing, customer, etc. You could also list specific tools in this field. Then for any given test area, or for the project as a whole, you can determine the percentage of bugs found by your automated tests.

There should also be a field for developers to enter the cause of the bug, when resolving it as fixed. This causal field could contain options such as bug regression, memory leak, cosmetic UI bug, typo, spec bug, etc. You could use this information to determine if there is any specific area on which to concentrate your automation efforts next time. For localization testing, I found that most of the bugs ended up being cosmetic UI problems, so I invested heavily in UI testing tools. For non-localization testing, the bug causes tend to be more evenly dispersed among all the causes we track.

28.9 My top ten list for a successful test automation strategy

Automation is a continuous process; you will never be 'complete.' I hope the preceding pages have given you an insight into the types of test tools and the test automation strategy that you need to adopt in your organization. To end this chapter, here is my top ten list. Follow this advice, and you will be well on your way to a successful test automation implementation.

1. Write a detailed test plan before doing anything – be very clear on your automation strategy and get buy-in from your management and peers.
2. Put together a test case management framework, so that each tester is writing to the same standards, and all tests are maintained and accessible.
3. Reduce maintenance – write common functions and modules, and reuse them everywhere.
4. Write meaningful test logs, and generate a summary report for all pass and fail results. Log everything.

5. Have tests run unattended, and capable of recovering from failure.

6. Leverage your tests across multiple languages, platforms, and configurations.

7. Introduce some randomness in your tests.

8. Start small, with tests that are run daily, e.g. build verification tests. Build on success.

9. Measure effectiveness of automation by number and rate of bugs found.

10. Use automation for stress testing – run tests on your product till it fails.

© Angela Smale, 1999.

Answer to DDP exercise (Chapter 8)

In Chapter 8, on p. 216, we gave an example incorrect calculation of the Defect Detection Percentage (DDP) as an exercise for the reader. The erroneous calculation is shown again in Table A.1 with the correct calculation. What had been calculated, instead of the DDP, was actually the percentage of the total number of defects. The total number of defects ever found was 397 (299 + 40 + 19 + 10 + 9 + the 20 found in live operation). The incorrect calculation divided the number of defects found at each stage by that total.

The first calculation was the 299 defects found in module and integration testing, divided by 397. Let's think in round numbers: 300/400 is 75%. This figure, however, is actually the correct calculation for the DDP for this first stage of testing, since it is the defects found here divided by any defects found anywhere.

For development testing, the incorrect calculation was 40/400, or 10%. This represents the defects found in this stage as a percentage of total defects. The DDP, however, should be the defects found at this stage (40) divided by all those found in this stage and afterwards (40 + 19 + 10 + 9 + 20), or approximately 100. Thus the DDP should be 40/100, or 40%.

Similarly for release testing (which found 5% of the total defects), the DDP is 19 divided by (19 + 10 + 9 + 20), or approximately 60; 20/60 is one third, or 33% (actually 19/58 is 32.7%, to be exact). The last two calculations are 10/39 = 25.6% (roughly 25%) and 9/29 = 31% (roughly 30%).

Note that there is never a DDP for the last set of defects (in this case live use). The number of defects from the last stage always helps to determine the DDP of all previous stages. (If it were to be calculated, it would always be 100%, but this is seriously misleading!)

Table A.1 Correct calculation of DDP.

Stage of testing	Number of defects	Incorrect calculation	DDP
Module and integration	299	75%	75%
Development testing	40	10%	40%
Release testing	19	5%	33%
User acceptance test	10	2.5%	25%
Pilot	9	2.5%	30%
Live use (1 month)	20	5%	

References

BACH, JAMES (1997) 'Test automation snake oil', *14th International Conference on Testing Computer Software,* June 1997, US Professional Development Institute.

BEIZER, BORIS (1990) *Software Testing Techniques,* 2nd edition. Van Nostrand Reinhold, New York.

BEIZER, BORIS (1995) *Black-Box Testing.* Wiley, New York.

BOULDIN, BARBARA (1989) *Agents of Change.* Prentice Hall, Englewood Cliffs, New Jersey.

FENTON, NORMAN E. AND LAWRENCE-PFLEEGER, SHARI (1997) *Software Metrics: A Rigorous and Practical Approach.* International Thomson Computer Press, London.

FRIEDL, JEFFREY E.F. (1997) *Mastering Regular Expressions: Powerful Techniques for PERL and Other Tools.* O'Reilly, Cambridge, Massachusetts.

GILB, TOM (1988) *Principles of Software Engineering Management.* Addison-Wesley, Wokingham.

GILB, TOM AND GRAHAM, DOROTHY (1993) *Software Inspection.* Addison-Wesley, Wokingham.

GRAHAM, DOROTHY and HERZLICH, PAUL (1995) *The CAST Report, Computer Aided Software Testing,* 3rd edition, Cambridge Market Intelligence, London.

HAYES, LINDA G. (1995) *The Automated Testing Handbook.* Software Testing Institute, Dallas, Texas.

HETZEL, BILL (1988) *The Complete Guide to Software Testing.* QED, Wellesley, Massachusetts.

HETZEL, BILL (1993) *Making Software Measurement Work.* QED, Wellesley, Massachusetts.

HUMPHREYS, WATT (1997) *Introduction to the Personal Software Process.* Addison Wesley, Harlow.

HUTCHESON, MARNIE (1995) Using S-curves to plan and track testing, *Unicom Seminar,* October 3, 1995.

IEEE (1992) *IEEE Standard 1209, Recommended Practice for the Evaluation and Selection of CASE Tools.* IEEE.

IEEE (1995) *IEEE Standard 1348, Recommended Practice for the Adoption of Computer-Aided Software Engineering (CASE) tools.* IEEE.

ISENBERG, HERB (1998) 'Multi level verification for automated testing systems', white paper, May 1, 1998.

JONES, CAPERS (1991) *Applied Software Measurement: Assuring Productivity and Quality.* McGraw-Hill, New York.

KANER, CEM (1997) Improving the maintainability of automated test suites. *Software QA* 4(4).

KANER, CEM; FALK, JACK AND NGUYEN, HUNG QUOC (1993) *Testing Computer Software,* 2nd edition. Van Nostrand Reinhold, New York.

KEMERER, CHRIS (1992) How the learning curve affects CASE tool adoption. *IEEE Software,* May.

KIT, ED (1995) *Software Testing in the Real World.* Addison Wesley, Wokingham.

KITCHENHAM, BARBARA (1996) 'DESMET: a methodology for evaluating software engineering methods and tools', Keele University Technical Report TR96-09, ISSN: 1353-7776, August [more detailed, more of the methodology].

KITCHENHAM, B. A., LINKMAN, S. G., AND LAW, D. (1997) 'DESMET: a methodology for evaluating software engineering methods and tools.' *IEE Computing and Control Journal,* June, 120–126 [overview of DESMET].

MARICK, BRIAN (1995) *The Craft of Software Testing.* Prentice Hall, Englewood Cliffs, New Jersey.

MYERS, GLENFORD (1979) *The Art of Software Testing.* Wiley, New York.

POSTON, ROBERT M. (1996) *Automating Specification-Based Software Testing.* IEEE Computer Society, Los Alamitos, California.

THOMAS, GRAHAM (1997) *Practical Test Monitoring.* British Computer Society Specialist Interest Group in Software Testing, September 12.

VOAS, JEFFREY M. AND MCGRAW, GARY (1998) *Software Fault Injection, Inoculating Programs Against Errors.* Wiley, New York.

Glossary

These terms relate to terms used in Part one of this book and are not necessarily used by the authors of the chapters in Part two.

Actual outcome Outputs and data states that are produced from test inputs.

AUT Application under test. *See* SUT.

Automated testware Testware used in automated testing, such as tool scripts.

Automator *See* Test automator.

Boundary value analysis A test case design technique in which test cases are designed to exercise boundary values at the extremes of equivalence partitions.

Breadth test A Test Suite that exercises the full scope of a system from a top-down perspective, but does not test any aspect in detail. *See also* Rollcall, Smoke test.

Bug *See* Defect.

Capture playback *See* Capture replay.

Capture replay The functionality of some test execution tools to record (capture) test inputs as a script, and to replay that script to exercise the software.

Clear-up The tasks required to be done after a test or set of tests has finished or stopped, in order to leave the system in a clean state for the next test or set of tests. Clear-up may be for a single test, a Test Set or a Test Suite. Clear-up is particularly important where a test has failed to complete.

Code-based test A test whose inputs are derived from the code being tested. For example, tests to extend branch coverage are based on the branches in the code that have not been tested so far.

Comparison The process of checking whether one thing or series of things matches another. Automated comparison looks for any differences between two sets of outcomes (normally the actual outcomes and expected outcomes).

Comparison process A series of one or more filters followed by a simple comparison.

Configuration item A standalone use-alone element of a system that is identified as a logical entity. A configuration item has a version number and is controlled by a configuration management system (manual or automated).

Data-driven A scripting technique that stores test inputs and expected outcomes as data, normally in a table or spreadsheet, so that a single control script can execute all of the tests in the data table.

Data Set A type of testware set that contains data files that are accessed by more than one test set. A Data Set also contains documentation about the data files.

Defect A manifestation of an error in software. A defect, if encountered, may cause a failure. (Note this is the BS7925-1 definition of fault.)

Defect Detection Percentage (DDP) The number of defects found by testing, divided by the total number of known defects, expressed as a percentage.

Defect Fix Percentage (DFP) The number of defects fixed divided by the total number of known defects, expressed as a percentage.

Depth test A test case that exercises some part of a system to a significant level of detail.

Dynamic comparison A comparison that is performed while a test case is executing by the comparison facility of a test execution tool. This may be used to check whether the correct data or messages have appeared on the screen.

Equivalence partition A set of data or software states for which the software's behavior is assumed to be the same, based on a specification of the software.

Equivalence partitioning A test case design technique in which tests are designed to exercise equivalence partitions.

Error A human action that produces an incorrect result (in the software or test) (from BS7925-1).

Error guessing A test case design technique where the experience of the tester is used to postulate what faults exist, and to design tests specifically to expose them (from BS7925-1).

Expected fail Test status given when the actual outcome of a test matches an expected outcome that contains known defects.

Expected outcome Outputs and data states that should result from executing a test or test case.

Exploratory testing Exercising software without a well-defined test oracle such as a specification. Rather than specifying expected outcomes, the tester selects test inputs and test data, and validates the actual outcome from a subjective perspective.

Fault *See* Defect. In this book we use the term defect as synonymous with the standard definition of fault.

Filter Automated processing applied to two sets of outcomes, expected outcome and actual outcome, for the purpose of simplifying the automated comparison of the outcomes. Example filter functions include sorting, replacing specific data with a generic term, and rounding.

Golden version A set of expected outcomes, often derived from a set of actual outcomes that have been validated by the tester. *See also* Reference testing.

Graphical user interface (GUI) A user interface using graphical components, such as windows, icons, pull-down menus, radio buttons, etc. under the control of either a keyboard or a mouse.

Interface-based test A test whose inputs are derived from an interface definition. For example, tests that activate every identifiable element in a GUI window are interface-based tests.

Keyword-driven A scripting technique that uses data files to contain not only test inputs and expected outcomes, but also keywords related to the application being tested. The keywords are interpreted by special supporting scripts that are called by the control script for the test.

Lateral testing A test design technique based on lateral thinking principles, to identify faults. *See also* Error guessing.

Library *See* Testware Library

Linear script A script that is executed sequentially with no control structures. A recorded script is a linear script.

Load testing Testing conducted to evaluate a system's capacity to function under extreme load conditions.

Manual test script *See* Test procedure.

Mutation testing A method to determine Test Suite thoroughness by measuring the extent to which a Test Suite can discriminate the program from slight variants (mutants) of the program (from BS7925-1).

Oracle A mechanism to produce the predicted outcomes to compare with the actual outcomes of the software under test (from BS7925-1).

Performance testing Testing conducted to evaluate the compliance of a system or component with specified performance requirements (from BS7925-1).

Post-execution comparison Any comparison that is performed after a test case has completed its execution. Often used to compare files or databases.

Post-processing Processing that is carried out after tests have been executed. Post-processing may include clear-up of data, moving actual outcomes to a different directory location, and running filters, for example. Post-processing may be done for a test, a Test Set or a Test Suite.

Precondition Environmental and state conditions which must be fulfilled before the software can be executed with a particular input value (from BS7925-1).

Pre-processing Processing that is carried out before tests are executed. Pre-processing may include set-up of data or deleting of previous actual outcome files, for example. Pre-processing may be done for a test, a Test Set or a Test Suite.

Record playback *See* Capture replay.

Reference testing A way of deriving expected outcomes by manually validating a set of actual outcomes. A less rigorous alternative to predicting expected outcomes in advance of test execution.

Regular expression A language for defining patterns of characters, used by utilities such as editors, programming environments, and specialized tools including some comparators. Some scripting languages support the use of regular expressions.

Robust test A test that compares a small amount of information, so that unexpected side effects are less likely to affect whether the test passes or fails.

Roll-call A Test Suite that includes one test for all identified aspects, such as menus or screens. A form of breadth test.

Script *See* Test script.

Script Set A type of testware set that contains test scripts that are accessed by more than one Test Set. A Script Set also may contain documentation about the scripts.

Sensitive test A test that compares a large amount of information, so that it is more likely to detect unexpected differences between the actual and expected outcomes of the test.

Set-up The tasks required to be done before a test or set of tests can be executed. Set-up may be for a single test, a Test Set or a Test Suite.

Shared script A script that is called by more than one other script. A shared script may be parameter driven.

Shelfware A tool that was purchased but is no longer used, i.e. it sits on a shelf.

Side effect defects Defects in unchanged software caused by or revealed by changes to other areas of software, found by regression testing.

Smoke test An automated Test Suite that is run on a regular basis, e.g. every night, as a prerequisite for more detailed testing. A roll-call breadth test could be run as a smoke test before depth testing was done in a part of a system.

Specification-based test A test whose inputs are derived from a specification. For example, black box tests such as those derived using equivalence partitioning and boundary value analysis are specification-based tests.

Stress testing Testing conducted to evaluate a system or component beyond the limits of its specified requirements (from BS7925-1).

Structured script A script that contains control structures such as if statements or loops, or that calls another script.

SUT Software under test or system under test. The software or system being tested.

Test An input, any preconditions, and an expected outcome. An item or event that can be verified.

Test automation regime A system of organizing the testware artifacts that defines where things should be stored and how they should be structured, and how various tasks should be carried out. The regime will define the techniques to be used for different types of automated tests (e.g. scripting, comparison, pre- and post-processing). It will also define the naming conventions, configuration items and directory structure. A good automation regime is effective and efficient. It will allow you to easily select what tests to run, it ensures that the tests take care of their own 'housekeeping' tasks, and it will ultimately make it easier to add a new automated test than to run that same test manually.

Test automator A person who builds and maintains the testware associated with automated tests.

Test case A set of tests performed in a sequence and related to a test objective.

Test case definition file A text file that gives all the necessary information about the testware artifacts needed to run a test, as well as information about the purpose of the test and configuration information. The test case definition file is normally part of a Test Set.

Test case specification A document that contains a description of test cases.

Test condition An item or event that could be verified by one or more tests.

Test data Data that exists (for example, in a database) before a test is executed, and that affects or is affected by the software under test.

Test design specification A document that contains a description of test conditions, the rationale for their selection, and their prioritization.

Test execution tool A software product which is able to execute other software using a test script.

Test input An entry or event which affects the software under test.

Test Library *See* Testware Library

Test objective The reason or purpose for tests being created.

Test oracle *See* Oracle.

Test outcome Outputs and data produced or affected by tests.

Test plan A document describing the scope, approach, resources, staffing, environment, and schedule of intended testing activities.

Test procedure A document providing detailed instructions for the [manual] execution of one or more test cases (from BS7925-1). Often called a 'manual test script.'

Test Result *See* Actual outcome.

Test script Data and/or instructions with a formal syntax typically held in a file and used by a test execution automation tool. A test script can implement one or more test cases, navigation, set-up or clear-down operations, or comparison. A test script intended for manual test execution is a test procedure.

Test Set A type of testware set that contains all the testware artifacts that are unique to one or more logically related test cases. It could contain test inputs, expected outcomes, test scripts, test data, documentation, and utilities (both source code and executables).

Test specification A document combining test design and test case specifications.

Test status The assessment of the result of running tests on software. If the actual outcomes match the expected outcomes, the test status is Passed. If not, test status is Failed. Additional test statuses are Expected Fail and Unknown.

Test Suite One or more test sets brought together to meet a test objective. For example, all the test sets relating to performance. A Test Suite is a self-contained environment in which to run a selection of tests taken from the Testware Library.

Test technique A formalized approach to choosing the test conditions that give a high probability of finding defects.

Test tree A physical implementation of a Test Suite.

Tester A person who identifies test conditions, designs test cases, and verifies test results. A tester may also build and execute tests and compare test results.

Testware The artifacts required to plan, design, and execute tests, such as documentation, scripts, inputs, expected outcomes, set-up and clear-up procedures, files, databases, environments, and any additional software or utilities used in testing.

Testware Library A repository of the master versions of all testware.

Testware Set A collection of tests or testware (scripts, data files, etc.) stored in the Testware Library as a configuration item. Testware sets can be Script Sets, Test Sets, Data Sets, or Utility Sets.

Unknown Test status given when it is not possible to assign a status of Pass, Fail or Expected Fail. For example, if actual outcomes do not match expected outcomes or expected fail outcomes, or if expected outcomes are missing.

Utility Set A type of testware set that contains utilities that are used by more than one test set. The Utility Set contains source files, any other files needed to produce an executable, and the executable program. Utility sets may also contain documentation and command files.

Validation The process of checking whether the software or system is doing the 'right thing.' This may include verification, but may also be based on subjective assessment.

Verification The process of checking whether the software or system conforms to a specified standard. Software execution is verified when its actual outcome matches expected outcome that has been determined to be correct. Note that verification may be informal, where a human tester looks at actual test outcomes and approves them as correct or not, based on knowledge in his or her head.

Volume testing Testing where the system is subjected to large volumes of data (from BS7925-1).

Index

Page numbers in bold indicate where the term is defined in the text.